T-SQL Fundamentals

Itzik Ben-Gan

T-SQL Fundamentals

Published with the authorization of Microsoft Corporation by:

Pearson Education, Inc.

Copyright © 2023 by Itzik Ben-Gan.

ISBN-13: 978-0-13-810210-4

ISBN-10: 0-13-810210-4

Library of Congress Control Number: 2023930537

4 2023

Trademarks

Warning and Disclaimer

Special Sales

For information about buying this title in bulk quantities, or for special sales opportunities (which may include electronic versions; custom cover designs; and content particular to your business, training goals, marketing focus, or branding interests), please contact our corporate sales department at corpsales@pearsoned.com or (800) 382-3419.

For government sales inquiries, please contact governmentsales@pearsoned.com.

For questions about sales outside the U.S., please contact intlcs@pearson.com.

Editor-in-Chief
Brett Bartow

Executive Editor
Loretta Yates

Associate Editor
Charvi Arora

Development Editor
Songlin Qiu

Managing Editor
Sandra Schroeder

Senior Project Editor
Tracey Croom

Copy Editor
Scout Festa

Indexer
Erika Milllen

Proofreader
Jen Hinchliffe

Technical Editor
Lilach Ben-Gan

Editorial Assistant
Cindy Teeters

Cover Illustration
sasimoto/Shutterstock

Cover Designer
Twist Creative, Seattle

Compositor
codeMantra

Pearson's Commitment to Diversity, Equity, and Inclusion

Pearson is dedicated to creating bias-free content that reflects the diversity of all learners. We embrace the many dimensions of diversity, including but not limited to race, ethnicity, gender, socioeconomic status, ability, age, sexual orientation, and religious or political beliefs.

Education is a powerful force for equity and change in our world. It has the potential to deliver opportunities that improve lives and enable economic mobility. As we work with authors to create content for every product and service, we acknowledge our responsibility to demonstrate inclusivity and incorporate diverse scholarship so that everyone can achieve their potential through learning. As the world's leading learning company, we have a duty to help drive change and live up to our purpose to help more people create a better life for themselves and to create a better world.

Our ambition is to purposefully contribute to a world where:

- Everyone has an equitable and lifelong opportunity to succeed through learning.

- Our educational products and services are inclusive and represent the rich diversity of learners.

- Our educational content accurately reflects the histories and experiences of the learners we serve.

- Our educational content prompts deeper discussions with learners and motivates them to expand their own learning (and worldview).

While we work hard to present unbiased content, we want to hear from you about any concerns or needs with this Pearson product so that we can investigate and address them.

- Please contact us with concerns about any potential bias at https://www.pearson.com/report-bias.html.

To Dato,
To live in hearts we leave behind,
Is not to die.

—Thomas Campbell

Contents at a Glance

Contents

Chapter 9　Temporal tables　343

Chapter 10　Transactions and concurrency　367

Chapter 11   SQL Graph   409

Acknowledgments

A number of people contributed to making this book a reality, either directly or indirectly, and deserve thanks and recognition. It's certainly possible I omitted some names unintentionally, and I apologize for this ahead of time.

To Lilach: You're the one who makes me want to be good at what I do. Besides being my inspiration in life, you always take an active role in my books, helping to review the text for the first time. In this book, you took a more official technical editing role, and I can't appreciate enough the errors you spotted, and the many ideas and suggestions for improvements.

To my siblings, Mickey and Ina: Thank you for the constant support and for accepting the fact that I'm away.

To Davide Mauri, Herbert Albert, Gianluca Hotz, and Dejan Sarka: Thanks for your valuable advice when I reached out asking for it.

To the editorial team at Pearson and related vendors. Loretta Yates, many thanks for being so good at what you do and for your positive attitude! Thanks to Charvi Arora for all your hard work and effort. Also, thanks to Songlin Qiu, Scout Festa, Karthik Orukaimani, and Tracey Croom for sifting through all the text and making sure it's polished.

To my friends from Lucient, Fernando G. Guerrero, Herbert Albert, Fritz Lechnitz, and many others. We've been working together for over two decades, and it's been quite a ride!

To members of the Microsoft SQL Server development team, Umachandar Jayachandran (UC), Conor Cunningham, Kevin Farlee, Craig Freedman, Kendal Van Dyke, Derek Wilson, Davide Mauri, Bob Ward, Buck Woody, and I'm sure many others. Thanks for creating such a great product, and thanks for all the time you spent meeting with me and responding to my emails, addressing my questions, and answering my requests for clarification.

To Aaron Bertrand, who besides being one of the most active and prolific SQL Server pros I know, does an amazing job editing the sqlperformance.com content, including my articles.

To Data Platform MVPs, past and present: Erland Sommarskog, Aaron Bertrand, Hugo Kornelis, Paul White, Alejandro Mesa, Tibor Karaszi, Simon Sabin, Denis Reznik, Tony Rogerson, and many others—and to the Data Platform MVP lead, Rie Merritt. This is a great program that I'm grateful for and proud to be part of. The level of expertise of this group is amazing, and I'm always excited when we all get to meet, both to share ideas and Just to catch up at a personal level.

Finally, to my students: Teaching about T-SQL is what drives me. It's my passion. Thanks for allowing me to fulfill my calling and for all the great questions that make me seek more knowledge.

About the Author

ITZIK BEN-GAN is a leading authority on T-SQL, regularly teaching, lecturing, and writing on the subject. He has delivered numerous training events around the world focused on T-SQL Querying, Query Tuning, and Programming. He is the author of several books including *T-SQL Fundamentals*, *T-SQL Querying*, and *T-SQL Window Functions*. Itzik has been a Microsoft Data Platform MVP (Most Valuable Professional) since 1999.

Introduction

This book walks you through your first steps in T-SQL (also known as *Transact-SQL*), which is the Microsoft SQL Server dialect of the ISO/IEC and ANSI standards for SQL. You'll learn the theory behind T-SQL querying and programming and how to develop T-SQL code to query and modify data, and you'll get a brief overview of programmable objects.

Although this book is intended for beginners, it's not merely a set of procedures for readers to follow. It goes beyond the syntactical elements of T-SQL and explains the logic behind the language and its elements.

Occasionally, the book covers subjects that might be considered advanced for readers who are new to T-SQL; therefore, you should consider those sections to be optional reading. If you feel comfortable with the material discussed in the book up to that point, you might want to tackle these more advanced subjects; otherwise, feel free to skip those sections and return to them after you gain more experience.

Many aspects of SQL are unique to the language and very different from other programming languages. This book helps you adopt the right state of mind and gain a true understanding of the language elements. You learn how to think in relational terms and follow good SQL programming practices.

The book is not version specific; it does, however, cover language elements that were introduced in recent versions of SQL Server, including SQL Server 2022. When I discuss language elements that were introduced recently, I specify the version in which they were added.

Besides being available as an on-premises, or box, flavor, SQL Server is also available as cloud-based flavors called Azure SQL Database and Azure SQL Managed Instance. The code samples in this book are applicable to both the box and cloud flavors of SQL Server.

To complement the learning experience, the book provides exercises you can use to practice what you learn. I cannot emphasize enough the importance of working on those exercises, so make sure not to skip them!

Who Should Read This Book

This book is intended for T-SQL developers, database administrators (DBAs), business intelligence (BI) practitioners, data scientists, report writers, analysts, architects, and SQL Server power users who just started working with SQL Server and who need to write queries and develop code using T-SQL.

This book covers fundamentals. It's mainly aimed at T-SQL practitioners with little or no experience. With that said, several readers of the previous editions of this book have mentioned that—even though they already had years of experience—they still found the book useful for filling in gaps in their knowledge.

This book assumes that you are familiar with basic concepts of relational database management systems.

Organization of This Book

This book starts with a theoretical background to T-SQL querying and programming in Chapter 1, laying the foundation for the rest of the book, and provides basic coverage of creating tables and defining data integrity. The book covers various aspects of querying and modifying data in Chapters 2 through 8, and holds a discussion of transactions and concurrency in Chapter 10. In Chapter 9 and Chapter 11 the book covers specialized topics including temporal tables and SQL Graph. Finally, the book provides a brief overview of programmable objects in Chapter 12.

Here's a list of the chapters along with a short description of the content in each chapter:

- Chapter 1, "Background to T-SQL querying and programming," provides the theoretical background for SQL, set theory, and predicate logic. It examines relational theory, describes SQL Server's architecture, and explains how to create tables and define data integrity.

- Chapter 2, "Single-table queries," covers various aspects of querying a single table by using the *SELECT* statement.

- Chapter 3, "Joins," covers querying multiple tables by using joins, including cross joins, inner joins, and outer joins.

- Chapter 4, "Subqueries," covers queries within queries, otherwise known as *subqueries*.

- Chapter 5, "Table expressions," covers derived tables, Common Table Expressions (CTEs), views, inline table-valued functions (iTVFs), and the *APPLY* operator.

- Chapter 6, "Set operators," covers the set operators *UNION, INTERSECT,* and *EXCEPT.*

- Chapter 7, "T-SQL for data analysis," covers window functions, pivoting, unpivoting, working with grouping sets, and handling time-series data.

- Chapter 8, "Data modification," covers inserting, updating, deleting, and merging data.

- Chapter 9, "Temporal tables," covers system-versioned temporal tables.

- Chapter 10, "Transactions and concurrency," covers concurrency of user connections that work with the same data simultaneously; it covers transactions, locks, blocking, isolation levels, and deadlocks.

- Chapter 11, "SQL Graph," covers modeling data using graph-based concepts such as nodes and edges. It includes creating, modifying, and querying graph-based data.

- Chapter 12, "Programmable objects," provides a brief overview of the T-SQL programming capabilities in SQL Server.

- The book also provides an appendix, "Getting started," to help you set up your environment, download the book's source code, install the *TSQLV6* sample database, start writing code against SQL Server, and learn how to get help by working with the product documentation.

System Requirements

The appendix, "Getting started," explains which editions of SQL Server 2022 you can use to work with the code samples included with this book. Each edition of SQL Server might have different hardware and software requirements, and those requirements are described in the product documentation, under "Hardware and Software Requirements for Installing SQL Server 2022," at the following URL: *https://learn.microsoft.com/en-us/sql/sql-server/install/hardware-and-software-requirements-for-installing-sql-server-2022*. The appendix also explains how to work with the product documentation.

If you're connecting to Azure SQL Database or Azure SQL Managed Instance, hardware and server software are handled by Microsoft, so those requirements are irrelevant in this case.

For the client tool to run the code samples against SQL Server, Azure SQL Database, and Azure SQL Managed Instance, you can use either SQL Server Management Studio (SSMS) or Azure Data Studio (ADS). You can download SSMS at *https://learn.microsoft.com/en-us/sql/ssms*. You can download Azure Data Studio at *https://learn.microsoft.com/en-us/sql/azure-data-studio*.

Code Samples

Most of the chapters in this book include exercises that let you interactively try out new material learned in the main text. All source code, including exercises and solutions, can be downloaded from the following webpage:

MicrosoftPressStore.com/TSQLFund4e/downloads

Follow the instructions to download the TSQLFundamentalsYYYYMMDD.zip file, where *YYYYMMDD* reflects the last update date of the source code.

Refer to the appendix, "Getting started," for details about the source code.

Errata & Book Support

We've made every effort to ensure the accuracy of this book and its companion content. You can access updates to this book—in the form of a list of submitted errata and their related corrections—at:

MicrosoftPressStore.com/TSQLFund4e/errata

If you discover an error that is not already listed, please submit it to us at the same page.

For additional book support and information, please visit *MicrosoftPressStore.com/Support*

Please note that product support for Microsoft software and hardware is not offered through the previous addresses. For help with Microsoft software or hardware, go to *http://support.microsoft.com*.

Stay in Touch

Let's keep the conversation going! We're on Twitter: *http://twitter.com/MicrosoftPress*.

CHAPTER 1

Background to T-SQL querying and programming

Y ou're about to embark on a journey to a land that is like no other—a land that has its own set of laws. If reading this book is your first step in learning Transact-SQL (T-SQL), you should feel like Alice—just before she started her adventures in Wonderland. For me, the journey has not ended; instead, it's an ongoing path filled with new discoveries. I envy you; some of the most exciting discoveries are still ahead of you!

I've been involved with T-SQL for many years: teaching, speaking, writing, and consulting about it. T-SQL is more than just a language—it's a way of thinking. In my first few books about T-SQL, I've written extensively on advanced topics, and for years I have postponed writing about fundamentals. This is not because T-SQL fundamentals are simple or easy—in fact, it's just the opposite. The apparent simplicity of the language is misleading. I could explain the language syntax elements in a superficial manner and have you writing queries within minutes. But that approach would only hold you back in the long run and make it harder for you to understand the essence of the language.

Acting as your guide while you take your first steps in this realm is a big responsibility. I wanted to make sure that I spent enough time and effort exploring and understanding the language before writing about its fundamentals. T-SQL is deep; learning the fundamentals the right way involves much more than just understanding the syntax elements and coding a query that returns the right output. You need to forget what you know about other programming languages and start thinking in terms of T-SQL.

Theoretical background

SQL stands for *Structured Query Language*. SQL is a standard language that was designed to query and manage data in relational database management systems (RDBMSs). An RDBMS is a database management system based on the relational model (a semantic model for representing data), which in turn is based on two mathematical branches: set theory and predicate logic. Many other programming languages and various aspects of computing evolved pretty much as a result of intuition. In contrast, to the degree that SQL is based on the relational model, it is based on a firm foundation—applied mathematics. T-SQL thus sits on wide and solid shoulders. Microsoft provides T-SQL as a dialect of, or an extension to, SQL in SQL Server—its on-premises RDBMS flavor, and in Azure SQL and Azure Synapse Analytics—its cloud-based RDBMS flavors.

> **Note** The term *Azure SQL* collectively refers to three different cloud offerings: Azure SQL Database, Azure SQL Managed Instance, and SQL Server on Azure VM. I describe the differences between these offerings later in the chapter.

This section provides a brief theoretical background about SQL, set theory and predicate logic, the relational model, and types of database systems. Because this book is neither a mathematics book nor a design/data-modeling book, the theoretical information provided here is informal and by no means complete. The goals are to give you a context for the T-SQL language and to deliver the key points that are integral to correctly understanding T-SQL later in the book.

Language independence

The relational model is language independent. That is, you can apply data management and manipulation following the relational model's principles with languages other than SQL—for example, with C# in an object model. Today it is common to see RDBMSs that support languages other than just a dialect of SQL—for example, the integration of the CLR, Java, Python, and R in SQL Server, with which you can handle tasks that historically you handled mainly with SQL, such as data manipulation.

Also, you should realize from the start that SQL deviates from the relational model in several ways. Some even say that a new language—one that more closely follows the relational model—should replace SQL. But to date, SQL is the de facto language used by virtually all leading RDBMSs.

> **See Also** For details about the deviations of SQL from the relational model, as well as how to use SQL in a relational way, see this book on the topic: *SQL and Relational Theory: How to Write Accurate SQL Code, 3rd Edition,* by C. J. Date (O'Reilly Media, 2015).

SQL

SQL is both an ANSI and ISO standard language based on the relational model, designed for querying and managing data in an RDBMS.

In the early 1970s, IBM developed a language called SEQUEL (short for Structured English QUEry Language) for its RDBMS product called System R. The name of the language was later changed from SEQUEL to SQL because of a trademark dispute. SQL first became an ANSI standard in 1986, and then an ISO standard in 1987. Since 1986, the American National Standards Institute (ANSI) and the International Organization for Standardization (ISO) have been releasing revisions for the SQL standard every few years. So far, the following standards have been released: SQL-86 (1986), SQL-89 (1989), SQL-92

(1992), SQL:1999 (1999), SQL:2003 (2003), SQL:2006 (2006), SQL:2008 (2008), SQL:2011 (2011), and SQL:2016 (2016). The SQL standard is made of multiple parts. Part 1 provides the framework and Part 2 defines the foundation with the core SQL elements. The other parts define standard extensions, such as SQL for XML, SQL-Java integration, and others.

Interestingly, SQL resembles English and is also very logical. Unlike many programming languages, which use an imperative programming paradigm, SQL uses a declarative one. That is, SQL requires you to specify *what* you want to get and not *how* to get it, letting the RDBMS figure out the physical mechanics required to process your request.

SQL has several categories of statements, including data definition language (DDL), data manipulation language (DML), and data control language (DCL). DDL deals with object definitions and includes statements such as *CREATE, ALTER,* and *DROP*. DML allows you to query and modify data and includes statements such as *SELECT, INSERT, UPDATE, DELETE, TRUNCATE,* and *MERGE*. It's a common misunderstanding that DML includes only data-modification statements, but as I mentioned, it also includes *SELECT*. Another common misunderstanding is that *TRUNCATE* is a DDL statement, but in fact it is a DML statement. DCL deals with permissions and includes statements such as *GRANT* and *REVOKE*. This book focuses on DML.

T-SQL is based on standard SQL, but it also provides some nonstandard/proprietary extensions. Moreover, T-SQL does not implement all of standard SQL. When describing a language element for the first time, I'll typically mention if it's nonstandard.

Set theory

Set theory, which originated with the mathematician Georg Cantor, is one of the mathematical branches on which the relational model is based. Cantor's definition of a set follows:

> By a "set" we mean any collection M into a whole of definite, distinct objects m
> (which are called the "elements" of M) of our perception or of our thought.

—GEORG CANTOR: HIS
MATHEMATICS AND
PHILOSOPHY OF THE INFINITE,
BY JOSEPH W. DAUBEN
(PRINCETON UNIVERSITY
PRESS, 2020)

Every word in the definition has a deep and crucial meaning. The definitions of a set and set membership are axioms that are not supported by proofs. Each element belongs to a universe, and either is or is not a member of the set.

Let's start with the word *whole* in Cantor's definition. A set should be considered a single entity. Your focus should be on the collection of objects as opposed to the individual objects that make up the collection. Later on, when you write T-SQL queries against tables in a database (such as a table of employees), you should think of the set of employees as a whole rather than the individual employees.

This might sound trivial and simple enough, but apparently many programmers have difficulty adopting this way of thinking.

The word *distinct* means that every element of a set must be unique. Jumping ahead to tables in a database, you can enforce the uniqueness of rows in a table by defining key constraints. Without a key, you won't be able to uniquely identify rows, and therefore the table won't qualify as a set. Rather, the table would be a *multiset* or a *bag*.

The phrase *of our perception or of our thought* implies that the definition of a set is subjective. Consider a classroom: one person might perceive a set of people, whereas another might perceive a set of students and a set of teachers. Therefore, you have a substantial amount of freedom in defining sets. When you design a data model for your database, the design process should carefully consider the subjective needs of the application to determine adequate definitions for the entities involved.

As for the word *object*, the definition of a set is not restricted to physical objects, such as cars or employees, but rather is relevant to abstract objects as well, such as prime numbers or lines.

What Cantor's definition of a set leaves out is probably as important as what it includes. Notice that the definition doesn't mention any order among the set elements. The order in which set elements are listed is not important. The formal notation for listing set elements uses curly brackets: {a, b, c}. Because order has no relevance, you can express the same set as *{b, a, c}* or *{b, c, a}*. Jumping ahead to the set of attributes (*columns* in SQL) that make up the heading of a relation (*table* in SQL), an element (in this case, an attribute) is supposed to be identified by name—not by ordinal position.

Similarly, consider the set of tuples (*rows* in SQL) that make up the body of the relation; an element (in this case a tuple) is identified by its key values—not by position. Many programmers have a hard time adapting to the idea that, with respect to querying tables, there is no order among the rows. In other words, a query against a table can return table rows in *any order* unless you explicitly request that the data be ordered in a specific way, perhaps for presentation purposes.

Predicate logic

Predicate logic, whose roots go back to ancient Greece, is another branch of mathematics on which the relational model is based. Dr. Edgar F. Codd, in creating the relational model, had the insight to connect predicate logic to both the management and querying of data. Loosely speaking, a *predicate* is a property or an expression that either holds or doesn't hold—in other words, is either true or false. The relational model relies on predicates to maintain the logical integrity of the data and define its structure. One example of a predicate used to enforce integrity is a constraint defined in a table called *Employees* that allows only employees with a salary greater than zero to be stored in the table. The predicate is "salary greater than zero" (T-SQL expression: *salary > 0*).

You can also use predicates when filtering data to define subsets, and more. For example, if you need to query the *Employees* table and return only rows for employees from the sales department, you use the predicate "department equals sales" in your query filter (T-SQL expression: *department = 'sales'*).

In set theory, you can use predicates to define sets. This is helpful because you can't always define a set by listing all its elements (for example, infinite sets), and sometimes for brevity it's more convenient to define a set based on a property. As an example of an infinite set defined with a predicate, the set of all prime numbers can be defined with the following predicate: "*x* is a positive integer greater than 1 that is divisible only by 1 and itself." For any specified value, the predicate is either true or not true. The set of all prime numbers is the set of all elements for which the predicate is true. As an example of a finite set defined with a predicate, the set {0, 1, 2, 3, 4, 5, 6, 7, 8, 9} can be defined as the set of all elements for which the following predicate holds true: "*x* is an integer greater than or equal to 0 and smaller than or equal to 9."

The relational model

The relational model is a semantic model for data management and manipulation and is based on set theory and predicate logic. As mentioned earlier, it was created by Dr. Edgar F. Codd, and later explained and developed by Chris Date, Hugh Darwen, and others. The first version of the relational model was proposed by Codd in 1969 in an IBM research report called "Derivability, Redundancy, and Consistency of Relations Stored in Large Data Banks." A revised version was proposed by Codd in 1970 in a paper called "A Relational Model of Data for Large Shared Data Banks," published in the journal *Communications of the ACM.*

The goal of the relational model is to enable consistent representation of data with minimal or no redundancy and without sacrificing completeness, and to define data integrity (enforcement of data consistency) as part of the model. An RDBMS is supposed to implement the relational model and provide the means to store, manage, enforce the integrity of, and query data. The fact that the relational model is based on a strong mathematical foundation means that given a certain data-model instance (from which a physical database will later be generated), you can tell with certainty when a design is flawed, rather than relying solely on intuition.

The relational model involves concepts such as propositions, predicates, relations, tuples, attributes, and more. For nonmathematicians, these concepts can be quite intimidating. The sections that follow cover some key aspects of the model in an informal, nonmathematical manner and explain how they relate to databases.

Propositions, predicates, and relations

The common belief that the term *relational* stems from relationships between tables is incorrect. "Relational" actually pertains to the mathematical term *relation*. In set theory, a relation is a representation of a set. In the relational model, a relation is a set of related information, with the counterpart in SQL being a table—albeit not an exact counterpart. A key point in the relational model is that a single relation should represent a single set (for example, *Customers*). Note that operations on relations (based on relational algebra) result in a relation (for example, an intersection between two relations). This is what's known as the *closure* property of the relational algebra, and is what enables the nesting of relational expressions.

Figure 1-1 shows an illustration of a relation called Employees. It compares the components of a relation in relational theory with those of a table in SQL.

Employees relation/table

Relational Theory	SQL Counterparts
Relation	Table
set of attributes	set of columns
set of tuples	multiset of rows

PK

empid INT	firstname VARCHAR(40)	lastname VARCHAR(40)	hiredate DATE
5	Sven	Mortensen	10/17/2021
8	Maria	Cameron	3/5/2022
3	Judy	Lew	4/1/2020
2	Don	Funk	8/14/2020
6	Paul	Suurs	10/17/2021
9	Patricia	Doyle	11/15/2022
1	Sara	Davis	5/1/2020
4	Yael	Peled	5/3/2021
7	Russell	King	1/2/2022

Heading — the first row (empid, firstname, lastname, hiredate)

Body — the data rows

FIGURE 1-1 Illustration of Employees relation

Be aware that creating a truly adequate visual representation of a relation is very difficult in practice, since the set of attributes making the heading of a relation has no order, and the same goes for the set of tuples making the body of a relation. In an illustration, it might seem like those elements do have order even though they don't. Just make sure to keep this in mind.

When you design a data model for a database, you represent all data with relations (tables). You start by identifying propositions that you will need to represent in your database. A proposition is an assertion or a statement that must be true or false. For example, the statement, "Employee Jiru Ben-Gan was born on June 22, 2003, and works in the Pet Food department" is a proposition. If this proposition is true, it will manifest itself as a row in a table of *Employees*. A false proposition simply won't manifest itself. This presumption is known as the *closed-world assumption (CWA)*.

The next step is to formalize the propositions. You do this by taking out the actual data (the body of the relation) and defining the structure (the heading of the relation)—for example, by creating predicates out of propositions. You can think of predicates as parameterized propositions. The heading of a relation comprises a set of attributes. Note the use of the term "set"; in the relational model, attributes are unordered and distinct. An attribute has a name and a type name, and is identified by name. For example, the heading of an *Employees* relation might consist of the following attributes (expressed as pairs of attribute names and type names): *employeeid* integer, *firstname* character string, *lastname* character string, *birthdate* date, and *departmentid* integer.

A *type* is one of the most fundamental building blocks for relations. A type constrains an attribute to a certain set of possible or valid values. For example, the type *INT* is the set of all integers in the range –2,147,483,648 to 2,147,483,647. A type is one of the simplest forms of a predicate in a database because it restricts the attribute values that are allowed. For example, the database would not accept a proposition where an employee birth date is February 31, 2003 (not to mention a birth date stated as something like "abc!"). Note that types are not restricted to base types such as integers or dates; a type can also be an enumeration of possible values, such as an enumeration of possible job positions. A type can be simple or complex. Probably the best way to think of a type is as a class—encapsulated data and the behavior supporting it. An example of a complex type is a geometry type that supports polygons.

Missing values

There's an aspect of the relational model and SQL that is the source of many passionate debates. Whether to support the notion of missing values and three-valued predicate logic. That is, in two-valued predicate logic, a predicate is either true or false. If a predicate is not true, it must be false. Use of two-valued predicate logic follows a mathematical law called "the law of excluded middle." However, some support the idea of three-valued predicate logic, taking into account cases where values are missing. A predicate involving a missing value yields neither *true* nor *false* as the result truth value—it yields *unknown*.

Take, for example, a *mobilephone* attribute of an *Employees* relation. Suppose that a certain employee's mobile phone number is missing. How do you represent this fact in the database? One option is to have the *mobilephone* attribute allow the use of a special marker for a missing value. Then a predicate used for filtering purposes, comparing the *mobilephone* attribute with some specific number, will yield *unknown* for the case with the missing value. Three-valued predicate logic refers to the three possible truth values that can result from a predicate—*true*, *false*, and *unknown*.

Some people believe that *NULLs* and three-valued predicate logic are nonrelational, whereas others believe that they are relational. Codd actually advocated for four-valued predicate logic, saying that there were two different cases of missing values: missing but applicable (A-Values marker), and missing but inapplicable (I-Values marker). An example of "missing but applicable" is when an employee has a mobile phone, but you don't know what the mobile phone number is. An example of "missing but inapplicable" is when an employee doesn't have a mobile phone at all. According to Codd, two special markers should be used to support these two cases of missing values. SQL doesn't make a distinction between the two cases for missing values that Codd does; rather, it defines the *NULL* marker to signify any kind of missing value. It also supports three-valued predicate logic. Support for *NULLs* and three-valued predicate logic in SQL is the source of a great deal of confusion and complexity, though one can argue that missing values are part of reality. In addition, the alternative—using only two-valued predicate logic and representing missing values with your own custom means—is not necessarily less problematic.

> **Note** As mentioned, a *NULL* is not a value but rather a marker for a missing value. Therefore, though unfortunately it's common, the use of the terminology *"NULL value"* is incorrect. The correct terminology is *"NULL marker"* or just *"NULL."* In the book, I typically use the latter because it's more common in the SQL community.

Constraints

One of the greatest benefits of the relational model is the ability to define data integrity as part of the model. Data integrity is achieved through rules called *constraints* that are defined in the data model and enforced by the RDBMS. The simplest methods of enforcing integrity are assigning an attribute type and "nullability" (whether it supports or doesn't support *NULLs*). Constraints are also enforced through the model itself; for example, the relation *Orders(orderid, orderdate, duedate, shipdate)* allows three distinct dates per order, whereas the relations *Employees(empid)* and *EmployeeChildren(empid, childname)* allow zero to countable infinity children per employee.

Other examples of constraints include the enforcement of *candidate keys,* which provide entity integrity, and *foreign keys,* which provide referential integrity. A candidate key is a key defined on one or more attributes of a relation. Based on a candidate key's attribute values you can uniquely identify a tuple (row). A constraint enforcing a candidate key prevents duplicates. You can identify multiple candidate keys in a relation. For example, in an *Employees* relation, you can have one candidate key based on *employeeid*, another on *SSN* (Social Security number), and others. Typically, you arbitrarily choose one of the candidate keys as the *primary key* (for example, *employeeid* in the *Employees* relation) and use that as the preferred way to identify a row. All other candidate keys are known as *alternate keys.*

Foreign keys are used to enforce referential integrity. A foreign key is defined on one or more attributes of a relation (known as the *referencing relation*) and references a candidate key in another (or possibly the same) relation. This constraint restricts the values in the referencing relation's foreign-key attributes to the values that appear in the referenced relation's candidate-key attributes. For example, suppose that the *Employees* relation has a foreign key defined on the attribute *departmentid*, which references the primary-key attribute *departmentid* in the *Departments* relation. This means that the values in *Employees.departmentid* are restricted to the values that appear in *Departments.departmentid.*

Normalization

The relational model also defines *normalization rules* (also known as *normal forms*). Normalization is a formal mathematical process to guarantee that each entity will be represented by a single relation. In a normalized database, you avoid anomalies during data modification and keep redundancy to a minimum without sacrificing completeness. If you follow entity relationship modeling (ERM) and represent each entity and its attributes, you probably won't need normalization; instead, you will apply normalization only to reinforce and ensure that the model is correct. You can find the definition of ERM in the following Wikipedia article: *https://en.wikipedia.org/wiki/Entity–relationship_model.*

The following sections briefly cover the first three normal forms (1NF, 2NF, and 3NF) introduced by Codd.

1NF

The first normal form says that the tuples (rows) in the relation (table) must be unique and attributes should be atomic. This is a redundant definition of a relation; in other words, if a table truly represents a relation, it is already in first normal form.

You enforce the uniqueness of rows in SQL by defining a primary key or unique constraint in the table.

You can operate on attributes only with operations that are defined as part of the attribute's type. Atomicity of attributes is subjective in the same way that the definition of a set is subjective. As an example, should an employee name in an *Employees* relation be expressed with one attribute (*fullname*), two attributes (*firstname* and *lastname*), or three attributes (*firstname*, *middlename*, and *lastname*)? The answer depends on the application. If the application needs to manipulate the parts of the employee's name separately (such as for search purposes), it makes sense to break them apart; otherwise, it doesn't.

In the same way that an attribute might not be atomic enough based on the needs of the applications that use it, an attribute might also be subatomic. For example, if an address attribute is considered atomic for the applications that use it, not including the city as part of the address would violate the first normal form.

This normal form is often misunderstood. Some people think that an attempt to mimic arrays violates the first normal form. An example would be defining a *YearlySales* relation with the following attributes: *salesperson*, *qty2020*, *qty2021*, and *qty2022*. However, in this example, you don't really violate the first normal form; you simply impose a constraint—restricting the data to three specific years: 2020, 2021, and 2022.

2NF

The second normal form involves two rules. One rule is that the data must meet the first normal form. The other rule addresses the relationship between nonkey and candidate-key attributes. For every candidate key, every nonkey attribute has to be fully functionally dependent on the entire candidate key. In other words, a nonkey attribute cannot be fully functionally dependent on part of a candidate key. To put it more informally, if you need to obtain any nonkey attribute value, you need to provide the values of all attributes of a candidate key from the same tuple. You can find any value of any attribute of any tuple if you know all the attribute values of a candidate key.

As an example of violating the second normal form, suppose that you define a relation called *Orders* that represents information about orders and order lines. (See Figure 1-2.) The *Orders* relation contains the following attributes: *orderid*, *productid*, *orderdate*, *qty*, *customerid*, and *companyname*. The primary key is defined on *orderid* and *productid*.

Orders	
PK	**orderid**
PK	**productid**
	orderdate
	qty
	customerid
	companyname

FIGURE 1-2 Data model before applying 2NF

The second normal form is violated in Figure 1-2 because there are nonkey attributes that depend on only part of a candidate key (the primary key, in this example). For example, you can find the *orderdate* of an order, as well as *customerid* and *companyname*, based on the *orderid* alone.

To conform to the second normal form, you would need to split your original relation into two relations: *Orders* and *OrderDetails* (as shown in Figure 1-3). The *Orders* relation would include the attributes *orderid*, *orderdate*, *customerid*, and *companyname*, with the primary key defined on *orderid*. The *OrderDetails* relation would include the attributes *orderid*, *productid*, and *qty*, with the primary key defined on *orderid* and *productid*.

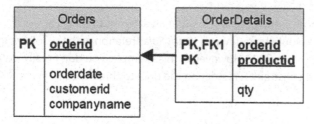

FIGURE 1-3 Data model after applying 2NF and before 3NF

3NF

The third normal form also has two rules. The data must meet the second normal form. Also, all nonkey attributes must be dependent on candidate keys nontransitively. Informally, this rule means that all nonkey attributes must be mutually independent. In other words, one nonkey attribute cannot be dependent on another nonkey attribute.

The *Orders* and *OrderDetails* relations described previously now conform to the second normal form. Remember that the *Orders* relation at this point contains the attributes *orderid*, *orderdate*, *customerid*, and *companyname*, with the primary key defined on *orderid*. Both *customerid* and *companyname* depend on the whole primary key—*orderid*. For example, you need the entire primary key to find the *customerid* representing the customer who placed the order. Similarly, you need the whole primary key to find the company name of the customer who placed the order. However, *customerid* and *companyname* are also dependent on each other. To meet the third normal form, you need to add a *Customers* relation (shown in Figure 1-4) with the attributes *customerid* (as the primary key) and *companyname*. Then you can remove the *companyname* attribute from the *Orders* relation.

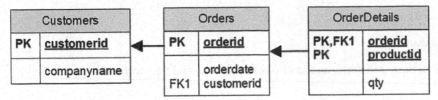

FIGURE 1-4 Data model after applying 3NF

Informally, 2NF and 3NF are commonly summarized as follows: "Every non-key attribute is dependent on the key, the whole key, and nothing but the key—so help me Codd."

There are higher normal forms beyond Codd's original first three normal forms that involve compound primary keys and temporal databases, but they are outside the scope of this book.

> **Note** SQL, as well as T-SQL, permits violating all the normal forms in real tables. It's the data modeler's prerogative and responsibility to design a normalized model.

Types of database workloads

Two main types of workloads use Microsoft RDBMS platforms and T-SQL to manage and manipulate the data: online transactional processing (OLTP) and data warehouses (DWs). The former can be implemented on SQL Server or Azure SQL. The latter can be implemented on SQL Server or Azure SQL, which use a symmetric multiprocessing (SMP) architecture; or, for more demanding workloads, on Synapse Azure Analytics, which uses a massively parallel processing (MPP) architecture. Figure 1-5 illustrates those workloads and systems and the transformation process that usually takes place between them.

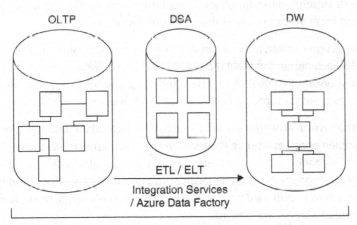

FIGURE 1-5 Classes of database systems

Here's a quick description of what each acronym represents:

- OLTP: online transactional processing

- DSA: data-staging area

- DW: data warehouse

- ETL / ELT: extract, transform, and load; or extract, load, and transform

Online transactional processing

Data is entered initially into an online transactional processing system. The primary focus of an OLTP system is data entry and not reporting—transactions mainly insert, update, and delete data. The relational model is targeted primarily at OLTP systems, where a normalized model provides both good performance for data entry and data consistency. In a normalized environment, each table represents a single entity and keeps redundancy to a minimum. When you need to modify a fact, you need to modify it in only one place. This results in optimized performance for data modifications and little chance for error.

However, an OLTP environment is not suitable for reporting purposes, because a normalized model usually involves many tables (one for each entity) with complex relationships. Even simple reports require joining many tables, resulting in complex and poorly performing queries.

You can implement an OLTP database in SQL Server or Azure SQL and both manage it and query it with T-SQL.

Data warehouses

A *data warehouse* (DW) is an environment designed for data-retrieval and reporting purposes. When it serves an entire organization, such an environment is called a *data warehouse*; when it serves only part of the organization (such as a specific department) or a subject matter area in the organization, it is called a *data mart*. The data model of a data warehouse is designed and optimized mainly to support data-retrieval needs. The model has intentional redundancy, fewer tables, and simpler relationships, ultimately resulting in simpler and more efficient queries than an OLTP environment.

The simplest data-warehouse design is called a *star schema*. The star schema includes several dimension tables and a fact table. Each dimension table represents a subject by which you want to analyze the data. For example, in a system that deals with orders and sales, you will probably want to analyze data by dimensions such as customers, products, employees, and time.

In a star schema, each dimension is implemented as a single table with redundant data. For example, a product dimension could be implemented as a single *ProductDim* table instead of three normalized tables: *Products*, *ProductSubCategories*, and *ProductCategories*. If you normalize a dimension table, which results in multiple tables representing that dimension, you get what's known as a *snowflake dimension*. A schema that contains snowflake dimensions is known as a *snowflake schema*. A star schema is considered a special case of a snowflake schema.

The fact table holds the facts and measures, such as quantity and value, for each relevant combination of dimension keys. For example, for each relevant combination of customer, product, employee, and day, the fact table would have a row containing the quantity and value. Note that data in a data warehouse is typically preaggregated to a certain level of granularity (such as a day), unlike data in an OLTP environment, which is usually recorded at the transaction level.

Historically, early versions of SQL Server mainly targeted OLTP environments, but eventually SQL Server also started targeting data-warehouse systems and data-analysis needs. You can implement a data warehouse in SQL Server or Azure SQL, which use a SMP architecture. You can implement a more demanding workload on Azure Synapse Analytics, which uses a MPP architecture. In any case, you query and manage the data warehouse with T-SQL.

The process that pulls data from source systems (OLTP and others), manipulates it, and loads it into the data warehouse is called *extract, transform, and load*, or *ETL*. Some of the integration solutions—especially cloud-based—extract the data, load it, and then transform it. In such a case, the process is known by the acronym *ELT*. Microsoft provides an on-premises tool called Microsoft SQL Server Integration Services (SSIS) to handle ETL/ELT needs, which comes with a SQL Server license. Microsoft also provides a serverless cloud service for ETL/ELT solutions called Azure Data Factory.

Often the ETL/ELT process will involve the use of a data-staging area (DSA) between the OLTP and the DW. The DSA can reside in a relational database, such as SQL Server or Azure SQL, or in Azure Data Lake Storage Gen2, and is used as the data-cleansing area.

SQL Server architecture

This section will introduce you to the SQL Server architecture, the on-premises and cloud RDBMS flavors that Microsoft offers, the entities involved—SQL Server Instances, databases, schemas, and database objects—and the purpose of each entity.

On-premises and cloud RDBMS flavors

Initially, Microsoft offered mainly one enterprise-level RDBMS—an on-premises flavor called Microsoft SQL Server. These days, Microsoft offers an overwhelming plethora of options as part of its data platform, which constantly keeps evolving. Within its data platform, Microsoft offers both on-premises, or box, solutions, and service-based cloud solutions.

On-premises

The on-premises RDBMS flavor that Microsoft offers is called Microsoft SQL Server, or just SQL Server. This is the traditional flavor, usually installed on the customer's premises. The customer is responsible for everything—getting the hardware, installing the software, patching, high availability and disaster recovery, security, and everything else.

The customer can install multiple instances of the product on the same server (more on this in the next section) and can write queries that interact with multiple databases. It is also possible to switch the connection between databases, unless one of them is a contained database (defined later).

The querying language used is T-SQL. You can run all the code samples and exercises in this book on an on-premises SQL Server implementation, if you want. See the Appendix for details about obtaining and installing SQL Server, as well as creating the sample database.

Cloud

Cloud computing provides compute and storage resources on demand from a shared pool of resources. Microsoft's RDBMS technologies can be provided both as private-cloud and public-cloud services. A *private cloud* is cloud infrastructure that services a single organization and usually uses virtualization technology. It's typically hosted locally at the customer site, and maintained by the IT group in the organization. It's about self-service agility, allowing the users to deploy resources on demand. It provides standardization and usage metering. The database engine is usually an on-premises engine, where T-SQL is used to manage and manipulate the data. SQL Server can run on either Windows or Linux, and therefore can be deployed on any private cloud, no matter the underlying OS platform.

As for the public cloud, the services are provided over the network and available to the public. Microsoft provides two forms of public RDBMS cloud services: infrastructure as a service (IaaS) and platform as a service (PaaS). With IaaS, you provision a virtual machine (VM) that resides in Microsoft's cloud infrastructure. This offering is known as SQL Server on Azure VM. As a starting point, you can choose between several preconfigured VMs that already have a certain version and edition of SQL Server installed on them, and follow best practices. The hardware is maintained by Microsoft, but you're responsible for maintaining and patching the software. It's essentially like maintaining your own SQL Server installation—one that happens to reside on Microsoft's hardware.

With PaaS, Microsoft provides the database cloud platform as a service. It's hosted in Microsoft's data centers. Hardware, software installation and maintenance, high availability and disaster recovery, and patching are all responsibilities of Microsoft. The customer is still responsible for index and query tuning, however.

Microsoft provides a number of PaaS database offerings. For OLTP systems as well as SMP-based data warehouses, it offers Azure SQL Database and Azure SQL Managed Instance. You can find a detailed comparison between these two PaaS offerings here: *https://learn.microsoft.com/en-us/azure/azure-sql/database/features-comparison*. You will find that, for example, with the former you cannot perform cross-database/three-part name queries and with the latter you can, as well as other differences. Generally, the latter gives you closer parity with the on-premises flavor.

As mentioned, Microsoft uses the term *Azure SQL* to collectively refer to the three SMP-based cloud offerings: SQL Server on Azure VM, Azure SQL Database, and Azure SQL Managed Instance.

Note that Azure SQL Database and Azure SQL Managed Instance share the same code base with the latest version of SQL Server. So most of the T-SQL language surface is the same in both the on-premises and cloud environments. Therefore, most of the T-SQL you'll learn about in this book is applicable to both environments. You can read about the differences that do exist—especially between SQL Server and Azure SQL Database—here: *https://learn.microsoft.com/en-us/azure/azure-sql/database/transact-sql-tsql-differences-sql-server*. You should also note that the update and deployment rate of the cloud flavors are faster than that of the on-premises SQL Server product. Therefore, some T-SQL features might be exposed in the cloud first before they show up in the on-premises product.

As mentioned, Microsoft also provides a MPP-based PaaS offering called Azure Synapse Analytics as a cloud native data warehousing solution, with a distributed processing engine, that you query and manage with T-SQL.

SQL Server instances

In the on-premises product, an instance of SQL Server, as illustrated in Figure 1-6, is an installation of a SQL Server database engine or service. You can install multiple instances of SQL Server on the same computer. Each instance is completely independent of the others in terms of security and the data that it manages, and in all other respects. At the logical level, two different instances residing on the same computer have no more in common than two instances residing on two separate computers. Of course, same-computer instances do share the server's physical resources, such as CPU, memory, and disk.

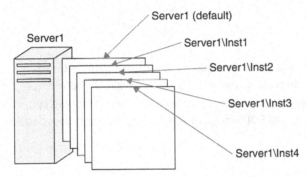

Server1 (default)

Server1

Server1\Inst1

Server1\Inst2

Server1\Inst3

Server1\Inst4

FIGURE 1-6 Multiple instances of SQL Server on the same computer

You can set up one of the multiple instances on a computer as the *default instance*, whereas all others must be *named instances*. You determine whether an instance is the default or a named one upon installation; you cannot change that decision later. To connect to a default instance, a client application needs to specify the computer's name or IP address. To connect to a named instance, the client needs to specify the computer's name or IP address, followed by a backslash (\), followed by the instance name (as provided upon installation). For example, suppose you have two instances of SQL Server installed on a computer called *Server1*. One of these instances was installed as the default instance, and the other was installed as a named instance called *Inst1*. To connect to the default instance, you need to specify only *Server1* as the server name. To connect to the named instance, you need to specify both the server and the instance name: *Server1\Inst1*.

There are various reasons why you might want to install multiple instances of SQL Server on the same computer, but I'll mention a couple of them here. One reason, mainly historic, is to save on support costs. For example, to test the functionality of features in response to support calls or reproduce errors that users encounter in the production environment, the support department needs local installations of SQL Server that mimic the user's production environment in terms of version, edition, and service pack of SQL Server. If an organization has multiple user environments, the support department needs multiple installations of SQL Server. Rather than having multiple computers, each hosting a different installation of SQL Server that must be supported separately, the support department can have one computer with multiple installed instances. Of course, nowadays you can meet the same needs with container or virtualization technologies. It's just that SQL Server instances were available before virtualization and container technologies took off.

As another example, consider people like me who teach and lecture about SQL Server. For us, it is convenient to be able to install multiple instances of SQL Server on the same laptop. This way, we can perform demonstrations against different versions of the product, showing differences in behavior between versions, and so on.

As a final example, also mainly historic, providers of database services sometimes need to guarantee their customers complete security separation of their data from other customers' data. At least in the past, the database provider could have a very powerful data center hosting multiple instances of SQL Server, rather than needing to maintain multiple less-powerful computers, each hosting a different instance. Nowadays, cloud solutions and advanced container and virtualization technologies make it possible to achieve similar goals.

Databases

You can think of a database as a container of objects such as tables, views, stored procedures, and other objects. Each instance of SQL Server can contain multiple databases, as illustrated in Figure 1-7. When you install SQL Server, the setup program creates several system databases that hold system data and serve internal purposes. After you install SQL Server, you can create your own user databases that will hold application data.

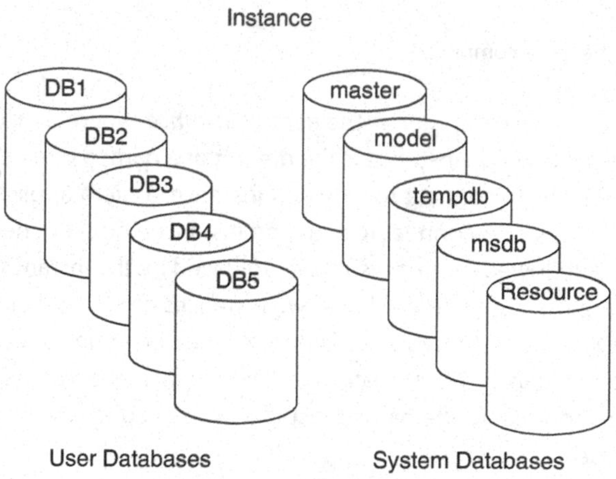

FIGURE 1-7 An example of multiple databases on a SQL Server instance

The system databases that the setup program creates include *master*, *msdb*, *model*, *tempdb*, and *Resource*. A description of each follows:

- **master** The *master* database holds instance-wide metadata information, the server configuration, information about all databases in the instance, and initialization information.

- **model** The *model* database is used as a template for new databases. Every new database you create is initially created as a copy of *model*. So if you want certain objects (such as user-defined data types) to appear in all new databases you create, or certain database properties to be configured in a certain way in all new databases, you need to create those objects and configure those properties in the *model* database. Note that changes you apply to the *model* database will not affect existing databases—only new databases you create in the future.

- **tempdb**   The *tempdb* database is where SQL Server stores temporary data such as work tables, sort and hash table data when it needs to persist those, row versioning information, and so on. SQL Server allows you to create temporary tables for your own use, and the physical location of those is in *tempdb*. Note that this database is destroyed and re-created as a copy of the *model* database every time you restart the instance of SQL Server.

- **msdb**   The *msdb* database is used mainly by a service called SQL Server Agent to store its data. SQL Server Agent is in charge of automation, which includes entities such as jobs, schedules, and alerts. SQL Server Agent is also the service in charge of replication. The *msdb* database also holds information related to other SQL Server features, such as Database Mail, Service Broker, backups, and more.

- **Resource**   The *Resource* database is a hidden, read-only database that holds the definitions of all system objects. When you query system objects in a database, they appear to reside in the *sys* schema of the local database, but in actuality their definitions reside in the *Resource* database.

In SQL Server and Azure SQL Managed Instance, you can connect directly to the system databases *master*, *model*, *tempdb*, and *msdb*. In Azure SQL Database, you can connect directly only to the system database *master*. If you create temporary tables or declare table variables (more on this topic in Chapter 12, "Programmable objects"), they are created in *tempdb*, but you cannot connect directly to *tempdb* and explicitly create user objects there.

You can create multiple user databases (up to 32,767) within an instance. A user database holds objects and data for an application.

You can define a property called *collation* at the database level that will determine default language support, case sensitivity, and sort order for character data in that database. If you do not specify a collation for the database when you create it, the new database will use the default collation of the instance (chosen upon installation).

To run T-SQL code against a database, a client application needs to connect to a SQL Server instance and be in the context of, or use, the relevant database. The application can still access objects from other databases by adding the database name as a prefix. That's the case with both SQL Server and Azure SQL Managed Instance. Azure SQL Database does not support cross-database/three-part name queries.

In terms of security, to be able to connect to a SQL Server instance, the database administrator (DBA) must create a *login* for you. The login can be tied to your Microsoft Windows credentials, in which case it is called a *Windows authenticated login*. With a Windows authenticated login, you can't provide login and password information when connecting to SQL Server, because you already provided those when you logged on to Windows. The login can be independent of your Windows credentials, in which case it's called a *SQL Server authenticated login*. When connecting to SQL Server using a SQL Server authenticated login, you will need to provide both a login name and a password.

The DBA needs to map your login to a *database user* in each database you are supposed to have access to. The database user is the entity that is granted permissions to objects in the database.

SQL Server supports a feature called *contained databases* that breaks the connection between a database user and an instance-level login. The user (Windows or SQL authenticated) is fully contained within the specific database and is not tied to a login at the instance level. When connecting to SQL Server, the user needs to specify the database he or she is connecting to, and the user cannot subsequently switch to other user databases.

So far, I've mainly mentioned the logical aspects of databases. If you're using Azure SQL Database or Azure SQL Managed Instance, your only concern is that logical layer. You do not deal with the physical layout of the database's data and log files, *tempdb*, and so on. But if you're using SQL Server (including SQL Server on Azure VM), you are responsible for the physical layer as well. Figure 1-8 shows a diagram of the physical database layout.

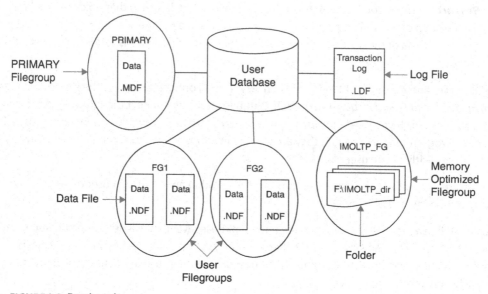

FIGURE 1-8 Database layout

The database is made up of data files, transaction log files, and optionally checkpoint files holding memory-optimized data (part of a feature called *In-Memory OLTP*, which I describe shortly). When you create a database, you can define various properties for data and log files, including the file name, location, initial size, maximum size, and an autogrowth increment. Each database must have at least one data file and at least one log file (the default in SQL Server). The data files hold object data, and the log files hold information that SQL Server needs to maintain transactions.

Although SQL Server can write to multiple data files in parallel, it can write to only one log file at a time, in a sequential manner. Therefore, unlike with data files, having multiple log files does not result in a performance benefit. You might need to add log files if the disk drive where the log resides runs out of space.

Data files are organized in logical groups called *filegroups*. A filegroup is the target for creating an object, such as a table or an index. The object data will be spread across the files that belong to the target filegroup. Filegroups are your way of controlling the physical locations of your objects. A database must have at least one filegroup called *PRIMARY*, and it can optionally have other user filegroups as well. The *PRIMARY* filegroup contains the primary data file (which has an .mdf extension) for the database, and the database's system catalog. You can optionally add secondary data files (which have an .ndf extension) to *PRIMARY*. User filegroups contain only secondary data files. You can decide which filegroup is marked as the default filegroup. Objects are created in the default filegroup when the object creation statement does not explicitly specify a different target filegroup.

File extensions .mdf, .ldf, and .ndf

The database file extensions .mdf and .ldf are straightforward. The extension *.mdf* stands for *Master Data File* (not to be confused with the *master* database), and *.ldf* stands for *Log Data File*. According to one anecdote, when discussing the extension for the secondary data files, one of the developers suggested, humorously, using .ndf to represent "Not Master Data File," and the idea was accepted.

The SQL Server database engine includes a memory-optimized engine called In-Memory OLTP. You can use this feature to integrate memory-optimized objects, such as memory-optimized tables and natively compiled modules (procedures, functions, and triggers), into your database. To do so, you need to create a filegroup in the database marked as containing memory-optimized data and, within it, at least one path to a folder. SQL Server stores checkpoint files with memory-optimized data in that folder, and it uses those to recover the data every time SQL Server is restarted.

Schemas and objects

When I said earlier that a database is a container of objects, I simplified things a bit. As illustrated in Figure 1-9, a database contains schemas, and schemas contain objects. You can think of a schema as a container of objects, such as tables, views, stored procedures, and others.

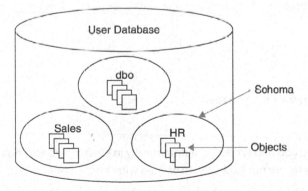

FIGURE 1-9 A database, schemas, and database objects

You can control permissions at the schema level. For example, you can grant a user SELECT permissions on a schema, allowing the user to query data from all objects in that schema. So security is one of the considerations for determining how to arrange objects in schemas.

The schema is also a namespace—it is used as a prefix to the object name. For example, suppose you have a table named *Orders* in a schema named *Sales*. The schema-qualified object name (also known as the *two-part object name*) is *Sales.Orders*. You can refer to objects in other databases by adding the database name as a prefix (*three-part object name*), and to objects in other instances by adding the instance name as a prefix (*four-part object name*). If you omit the schema name when referring to an object, SQL Server will apply a process to resolve the schema name, such as checking whether the object exists in the user's default schema and, if the object doesn't exist, checking whether it exists in the *dbo* schema. Microsoft recommends that when you refer to objects in your code you always use the two-part object names. If multiple objects with the same name exist in different schemas, you might end up getting a different object than the one you wanted.

Creating tables and defining data integrity

This section describes the fundamentals of creating tables and defining data integrity using T-SQL. Feel free to run the included code samples in your environment.

> ## More Info
>
> If you don't know yet how to run code against SQL Server, the Appendix will help you get started.

As mentioned earlier, DML rather than DDL is the focus of this book. Still, you need to understand how to create tables and define data integrity. I won't go into great detail here, but I'll provide a brief description of the essentials.

Before you look at the code for creating a table, remember that tables reside within schemas, and schemas reside within databases. The examples use the book's sample database, *TSQLV6*, and a schema called *dbo*.

> ## More Info
>
> See the Appendix for details on creating the sample database.

The examples here use a schema named *dbo* that is created automatically in every database and is also used as the default schema for users who are not explicitly associated with a different schema.

Creating tables

The following code creates a table named *Employees* in the *dbo* schema in the *TSQLV6* database:

```
USE TSQLV6;

DROP TABLE IF EXISTS dbo.Employees;

CREATE TABLE dbo.Employees
(
  empid     INT         NOT NULL,
  firstname VARCHAR(30) NOT NULL,
  lastname  VARCHAR(30) NOT NULL,
  hiredate  DATE        NOT NULL,
  mgrid     INT         NULL,
  ssn       VARCHAR(20) NOT NULL,
  salary    MONEY       NOT NULL
);
```

The *USE* statement sets the current database context to that of *TSQLV6*. It is important to incorporate the *USE* statement in scripts that create objects to ensure that SQL Server creates the objects in the specified database. In SQL Server and Azure SQL Managed Instance, the *USE* statement can actually change the database context from one to another. In Azure SQL Database, you cannot switch between different databases, but the *USE* statement will not fail as long as you are already connected to the target database. So even in Azure SQL Database, I recommend having the *USE* statement to ensure that you are connected to the right database when creating your objects.

The *DROP TABLE IF EXISTS* statement (aka DIE) drops the *Employees* table if it already exists in the current database. Of course, you can choose a different treatment, such as not creating the object if it already exists.

You use the *CREATE TABLE* statement to define a table. You specify the name of the table and, in parentheses, the definition of its attributes (columns).

Notice the use of the two-part name *dbo.Employees* for the table name, as recommended earlier. If you omit the schema name, for ad-hoc queries SQL Server will assume the default schema associated with the database user running the code. For queries in stored procedures, SQL Server will assume the schema associated with the procedure's owner.

For each attribute, you specify the attribute name, data type, and whether the value can be *NULL* (which is called *nullability*).

In the *Employees* table, the attributes *empid* (employee ID) and *mgrid* (manager ID) are each defined with the *INT* (four-byte integer) data type; the *firstname*, *lastname*, and *ssn* (US Social Security number) are defined as *VARCHAR* (variable-length character string with the specified maximum supported number of characters); *hiredate* is defined as *DATE* and *salary* is defined as *MONEY*.

If you don't explicitly specify whether a column allows or disallows *NULLs*, SQL Server will have to rely on defaults. Standard SQL dictates that when a column's nullability is not specified, the assumption should be *NULL* (allowing *NULLs*), but SQL Server has settings that can change that behavior. I recommend that you be explicit and not rely on defaults. Also, I recommend defining a column as *NOT NULL* unless you have a compelling reason to support *NULLs*. If a column is not supposed to allow *NULLs* and you don't enforce this with a *NOT NULL* constraint, you can rest assured that *NULLs* will occur. In the *Employees* table, all columns are defined as *NOT NULL* except for the *mgrid* column. A *NULL* in the *mgrid* column would represent the fact that the employee has no manager, as in the case of the CEO of the organization.

Coding style

You should be aware of a few general notes regarding coding style, the use of white spaces (space, tab, new line, and so on), and semicolons. My advice is that you use a style that you and your fellow developers feel comfortable with. What ultimately matters most is the consistency, readability, and maintainability of your code. I have tried to reflect these aspects in my code throughout the book.

T-SQL lets you use white spaces quite freely in your code. You can take advantage of white spaces to facilitate readability. For example, I could have written the code in the previous section as a single line. However, the code wouldn't have been as readable as when it is broken into multiple lines that use indentation.

The practice of using a semicolon to terminate statements is standard and, in fact, is a requirement in several other database platforms. T-SQL requires the semicolon only in particular cases—but in cases where it's not required, it's still allowed. I recommend that you adopt the practice of terminating all statements with a semicolon. Not only will doing this improve the readability of your code, but in some cases it can save you some grief. (When a semicolon is required and is *not* specified, the error message SQL Server produces is not always clear.)

Note The SQL Server documentation indicates that not terminating T-SQL statements with a semicolon is a deprecated feature. That's one more reason to get into the habit of terminating all your statements with a semicolon, even where it's currently not required.

Defining data integrity

As mentioned earlier, one of the great benefits of the relational model is that data integrity is an integral part of it. Data integrity enforced as part of the model—namely, as part of the table definitions—is considered *declarative data integrity*. Data integrity enforced with code—such as with stored procedures or triggers—is considered *procedural data integrity*.

Data type and nullability choices for attributes and even the data model itself are examples of declarative data integrity constraints. In this section, I describe other examples of declarative constraints: primary key, unique, foreign key, check, and default constraints. You can define such constraints when creating a table as part of the *CREATE TABLE* statement, or you can define them for already created tables by using an *ALTER TABLE* statement. All types of constraints except for default constraints can be defined as *composite constraints*—that is, based on more than one attribute.

Primary key constraints

A primary key constraint enforces the uniqueness of rows and also disallows *NULLs* in the constraint attributes. Each unique combination of values in the constraint attributes can appear only once in the table—in other words, only in one row. An attempt to define a primary key constraint on a column that allows *NULLs* will be rejected by the RDBMS. Each table can have only one primary key.

Here's an example of defining a primary key constraint on the *empid* attribute in the *Employees* table that you created earlier:

```
ALTER TABLE dbo.Employees
  ADD CONSTRAINT PK_Employees
  PRIMARY KEY(empid);
```

With this primary key in place, you can be assured that all *empid* values will be unique and known. An attempt to insert or update a row such that the constraint would be violated will be rejected by the RDBMS and result in an error.

To enforce the uniqueness of the logical primary key constraint, SQL Server will create a unique index behind the scenes. A *unique index* is a physical object used by SQL Server to enforce uniqueness. Indexes (not necessarily unique ones) are also used to speed up queries by avoiding sorting and unnecessary full table scans (similar to indexes in books).

Unique constraints

A unique constraint enforces the uniqueness of rows, allowing you to implement the concept of alternate keys from the relational model in your database. Unlike with primary keys, you can define multiple unique constraints within the same table. Also, a unique constraint is not restricted to columns defined as *NOT NULL*. More on the specifics of *NULL*-handling shortly.

The following code defines a unique constraint on the *ssn* column in the *Employees* table:

```
ALTER TABLE dbo.Employees
  ADD CONSTRATNT UNQ_Employees_ssn
  UNIQUE(ssn);
```

As with a primary key constraint, SQL Server will create a unique index behind the scenes as the physical mechanism to enforce the logical unique constraint.

For the purpose of enforcing a unique constraint, SQL Server handles *NULLs* just like non-*NULL* values. Consequently, for example, a single-column unique constraint allows only one *NULL* in the constrained column. However, the SQL standard defines *NULL*-handling by a unique constraint differently, like so: *"A unique constraint on T is satisfied if and only if there do not exist two rows R1 and R2 of T such that R1 and R2 have the same non-NULL values in the unique columns."* In other words, only the non-*NULL* values are compared to determine whether duplicates exist. Consequently, a standard single-column unique constraint would allow multiple *NULLs* in the constrained column. To emulate a standard single-column unique constraint in SQL Server you can use a unique filtered index that filters only non-*NULL* values. For example, suppose that the column *ssn* allowed *NULLs,* and you wanted to create such an index instead of a unique constraint. You would have used the following code:

```
CREATE UNIQUE INDEX idx_ssn_notnull ON dbo.Employees(ssn) WHERE ssn IS NOT NULL;
```

The index is defined as a unique one, and the filter excludes *NULLs* from the index, so duplicate *NULLs* will be allowed in the underlying table, whereas duplicate non-*NULL* values won't be allowed.

Emulating a standard composite unique constraint in SQL Server is a bit more involved and may not be of common knowledge. You can find the details in the following article: *https://sqlperformance. com/2020/03/t-sql-queries/null-complexities-part-4-missing-standard-unique-constraint.*

Foreign key constraints

A foreign key enforces referential integrity. This constraint is defined on one or more attributes in what's called the *referencing* table and points to candidate key (primary key or unique constraint) attributes in what's called the *referenced* table. Note that the referencing and referenced tables can be one and the same. The foreign key's purpose is to restrict the values allowed in the foreign key columns to those that exist in the referenced columns.

The following code creates a table called *Orders* with a primary key defined on the *orderid* column:

```
DROP TABLE IF EXISTS dbo.Orders;

CREATE TABLE dbo.Orders
(
  orderid   INT         NOT NULL,
  empid     INT         NOT NULL,
  custid    VARCHAR(10) NOT NULL,
  orderts   DATETIME2   NOT NULL,
  qty       INT         NOT NULL,
  CONSTRAINT PK_Orders
    PRIMARY KEY(orderid)
);
```

Suppose you want to enforce an integrity rule that restricts the values supported by the *empid* column in the *Orders* table to the values that exist in the *empid* column in the *Employees* table. You can achieve this by defining a foreign key constraint on the *empid* column in the *Orders* table pointing to the *empid* column in the *Employees* table, like so:

```
ALTER TABLE dbo.Orders
  ADD CONSTRAINT FK_Orders_Employees
  FOREIGN KEY(empid)
  REFERENCES dbo.Employees(empid);
```

Similarly, if you want to restrict the values supported by the *mgrid* column in the *Employees* table to the values that exist in the *empid* column of the same table, you can do so by adding the following foreign key:

```
ALTER TABLE dbo.Employees
  ADD CONSTRAINT FK_Employees_Employees
  FOREIGN KEY(mgrid)
  REFERENCES dbo.Employees(empid);
```

Note that *NULLs* are allowed in the foreign key columns (*mgrid* in the last example) even if there are no *NULLs* in the referenced candidate key columns.

The preceding two examples are basic definitions of foreign keys that enforce a referential action called *no action*. No action means that attempts to delete rows from the referenced table or update the referenced candidate key attributes will be rejected if related rows exist in the referencing table. For example, if you try to delete an employee row from the *Employees* table when there are related orders in the *Orders* table, the RDBMS will reject such an attempt and produce an error.

You can define the foreign key with actions that will compensate for such attempts (to delete rows from the referenced table or update the referenced candidate key attributes when related rows exist in the referencing table). You can define the options *ON DELETE* and *ON UPDATE* with actions such as *CASCADE*, *SET DEFAULT*, and *SET NULL* as part of the foreign key definition. *CASCADE* means that the operation (delete or update) will be cascaded to related rows. For example, *ON DELETE CASCADE* means that when you delete a row from the referenced table, the RDBMS will delete the related rows from the referencing table. *SET DEFAULT* and *SET NULL* mean that the compensating action will set the foreign key attributes of the related rows to the column's default value or *NULL*, respectively. Note that regardless of which action you choose, the referencing table will have orphaned rows only in the case of the exception with *NULLs* in the referencing column that I mentioned earlier. Parent rows with no related child rows are always allowed.

Check constraints

You can use a *check constraint* to define a predicate that a row must meet to be entered into the table or to be modified. For example, the following check constraint ensures that the salary column in the *Employees* table will support only positive values:

```
ALTER TABLE dbo.Employees
  ADD CONSTRAINT CHK_Employees_salary
  CHECK(salary > 0.00);
```

An attempt to insert or update a row with a nonpositive salary value will be rejected by the RDBMS. Note that a check constraint rejects an attempt to insert or update a row when the predicate evaluates to *FALSE*. The modification will be accepted when the predicate evaluates to either *TRUE* or *UNKNOWN*. For example, salary –1000 will be rejected, whereas salaries 50000 and *NULL* will both be accepted (if the column allowed *NULLs*). As mentioned earlier, SQL is based on three-valued logic, which results in two actual actions. With a check constraint, the row is either accepted or rejected.

When adding check and foreign key constraints, you can specify an option called *WITH NOCHECK* that tells the RDBMS you want it to bypass constraint checking for existing data. This is considered a bad practice because you cannot be sure your data is consistent. You can also disable or enable existing check and foreign key constraints.

Default constraints

A default constraint is associated with a particular attribute. It's an expression that is used as the default value when an explicit value is not specified for the attribute when you insert a row. For example, the following code defines a default constraint for the *orderts* attribute (representing the order's time stamp):

```
ALTER TABLE dbo.Orders
  ADD CONSTRAINT DFT_Orders_orderts
  DEFAULT(SYSDATETIME()) FOR orderts;
```

The default expression invokes the *SYSDATETIME* function, which returns the current date and time value. After this default expression is defined, whenever you insert a row into the *Orders* table and do not explicitly specify a value in the *orderts* attribute, SQL Server will set the attribute value to *SYSDATETIME*.

When you're done, run the following code for cleanup:

```
DROP TABLE IF EXISTS dbo.Orders, dbo.Employees;
```

Conclusion

This chapter provided a brief background to T-SQL querying and programming. It presented a theoretical background, explaining the strong foundations that T-SQL is based on. It gave an overview of the SQL Server architecture and concluded with sections that demonstrated how to use T-SQL to create tables and define data integrity. I hope that by now you see that there's something special about SQL, and that it's not just a language that can be learned as an afterthought. This chapter equipped you with fundamental concepts—the actual journey is just about to begin.

CHAPTER 2

Single-table queries

This chapter introduces you to the fundamentals of the *SELECT* statement, focusing for now on queries against a single table. The chapter starts by describing logical query processing—namely, the conceptual interpretation of queries. The chapter then covers other aspects of single-table queries, including predicates and operators, *CASE* expressions, *NULLs*, all-at-once operations, manipulating character data and date and time data, and querying metadata. Many of the code samples and exercises in this book use a sample database called *TSQLV6*. You can find the instructions for downloading and installing this sample database in the Appendix, "Getting started."

Elements of the *SELECT* statement

The purpose of a *SELECT* statement is to query tables, apply some logical manipulation, and return a result. In this section, I talk about the phases involved in logical query processing. I describe the logical order in which the different query clauses are processed and what happens in each phase.

Note that by "logical query processing," I'm referring to the conceptual way in which standard SQL defines how a query should be processed and the final result achieved. Don't be alarmed if some logical processing phases that I describe here seem inefficient. The database engine doesn't have to follow logical query processing to the letter; rather, it is free to physically process a query differently by rearranging processing phases, as long as the final result would be the same as that dictated by logical query processing. The database engine's query optimizer can—and in fact, often does—apply many transformation rules and shortcuts in the physical processing of a query as part of query optimization.

To describe logical query processing and the various *SELECT* query clauses, I use the query in Listing 2-1 as an example.

LISTING 2-1 Sample query

```
USE TSQLV6;

SELECT empid, YEAR(orderdate) AS orderyear, COUNT(*) AS numorders
FROM Sales.Orders
WHERE custid = 71
GROUP BY empid, YEAR(orderdate)
HAVING COUNT(*) > 1
ORDER BY empid, orderyear;
```

This query filters orders that were placed by customer 71, groups those orders by employee and order year, and then filters only groups of employees and years that have more than one order. For the remaining groups, the query presents the employee ID, order year, and count of orders, sorted by the employee ID and order year. For now, don't worry about understanding how this query does what it does; I'll explain the query clauses one at a time.

The code starts with a *USE* statement that ensures that the database context of your session is the *TSQLV6* sample database. If your session is already in the context of the database you need to query, the *USE* statement is not required.

Before I get into the details of each phase of the *SELECT* statement, notice the order in which the query clauses are logically processed. In most programming languages, the lines of code are processed in the order that they are written. In SQL, things are different. Even though the *SELECT* clause appears first in the query, it is logically processed almost last. The clauses are logically processed in the following order:

1. *FROM*

2. *WHERE*

3. *GROUP BY*

4. *HAVING*

5. *SELECT*

6. *ORDER BY*

So even though syntactically the sample query in Listing 2-1 starts with a *SELECT* clause, logically its clauses are processed in the following order:

```
FROM Sales.Orders
WHERE custid = 71
GROUP BY empid, YEAR(orderdate)
HAVING COUNT(*) > 1
SELECT empid, YEAR(orderdate) AS orderyear, COUNT(*) AS numorders
ORDER BY empid, orderyear
```

Or, to present it in a more readable manner, here's what the statement does:

1. Queries the rows *from* the *Sales.Orders* table

2. Filters only orders *where* the customer ID is equal to 71

3. *Groups* the orders *by* employee ID and order year

4. Filters only groups (employee ID and order year) *having* more than one order

5. *Selects* (returns) for each group the employee ID, order year, and number of orders

6. *Orders* (sorts) the rows in the output *by* employee ID and order year

You cannot write the query in correct logical order. You have to start with the *SELECT* clause, as shown in Listing 2-1. There's reason behind this discrepancy between the keyed-in order and the logical processing order of the clauses. The designers of SQL envisioned a declarative language with which you provide your request in an English-like manner. Consider an instruction made by one human to another in English, such as "Bring me the car keys from the top-left drawer in the kitchen." Notice that you start the instruction with the object and then indicate the location where the object resides. But if you were to express the same instruction to a robot, or a computer program, you would have to start with the location before indicating what can be obtained from that location. Your instruction might have been something like "Go to the kitchen; open the top-left drawer; grab the car keys; bring them to me." The keyed-in order of the query clauses is similar to English—it starts with the *SELECT* clause. Logical query processing order is similar to how you provide instructions to a computer program—with the *FROM* clause processed first.

Now that you understand the order in which the query clauses are logically processed, the next sections explain the details of each phase.

When discussing logical query processing, I refer to query *clauses* and query *phases* (the *WHERE* clause and the *WHERE* phase, for example). A query clause is a syntactical component of a query, so when discussing the syntax of a query element I usually use the term *clause*—for example, "In the *WHERE* clause, you specify a predicate." When discussing the logical manipulation taking place as part of logical query processing, I usually use the term *phase*—for example, "The *WHERE* phase returns rows for which the predicate evaluates to *TRUE*."

Recall my recommendation from the previous chapter regarding the use of a semicolon to terminate statements. At the moment, Microsoft SQL Server doesn't require you to terminate all statements with a semicolon. This is a requirement only in particular cases where the parsing of the code might otherwise be ambiguous. However, I recommend you terminate all statements with a semicolon because it is standard, it improves the code readability, and it is likely that T-SQL will require this in more—if not all—cases in the future. Currently, when a semicolon is not required, adding one doesn't hurt.

The *FROM* clause

The *FROM* clause is the very first query clause that is logically processed. In this clause, you specify the names of the tables you want to query and table operators that operate on those tables. This chapter doesn't get into table operators; I describe those in Chapters 3, 5, and 7. For now, you can just consider the *FROM* clause to be simply where you specify the name of the table you want to query. The sample query in Listing 2-1 queries the *Orders* table in the *Sales* schema, finding 830 rows.

```
FROM Sales.Orders
```

Recall the recommendation I gave in the previous chapter to always schema-qualify object names in your code. When you don't specify the schema name explicitly, SQL Server must resolve it implicitly based on its implicit name-resolution rules. This can result in SQL Server choosing a different object than the one you intended. By being explicit, your code is safer in the sense that you ensure that you get the object you intended to get.

To return all rows from a table with no special manipulation, all you need is a query with a *FROM* clause in which you specify the table you want to query, and a *SELECT* clause in which you specify the attributes you want to return. For example, the following statement queries all rows from the *Orders* table in the *Sales* schema, selecting the attributes *orderid, custid, empid, orderdate,* and *freight.*

```
SELECT orderid, custid, empid, orderdate, freight
FROM Sales.Orders;
```

> **Note** This code doesn't include a *USE TSQLV6* statement. I'm assuming that you're still connected to the *TSQLV6* sample database. But of course, you should always make sure that you're connected to the right database before running your code.

The output of this statement is shown here in abbreviated form:

```
orderid      custid      empid        orderdate   freight
-----------  ----------- -----------  ----------  ----------------------
10248        85          5            2020-07-04  32.38
10249        79          6            2020-07-05  11.61
10250        34          4            2020-07-08  65.83
10251        84          3            2020-07-08  41.34
10252        76          4            2020-07-09  51.30
10253        34          3            2020-07-10  58.17
10254        14          5            2020-07-11  22.98
10255        68          9            2020-07-12  148.33
10256        88          3            2020-07-15  13.97
10257        35          4            2020-07-16  81.91
...

(830 rows affected)
```

Note that if your default *Results To* mode in SSMS is *Results to Grid,* the query output will appear under the Results tab and the message indicating how many rows were affected will appear under the Messages tab.

Although it might seem that the output of the query is returned in a particular order, this is not guaranteed. I'll elaborate on this point later in this chapter, in the sections "The *SELECT* clause" and "The *ORDER BY* clause."

Delimiting identifier names

As long as the identifiers in your query comply with rules for the format of regular identifiers, you don't need to delimit the identifier names used for schemas, tables, and columns. The rules for the format of regular identifiers can be found at the following URL: *https://learn.microsoft.com/en-us/sql/relational-databases/databases/database-identifiers*. If an identifier is irregular—for example, if it has embedded spaces or special characters, starts with a digit, or is a reserved keyword—you have to delimit it. There are a couple of ways to delimit identifiers in T-SQL. One is the standard SQL form using double quotes—for example, *"Order Details"*. Another is the T-SQL-specific form using square brackets—for example, *[Order Details]*.

With regular identifiers, delimiting is optional. For example, a table called *OrderDetails* residing in the *Sales* schema can be referred to as *Sales.OrderDetails* or *"Sales"."OrderDetails"* or *[Sales].[OrderDetails]*. My personal preference is not to use delimiters when they are not required, because they tend to clutter the code. Also, when you're in charge of assigning identifiers, I recommend always using regular ones—for example, *OrderDetails* instead of *Order Details*.

The *WHERE* clause

In the *WHERE* clause, you specify a predicate, or logical expression, to filter the rows returned by the *FROM* phase. Only rows for which the logical expression evaluates to *TRUE* are returned by the *WHERE* phase to the subsequent logical query processing phase. In the sample query in Listing 2-1, the *WHERE* phase filters only orders placed by customer 71:

```
FROM Sales.Orders
WHERE custid = 71
```

Out of the 830 rows returned by the *FROM* phase, the *WHERE* phase filters only the 31 rows where the customer ID is equal to 71. To see which rows you get back after applying the filter *custid = 71*, run the following query:

```
SELECT orderid, empid, orderdate, freight
FROM Sales.Orders
WHERE custid = 71;
```

This query generates the following output:

```
orderid     empid        orderdate   freight
----------- ------------ ----------- --------
10324       9            2020-10-08  214.27
10393       1            2020-12-25  126.56
10398       2            2020-12-30  89.16
10440       4            2021-02-10  86.53
10452       8            2021-02-20  140.26
10510       6            2021-04-18  367.63
10555       6            2021-06-02  252.49
10603       8            2021-07-18  48.77
10607       5            2021-07-22  200.24
10612       1            2021-07-28  544.08
```

```
10627      8          2021-08-11 107.46
10657      2          2021-09-04 352.69
10678      7          2021-09-23 388.98
10700      3          2021-10-10 65.10
10711      5          2021-10-21 52.41
10713      1          2021-10-22 167.05
10714      5          2021-10-22 24.49
10722      8          2021-10-29 74.58
10748      3          2021-11-20 232.55
10757      6          2021-11-27 8.19
10815      2          2022-01-05 14.62
10847      4          2022-01-22 487.57
10882      4          2022-02-11 23.10
10894      1          2022-02-18 116.13
10941      7          2022-03-11 400.81
10983      2          2022-03-27 657.54
10984      1          2022-03-30 211.22
11002      4          2022-04-06 141.16
11030      7          2022-04-17 830.75
11031      6          2022-04-17 227.22
11064      1          2022-05-01 30.09
```

```
(31 rows affected)
```

The *WHERE* clause has significance when it comes to query performance. Based on what you have in the filter expression, SQL Server evaluates the use of indexes to access the required data. By using indexes, SQL Server can sometimes get the required data with much less work compared to applying full table scans. Query filters also reduce the network traffic created by returning all possible rows to the caller and filtering on the client side.

Earlier, I mentioned that only rows for which the logical expression evaluates to *TRUE* are returned by the *WHERE* phase. Always keep in mind that T-SQL uses three-valued predicate logic, where logical expressions can evaluate to *TRUE*, *FALSE*, or *UNKNOWN*. With three-valued logic, saying "returns *TRUE*" is not the same as saying "does not return *FALSE*." The *WHERE* phase returns rows for which the logical expression evaluates to *TRUE*, and it doesn't return rows for which the logical expression evaluates to *FALSE* or *UNKNOWN*. I elaborate on this point later in this chapter in the section "*NULLs.*"

The *GROUP BY* clause

You can use the *GROUP BY* phase to arrange the rows returned by the previous logical query processing phase in groups. The groups are determined by the elements, or expressions, you specify in the *GROUP BY* clause. For example, the *GROUP BY* clause in the query in Listing 2-1 has the elements *empid* and *YEAR(orderdate)*:

```
FROM Sales.Orders
WHERE custid = 71
GROUP BY empid, YEAR(orderdate)
```

This means that the *GROUP BY* phase produces a group for each distinct combination of employee-ID and order-year values that appears in the data returned by the *WHERE* phase. The expression *YEAR(orderdate)* invokes the *YEAR* function to return only the year part from the *orderdate* column.

The *WHERE* phase returned 31 rows, within which there are 16 distinct combinations of employee-ID and order-year values, as shown here:

```
empid       YEAR(orderdate)
----------- ----------------
1           2020
1           2021
1           2022
2           2020
2           2021
2           2022
3           2021
4           2021
4           2022
5           2021
6           2021
6           2022
7           2021
7           2022
8           2021
9           2020
```

Thus, the *GROUP BY* phase creates 16 groups and associates each of the 31 rows returned from the *WHERE* phase with the relevant group.

If the query is a grouped query, all phases subsequent to the *GROUP BY* phase—including *HAVING*, *SELECT*, and *ORDER BY*—operate on groups as opposed to operating on individual rows. Each group is ultimately represented by a single row in the final result of the query. All expressions you specify in clauses that are processed in phases subsequent to the *GROUP BY* phase are required to guarantee returning a scalar (single value) per group.

Expressions based on elements that participate in the *GROUP BY* clause meet the requirement because, by definition, each such element represents a distinct value per group. For example, in the group for employee ID 8 and order year 2021, there's only one distinct employee-ID value (8) and only one distinct order-year value (2021). Therefore, you're allowed to refer to the expressions *empid* and *YEAR(orderdate)* in clauses that are processed in phases subsequent to the *GROUP BY* phase, such as the *SELECT* clause. The following query, for example, returns 16 rows for the 16 groups of employee-ID and order-year values:

```
SELECT empid, YEAR(orderdate) AS orderyear
FROM Sales.Orders
WHERE custid = 71
GROUP BY empid, YEAR(orderdate);
```

This query returns the following output:

```
empid       orderyear
----------- -----------
1           2020
1           2021
1           2022
2           2020
2           2021
```

```
2           2022
3           2021
4           2021
4           2022
5           2021
6           2021
6           2022
7           2021
7           2022
8           2021
9           2020
```

```
(16 rows affected)
```

Elements that do not participate in the *GROUP BY* clause are allowed only as inputs to an aggregate function such as *COUNT, SUM, AVG, MIN,* or *MAX*. For example, the following query returns the total freight and number of orders per employee and order year:

```
SELECT
  empid,
  YEAR(orderdate) AS orderyear,
  SUM(freight) AS totalfreight,
  COUNT(*) AS numorders
FROM Sales.Orders
WHERE custid = 71
GROUP BY empid, YEAR(orderdate);
```

This query generates the following output:

```
empid       orderyear   totalfreight            numorders
----------- ----------- ----------------------- -----------
1           2020        126.56                  1
2           2020        89.16                   1
9           2020        214.27                  1
1           2021        711.13                  2
2           2021        352.69                  1
3           2021        297.65                  2
4           2021        86.53                   1
5           2021        277.14                  3
6           2021        628.31                  3
7           2021        388.98                  1
8           2021        371.07                  4
1           2022        357.44                  3
2           2022        672.16                  2
4           2022        651.83                  3
6           2022        227.22                  1
7           2022        1231.56                 2
```

```
(16 rows affected)
```

The expression *SUM(freight)* returns the sum of all freight values in each group, and the function *COUNT(*)* returns the count of rows in each group—which in this case means the number of orders. If you try to refer to an attribute that does not participate in the *GROUP BY* clause (such as *freight*) and not as an input to an aggregate function in any clause that is processed after the *GROUP BY* clause, you get an error—in such a case, there's no guarantee that the expression will return a single value per group. For example, the following query will fail:

```
SELECT empid, YEAR(orderdate) AS orderyear, freight
FROM Sales.Orders
WHERE custid = 71
GROUP BY empid, YEAR(orderdate);
```

SQL Server produces the following error:

```
Msg 8120, Level 16, State 1, Line 1
Column 'Sales.Orders.freight' is invalid in the select list because it is not contained in
either an aggregate function or the GROUP BY clause.
```

Note that all aggregate functions that are applied to an input expression ignore *NULLs*. The *COUNT(*)* function isn't applied to any input expression; it just counts rows irrespective of what those rows contain. For example, consider a group of five rows with the values *30, 10, NULL, 10, 10* in a column called *qty*. The expression *COUNT(*)* returns 5 because there are five rows in the group, whereas *COUNT(qty)* returns 4 because there are four known (non-*NULL*) values.

If you want to handle only distinct (unique) occurrences of known values, specify the *DIS-TINCT* keyword before the input expression to the aggregate function. For example, the expression *COUNT(DISTINCT qty)* returns 2, because there are two distinct known values (30 and 10). The *DISTINCT* keyword can be used with other functions as well. For example, although the expression *SUM(qty)* returns 60, the expression *SUM(DISTINCT qty)* returns 40. The expression *AVG(qty)* returns 15, whereas the expression *AVG(DISTINCT qty)* returns 20. As an example of using the *DISTINCT* option with an aggregate function in a complete query, the following code returns the number of distinct customers handled by each employee in each order year:

```
SELECT
  empid,
  YEAR(orderdate) AS orderyear,
  COUNT(DISTINCT custid) AS numcusts
FROM Sales.Orders
GROUP BY empid, YEAR(orderdate);
```

This query generates the following output:

```
empid       orderyear   numcusts
----------- ----------- -----------
1           2020        22
2           2020        15
3           2020        16
4           2020        26
5           2020        10
6           2020        15
7           2020        11
8           2020        19
9           2020        5
1           2021        40
2           2021        35
3           2021        46
```

```
4          2021          57
5          2021          13
6          2021          24
7          2021          30
8          2021          36
9          2021          16
1          2022          32
2          2022          34
3          2022          30
4          2022          33
5          2022          11
6          2022          17
7          2022          21
8          2022          23
9          2022          16

(27 rows affected)
```

The aggregate functions that are covered in this section, including the *MAX* and *MIN* functions, are grouped aggregate functions. They operate on sets of rows that are defined by the query's grouping. However, sometimes you need to apply maximum and minimum calculations across columns. Starting with SQL Server 2022, this is achievable with the functions *GREATEST* and *LEAST*. You can find details later in the chapter under "The *GREATEST* and *LEAST* functions."

The *HAVING* clause

Whereas the *WHERE* clause is a row filter, the *HAVING* clause is a group filter. Only groups for which the *HAVING* predicate evaluates to *TRUE* are returned by the *HAVING* phase to the next logical query processing phase. Groups for which the predicate evaluates to *FALSE* or *UNKNOWN* are discarded.

Because the *HAVING* clause is processed after the rows have been grouped, you can refer to aggregate functions in the *HAVING* filter predicate. For example, in the query from Listing 2-1, the *HAVING* clause has the predicate *COUNT(*) > 1*, meaning that the *HAVING* phase filters only groups (employee and order year) with more than one row. The following fragment of the Listing 2-1 query shows the steps that have been processed so far:

```
FROM Sales.Orders
WHERE custid = 71
GROUP BY empid, YEAR(orderdate)
HAVING COUNT(*) > 1
```

Recall that the *GROUP BY* phase created 16 groups of employee ID and order year. Seven of those groups have only one row, so after the *HAVING* clause is processed, nine groups remain. Run the following query to return those nine groups:

```
SELECT empid, YEAR(orderdate) AS orderyear
FROM Sales.Orders
WHERE custid = 71
GROUP BY empid, YEAR(orderdate)
HAVING COUNT(*) > 1;
```

This query returns the following output:

```
empid       orderyear
----------- -----------
1           2021
3           2021
5           2021
6           2021
8           2021
1           2022
2           2022
4           2022
7           2022

(9 rows affected)
```

The *SELECT* clause

The *SELECT* clause is where you specify the attributes (columns) you want to return in the result table of the query. You can base the expressions in the *SELECT* list on attributes from the queried tables, with or without further manipulation.

For example, the *SELECT* list in Listing 2-1 has the following expressions: *empid*, *YEAR(orderdate)*, and *COUNT(*)*. If an expression refers to an attribute with no manipulation, such as *empid*, the name of the target attribute is the same as the name of the source attribute. You can optionally assign your own name to the target attribute by using the *AS* clause—for example, *empid AS employee_id*. Expressions that do apply manipulation, such as *YEAR(orderdate)*, or that are not based on a source attribute, such as a call to the function *SYSDATETIME*, won't have a name unless you alias them. T-SQL allows a query to return anonymous result columns in certain cases, but the relational model doesn't. I recommend that you always ensure that all result columns have names by aliasing the ones that would otherwise be anonymous. In this respect, the result table returned from the query would be considered relational.

In addition to supporting the *AS* clause, T-SQL supports a couple of other forms with which you can alias expressions. To me, the *AS* clause seems the most readable and intuitive form; therefore, I recommend using it. I will cover the other forms for the sake of completeness and also to describe an elusive bug related to one of them.

In addition to supporting the form *<expression> AS <alias>*, T-SQL also supports the forms *<alias> = <expression>* ("alias equals expression") and *<expression> <alias>* ("expression space alias"). An example of the former is *orderyear = YEAR(orderdate)*, and an example of the latter is *YEAR(orderdate) orderyear*. I find the latter particularly unclear and recommend avoiding it, although unfortunately this form is very common in people's code. Keep in mind that often code that you write needs to be reviewed and maintained by other developers, or even by yourself at a later date, so code clarity is very important.

Note that if by mistake you miss a comma between two column names in the *SELECT* list, your code won't fail. Instead, SQL Server will assume the second name is an alias for the first column name. As an example, suppose you want to query the columns *orderid* and *orderdate* from the *Sales.Orders* table and you miss the comma between them, as follows:

```
SELECT orderid orderdate
FROM Sales.Orders;
```

This query is considered syntactically valid, as if you intended to alias the *orderid* column as *order-date*. In the output, you will get only one column holding the order IDs, with the alias *orderdate*:

```
orderdate
-----------
10248
10249
10250
10251
10252
...
```

```
(830 rows affected)
```

If you're accustomed to using the syntax with the space between an expression and its alias, it will be harder for you to detect such bugs.

With the addition of the *SELECT* phase, the following query clauses from the query in Listing 2-1 have been processed so far:

```
SELECT empid, YEAR(orderdate) AS orderyear, COUNT(*) AS numorders
FROM Sales.Orders
WHERE custid = 71
GROUP BY empid, YEAR(orderdate)
HAVING COUNT(*) > 1
```

The *SELECT* clause produces the result table of the query. In the case of the query in Listing 2-1, the heading of the result table has the attributes *empid*, *orderyear*, and *numorders*, and the body has nine rows (one for each group). Run the following query to return those nine rows:

```
SELECT empid, YEAR(orderdate) AS orderyear, COUNT(*) AS numorders
FROM Sales.Orders
WHERE custid = 71
GROUP BY empid, YEAR(orderdate)
HAVING COUNT(*) > 1;
```

This query generates the following output:

```
empid       orderyear   numorders
----------- ----------- -----------
1           2021        2
3           2021        2
5           2021        3
6           2021        3
8           2021        4
1           2022        3
2           2022        2
4           2022        3
7           2022        2
```

```
(9 rows affected)
```

Remember that the *SELECT* clause is processed after the *FROM, WHERE, GROUP BY*, and *HAVING* clauses. This means that aliases assigned to expressions in the *SELECT* clause do not exist as far as clauses that are processed before the *SELECT* clause are concerned. It's a typical mistake to try and refer to expression aliases in clauses that are processed before the *SELECT* clause, such as in the following example in which the attempt is made in the *WHERE* clause:

```
SELECT orderid, YEAR(orderdate) AS orderyear
FROM Sales.Orders
WHERE orderyear > 2021;
```

At first glance, this query might seem valid, but if you consider that the column aliases are created in the *SELECT* phase—which is processed after the *WHERE* phase—you can see that the reference to the *orderyear* alias in the *WHERE* clause is invalid. Consequently, SQL Server produces the following error:

```
Msg 207, Level 16, State 1, Line 3
Invalid column name 'orderyear'.
```

Amusingly, a lecture attendee once asked me in all seriousness when Microsoft is going to fix this bug. As you can gather from this chapter, this behavior is not a bug; rather, it is by design. Also, it was not defined by Microsoft; it was defined by the SQL standard.

One way around this problem is to repeat the expression *YEAR(orderdate)* in both the *WHERE* and *SELECT* clauses:

```
SELECT orderid, YEAR(orderdate) AS orderyear
FROM Sales.Orders
WHERE YEAR(orderdate) > 2021;
```

A similar problem can happen if you try to refer to an expression alias in the *HAVING* clause, which is also processed before the *SELECT* clause:

```
SELECT empid, YEAR(orderdate) AS orderyear, COUNT(*) AS numorders
FROM Sales.Orders
WHERE custid = 71
GROUP BY empid, YEAR(orderdate)
HAVING numorders > 1;
```

This query fails with an error saying that the column name *numorders* is invalid. Just like in the previous example, the workaround here is to repeat the expression *COUNT(*)* in both clauses:

```
SELECT empid, YEAR(orderdate) AS orderyear, COUNT(*) AS numorders
FROM Sales.Orders
WHERE custid = 71
GROUP BY empid, YEAR(orderdate)
HAVING COUNT(*) > 1;
```

In relational theory, a relational expression is applied to one or more input relations using operators from relational algebra, and returns a relation as output. This is what's known as the *closure property* of the relational algebra, and what allows nesting of relational expressions. Think in terms similar to an integer expression such as 2 + 4. The operands are integers and the result is an integer. Thanks to the closure property of algebra, you can nest such an expression in a more elaborate one—for example, (2 + 4) * 7. Given that the counterpart to a relation in SQL is a table, the counterpart to a relational expression in SQL is a *table expression*. For example, the query above without the terminator (semicolon) is a table expression, of which the result is conceptually a table result, and hence can be nested. With the terminator it is a *SELECT* statement whose result table is returned to the caller.

Recall that a relation's body is a set of tuples, and a set has no duplicates. Unlike relational theory, which is based on mathematical set theory, SQL is based on multiset theory. The mathematical term *multiset*, or *bag*, is similar in some aspects to a set, but it does allow duplicates. A table in SQL isn't required to have a key. Without a key, the table can have duplicate rows and therefore isn't relational. Even if the table does have a key, a *SELECT* query against the table can still return duplicate rows. SQL query results do not have keys. As an example, the *Orders* table does have a primary key defined on the *orderid* column. Still, the query in Listing 2-2 against the *Orders* table returns duplicate rows.

LISTING 2-2 Query returning duplicate rows

```
SELECT empid, YEAR(orderdate) AS orderyear
FROM Sales.Orders
WHERE custid = 71;
```

This query generates the following output:

```
empid       orderyear
----------- -----------
9           2020
1           2020
2           2020
4           2021
8           2021
6           2021
6           2021
8           2021
5           2021
1           2021
8           2021
2           2021
7           2021
3           2021
5           2021
1           2021
5           2021
8           2021
3           2021
6           2021
2           2022
4           2022
4           2022
1           2022
7           2022
2           2022
1           2022
4           2022
7           2022
6           2022
1           2022
```

```
(31 rows affected)
```

SQL provides the means to remove duplicates using the *DISTINCT* clause (as shown in Listing 2-3) and, in this sense, return a relational result.

LISTING 2-3 Query with a *DISTINCT* clause

```
SELECT DISTINCT empid, YEAR(orderdate) AS orderyear
FROM Sales.Orders
WHERE custid = 71;
```

Note that the *DISTINCT* clause here applies to the combination of *empid* and *orderyear*.

This query generates the following output:

```
empid       orderyear
----------- -----------
1           2020
1           2021
1           2022
2           2020
2           2021
2           2022
3           2021
4           2021
4           2022
5           2021
6           2021
6           2022
7           2021
7           2022
8           2021
9           2020

(16 rows affected)
```

Of the 31 rows in the multiset returned by the query in Listing 2-2, 16 rows are in the set returned by the query in Listing 2-3 after the removal of duplicates.

SQL allows specifying an asterisk (*) in the *SELECT* list to request all attributes from the queried tables instead of listing them explicitly, as in the following example:

```
SELECT *
FROM Sales.Shippers;
```

Such use of an asterisk is considered a bad programming practice in most cases. It is recommended that you explicitly list all attributes you need.

Unlike with the relational model, SQL keeps ordinal positions for columns based on the order in which you specified them in the *CREATE TABLE* statement. By specifying *SELECT* *, you're guaranteed to get the columns ordered in the output based on their ordinal positions. Client applications can refer to columns in the result by their ordinal positions (a bad practice in its own right) instead of by name. Then any schema changes applied to the table—such as adding or removing columns, rearranging their order, and so on—might result in failures in the client application or, even worse, in application bugs that will go unnoticed. By explicitly specifying the attributes you need, you always get the right ones, as long as the columns exist in the table. If a column referenced by the query was dropped from the table, you get an error and can fix your code accordingly.

People often wonder whether there's any performance difference between specifying an asterisk and explicitly listing column names. There is some extra work involved in resolving column names when the asterisk is used, but the cost is negligible compared to other costs involved in the processing of a query. Because listing column names explicitly is the recommended practice anyway, it's a win-win situation.

Curiously, you are not allowed to refer to column aliases created in the *SELECT* clause in other expressions within the same *SELECT* clause. That's the case even if the expression that tries to use the alias appears to the right of the expression that created it. For example, the following attempt is invalid:

```
SELECT orderid,
  YEAR(orderdate) AS orderyear,
  orderyear + 1 AS nextyear
FROM Sales.Orders;
```

I'll explain the reason for this restriction later in this chapter, in the section "All-at-once operations." As explained earlier in this section, one of the ways around this problem is to repeat the expression:

```
SELECT orderid,
  YEAR(orderdate) AS orderyear,
  YEAR(orderdate) + 1 AS nextyear
FROM Sales.Orders;
```

The *ORDER BY* clause

You use the *ORDER BY* clause to sort the rows in the output for presentation purposes. In terms of logical query processing, *ORDER BY* comes after *SELECT*. The sample query shown in Listing 2-4 orders the rows in the output by employee ID and order year.

LISTING 2-4 Query demonstrating the *ORDER BY* clause

```
SELECT empid, YEAR(orderdate) AS orderyear, COUNT(*) AS numorders
FROM Sales.Orders
WHERE custid = 71
GROUP BY empid, YEAR(orderdate)
HAVING COUNT(*) > 1
ORDER BY empid, orderyear;
```

This query generates the following output:

```
empid       orderyear   numorders
----------- ----------- -----------
1           2021        2
1           2022        3
2           2022        2
3           2021        2
4           2022        3
5           2021        3
```

6	2021	3
7	2022	2
8	2021	4

```
(9 rows affected)
```

This time, presentation ordering in the output is guaranteed—unlike with queries that don't have a presentation *ORDER BY* clause.

One of the most important points to understand about SQL is that a table—be it an existing table in the database or a table result returned by a query—has no guaranteed order. That's because a table is supposed to represent a set of rows (or multiset, if it has duplicates), and a set has no order. This means that when you query a table without specifying an *ORDER BY* clause, SQL Server is free to return the rows in the output in any order. The only way for you to guarantee the presentation order in the result is with an *ORDER BY* clause. However, you should realize that if you do specify an *ORDER BY* clause, the result can't qualify as a table, because it is ordered. Standard SQL calls such a result a *cursor*.

You're probably wondering why it matters whether a query returns a table or a cursor. Some language elements and operations in SQL expect to work with table results of queries and not with cursors. Examples include named table expressions and set operators, which I cover in detail in Chapter 5, "Table expressions," and Chapter 6, "Set operators."

Notice in the query in Listing 2-4 that the *ORDER BY* clause refers to the column alias *orderyear*, which was created in the *SELECT* phase. The *ORDER BY* phase is the only phase in which you can refer to column aliases created in the *SELECT* phase, because it is the only phase processed after the *SELECT* phase. Note that if you define a column alias that is the same as an underlying column name, as in *1 - col1 AS col1*, and refer to that alias in the *ORDER BY* clause, the new column is the one considered for ordering.

When you want to order the rows by some expression in an ascending order, you either specify *ASC* right after the expression, as in *orderyear ASC*, or don't specify anything after the expression, because *ASC* is the default. If you want to sort in descending order, you need to specify *DESC* after the expression, as in *orderyear DESC*.

With T-SQL, you can specify ordinal positions of columns in the *ORDER BY* clause, based on the order in which the columns appear in the *SELECT* list. For example, in the query in Listing 2-4, instead of using

```
ORDER BY empid, orderyear
```

you could use

```
ORDER BY 1, 2
```

However, this is considered a bad programming practice for a few reasons. First, in the relational model, attributes don't have ordinal positions and need to be referred to by name. Second, when you make revisions to the *SELECT* clause, you might forget to make the corresponding revisions in the *ORDER BY* clause. When you use column names, your code is safe from this type of mistake. Third, using the attribute names is more readable.

With T-SQL, you can also specify elements in the *ORDER BY* clause that do not appear in the *SELECT* clause, meaning you can sort by something you don't necessarily want to return. That's at least the case when you don't also specify the *DISTINCT* clause. For example, the following query sorts the employee rows by hire date without returning the *hiredate* attribute:

```
SELECT empid, firstname, lastname, country
FROM HR.Employees
ORDER BY hiredate;
```

However, when the *DISTINCT* clause is specified, you are restricted in the *ORDER BY* list only to elements that appear in the *SELECT* list. The reasoning behind this restriction is that when *DISTINCT* is specified, a single result row might represent multiple source rows; therefore, it might not be clear which of the values in the multiple rows should be used. Consider the following invalid query:

```
SELECT DISTINCT country
FROM HR.Employees
ORDER BY empid;
```

If you try running it, you get the following error:

```
Msg 145, Level 15, State 1, Line 157
ORDER BY items must appear in the select list if SELECT DISTINCT is specified.
```

There are nine employees in the *Employees* table—five from the United States and four from the United Kingdom. If you omit the invalid *ORDER BY* clause from this query, you get two rows back—one for each distinct country. Because each country appears in multiple rows in the source table, and each such row has a different employee ID, the meaning of *ORDER BY empid* is not really defined.

The *TOP* and *OFFSET-FETCH* filters

Earlier in this chapter I covered the filtering clauses *WHERE* and *HAVING*, which are based on predicates. In this section I cover the filtering clauses *TOP* and *OFFSET-FETCH*, which are based on number of rows and ordering.

The *TOP* filter

The *TOP* filter is a proprietary T-SQL feature you can use to limit the number or percentage of rows your query returns. It relies on two elements as part of its specification: one is the number or percent of rows to return, and the other is the ordering. For example, to return from the *Orders* table the five most recent orders, you specify *TOP (5)* in the *SELECT* clause and *orderdate DESC* in the *ORDER BY* clause, as shown in Listing 2-5.

LISTING 2-5 Query demonstrating the *TOP* filter

```
SELECT TOP (5) orderid, orderdate, custid, empid
FROM Sales.Orders
ORDER BY orderdate DESC;
```

This query returns the following output:

```
orderid      orderdate   custid      empid
-----------  ----------  ----------  -----------
11077        2022-05-06  65          1
11076        2022-05-06  9           4
11075        2022-05-06  68          8
11074        2022-05-06  73          7
11073        2022-05-05  58          2

(5 rows affected)
```

Note that the *TOP* filter is handled after *DISTINCT*. This means that if *DISTINCT* is specified in the *SELECT* clause, the *TOP* filter is evaluated after duplicate rows have been removed.

Also note that when the *TOP* filter is specified, the *ORDER BY* clause serves a dual purpose in the query. One purpose is to define the presentation ordering for the rows in the query result. Another purpose is to define for the *TOP* option which rows to filter. For example, the query in Listing 2-5 returns the five rows with the most recent *orderdate* values and presents the rows in the output in *orderdate DESC* ordering.

If you're confused about whether a *TOP* query returns a table result or a cursor, you have every reason to be. Normally, a query with an *ORDER BY* clause returns a cursor—not a table result. But what if you need to filter rows with the *TOP* option based on some ordering but still return a table result? Also, what if you need to filter rows with the *TOP* option based on one order but present the output rows in another order?

To achieve this, you have to use a named table expression, but I'll save the discussion about table expressions for Chapter 5. Suffice to say for now that the design of the *TOP* filter is a bit confusing. It would have been nice if the *TOP* filter had its own ordering specification that is separate from the presentation ordering specification in the query. Unfortunately, that ship has sailed.

You can use the *TOP* option with the *PERCENT* keyword, in which case SQL Server calculates the number of rows to return based on a percentage of the number of qualifying rows, rounded up. For example, the following query requests the top 1 percent of the most recent orders:

```
SELECT TOP (1) PERCENT orderid, orderdate, custid, empid
FROM Sales.Orders
ORDER BY orderdate DESC;
```

This query generates the following output:

```
orderid      orderdate   custid      empid
-----------  ----------  ----------  -----------
11074        2022-05-06  73          7
11075        2022-05-06  68          8
11076        2022-05-06  9           4
11077        2022-05-06  65          1
11070        2022-05-05  44          2
11071        2022-05-05  46          1
11072        2022-05-05  20          4
11073        2022-05-05  58          2
11067        2022-05-04  17          1

(9 rows affected)
```

The query returns nine rows because the *Orders* table has 830 rows, and 1 percent of 830, rounded up, is 9.

In the query in Listing 2-5, you might have noticed that the *ORDER BY* list is not unique (because no primary key or unique constraint is defined on the *orderdate* column). In other words, the ordering is not *strict total ordering*. Multiple rows can have the same order date. In such a case, the ordering among rows with the same order date is undefined. This fact makes the query nondeterministic—more than one result can be considered correct. In case of ties, SQL Server filters rows based on optimization choices and physical access order.

Note that you can even use the *TOP* filter in a query without an *ORDER BY* clause. In such a case, the ordering is completely undefined—SQL Server returns whichever *n* rows it happens to physically access first, where *n* is the requested number of rows.

Notice in the output for the query in Listing 2-5 that the minimum order date in the rows returned is May 5, 2022, and one row in the output has that date. Other rows in the table might have the same order date, and with the existing non-unique *ORDER BY* list, there is no guarantee which one will be returned.

If you want the query to be deterministic, you need strict total ordering; in other words, add a tiebreaker. For example, you can add *orderid DESC* to the *ORDER BY* list as shown in Listing 2-6 so that, in case of ties, the row with the greater order ID value will be preferred.

LISTING 2-6 Query demonstrating *TOP* with unique *ORDER BY* list

```
SELECT TOP (5) orderid, orderdate, custid, empid
FROM Sales.Orders
ORDER BY orderdate DESC, orderid DESC;
```

This query returns the following output:

```
orderid      orderdate  custid       empid
-----------  ---------- -----------  -----------
11077        2022-05-06 65           1
11076        2022-05-06 9            4
11075        2022-05-06 68           8
11074        2022-05-06 73           7
11073        2022-05-05 58           2

(5 rows affected)
```

If you examine the results of the queries from Listings 2-5 and 2-6, you'll notice that they seem to be the same. The important difference is that the result shown in the query output for Listing 2-5 is one of several possible valid results for this query, whereas the result shown in the query output for Listing 2-6 is the only possible valid result.

Instead of adding a tiebreaker to the *ORDER BY* list, you can request to return all ties. For example, you can ask that, in addition to the five rows you get back from the query in Listing 2-5, all other rows from the table be returned that have the same sort value (order date, in this case) as the last one found (May 5, 2022, in this case). You achieve this by adding the *WITH TIES* option, as shown in the following query:

```
SELECT TOP (5) WITH TIES orderid, orderdate, custid, empid
FROM Sales.Orders
ORDER BY orderdate DESC;
```

This query returns the following output:

```
orderid      orderdate   custid      empid
-----------  ----------  ----------  -----------
11077        2022-05-06  65          1
11076        2022-05-06  9           4
11075        2022-05-06  68          8
11074        2022-05-06  73          7
11073        2022-05-05  58          2
11072        2022-05-05  20          4
11071        2022-05-05  46          1
11070        2022-05-05  44          2

(8 rows affected)
```

Notice that the output has eight rows, even though you specified *TOP (5)*. SQL Server first returned the *TOP (5)* rows based on *orderdate DESC* ordering, and it also returned all other rows from the table that had the same *orderdate* value as in the last of the five rows that were accessed. Using the *WITH TIES* option, the selection of rows is deterministic, but the presentation order among rows with the same order date isn't.

The *OFFSET-FETCH* filter

The *TOP* filter is very useful, but it has two shortcomings—it's not standard, and it doesn't support a skipping capability. T-SQL also supports a standard, *TOP*-like filter, called *OFFSET FETCH*, which does support a skipping option. This makes it very useful for paging purposes.

According to the SQL standard, the *OFFSET-FETCH* filter is considered an extension to the *ORDER BY* clause. With the *OFFSET* clause you indicate how many rows to skip, and with the *FETCH* clause you indicate how many rows to filter after the skipped rows. As an example, consider the following query:

```
SELECT orderid, orderdate, custid, empid
FROM Sales.Orders
ORDER BY orderdate, orderid
OFFSET 50 ROWS FETCH NEXT 25 ROWS ONLY;
```

This query generates the following output:

```
orderid      orderdate   custid      empid
-----------  ----------  ----------  -----------
10298        2020-09-05  37          6
10299        2020-09-06  67          4
10300        2020-09-09  49          2
10301        2020-09-09  86          8
```

```
10302           2020-09-10 76           4
10303           2020-09-11 30           7
10304           2020-09-12 80           1
10305           2020-09-13 55           8
10306           2020-09-16 69           1
10307           2020-09-17 48           2
10308           2020-09-18 2            7
10309           2020-09-19 37           3
10310           2020-09-20 77           8
10311           2020-09-20 18           1
10312           2020-09-23 86           2
10313           2020-09-24 63           2
10314           2020-09-25 65           1
10315           2020-09-26 38           4
10316           2020-09-27 65           1
10317           2020-09-30 48           6
10318           2020-10-01 38           8
10319           2020-10-02 80           7
10320           2020-10-03 87           5
10321           2020-10-03 38           3
10322           2020-10-04 58           7

(25 rows affected)
```

The query orders the rows from the *Orders* table based on the *orderdate* and *orderid* attributes (from least recent to most recent, with *orderid* as the tiebreaker). Based on this ordering, the *OFFSET* clause skips the first 50 rows and the *FETCH* clause filters the next 25 rows only.

Note that a query that uses *OFFSET-FETCH* must have an *ORDER BY* clause. Also, contrary to the SQL standard, T-SQL doesn't support the *FETCH* clause without the *OFFSET* clause. If you do not want to skip any rows but do want to filter rows with the *FETCH* clause, you must indicate that by using *OFFSET 0 ROWS*. However, *OFFSET* without *FETCH* is allowed. In such a case, the query skips the indicated number of rows and returns all remaining rows in the result.

There are interesting language aspects to note about the syntax for the *OFFSET-FETCH* filter. The singular and plural forms *ROW* and *ROWS* are interchangeable. The idea behind this is to allow you to phrase the filter in an intuitive, English-like manner. For example, suppose you want to fetch only one row; though it would be syntactically valid, it would nevertheless look strange if you specified *FETCH 1 ROWS*. Therefore, you're allowed to use the form *FETCH 1 ROW*. The same principle applies to the *OFFSET* clause. Also, if you're not skipping any rows (*OFFSET 0 ROWS*), you might find the term "first" more suitable than "next." Hence, the forms *FIRST* and *NEXT* are interchangeable.

As you can see, the *OFFSET-FETCH* filter is more flexible than the *TOP* filter in the sense that it supports a skipping capability. However, the T-SQL implementation of the *OFFSET-FETCH* filter doesn't yet support the *PERCENT* and *WITH TIES* options that *TOP* does. Curiously, the SQL standard specification for the *OFFSET-FETCH* filter does support these options. In fact, the option *ONLY* is the alternative to *WITH TIES*. According to the standard, you must specify one of the two options. That's why even though T-SQL supports only the *ONLY* option for now, you still have to specify it. In case you were wondering…

A quick look at window functions

A window function is a function that, for each row in the underlying query, operates on a window (set) of rows that is derived from the underlying query result, and computes a scalar (single) result value. The window of rows is defined with an *OVER* clause. Window functions are profound; you can use them to address a wide variety of needs, such as to perform data-analysis calculations. T-SQL supports several categories of window functions, and each category has several functions. Window functions are defined by the SQL standard, and T-SQL supports a subset of the features from the standard.

At this point in the book, it could be premature to get into too much detail. For now, I'll just provide a glimpse into the concept and demonstrate it by using the *ROW_NUMBER* window function. Later in the book (in Chapter 7, "T-SQL for data analysis"), I provide more details.

As mentioned, a window function operates on a set of rows exposed to it by the *OVER* clause. For each row in the underlying query, the *OVER* clause exposes to the function a subset of the rows from the underlying query's result set. The *OVER* clause can restrict the rows in the window by using an optional window partition clause (*PARTITION BY*). It can define ordering for the calculation (if relevant) using a window order clause (*ORDER BY*)—not to be confused with the query's presentation *ORDER BY* clause.

Consider the following query as an example:

```
SELECT orderid, custid, val,
  ROW_NUMBER() OVER(PARTITION BY custid
                    ORDER BY val) AS rownum
FROM Sales.OrderValues
ORDER BY custid, val;
```

This query generates the following output, shown here in abbreviated form:

```
orderid      custid       val                                            rownum
-----------  -----------  ---------------------------------------------  --------------------
10702        1            330.00                                         1
10952        1            471.20                                         2
10643        1            814.50                                         3
10835        1            845.80                                         4
10692        1            878.00                                         5
11011        1            933.50                                         6
10308        2            88.80                                          1
10759        2            320.00                                         2
10625        2            479.75                                         3
10926        2            514.40                                         4
10682        3            375.50                                         1
...

(830 rows affected)
```

The *ROW_NUMBER* function assigns unique sequential incrementing integers to the rows in the result within the respective partition, based on the indicated ordering. The *OVER* clause in this example function partitions the window by the *custid* attribute. In other words, it creates a separate partition for each distinct *custid* value; hence, the row numbers are unique to each customer. The *OVER* clause also defines ordering in the window by the *val* attribute, so the sequential row numbers are incremented within the partition based on the values in this attribute.

Note that the *ROW_NUMBER* function must produce unique values within each partition. This means that even when the ordering value doesn't increase, the row number still must increase. Therefore, if the *ROW_NUMBER* function's *ORDER BY* list is non-unique, as in the preceding example, the calculation is nondeterministic. That is, more than one correct result is possible. If you want to make a row number calculation deterministic, you must add elements to the *ORDER BY* list to make it unique. For example, in our sample query you can achieve this by adding the *orderid* attribute as a tiebreaker.

Window ordering should not be confused with presentation ordering; it does not prevent the result from being relational. Also, specifying window ordering in a window function doesn't give you any presentation-ordering guarantees. If you need to guarantee presentation ordering, you must add a presentation *ORDER BY* clause, as I did in the last query.

Note that expressions in the *SELECT* list are evaluated before the *DISTINCT* clause (if one exists). This rule also applies to expressions based on window functions that appear in the *SELECT* list. I explain the significance of this fact in Chapter 7.

To put it all together, the following list presents the logical order in which all clauses discussed so far are processed:

- *FROM*

- *WHERE*

- *GROUP BY*

- *HAVING*

- *SELECT*

    - Expressions
    - *DISTINCT*

- *ORDER BY*

    - *TOP/OFFSET-FETCH*

Predicates and operators

T-SQL has language elements in which predicates can be specified—for example, query filters such as *WHERE* and *HAVING*, the *JOIN* operator's *ON* clause, *CHECK* constraints, and others. Remember that predicates are logical expressions that evaluate to *TRUE*, *FALSE*, or *UNKNOWN*. You can combine predicates by using logical operators such as *AND* (forming a combination known as a *conjunction of predicates*) and *OR* (known as a *disjunction of predicates*). You can also involve other types of operators, such as comparison operators, in your expressions.

Examples of predicates supported by T-SQL include *IN*, *BETWEEN*, and *LIKE*. You use the *IN* predicate to check whether a value, or scalar expression, is equal to at least one of the elements in a set. For example, the following query returns orders in which the order ID is equal to 10248, 10249, or 10250:

```
SELECT orderid, empid, orderdate
FROM Sales.Orders
WHERE orderid IN(10248, 10249, 10250);
```

You use the *BETWEEN* predicate to check whether a value falls within a specified range, inclusive of the two delimiters of the range. For example, the following query returns all orders in the inclusive range 10300 through 10310:

```
SELECT orderid, empid, orderdate
FROM Sales.Orders
WHERE orderid BETWEEN 10300 AND 10310;
```

With the *LIKE* predicate, you can check whether a character string value meets a specified pattern. For example, the following query returns employees whose last names start with the letter *D*:

```
SELECT empid, firstname, lastname
FROM HR.Employees
WHERE lastname LIKE N'D%';
```

Later in this chapter, I'll elaborate on pattern matching and the *LIKE* predicate.

Notice the use of the letter *N* to prefix the string *'D%'*; it stands for *National* and is used to denote that a character string is of a Unicode data type (*NCHAR* or *NVARCHAR*), as opposed to a regular character data type (*CHAR* or *VARCHAR*). Because the data type of the *lastname* attribute is *NVARCHAR(40)*, the letter *N* is used to prefix the string. Later in this chapter, in the section "Working with character data," I elaborate on the treatment of character strings.

T-SQL supports the following comparison operators: =, >, <, >=, <=, <>, !=, !>, and !<, of which the last three are not standard. Because the nonstandard operators have standard alternatives (such as <> instead of !=), I recommend you avoid using nonstandard operators. For example, the following query returns all orders placed on or after January 1, 2022:

```
SELECT orderid, empid, orderdate
FROM Sales.Orders
WHERE orderdate >= '20220101';
```

If you need to combine logical expressions, you can use the logical operators *OR* and *AND*. If you want to negate an expression, you can use the *NOT* operator. For example, the following query returns orders placed on or after January 1, 2022, that were handled by an employee whose ID is other than 1, 3, and 5:

```
SELECT orderid, empid, orderdate
FROM Sales.Orders
WHERE orderdate >= '20220101'
  AND empid NOT IN(1, 3, 5);
```

T-SQL supports the four obvious arithmetic operators: +, –, *, and /. It also supports the % operator (modulo), which returns the remainder of integer division. For example, the following query calculates the net value as a result of arithmetic manipulation of the *quantity*, *unitprice*, and *discount* attributes:

```
SELECT orderid, productid, qty, unitprice, discount,
  qty * unitprice * (1 - discount) AS val
FROM Sales.OrderDetails;
```

Note that the data type of a scalar expression involving two operands is determined in T-SQL by the operand with the higher data-type precedence. If both operands are of the same data type, the result of the expression is of the same data type as well. For example, a division between two integers (*INT*) yields an integer. The expression 5/2 returns the integer 2 and not the numeric 2.5. This is not a problem when you are dealing with constants, because you can always specify the values as numeric ones with a decimal point. But when you are dealing with, say, two integer columns, as in *col1/col2*, you need to cast the operands to the appropriate type if you want the calculation to be a numeric one: *CAST(col1 AS NUMERIC(12, 2))/CAST(col2 AS NUMERIC(12, 2))*. The data type *NUMERIC(12, 2)* has a precision of 12 and a scale of 2, meaning that it has 12 digits in total, 2 of which are after the decimal point.

If the two operands are of different types, the one with the lower precedence is promoted to the one that is higher. For example, in the expression 5/2.0, the first operand is *INT* and the second is *NUMERIC*. Because *NUMERIC* is considered higher than *INT*, the *INT* operand 5 is implicitly converted to the *NUMERIC* 5.0 before the arithmetic operation, and you get the result 2.5.

You can find information about data types, their precedence, and related information in the product documentation here: *https://learn.microsoft.com/en-us/sql/t-sql/data-types/data-types-transact-sql*.

When multiple operators appear in the same expression, SQL Server evaluates them based on operator precedence rules. The following list describes the precedence among operators, from highest to lowest:

1. ( ) (Parentheses)

2. * (Multiplication), / (Division), % (Modulo)

3. + (Positive), – (Negative), + (Addition), + (Concatenation), – (Subtraction)

4. =, >, <, >=, <=, <>, !=, !>, !< (Comparison operators)

5. *NOT*

6. *AND*

7. *BETWEEN, IN, LIKE, OR*

8. = (Assignment)

For example, in the following query, *AND* has precedence over *OR*:

```
SELECT orderid, custid, empid, orderdate
FROM Sales.Orders
WHERE
      custid = 1
  AND empid IN(1, 3, 5)
  OR  custid = 85
  AND empid IN(2, 4, 6);
```

The query returns orders that were either "placed by customer 1 and handled by employees 1, 3, or 5" or "placed by customer 85 and handled by employees 2, 4, or 6."

Parentheses have the highest precedence, so they give you full control. For the sake of other people who need to review or maintain your code and for readability purposes, it's a good practice to use parentheses even when they are not required. The same is true with indentation. For example, the following query is the logical equivalent of the previous query, only its meaning is much clearer:

```
SELECT orderid, custid, empid, orderdate
FROM Sales.Orders
WHERE
      (      custid = 1
        AND empid IN(1, 3, 5) )
   OR
      (      custid = 85
        AND empid IN(2, 4, 6) );
```

Using parentheses to force precedence with logical operators is similar to using parentheses with arithmetic operators. For example, without parentheses in the following expression, multiplication precedes addition:

```
SELECT 10 + 2 * 3;
```

Therefore, this expression returns 16. You can use parentheses to force the addition to be calculated first:

```
SELECT (10 + 2) * 3;
```

This time, the expression returns 36.

This is of course obvious and intuitive to most people. In a very similar manner, parentheses can be used to force desired precedence of a number of other T-SQL elements, including set operators, as you will see later in the book.

CASE expressions

A *CASE* expression is a scalar expression that returns a value based on conditional logic. It is based on the SQL standard. Note that *CASE* is an expression and not a statement; that is, it doesn't take action such as controlling the flow of your code. Instead, it returns a value. Because *CASE* is a scalar expression, it is allowed wherever scalar expressions are allowed, such as in the *SELECT*, *WHERE*, *HAVING*, and *ORDER BY* clauses and in *CHECK* constraints.

There are two forms of *CASE* expressions: *simple* and *searched*. You use the simple form to compare one value or scalar expression with a list of possible values and return a value for the first match. If no value in the list is equal to the tested value, the *CASE* expression returns the value that appears in the *ELSE* clause (if one exists). If the *CASE* expression doesn't have an *ELSE* clause, it defaults to *ELSE NULL*.

For example, the following query against the *Production.Products* table uses a *CASE* expression to compute the product count parity (whether the count is odd or even) per category:

```
SELECT supplierid, COUNT(*) AS numproducts,
  CASE COUNT(*) % 2
    WHEN 0 THEN 'Even'
    WHEN 1 THEN 'Odd'
    ELSE 'Unknown'
  END AS countparity
FROM Production.Products
GROUP BY supplierid;
```

This query produces the following output, shown in abbreviated form:

```
supplierid  numproducts countparity
----------- ----------- -----------
1           3           Even
2           4           Odd
3           3           Even
4           3           Even
5           2           Odd
6           3           Even
7           5           Even
8           4           Odd
9           2           Odd
10          1           Even
...

(29 rows affected)
```

The simple *CASE* expression has a single test value or expression right after the *CASE* keyword (COUNT(*) % 2 in this query) that is compared with a list of possible values or expressions, in the *WHEN* clauses (0 and 1 in this query). The *THEN* expression that is associated with the first match is returned. The *ELSE* expression is returned if the input expression isn't equal to any of the *WHEN* expressions. If an *ELSE* clause isn't specified, ELSE NULL is assumed. In our specific query, the input expression will always evaluate to either 0 or 1, so the *ELSE* clause will never be activated. I added it just so that you can see the full possibilities of the syntax.

The searched *CASE* expression is more flexible in the sense that you can specify predicates in the *WHEN* clauses rather than being restricted to using equality comparisons. The searched *CASE* expression returns the value in the *THEN* clause that is associated with the first *WHEN* predicate that evaluates to *TRUE*. If none of the *WHEN* predicates evaluates to *TRUE*, the *CASE* expression returns the value that appears in the *ELSE* clause (or *NULL* if an *ELSE* clause is not present). For example, the following query produces a value category description based on whether the value is less than 1,000.00, between 1,000.00 and 3,000.00, or greater than 3,000.00:

```
SELECT orderid, custid, val,
  CASE
    WHEN val < 1000.00  THEN 'Less than 1000'
    WHEN val <= 3000.00 THEN 'Between 1000 and 3000'
    WHEN val > 3000.00  THEN 'More than 3000'
    ELSE 'Unknown'
  END AS valuecategory
FROM Sales.OrderValues;
```

This query generates the following output, shown here in abbreviated form:

```
orderid     custid      val      valuecategory
----------- ----------- -------- ---------------------
10248       85          440.00   Less than 1000
10249       79          1863.40  Between 1000 and 3000
10250       34          1552.60  Between 1000 and 3000
10251       84          654.06   Less than 1000
10252       76          3597.90  More than 3000
10253       34          1444.80  Between 1000 and 3000
10254       14          556.62   Less than 1000
10255       68          2490.50  Between 1000 and 3000
10256       88          517.80   Less than 1000
10257       35          1119.90  Between 1000 and 3000
...

(830 rows affected)
```

You can see that every simple *CASE* expression can be converted to the searched *CASE* form, but the reverse is not true.

T-SQL supports some functions you can consider abbreviations of the *CASE* expression: *ISNULL, COALESCE, IIF,* and *CHOOSE*. Note that of the four, only *COALESCE* is standard.

The *ISNULL* function accepts two arguments as input and returns the first that is not *NULL*, or *NULL* if both are *NULL*. For example *ISNULL(col1, '')* returns the *col1* value if it isn't *NULL* and an empty string if it is *NULL*. The *COALESCE* function is similar, only it supports two or more arguments and returns the first that isn't *NULL*, or *NULL* if all are *NULL*.

> **See Also** It's a common question whether you should use *ISNULL* or *COALESCE*. I cover the topic in detail in the following article: *https://www.itprotoday.com/sql-server/coalesce-vs-isnull.*

The nonstandard *IIF* and *CHOOSE* functions were added to T-SQL to support easier migrations from Microsoft Access. The function *IIF(<logical_expression>, <expr1>, <expr2>)* returns *expr1* if *logical_expression* is *TRUE,* and it returns *expr2* otherwise. For example, the expression *IIF(col1 <> 0, col2/col1, NULL)* returns the result of *col2/col1* if *col1* is not zero; otherwise, it returns a *NULL*. The function *CHOOSE(<index>, <expr1>, <expr2>, ..., <exprn>)* returns the expression from the list in the specified index. For example, the expression *CHOOSE(3, col1, col2, col3)* returns the value of *col3*. Of course, actual expressions that use the *CHOOSE* function tend to be more dynamic—for example, relying on user input.

So far, I've just used a few examples to familiarize you with the *CASE* expression and related functions. Even though it might not be apparent at this point from these examples, the *CASE* expression is an extremely powerful and useful language element.

NULLs

As explained in Chapter 1, "Background to T-SQL querying and programming," SQL supports the *NULL* marker to represent missing values and uses three-valued predicate logic, meaning that predicates can evaluate to *TRUE*, *FALSE*, or *UNKNOWN*. T-SQL follows the standard in this respect. Treatment of *NULLs* and *UNKNOWN* in SQL can be confusing because intuitively people are more accustomed to thinking in terms of two-valued logic (*TRUE* and *FALSE*). To add to the confusion, different language elements in SQL treat *NULLs* and *UNKNOWN* inconsistently.

Let's start with three-valued predicate logic. A logical expression involving only non-*NULL* values evaluates to either *TRUE* or *FALSE*. When the logical expression involves a *NULL*, it evaluates to *UNKNOWN*. That's at least the case with most operators. For example, consider the predicate *salary > 0*. When *salary* is equal to 1,000, the expression evaluates to *TRUE*. When *salary* is equal to –1,000, the expression evaluates to *FALSE*. When *salary* is *NULL*, the expression evaluates to *UNKNOWN*.

SQL treats *TRUE* and *FALSE* in an intuitive and probably expected manner. For example, if the predicate *salary > 0* appears in a query filter (such as in a *WHERE* or *HAVING* clause), rows or groups for which the expression evaluates to *TRUE* are returned, whereas those for which the expression evaluates to *FALSE* are discarded. Similarly, if the predicate *salary > 0* appears in a *CHECK* constraint in a table, *INSERT* or *UPDATE* statements for which the expression evaluates to *TRUE* for all rows are accepted, whereas those for which the expression evaluates to *FALSE* for any row are rejected.

SQL has different treatments for *UNKNOWN* in different language elements (and for some people, not necessarily the expected treatments). The treatment SQL has for query filters is "accept *TRUE*," meaning that both *FALSE* and *UNKNOWN* are discarded. Conversely, the definition of the treatment SQL has for *CHECK* constraints is "reject *FALSE*," meaning that both *TRUE* and *UNKNOWN* are accepted. Had SQL used two-valued predicate logic, there wouldn't have been a difference between the definitions "accept *TRUE*" and "reject *FALSE*." But with three-valued predicate logic, "accept *TRUE*" rejects *UNKNOWN*, whereas "reject *FALSE*" accepts it. With the predicate *salary > 0* from the previous example, a *NULL* salary would cause the expression to evaluate to *UNKNOWN*. If this predicate appears in a query's *WHERE* clause, a row with a *NULL* salary will be discarded. If this predicate appears in a *CHECK* constraint in a table, a row with a *NULL* salary will be accepted.

One of the tricky aspects of the truth value *UNKNOWN* is that when you negate it, you still get *UNKNOWN*. For example, given the predicate *NOT (salary > 0)*, when salary is *NULL*, *salary > 0* evaluates to *UNKNOWN*, and *NOT UNKNOWN* remains *UNKNOWN*.

What some people find surprising is that an expression comparing two *NULLs* (*NULL = NULL*) evaluates to *UNKNOWN*. The reasoning for this from SQL's perspective is that a *NULL* represents a missing value, and you can't really tell whether one missing value is equal to another. Therefore, SQL provides you with the predicates *IS NULL* and *IS NOT NULL*, which you should use instead of *= NULL* and *<> NULL*.

SQL Server 2022 introduces support for the standard distinct predicate, which uses two-valued logic when comparing elements, essentially treating *NULLs* like non-*NULL* values. The distinct predicate has the following syntax:

```
comparand1 IS [NOT] DISTINCT FROM comparand2
```

The *IS NOT DISTINCT FROM* predicate is similar to the equality (=) operator, only it evaluates to *TRUE* when comparing two *NULLs*, and to *FALSE* when comparing a *NULL* with a non-*NULL* value. The *IS DISTINCT FROM* predicate is similar to the different than (<>) operator, only it evaluates to *FALSE* when comparing two *NULLs*, and to *TRUE* when comparing a *NULL* with a non-*NULL* value. It might sound a bit confusing that this predicate uses negative form (with a *NOT*) to apply a positive comparison and a positive form (without a *NOT*) to apply a negative comparison, but if you think about it, that's similar to how we speak in English when describing distinctness.

To make things a bit more tangible, I'll demonstrate the ramifications of three-valued logic with examples. The *Sales.Customers* table has three attributes, called *country*, *region*, and *city*, where the customer's location information is stored. All locations have existing countries and cities. Some have existing regions (such as *country*: USA, *region*: WA, *city*: Seattle), yet for some the *region* element is missing but inapplicable (such as *country*: UK, *region*: NULL, *city*: London). Consider the following query, which attempts to return all customers where the region is equal to WA:

```
SELECT custid, country, region, city
FROM Sales.Customers
WHERE region = N'WA';
```

This query generates the following output:

custid	country	region	city
43	USA	WA	Walla Walla
82	USA	WA	Kirkland
89	USA	WA	Seattle

Out of the 91 rows in the *Customers* table, the query returns the three rows where the *region* attribute is equal to WA. The query returns neither rows in which the value in the *region* attribute is present and different than WA (the predicate evaluates to *FALSE*) nor those where the *region* attribute is *NULL* (the predicate evaluates to *UNKNOWN*). Most people would consider this result the expected one.

In this case, when comparing the column *region* with the constant *N'WA'*, there's no real reason to use the distinct predicate, since the end result is the same as with the equality operator. So the following query returns the same result as the last one:

```
SELECT custid, country, region, city
FROM Sales.Customers
WHERE region IS NOT DISTINCT FROM N'WA';
```

For the three customers from WA, the predicate evaluates to *TRUE*. For the remaining customers, the predicate evaluates to *FALSE*. The result is that you get only the three customers from WA, like with the previous query.

Using the distinct predicate as an alternative to the equality operator becomes important when you compare two columns, or a column with a variable, or an input parameter that you pass to a stored procedure or a user-defined function. You can find details about variables, parameters, stored procedures, and user-defined functions in Chapter 12. But just for the sake of the example, suppose that you have a query within a stored procedure that accepts the region as an input parameter called *@region*, and the query needs to return customers from the input region, even if it's *NULL*. Using the equality operator will not give you the correct result when the input is *NULL*. Without the distinct predicate, you would need to write an elaborate filter predicate, like so (don't actually try running this, since the definition of the hosting stored procedure is missing):

```
SELECT custid, country, region, city
FROM Sales.Customers
WHERE region = @region
  OR (region IS NULL AND @region IS NULL);
```

Instead, using the distinct predicate, the logically equivalent query looks like this:

```
SELECT custid, country, region, city
FROM Sales.Customers
WHERE region IS NOT DISTINCT FROM @region;
```

Now let's examine an example looking for difference. The following query attempts to return all customers for whom the region is different than WA:

```
SELECT custid, country, region, city
FROM Sales.Customers
WHERE region <> N'WA';
```

This query generates the following output:

```
custid       country           region            city
-----------  ----------------  ----------------  ----------------
10           Canada            BC                Tsawassen
15           Brazil            SP                Sao Paulo
21           Brazil            SP                Sao Paulo
31           Brazil            SP                Campinas
32           USA               OR                Eugene
33           Venezuela         DF                Caracas
34           Brazil            RJ                Rio de Janeiro
35           Venezuela         Táchira           San Cristóbal
36           USA               OR                Elgin
37           Ireland           Co. Cork          Cork
38           UK                Isle of Wight     Cowes
42           Canada            BC                Vancouver
45           USA               CA                San Francisco
46           Venezuela         Lara              Barquisimeto
47           Venezuela         Nueva Esparta     I. de Margarita
48           USA               OR                Portland
```

51	Canada	Québec	Montréal
55	USA	AK	Anchorage
61	Brazil	RJ	Rio de Janeiro
62	Brazil	SP	Sao Paulo
65	USA	NM	Albuquerque
67	Brazil	RJ	Rio de Janeiro
71	USA	ID	Boise
75	USA	WY	Lander
77	USA	OR	Portland
78	USA	MT	Butte
81	Brazil	SP	Sao Paulo
88	Brazil	SP	Resende

(28 rows affected)

If you expected to get 88 rows back (91 rows in the table minus 3 returned by the previous query), you might find this result (with just 28 rows) surprising. But remember that a query filter "accepts *TRUE*," meaning that it rejects both *FALSE* and *UNKNOWN*. So this query returned rows in which the *region* value was present and different than WA. It returned neither rows in which the *region* value was equal to WA nor rows in which *region* was *NULL*. You will get the same output if you use the predicate *NOT (region = N'WA')*. That's because in the rows where *region* is *NULL* the expression *region = N'WA'* evaluates to *UNKNOWN*, and *NOT (region = N'WA')* evaluates to *UNKNOWN* also.

If you want to return all rows for which *region* is *NULL*, do not use the predicate *region = NULL*, because the expression evaluates to *UNKNOWN* in all rows—both those in which the value is present and those in which the value is missing (is *NULL*). The following query returns an empty set:

```
SELECT custid, country, region, city
FROM Sales.Customers
WHERE region = NULL;
```

custid	country	region	city

(0 rows affected)

Instead, you should use the *IS NULL* predicate:

```
SELECT custid, country, region, city
FROM Sales.Customers
WHERE region IS NULL;
```

This query generates the following output, shown in abbreviated form:

custid	country	region	city
1	Germany	NULL	Berlin
2	Mexico	NULL	México D.F.
3	Mexico	NULL	México D.F.
4	UK	NULL	London
5	Sweden	NULL	Luleå
6	Germany	NULL	Mannheim
7	France	NULL	Strasbourg

```
8          Spain          NULL          Madrid
9          France         NULL          Marseille
11         UK             NULL          London
...
```

```
(60 rows affected)
```

If you want to return all rows for which the *region* attribute is different than WA, including those in which the value is missing, you need to include an explicit test for *NULLs*, like this:

```
SELECT custid, country, region, city
FROM Sales.Customers
WHERE region <> N'WA'
   OR region IS NULL;
```

This query generates the following output, shown in abbreviated form:

```
custid      country          region            city
----------- ---------------- ----------------  ----------------
1           Germany          NULL              Berlin
2           Mexico           NULL              México D.F.
3           Mexico           NULL              México D.F.
4           UK               NULL              London
5           Sweden           NULL              Luleå
6           Germany          NULL              Mannheim
7           France           NULL              Strasbourg
8           Spain            NULL              Madrid
9           France           NULL              Marseille
10          Canada           BC                Tsawassen
...
```

```
(88 rows affected)
```

Using the distinct predicate, you could think of the request as returning customers for which *region* is distinct from WA, using the following query:

```
SELECT custid, country, region, city
FROM Sales.Customers
WHERE region IS DISTINCT FROM N'WA';
```

This query is the logical equivalent of the previous query, but a bit less verbose.

For a parameterized query looking for difference, the version without the distinct predicate is even more verbose. It looks like this (again, don't actually try running this query, since the definition of the hosting stored procedure is missing):

```
SELECT custid, country, region, city
FROM Sales.Customers
WHERE region <> @region
   OR (region IS NULL AND @region IS NOT NULL)
   OR (region IS NOT NULL AND @region IS NULL);
```

Using the distinct predicate, the parameterized query is much simpler:

```
SELECT custid, country, region, city
FROM Sales.Customers
WHERE region IS DISTINCT FROM @region;
```

SQL also treats *NULLs* inconsistently in different language elements for comparison and sorting purposes. Some elements treat two *NULLs* as equal to each other, and others treat them as different.

For example, for grouping and sorting purposes, two *NULLs* are considered equal. That is, the *GROUP BY* clause arranges all *NULLs* in one group just like present values, and the *ORDER BY* clause sorts all *NULLs* together. Standard SQL leaves it to the product implementation to determine whether *NULLs* sort before present values or after them, but it must be consistent within the implementation. T-SQL sorts *NULLs* before present values when using ascending ordering.

As mentioned, query filters "accept *TRUE*." An expression comparing two *NULLs* yields *UNKNOWN*; therefore, such a row is filtered out.

For the purposes of enforcing a *UNIQUE* constraint, standard SQL enforces uniqueness only among the non-*NULL* values. As a result, for example, a *UNIQUE* constraint on a single *NULL*-able *column* allows multiple *NULLs* in that column. Conversely, in T-SQL, a *UNIQUE* constraint handles *NULLs* like non-*NULL* values, as if two *NULLs* are equal (allowing only one *NULL*). You can find more information on the standard *UNIQUE* constraint and how to implement similar functionality in T-SQL in the following article: *https://sqlperformance.com/2020/03/t-sql-queries/ null-complexities-part-4-missing-standard-unique-constraint*.

The complexity in handling *NULLs* often results in logical errors. Therefore, you should think about them in every query you write. If the default treatment is not what you want, you must intervene explicitly; otherwise, just ensure that the default behavior is, in fact, what you want.

The information provided in this section about *NULLs* should be sufficient background for the remainder of this book. However, if you find this topic interesting and would like to delve into it more deeply, including optimization considerations, you can find more info in the following four-part series:

- "NULL complexities – Part 1" at *https://sqlperformance.com/2019/12/t-sql-queries/ null-complexities-part-1*

- "NULL Complexities – Part 2" at *https://sqlperformance.com/2020/01/t-sql-queries/ null-complexities-part-2*

- "NULL complexities – Part 3, Missing standard features and T-SQL alternatives" at *https://sqlperformance.com/2020/02/t-sql-queries/ null-complexities-part-3-missing-standard-features-and-t-sql-alternatives*

- "NULL complexities – Part 4, Missing standard unique constraint" at *https://sqlperformance. com/2020/03/t-sql-queries/null-complexities-part-4-missing-standard-unique-constraint*

The *GREATEST* and *LEAST* functions

In the section "The *GROUP BY* clause" I covered grouped aggregate functions, including the *MAX* and *MIN* functions. Recall that these functions operate on sets of rows that are defined by the query's grouping set—the elements that you group by. However, sometimes you need to apply maximum and minimum calculations across columns, or across a set of expressions, per row. Starting with SQL Server 2022, such needs are achievable with the functions *GREATEST* and *LEAST*, which are the row-level alternatives to *MAX* and *MIN*, respectively.

These functions are straightforward and intuitive to use, so I'll jump straight to an example. The following query retrieves the orders that were placed by customer 8, and uses the *GREATEST* and *LEAST* functions to calculate, per order, the latest and earliest dates among the order's required date and shipped date:

```
SELECT orderid, requireddate, shippeddate,
  GREATEST(requireddate, shippeddate) AS latestdate,
  LEAST(requireddate, shippeddate) AS earliestdate
FROM Sales.Orders
WHERE custid = 8;
```

Assuming you're running this code against SQL Server 2022 or later, or Azure SQL Database, this query generates the following output:

```
orderid     requireddate  shippeddate  latestdate  earliestdate
----------- ------------- ------------ ----------- -------------
10326       2020-11-07    2020-10-14   2020-11-07  2020-10-14
10801       2022-01-26    2021-12-31   2022-01-26  2021-12-31
10970       2022-04-07    2022-04-24   2022-04-24  2022-04-07
```

As you can see in this example, the *GREATEST* and *LEAST* functions are not limited to numeric input arguments. In this sense they are similar to *MAX* and *MIN*. If the inputs are of mixed data types, the one with the strongest data type precedence forces implicit conversion of the ones with the weaker types, and determines the type of the result.

These functions support any number of input arguments between 1 and 254. *NULL* inputs are ignored, but if all inputs are *NULL*, the result is *NULL*.

In earlier versions of SQL Server, if you had only two input arguments, you could handle such needs with *CASE* expressions, like so:

```
SELECT orderid, requireddate, shippeddate,
  CASE
    WHEN requireddate > shippeddate OR shippeddate IS NULL THEN requireddate
    ELSE shippeddate
  END AS latestdate,
  CASE
    WHEN requireddate < shippeddate OR shippeddate IS NULL THEN requireddate
    ELSE shippeddate
  END AS earliestdate
FROM Sales.Orders
WHERE custid = 8;
```

Beyond two inputs, solving such needs using *CASE* expressions results in very convoluted code. Try it, for example, by adding the *orderdate* column to the mix. So usually people opt for more advanced alternative solutions that utilize unpivoting techniques with the *UNPIVOT* or *APPLY* operators. I cover both operators in later chapters in this book. Once the *GREATEST* and *LEAST* functions became available, it became so easy to handle such needs.

All-at-once operations

SQL supports a concept called *all-at-once operations*, which means that all expressions that appear in the same logical query processing phase are evaluated logically at the same point in time. The reason for this is that all expressions that appear in the same logical phase are treated as a set, and as mentioned earlier, a set has no order to its elements.

This concept explains why, for example, you cannot refer to column aliases assigned in the *SELECT* clause within the same *SELECT* clause. Consider the following query:

```
SELECT
  orderid,
  YEAR(orderdate) AS orderyear,
  orderyear + 1 AS nextyear
FROM Sales.Orders;
```

The reference to the column alias *orderyear* in the third expression in the *SELECT* list is invalid, even though the referencing expression appears after the one in which the alias is assigned. The reason is that logically there is no order of evaluation of the expressions in the *SELECT* clause—it is a set of expressions. Conceptually, all the expressions are evaluated at the same point in time. Therefore, this query generates the following error:

```
Msg 207, Level 16, State 1, Line 4
Invalid column name 'orderyear'.
```

Here's another example for the ramifications of all-at-once operations: Suppose you have a table called *T1* with two integer columns called *col1* and *col2*, and you want to return all rows for which *col2/col1* is greater than 2. Because there might be rows in the table in which *col1* is zero, you need to ensure that the division doesn't take place in those cases—otherwise, the query would fail because of a divide-by-zero error. So you write a query using the following format:

```
SELECT col1, col2
FROM dbo.T1
WHERE col1 <> 0 AND col2/col1 > 2;
```

You might very well assume SQL Server evaluates the expressions from left to right, and that if the expression *col1 <> 0* evaluates to *FALSE*, SQL Server will short-circuit—that is, that it won't bother to evaluate the expression *col2/col1 > 2* because at this point it is known that the whole expression is *FALSE*. So you might think that this query should never produce a divide-by-zero error.

SQL Server does support short circuits, but because of the all-at-once operations concept, it is free to process the expressions in the *WHERE* clause in any order. SQL Server usually makes decisions like this based on cost estimations. You can see that if SQL Server decides to process the expression *col2/col1 > 2* first, this query might fail because of a divide-by-zero error.

You have several ways to avoid a failure here. For example, the order in which the *WHEN* clauses of a *CASE* expression are evaluated is guaranteed. So you could revise the query as follows:

```
SELECT col1, col2
FROM dbo.T1
WHERE
  CASE
    WHEN col1 = 0 THEN 'no' -- or 'yes' if row should be returned
    WHEN col2/col1 > 2 THEN 'yes'
    ELSE 'no'
  END = 'yes';
```

In rows where *col1* is equal to zero, the first *WHEN* clause evaluates to *TRUE* and the *CASE* expression returns the string *'no'*. (Replace *'no'* with *'yes'* if you want to return the row when *col1* is equal to zero.) Only if the first *CASE* expression does not evaluate to *TRUE*—meaning that *col1* is not 0—does the second *WHEN* clause check whether the expression *col2/col1 > 2* evaluates to *TRUE*. If it does, the *CASE* expression returns the string *'yes'*. In all other cases, the *CASE* expression returns the string *'no'*. The predicate in the *WHERE* clause returns *TRUE* only when the result of the *CASE* expression is equal to the string *'yes'*. This means that there will never be an attempt here to divide by zero.

This workaround turned out to be quite convoluted. In this particular case, you can use a mathematical workaround that avoids division altogether:

```
SELECT col1, col2
FROM dbo.T1
WHERE (col1 > 0 AND col2 > 2*col1) OR (col1 < 0 AND col2 < 2*col1);
```

I included this example to explain the unique and important concept of all-at-once operations and to elaborate on the fact that SQL Server guarantees the processing order of the *WHEN* clauses in a *CASE* expression.

If you feel like you need some practice with the topics covered thus far before continuing, you should be able to work on exercises 4, 6, 8, 9, and 10. You can find those at the end of this chapter.

Working with character data

In this section, I cover query manipulation of character data—including data types, collation, and operators and functions—and pattern matching.

Data types

SQL Server supports two kinds of character data type pairs; we will refer to them as the *regular* kind and the *N*-kind. The regular kind pair includes *CHAR* and *VARCHAR*, and the *N*-kind includes *NCHAR* and *NVARCHAR*. As you could probably guess, I refer to the latter pair as the *N*-kind because the names of the data types of this kind have the letter *N* (for National) as a prefix.

The differences between the two pair kinds can be a bit confusing—especially when you're just getting started with T-SQL. Each of the type pairs can support different character encoding systems, and can result in different encoded byte lengths and on-disk storage sizes, based on the effective collation of the data (more on collation shortly) and the character code range in use.

Prior to SQL Server 2019, the regular types did not support the full range of Unicode characters, rather only the subset of characters that was supported by the code page of the effective collation. SQL Server 2019 introduced UTF-8 character encoding support for the regular types (when the effective collation name ends with UTF8), giving you support for the full range of Unicode characters.

As for the *N*-kind types, when you use with those a so-called supplementary character-enabled collation (the collation name has *SC* in it), they use the UTF-16 encoding system and support the full range of Unicode characters. Otherwise, they support only the subset of characters from the UCS-2 character encoding system.

Back to size; when using one of the regular types and specifying a size in parentheses—for example, *VARCHAR(10)*—you specify the size in bytes. This size may translate to support for 10 characters, but not necessarily, since some characters in certain encoding systems require more than one byte. When using the *N*-kind types and specifying a size in parentheses—for example, *NVARCHAR(10)*—you specify the size in byte pairs, so in this example that's 10 byte pairs, or 20 bytes. Again, this size may translate to support for 10 characters, but not necessarily, since some characters in certain encoding systems require more than one byte pair.

If you're using mostly English characters in the ASCII code range 0–127, the regular types with a UTF-8 collation will give you storage benefits, since they require 1 byte per character in this range. That's compared to the *N*-types with a UTF-16 collation, which require one byte pair (two bytes) per character in this range. But for some character code point ranges, the *N*-types can actually be more economical, such as with East Asian script.

The two pair kinds (the regular pair and the *N*-types pair) also differ in the way you express literals. When expressing a regular character type literal, you simply use single quotes: *'This is a literal'*. When expressing an *N*-type character literal, you need to specify the character *N* as a prefix: *N'This is a literal'*.

In hope that you won't abandon the book before getting to much more exciting T-SQL topics, I'll defer you to the product documentation for more details on the differences between the two pair kinds:

- Collation and Unicode support at *https://learn.microsoft.com/en-us/sql/relational-databases/ collations/collation-and-unicode-support*

- char and varchar at *https://learn.microsoft.com/en-us/sql/t-sql/data-types/ char-and-varchar-transact-sql*

- nchar and nvarchar at *https://learn.microsoft.com/en-us/sql/t-sql/data-types/ nchar-and-nvarchar-transact-sql*

Any data type without the *VAR* element (*CHAR*, *NCHAR*) in its name has a fixed length, which means that SQL Server preserves the maximum space in the row based on the column's defined size and not on the actual user data that is stored. For example, when a column is defined as *CHAR(25)*, SQL Server preserves 25 bytes of space in the row regardless of the length of the stored character string. Because no expansion of the row is required when the strings are expanded, fixed-length data types are more suited for write-focused systems. But because storage consumption is not optimal with fixed-length strings, you pay more when reading data.

A data type with the *VAR* element (*VARCHAR, NVARCHAR*) in its name has a variable length, which means that SQL Server uses as much storage space in the row as required to store the actual character string, plus two extra bytes for offset data. For example, when a column is defined as *VARCHAR(25)*, the maximum number of bytes supported is 25, but in practice, the user data in the character string determines the actual amount of storage. Because storage consumption for these data types is less than that for fixed-length types, read operations are faster. However, updates might result in row expansion, which might result in data movement outside the current page. Therefore, updates of data having variable-length data types are less efficient than updates of data having fixed-length data types.

> **Note** If compression is used, the storage requirements change. For details about compression, see "Data Compression" in the product documentation at *https://learn. microsoft.com/en-us/sql/relational-databases/data-compression/data-compression*.

You can also define the variable-length data types with the *MAX* specifier instead of a maximum number of bytes or byte pairs. When the column is defined with the *MAX* specifier, each single value can reach a size of up to 2 GB. Any value with a size up to a certain threshold (8,000 bytes by default) can be stored inline in the row. Any value with a size above the threshold is stored external to the row as a large object (LOB).

Later in this chapter, in the "Querying metadata" section, I explain how you can obtain metadata information about objects in the database, including the data types of columns.

Collation

Collation is a property of character data that encapsulates several aspects: language support, sort order, case sensitivity, accent sensitivity, and more. To get the set of supported collations and their descriptions, you can query the table function *fn_helpcollations* as follows:

```
SELECT name, description
FROM sys.fn_helpcollations();
```

For example, the following list explains the collation *Latin1_General_CI_AS*:

- **Latin1_General** Code page 1252 is used. (This supports English and German characters, as well as characters used by most Western European countries.)

- **Dictionary sorting** Sorting and comparison of character data are based on dictionary order (A and a < B and b).

You can tell that dictionary order is used because that's the default when no other ordering is defined explicitly. More specifically, the element *BIN* doesn't explicitly appear in the collation name. If the element *BIN* appeared, it would mean that the sorting and comparison of character data was based on the binary representation of characters (A < B < a < b).

- **CI**   The data is case insensitive (a = A).

- **AS**   The data is accent sensitive (à <> ä).

In an on-premises SQL Server implementation and Azure SQL Managed Instance, collation can be defined at four different levels: instance, database, column, and expression. The lowest level is the effective one that is used. In Azure SQL Database, collation can be defined at the database, column, and expression levels. There are some specialized aspects of collation in contained databases. (For details, see *https://learn.microsoft.com/en-us/sql/relational-databases/databases/contained-database-collations*.)

The collation of the instance is chosen as part of the setup program. It determines the collations of all system databases and is used as the default for user databases.

When you create a user database, you can specify a collation for the database by using the *COLLATE* clause. If you don't, the instance's collation is assumed by default.

The database collation determines the collation of the metadata of objects in the database and is used as the default for user table columns. I want to emphasize the importance of the fact that the database collation determines the collation of the metadata, including object and column names. For example, if the database collation is case insensitive, you can't create two tables called *T1* and *t1* within the same schema, but if the database collation is case sensitive, you can do that. Note, though, that the collation aspects of variable and parameter identifiers are determined by the instance and not the database collation, regardless of the database you are connected to when declaring them. For example, if your instance has a case-insensitive collation and your database has a case-sensitive collation, you won't be able to define two variables or parameters named @p and @P in the same scope. Such an attempt will result in an error saying that the variable name has already been declared.

You can explicitly specify a collation for a column as part of its definition by using the *COLLATE* clause. If you don't, the database collation is assumed by default.

You can convert the collation of an expression by using the *COLLATE* clause. For example, in a case-insensitive environment, the following query uses a case-insensitive comparison:

```
SELECT empid, firstname, lastname
FROM HR.Employees
WHERE lastname = N'davis';
```

The query returns the row for Sara Davis, even though the casing doesn't match, because the effective casing is insensitive:

```
empid       firstname  lastname
----------- ---------- --------------------
1           Sara       Davis
```

If you want to make the filter case sensitive even though the column's collation is case insensitive, you can convert the collation of the expression:

```
SELECT empid, firstname, lastname
FROM HR.Employees
WHERE lastname COLLATE Latin1_General_CS_AS = N'davis';
```

This time the query returns an empty set because no match is found when a case-sensitive comparison is used.

Quoted identifiers

In standard SQL, single quotes are used to delimit literal character strings (for example, *'literal'*) and double quotes are used to delimit irregular identifiers such as table or column names that include a space or start with a digit (for example, *"Irregular Identifier"*). In T-SQL, there's a setting called *QUOTED_IDENTIFIER* that controls the meaning of double quotes. You can apply this setting either at the database level by using the *ALTER DATABASE* command or at the session level by using the *SET* command. When the setting is turned on, the behavior is determined according to standard SQL, meaning that double quotes are used to delimit identifiers. When the setting is turned off, the behavior is nonstandard, and double quotes are used to delimit literal character strings. It is strongly recommended that you follow best practices and use standard behavior (with the setting on). Most database interfaces, including OLE DB and ODBC, turn this setting on by default.

Tip As an alternative to using double quotes to delimit identifiers, T-SQL also supports square brackets (for example, *[Irregular Identifier]*).

Note Regarding single quotes that are used to delimit literal character strings, if you want to incorporate a single quote character as part of the string, you need to specify two single quotes. For example, to express the literal *abc'de*, specify **'abc''de'**.

As mentioned earlier, if you want to use the UTF8 encoding system with the regular character string types, you need to choose a collation that has UTF8 in the name.

Operators and functions

This section covers string concatenation and functions that operate on character strings. For string concatenation, T-SQL provides the plus-sign (+) operator and the *CONCAT* and *CONCAT_WS* functions. For other operations on character strings, T-SQL provides several functions, including *SUB-STRING, LEFT, RIGHT, LEN, DATALENGTH, CHARINDEX, PATINDEX, REPLACE, TRANSLATE, REPLICATE, STUFF, UPPER, LOWER, RTRIM, LTRIM, TRIM, FORMAT, COMPRESS, DECOMPRESS, STRING_SPLIT*, and

STRING_AGG. In the following sections, I describe these commonly used operators and functions. Note that there is no SQL standard functions library—they are all implementation-specific.

String concatenation (plus-sign [+] operator and *CONCAT* and *CONCAT_WS* functions)

T-SQL provides the plus-sign (+) operator and the *CONCAT* and *CONCAT_WS* functions to concatenate strings. For example, the following query against the *Employees* table produces the *fullname* result column by concatenating *firstname*, a space, and *lastname*:

```
SELECT empid, firstname + N' ' + lastname AS fullname
FROM HR.Employees;
```

This query produces the following output:

```
empid       fullname
----------- --------------------------------
1           Sara Davis
2           Don Funk
3           Judy Lew
4           Yael Peled
5           Sven Mortensen
6           Paul Suurs
7           Russell King
8           Maria Cameron
9           Patricia Doyle
```

Standard SQL dictates that a concatenation with a *NULL* should yield a *NULL*. This is the default behavior of T-SQL. For example, consider the query against the *Customers* table shown in Listing 2-7.

LISTING 2-7 Query demonstrating string concatenation

```
SELECT custid, country, region, city,
country + N',' + region + N',' + city AS location
FROM Sales.Customers;
```

Some of the rows in the *Customers* table have a *NULL* in the region column. For those, SQL Server returns by default a *NULL* in the location result column:

```
custid      country             region  city             location
----------- ------------------- ------- ---------------- ----------------------
1           Germany             NULL    Berlin           NULL
2           Mexico              NULL    México D.F.      NULL
3           Mexico              NULL    México D.F.      NULL
4           UK                  NULL    London           NULL
5           Sweden              NULL    Luleå            NULL
6           Germany             NULL    Mannheim         NULL
7           France              NULL    Strasbourg       NULL
8           Spain               NULL    Madrid           NULL
9           France              NULL    Marseille        NULL
10          Canada              BC      Tsawwassen       Canada,BC,Tsawwassen
11          UK                  NULL    London           NULL
12          Argentina           NULL    Buenos Aires     NULL
```

```
13          Mexico        NULL    México D.F.    NULL
14          Switzerland   NULL    Bern           NULL
15          Brazil        SP      Sao Paulo      Brazil,SP,Sao Paulo
16          UK            NULL    London         NULL
17          Germany       NULL    Aachen         NULL
18          France        NULL    Nantes         NULL
19          UK            NULL    London         NULL
20          Austria       NULL    Graz           NULL
...

(91 rows affected)
```

To treat a *NULL* as an empty string—or more accurately, to substitute a *NULL* with an empty string—you can use the *COALESCE* function. This function accepts a list of input values and returns the first that is not *NULL*. Here's how you can revise the query from Listing 2-7 to programmatically substitute *NULLs* with empty strings:

```
SELECT custid, country, region, city,
  country + COALESCE(N',' + region, N'') + N',' + city AS location
FROM Sales.Customers;
```

In this example, when *region* is *NULL*, N',' + *region* will also be *NULL* and the *COALESCE* function will return an empty string.

T-SQL supports a function called *CONCAT*, which accepts a list of inputs for concatenation and automatically substitutes NULLs with empty strings. For example, the expression *CONCAT('a', NULL, 'b')* returns the string 'ab'.

Here's how to use the *CONCAT* function to concatenate the customer's location elements, replacing *NULLs* with empty strings:

```
SELECT custid, country, region, city,
  CONCAT(country, N',' + region, N',' + city) AS location
FROM Sales.Customers;
```

T-SQL also supports a function called *CONCAT_WS*, which accepts the separator as the first parameter, specifying it only once, and then the list of inputs for concatenation. This saves you the need to explicitly repeat all separator occurrences. Besides the simplified expressions, using this function also gives you support for a larger number of inputs. That's because both functions support a maximum of 254 inputs, and the explicitly specified separators are counted as inputs. *CONCAT_WS* also automatically substitutes *NULLs* with empty strings.

Here's how to use the *CONCAT_WS* function to concatenate the customer's location elements:

```
SELECT custid, country, region, city,
  CONCAT_WS(N',', country, region, city) AS location
FROM Sales.Customers;
```

The *SUBSTRING* function

The *SUBSTRING* function extracts a substring from a string.

SUBSTRING(*string*, *start*, *length*)

This function operates on the input *string* and extracts a substring starting at position *start* that is *length* characters long. For example, the following code returns the output 'abc':

```
SELECT SUBSTRING('abcde', 1, 3);
```

If the value of the third argument exceeds the end of the input string, the function returns everything until the end without raising an error. This can be convenient when you want to return everything from a certain point until the end of the string—you can simply specify the maximum length of the data type or a value representing the full length of the input string.

The *LEFT* and *RIGHT* functions

The *LEFT* and *RIGHT* functions are abbreviations of the *SUBSTRING* function, returning a requested number of characters from the left or right end of the input string.

Syntax

LEFT(*string*, *n*), RIGHT(*string*, *n*)

The first argument, *string*, is the string the function operates on. The second argument, *n*, is the number of characters to extract from the left or right end of the string. For example, the following code returns the output 'cde':

```
SELECT RIGHT('abcde', 3);
```

The *LEN* and *DATALENGTH* functions

The *LEN* function returns the number of characters in the input string.

Syntax

LEN(*string*)

Note that this function returns the number of characters in the input string and not necessarily the number of bytes used to represent it. For example, with regular character types, when using English characters in the ASCII 0–127 code range, both numbers are the same because each character is represented with 1 byte. With *N*-kind character types, the same characters are represented with 2 bytes; therefore, the number of characters is half the number of bytes. To get the number of bytes, use the *DATALENGTH* function instead of *LEN*. For example, the following code returns 5:

```
SELECT LEN(N'abcde');
```

The following code returns 10:

```
SELECT DATALENGTH(N'abcde');
```

Another difference between *LEN* and *DATALENGTH* is that the former excludes trailing spaces but the latter doesn't.

The *CHARINDEX* function

The *CHARINDEX* function returns the position of the first occurrence of a substring within a string.

Syntax

CHARINDEX(*substring*, *string*[, *start_pos*])

This function returns the position of the first argument, *substring*, within the second argument, *string*. You can optionally specify a third argument, *start_pos*, to tell the function the position from which to start looking. If you don't specify the third argument, the function starts looking from the first character. If the substring is not found, the function returns 0. For example, the following code returns the first position of a space in *'Itzik Ben-Gan'*, so it returns the output 6:

```
SELECT CHARINDEX(' ', 'Itzik Ben-Gan');
```

The *PATINDEX* function

The *PATINDEX* function returns the position of the first occurrence of a pattern within a string.

Syntax

PATINDEX(*pattern*, *string*)

The argument *pattern* uses similar patterns to those used by the *LIKE* predicate in T-SQL. I'll explain patterns and the *LIKE* predicate later in this chapter, in the section "The *LIKE* predicate." Even though I haven't explained yet how patterns are expressed in T-SQL, I include the following example here to show how to find the position of the first occurrence of a digit within a string:

```
SELECT PATINDEX('%[0-9]%', 'abcd123efgh');
```

This code returns the output 5.

The *REPLACE* function

The *REPLACE* function replaces all occurrences of a substring with another.

Syntax

REPLACE(*string*, *substring1*, *substring2*)

The function replaces all occurrences of *substring1* in *string* with *substring2*. For example, the following code substitutes all occurrences of a dash in the input string with a colon:

```
SELECT REPLACE('1-a 2-b', '-', ':');
```

This code returns the output '1:a 2:b'.

You can use the *REPLACE* function to count the number of occurrences of a character within a string. To do this, you replace all occurrences of the character with an empty string (zero characters) and calculate the original length of the string minus the new length. For example, the following query returns, for each employee, the number of times the character *e* appears in the *lastname* attribute:

```
SELECT empid, lastname,
  LEN(lastname) - LEN(REPLACE(lastname, 'e', '')) AS numoccur
FROM HR.Employees;
```

This query generates the following output:

```
empid        lastname               numoccur
-----------  ---------------------  -----------
8            Cameron                1
1            Davis                  0
9            Doyle                  1
2            Funk                   0
7            King                   0
3            Lew                    1
5            Mortensen              2
4            Peled                  2
6            Suurs                  0
```

The *TRANSLATE* function

The *TRANSLATE* function replaces in the *string* parameter all occurrences of the individual characters in the *characters* parameter with the respective individual characters in the *translations* parameter.

Syntax

TRANSLATE(*string, characters, translations*)

You can think of the *TRANSLATE* function as a more flexible version of the *REPLACE* function, allowing much simpler expressions when multiple single-character replacements are needed. This is especially important when you need to swap between characters in a string. For example, suppose that you're given an input string such as '123.456.789,00' representing an amount in Spanish format. You need to convert it to US format by swapping all dots and commas, which should result in 123,456,789.00 for this sample value.

When using *REPLACE* as opposed to *TRANSLATE*, it's common to fall into a classic swap trap that results in the substitution of all of the occurrences of only one of the characters with the other, due to the sequential manner in which nested replacements are done. Here's an example for an expression that involves such a bug:

```
SELECT REPLACE(REPLACE('123.456.789,00', '.', ','), ',', '.');
```

First all dots are substituted with commas. At this point, there are only commas in the string. Then you replace all occurrences of commas with dots. This code returns the output '123.456.789.00'.

To avoid the bug while still using the *REPLACE* function, you need to add an in-between replacement that temporarily substitutes one of the characters in the intended swap with a third character that is not in use in the input string, like so:

```
SELECT REPLACE(REPLACE(REPLACE('123.456.789,00', '.', '~'), ',', '.'), '~', ',');
```

This time the output is the correct one: '123,456,789.00'.

That's messy. Imagine how much more complex this becomes if you need to apply multiple character pair swaps. Using the *TRANSLATE* function this task is a no-brainer. Here's the expression that you need to use:

```
SELECT TRANSLATE('123.456.789,00', '.,', ',.');
```

Pay attention to the syntax of this function. You do not list pairs of characters and their translation but rather you first list all the characters that need to be changed and then you list all their translations.

You get the correct output: '123,456,789.00'.

The *REPLICATE* function

The *REPLICATE* function replicates a string a requested number of times.

Syntax

REPLICATE(*string, n*)

For example, the following code replicates the string 'abc' three times, returning the string 'abcabcabc':

```
SELECT REPLICATE('abc', 3);
```

The next example demonstrates the use of the *REPLICATE* function, along with the *RIGHT* function and string concatenation. The following query against the *Production.Suppliers* table generates a 10-digit string representation of the supplier ID integer with leading zeros:

```
SELECT supplierid,
  RIGHT(REPLICATE('0', 9) + CAST(supplierid AS VARCHAR(10)), 10) AS strsupplierid
FROM Production.Suppliers;
```

The expression producing the result column *strsupplierid* replicates the character *0* nine times (producing the string '000000000') and concatenates the string representation of the supplier ID. The *CAST* function converts the original integer supplier ID to a character string data type (*VARCHAR*). Finally, the *RIGHT* function extracts the 10 rightmost characters of the result string. Here's the output of this query, shown in abbreviated form:

```
supplierid  strsupplierid
----------- -------------
29          0000000029
28          0000000028
4           0000000004
```

```
21          0000000021
2           0000000002
22          0000000022
14          0000000014
11          0000000011
25          0000000025
7           0000000007
. . .
```

```
(29 rows affected)
```

Note that T-SQL supports a function called *FORMAT* that you can use to achieve such formatting needs much more easily, though at a higher cost. I'll describe it later in this section.

The *STUFF* function

You use the *STUFF* function to remove a substring from a string and insert a new substring instead.

Syntax

STUFF(*string, pos, delete_length, insert_string*)

This function operates on the input parameter *string*. It deletes as many characters as the number specified in the *delete_length* parameter, starting at the character position specified in the *pos* input parameter. The function inserts the string specified in the *insert_string* parameter in position *pos*. For example, the following code operates on the string 'xyz', removes one character from the second character position, and inserts the substring 'abc' instead:

```
SELECT STUFF('xyz', 2, 1, 'abc');
```

The output of this code is 'xabcz'.

If you just want to insert a string without deleting anything, you can specify a length of 0 as the third argument. If you only want to delete a substring but not insert anything instead, specify a *NULL* as the fourth argument.

The *UPPER* and *LOWER* functions

The *UPPER* and *LOWER* functions return the input string with all uppercase or lowercase characters, respectively.

Syntax

UPPER(*string*), LOWER(*string*)

For example, the following code returns 'ITZIK BEN-GAN':

```
SELECT UPPER('Itzik Ben-Gan');
```

The following code returns 'itzik ben-gan':

```
SELECT LOWER('Itzik Ben-Gan');
```

The *RTRIM*, *LTRIM*, and *TRIM* functions

The various trim functions allow you to remove leading, trailing, or both leading and trailing characters from an input string. These functions were enhanced in SQL Server 2022 to provide more functionality. I'll start with their syntax prior to SQL Server 2022 and then describe the enhancements.

The *RTRIM* and *LTRIM* functions return the input string with leading or trailing spaces removed, respectively.

Syntax

RTRIM(*string*), LTRIM(*string*)

If you want to remove both leading and trailing spaces, one option is to use the result of *LTRIM* as the input to *RTRIM*, or the other way around. For example, the following code removes both leading and trailing spaces from the input string, returning 'abc':

```
SELECT RTRIM(LTRIM('   abc   '));
```

A simpler option is to use the *TRIM* function, which removes both leading and trailing spaces, like so:

```
SELECT TRIM('   abc   ');
```

But wait, there's more! The *TRIM* function has more sophisticated capabilities. Let's start with the function's syntax.

Syntax

TRIM([*characters* FROM] *string*)

If you provide just the input *string*, the *TRIM* function indeed removes only leading and trailing spaces. However, observe that there's an optional *characters* input (square brackets in syntax definition means that the syntax element is optional), which allows you to be specific about the list of individual characters that you want to trim from the start and end of the input *string*.

Attempting to trim nonspace characters from the edges of an input string can be quite tricky without this optional input, especially if those characters can appear in other places beyond the beginning and end. For example, suppose that you need to remove all leading and trailing slashes (both forward and backward) from an input string. I'll use the following value as my sample input value:

'//\\ remove leading and trailing backward (\) and forward (/) slashes \\//'

Here's the correct desired result value after trimming:

' remove leading and trailing backward (\) and forward (/) slashes '

Notice that the output should keep the leading and trailing spaces.

If *TRIM* didn't allow you to be specific about the characters to trim, you would need to use a complex expression, such as the following:

```
SELECT
  TRANSLATE(TRIM(TRANSLATE(TRIM(TRANSLATE(
    '//\\ remove leading and trailing backward (\) and forward (/) slashes \\//',
    ' /', '~ ')), ' \', '^ ')), ' ^~', '\/ ')
  AS outputstring;
```

Here you start by using the *TRANSLATE* function to substitute all spaces with a temporary character (~) and forward slashes with spaces. You then use the *TRIM* function to trim leading and trailing spaces from the result. This results in trimming leading and trailing forward slashes, temporarily using ~ instead of the original spaces. This part results in the following value:

'\\~remove~leading~and~trailing~backward~(\)~and~forward~( )~slashes~\\'

Next, you use the *TRANSLATE* function to substitute all spaces with another temporary character (^) and backward slashes with spaces, and the *TRIM* function to trim leading and trailing spaces from the result. This part removes leading and trailing backward slashes, temporarily using ^ instead of the intermediate spaces. This part results in the following value:

'~remove~leading~and~trailing~backward~( )~and~forward~(^)~slashes~'

Finally, you use the *TRANSLATE* function to substitute spaces with backward slashes, ^ with forward slashes, and ~ with spaces, generating the desired result:

' remove leading and trailing backward (\) and forward (/) slashes '

Using the *TRIM* function with the optional *characters* input, the task becomes a no-brainer:

```
SELECT TRIM( '/\'
              FROM '//\\ remove leading and trailing backward (\) and forward (/) slashes \\//' )
        AS outputstring;
```

As mentioned, the various trim functions were enhanced in SQL Server 2022 to provide more functionality. Here's the enhanced *TRIM* function's syntax:

TRIM([LEADING | TRAILING | BOTH] [*characters* FROM] *string*)

As you can see, instead of always trimming both leading and trailing characters, which is the default, you can now be explicit about whether you want to trim leading characters, trailing characters, or both leading and trailing characters.

As for the *RTRIM* and *LTRIM* functions, here's their enhanced syntax:

RTRIM (*string* , [*characters*]), LTRIM (*string* , [*characters*])

The enhancement is the optional *characters* input, which allows you to specify special characters that you want to remove instead of the default spaces, similar to the optional *characters* input that you can specify with the *TRIM* function.

With the above enhancements, there's really no need for three separate functions anymore. It's sufficient to use *TRIM* alone, adding the keyword *LEADING* (instead of using *LTRIM*) or *TRAILING* (instead of using *RTRIM*). Or in more detail, instead of using:

RTRIM (*string* , [*characters*])

You can use:

TRIM(TRAILING [*characters* FROM] *string*)

And instead of using:

LTRIM (*string* , [*characters*])

You can use:

TRIM(LEADING [*characters* FROM] *string*)

Of course, you might still opt to use *RTRIM* and *LTRIM* to benefit from their code brevity.

The *FORMAT* function

You use the *FORMAT* function to format an input value as a character string based on a Microsoft .NET format string and an optional culture specification.

Syntax

FORMAT(*input* , *format_string, culture*)

There are numerous possibilities for formatting inputs using both standard and custom format strings. The article at *https://learn.microsoft.com/en-us/dotnet/standard/base-types/formatting-types* provides more information. But just as a simple example, recall the convoluted expression used earlier to format a number as a 10-digit string with leading zeros. By using *FORMAT*, you can achieve the same task with either the custom format string '0000000000' or the standard one, 'd10'. As an example, the following code returns '0000001759':

```
SELECT FORMAT(1759, '000000000');
```

> **Note** The *FORMAT* function is usually more expensive than alternative T-SQL functions that you use to format values. You should generally refrain from using it unless you are willing to accept the performance penalty. As an example, I ran a query against a table with 1,000,000 rows to compute the 10-digit string representation of one of the integer columns. The query took close to a minute to complete on my computer with the *FORMAT* function compared to under a second with the alternative method using the *REPLICATE* and *RIGHT* functions.

The COMPRESS and DECOMPRESS functions

The *COMPRESS* and *DECOMPRESS* functions use the GZIP algorithm to compress and decompress the input, respectively.

Syntax

COMPRESS(*string*), DECOMPRESS(*string*)

The *COMPRESS* function accepts a character or binary string as input and returns a compressed *VARBINARY(MAX)* typed value. Here's an example for using the function with a constant as input:

```
SELECT COMPRESS(N'This is my cv. Imagine it was much longer.');
```

The result is a binary value holding the compressed form of the input string.

If you want to store the compressed form of input values in a column in a table, you need to apply the *COMPRESS* function to the input value and store the result in the table. You can do this as part of the *INSERT* statement that adds the row to the target table. (For information about data modification, see Chapter 8.) For example, suppose you have a table called *EmployeeCVs* in your database, with columns called *empid* and *cv*. The column *cv* holds the compressed form of the employee's résumé and is defined as *VARBINARY(MAX)*. Suppose you have a stored procedure called *AddEmpCV* that accepts input parameters called *@empid* and *@cv*. (For information about stored procedures, see Chapter 12.) The parameter *@cv* is the uncompressed form of the input employee's résumé and is defined as *NVARCHAR(MAX)*. The procedure is responsible for inserting a new row into the table with the compressed employee résumé information. The *INSERT* statement within the stored procedure might look like this:

```
INSERT INTO dbo.EmployeeCVs( empid, cv ) VALUES( @empid, COMPRESS(@cv) );
```

The *DECOMPRESS* function accepts a binary string as input and returns a decompressed *VARBINARY(MAX)* typed value. Note that if the value you originally compressed was of a character string type, you will need to explicitly cast the result of the *DECOMPRESS* function to the target type. As an example, the following code doesn't return the original input value; rather, it returns a binary value:

```
SELECT DECOMPRESS(COMPRESS(N'This is my cv. Imagine it was much longer.'));
```

To get the original value, you need to cast the result to the target character string type, like so:

```
SELECT
  CAST(
    DECOMPRESS(COMPRESS(N'This is my cv. Imagine it was much longer.'))
      AS NVARCHAR(MAX));
```

Consider the *EmployeeCVs* table from the earlier example. To return the uncompressed form of the employee résumés, you use the following query (don't run this code, because this table doesn't actually exist):

```
SELECT empid, CAST(DECOMPRESS(cv) AS NVARCHAR(MAX)) AS cv
FROM dbo.EmployeeCVs;
```

The *STRING_SPLIT* function

The *STRING_SPLIT* table function splits an input string with a separated list of values into the individual elements.

Syntax

SELECT value FROM STRING_SPLIT(*string, separator*[, *enable_ordinal*]);

Unlike the string functions described so far, which are all scalar functions, the *STRING_SPLIT* function is a table function. It accepts as inputs a string with a separated list of values, a separator, and starting with SQL Server 2022 also an optional input flag that indicates whether to return an ordinal position column. The function returns a table result with a string column called *value* with the individual elements, and if the flag was enabled, also an integer column called *ordinal* with the element's ordinal position. If you need the elements to be returned with a data type other than a character string, you will need to cast the *value* column to the target type. For example, the following code accepts the input string '10248,10249,10250' and separator ',' and it returns a table result aliased as S with the individual elements:

```
SELECT CAST(value AS INT) AS myvalue
FROM STRING_SPLIT('10248,10249,10250', ',') AS S;
```

In this example, the input list contains values representing order IDs. Because the IDs are supposed to be integers, the query converts the *value* column to the *INT* data type. Here's the output of this code:

```
myvalue
-----------
10248
10249
10250
```

In case you're using SQL Server 2022 or later, here's an example with the ordinal flag enabled:

```
SELECT CAST(value AS INT) AS myvalue, ordinal
FROM STRING_SPLIT('10248,10249,10250', ',', 1) AS S;
```

This code generates the following output:

```
myvalue      ordinal
-----------  --------
10248        1
10249        2
10250        3
```

A common use case for such splitting logic is passing a separated list of values representing keys, such as order IDs, to a stored procedure or user-defined function and returning the rows from some table, such as Orders, that have the input keys. This is achieved by joining the *STRING_SPLIT* function with the target table and matching the keys from both sides.

The *STRING_AGG* function

The *STRING_AGG* aggregate function concatenates the values of the input expression in the aggregated group. You can think of it as the inverse of the *STRING_SPLIT* function.

Syntax

STRING_AGG(*input , separator*) [WITHIN GROUP(*order_specification*)]

The function concatenates the values of the *input* argument expression in the target group, separated by the *separator* argument. To guarantee the order of concatenation, you must specify the optional *WITHIN GROUP* clause along with the desired ordering specification. As an example, the following query returns the order IDs for each customer, ordered by recency, using a comma as a separator:

```
SELECT custid,
  STRING_AGG(CAST(orderid AS VARCHAR(10)), ',')
    WITHIN GROUP(ORDER BY orderdate DESC, orderid DESC) AS custorders
FROM Sales.Orders
GROUP BY custid;
```

This query generates the following output, shown here in abbreviated form:

```
custid      custorders
----------- --------------------------------------------
1           11011,10952,10835,10702,10692,10643
2           10926,10759,10625,10308
3           10856,10682,10677,10573,10535,10507,10365
...

(89 rows affected)
```

Note that if *input* is of a *VARCHAR* datatype, the output is *VARCHAR* as well; otherwise, it's *NVARCHAR*, with implicit conversion if needed. The input *orderid* column is of an *INT* datatype, so the code implicitly converts it to *VARCHAR* to ensure a *VARCHAR* output. In terms of size, if *input* is typed as *VARCHAR(MAX)* or *NVARCHAR(MAX)*, the output is *MAX* as well. If *input* is of a limited sized type (1...8000 with *VARCHAR* and 1...4000 with *NVARCHAR*), the output is of the respective type with the highest supported limited size (8000 for *VARCHAR* and 4000 for *NVARCHAR*).

The *LIKE* predicate

T-SQL provides a predicate called *LIKE* that you can use to check whether a character string matches a specified pattern. Similar patterns are used by the *PATINDEX* function described earlier. The following section describes the wildcards supported in the patterns and demonstrates their use.

The % (percent) wildcard

The percent sign represents a string of any size, including an empty string. For example, the following query returns employees where the last name starts with *D*:

```
SELECT empid, lastname
FROM HR.Employees
WHERE lastname LIKE N'D%';
```

This query returns the following output:

```
empid        lastname
-----------  --------------------
1            Davis
9            Doyle
```

Note that often you can use functions such as *SUBSTRING* and *LEFT* instead of the *LIKE* predicate to represent the same meaning. But the *LIKE* predicate tends to get optimized better—especially when the pattern starts with a known prefix.

The _ (underscore) wildcard

An underscore represents a single character. For example, the following query returns employees where the second character in the last name is *e:*

```
SELECT empid, lastname
FROM HR.Employees
WHERE lastname LIKE N'_e%';
```

This query returns the following output:

```
empid        lastname
-----------  --------------------
3            Lew
4            Peled
```

The [*<list of characters>*] wildcard

Square brackets with a list of characters (such as *[ABC]*) represent a single character that must be one of the characters specified in the list. For example, the following query returns employees where the first character in the last name is *A*, *B*, or *C*:

```
SELECT empid, lastname
FROM HR.Employees
WHERE lastname LIKE N'[ABC]%';
```

This query returns the following output:

```
empid        lastname
-----------  --------------------
8            Cameron
```

The [*<character>-<character>*] wildcard

Square brackets with a character range (such as *[A–E]*) represent a single character that must be within the specified range. For example, the following query returns employees where the first character in the last name is a letter in the range *A* through *E*, inclusive, taking the collation into account:

```
SELECT empid, lastname
FROM HR.Employees
WHERE lastname LIKE N'[A-E]%';
```

This query returns the following output:

```
empid        lastname
-----------  --------------------
8            Cameron
1            Davis
9            Doyle
```

The [^<character list or range>] wildcard

Square brackets with a caret sign (^) followed by a character list or range (such as [^A–E]) represent a single character that is not in the specified character list or range. For example, the following query returns employees where the first character in the last name is not a letter in the range A through E:

```
SELECT empid, lastname
FROM HR.Employees
WHERE lastname LIKE N'[^A-E]%';
```

This query returns the following output:

```
empid        lastname
-----------  --------------------
2            Funk
7            King
3            Lew
5            Mortensen
4            Peled
6            Suurs
```

The ESCAPE character

If you want to search for a character that is also used as a wildcard (such as %, _, [, or]), you can use an escape character. Specify a character that you know for sure doesn't appear in the data as the escape character in front of the character you are looking for, and specify the keyword ESCAPE followed by the escape character right after the pattern. For example, to check whether a column called col1 contains an underscore, use col1 LIKE '%!_%' ESCAPE '!'.

For the wildcards %, _, and [, you can use square brackets instead of an escape character. For example, instead of col1 LIKE '%!_%' ESCAPE '!', you can use col1 LIKE '%[_]%'.

If you want to do some practice related to character data at this point, try working on exercises 3 and 5 at the end of this chapter.

Working with date and time data

Working with date and time data in SQL Server is not trivial. You will face several challenges in this area, such as expressing literals in a language-neutral manner and working with date and time separately.

In this section, I first introduce the date and time data types supported by SQL Server, then I explain the recommended way to work with those types, and finally I cover date- and time-related functions.

Date and time data types

T-SQL supports six date and time data types: *DATETIME* and *SMALLDATETIME*, which are considered legacy types, as well as *DATE, TIME, DATETIME2*, and *DATETIMEOFFSET*. The legacy types *DATETIME* and *SMALLDATETIME* include date and time components that are inseparable. The two types differ in their storage requirements, their supported date range, and their precision. The *DATE* and *TIME* data types provide a separation between the date and time components if you need it. The *DATETIME2* data type has a bigger date range and better precision than the legacy types. The *DATETIMEOFFSET* data type is similar to *DATETIME2*, but it also includes the offset from UTC.

Table 2-1 lists details about date and time data types, including storage requirements, supported date range, precision, and recommended entry format.

TABLE 2-1 Date and time data types

Data type	Storage (bytes)	Date range	Precision	Recommended entry format and example
DATETIME	8	January 1, 1753, through December 31, 9999	3 1/3 milliseconds	'YYYYMMDD hh:mm:ss.nnn' '20220212 12:30:15.123'
SMALLDATETIME	4	January 1, 1900, through June 6, 2079	1 minute	'YYYYMMDD hh:mm' '20220212 12:30'
DATE	3	January 1, 0001, through December 31, 9999	1 day	'YYYY-MM-DD' '2022-02-12'
TIME	3 to 5	N/A	100 nanoseconds	'hh:mm:ss.nnnnnnn' '12:30:15.1234567'
DATETIME2	6 to 8	January 1, 0001, through December 31, 9999	100 nanoseconds	'YYYY-MM-DD hh:mm:ss.nnnnnnn' '2022-02-12 12:30:15.1234567'
DATETIMEOFFSET	8 to 10	January 1, 0001, through December 31, 9999	100 nanoseconds	'YYYY-MM-DD hh:mm:ss.nnnnnnn [+|-]hh:mm' '2022-02-12 12:30:15.1234567 +02:00'

The storage requirements for the last three data types in Table 2-1 (*TIME, DATETIME2*, and *DATE-TIMEOFFSET*) depend on the precision you choose. You specify a fractional-second precision as an integer in the range 0 to 7. For example, *TIME(0)* means 0 fractional-second precision—in other words, one-second precision. *TIME(3)* means one-millisecond precision, and *TIME(7)* means 100-nanosecond precision. If you don't specify a fractional-second precision, SQL Server assumes 7 by default. When converting a value to a data type with a lower precision, it gets rounded to the closest expressible value in the target precision.

Literals

When you need to specify a literal (constant) of a date and time data type, you should consider several things. First, though it might sound a bit strange, T-SQL doesn't provide the means to express a date and time literal; instead, you can specify a literal of a different type that can be converted—explicitly or implicitly—to a date and time data type. It is a best practice to use character strings to express date and time values, as shown in the following example:

```
SELECT orderid, custid, empid, orderdate
FROM Sales.Orders
WHERE orderdate = '20220212';
```

SQL Server recognizes the literal '20220212' as a character-string literal of a *VARCHAR* datatype, and not as a date and time literal; however, because the expression involves operands of two different types, one operand needs to be implicitly converted to the other's type. Normally, implicit conversion between types is based on what's called *data-type precedence*. SQL Server defines precedence among data types and will usually implicitly convert the operand that has a lower data-type precedence to the one that has higher precedence. In this example, the *VARCHAR* literal is converted to the column's data type (*DATE*) because character strings are considered lower in terms of data-type precedence with respect to date and time data types. Implicit conversion rules are not always that simple. In fact, different rules are applied with filters and in other expressions, but for the purposes of this discussion, I'll keep things simple. For the complete description of data-type precedence, see "Data Type Precedence" in the product documentation.

The point I'm trying to make is that in the preceding example, implicit conversion takes place behind the scenes. This query is logically equivalent to the following one, which explicitly converts the character string to a *DATE* data type:

```
SELECT orderid, custid, empid, orderdate
FROM Sales.Orders
WHERE orderdate = CAST('20220212' AS DATE);
```

Note that some character-string formats of date and time literals are language dependent, meaning that when you convert them to a date and time data type, SQL Server might interpret the value differently based on the language setting in effect in the session. Each login defined by the database administrator has a default language associated with it, and unless it is changed explicitly, that language becomes the effective language in the session. You can override the default language in your session by using the *SET LANGUAGE* command, but this is generally not recommended, because some aspects of the code might rely on the user's default language.

The effective language in the session sets several language-related settings behind the scenes. Among them is one called *DATEFORMAT*, which determines how SQL Server interprets the literals you enter when they are converted from a character-string type to a date and time type. The *DATEFORMAT* setting is expressed as a combination of the characters *d*, *m*, and *y*. For example, the *us_english* language setting sets the *DATEFORMAT* to *mdy*, whereas the *British* language setting sets the *DATEFORMAT* to *dmy*. You can override the *DATEFORMAT* setting in your session by using the *SET DATEFORMAT* command, but as mentioned earlier, changing language-related settings is generally not recommended.

Consider, for example, the literal '02/12/2022'. SQL Server can interpret the date as either February 12, 2022 or December 2, 2022 when you convert this literal to one of the following types: *DATETIME*, *SMALLDATETIME*, *DATE*, *DATETIME2*, or *DATETIMEOFFSET*. The effective *LANGUAGE/DATEFORMAT* setting is the determining factor. To demonstrate different interpretations of the same character-string literal, run the following code:

```
SET LANGUAGE British;
SELECT CAST('02/12/2022' AS DATE);

SET LANGUAGE us_english;
SELECT CAST('02/12/2022' AS DATE);
```

Notice in the output that the literal was interpreted differently in the two different language environments:

```
Changed language setting to British.

----------
2022-12-02

Changed language setting to us_english.

----------
2022-02-12
```

Note that the *LANGUAGE/DATEFORMAT* setting affects only the way the values you enter are interpreted; these settings have no impact on the format used in the output for presentation purposes. Output format is determined by the database interface used by the client tool (such as ODBC) and not by the *LANGUAGE/DATEFORMAT* setting. For example, OLE DB and ODBC present *DATE* values in the format '*YYYY-MM-DD*'.

Because the code you write might end up being used by international users with different language settings for their logins, understanding that some formats of literals are language dependent is crucial. It is strongly recommended that you phrase your literals in a language-neutral manner. Language-neutral formats are always interpreted by SQL Server the same way and are not affected by language-related settings.

Table 2-2 provides literal formats that are considered neutral for each of the date and time types.

TABLE 2-2 Language-neutral date and time data type formats

Data type	Recommended entry format	Example
DATETIME	'YYYYMMDD hh:mm:ss.nnn'	'20220212 12:30:15.123'
	'YYYY-MM-DDThh:mm:ss.nnn'	'2022-02-12T12:30:15.123'
	'YYYYMMDD'	'20220212'
SMALLDATETIME	'YYYYMMDD hh:mm'	'20220212 12:30'
	'YYYY-MM-DDThh:mm'	'2022-02-12T12:30'
	'YYYYMMDD'	'20220212'
DATE	'YYYYMMDD'	'20220212'
	'YYYY-MM-DD'	'2022-02-12'

Data type	Recommended entry format	Example
DATETIME2	'YYYYMMDD hh:mm:ss.nnnnnnn' 'YYYY-MM-DD hh:mm:ss.nnnnnnn' 'YYYY-MM-DDThh:mm:ss.nnnnnnn' 'YYYYMMDD' 'YYYY-MM-DD'	'20220212 12:30:15.1234567' '2022-02-12 12:30:15.1234567' '2022-02-12T12:30:15.1234567' '20220212' '2022-02-12'
DATETIMEOFFSET	'YYYYMMDD hh:mm:ss.nnnnnnn [+|-]hh:mm' 'YYYY-MM-DD hh:mm:ss.nnnnnnn [+|-]hh:mm' 'YYYYMMDD' 'YYYY-MM-DD'	'20220212 12:30:15.1234567 +02:00' '2022-02-12 12:30:15.1234567 +02:00' '20220212' '2022-02-12'
TIME	'hh:mm:ss.nnnnnnn'	'12:30:15.1234567'

Note a couple of things about Table 2-2. With all types that include both date and time components, if you don't specify a time part in your literal, SQL Server assumes midnight. If you don't specify an offset from UTC, SQL Server assumes 00:00. Also note that the formats 'YYYY-MM-DD' and 'YYYY-MM-DD hh:mm...' are language dependent when converted to *DATETIME* or *SMALLDATETIME* and language neutral when converted to *DATE*, *DATETIME2*, and *DATETIMEOFFSET*.

For example, notice in the following code that the language setting has no impact on how a literal expressed with the format 'YYYYMMDD' is interpreted when it is converted to *DATE*:

```
SET LANGUAGE British;
SELECT CAST('20220212' AS DATE);

SET LANGUAGE us_english;
SELECT CAST('20220212' AS DATE);
```

The output shows that the literal was interpreted in both cases as February 12, 2022:

```
Changed language setting to British.

----------
2022-02-12

Changed language setting to us_english.

----------
2022-02-12
```

I can't emphasize enough that using language-neutral formats such as 'YYYYMMDD' is a best practice, because such formats are interpreted the same way regardless of the *LANGUAGE/DATEFORMAT* settings.

If you insist on using a language-dependent format to express literals, there are two options available to you. One is to use the *CONVERT* function to explicitly convert the character-string literal to the requested data type and, in the third argument, specify a number representing the style you used. The product documentation has a table with all the style numbers and the formats they represent. You can find it under the topic "The *CAST* and *CONVERT* Functions." For example, if you want to specify the literal '02/12/2022' with the format *MM/DD/YYYY*, use style number 101, as shown here:

```
SELECT CONVERT(DATE, '02/12/2022', 101);
```

The literal is interpreted as February 12, 2022, regardless of the language setting that is in effect.

If you want to use the format *DD/MM/YYYY*, use style number 103:

```
SELECT CONVERT(DATE, '02/12/2022', 103);
```

This time, the literal is interpreted as December 2, 2022.

Another option is to use the *PARSE* function. By using this function, you can parse a value as a requested type and indicate the culture. For example, the following is the equivalent of using *CONVERT* with style 101 (US English):

```
SELECT PARSE('02/12/2022' AS DATE USING 'en-US');
```

The following is equivalent to using *CONVERT* with style 103 (British English):

```
SELECT PARSE('02/12/2022' AS DATE USING 'en-GB');
```

> **Note** The *PARSE* function is significantly more expensive than the *CONVERT* function; therefore, it is generally recommended you refrain from using it.

Working with date and time separately

If you need to work with only dates or only times, it's recommended that you use the *DATE* and *TIME* data types, respectively. Adhering to this guideline can become challenging if you need to restrict yourself to using only the legacy types *DATETIME* and *SMALLDATETIME* for reasons such as compatibility with older systems. The challenge is that the legacy types contain both the date and time components. The best practice in such a case says that when you want to work only with dates, you store the date with a value of midnight in the time part. When you want to work only with times, you store the time with the base date January 1, 1900.

To demonstrate working with date and time separately, I'll use a table called *Sales.Orders2*, which has a column called *orderdate* of a *DATETIME* data type. Run the following code to create the *Sales.Orders2* table by copying data from the *Sales.Orders* table and casting the source *orderdate* column, which is of a *DATE* type, to *DATETIME*:

```
DROP TABLE IF EXISTS Sales.Orders2;

SELECT orderid, custid, empid, CAST(orderdate AS DATETIME) AS orderdate
INTO Sales.Orders2
FROM Sales.Orders;
```

Don't worry if you're not yet familiar with the *SELECT INTO* statement; I describe it in Chapter 8.

As mentioned, the *orderdate* column in the *Sales.Orders2* table is of a *DATETIME* data type, but because only the date component is actually relevant, all values contain midnight as the time. When you need to filter only orders from a certain date, you don't have to use a range filter. Instead, you can use the equality operator, like this:

```
SELECT orderid, custid, empid, orderdate
FROM Sales.Orders2
WHERE orderdate = '20220212';
```

When SQL Server converts a character-string literal that has only a date to *DATETIME*, it assumes midnight by default. Because all values in the *orderdate* column contain midnight in the time component, all orders placed on the requested date will be returned. Note that you can use a *CHECK* constraint to ensure that only midnight is used as the time part:

```
ALTER TABLE Sales.Orders2
  ADD CONSTRAINT CHK_Orders2_orderdate
  CHECK( CONVERT(CHAR(12), orderdate, 114) = '00:00:00:000' );
```

The *CONVERT* function extracts the time-only portion of the *orderdate* value as a character string using style 114. The *CHECK* constraint verifies that the string represents midnight.

If the time component is stored with nonmidnight values, you can use a range filter like this:

```
SELECT orderid, custid, empid, orderdate
FROM Sales.Orders2
WHERE orderdate >= '20220212'
  AND orderdate < '20220213';
```

If you want to work only with times using the legacy types, you can store all values with the base date of January 1, 1900. When SQL Server converts a character-string literal that contains only a time component to *DATETIME* or *SMALLDATETIME*, SQL Server assumes that the date is the base date. For example, run the following code:

```
SELECT CAST('12:30:15.123' AS DATETIME);
```

You get the following output:

```
-----------------------
1900-01-01 12:30:15.123
```

Suppose you have a table with a column called *tm* of a *DATETIME* data type and you store all values by using the base date. Again, this can be enforced with a *CHECK* constraint. To return all rows for which the time value is 12:30:15.123, you use the filter *WHERE tm = '12:30:15.123'*. Because you did not specify a date component, SQL Server assumes the date is the base date when it implicitly converts the character string to a *DATETIME* data type.

If you want to work only with dates or only with times using the legacy types, but the input values you get include both date and time components, you need to apply some manipulation to the input values to "zero" the irrelevant part. That is, set the time component to midnight if you want to work only with dates, and set the date component to the base date if you want to work only with times. I'll explain how you can achieve this shortly, in the "Date and time functions" section.

Run the following code for cleanup:

```
DROP TABLE IF EXISTS Sales.Orders2;
```

Filtering date ranges

When you need to filter a range of dates, such as a whole year or a whole month, it seems natural to use functions such as *YEAR* and *MONTH*. For example, the following query returns all orders placed in the year 2021:

```
SELECT orderid, custid, empid, orderdate
FROM Sales.Orders
WHERE YEAR(orderdate) = 2021;
```

However, you should be aware that in most cases, when you apply manipulation to the filtered column, such as providing it as input to the *YEAR* function like in the example above, SQL Server cannot use an index in an efficient manner. This is probably hard to understand without some background about indexes and query tuning, which are outside the scope of this book. For now, just keep this general point in mind: To have the potential to use an index efficiently, you should refrain from manipulating the filtered column. To achieve this, you can revise the filter predicate from the last query like this:

```
SELECT orderid, custid, empid, orderdate
FROM Sales.Orders
WHERE orderdate >= '20210101' AND orderdate < '20220101';
```

Similarly, instead of using functions to filter orders placed in a particular month, like this:

```
SELECT orderid, custid, empid, orderdate
FROM Sales.Orders
WHERE YEAR(orderdate) = 2022 AND MONTH(orderdate) = 2;
```

use a range filter, like the following:

```
SELECT orderid, custid, empid, orderdate
FROM Sales.Orders
WHERE orderdate >= '20220201' AND orderdate < '20220301';
```

Date and time functions

In this section, I describe functions that operate on date and time data types, including *GETDATE, CURRENT_TIMESTAMP, GETUTCDATE, SYSDATETIME, SYSUTCDATETIME, SYSDATETIMEOFFSET, CAST, CONVERT, PARSE, SWITCHOFFSET, TODATETIMEOFFSET, AT TIME ZONE, DATEADD, DATEDIFF* and *DATEDIFF_BIG, DATEPART, YEAR, MONTH, DAY, DATENAME, DATETRUNC, DATE_BUCKET, ISDATE,* various *FROMPARTS* functions, *EOMONTH,* and *GENERATE_SERIES.*

Current date and time

The following *niladic* (parameterless) functions return the current date and time values in the system where the SQL Server instance resides: *GETDATE, CURRENT_TIMESTAMP, GETUTCDATE, SYSDATETIME, SYSUTCDATETIME,* and *SYSDATETIMEOFFSET.*

Table 2-3 provides the description of these functions.

TABLE 2-3 Functions returning current date and time

Function	Return type	Description
GETDATE	*DATETIME*	Current date and time
CURRENT_TIMESTAMP	*DATETIME*	Same as GETDATE but SQL-compliant
GETUTCDATE	*DATETIME*	Current date and time in UTC
SYSDATETIME	*DATETIME2*	Current date and time
SYSUTCDATETIME	*DATETIME2*	Current date and time in UTC
SYSDATETIMEOFFSET	*DATETIMEOFFSET*	Current date and time, including the offset from UTC

Note that you need to specify empty parentheses with all functions that should be specified without parameters, except the standard function *CURRENT_TIMESTAMP*, which requires no parentheses. Also, because *CURRENT_TIMESTAMP* and *GETDATE* return the same thing but only the former is standard, it is recommended that you use the former. This is a practice I try to follow in general—when I have several options that do the same thing with no functional or performance difference, and one is standard but others aren't, my preference is to use the standard option.

The following code demonstrates using the current date and time functions:

```
SELECT
  GETDATE()            AS [GETDATE],
  CURRENT_TIMESTAMP    AS [CURRENT_TIMESTAMP],
  GETUTCDATE()         AS [GETUTCDATE],
  SYSDATETIME()        AS [SYSDATETIME],
  SYSUTCDATETIME()     AS [SYSUTCDATETIME],
  SYSDATETIMEOFFSET()  AS [SYSDATETIMEOFFSET];
```

Notice that the code uses square brackets here to define delimited identifiers for the target column names, since they are reserved keywords. See the note on delimited identifiers earlier in this chapter if you need a reminder.

As you probably noticed, none of the functions return only the current system date or only the current system time. However, you can get those easily by converting *CURRENT_TIMESTAMP* or *SYSDATE-TIME* to *DATE* or *TIME*, like this:

```
SELECT
  CAST(SYSDATETIME() AS DATE) AS [current_date],
  CAST(SYSDATETIME() AS TIME) AS [current_time];
```

The *CAST, CONVERT,* and *PARSE* functions and their *TRY_* counterparts

The *CAST, CONVERT,* and *PARSE* functions are used to convert an input value to some target type. If the conversion succeeds, the functions return the converted value; otherwise, they cause the query to fail. The three functions have counterparts called *TRY_CAST, TRY_CONVERT,* and *TRY_PARSE,* respectively. Each version with the prefix TRY_ accepts the same input as its counterpart and applies the same conversion; the difference is that if the input isn't convertible to the target type, the function returns a *NULL* instead of failing the query.

Syntax

CAST(*value* AS *datatype*)

TRY_CAST(*value* AS *datatype*)

CONVERT(*datatype, value* [, *style_number*])

TRY_CONVERT(*datatype, value* [, *style_number*])

PARSE(*value* AS *datatype* [USING *culture*])

TRY_PARSE(*value* AS *datatype* [USING *culture*])

All three base functions convert the input *value* to the specified target *datatype*. In some cases, *CONVERT* has a third argument with which you can specify the style of the conversion. For example, when you are converting from a character string to one of the date and time data types (or the other way around), the style number indicates the format of the string. For example, style 101 indicates 'MM/DD/YYYY', and style 103 indicates 'DD/MM/YYYY'. You can find the full list of style numbers and their meanings in the product documentation under "*CAST* and *CONVERT*." Similarly, where applicable, the *PARSE* function supports the indication of a culture—for example, '*en-US*' for US English and '*en-GB*' for British English.

As mentioned earlier, when you are converting from a character string to one of the date and time data types, some of the string formats are language dependent. I recommend either using one of the language-neutral formats or using the *CONVERT* function and explicitly specifying the style number. This way, your code is interpreted the same way regardless of the language of the login running it.

Note that *CAST* is standard and *CONVERT* and *PARSE* aren't, so unless you need to use the style number or culture, it is recommended that you use the *CAST* function.

Following are a few examples of using the *CAST*, *CONVERT*, and *PARSE* functions with date and time data types. The following code converts the character string literal '20220212' to a *DATE* data type:

```
SELECT CAST('20220212' AS DATE);
```

The following code converts the current system date and time value to a *DATE* data type, practically extracting only the current system date:

```
SELECT CAST(SYSDATETIME() AS DATE);
```

The following code converts the current system date and time value to a *TIME* data type, practically extracting only the current system time:

```
SELECT CAST(SYSDATETIME() AS TIME);
```

As suggested earlier, if you need to work with the *DATETIME* or *SMALLDATETIME* types (for example, to be compatible with legacy systems) and want to represent only a date or only a time, you can set the irrelevant part to a specific value. To work only with dates, you set the time to midnight. To work only with time, you set the date to the base date January 1, 1900.

The following code converts the current date and time value to *CHAR(8)* by using style 112 ('YYYYMMDD'):

```
SELECT CONVERT(CHAR(8), CURRENT_TIMESTAMP, 112);
```

For example, if the current date is February 12, 2022, this code returns '20220212'. You then convert the character string back to *DATETIME* and get the current date at midnight:

```
SELECT CONVERT(DATETIME, CONVERT(CHAR(8), CURRENT_TIMESTAMP, 112), 112);
```

Similarly, to zero the date portion to the base date, you can first convert the current date and time value to *CHAR(12)* by using style 114 ('hh:mm:ss.nnn'):

```
SELECT CONVERT(CHAR(12), CURRENT_TIMESTAMP, 114);
```

When the code is converted back to *DATETIME*, you get the current time on the base date:

```
SELECT CONVERT(DATETIME, CONVERT(CHAR(12), CURRENT_TIMESTAMP, 114), 114);
```

As for using the *PARSE* function, here are a couple of examples:

```
SELECT PARSE('02/12/2022' AS DATETIME USING 'en-US');
SELECT PARSE('02/12/2022' AS DATETIME USING 'en-GB');
```

The first example parses the input string by using a US English culture, and the second one does so by using a British English culture.

As a reminder, the *PARSE* function is significantly more expensive than the *CONVERT* function; therefore, I recommend you use the latter.

The *SWITCHOFFSET* function

The *SWITCHOFFSET* function adjusts an input *DATETIMEOFFSET* value to a specified target offset from UTC. Note that you need to take into account whether daylight saving time is in effect or not for your input value with your target offset.

Syntax

SWITCHOFFSET(*datetimeoffset_value, UTC_offset*)

For example, the following code adjusts the current system *datetimeoffset* value to offset –05:00.

```
SELECT SWITCHOFFSET(SYSDATETIMEOFFSET(), '-05:00');
```

So if the current system *datetimeoffset* value is February 12, 2022 10:00:00.0000000 –08:00, this code returns the value February 12, 2022 13:00:00.0000000 –05:00.

The following code adjusts the current *datetimeoffset* value to UTC:

```
SELECT SWITCHOFFSET(SYSDATETIMEOFFSET(), '+00:00');
```

Assuming the aforementioned current *datetimeoffset* value, this code returns the value February 12, 2022 18:00:00.0000000 +00:00.

The *TODATETIMEOFFSET* function

The *TODATETIMEOFFSET* function constructs a *DATETIMEOFFSET* typed value from a local date and time value and an offset from UTC.

Syntax

TODATETIMEOFFSET(*local_date_and_time_value, UTC_offset*)

This function is different from *SWITCHOFFSET* in that its first input is a local date and time value without an offset component. This function simply merges the input date and time value with the specified offset to create a new *datetimeoffset* value.

You will typically use this function when migrating non-offset-aware data to offset-aware data. Imagine you have a table holding local date and time values in an attribute called *dt* of a *DATETIME2* or *DATETIME* data type and holding the offset in an attribute called *theoffset*. You then decide to merge the two to one offset-aware attribute called *dto*. You alter the table and add the new attribute. Then you update it to the result of the expression *TODATETIMEOFFSET(dt, theoffset)*. Then you can drop the two existing attributes *dt* and *theoffset*.

The *AT TIME ZONE* function

The *AT TIME ZONE* function accepts an input date and time value and converts it to a *datetimeoffset* value that corresponds to the specified target time zone.

Syntax

dt_val AT TIME ZONE *time_zone*

The input *dt_val* can be of the following data types: *DATETIME, SMALLDATETIME, DATETIME2*, and *DATETIMEOFFSET*. The input *time_zone* can be any of the supported Windows time-zone names as they appear in the *name* column in the *sys.time_zone_info* view. Use the following query to see the available time zones, their current offset from UTC, and whether it's currently daylight saving time (DST):

```
SELECT name, current_utc_offset, is_currently_dst
FROM sys.time_zone_info;
```

Regarding *dt_val*: when using any of the three non-*datetimeoffset* types (*DATETIME, SMALLDATE-TIME*, and *DATETIME2*), the *AT TIME ZONE* function assumes the input value is already in the target time zone. As a result, it behaves similar to the *TODATETIMEOFFSET* function, except the offset isn't necessarily fixed. It depends on whether DST applies. Take the time zone Pacific Standard Time as an example. When it's not DST, the offset from UTC is –08:00; when it is DST, the offset is –07:00. The following code demonstrates the use of this function with non-*datetimeoffset* inputs:

```
SELECT
  CAST('20220212 12:00:00.0000000' AS DATETIME2)
    AT TIME ZONE 'Pacific Standard Time' AS val1,
  CAST('20220812 12:00:00.0000000' AS DATETIME2)
    AT TIME ZONE 'Pacific Standard Time' AS val2;
```

This code generates the following output:

```
val1                                val2
----------------------------------- -----------------------------------
2022-02-12 12:00:00.0000000 -08:00  2022-08-12 12:00:00.0000000 -07:00
```

The first value happens when DST doesn't apply; hence, offset –08:00 is assumed. The second value happens during DST; hence, offset –07:00 is assumed. Here there's no ambiguity.

There are two tricky cases: when switching to DST and when switching from DST. For example, in Pacific Standard Time, when switching to DST the clock is advanced by an hour, so there's an hour that doesn't exist. If you specify a nonexisting time during that hour as input to the function, the input time is advanced by an hour, and the offset after the change (–07:00) is assumed. When switching from DST, the clock retreats by an hour, so there's an hour that repeats itself. If you specify a time during that hour, the input time is not changed, and the offset after the change is assumed (that is, the offset –08:00 is used).

When the input *dt_val* is a *datetimeoffset* value, the *AT TIME ZONE* function behaves more similarly to the *SWITCHOFFSET* function. Again, however, the target offset isn't necessarily fixed. T-SQL uses the Windows time-zone-conversion rules to apply the conversion. The following code demonstrates the use of the function with *datetimeoffset* inputs:

```
SELECT
  CAST('20220212 12:00:00.0000000 -05:00' AS DATETIMEOFFSET)
    AT TIME ZONE 'Pacific Standard Time' AS val1,
  CAST('20220812 12:00:00.0000000 -04:00' AS DATETIMEOFFSET)
    AT TIME ZONE 'Pacific Standard Time' AS val2;
```

The input values reflect the time zone Eastern Standard Time. Both have noon in the time component. The first value occurs when DST doesn't apply (offset is –05:00), and the second one occurs when DST does apply (that is, the offset is –04:00). Both values are converted to the time zone Pacific Standard Time (the offset –08:00 when DST doesn't apply and –07:00 when it does). In both cases, the time needs to retreat by three hours to 9:00 AM. You get the following output.

```
val1                                val2
----------------------------------- -----------------------------------
2022-02-12 09:00:00.0000000 -08:00  2022-08-12 09:00:00.0000000 -07:00
```

There's another interesting use case for the *AT TIME ZONE* function. If you're connected to Azure SQL Database, the time zone used there is always UTC. Also, irrespective of the platform you're using, what if you need to compute the local date and time in a desired target time zone? This can be easily achieved by applying the *AT TIME ZONE* function to the result of the *SYSDATETIMEOFFSET* function and specifying the desired target time zone name. For example, the following expression will give you the current time in Pacific Time terms irrespective of the time zone setting of your target system:

```
SELECT SYSDATETIMEOFFSET() AT TIME ZONE 'Pacific Standard Time';
```

The *DATEADD* function

You use the *DATEADD* function to add a specified number of units of a specified date part to an input date and time value.

Syntax

DATEADD(*part, n, dt_val*)

Valid values for the *part* input include *year, quarter, month, dayofyear, day, week, weekday, hour, minute, second, millisecond, microsecond,* and *nanosecond.* You can also specify the part in abbreviated form, such as *yy* instead of *year.* Refer to the product documentation for details.

The return type for a date and time input is the same type as the input's type. If this function is given a string literal as input, the output is *DATETIME.*

For example, the following code adds one year to February 12, 2022:

```
SELECT DATEADD(year, 1, '20220212');
```

This code returns the following output:

```
-----------------------
2023-02-12 00:00:00.000
```

In case you're curious about the difference between the parts *day, weekday,* and *dayofyear,* they all have the same meaning for the functions *DATEADD* and *DATEDIFF.* For example, with the *DATEADD* function, any of the three parts will result in adding *n* days to *dt_val.* However, these parts do have different meanings for other functions, such as *DATEPART* and *DATENAME,* which will be described shortly.

The *DATEDIFF* and *DATEDIFF_BIG* Functions

The *DATEDIFF* and *DATEDIFF_BIG* functions return the difference between two date and time values in terms of a specified date part. The former returns a value typed as *INT* (a 4-byte integer), and the latter returns a value typed as *BIGINT* (an 8-byte integer).

Syntax

DATEDIFF(*part, dt_val1, dt_val2*), DATEDIFF_BIG(*part, dt_val1, dt_val2*)

For example, the following code returns the difference in terms of days between two values:

```
SELECT DATEDIFF(day, '20210212', '20220212');
```

This code returns the output 365.

There are certain differences that result in an integer that is greater than the maximum INT value (2,147,483,647). For example, the difference in milliseconds between January 1, 0001 and February 12, 2022 is 63,780,220,800,000. You can't use the *DATEDIFF* function to compute such a difference, but you can achieve this with the *DATEDIFF_BIG* function:

```
SELECT DATEDIFF_BIG(millisecond, '00010101', '20220212');
```

If you need to compute the beginning of the day that corresponds to an input date and time value, you can simply cast the input value to the *DATE* type and then cast the result to the target type. Try it! But with a bit more sophisticated use of the *DATEADD* and *DATEDIFF* functions, you can compute the beginning or end of different parts (day, month, quarter, year) that correspond to the input value. For example, use the following code to compute the beginning of the day that corresponds to the input date and time value:

```
SELECT
  DATEADD(
    day,
    DATEDIFF(day, '19000101', SYSDATETIME()), '19000101');
```

This is achieved by first using the *DATEDIFF* function to calculate the difference in terms of whole days between an anchor date at midnight ('19000101' in this case) and the current date and time (call that difference *diff*). Then the *DATEADD* function is used to add *diff* days to the anchor. You get the current system date at midnight.

Of course, it could be much easier to cast the input value to *DATE* and then back to *DATETIME2*. However, the more complex expression is more flexible in that you can use it to compute the beginning of other parts.

If you use this expression with a month part instead of a day and make sure to use an anchor that is the first day of a month (as in this example), you get the first day of the current month:

```
SELECT
  DATEADD(
    month,
    DATEDIFF(month, '19000101', SYSDATETIME()), '19000101');
```

Similarly, by using a year part and an anchor that is the first day of a year, you get back the first day of the current year.

Starting with SQL Server 2022 you can compute the beginning of a requested part (year, month, day, and so on) much more easily using a new function called *DATETRUNC*. I'll describe and demonstrate how to use this function shortly.

If you want the last day of the month or year, simply use an anchor that is the last day of a month or year. For example, the following expression returns the last day of the current year:

```
SELECT
  DATEADD(
    year,
    DATEDIFF(year, '18991231', SYSDATETIME()), '18991231');
```

Using a similar expression with the month part, you can get the last day of the month, but it's much easier to achieve this using the function *EOMONTH* instead. Unfortunately, there are no similar functions to get the end of quarter and year, so you will need to use a computation for those such as the one just shown.

The *DATEPART* function

The *DATEPART* function returns an integer representing a requested part of a date and time value.

Syntax

DATEPART(*part*, *dt_val*)

Valid values for the *part* argument include *year, quarter, month, dayofyear, day, week, weekday, hour, minute, second, millisecond, microsecond, nanosecond, tzoffset* (time zone offset), and *iso_week* (ISO-based week number). As mentioned, you can use abbreviations for the date and time parts, such as *yy* instead of *year*, *mm* instead of *month*, *dd* instead of *day*, and so on.

For example, the following code returns the month part of the input value:

```
SELECT DATEPART(month, '20220212');
```

This code returns the integer 2.

For this function, the parts *day*, *weekday*, and *dayofyear*, have different meanings. The part *day* means the number of the day of the month. The part *weekday* means the number of the day of the week. The part *dayofyear* means the number of the day of the year.

The following example extracts all three parts from an input date:

```
SELECT
  DATEPART(day, '20220212') AS part_day,
  DATEPART(weekday, '20220212') AS part_weekday,
  DATEPART(dayofyear, '20220212') AS part_dayofyear;
```

This code generates the following output, assuming *us_english* as the language, defining Sunday as the first day of the week:

```
part_day    part_weekday part_dayofyear
----------- ------------ ---------------
12          7            43
```

The *YEAR*, *MONTH*, and *DAY* functions

The *YEAR*, *MONTH*, and *DAY* functions are abbreviations for the *DATEPART* function returning the integer representation of the year, month, and day parts of an input date and time value.

Syntax

YEAR(*dt_val*)

MONTH(*dt_val*)

DAY(*dt_val*)

For example, the following code extracts the day, month, and year parts of an input value:

```
SELECT
  DAY('20220212') AS theday,
  MONTH('20220212') AS themonth,
  YEAR('20220212') AS theyear;
```

This code returns the following output:

```
theday      themonth    theyear
----------- ----------- -----------
12          2           2022
```

The *DATENAME* function

The *DATENAME* function returns a character string representing a part of a date and time value.

Syntax

DATENAME(*dt_val*, *part*)

This function is similar to *DATEPART* and, in fact, has the same options for the *part* input. However, when relevant, it returns the name of the requested part rather than the number. For example, the following code returns the month name of the given input value:

```
SELECT DATENAME(month, '20220212');
```

Recall that *DATEPART* returned the integer 2 for this input. *DATENAME* returns the name of the month, which is language dependent. If your session's language is one of the English languages (such as US English or British English), you get back the value 'February'. If your session's language is Italian, you get back the value 'febbraio'. If a part is requested that has no name and only a numeric value (such as *year*), the *DATENAME* function returns its numeric value as a character string. For example, the following code returns '2022':

```
SELECT DATENAME(year, '20220212');
```

The *DATETRUNC* function

The *DATETRUNC* function truncates, or floors, the input date and time value to the beginning of the specified part. This function was introduced in SQL Server 2022.

Syntax

DATETRUNC(*part, dt_val*)

If *dt_val* is of a date and time type, the output truncated value will be of the same type and fractional time scale as the input. If *dt_val* is of a character string type, the output will be of the type *DATETIME2(7)*.

Valid values for the *part* argument include *year, quarter, month, dayofyear, day, week, iso_week, hour, minute, second, millisecond,* and *microsecond.* As with other functions, you can use abbreviations for the date and time parts, such as *yy* instead of *year, mm* instead of *month, dd* instead of *day,* and so on.

For example, the following code returns the beginning of month date corresponding to the input value, at midnight, as a *DATETIME2(7)*-typed value:

```
SELECT DATETRUNC(month, '20220212');
```

This code returns the following output:

```
---------------------------
2022-02-01 00:00:00.0000000
```

For this function, the parts *day* and *dayofyear* have the same meaning, which is the beginning of the day (at midnight) that corresponds to the input date and time value.

SQL Server 2022 also introduces a function called *DATE_BUCKET*, which for most input parts can be considered a more sophisticated version of *DATETRUNC*. The *DATE_BUCKET* function returns the beginning of the date and time bucket corresponding to an input value, based on indicated part, width, and origin values. One of the main uses of this function is in the context of what's known as time series data. Since this is a pretty big topic, I cover time series and the use of this function in Chapter 7 as part of the coverage of data analysis topics.

The *ISDATE* function

The *ISDATE* function accepts a character string as input and returns 1 if it is convertible to a date and time data type and 0 if it isn't.

Syntax

ISDATE(*string*)

For example, the following code returns 1:

```
SELECT ISDATE('20220212');
```

And the following code returns 0:

```
SELECT ISDATE('20220230');
```

The *FROMPARTS* functions

The *FROMPARTS* functions accept integer inputs representing parts of a date and time value and construct a value of the requested type from those parts.

Syntax

DATEFROMPARTS (*year, month, day*)

DATETIME2FROMPARTS (*year, month, day, hour, minute, seconds, fractions, precision*)

DATETIMEFROMPARTS (*year, month, day, hour, minute, seconds, milliseconds*)

DATETIMEOFFSETFROMPARTS (*year, month, day, hour, minute, seconds, fractions, hour_offset, minute_offset, precision*)

SMALLDATETIMEFROMPARTS (*year, month, day, hour, minute*)

TIMEFROMPARTS (*hour, minute, seconds, fractions, precision*)

These functions make it easier for programmers to construct date and time values from the different components, and they also simplify migrating code from other environments that already support similar functions. The following code demonstrates the use of these functions:

```
SELECT
  DATEFROMPARTS(2022, 02, 12),
  DATETIME2FROMPARTS(2022, 02, 12, 13, 30, 5, 1, 7),
  DATETIMEFROMPARTS(2022, 02, 12, 13, 30, 5, 997),
  DATETIMEOFFSETFROMPARTS(2022, 02, 12, 13, 30, 5, 1, -8, 0, 7),
  SMALLDATETIMEFROMPARTS(2022, 02, 12, 13, 30),
  TIMEFROMPARTS(13, 30, 5, 1, 7);
```

The *EOMONTH* function

The *EOMONTH* function accepts an input date and time value and returns the respective end-of-month date as a *DATE* typed value. The function also supports an optional second argument indicating how many months to add (or subtract, if negative).

Syntax

EOMONTH(*input* [, *months_to_add*])

For example, the following code returns the end of the current month:

```
SELECT EOMONTH(SYSDATETIME());
```

The following query returns orders placed on the last day of the month:

```
SELECT orderid, orderdate, custid, empid
FROM Sales.Orders
WHERE orderdate = EOMONTH(orderdate);
```

There's an alternative expression for computing the last day of the month that corresponds to the input date value:

```
DATEADD(month, DATEDIFF(month, '18991231', date_val), '18991231')
```

Don't be alarmed if it feels a bit over your head at this point. It is a more complex technique, but it has the advantage that you can use it to compute the beginning or end of other parts (day, month, quarter, year).

This expression first calculates the difference in terms of whole months between an anchor last day of some month (December 31, 1899, in this case) and the specified date. Call this difference *diff*. By adding *diff* months to the anchor date, you get the last day of the target month. Here's the full solution query, returning only orders that were placed on the last day of the month:

```
SELECT orderid, orderdate, custid, empid
FROM Sales.Orders
WHERE orderdate = DATEADD(month, DATEDIFF(month, '18991231', orderdate), '18991231');
```

The *GENERATE_SERIES* function

The *GENERATE_SERIES* function is a table function that returns a sequence of numbers in the requested range. This function was introduced in SQL Server 2022. You specify as inputs the range start and stop values, and optionally the step value if you want it to be different than the default (1 for an increasing range and –1 for a decreasing range). You get the result sequence of numbers in a result column called *value*. You can then easily convert the sequence of numbers to a sequence of date and time values if you need to.

Syntax

SELECT value FROM GENERATE_SERIES(*start_value, stop_value*[, *step_value*]);

The *start_value* and *stop_value* inputs can be of any of the types *TINYINT, SMALLINT, INT, BIGINT, DECIMAL,* or *NUMERIC,* and the two must have matching types. The type of the result column *value* is the same as the type of the inputs *start_value* and *stop_value*.

For example, the following code returns a sequence of integers between 1 and 10:

```
SELECT value
FROM GENERATE_SERIES( 1, 10 ) AS N;
```

This code generates the following output:

```
value
-----------
1
2
3
4
5
6
7
8
9
10
```

With a bit of date and time manipulation you can convert the numbers returned from the function to date and time values. As an example, the following code generates a sequence of all dates in the year 2022:

```
DECLARE @startdate AS DATE = '20220101', @enddate AS DATE = '20221231';

SELECT DATEADD(day, value, @startdate) AS dt
FROM GENERATE_SERIES( 0, DATEDIFF(day, @startdate, @enddate) ) AS N;
```

The code starts by declaring local variables called *@startdate* and *@enddate*, and assigning to those the start and end dates, respectively, of the year 2022. If you're not already familiar with variables and parameters in T-SQL, you can find details about those in Chapter 12.

The code then invokes the *GENERATE_SERIES* function, passing the value 0 as the input start value, and the result of the difference in terms of days between *@startdate* and *@enddate* as the input stop value. In the *SELECT* list, the code computes the result date in a column called *dt* by adding *value* days to *@startdate*.

This code generates the following output, shown here in abbreviated form:

```
dt
----------
2022-01-01
2022-01-02
2022-01-03
2022-01-04
2022-01 05
...
2022-12-27
2022-12-28
2022-12-29
2022-12-30
2022-12-31

(365 rows affected)
```

If you want to do some practice related to date and time at this point, try working on exercises 1, 2, and 7 at the end of this chapter.

Querying metadata

SQL Server provides tools for getting information about the metadata of objects, such as information about tables in a database and columns in a table. Those tools include catalog views, information schema views, and system stored procedures and functions. This area is documented well in the product documentation in the "Querying the SQL Server System Catalog" section, so I won't cover it in great detail here. I'll just give a couple of examples of each metadata tool to give you a sense of what's available and get you started.

Catalog views

Catalog views provide detailed information about objects in the database, including information that is specific to SQL Server. For example, if you want to list the tables in a database along with their schema names, you can query the *sys.tables* view as follows:

```
USE TSQLV6;

SELECT SCHEMA_NAME(schema_id) AS table_schema_name, name AS table_name
FROM sys.tables;
```

The *SCHEMA_NAME* function is used to convert the schema ID integer to its name. This query returns the following output:

```
table_schema_name    table_name
------------------    --------------
HR                    Employees
Production            Suppliers
Production            Categories
Production            Products
Sales                 Customers
Sales                 Shippers
Sales                 Orders
Sales                 OrderDetails
Stats                 Tests
Stats                 Scores
dbo                   Nums
```

To get information about columns in a table, you can query the *sys.columns* table. For example, the following code returns information about columns in the *Sales.Orders* table, including column names, data types (with the system type ID translated to a name by using the *TYPE_NAME* function), maximum length, collation name, and nullability:

```
SELECT
  name AS column_name,
  TYPE_NAME(system_type_id) AS column_type,
  max_length,
  collation_name,
  is_nullable
FROM sys.columns
WHERE object_id = OBJECT_ID(N'Sales.Orders');
```

This query returns the following output:

```
column_name     column_type   max_length  collation_name          is_nullable
---------------  ------------  ----------  ----------------------  -----------
orderid         int           4           NULL                    0
custid          int           4           NULL                    1
empid           int           4           NULL                    0
orderdate       date          3           NULL                    0
requireddate    date          3           NULL                    0
shippeddate     date          3           NULL                    1
```

shipperid	int	4	NULL	0
freight	money	8	NULL	0
shipname	nvarchar	80	Latin1_General_CI_AS	0
shipaddress	nvarchar	120	Latin1_General_CI_AS	0
shipcity	nvarchar	30	Latin1_General_CI_AS	0
shipregion	nvarchar	30	Latin1_General_CI_AS	1
shippostalcode	nvarchar	20	Latin1_General_CI_AS	1
shipcountry	nvarchar	30	Latin1_General_CI_AS	0

Information schema views

SQL Server supports a set of views that reside in a schema called *INFORMATION_SCHEMA* and provide metadata information in a standard manner. That is, the views are defined in the SQL standard, so naturally they don't cover metadata aspects or objects specific to SQL Server (such as indexing).

For example, the following query against the *INFORMATION_SCHEMA.TABLES* view lists the base tables in the current database along with their schema names:

```
SELECT TABLE_SCHEMA, TABLE_NAME
FROM INFORMATION_SCHEMA.TABLES
WHERE TABLE_TYPE = N'BASE TABLE';
```

The following query against the *INFORMATION_SCHEMA.COLUMNS* view provides most of the available information about columns in the *Sales.Orders* table:

```
SELECT
  COLUMN_NAME, DATA_TYPE, CHARACTER_MAXIMUM_LENGTH,
  COLLATION_NAME, IS_NULLABLE
FROM INFORMATION_SCHEMA.COLUMNS
WHERE TABLE_SCHEMA = N'Sales'
  AND TABLE_NAME = N'Orders';
```

System stored procedures and functions

System stored procedures and functions internally query the system catalog and return more "digested" metadata information. Again, you can find the full list of objects and their detailed descriptions in the product documentation, but here are a few examples.

The *sp_tables* stored procedure returns a list of objects (such as tables and views) that can be queried in the current database:

```
EXEC sys.sp_tables;
```

The *sp_help* procedure accepts an object name as input and returns multiple result sets with general information about the object, and also information about columns, indexes, constraints, and more. For example, the following code returns detailed information about the *Orders* table:

```
EXEC sys.sp_help
  @objname = N'Sales.Orders';
```

The *sp_columns* procedure returns information about columns in an object. For example, the following code returns information about columns in the *Orders* table:

```
EXEC sys.sp_columns
  @table name = N'Orders',
  @table_owner = N'Sales';
```

The *sp_helpconstraint* procedure returns information about constraints in an object. For example, the following code returns information about constraints in the *Orders* table:

```
EXEC sys.sp_helpconstraint
  @objname = N'Sales.Orders';
```

One set of functions returns information about properties of entities such as the SQL Server instance, database, object, column, and so on. The *SERVERPROPERTY* function returns the requested property of the current instance. For example, the following code returns the collation of the current instance:

```
SELECT
  SERVERPROPERTY('Collation');
```

The *DATABASEPROPERTYEX* function returns the requested property of the specified database name. For example, the following code returns the collation of the *TSQLV6* database:

```
SELECT
  DATABASEPROPERTYEX(N'TSQLV6', 'Collation');
```

The *OBJECTPROPERTY* function returns the requested property of the specified object name. For example, the output of the following code indicates whether the *Orders* table has a primary key:

```
SELECT
  OBJECTPROPERTY(OBJECT_ID(N'Sales.Orders'), 'TableHasPrimaryKey');
```

Notice the nesting of the function *OBJECT_ID* within *OBJECTPROPERTY*. The *OBJECTPROPERTY* function expects an object ID and not a name, so the *OBJECT_ID* function is used to return the ID of the *Orders* table.

The *COLUMNPROPERTY* function returns the requested property of a specified column. For example, the output of the following code indicates whether the *shipcountry* column in the *Orders* table is nullable:

```
SELECT
  COLUMNPROPERTY(OBJECT_ID(N'Sales.Orders'), N'shipcountry', 'AllowsNull');
```

Conclusion

This chapter introduced you to the *SELECT* statement, logical query processing, and various other aspects of single-table queries. I covered quite a few subjects here, including many new and unique concepts. If you're new to T-SQL, you might feel overwhelmed at this point. But remember that this chapter introduces some of the most important points about SQL that might be hard to digest at the beginning. If some of the concepts weren't completely clear, you might want to revisit sections from this chapter later on, after you've had a chance to sleep on it.

For an opportunity to practice what you learned and absorb the material better, I recommend going over the chapter exercises.

Exercises

This section provides exercises to help you familiarize yourself with the subjects discussed in Chapter 2. Solutions to the exercises appear in the section that follows.

You can find instructions for downloading and installing the *TSQLV6* sample database in the Appendix.

Exercise 1

Write a query against the *Sales.Orders* table that returns orders placed in June 2021:

- Tables involved: *TSQLV6* database and the *Sales.Orders* table

- Desired output (abbreviated):

```
orderid     orderdate   custid       empid
----------- ----------- ----------- -----------
10555       2021-06-02  71           6
10556       2021-06-03  73           2
10557       2021-06-03  44           9
10558       2021-06-04  4            1
10559       2021-06-05  7            6
10560       2021-06-06  25           8
10561       2021-06-06  24           2
10562       2021-06-09  66           1
10563       2021-06-10  67           2
10564       2021-06-10  65           4
...

(30 rows affected)
```

Exercise 2

Write a query against the *Sales.Orders* table that returns orders placed on the day before the last day of the month:

- Tables involved: *TSQLV6* database and the *Sales.Orders* table

- Desired output (abbreviated):

```
orderid     orderdate   custid       empid
----------- ----------- ----------- -----------
10268       2020-07-30  33           8
10294       2020-08-30  65           4
```

```
10342          2020-10-30 25          4
10368          2020-11-29 20          2
10398          2020-12-30 71          2
10430          2021-01-30 20          4
10431          2021-01-30 10          4
10459          2021-02-27 84          4
10520          2021-04-29 70          7
10521          2021-04-29 12          8
...

(30 rows affected)
```

Exercise 3

Write a query against the *HR.Employees* table that returns employees with a last name containing the letter *e* twice or more:

- Tables involved: *TSQLV6* database and the *HR.Employees* table

- Desired output:

```
empid        firstname  lastname
-----------  ---------- --------------------
4            Yael       Peled
5            Sven       Mortensen

(2 rows affected)
```

Exercise 4

Write a query against the *Sales.OrderDetails* table that returns orders with a total value (quantity * unitprice) greater than 10,000, sorted by total value, descending:

- Tables involved: *TSQLV6* database and the *Sales.OrderDetails* table

- Desired output:

```
orderid      totalvalue
-----------  ---------------------
10865        17250.00
11030        16321.90
10981        15810.00
10372        12281.20
10424        11493.20
10817        11490.70
10889        11380.00
10417        11283.20
10897        10835.24
10353        10741.60
10515        10588.50
10479        10495.60
10540        10191.70
10691        10164.80

(14 rows affected)
```

Exercise 5

To check the validity of the data, write a query against the *HR.Employees* table that returns employees with a last name that starts with a lowercase English letter in the range a through z. Remember that the collation of the sample database is case insensitive (*Latin1_General_CI_CP1_AS* if you didn't choose an explicit collation during the SQL Server installation, or *Latin1_General_CI_AS* if you chose Windows collation, Case Insensitive, Accent Sensitive):

- Tables involved: *TSQLV6* database and the *HR.Employees* table

- Desired output is an empty set:

```
empid       lastname
----------- --------------------

(0 rows affected))
```

Exercise 6

Explain the difference between the following two queries:

```
-- Query 1
SELECT empid, COUNT(*) AS numorders
FROM Sales.Orders
WHERE orderdate < '20220501'
GROUP BY empid;

-- Query 2
SELECT empid, COUNT(*) AS numorders
FROM Sales.Orders
GROUP BY empid
HAVING MAX(orderdate) < '20220501';
```

- Tables involved: *TSQLV6* database and the *Sales.Orders* table

Exercise 7

Write a query against the *Sales.Orders* table that returns the three shipped-to countries with the highest average freight for orders placed in 2021:

- Tables involved: *TSQLV6* database and the *Sales.Orders* table

- Desired output:

```
shipcountry     avgfreight
--------------- ----------------------
Austria         178.3642
Switzerland     117.1775
Sweden          105.16

(3 rows affected)
```

Exercise 8

Write a query against the *Sales.Orders* table that calculates row numbers for orders based on order date ordering (using the order ID as the tiebreaker) for each customer separately:

- Tables involved: *TSQLV6* database and the *Sales.Orders* table

- Desired output (abbreviated):

```
custid      orderdate  orderid      rownum
----------- ---------- -----------  --------------------
1           2021-08-25 10643        1
1           2021-10-03 10692        2
1           2021-10-13 10702        3
1           2022-01-15 10835        4
1           2022-03-16 10952        5
1           2022-04-09 11011        6
2           2020-09-18 10308        1
2           2021-08-08 10625        2
2           2021-11-28 10759        3
2           2022-03-04 10926        4
...

(830 rows affected)
```

Exercise 9

Using the *HR.Employees* table, write a *SELECT* statement that returns for each employee the gender based on the title of courtesy. For 'Ms.' and 'Mrs.' return 'Female'; for 'Mr.' return 'Male'; and in all other cases (for example, 'Dr.') return 'Unknown':

- Tables involved: *TSQLV6* database and the *HR.Employees* table

- Desired output:

```
empid  firstname   lastname    titleofcourtesy   gender
------ ----------  ----------  ---------------   -------
1      Sara        Davis       Ms.               Female
2      Don         Funk        Dr.               Unknown
3      Judy        Lew         Ms.               Female
4      Yael        Peled       Mrs.              Female
5      Sven        Mortensen   Mr.               Male
6      Paul        Suurs       Mr.               Male
7      Russell     King        Mr.               Male
8      Maria       Cameron     Ms.               Female
9      Patricia    Doyle       Ms.               Female

(9 rows affected)
```

Exercise 10

Write a query against the *Sales.Customers* table that returns for each customer the customer ID and region. Sort the rows in the output by region, ascending, having *NULLs* sort last (after non-*NULL* values). Note that the default sort behavior for *NULLs* in T-SQL is to sort first (before non-*NULL* values):

- Tables involved: *TSQLV6* database and the *Sales.Customers* table

- Desired output (abbreviated):

```
custid       region
-----------  ---------------
55           AK
10           BC
42           BC
45           CA
37           Co. Cork
33           DF
71           ID
38           Isle of Wight
46           Lara
78           MT
...
1            NULL
2            NULL
3            NULL
4            NULL
5            NULL
6            NULL
7            NULL
8            NULL
9            NULL
11           NULL
...

(91 rows affected)
```

Solutions

This section provides the solutions to the exercises for this chapter, accompanied by explanations where needed.

Exercise 1

You might have considered using the *YEAR* and *MONTH* functions in the *WHERE* clause of your solution query, like this:

```
USE TSQLV6;

SELECT orderid, orderdate, custid, empid
FROM Sales.Orders
WHERE YEAR(orderdate) = 2021 AND MONTH(orderdate) = 6;
```

This solution is valid and returns the correct result. However, I explained that if you apply manipulation to the filtered column, in most cases SQL Server can't use an index efficiently. Therefore, I advise using a range filter instead:

```
SELECT orderid, orderdate, custid, empid
FROM Sales.Orders
WHERE orderdate >= '20210601'
  AND orderdate < '20210701';
```

Exercise 2

You can use the *EOMONTH* and *DATEADD* functions to address this task, like this:

```
SELECT orderid, orderdate, custid, empid
FROM Sales.Orders
WHERE orderdate = DATEADD(day, -1, EOMONTH(orderdate));
```

Using the *EOMONTH* function you compute the end of month date that corresponds to the *orderdate* value. Then, using the *DATEADD* function, you subtract one day from the end of month date.

Exercise 3

This exercise involves using pattern matching with the *LIKE* predicate. Remember that the percent sign (%) represents a character string of any size, including an empty string. Therefore, you can use the pattern '%e%e%' to express at least two occurrences of the character *e* anywhere in the string. Here's the full solution query:

```
SELECT empid, firstname, lastname
FROM HR.Employees
WHERE lastname LIKE '%e%e%';
```

Exercise 4

This exercise is quite tricky, and if you managed to solve it correctly, you should be proud of yourself. A subtle requirement in the request might be overlooked or interpreted incorrectly. Observe that the request said "return orders with *total value* greater than 10,000" and not "return orders with *value* greater than 10,000." In other words, it's not the individual order line row that is supposed to meet the requirement. Instead, the group of all order lines within the order should meet the requirement. This means that the query shouldn't have a filter in the *WHERE* clause like this:

```
WHERE quantity * unitprice > 10000
```

Rather, the query should group the data by the *orderid* attribute and have a filter in the *HAVING* clause, like this:

```
HAVING SUM(quantity*unitprice) > 10000
```

Here's the complete solution query:

```
SELECT orderid, SUM(qty*unitprice) AS totalvalue
FROM Sales.OrderDetails
GROUP BY orderid
HAVING SUM(qty*unitprice) > 10000
ORDER BY totalvalue DESC;
```

Exercise 5

You might have tried addressing the task using a query such as the following:

```
SELECT empid, lastname
FROM HR.Employees
WHERE lastname COLLATE Latin1_General_CS_AS LIKE N'[a-z]%';
```

The expression in the *WHERE* clause uses the *COLLATE* clause to convert the current case-insensitive collation of the *lastname* column to a case-sensitive one. The *LIKE* predicate then checks that the case-sensitive last name starts with a letter in the range a through z. The tricky part here is that the specified collation uses dictionary sort order, in which the lowercase and uppercase forms of each letter appear next to each other and not in separate groups. The sort order looks like this:

```
a
A
b
B
c
C
. . .
x
X
y
Y
z
Z
```

You realize that all the lowercase letters a through z, as well as the uppercase letters A through Y (excluding Z), qualify. Therefore, if you run the preceding query, you get the following output:

```
empid       lastname
----------- --------------------
8           Cameron
1           Davis
9           Doyle
2           Funk
7           King
3           Lew
5           Mortensen
4           Peled
6           Suurs
```

To look only for the lowercase letters a through z, one solution is to list them explicitly in the LIKE pattern, like this:

```
SELECT empid, lastname
FROM HR.Employees
WHERE lastname COLLATE Latin1_General_CS_AS LIKE N'[abcdefghijklmnopqrstuvwxyz]%';
```

Naturally, there are other possible solutions. For example, using a binary collation and then a simplified range of letters, like so:

```
SELECT empid, lastname
FROM HR.Employees
WHERE lastname COLLATE Latin1_General_BIN LIKE N'[a-z]%';
```

I'd like to thank Paul White, who enlightened me when I fell into this trap myself in the past.

Exercise 6

The *WHERE* clause is a row filter, whereas the *HAVING* clause is a group filter. Query 1 filters only orders placed before May 2022, groups them by the employee ID, and returns the number of orders each employee handled among the filtered ones. In other words, it computes how many orders each employee handled prior to May 2022. The query doesn't include orders placed in May 2022 or later in the count. An employee will show up in the output as long as he or she handled orders prior to May 2022, regardless of whether the employee handled orders since May 2022. Here's the output of Query 1:

```
empid       numorders
----------- -----------
9           43
3           127
6           67
7           70
1           118
4           154
5           42
2           94
8           101
```

Query 2 groups all orders by the employee ID, and then filters only groups having a maximum date of activity prior to May 2022. Then it computes the order count in each employee group. The query discards the entire employee group if the employee handled any orders since May 2022. In a sentence, this query returns for employees who didn't handle any orders since May 2022 the total number of orders they handled. This query generates the following output:

```
empid       numorders
----------- -----------
9           43
3           127
6           67
5           42
```

Take employee 1 as an example. This employee had activity both before and since May 2022. The first query result includes this employee, but the order count reflects only the orders the employee handled prior to May 2022. The second query result doesn't include this employee at all.

Exercise 7

Because the request involves activity in the year 2021, the query should have a *WHERE* clause with the appropriate date-range filter (*orderdate >= '20210101' AND orderdate < '20220101'*). Note that *orderdate >= '20210101'* is not necessarily the same as *orderdate > '20201231'*, since if *orderdate* is of a type that has both date and time elements and not just a date element, an order placed after midnight but still on December 31, 2020, will be included in the range.

Because the request involves average freight values per shipping country and the table can have multiple rows per country, the query should group the rows by country and calculate the average freight. To get the three countries with the highest average freights, the query should specify *TOP (3)*, based on the order of average freight descending. Here's the complete solution query:

```
SELECT TOP (3) shipcountry, AVG(freight) AS avgfreight
FROM Sales.Orders
WHERE orderdate >= '20210101' AND orderdate < '20220101'
GROUP BY shipcountry
ORDER BY avgfreight DESC;
```

Remember that you can use the standard *OFFSET-FETCH* filter instead of the proprietary *TOP* filter. Here's the revised solution using *OFFSET-FETCH*:

```
SELECT shipcountry, AVG(freight) AS avgfreight
FROM Sales.Orders
WHERE orderdate >= '20210101' AND orderdate < '20220101'
GROUP BY shipcountry
ORDER BY avgfreight DESC
OFFSET 0 ROWS FETCH NEXT 3 ROWS ONLY;
```

Exercise 8

Because the exercise requests that the row number calculation be done for each customer separately, the expression should partition the window by *custid* (*PARTITION BY custid*). In addition, the request was to use ordering based on the *orderdate* column, with the *orderid* column as a tiebreaker (*ORDER BY orderdate, orderid*). Here's the complete solution query:

```
SELECT custid, orderdate, orderid,
  ROW_NUMBER() OVER(PARTITION BY custid ORDER BY orderdate, orderid) AS rownum
FROM Sales.Orders
ORDER BY custid, rownum;
```

Remember not to confuse the *ORDER BY* of the *OVER* clause with the *ORDER BY* for presentation. In the latter you only had to include *custid* and *rownum*, since the ordering of *rownum* was already based on *orderdate* and *orderid*.

Exercise 9

You can handle the conditional logic in this exercise with a *CASE* expression. Using the simple *CASE* expression form, you specify the *titleofcourtesy* attribute right after the *CASE* keyword; list each possible title of courtesy in a separate *WHEN* clause followed by the *THEN* clause and the gender; and in the *ELSE* clause, specify *'Unknown'*.

```
SELECT empid, firstname, lastname, titleofcourtesy,
  CASE titleofcourtesy
    WHEN 'Ms.'  THEN 'Female'
    WHEN 'Mrs.' THEN 'Female'
    WHEN 'Mr.'  THEN 'Male'
    ELSE             'Unknown'
  END AS gender
FROM HR.Employees;
```

You can also use the searched *CASE* form with two predicates—one to handle all cases in which the gender is female and one for all cases in which the gender is male—and an *ELSE* clause with *'Unknown'*.

```
SELECT empid, firstname, lastname, titleofcourtesy,
  CASE
    WHEN titleofcourtesy IN('Ms.', 'Mrs.') THEN 'Female'
    WHEN titleofcourtesy = 'Mr.'           THEN 'Male'
    ELSE                     'Unknown'
  END AS gender
FROM HR.Employees;
```

Exercise 10

By default, SQL Server sorts *NULLs* before non-*NULL* values. To get *NULLs* to sort last, you can use a *CASE* expression that returns 1 when the *region* column is *NULL* and 0 when it is not *NULL*. Specify this *CASE* expression as the first sort column and the *region* column as the second. This way, non-*NULLs* sort correctly among themselves first, followed by *NULLs*. Here's the complete solution query:

```
SELECT custid, region
FROM Sales.Customers
ORDER BY
  CASE WHEN region IS NULL THEN 1 ELSE 0 END, region;
```

CHAPTER 3

Joins

The *FROM* clause of a query is the first clause to be logically processed, and within the *FROM* clause, table operators operate on input tables. T-SQL supports four table operators: *JOIN, APPLY, PIVOT,* and *UNPIVOT.* The *JOIN* table operator is standard, whereas *APPLY, PIVOT,* and *UNPIVOT* are T-SQL extensions to the standard. Each table operator acts on tables provided to it as input, applies a set of logical query processing phases, and returns a table result. This chapter focuses on the *JOIN* table operator. The *APPLY* operator will be covered in Chapter 5, "Table expressions," and the *PIVOT* and *UNPIVOT* operators will be covered in Chapter 7, "T-SQL for data analysis."

A *JOIN* table operator operates on two input tables. The three fundamental types of joins are cross joins, inner joins, and outer joins. These three types of joins differ in how they apply their logical query processing phases; each type applies a different set of phases. A cross join applies only one phase—Cartesian Product. An inner join applies two phases—Cartesian Product and Filter. An outer join applies three phases—Cartesian Product, Filter, and Add Outer Rows. This chapter explains in detail each of the join types and the phases involved.

Logical query processing describes a generic series of logical steps that for any specified query produces the correct result, whereas *physical query processing* is the way the query is processed by the RDBMS engine in practice. Some phases of logical query processing of joins might sound inefficient, but remember that the query will be optimized by the physical implementation. It's important to stress the term *logical* in *logical query processing.* The steps in the process apply operations to the input tables based on relational algebra. The database engine does not have to follow logical query processing phases literally, as long as it can guarantee that the result that it produces is the same as that dictated by logical query processing. The query optimizer often applies shortcuts when it knows it can still produce the correct result. Even though this book's focus is on understanding the logical aspects of querying, I want to stress this point to avoid performance-related concerns.

Cross joins

The cross join is the simplest type of join. It implements only one logical query processing phase—a Cartesian Product. This phase operates on the two tables provided as inputs and produces a Cartesian product of the two. That is, each row from one input is matched with all rows from the other. So if you have m rows in one table and n rows in the other, you get $m \times n$ rows in the result.

T-SQL supports two standard syntaxes for cross joins: the SQL-92 and SQL-89 syntaxes. I recommend you use the SQL-92 syntax for reasons I'll describe shortly. It's also the main syntax I use throughout the book. For the sake of completeness, I describe both syntaxes in this section.

SQL-92 syntax

The following query applies a cross join between the *Customers* and *Employees* tables (using the SQL-92 syntax) in the *TSQLV6* database, and returns the *custid* and *empid* attributes in the result set:

```
USE TSQLV6;

SELECT C.custid, E.empid
FROM Sales.Customers AS C
  CROSS JOIN HR.Employees AS E;
```

Because there are 91 rows in the *Customers* table and 9 rows in the *Employees* table, this query produces a result set with 819 rows, as shown here in abbreviated form:

```
custid      empid
----------- -----------
1           2
2           2
3           2
4           2
5           2
6           2
7           2
8           2
9           2
11          2
...

(819 rows affected)
```

When you use the SQL-92 syntax, you specify the CROSS JOIN keywords between the two tables involved in the join.

Notice that in the *FROM* clause of the preceding query, I assigned the aliases *C* and *E* to the *Customers* and *Employees* tables, respectively. If assigned, the table aliases should be used instead of the original table names as a prefix to the column name as in *table_alias.column_name* in table-qualified column references. The purpose of the prefixes is to facilitate the identification of columns in an unambiguous manner when the same column name appears in both tables. In unambiguous cases, column prefixes are optional. However, it's a good practice to always use column prefixes for the sake of clarity. Also note that if you assign an alias to a table, it's invalid to use the full table name as a column prefix; in ambiguous cases, you have to use the table alias as a prefix.

SQL-89 syntax

T-SQL also supports an older syntax for cross joins that was introduced in SQL-89. In this syntax, you simply specify a comma between the table names, like this:

```
SELECT C.custid, E.empid
FROM Sales.Customers AS C, HR.Employees AS E;
```

There is no logical or performance difference between the two syntaxes. Both are integral parts of the SQL standard, and both are fully supported by T-SQL. I'm not aware of any plans to deprecate the older syntax in the SQL standard or in T-SQL. However, I recommend using the SQL-92 syntax for reasons that will become clear after I explain inner and outer joins.

Self cross joins

You can join multiple instances of the same table. This capability is known as a *self join* and is supported with all fundamental join types (cross joins, inner joins, and outer joins). For example, the following query performs a self cross join between two instances of the *Employees* table:

```
SELECT
  E1.empid, E1.firstname, E1.lastname,
  E2.empid, E2.firstname, E2.lastname
FROM HR.Employees AS E1
  CROSS JOIN HR.Employees AS E2;
```

This query produces all possible pairs of employees. Because the *Employees* table has 9 rows, this query returns 81 rows, as shown here in abbreviated form:

```
empid       firstname   lastname               empid       firstname   lastname
----------- ----------- ---------------------- ----------- ----------- ----------------------
1           Sara        Davis                  1           Sara        Davis
2           Don         Funk                   1           Sara        Davis
3           Judy        Lew                    1           Sara        Davis
4           Yael        Peled                  1           Sara        Davis
5           Sven        Mortensen              1           Sara        Davis
6           Paul        Suurs                  1           Sara        Davis
7           Russell     King                   1           Sara        Davis
8           Maria       Cameron                1           Sara        Davis
9           Patricia    Doyle                  1           Sara        Davis
1           Sara        Davis                  2           Don         Funk
2           Don         Funk                   2           Don         Funk
3           Judy        Lew                    2           Don         Funk
4           Yael        Peled                  2           Don         Funk
5           Sven        Mortensen              2           Don         Funk
6           Paul        Suurs                  2           Don         Funk
7           Russell     King                   2           Don         Funk
8           Maria       Cameron                2           Don         Funk
9           Patricia    Doyle                  2           Don         Funk
...

(81 rows affected)
```

In a self join, aliasing tables is not optional. Without table aliases, all column names in the result of the join would be ambiguous.

Producing tables of numbers

One situation in which cross joins can be handy is when they are used to produce a result set with a sequence of integers (1, 2, 3, and so on). Such a sequence of numbers is an extremely powerful tool that I use for many purposes. By using cross joins, you can produce the sequence of integers in a very efficient manner.

You can start by creating a table called *Digits* with a column called *digit*, and populate the table with 10 rows with the digits 0 through 9. Run the following code to create the *Digits* table in the *TSQLV6* database and populate it with the 10 digits:

```
USE TSQLV6;

DROP TABLE IF EXISTS dbo.Digits;

CREATE TABLE dbo.Digits(digit INT NOT NULL PRIMARY KEY);

INSERT INTO dbo.Digits(digit)
  VALUES (0),(1),(2),(3),(4),(5),(6),(7),(8),(9);

SELECT digit FROM dbo.Digits;
```

This code also uses an *INSERT* statement to populate the *Digits* table. If you're not familiar with the syntax of the *INSERT* statement, see Chapter 8, "Data modification," for details.

This code generates the following output:

```
digit
-----------
0
1
2
3
4
5
6
7
8
9
```

Suppose you need to write a query that produces a sequence of integers in the range 1 through 1,000. You apply cross joins between three instances of the *Digits* table, each representing a different power of 10 (1, 10, 100). By multiplying three instances of the same table, each instance with 10 rows, you get a result set with 1,000 rows. To produce the actual number, multiply the digit from each instance by the power of 10 it represents, sum the results, and add 1. Here's the complete query:

```
SELECT D3.digit * 100 + D2.digit * 10 + D1.digit + 1 AS n
FROM        dbo.Digits AS D1
  CROSS JOIN dbo.Digits AS D2
  CROSS JOIN dbo.Digits AS D3
ORDER BY n;
```

This query returns the following output, shown here in abbreviated form:

```
n
-----------
1
2
3
4
5
6
7
8
9
10
...
998
999
1000

(1000 rows affected)
```

This was an example that produces a sequence of 1,000 integers. If you need more numbers, you can add more instances of the *Digits* table to the query. For example, if you need to produce a sequence of 1,000,000 rows, you need to join six instances.

Note that the above technique is useful if you're using older versions than SQL Server 2022. Recall from Chapter 2 that starting with SQL Server 2022, you can generate a sequence of integers easily with the *GENERATE_SERIES* function.

Inner joins

An inner join applies two logical query processing phases—it applies a Cartesian product between the two input tables like in a cross join, and then it filters rows based on a predicate you specify. Like cross joins, inner joins have two standard syntaxes: SQL-92 and SQL-89.

SQL-92 syntax

Using the SQL-92 syntax, you specify the INNER JOIN keywords between the table names. The INNER keyword is optional, so you can specify the JOIN keyword alone. You specify the predicate that is used to filter rows in a designated clause called *ON*. This predicate is also known as the *join condition*.

For example, the following query performs an inner join between the *Employees* and *Orders* tables in the *TSQLV6* database, matching employees and orders based on the predicate *E.empid = O.empid*:

```
USE TSQLV6;

SELECT E.empid, E.firstname, E.lastname, O.orderid
FROM HR.Employees AS E
  INNER JOIN Sales.Orders AS O
    ON E.empid = O.empid;
```

This query produces the following result set, shown here in abbreviated form:

```
empid        firstname   lastname                ordered
-----------  ----------  --------------------    -----------
1            Sara        Davis                   10258
1            Sara        Davis                   10270
1            Sara        Davis                   10275
1            Sara        Davis                   10285
1            Sara        Davis                   10292
...
2            Don         Funk                    10265
2            Don         Funk                    10277
2            Don         Funk                    10280
2            Don         Funk                    10295
2            Don         Funk                    10300
...
```

```
(830 rows affected)
```

For most people, the easiest way to think of such an inner join is as matching each employee row with all order rows that have the same employee ID as in the employee row. This is a simplified way to think of the join. The more formal way to think of it is based on relational algebra. First, the join performs a Cartesian product between the two tables (9 employee rows × 830 order rows = 7,470 rows). Then, the join filters rows based on the predicate *E.empid = O.empid*, eventually returning 830 rows. As mentioned earlier, that's just the logical way that the join is processed; in practice, physical processing of the query by the database engine can be different.

Recall the discussion from previous chapters about the three-valued predicate logic used by SQL. As with the *WHERE* and *HAVING* clauses, the *ON* clause also returns only rows for which the predicate evaluates to *TRUE*, and it does not return rows for which the predicate evaluates to *FALSE* or *UNKNOWN*.

In the *TSQLV6* database, all employees have related orders, so all employees show up in the output. However, had there been employees with no related orders, they would have been discarded by the filter phase. The same would apply to orders with no related employees, although a foreign-key relationship combined with the fact that the *empid* column in *Orders* disallows *NULLs* forbids those in our sample database.

SQL-89 syntax

Similar to cross joins, inner joins can be expressed by using the SQL-89 syntax. You specify a comma between the table names just as in a cross join, and you specify the join condition in the query's *WHERE* clause, like this:

```
SELECT E.empid, E.firstname, E.lastname, O.orderid
FROM HR.Employees AS E, Sales.Orders AS O
WHERE E.empid = O.empid;
```

Note that the SQL-89 syntax has no *ON* clause.

Again, both syntaxes are standard, fully supported by T-SQL, and interpreted in the same way by the database engine, so you shouldn't expect any performance difference between them. But one syntax is safer, as explained in the next section.

Inner join safety

I strongly recommend that you stick to the SQL-92 join syntax for a couple of reasons. For one, that's the only standard syntax that supports all three fundamental join types—cross, inner, and outer. Also, it's less prone to errors. Suppose you intend to write an inner join query, and by mistake you forget to specify the join condition. With the SQL-92 syntax, the query becomes invalid, and the parser generates an error. For example, try to run the following code:

```
SELECT E.empid, E.firstname, E.lastname, O.orderid
FROM HR.Employees AS E
  INNER JOIN Sales.Orders AS O;
```

You get the following error:

```
Msg 102, Level 15, State 1, Line 74
Incorrect syntax near ';'.
```

Even though it might not be immediately obvious from the error message that the error involves a missing join condition—that is, an *ON* clause—you will figure it out eventually and fix the query. However, if you forget to specify the join condition when you're using the SQL-89 syntax, you get a valid query that performs a cross join:

```
SELECT E.empid, E.firstname, E.lastname, O.orderid
FROM HR.Employees AS E, Sales.Orders AS O;
```

Because the query doesn't fail, the logical error might go unnoticed for a while, and users of your application might end up relying on incorrect results. It's unlikely that a programmer would forget to specify the join condition with such short and simple queries; however, most production queries are much more complicated and have multiple tables, filters, and other query elements. In those cases, the likelihood of forgetting to specify a join condition increases.

If I've convinced you that it's important to use the SQL-92 syntax for inner joins, you might wonder whether the recommendation holds for cross joins. Because no join condition is involved, you might think that both syntaxes are just as good. However, I recommend sticking to the SQL-92 syntax for consistency. As mentioned, it's the only standard syntax that supports all three fundamental join types. Trying to mix the two join styles when using multiple joins in the same query can result in awkward code that is less readable and is hard to maintain.

More join examples

This section covers further join considerations before we start delving into outer joins: composite joins, non-equi joins, and multi-join queries.

Composite joins

A *composite join* is simply a join for which you need to match multiple attributes from each side. You usually need such a join when a primary key–foreign key relationship is based on more than one attribute. For example, suppose you have a foreign key defined on *dbo.Table2*, columns *col1*, *col2*, referencing *dbo.Table1*, columns *col1*, *col2*, and you need to write a query that joins the two based on this relationship. The *FROM* clause of the query would look like this:

```
FROM dbo.Table1 AS T1
  INNER JOIN dbo.Table2 AS T2
    ON T1.col1 = T2.col1
    AND T1.col2 = T2.col2
```

For a more tangible example, suppose you need to audit updates to column values against the *OrderDetails* table in the *TSQLV6* database. You create a custom auditing table called *OrderDetailsAudit*:

```
USE TSQLV6;

DROP TABLE IF EXISTS Sales.OrderDetailsAudit;

CREATE TABLE Sales.OrderDetailsAudit
(
  lsn        INT NOT NULL IDENTITY,
  orderid    INT NOT NULL,
  productid  INT NOT NULL,
  dt         DATETIME NOT NULL,
  loginname  sysname NOT NULL,
  columnname sysname NOT NULL,
  oldval     SQL_VARIANT,
  newval     SQL_VARIANT,
  CONSTRAINT PK_OrderDetailsAudit PRIMARY KEY(lsn),
  CONSTRAINT FK_OrderDetailsAudit_OrderDetails
    FOREIGN KEY(orderid, productid)
    REFERENCES Sales.OrderDetails(orderid, productid)
);
```

Each audit row stores a log serial number (*lsn*), the key of the modified row (*orderid, productid*), the name of the modified column (*columnname*), the old value (*oldval*), the new value (*newval*), when the change took place (*dt*), and who made the change (*loginname*). The table has a foreign key defined on the attributes *orderid, productid*, referencing the primary key of the *OrderDetails* table, which is defined on the attributes *orderid, productid*. Assume you already have in place the process that logs changes in the *OrderDetailsAudit* table whenever columns are updated in the *OrderDetails* table.

You need to write a query against the *OrderDetails* and *OrderDetailsAudit* tables that returns information about all value changes that took place in the column *qty*. In each result row, you need to return the current value from the *OrderDetails* table and the values before and after the change from the *OrderDetailsAudit* table. You need to join the two tables based on a primary key–foreign key relationship, like this:

```
SELECT OD.orderid, OD.productid, OD.qty,
  ODA.dt, ODA.loginname, ODA.oldval, ODA.newval
FROM Sales.OrderDetails AS OD
  INNER JOIN Sales.OrderDetailsAudit AS ODA
    ON OD.orderid = ODA.orderid
    AND OD.productid = ODA.productid
WHERE ODA.columnname = N'qty';
```

Because the relationship is based on multiple attributes, the join condition is composite.

Non-equi joins

When a join condition involves only an equality operator, the join is said to be an *equi join*. When a join condition involves any operator besides equality, the join is said to be a *non-equi join*.

> **Note** Standard SQL supports a concept called *natural join*, which represents an inner join based on a match between columns with the same name in both sides. For example, *T1 NATURAL JOIN T2* joins the rows between *T1* and *T2* based on a match between the columns with the same names on both sides. T-SQL doesn't have an implementation of a natural join. A join that has an explicit join predicate that is based on a binary operator (equality or inequality) is known as a *theta join*. So both equi joins and non-equi joins are types of theta joins.

As an example of a non-equi join, the following query joins two instances of the *Employees* table to produce unique pairs of employees:

```
SELECT
  E1.empid, E1.firstname, E1.lastname,
  E2.empid, E2.firstname, E2.lastname
FROM HR.Employees AS E1
  INNER JOIN HR.Employees AS E2
    ON E1.empid < E2.empid;
```

Notice the predicate specified in the *ON* clause. The purpose of the query is to produce unique pairs of employees. Had a cross join been used, the result would have included self pairs (for example, 1 with 1) and also mirrored pairs (for example, 1 with 2 and also 2 with 1). Using an inner join with a join condition that says the key on the left side must be smaller than the key on the right side eliminates the two inapplicable cases. Self pairs are eliminated because both sides are equal. With mirrored pairs, only one of the two cases qualifies because, of the two cases, only one will have a left key that is smaller than the right key. In this example, of the 81 possible pairs of employees a cross join would have returned, this query returns the 36 unique pairs shown here:

empid	firstname	lastname	empid	firstname	lastname
1	Sara	Davis	2	Don	Funk
1	Sara	Davis	3	Judy	Lew
2	Don	Funk	3	Judy	Lew
1	Sara	Davis	4	Yael	Peled
2	Don	Funk	4	Yael	Peled
3	Judy	Lew	4	Yael	Peled
1	Sara	Davis	5	Sven	Mortensen
2	Don	Funk	5	Sven	Mortensen
3	Judy	Lew	5	Sven	Mortensen
4	Yael	Peled	5	Sven	Mortensen
1	Sara	Davis	6	Paul	Suurs
2	Don	Funk	6	Paul	Suurs
3	Judy	Lew	6	Paul	Suurs
4	Yael	Peled	6	Paul	Suurs
5	Sven	Mortensen	6	Paul	Suurs
1	Sara	Davis	7	Russell	King
2	Don	Funk	7	Russell	King
3	Judy	Lew	7	Russell	King
4	Yael	Peled	7	Russell	King
5	Sven	Mortensen	7	Russell	King
6	Paul	Suurs	7	Russell	King
1	Sara	Davis	8	Maria	Cameron
2	Don	Funk	8	Maria	Cameron
3	Judy	Lew	8	Maria	Cameron
4	Yael	Peled	8	Maria	Cameron
5	Sven	Mortensen	8	Maria	Cameron
6	Paul	Suurs	8	Maria	Cameron
7	Russell	King	8	Maria	Cameron
1	Sara	Davis	9	Patricia	Doyle
2	Don	Funk	9	Patricia	Doyle
3	Judy	Lew	9	Patricia	Doyle
4	Yael	Peled	9	Patricia	Doyle
5	Sven	Mortensen	9	Patricia	Doyle
6	Paul	Suurs	9	Patricia	Doyle
7	Russell	King	9	Patricia	Doyle
8	Maria	Cameron	9	Patricia	Doyle

(36 rows affected)

If it's still not clear to you what this query does, try to process it one step at a time with a smaller set of employees. For example, suppose the *Employees* table contained only employees 1, 2, and 3. First, produce the Cartesian product of two instances of the table:

E1.empid	E2.empid
1	1
1	2
1	3
2	1
2	2
2	3
3	1
3	2
3	3

Next, filter the rows based on the predicate *E1.empid < E2.empid*, and you are left with only three rows:

```
E1.empid      E2.empid
------------- -------------
1             2
1             3
2             3
```

Multi-join queries

A join table operator operates only on two tables, but a single query can have multiple joins. In general, when more than one table operator appears in the *FROM* clause, the table operators are logically processed in written order. That is, the result table of the first table operator is treated as the left input to the second table operator; the result of the second table operator is treated as the left input to the third table operator; and so on. So if there are multiple joins in the *FROM* clause, the first join operates on two base tables, but all other joins get the result of the preceding join as their left input. With cross joins and inner joins, the database engine can (and often does) internally rearrange join ordering for optimization purposes because it won't have an impact on the correctness of the result of the query.

As an example, the following query joins the *Customers* and *Orders* tables to match customers with their orders, and then it joins the result of the first join with the *OrderDetails* table to match orders with their order lines:

```
SELECT
    C.custid, C.companyname, O.orderid,
    OD.productid, OD.qty
FROM Sales.Customers AS C
    INNER JOIN Sales.Orders AS O
      ON C.custid = O.custid
    INNER JOIN Sales.OrderDetails AS OD
      ON O.orderid = OD.orderid;
```

This query returns the following output, shown here in abbreviated form:

```
custid      companyname           orderid      productid      qty
----------- --------------------- ------------ -------------- ------
85          Customer ENQZT        10248        11             12
85          Customer ENQZT        10248        42             10
85          Customer ENQZT        10248        72             5
79          Customer FAPSM        10249        14             9
79          Customer FAPSM        10249        51             40
34          Customer IBVRG        10250        41             10
34          Customer IBVRG        10250        51             35
34          Customer IBVRG        10250        65             15
84          Customer NRCSK        10251        22             6
84          Customer NRCSK        10251        57             15
...

(2155 rows affected)
```

Outer joins

In this section I cover outer joins. I start with the fundamentals of outer joins and the logical query processing phases that they involve. I then continue with further outer join considerations, such as including missing values, filtering attributes from the nonpreserved side of the join, using outer joins in multi-join queries, and using the *COUNT* aggregate function with outer joins.

Outer joins, described

Outer joins were introduced in SQL-92 and, unlike inner joins and cross joins, have only one standard syntax—the one in which the JOIN keyword is specified between the table names and the join condition is specified in the *ON* clause. Outer joins apply the two logical processing phases that inner joins apply (Cartesian Product and the *ON* filter), plus a third phase called Adding Outer Rows that is unique to this type of join.

In an outer join, you mark a table as a *preserved* table by using the keywords LEFT OUTER JOIN, RIGHT OUTER JOIN, or FULL OUTER JOIN between the table names. The OUTER keyword is optional. The LEFT keyword means that the rows of the left table (the one to the left of the JOIN keyword) are preserved; the RIGHT keyword means that the rows in the right table are preserved; and the FULL keyword means that the rows in both the left and right tables are preserved. The third logical query processing phase of an outer join identifies the rows from the preserved table that did not find matches in the other table based on the *ON* predicate. This phase adds those rows to the result table produced by the first two phases of the join, and it uses *NULLs* as placeholders for the attributes from the nonpreserved side of the join in those outer rows.

A good way to understand outer joins is through an example. The following query joins the *Customers* and *Orders* tables, based on a match between the customer's customer ID and the order's customer ID, to return customers and their orders. The join type is a left outer join; therefore, the query also returns customers who did not place any orders:

```
SELECT C.custid, C.companyname, O.orderid
FROM Sales.Customers AS C
  LEFT OUTER JOIN Sales.Orders AS O
    ON C.custid = O.custid;
```

This query returns the following output, shown here in abbreviated form:

```
custid       companyname       ordered
-----------  ----------------  -----------
1            Customer NRZBB    10643
1            Customer NRZBB    10692
1            Customer NRZBB    10702
1            Customer NRZBB    10835
1            Customer NRZBB    10952
...
21           Customer KIDPX    10414
21           Customer KIDPX    10512
```

```
21          Customer KIDPX   10581
21          Customer KIDPX   10650
21          Customer KIDPX   10725
22          Customer DTDMN   NULL
23          Customer WVFAF   10408
23          Customer WVFAF   10480
23          Customer WVFAF   10634
23          Customer WVFAF   10763
23          Customer WVFAF   10789
...
56          Customer QNIVZ   10684
56          Customer QNIVZ   10766
56          Customer QNIVZ   10833
56          Customer QNIVZ   10999
56          Customer QNIVZ   11020
57          Customer WVAXS   NULL
58          Customer AHXHT   10322
58          Customer AHXHT   10354
58          Customer AHXHT   10474
58          Customer AHXHT   10502
58          Customer AHXHT   10995
...
91          Customer CCFIZ   10792
91          Customer CCFIZ   10870
91          Customer CCFIZ   10906
91          Customer CCFIZ   10998
91          Customer CCFIZ   11044
```

(832 rows affected)

Two customers in the *Customers* table did not place any orders. Their IDs are 22 and 57. Observe that in the output of the query, both customers are returned with *NULLs* in the attributes from the *Orders* table. Logically, the rows for these two customers were discarded by the second phase of the join (the filter based on the *ON* predicate), but the third phase added those as outer rows. Had the join been an inner join, these two rows would not have been returned. These two rows are added to preserve all the rows of the left table.

It might help to think of the result of an outer join as having two kinds of rows with respect to the preserved side—inner rows and outer rows. Inner rows are rows that have matches on the other side based on the *ON* predicate, and outer rows are rows that don't. An inner join returns only inner rows, whereas an outer join returns both inner and outer rows.

A common question about outer joins that is the source of a lot of confusion is whether to specify a predicate in the *ON* or *WHERE* clause of a query. You can see that with respect to rows from the preserved side of an outer join, the filter based on the *ON* predicate is not final. In other words, the *ON* predicate does not determine whether a row will show up in the output, only whether it will be matched with rows from the other side. So when you need to express a predicate that is not final— meaning a predicate that determines which rows to *match* from the nonpreserved side—specify the predicate in the *ON* clause. When you need a filter to be applied after outer rows are produced, and you want the filter to be final, specify the predicate in the *WHERE* clause. Conceptually, the *WHERE* clause is processed after the *FROM* clause—specifically, after all table operators have been processed and (in the case of outer joins) after all outer rows have been produced. To recap, in the *ON* clause you specify nonfinal, or *matching*, predicates. In the *WHERE* clause you specify final, or *filtering*, predicates.

Suppose you need to return only customers who did not place any orders or, more technically speaking, you need to return only outer rows. You can use the previous query as your basis, adding a *WHERE* clause that filters only outer rows. Remember that outer rows are identified by the *NULLs* in the attributes from the nonpreserved side of the join. So you can filter only the rows in which one of the attributes on the nonpreserved side of the join is *NULL*, like this:

```
SELECT C.custid, C.companyname
FROM Sales.Customers AS C
  LEFT OUTER JOIN Sales.Orders AS O
    ON C.custid = O.custid
WHERE O.orderid IS NULL;
```

This query returns only two rows, with customers 22 and 57:

```
custid       companyname
-----------  ----------------
22           Customer DTDMN
57           Customer WVAXS

(2 rows affected)
```

Notice a couple of important things about this query. Recall the discussions about *NULLs* earlier in the book: When looking for a *NULL*, you should use the operator *IS NULL* and not an equality operator. You do this because when an equality operator compares something with a *NULL*, it always returns *UNKNOWN*—even when it's comparing two *NULLs*. Also, the choice of which attribute from the non-preserved side of the join to filter is important. You should choose an attribute that can have a *NULL* only when the row is an outer row and not otherwise (for example, not a *NULL* originating from the base table). For this purpose, three cases are safe to consider: a primary key column, a join column, and a column defined as *NOT NULL*. A primary key column cannot be *NULL*; therefore, a *NULL* in such a column can only mean that the row is an outer row. If a row has a *NULL* in the join column, that row is filtered out by the second phase of the join, so a *NULL* in such a column can only mean that it's an outer row. And obviously, a *NULL* in a column that is defined as *NOT NULL* can only mean that the row is an outer row.

Including missing values

You can use outer joins to identify and include missing values when querying data. For example, suppose you need to query all orders from the *Orders* table in the *TSQLV6* database. You need to ensure that you get at least one row in the output for each date in the range January 1, 2020 through December 31, 2022. You don't want to do anything special with dates within the range that have orders, but you do want the output to include the dates with no orders, with *NULLs* as placeholders in the attributes of the order.

To solve the problem, you can first write a query that returns a sequence of all dates in the requested period. You can then perform a left outer join between that set and the *Orders* table. This way, the result also includes the missing dates.

To produce a sequence of dates in a given range, I usually use an auxiliary table of numbers. I create a table called *dbo.Nums* with a column called *n*, and populate it with a sequence of integers (1, 2, 3, and so on). I find that an auxiliary table of numbers is an extremely powerful general-purpose tool I end up using to solve many problems. You need to create it only once in the database and populate it with as many numbers as you might need. The *TSQLV6* sample database already has such an auxiliary table.

As the first step in the solution, you need to produce a sequence of all dates in the requested range. You can achieve this by querying the *Nums* table and filtering as many numbers as the number of days in the requested date range. You can use the *DATEDIFF* function to calculate that number. By adding *n – 1* days to the starting point of the date range (January 1, 2020), you get the actual date in the sequence. Here's the solution query:

```
SELECT DATEADD(day, n-1, CAST('20200101' AS DATE)) AS orderdate
FROM dbo.Nums
WHERE n <= DATEDIFF(day, '20200101', '20221231') + 1
ORDER BY orderdate;
```

This query returns a sequence of all dates in the range January 1, 2020 through December 31, 2022, as shown here in abbreviated form:

```
orderdate
-----------
2020-01-01
2020-01-02
2020-01-03
2020-01-04
2020-01-05
...
2022-12-27
2022-12-28
2022-12-29
2022-12-30
2022-12-31

(1096 rows affected)
```

The next step is to extend the previous query, adding a left outer join between *Nums* and the *Orders* tables. The join condition compares the order date produced from the *Nums* table and the *orderdate* from the *Orders* table by using the expression *DATEADD(day, Nums.n – 1, CAST('20200101' AS DATE))*, like this:

```
SELECT DATEADD(day, Nums.n - 1, CAST('20200101' AS DATE)) AS orderdate,
    O.orderid, O.custid, O.empid
FROM dbo.Nums
  LEFT OUTER JOIN Sales.Orders AS O
    ON DATEADD(day, Nums.n - 1, CAST('20200101' AS DATE)) = O.orderdate
WHERE Nums.n <= DATEDIFF(day, '20200101', '20221231') + 1
ORDER BY orderdate;
```

This query produces the following output, shown here in abbreviated form:

```
orderdate    orderid    custid    empid
-----------  ---------- --------- ----------
2020-01-01   NULL       NULL      NULL
2020-01-02   NULL       NULL      NULL
2020-01-03   NULL       NULL      NULL
2020-01-04   NULL       NULL      NULL
2020-01-05   NULL       NULL      NULL
...
2020-06-29   NULL       NULL      NULL
2020-06-30   NULL       NULL      NULL
2020-07-01   NULL       NULL      NULL
2020-07-02   NULL       NULL      NULL
2020-07-03   NULL       NULL      NULL
2020-07-04   10248      85        5
2020-07-05   10249      79        6
2020-07-06   NULL       NULL      NULL
2020-07-07   NULL       NULL      NULL
2020-07-08   10250      34        4
2020-07-08   10251      84        3
2020-07-09   10252      76        4
2020-07-10   10253      34        3
2020-07-11   10254      14        5
2020-07-12   10255      68        9
2020-07-13   NULL       NULL      NULL
2020-07-14   NULL       NULL      NULL
2020-07-15   10256      88        3
2020-07-16   10257      35        4
...
2008-12-2    NULL       NULL      NULL
2008-12-2    NULL       NULL      NULL
2008-12-2    NULL       NULL      NULL
2008-12-3    NULL       NULL      NULL
2008-12-3    NULL       NULL      NULL

(1446 rows affected)
```

Dates that do not appear as order dates in the *Orders* table appear in the output of the query with *NULLs* in the order attributes.

Note that starting with SQL Server 2022, you can use the *GENERATE_SERIES* function described in Chapter 2 instead of the *dbo.Nums* table.

Filtering attributes from the nonpreserved side of an outer join

When you need to review code involving outer joins to look for logical bugs, one of the things you should examine is the *WHERE* clause. If the predicate in the *WHERE* clause refers to an attribute from the nonpreserved side of the join using an expression in the form *<attribute> <operator> <value>*, it's usually an indication of a bug. This is because attributes from the nonpreserved side of the join are *NULLs* in outer rows, and an expression in the form *NULL <operator> <value>* yields *UNKNOWN* (unless it's the *IS NULL* operator explicitly looking for *NULLs*, or the distinct predicate *IS [NOT] DISTINCT FROM*). Recall that a *WHERE* clause filters *UNKNOWN* out. Such a predicate in the *WHERE* clause causes all outer rows to be filtered out. Effectively, the join becomes an inner join. So the programmer made a mistake either in the join type or in the predicate.

If this is not clear yet, the following example might help. Consider the following query:

```
SELECT C.custid, C.companyname, O.orderid, O.orderdate
FROM Sales.Customers AS C
  LEFT OUTER JOIN Sales.Orders AS O
    ON C.custid = O.custid
WHERE O.orderdate >= '20220101';
```

The query performs a left outer join between the *Customers* and *Orders* tables. Prior to applying the *WHERE* filter, the join operator returns inner rows for customers who placed orders and outer rows for customers who didn't place orders, with *NULLs* in the order attributes. The predicate *O.orderdate >= '20220101'* in the *WHERE* clause evaluates to *UNKNOWN* for all outer rows, because those have a *NULL* in the *O.orderdate* attribute. All outer rows are eliminated by the *WHERE* filter, as you can see in the output of the query, shown here in abbreviated form:

```
custid      companyname       orderid    orderdate
----------- ----------------- ---------- ----------
1           Customer NRZBB    10835      2022-01-15
1           Customer NRZBB    10952      2022-03-16
1           Customer NRZBB    11011      2022-04-09
2           Customer MLTDN    10926      2022-03-04
3           Customer KBUDE    10856      2022-01-28
...
90          Customer XBBVR    10910      2022-02-26
91          Customer CCFIZ    10906      2022-02-25
91          Customer CCFIZ    10870      2022-02-04
91          Customer CCFIZ    10998      2022-04-03
91          Customer CCFIZ    11044      2022-04-23

(270 rows affected)
```

This means that the use of an outer join here was futile, as the query did not return customers who did not place orders. The programmer made a mistake either in using an outer join or in specifying the predicate in the *WHERE* clause.

Using outer joins in a multi-join query

Recall the discussion about all-at-once operations in Chapter 2, "Single-table queries." The concept describes the fact that all expressions that appear in the same logical query processing phase are evaluated as a set, at the same point in time. However, this concept is not applicable to the processing of table operators in the *FROM* phase. Table operators are logically evaluated in written order. Rearranging the order in which outer joins are processed might result in different output, so you cannot rearrange them at will.

Some interesting bugs have to do with the logical order in which outer joins are processed. For example, a common bug could be considered a variation of the bug in the previous section. Suppose you write a multi-join query with an outer join between two tables, followed by an inner join with a third table. If the predicate in the inner join's *ON* clause compares an attribute from the nonpreserved side of the outer join and an attribute from the third table, all outer rows are discarded. Remember that outer rows have *NULLs* in the attributes from the nonpreserved side of the join, and comparing a *NULL* with anything yields *UNKNOWN. UNKNOWN* is filtered out by the *ON* filter. In other words, such a predicate nullifies the outer join, effectively turning it into an inner join. For example, consider the following query:

```
SELECT C.custid, O.orderid, OD.productid, OD.qty
FROM Sales.Customers AS C
  LEFT OUTER JOIN Sales.Orders AS O
    ON C.custid = O.custid
  INNER JOIN Sales.OrderDetails AS OD
    ON O.orderid = OD.orderid;
```

The first join is an outer join returning customers and their orders and also customers who did not place any orders. The outer rows representing customers with no orders have *NULLs* in the order attributes. The second join matches order lines from the *OrderDetails* table with rows from the result of the first join, based on the predicate *O.orderid = OD.orderid*; however, in the rows representing customers with no orders, the *O.orderid* attribute is *NULL*. Therefore, the predicate evaluates to *UNKNOWN*, and those rows are discarded. The output shown here in abbreviated form doesn't contain customers 22 and 57, the two customers who did not place orders:

```
custid        orderid        productid    qty
-----------   -----------    -----------  ------
85            10248          11           12
85            10248          42           10
85            10248          72           5
79            10249          14           9
79            10249          51           40
...
65            11077          64           2
65            11077          66           1
65            11077          73           2
65            11077          75           4
65            11077          77           2
```

```
(2155 rows affected)
```

Generally, outer rows are dropped whenever any kind of outer join (left, right, or full) is followed by a subsequent inner join or right outer join. That's assuming, of course, that the join condition compares the *NULLs* from the left side with something from the right side.

There are several ways to get around the problem if you want to return customers with no orders in the output. One option is to use a left outer join in the second join as well:

```
SELECT C.custid, O.orderid, OD.productid, OD.qty
FROM Sales.Customers AS C
  LEFT OUTER JOIN Sales.Orders AS O
    ON C.custid = O.custid
  LEFT OUTER JOIN Sales.OrderDetails AS OD
    ON O.orderid = OD.orderid;
```

This way, the outer rows produced by the first join aren't filtered out, as you can see in the output, shown here in abbreviated form:

```
custid       orderid      productid    qty
----------   ----------   ----------   ------
85           10248        11           12
85           10248        42           10
85           10248        72           5
79           10249        14           9
79           10249        51           40
...
65           11077        64           2
65           11077        66           1
65           11077        73           2
65           11077        75           4
65           11077        77           2
22           NULL         NULL         NULL
57           NULL         NULL         NULL
```

```
(2157 rows affected)
```

This solution is usually not a good one, because it preserves all rows from *Orders*. What if there were rows in *Orders* that didn't have matches in *OrderDetails*, and you wanted those rows to be discarded. What you want is an inner join between *Orders* and *OrderDetails*.

A second option is to use an inner join between *Orders* and *OrderDetails*, and then join the result with the *Customers* table using a right outer join:

```
SELECT C.custid, O.orderid, OD.productid, OD.qty
FROM Sales.Orders AS O
  INNER JOIN Sales.OrderDetails AS OD
    ON O.orderid = OD.orderid
  RIGHT OUTER JOIN Sales.Customers AS C
    ON O.custid = C.custid;
```

This way, the outer rows are produced by the last join and are not filtered out.

A third option is to consider the inner join between *Orders* and *OrderDetails* as its own unit. Then, apply a left outer join between the *Customers* table and that unit. Though not required, it's recommended to use parentheses to encapsulate the independent unit for clarity. The query would look like this:

```
SELECT C.custid, O.orderid, OD.productid, OD.qty
FROM Sales.Customers AS C
  LEFT OUTER JOIN
      (Sales.Orders AS O
        INNER JOIN Sales.OrderDetails AS OD
          ON O.orderid = OD.orderid)
    ON C.custid = O.custid;
```

What you're doing here is essentially nesting one join within another. Indeed, some in the SQL community refer to this technique as *nested joins*.

Using the *COUNT* aggregate with outer joins

Another common bug involves using *COUNT* with outer joins. When you group the result of an outer join and use the *COUNT(*)* aggregate, the aggregate takes into consideration both inner rows and outer rows, because it counts rows regardless of their contents. Usually, you're not supposed to take outer rows into consideration for the purposes of counting. For example, the following query is supposed to return the count of orders for each customer:

```
SELECT C.custid, COUNT(*) AS numorders
FROM Sales.Customers AS C
  LEFT OUTER JOIN Sales.Orders AS O
    ON C.custid = O.custid
GROUP BY C.custid;
```

Customers such as 22 and 57, who did not place orders, each have an outer row in the result of the join; therefore, they show up in the output with a count of 1:

```
custid      numorders
----------- -----------
1           6
2           4
3           7
4           13
5           18
...
22          1
...
57          1
...
87          15
88          9
89          14
90          7
91          7

(91 rows affected)
```

The *COUNT(*)* aggregate function cannot detect whether a row really represents an order. To fix the problem, you should use *COUNT(<column>)* instead of *COUNT(*)* and provide a column from the nonpreserved side of the join. This way, the *COUNT()* aggregate ignores outer rows because they have a *NULL* in that column. Remember to use a column that can only be *NULL* in case the row is an outer row—for example, the primary key column *orderid*:

```
SELECT C.custid, COUNT(O.orderid) AS numorders
FROM Sales.Customers AS C
  LEFT OUTER JOIN Sales.Orders AS O
    ON C.custid = O.custid
GROUP BY C.custid;
```

Notice in the output that customers 22 and 57 now show up with a count of 0:

```
custid       numorders
-----------  -----------
1            6
2            4
3            7
4            13
5            18
...
22           0
...
57           0
...
87           15
88           9
89           14
90           7
91           7

(91 rows affected)
```

Conclusion

This chapter covered the *JOIN* table operator. It described the logical query processing phases involved in the three fundamental types of joins: cross joins, inner joins, and outer joins. The chapter also covered further join examples, including composite joins, non-equi joins, and multi-join queries. To practice what you learned, go over the exercises for this chapter.

Exercises

This section provides exercises to help you familiarize yourself with the subjects discussed in this chapter. All exercises involve querying objects in the *TSQLV6* database.

Exercise 1-1

Write a query that generates five copies of each employee row:

- Tables involved: *HR.Employees* and *dbo.Nums*

- Desired output:

```
empid        firstname  lastname              n
-----------  ---------- --------------------  -----------
1            Sara       Davis                 1
2            Don        Funk                  1
3            Judy       Lew                   1
4            Yael       Peled                 1
```

```
5          Sven       Mortensen      1
6          Paul       Suurs          1
7          Russell    King           1
8          Maria      Cameron        1
9          Patricia   Doyle          1
1          Sara       Davis          2
2          Don        Funk           2
3          Judy       Lew            2
4          Yael       Peled          2
5          Sven       Mortensen      2
6          Paul       Suurs          2
7          Russell    King           2
8          Maria      Cameron        2
9          Patricia   Doyle          2
1          Sara       Davis          3
2          Don        Funk           3
3          Judy       Lew            3
4          Yael       Peled          3
5          Sven       Mortensen      3
6          Paul       Suurs          3
7          Russell    King           3
8          Maria      Cameron        3
9          Patricia   Doyle          3
1          Sara       Davis          4
2          Don        Funk           4
3          Judy       Lew            4
4          Yael       Peled          4
5          Sven       Mortensen      4
6          Paul       Suurs          4
7          Russell    King           4
8          Maria      Cameron        4
9          Patricia   Doyle          4
1          Sara       Davis          5
2          Don        Funk           5
3          Judy       Lew            5
4          Yael       Peled          5
5          Sven       Mortensen      5
6          Paul       Suurs          5
7          Russell    King           5
8          Maria      Cameron        5
9          Patricia   Doyle          5

(45 rows affected)
```

Exercise 1-2

Write a query that returns a row for each employee and day in the range June 12, 2022 through June 16, 2022:

- Tables involved: *HR.Employees* and *dbo.Nums*

- Desired output:

```
empid       dt
----------- -----------
1           2022-06-12
1           2022-06-13
1           2022-06-14
1           2022-06-15
1           2022-06-16
```

```
2        2022-06-12
2        2022-06-13
2        2022-06-14
2        2022-06-15
2        2022-06-16
3        2022-06-12
3        2022-06-13
3        2022-06-14
3        2022-06-15
3        2022-06-16
4        2022-06-12
4        2022-06-13
4        2022-06-14
4        2022-06-15
4        2022-06-16
5        2022-06-12
5        2022-06-13
5        2022-06-14
5        2022-06-15
5        2022-06-16
6        2022-06-12
6        2022-06-13
6        2022-06-14
6        2022-06-15
6        2022-06-16
7        2022-06-12
7        2022-06-13
7        2022-06-14
7        2022-06-15
7        2022-06-16
8        2022-06-12
8        2022-06-13
8        2022-06-14
8        2022-06-15
8        2022-06-16
9        2022-06-12
9        2022-06-13
9        2022-06-14
9        2022-06-15
9        2022-06-16

(45 rows affected)
```

Exercise 2

Explain what's wrong in the following query, and provide a correct alternative:

```
SELECT Customers.custid, Customers.companyname, Orders.orderid, Orders.orderdate
FROM Sales.Customers AS C
  INNER JOIN Sales.Orders AS O
  ON Customers.custid = Orders.custid;
```

Exercise 3

Return US customers, and for each customer return the total number of orders and total quantities:

- Tables involved: *Sales.Customers*, *Sales.Orders*, and *Sales.OrderDetails*

- Desired output:

```
custid        numorders     totalqty
-----------   -----------   -----------
32            11            345
36            5             122
43            2             20
45            4             181
48            8             134
55            10            603
65            18            1383
71            31            4958
75            9             327
77            4             46
78            3             59
82            3             89
89            14            1063

(13 rows affected)
```

Exercise 4

Return customers and their orders, including customers who placed no orders:

- Tables involved: *Sales.Customers* and *Sales.Orders*

- Desired output (abbreviated):

```
custid        companyname        orderid       orderdate
-----------   ----------------   -----------   -----------
85            Customer ENQZT     10248         2020-07-04
79            Customer FAPSM     10249         2020-07-05
34            Customer IBVRG     10250         2020-07-08
84            Customer NRCSK     10251         2020-07-08
...
73            Customer JMIKW     11074         2022-05-06
68            Customer CCKOT     11075         2022-05-06
9             Customer RTXGC     11076         2022-05-06
65            Customer NYUHS     11077         2022-05-06
22            Customer DTDMN     NULL          NULL
57            Customer WVAXS     NULL          NULL

(832 rows affected)
```

Exercise 5

Return customers who placed no orders:

- Tables involved: *Sales.Customers* and *Sales.Orders*

- Desired output:

```
custid        companyname
-----------   ----------------
22            Customer DTDMN
57            Customer WVAXS

(2 rows affected)
```

Exercise 6

Return customers with orders placed on February 12, 2022, along with their orders:

- Tables involved: *Sales.Customers* and *Sales.Orders*

- Desired output:

```
custid       companyname      orderid      orderdate
-----------  ----------------  -----------  ----------
48           Customer DVFMB   10883        2022-02-12
45           Customer QXPPT   10884        2022-02-12
76           Customer SFOGW   10885        2022-02-12

(3 rows affected)
```

Exercise 7

Write a query that returns all customers, but matches them with their respective orders only if they were placed on February 12, 2022:

- Tables involved: *Sales.Customers* and *Sales.Orders*

- Desired output (abbreviated):

```
custid       companyname      orderid      orderdate
----------   ----------------  -----------  ----------
72           Customer AHPOP   NULL         NULL
58           Customer AHXHT   NULL         NULL
25           Customer AZJED   NULL         NULL
18           Customer BSVAR   NULL         NULL
91           Customer CCFIZ   NULL         NULL
68           Customer CCKOT   NULL         NULL
49           Customer CQRAA   NULL         NULL
24           Customer CYZTN   NULL         NULL
22           Customer DTDMN   NULL         NULL
48           Customer DVFMB   10883        2022-02-12
10           Customer EEALV   NULL         NULL
40           Customer EFFTC   NULL         NULL
85           Customer ENQZT   NULL         NULL
```

```
82          Customer EYHKM  NULL     NULL
79          Customer FAPSM  NULL     NULL
...
51          Customer PVDZC  NULL     NULL
52          Customer PZNLA  NULL     NULL
56          Customer QNTV7  NULL     NULL
8           Customer QUHWH  NULL     NULL
67          Customer QVEPD  NULL     NULL
45          Customer QXPPT  10884    2022-02-12
7           Customer QXVLA  NULL     NULL
60          Customer QZURI  NULL     NULL
19          Customer RFNQC  NULL     NULL
9           Customer RTXGC  NULL     NULL
76          Customer SFOGW  10885    2022-02-12
69          Customer SIUIH  NULL     NULL
86          Customer SNXOJ  NULL     NULL
88          Customer SRQVM  NULL     NULL
54          Customer TDKEG  NULL     NULL
20          Customer THHDP  NULL     NULL
...

(91 rows affected)
```

Exercise 8

Explain why the following query isn't a correct solution query for Exercise 7:

```
SELECT C.custid, C.companyname, O.orderid, O.orderdate
FROM Sales.Customers AS C
  LEFT OUTER JOIN Sales.Orders AS O
    ON O.custid = C.custid
WHERE O.orderdate = '20220212'
  OR O.orderid IS NULL;
```

Exercise 9

Return all customers, and for each return a Yes/No value depending on whether the customer placed orders on February 12, 2022:

- Tables involved: *Sales.Customers* and *Sales.Orders*

- Desired output (abbreviated):

```
custid       companyname       HasOrderOn20220212
-----------  ----------------  --------------------
...
40           Customer EFFTC    No
41           Customer XIIWM    No
42           Customer IAIJK    No
43           Customer UISOJ    No
44           Customer OXFRU    No
45           Customer QXPPT    Yes
46           Customer XPNIK    No
47           Customer PSQUZ    No
48           Customer DVFMB    Yes
```

```
49        Customer CQRAA   No
50        Customer JYPSC   No
51        Customer PVDZC   No
52        Customer PZNLA   No
53        Customer GCJSG   No
...

(91 rows affected)
```

Solutions

This section provides solutions to the exercises for this chapter.

Exercise 1-1

Producing multiple copies of rows can be achieved with a cross join. If you need to produce five copies of each employee row, you need to perform a cross join between the *Employees* table and a table that has five rows; alternatively, you can perform a cross join between *Employees* and a table that has more than five rows, but filter only five from that table in the *WHERE* clause. The *Nums* table is convenient for this purpose. Simply join *Employees* and *Nums*, and filter from *Nums* as many rows as the number of requested copies (five, in this case). Here's the solution query:

```
SELECT E.empid, E.firstname, E.lastname, N.n
FROM HR.Employees AS E
    CROSS JOIN dbo.Nums AS N
WHERE N.n <= 5
ORDER BY n, empid;
```

Exercise 1-2

This exercise is an extension of the previous exercise. Instead of being asked to produce a predetermined constant number of copies of each employee row, you are asked to produce a copy for each day in a certain date range. So here you need to calculate the number of days in the requested date range by using the *DATEDIFF* function, and refer to the result of that expression in the query's *WHERE* clause instead of referring to a constant. To produce the dates, simply add *n* – 1 days to the date that starts the requested range. Here's the solution query:

```
SELECT E.empid,
    DATEADD(day, D.n - 1, CAST('20220612' AS DATE)) AS dt
FROM HR.Employees AS E
    CROSS JOIN dbo.Nums AS D
WHERE D.n <= DATEDIFF(day, '20220612', '20220616') + 1
ORDER BY empid, dt;
```

The *DATEDIFF* function returns *4* because there is a four-day difference between June 12, 2022 and June 16, 2022. Add 1 to the result, and you get 5 for the five days in the range. So the *WHERE* clause filters five rows from *Nums* where *n* is less than or equal to 5. By adding $n - 1$ days to June 12, 2022, you get all dates in the range June 12, 2022 through June 16, 2022.

Exercise 2

The first step in the processing of the JOIN table operator assigns to the *Customers* and *Orders* tables the shorter aliases *C* and *O*, respectively. The aliasing effectively renames the tables for the purposes of the query. In all subsequent phases of logical query processing, the original table names are not accessible; rather, only the shorter aliases are. You have two options to fix the query. One is to avoid aliasing and use the original table names as prefixes, like so:

```
SELECT Customers.custid, Customers.companyname, Orders.orderid, Orders.orderdate
FROM Sales.Customers
  INNER JOIN Sales.Orders
    ON Customers.custid = Orders.custid;
```

Another solution is to keep the aliases, but to make sure to use the aliases as prefixes, like so:

```
SELECT C.custid, C.companyname, O.orderid, O.orderdate
FROM Sales.Customers AS C
  INNER JOIN Sales.Orders AS O
    ON C.custid = O.custid;
```

Exercise 3

This exercise requires you to write a query that joins three tables: *Customers*, *Orders*, and *OrderDetails*. The query should use the *WHERE* clause to filter only rows where the customer's country is the United States. Because you are asked to return aggregates per customer, the query should group the rows by customer ID. You need to resolve a tricky issue here to return the right number of orders for each customer. Because of the join between *Orders* and *OrderDetails*, you don't get only one row per order—you get one row per order line. So if you use *COUNT(*)* or even *COUNT(O.orderid)*, in the *SELECT* list, you get back the number of order lines for each customer and not the number of orders.

To resolve this issue, you need to take each order into consideration only once. You can do this by using *COUNT(DISTINCT O.orderid)* instead of *COUNT(*)*. The total quantities don't create any special issues, because the quantity is associated with the order line and not the order. Here's the solution query:

```
SELECT C.custid, COUNT(DISTINCT O.orderid) AS numorders, SUM(OD.qty) AS totalqty
FROM Sales.Customers AS C
  INNER JOIN Sales.Orders AS O
    ON O.custid = C.custid
  INNER JOIN Sales.OrderDetails AS OD
    ON OD.orderid = O.orderid
WHERE C.country = N'USA'
GROUP BY C.custid;
```

Exercise 4

To get both customers who placed orders and customers who didn't place orders in the result, you need to use an outer join, like this:

```
SELECT C.custid, C.companyname, O.orderid, O.orderdate
FROM Sales.Customers AS C
  LEFT OUTER JOIN Sales.Orders AS O
    ON O.custid = C.custid;
```

This query returns 832 rows (including customers 22 and 57, who didn't place orders). An inner join between the tables would return only 830 rows, without those customers.

Exercise 5

This exercise is an extension of the previous one. To return only customers who didn't place orders, you need to add a *WHERE* clause to the query that filters only outer rows—namely, rows that represent customers with no orders. Outer rows have *NULLs* in the attributes from the nonpreserved side of the join (*Orders*). But to make sure that the *NULL* is a placeholder for an outer row and not a *NULL* that originated from the table, it's recommended that you refer to an attribute that is the primary key, or the join column, or one defined as not allowing *NULLs*. Here's the solution query, which refers to the primary key of the *Orders* table in the *WHERE* clause:

```
SELECT C.custid, C.companyname
FROM Sales.Customers AS C
  LEFT OUTER JOIN Sales.Orders AS O
    ON O.custid = C.custid
WHERE O.orderid IS NULL;
```

This query returns only two rows, for customers 22 and 57, who didn't place orders.

Exercise 6

This exercise involves writing a query that performs an inner join between *Customers* and *Orders* and filters only rows in which the order date is February 12, 2022:

```
SELECT C.custid, C.companyname, O.orderid, O.orderdate
FROM Sales.Customers AS C
  INNER JOIN Sales.Orders AS O
    ON O.custid = C.custid
WHERE O.orderdate = '20220212';
```

The *WHERE* clause filtered out customers who didn't place orders on February 12, 2022, but that was the request.

Exercise 7

This exercise builds on the previous one. The trick here is to realize two things. First, you need an outer join because you are supposed to preserve all customers, even if they don't have matching orders. Second, the predicate based on the order date is a nonfinal matching predicate; as such, it must appear in the *ON* clause and not the *WHERE* clause. Remember that the *WHERE* clause is a final filter that is applied after outer rows are added. Your goal is to match orders to customers only if the order was placed by the customer on February 12, 2022. You still want to get customers who didn't place orders on that date in the output. Hence, the *ON* clause should match customers and orders based on both an equality between the customer's customer ID and the order's customer ID, and on the order date being February 12, 2022. Here's the solution query:

```
SELECT C.custid, C.companyname, O.orderid, O.orderdate
FROM Sales.Customers AS C
  LEFT OUTER JOIN Sales.Orders AS O
    ON O.custid = C.custid
    AND O.orderdate = '20220212';
```

Exercise 8

The outer join matches all customers with their respective orders, and it preserves also customers who didn't place any orders. Customers without orders have *NULLs* in the order attributes. Then the *WHERE* filter keeps only rows where the order date is February 12, 2022 or the order ID is NULL (a customer without orders at all). The filter discards customers who didn't place orders on February 12, 2022 but did place orders on other dates, and according to Exercise 7 the query is supposed to return all customers. Here's the output of the incorrect query:

```
custid       companyname      orderid       orderdate
-----------  ---------------- -----------   ----------
48           Customer DVFMB   10883         2022-02-12
45           Customer QXPPT   10884         2022-02-12
76           Customer SFOGW   10885         2022-02-12
22           Customer DTDMN   NULL          NULL
57           Customer WVAXS   NULL          NULL

(5 rows affected)
```

The first three rows represent orders that were placed on February 12, 2022. The last two rows represent customers who didn't place orders at all. Observe that many of the 91 customers from the *Customers* table are missing. As mentioned, those are customers who didn't place orders on February 12, 2022, but did place orders on other dates.

Exercise 9

This exercise is an extension of Exercise 7. Here, instead of returning matching orders, you just need to return a Yes/No value indicating whether there is a matching order. Remember that in an outer join, a nonmatch is identified as an outer row with *NULLs* in the attributes of the nonpreserved side. So you can use a *CASE* expression that checks whether the current row is not an outer one, in which case it returns *Yes*; otherwise, it returns *No*. Because technically you can have more than one match per customer, you should add a *DISTINCT* clause to the *SELECT* list. This way, you get only one row back for each customer. Here's the solution query:

```
SELECT DISTINCT C.custid, C.companyname,
  CASE WHEN O.orderid IS NOT NULL THEN 'Yes' ELSE 'No' END AS HasOrderOn20220212
FROM Sales.Customers AS C
  LEFT OUTER JOIN Sales.Orders AS O
    ON O.custid = C.custid
    AND O.orderdate = '20220212';
```

CHAPTER 4

Subqueries

SQL supports writing queries within queries, or *nesting* queries. The outermost query is a query whose result set is returned to the caller and is known as the *outer query*. The inner query is a query whose result set is used by the outer query and is known as a *subquery*. The inner query acts in place of an expression that is based on constants or variables and is evaluated at run time. Unlike the results of expressions that use constants, the result of a subquery can change, because of changes in the queried tables. When you use subqueries, you avoid the need for separate steps in your solutions that store intermediate query results in variables.

A subquery can be either self-contained or correlated. A self-contained subquery has no dependency on tables from the outer query, whereas a correlated subquery does. A subquery can be single-valued, multivalued, or table-valued. That is, a subquery can return a single value, multiple values, or a whole table result.

This chapter focuses on subqueries that return a single value (scalar subqueries) and subqueries that return multiple values (multivalued subqueries). I'll cover subqueries that return whole tables (table subqueries) later in the book in Chapter 5, "Table expressions."

Both self-contained and correlated subqueries can return a scalar or multiple values. I'll first describe self-contained subqueries and demonstrate both scalar and multivalued examples. Then I'll describe correlated subqueries.

Again, exercises at the end of the chapter can help you practice what you learned.

Self-contained subqueries

Self-contained subqueries are subqueries that are independent of the tables in the outer query. Self-contained subqueries are convenient to debug, because you can always highlight the inner query, run it, and ensure that it does what it's supposed to do. Logically, the subquery code is evaluated only once before the outer query is evaluated, and then the outer query uses the result of the subquery. The following sections take a look at some concrete examples of self-contained subqueries.

Self-contained scalar subquery examples

A scalar subquery is a subquery that returns a single value. Such a subquery can appear anywhere in the outer query where a single-valued expression can appear (such as *WHERE* or *SELECT*).

For example, suppose you need to query the *Orders* table in the *TSQLV6* database and return information about the order that has the maximum order ID in the table. You could accomplish the task by using a variable. The code could retrieve the maximum order ID from the *Orders* table and store the result in a variable. Then the code could query the *Orders* table and filter the order where the order ID is equal to the value stored in the variable. The following code demonstrates this technique:

```
USE TSQLV6;

DECLARE @maxid AS INT = (SELECT MAX(orderid)
                         FROM Sales.Orders);

SELECT orderid, orderdate, empid, custid
FROM Sales.Orders
WHERE orderid = @maxid;
```

This query returns the following output:

```
orderid      orderdate   empid         custid
-----------  ----------- ------------- -----------
11077        2022-05-06  1             65
```

You can substitute the variable with a scalar self-contained subquery, like so:

```
SELECT orderid, orderdate, empid, custid
FROM Sales.Orders
WHERE orderid = (SELECT MAX(O.orderid)
                 FROM Sales.Orders AS O);
```

For a scalar subquery to be valid, it must return no more than one value. If a scalar subquery returns more than one value, it fails at run time. With the sample data in the *TSQLV6* database, the following query runs successfully:

```
SELECT orderid
FROM Sales.Orders
WHERE empid =
  (SELECT E.empid
   FROM HR.Employees AS E
   WHERE E.lastname LIKE N'C%');
```

The purpose of this query is to return orders placed by employees whose last name starts with the letter C. The subquery returns employee IDs of all employees whose last names start with the letter C. The outer query returns the orders where the employee ID is equal to the result of the subquery. Because an equality operator expects scalar operands on both sides, the subquery is considered scalar. Because the subquery can potentially return more than one value, the choice of using an equality predicate here is wrong. If the subquery returns more than one value, the query fails.

This query happens to run without failure because currently the *Employees* table contains only one employee whose last name starts with *C* (Maria Cameron with employee ID 8). This query returns the following output, shown here in abbreviated form:

```
orderid
-----------
10262
10268
10276
10278
10279
...
11054
11056
11065
11068
11075

(104 rows affected)
```

If the subquery returns more than one value, the query fails. For example, try running the query with employees whose last names start with *D*:

```
SELECT orderid
FROM Sales.Orders
WHERE empid =
  (SELECT E.empid
   FROM HR.Employees AS E
   WHERE E.lastname LIKE N'D%');
```

Apparently, two employees have a last name starting with *D* (Sara Davis and Patricia Doyle). Therefore, the query fails at run time with the following error:

```
Msg 512, Level 16, State 1, Line 40
Subquery returned more than 1 value. This is not permitted when the subquery follows =, !=, <,
<= , >, >= or when the subquery is used as an expression.
```

If a scalar subquery returns no value, the empty result is converted to a *NULL*. Recall that a comparison with a *NULL* yields *UNKNOWN* and that query filters do not return a row for which the filter expression evaluates to *UNKNOWN*. For example, the *Employees* table currently has no employees whose last names start with *A*; therefore, the following query returns an empty set:

```
SELECT orderid
FROM Sales.Orders
WHERE empid =
  (SELECT E.empid
   FROM HR.Employees AS E
   WHERE E.lastname LIKE N'A%');
```

Self-contained multivalued subquery examples

A multivalued subquery is a subquery that returns multiple values as a single column. Some predicates, such as the *IN* predicate, operate on a multivalued subquery.

Note SQL supports other predicates that operate on a multivalued subquery; those are *SOME*, *ANY*, and *ALL*. They are rarely used and therefore are not covered in this book.

The form of the *IN* predicate is

<scalar_expression> IN (<multivalued subquery>)

The predicate evaluates to *TRUE* if *scalar_expression* is equal to any of the values returned by the subquery. Recall the request in the previous section—returning orders that were handled by employees with a last name starting with a certain letter. Because more than one employee can have a last name starting with the same letter, this request should be handled with the *IN* predicate and not with an equality operator. For example, the following query returns orders placed by employees with a last name starting with *D*:

```
SELECT orderid
FROM Sales.Orders
WHERE empid IN
  (SELECT E.empid
   FROM HR.Employees AS E
   WHERE E.lastname LIKE N'D%');
```

Because this solution uses the *IN* predicate, this query is valid with any number of values returned—none, one, or more. This query returns the following output, shown here in abbreviated form:

```
orderid
-----------
10258
10270
10275
10285
10292
...
10978
11016
11017
11022
11058

(166 rows affected)
```

You might wonder why you don't implement this task by using a join instead of subqueries, like this:

```
SELECT O.orderid
FROM HR.Employees AS E
  INNER JOIN Sales.Orders AS O
    ON E.empid = O.empid
WHERE E.lastname LIKE N'D%';
```

Similarly, you're likely to stumble into many other querying tasks you can solve with either subqueries or joins. I don't know of a reliable rule of thumb that says a subquery is better than a join or the other way around. In some cases the database engine optimizes both the same way, sometimes joins perform better, and sometimes subqueries perform better. My approach is to first write a solution query that is intuitive and then, if performance is not satisfactory, try query revisions among other tuning methods. Such query revisions might include using joins instead of subqueries or the other way around. Also, consider keeping the different query rewrites; future changes in the database engine or the data might result in a different query being faster.

As another example of using multivalued subqueries, suppose you need to write a query that returns orders placed by customers from the United States. You can write a query against the *Orders* table that returns orders where the customer ID is in the set of customer IDs of customers from the United States. You can implement the last part in a self-contained, multivalued subquery. Here's the complete solution query:

```
SELECT custid, orderid, orderdate, empid
FROM Sales.Orders
WHERE custid IN
  (SELECT C.custid
   FROM Sales.Customers AS C
   WHERE C.country = N'USA');
```

This query returns the following output, shown here in abbreviated form:

```
custid      orderid      orderdate    empid
----------- -----------  -----------  -----------
65          10262        2020-07-22   8
89          10269        2020-07-31   5
75          10271        2020-08-01   6
65          10272        2020-08-02   6
65          10294        2020-08-30   4
...
32          11040        2022-04-22   4
32          11061        2022-04-30   4
71          11064        2022-05-01   1
89          11066        2022-05-01   7
65          11077        2022-05-06   1

(122 rows affected)
```

As with any other predicate, you can negate the *IN* predicate with the *NOT* operator. For example, the following query returns customers who did not place any orders:

```
SELECT custid, companyname
FROM Sales.Customers
WHERE custid NOT IN
  (SELECT O.custid
   FROM Sales.Orders AS O);
```

Note that it's considered a best practice to qualify the subquery, namely to add a filter, to exclude *NULLs*. I didn't do this here because I didn't explain the reason for this recommendation. I'll explain it later, in the section "*NULL* trouble."

The subquery returns the IDs of all customers that appear in the *Orders* table. In other words, it returns only the IDs of customers who placed orders. The outer query returns customers with IDs that do not appear in the result of the subquery—in other words, customers who did not place orders. This query returns the following output:

```
custid       companyname
-----------  -----------------
22           Customer DTDMN
57           Customer WVAXS
```

You might wonder whether specifying a *DISTINCT* clause in the subquery can help performance, because the same customer ID can occur more than once in the *Orders* table. The database engine is smart enough to consider removing duplicates without you asking it to do so explicitly, so this isn't something you need to worry about.

The last example in this section demonstrates the use of multiple self-contained subqueries in the same query—both single-valued and multivalued. Before I describe the task, run the following code to create a table called *dbo.Orders* in the *TSQLV6* database, and populate it with even-numbered order IDs from the *Sales.Orders* table:

```
USE TSQLV6;
DROP TABLE IF EXISTS dbo.Orders;
CREATE TABLE dbo.Orders(orderid INT NOT NULL CONSTRAINT PK_Orders PRIMARY KEY);

INSERT INTO dbo.Orders(orderid)
  SELECT orderid
  FROM Sales.Orders
  WHERE orderid % 2 = 0;
```

I describe the *INSERT* statement in more detail in Chapter 8, "Data modification," so don't worry if you're not familiar with it yet.

You need to write a query that returns all individual order IDs that are missing between the minimum and maximum ones in the table. It can be quite complicated to solve this task with a query without any helper tables or functions. You might find the *Nums* table introduced in Chapter 3, "Joins," useful here. Remember that the *Nums* table contains a sequence of integers, starting with 1, with no gaps. Recall that starting with SQL Server 2022, you can alternatively use the *GENERATE_SERIES* function described in Chapter 2 to generate a sequence of numbers. But in this example I'll use the *Nums* table. To return all missing order IDs, query the *Nums* table and filter only numbers that are between the minimum and maximum ones in the *dbo.Orders* table, and that do not appear as order IDs in the *Orders* table. You can use scalar self-contained subqueries to return the minimum and maximum order IDs and a multivalued self-contained subquery to return the set of all existing order IDs. Here's the complete solution query:

```
SELECT n
FROM dbo.Nums
WHERE n BETWEEN (SELECT MIN(O.orderid) FROM dbo.Orders AS O)
            AND (SELECT MAX(O.orderid) FROM dbo.Orders AS O)
  AND n NOT IN (SELECT O.orderid FROM dbo.Orders AS O);
```

Because the code that populated the *dbo.Orders* table filtered only even-numbered order IDs, this query returns all odd-numbered values between the minimum and maximum order IDs in the *Orders* table. The output of this query is shown here in abbreviated form:

```
n
-----------
10249
10251
10253
10255
10257
...
11067
11069
11071
11073
11075

(414 rows affected)
```

When you're done, run the following code for cleanup:

```
DROP TABLE IF EXISTS dbo.Orders;
```

Correlated subqueries

Correlated subqueries are subqueries that refer to attributes from the tables that appear in the outer query. This means the subquery is dependent on the outer query and cannot be invoked as a standalone query. Logically, the subquery is evaluated separately for each outer row in the logical query processing step in which it appears. For example, the query in Listing 4-1 returns orders with the maximum order ID for each customer.

LISTING 4-1 Correlated subquery

```
USE TSQLV6;

SELECT custid, orderid, orderdate, empid
FROM Sales.Orders AS O1
WHERE orderid =
  (SELECT MAX(O2.orderid)
   FROM Sales.Orders AS O2
   WHERE O2.custid = O1.custid);
```

The outer query is issued against an instance of the *Orders* table called *O1*; it filters orders where the order ID is equal to the value returned by the subquery. The subquery filters orders from a second instance of the *Orders* table called *O2*, where the inner customer ID is equal to the outer customer ID, and returns the maximum order ID from those filtered orders. In other words, for each row in *O1*, the subquery returns the maximum order ID for the current customer. If the outer order ID and the order

ID returned by the subquery match, the query returns the outer row. This query returns the following output, shown here in abbreviated form:

```
custid       orderid      orderdate   empid
-----------  -----------  ----------  -----------
91           11044        2022-04-23  4
90           11005        2022-04-07  2
89           11066        2022-05-01  7
88           10935        2022-03-09  4
87           11025        2022-04-15  6
...
5            10924        2022-03-04  3
4            11016        2022-04-10  9
3            10856        2022-01-28  3
2            10926        2022-03-04  4
1            11011        2022-04-09  3

(89 rows affected)
```

Because of the dependency on the outer query, correlated subqueries are usually harder to figure out than self-contained subqueries. To simplify things, I suggest you focus your attention on a single row in the outer table and think about the logical processing that takes place in the inner query for that row. For example, focus your attention on the following row from the table in the outer query, which has order ID 10248:

```
custid       orderid      orderdate                    empid
-----------  -----------  ---------------------------  -----------
85           10248        2020-07-04 00:00:00.000      5
```

When the subquery is evaluated for this row, the correlation to *O1.custid* means *85*. If you substitute the correlation manually with *85*, you get the following:

```
SELECT MAX(O2.orderid)
FROM Sales.Orders AS O2
WHERE O2.custid = 85;
```

This query returns the order ID 10739. The outer row's order ID—10248—is compared with the inner one—10739—and because there's no match in this case, the outer row is filtered out. The subquery returns the same value for all rows in *O1* with the same customer ID, and only in one case is there a match—when the outer row's order ID is the maximum for the current customer. Thinking in such terms will make it easier for you to grasp the concept of correlated subqueries.

The fact that correlated subqueries are dependent on the outer query makes it harder to troubleshoot problems with them compared to self-contained subqueries. You can't just highlight the subquery portion and run it. For example, if you try to highlight and run the subquery portion in Listing 4-1, you get the following error:

```
Msg 4104, Level 16, State 1, Line 119
The multi-part identifier "O1.custid" could not be bound.
```

This error indicates that the identifier *O1.custid* cannot be bound to an object in the query, because *O1* is not defined in the query. It is defined only in the context of the outer query. To troubleshoot correlated subqueries, you need to substitute the correlation with a constant, and after ensuring the code is correct, substitute the constant with the correlation.

As another example, suppose you need to query the *Sales.OrderValues* view and return for each order the percentage of the current order value out of the customer total. In Chapter 7, "T-SQL for data analysis," I provide a solution to this task that uses window functions; here I'll explain how to solve the task by using subqueries. It's always a good idea to try to come up with several solutions to each task, because the different solutions will usually vary in complexity and performance.

You can write an outer query against one instance of the *OrderValues* view called *O1*. In the *SELECT* list, divide the current value by the result of a correlated subquery against a second instance of *OrderValues* called *O2* that returns the current customer's total. Here's the complete solution query:

```
SELECT orderid, custid, val,
    CAST(100. * val / (SELECT SUM(O2.val)
                       FROM Sales.OrderValues AS O2
                       WHERE O2.custid = O1.custid)
        AS NUMERIC(5,2)) AS pct
FROM Sales.OrderValues AS O1
ORDER BY custid, orderid;
```

The *CAST* function is used to convert the datatype of the expression to *NUMERIC* with a precision of 5 (the total number of digits) and a scale of 2 (the number of digits after the decimal point).

This query returns the following output, shown here in abbreviated form:

```
orderid     custid      val         pct
----------- ----------- ----------- ------
10643       1           814.50      19.06
10692       1           878.00      20.55
10702       1           330.00      7.72
10835       1           845.80      19.79
10952       1           471.20      11.03
11011       1           933.50      21.85
10308       2           88.80       6.33
10625       2           479.75      34.20
10759       2           320.00      22.81
10926       2           514.40      36.67
...

(830 rows affected)
```

The *EXISTS* predicate

T-SQL supports a predicate called *EXISTS*, which accepts a subquery as input and returns *TRUE* if the subquery returns any rows and *FALSE* otherwise. For example, the following query returns customers from Spain who placed orders:

```
SELECT custid, companyname
FROM Sales.Customers AS C
WHERE country = N'Spain'
  AND EXISTS
    (SELECT * FROM Sales.Orders AS O
     WHERE O.custid = C.custid);
```

The outer query against the *Customers* table filters only customers from Spain for whom the *EXISTS* predicate returns *TRUE*. The *EXISTS* predicate returns *TRUE* if the current customer has related orders in the *Orders* table.

One of the benefits of using the *EXISTS* predicate is that you can intuitively phrase queries that sound like English. For example, this query can be read just as you would say it in ordinary English: Return customers from Spain if they have any orders where the order's customer ID is the same as the customer's customer ID.

This query returns the following output:

```
custid       companyname
-----------  -----------------
8            Customer QUHWH
29           Customer MDLWA
30           Customer KSLQF
69           Customer SIUIH
```

As with other predicates, you can negate the *EXISTS* predicate with the *NOT* operator. For example, the following query returns customers from Spain who did not place orders:

```
SELECT custid, companyname
FROM Sales.Customers AS C
WHERE country = N'Spain'
  AND NOT EXISTS
    (SELECT * FROM Sales.Orders AS O
     WHERE O.custid = C.custid);
```

This query returns the following output:

```
custid       companyname
-----------  -----------------
22           Customer DTDMN
```

Even though this book's focus is on logical query processing and not performance, I thought you might be interested to know that the *EXISTS* predicate lends itself to good optimization. That is, the database engine knows that it's enough to determine whether the subquery returns at least one row or none, and it doesn't need to process all qualifying rows. You can think of this capability as a kind of short-circuit evaluation. The same applies to the *IN* predicate.

Even though in most cases the use of star (*) is considered a bad practice, with *EXISTS* it isn't. The predicate cares only about the existence of matching rows, regardless of what you have in the *SELECT* list. The database engine knows this and—for example, for index selection purposes—ignores the subquery's *SELECT* list. Some minor extra cost might be incurred in the resolution process, where Microsoft SQL Server expands the * against metadata info—for example, to check that you have permissions to query all columns. But this cost is so minor you'll probably barely notice it. My opinion is that queries should be natural and intuitive unless there's a compelling reason to sacrifice this aspect of the code. I find the form *EXISTS(SELECT * FROM . . .)* much more intuitive than *EXISTS(SELECT 1 FROM . . .)*. Saving the minor extra cost associated with the resolution of * is not worth the cost of sacrificing the readability of the code.

Finally, another aspect of *EXISTS* that is worth mentioning is that, unlike most predicates in T-SQL, *EXISTS* uses two-valued logic and not three-valued logic. If you think about it, there's no situation where it's unknown whether a query returns any rows.

Returning previous or next values

Suppose you need to query the *Orders* table in the *TSQLV6* database and return, for each order, information about the current order and also the previous order ID. The tricky part is that the concept of "previous" implies order, and rows in a table have no order. One way to achieve this objective is with a T-SQL expression that means "the maximum value that is smaller than the current value." You could use the following T-SQL expression, which is based on a correlated subquery, for this:

```
SELECT orderid, orderdate, empid, custid,
  (SELECT MAX(O2.orderid)
   FROM Sales.Orders AS O2
   WHERE O2.orderid < O1.orderid) AS prevorderid
FROM Sales.Orders AS O1;
```

This query produces the following output, shown here in abbreviated form:

```
orderid      orderdate    empid       custid       prevorderid
-----------  -----------  ----------  -----------  -----------
10248        2020-07-04   5           85           NULL
10249        2020-07-05   6           79           10248
10250        2020-07-08   4           34           10249
10251        2020-07-08   3           84           10250
10252        2020-07-09   4           76           10251
...
11073        2022-05-05   2           58           11072
11074        2022-05-06   7           73           11073
11075        2022-05-06   8           68           11074
11076        2022-05-06   4           9            11075
11077        2022-05-06   1           65           11076

(830 rows affected)
```

Notice that because there's no order before the first order, the subquery returned a *NULL* for the first order.

Similarly, you can phrase the concept of "next" as "the minimum value that is greater than the current value." Here's a query that returns for each order the next order ID:

```
SELECT orderid, orderdate, empid, custid,
  (SELECT MIN(O2.orderid)
   FROM Sales.Orders AS O2
   WHERE O2.orderid > O1.orderid) AS nextorderid
FROM Sales.Orders AS O1;
```

This query produces the following output, shown here in abbreviated form:

```
orderid      orderdate    empid    custid        nextorderid
-----------  -----------  -------  -----------   -----------
10248        2020-07-04   5        85            10249
10249        2020-07-05   6        79            10250
10250        2020-07-08   4        34            10251
10251        2020-07-08   3        84            10252
10252        2020-07-09   4        76            10253
...
11073        2022-05-05   2        58            11074
11074        2022-05-06   7        73            11075
11075        2022-05-06   8        68            11076
11076        2022-05-06   4        9             11077
11077        2022-05-06   1        65            NULL

(830 rows affected)
```

Notice that because there's no order after the last order, the subquery returned a *NULL* for the last order.

Note that T-SQL supports window functions called *LAG* and *LEAD* that you use to obtain elements from a previous or next row much more easily. I cover these and other window functions in Chapter 7.

Using running aggregates

Running aggregates are aggregates that accumulate values based on some order. In this section, I use the *Sales.OrderTotalsByYear* view to demonstrate a technique that calculates those. I explain what views are in Chapter 5. For now, just think of a view as being the same as a table. The view has total order quantities by year. Query the view to examine its contents:

```
SELECT orderyear, qty
FROM Sales.OrderTotalsByYear;
```

You get the following output:

```
orderyear    qty
-----------  -----------
2022         16247
2020         9581
2021         25489
```

Suppose you need to compute for each year the running total quantity up to and including that year's. For the earliest year recorded in the view (2020), the running total is equal to that year's quantity. For the second year (2021), the running total is the sum of the first year plus the second year, and so on.

You query one instance of the view (call it *O1*) to return for each year the current year and quantity. You use a correlated subquery against a second instance of the view (call it *O2*) to calculate the running-total quantity. The subquery should filter all rows in *O2* where the order year is smaller than or equal to the current year in *O1*, and sum the quantities from *O2*. Here's the solution query:

```
SELECT orderyear, qty,
  (SELECT SUM(O2.qty)
   FROM Sales.OrderTotalsByYear AS O2
   WHERE O2.orderyear <= O1.orderyear) AS runqty
FROM Sales.OrderTotalsByYear AS O1
ORDER BY orderyear;
```

This query returns the following output:

```
orderyear   qty           runqty
----------  -----------   -----------
2020        9581          9581
2021        25489         35070
2022        16247         51317
```

Note that T-SQL supports window aggregate functions, which you can use to compute running totals much more easily and efficiently. As mentioned, I discuss those in Chapter 7.

Dealing with misbehaving subqueries

This section introduces cases in which the use of subqueries involves bugs, and it provides best practices that can help you avoid those bugs.

NULL trouble

Remember that T-SQL uses three-valued logic because of its support for *NULLs*. In this section, I discuss problems that can evolve when you forget about *NULLs* and the three-valued logic.

Consider the following query, which is supposed to return customers who did not place orders:

```
SELECT custid, companyname
FROM Sales.Customers
WHERE custid NOT IN(SELECT O.custid
                    FROM Sales.Orders AS O);
```

With the current sample data in the *Orders* table, the query seems to work the way you expect it to, and indeed, it returns the following two customers:

```
custid       companyname
-----------  -----------------
22           Customer DTDMN
57           Customer WVAXS
```

Next, run the following code to insert a new order into the *Orders* table with a *NULL* customer ID:

```
INSERT INTO Sales.Orders
  (custid, empid, orderdate, requireddate, shippeddate, shipperid,
   freight, shipname, shipaddress, shipcity, shipregion,
   shippostalcode, shipcountry)
  VALUES(NULL, 1, '20220212', '20220212',
         '20220212', 1, 123.00, N'abc', N'abc', N'abc',
         N'abc', N'abc', N'abc');
```

Next, run the previous query again:

```
SELECT custid, companyname
FROM Sales.Customers
WHERE custid NOT IN(SELECT O.custid
                    FROM Sales.Orders AS O);
```

This time, the query returns an empty set. Keeping in mind what you read in the section about *NULLs* in Chapter 2, "Single-table queries," try to explain why this query returns an empty set. Also try to think of ways to get customers 22 and 57 in the output.

Obviously, the culprit here is the *NULL* customer ID you added to the *Orders* table. The *NULL* is one of the elements returned by the subquery.

Let's start with the part that does behave like you expect it to. The *IN* predicate returns *TRUE* for a customer who placed orders (for example, customer 85), because such a customer is returned by the subquery. The *NOT* operator negates the *IN* predicate; hence, the *NOT TRUE* becomes *FALSE*, and the customer is discarded. The expected behavior here is that if a customer ID is known to appear in the *Orders* table, you know with certainty that you do not want to return it. However (take a deep breath), if a customer ID from *Customers* doesn't appear in the set of non-*NULL* customer IDs in *Orders*, and there's also a *NULL* customer ID in *Orders*, you can't tell with certainty that the customer is there—and similarly you can't tell with certainty that it's not there. Confused? I hope I can clarify this explanation with an example.

The *IN* predicate returns *UNKNOWN* for a customer such as 22 that does not appear in the set of known customer IDs in *Orders*. That's because when you compare it with known customer IDs you get *FALSE*, and when you compare it with a *NULL* you get *UNKNOWN*. *FALSE OR UNKNOWN* yields *UNKNOWN*. Consider the expression *22 NOT IN (1, 2, <other non-22 values>, NULL)*. This expression can be rephrased as *NOT 22 IN (1, 2, ..., NULL)*. You can expand this expression to *NOT (22 = 1 OR 22 = 2 OR ... OR 22 = NULL)*. Evaluate each individual expression in the parentheses to its truth value and you get *NOT (FALSE OR FALSE OR ... OR UNKNOWN)*, which translates to *NOT UNKNOWN*, which evaluates to *UNKNOWN*.

The logical meaning of *UNKNOWN* here, before you apply the *NOT* operator, is that it can't be determined whether the customer ID appears in the set, because the *NULL* could represent that customer ID. The tricky part here is that negating the *UNKNOWN* with the *NOT* operator still yields *UNKNOWN*. This means that in a case where it is unknown whether a customer ID appears in a set, it is also unknown whether it doesn't appear in the set. Remember that a query filter discards rows that get *UNKNOWN* in the result of the predicate.

In short, when you use the *NOT IN* predicate against a subquery that returns at least one *NULL*, the query always returns an empty set. So what practices can you follow to avoid such trouble? First, when a column is not supposed to allow *NULLs*, be sure to define it as *NOT NULL*. Second, in all queries you write, you should consider *NULLs* and the three-valued logic. Think explicitly about whether the query might process *NULLs*, and if so, whether SQL's treatment of *NULLs* is correct for you. When it isn't, you need to intervene. For example, our query returns an empty set because of the comparison with the *NULL*. If you want to check whether a customer ID appears only in the set of known values, you should exclude the *NULLs*—either explicitly or implicitly. To exclude them explicitly, add the predicate *O.custid IS NOT NULL* to the subquery, like this:

```
SELECT custid, companyname
FROM Sales.Customers
WHERE custid NOT IN(SELECT O.custid
                    FROM Sales.Orders AS O
                    WHERE O.custid IS NOT NULL);
```

You can also exclude the *NULLs* implicitly by using the *NOT EXISTS* predicate instead of *NOT IN*, like this:

```
SELECT custid, companyname
FROM Sales.Customers AS C
WHERE NOT EXISTS
  (SELECT *
   FROM Sales.Orders AS O
   WHERE O.custid = C.custid);
```

Recall that unlike *IN*, *EXISTS* uses two-valued predicate logic. *EXISTS* always returns *TRUE* or *FALSE* and never *UNKNOWN*. When the subquery stumbles into a *NULL* in *O.custid*, the expression evaluates to *UNKNOWN* and the row is filtered out. As far as the *EXISTS* predicate is concerned, the *NULL* cases are eliminated naturally, as though they weren't there. So *EXISTS* ends up handling only known customer IDs. Therefore, it's safer to use *NOT EXISTS* than *NOT IN*.

When you're done, run the following code for cleanup:

```
DELETE FROM Sales.Orders WHERE custid IS NULL;
```

Substitution errors in subquery column names

Logical bugs in your code can sometimes be elusive. In this section, I cover a bug related to an innocent substitution error in a subquery column name. After explaining the bug, I provide best practices that can help you avoid it.

The examples in this section query a table called *MyShippers* in the *Sales* schema. Run the following code to create and populate this table:

```
DROP TABLE IF EXISTS Sales.MyShippers;

CREATE TABLE Sales.MyShippers
(
  shipper_id  INT          NOT NULL,
  companyname NVARCHAR(40) NOT NULL,
  phone       NVARCHAR(24) NOT NULL,
  CONSTRAINT PK_MyShippers PRIMARY KEY(shipper_id)
);

INSERT INTO Sales.MyShippers(shipper_id, companyname, phone)
  VALUES(1, N'Shipper GVSUA', N'(503) 555-0137'),
        (2, N'Shipper ETYNR', N'(425) 555-0136'),
        (3, N'Shipper ZHISN', N'(415) 555-0138');
```

Consider the following query, which is supposed to return shippers who shipped orders to customer 43:

```
SELECT shipper_id, companyname
FROM Sales.MyShippers
WHERE shipper_id IN
  (SELECT shipper_id
   FROM Sales.Orders
   WHERE custid = 43);
```

This query produces the following output:

```
shipper_id  companyname
----------- ---------------
1           Shipper GVSUA
2           Shipper ETYNR
3           Shipper ZHISN
```

Only shippers 2 and 3 shipped orders to customer 43, but for some reason this query returned all shippers from the *MyShippers* table. Examine the query carefully and also the schemas of the tables involved, and see if you can explain what's going on.

It turns out that the column name in the *Orders* table holding the shipper ID is called not *shipper_id*, but rather *shipperid* (no underscore). The column in the *MyShippers* table is called *shipper_id*, with an underscore. The resolution, or binding, of nonprefixed column names works in the context of a subquery from the inner scope outward. In our example, SQL Server first looks for the column *shipper_id* in the table in the inner query, *Orders*. Such a column is not found there, so SQL Server looks for it in the table in the outer query, *MyShippers*. Such a column is found in *MyShippers*, so that is the one used.

You can see that what was supposed to be a self-contained subquery unintentionally became a correlated subquery. As long as the *Orders* table has at least one row, all rows from the *MyShippers* table find a match when comparing the outer shipper ID with the very same shipper ID.

Some argue that this behavior is a bug in SQL Server. It is indeed a bug, but not in SQL Server. It's a bug in the developer's code. This behavior is by design in the SQL standard, and Microsoft just followed the standard here. The thinking in the standard is to allow you to refer to column names from the outer table without a prefix as long as they are unambiguous (that is, as long as they appear only in one of the tables).

This problem is more common in environments that do not use consistent attribute names across tables. Sometimes the names are only slightly different, as in this case—*shipperid* in one table and *shipper_id* in another. That's enough for the bug to manifest itself.

You can follow a couple of best practices to avoid such problems:

- Use consistent attribute names across tables.

- Prefix column names in subqueries with the source table name or alias (if you assigned one).

This way, the resolution process looks for the column only in the specified table. If it doesn't exist there, you get a resolution error. For example, try running the following code:

```
SELECT shipper_id, companyname
FROM Sales.MyShippers
WHERE shipper_id IN
  (SELECT O.shipper_id
   FROM Sales.Orders AS O
   WHERE O.custid = 43);
```

You get the following resolution error:

```
Msg 207, Level 16, State 1, Line 274
Invalid column name 'shipper_id'.
```

After getting this error, you identify the problem and correct the query:

```
SELECT shipper_id, companyname
FROM Sales.MyShippers
WHERE shipper_id IN
  (SELECT O.shipperid
   FROM Sales.Orders AS O
   WHERE O.custid = 43);
```

This time, the query returns the expected result:

```
shipper_id  companyname
----------- ---------------
2           Shipper ETYNR
3           Shipper ZHISN
```

When you're done, run the following code for cleanup:

```
DROP TABLE IF EXISTS Sales.MyShippers;
```

Conclusion

This chapter covered subqueries. It discussed self-contained subqueries, which are independent of their outer queries, and correlated subqueries, which are dependent on their outer queries. Regarding the results of subqueries, I discussed scalar and multivalued subqueries. The chapter also covered returning previous and next values, using running aggregates, and dealing with misbehaving subqueries. Remember to always think about the three-valued logic and the importance of prefixing column names in subqueries with the source table alias.

Exercises

This section provides exercises to help you familiarize yourself with the subjects discussed in this chapter. The sample database *TSQLV6* is used in all exercises in this chapter.

Note that any given task in SQL can be solved in many different ways. For example, many of the tasks that you will see in this chapter can be solved either with joins or with subqueries. The idea is for you to primarily practice the tools and techniques that you learned about in the current chapter. So naturally, in a chapter focusing on subqueries the expectation from you is to solve the tasks using subqueries.

Exercise 1

Write a query that returns all orders placed on the last day of activity that can be found in the *Orders* table:

- Table involved: *Sales.Orders*

- Desired output:

```
orderid     orderdate    custid      empid
----------- -----------  ----------- -----------
11077       2022-05-06   65          1
11076       2022-05-06   9           4
11075       2022-05-06   68          8
11074       2022-05-06   73          7
```

Exercise 2

Write a query that returns all orders placed by the customer(s) who placed the highest number of orders. Note that more than one customer might have the same number of orders:

- Table involved: *Sales.Orders*

- Desired output:

```
custid      orderid     orderdate    empid
----------- ----------- -----------  -----------
71          10324       2020-10-08   9
71          10393       2020-12-25   1
71          10398       2020-12-30   2
```

71	10440	2021-02-10	4
71	10452	2021-02-20	8
71	10510	2021-04-18	6
71	10555	2021-06-02	6
71	10603	2021-07-18	8
71	10607	2021-07-22	5
71	10612	2021-07-28	1
71	10627	2021-08-11	8
71	10657	2021-09-04	2
71	10678	2021-09-23	7
71	10700	2021-10-10	3
71	10711	2021-10-21	5
71	10713	2021-10-22	1
71	10714	2021-10-22	5
71	10722	2021-10-29	8
71	10748	2021-11-20	3
71	10757	2021-11-27	6
71	10815	2022-01-05	2
71	10847	2022-01-22	4
71	10882	2022-02-11	4
71	10894	2022-02-18	1
71	10941	2022-03-11	7
71	10983	2022-03-27	2
71	10984	2022-03-30	1
71	11002	2022-04-06	4
71	11030	2022-04-17	7
71	11031	2022-04-17	6
71	11064	2022-05-01	1

```
(31 rows affected)
```

Exercise 3

Write a query that returns employees who did not place orders on or after May 1, 2022:

- Tables involved: *HR.Employees* and *Sales.Orders*

- Desired output:

```
empid       firstname   lastname
----------- ----------- --------------------
3           Judy        Lew
5           Sven        Mortensen
6           Paul        Suurs
9           Patricia    Doyle
```

Exercise 4

Write a query that returns countries where there are customers but not employees:

- Tables involved: *Sales.Customers* and *HR.Employees*

- Desired output:

```
country
---------------
Argentina
Austria
Belgium
```

```
Brazil
Canada
Denmark
Finland
France
Germany
Ireland
Italy
Mexico
Norway
Poland
Portugal
Spain
Sweden
Switzerland
Venezuela

(19 rows affected)
```

Exercise 5

Write a query that returns for each customer all orders placed on the customer's last day of activity:

- Table involved: *Sales.Orders*

- Desired output:

```
custid       orderid       orderdate      empid
-----------  -----------   -----------    -----------
1            11011         2022-04-09     3
2            10926         2022-03-04     4
3            10856         2022-01-28     3
4            11016         2022-04-10     9
5            10924         2022-03-04     3
...
87           11025         2022-04-15     6
88           10935         2022-03-09     4
89           11066         2022-05-01     7
90           11005         2022-04-07     2
91           11044         2022-04-23     4

(90 rows affected)
```

Exercise 6

Write a query that returns customers who placed orders in 2021 but not in 2022:

- Tables involved: *Sales.Customers* and *Sales.Orders*

- Desired output:

```
custid       companyname
-----------  ----------------
21           Customer KIDPX
23           Customer WVFAF
33           Customer FVXPQ
36           Customer LVJSO
43           Customer UISOJ
```

```
51       Customer PVDZC
85       Customer ENQZT

(7 rows affected)
```

Exercise 7

Write a query that returns customers who ordered product 12:

- Tables involved: *Sales.Customers*, *Sales.Orders*, and *Sales.OrderDetails*

- Desired output:

```
custid      companyname
----------- -----------------
48          Customer DVFMB
39          Customer GLLAG
71          Customer LCOUJ
65          Customer NYUHS
44          Customer OXFRU
51          Customer PVDZC
86          Customer SNXOJ
20          Customer IHHDP
90          Customer XBBVR
46          Customer XPNIK
31          Customer YJCBX
87          Customer ZHYOS

(12 rows affected)
```

Exercise 8

Write a query that calculates a running-total quantity for each customer and month:

- Table involved: *Sales.CustOrders*

- Desired output:

```
custid      ordermonth  qty         runqty
----------- ----------- ----------- -----------
1           2021-08-01  38          38
1           2021-10-01  41          79
1           2022-01 01  17          96
1           2022-03-01  18          114
1           2022-04-01  60          174
2           2020-09-01  6           6
2           2021-08-01  18          24
2           2021-11-01  10          34
2           2022-03-01  29          63
3           2020-11-01  24          24
3           2021-04-01  30          54
3           2021-05-01  80          134
3           2021-06-01  83          217
3           2021-09-01  102         319
3           2022-01-01  40          359
...

(636 rows affected)
```

Exercise 9

Explain the difference between *IN* and *EXISTS*.

Exercise 10

Write a query that returns for each order the number of days that passed since the same customer's previous order. To determine recency among orders, use *orderdate* as the primary sort element and *orderid* as the tiebreaker:

- Table involved: *Sales.Orders*

- Desired output:

```
custid      orderdate   orderid      diff
----------- ----------  -----------  -----------
1           2021-08-25  10643        NULL
1           2021-10-03  10692        39
1           2021-10-13  10702        10
1           2022-01-15  10835        94
1           2022-03-16  10952        60
1           2022-04-09  11011        24
2           2020-09-18  10308        NULL
2           2021-08-08  10625        324
2           2021-11-28  10759        112
2           2022-03-04  10926        96
...

(830 rows affected)
```

Solutions

This section provides solutions to the exercises in the preceding section.

Exercise 1

You can write a self-contained subquery that returns the maximum order date from the *Orders* table. You can refer to the subquery in the *WHERE* clause of the outer query to return all orders that were placed on the last day of activity. Here's the solution query:

```
USE TSQLV6;

SELECT orderid, orderdate, custid, empid
FROM Sales.Orders
WHERE orderdate =
  (SELECT MAX(O.orderdate) FROM Sales.Orders AS O);
```

Exercise 2

This task is best solved in multiple steps. First, you can write a query that returns the customer or customers who placed the highest number of orders. You can achieve this by grouping the orders by customer, ordering the customers by *COUNT(*)* descending, and using the *TOP (1) WITH TIES* option to return the IDs of the customers who placed the highest number of orders. If you don't remember how to use the *TOP* option, refer to Chapter 2. Here's the query that solves the first step:

```
SELECT TOP (1) WITH TIES O.custid
FROM Sales.Orders AS O
GROUP BY O.custid
ORDER BY COUNT(*) DESC;
```

This query returns customer ID 71, which is the ID of the customer who placed the highest number of orders, 31. With the sample data stored in the *Orders* table, only one customer placed the maximum number of orders. But the query uses the *WITH TIES* option to return all IDs of customers who placed the maximum number of orders, in case there is more than one.

The next step is to write a query against the *Orders* table, returning all orders where the customer ID appears in the result of the subquery:

```
SELECT custid, orderid, orderdate, empid
FROM Sales.Orders
WHERE custid IN
  (SELECT TOP (1) WITH TIES O.custid
   FROM Sales.Orders AS O
   GROUP BY O.custid
   ORDER BY COUNT(*) DESC);
```

Exercise 3

You can write a self-contained subquery against the *Orders* table that filters orders placed on or after May 1, 2022, and returns only the employee IDs from those orders. Write an outer query against the *Employees* table returning employees whose IDs do not appear in the result of the subquery. Here's the complete solution query:

```
SELECT empid, firstname, lastname
FROM HR.Employees
WHERE empid NOT IN
  (SELECT O.empid
   FROM Sales.Orders AS O
   WHERE O.orderdate >= '20220501');
```

Exercise 4

You can write a self-contained subquery against the *Employees* table, returning the country column. Write an outer query against the *Customers* table that filters only customers with a country that does not appear in the result of the subquery. In the *SELECT* list of the outer query, specify *DISTINCT country* to remove duplicates. Here's the complete solution query:

```
SELECT DISTINCT country
FROM Sales.Customers
WHERE country NOT IN
  (SELECT E.country FROM HR.Employees AS E);
```

Exercise 5

This exercise is similar to Exercise 1, except that in that exercise, you were asked to return orders placed on the last day of activity in general; in this exercise, you were asked to return orders placed on the last day of activity for the customer. The solutions for both exercises are similar, but here you need to correlate the subquery to match the inner customer ID with the outer customer ID, like this:

```
SELECT custid, orderid, orderdate, empid
FROM Sales.Orders AS O1
WHERE orderdate =
  (SELECT MAX(O2.orderdate)
   FROM Sales.Orders AS O2
   WHERE O2.custid = O1.custid)
ORDER BY custid;
```

You're not comparing the outer row's order date with the general maximum order date; instead, you're comparing it with the maximum order date for the current customer.

Exercise 6

You can solve this task by querying the *Customers* table and using *EXISTS* and *NOT EXISTS* predicates with correlated subqueries. The *EXISTS* predicate returns *TRUE* if orders were placed by the current customer in 2021. The *NOT EXISTS* predicate returns *TRUE* only if no orders were placed by the current customer in 2022. Here's the complete solution query:

```
SELECT custid, companyname
FROM Sales.Customers AS C
WHERE EXISTS
  (SELECT *
   FROM Sales.Orders AS O
   WHERE O.custid = C.custid
     AND O.orderdate >= '20210101'
     AND O.orderdate < '20220101')
  AND NOT EXISTS
  (SELECT *
   FROM Sales.Orders AS O
   WHERE O.custid = C.custid
     AND O.orderdate >= '20220101'
     AND O.orderdate < '20230101');
```

Exercise 7

You can solve this exercise by nesting *EXISTS* predicates with correlated subqueries. You write the outermost query against the *Customers* table. In the *WHERE* clause of the outer query, you can use the *EXISTS* predicate with a correlated subquery against the *Orders* table to filter only the current customer's orders. In the filter of the subquery against the *Orders* table, you can use a nested *EXISTS* predicate with a subquery against the *OrderDetails* table that filters only order details with product ID 12. This way, only customers who placed orders that contain product 12 in their order details are returned. Here's the complete solution query:

```
SELECT custid, companyname
FROM Sales.Customers AS C
WHERE EXISTS
  (SELECT *
   FROM Sales.Orders AS O
   WHERE O.custid = C.custid
     AND EXISTS
       (SELECT *
        FROM Sales.OrderDetails AS OD
        WHERE OD.orderid = O.orderid
          AND OD.ProductID = 12));
```

Exercise 8

You can handle this task with a correlated subquery. Use the outer query against *CustOrders* (aliased as *O1*) to return the current customer, month, and quantity information. Use the correlated subquery against a second instance of *CustOrders* (aliased as *O2*). Aggregate all quantities from *O2* for the current customer in *O1* where the month from *O2* is on or before the current month in *O1*. Here's the complete solution query:

```
SELECT custid, ordermonth, qty,
  (SELECT SUM(O2.qty)
   FROM Sales.CustOrders AS O2
   WHERE O2.custid = O1.custid
     AND O2.ordermonth <= O1.ordermonth) AS runqty
FROM Sales.CustOrders AS O1
ORDER BY custid, ordermonth;
```

Exercise 9

Whereas the *IN* predicate uses three-valued logic, the *EXISTS* predicate uses two-valued logic. When no *NULLs* are involved in the data, *IN* and *EXISTS* give you the same meaning in both their positive and negative forms (with *NOT*). When *NULLs* are involved, *IN* and *EXISTS* give you the same meaning in their positive form but not in their negative form. In the positive form, when looking for a value that appears in the set of known values in the subquery, both return *TRUE*, and when looking for a value that doesn't appear in the set of known values, both return *FALSE*. In the negative forms (with *NOT*), when looking for a value that appears in the set of known values, both return *FALSE*; however, when looking for a value that doesn't appear in the set of known values, *NOT IN* returns *UNKNOWN* (outer row is discarded), whereas *NOT EXISTS* returns *TRUE* (outer row returned).

This is best understood through an example. See the section "*NULL* trouble" earlier in this chapter for a good example.

Exercise 10

You can handle the task in two steps:

1. Write a query that computes the date of the customer's previous order.

2. Compute the difference between the date returned by the first step and the current order date.

Here's the solution query that handles the first step:

```
SELECT custid, orderdate, orderid,
  (SELECT TOP (1) O2.orderdate
   FROM Sales.Orders AS O2
   WHERE O2.custid = O1.custid
     AND (    O2.orderdate = O1.orderdate AND O2.orderid < O1.orderid
           OR O2.orderdate < O1.orderdate )
   ORDER BY O2.orderdate DESC, O2.orderid DESC) AS prevdate
FROM Sales.Orders AS O1
ORDER BY custid, orderdate, orderid;
```

To get a previous order date, the solution uses a correlated subquery with the TOP filter. The subquery filters only orders where the inner customer ID is equal to the outer customer ID. It also filters only orders where either "the inner order date is equal to the outer order date and the inner order ID is smaller than the outer order ID" or "the inner order date is earlier than the outer order date." The remaining orders are the ones considered earlier than the current customer's order. Using the *TOP (1)* filter based on the ordering of *orderdate DESC, orderid DESC*, you get the date of the customer's previous order. This step returns the following output:

```
custid      orderdate  orderid      prevdate
----------- ---------- -----------  ----------
1           2021-08-25 10643         NULL
1           2021-10-03 10692         2021-08-25
1           2021-10-13 10702         2021-10-03
1           2022-01-15 10835         2021-10-13
1           2022-03-16 10952         2022-01-15
1           2022-04-09 11011         2022-03-16
2           2020-09-18 10308         NULL
2           2021-08-08 10625         2020-09-18
2           2021-11-28 10759         2021-08-08
2           2022-03-04 10926         2021-11-28
...

(830 rows affected)
```

If you're wondering why you don't rely on only *orderid* ordering, the reason is that companies typically support a concept of *late arrivals*. That's when an order was placed in the past but registered in the system at a later point. When the order is added to the system, it gets the highest order ID at that point but it doesn't have the most recent order date. So recency is determined first based on orderdate ordering, and then order ID is used as the tiebreaker. That's why the subquery's *WHERE* clause is so complex, and why the TOP filter's ordering is based on *orderdate DESC, orderid DESC* and not just *orderid DESC*.

As the second step, use the *DATEDIFF* function to compute the difference in terms of days between the previous order date returned by the subquery and the current order date. Here's the complete solution query:

```
SELECT custid, orderdate, orderid,
  DATEDIFF(day,
    (SELECT TOP (1) O2.orderdate
     FROM Sales.Orders AS O2
     WHERE O2.custid = O1.custid
       AND (    O2.orderdate = O1.orderdate AND O2.orderid < O1.orderid
            OR O2.orderdate < O1.orderdate )
     ORDER BY O2.orderdate DESC, O2.orderid DESC),
    orderdate) AS diff
FROM Sales.Orders AS O1
ORDER BY custid, orderdate, orderid;
```

CHAPTER 5

Table expressions

This chapter focuses on named table expressions. A table expression is an expression—typically a query—that conceptually returns a table result and as such can be nested as an operand of another table expression. Recall that a table in SQL is the counterpart to a relation in relational theory. A table expression is therefore SQL's counterpart to a relational expression. A relational expression in relational theory is an expression that returns a relation and as such can be nested as an operand of another relational expression. A named table expression is then a table expression that you assign with a name, and interact with like you do with a base table. For example, you can use named table expressions in data-manipulation statements much like you use base tables. T-SQL supports four types of named table expressions: derived tables, common table expressions (CTEs), views, and inline table-valued functions (inline TVFs). The focus of this chapter is on using *SELECT* queries against named table expressions; Chapter 8, "Data modification," covers modifications involving table expressions.

Table expressions are not physically materialized anywhere—they are virtual. When you query a table expression, the inner query gets unnested. In other words, the outer query and the inner query are merged into one query directly against the underlying objects. The benefits of using table expressions are typically related to logical aspects of your code and not to performance. For example, you can use table expressions to simplify your solutions by using a modular approach. Table expressions also help you circumvent certain restrictions in the language, such as the inability to refer to column aliases assigned in the *SELECT* clause in query clauses that are logically processed before the *SELECT* clause.

This chapter also introduces the *APPLY* table operator as it is used in conjunction with a table expression. I explain how to use this operator to apply a table expression to each row of another table.

Derived tables

Derived tables are defined in the *FROM* clause of an outer query. Their scope of existence is the outer query. As soon as the outer query is finished, the derived table is gone.

You specify the query that defines the derived table within parentheses, followed by the *AS* clause and the derived table name. For example, the following code defines a derived table called *USACusts* based on a query that returns all customers from the United States, and the outer query selects all rows from the derived table:

```
USE TSQLV6;

SELECT *
FROM (SELECT custid, companyname
      FROM Sales.Customers
      WHERE country = N'USA') AS USACusts;
```

In this particular case, which is a simple example of the basic syntax, a derived table is not needed, because the outer query doesn't apply any manipulation.

The code in this basic example returns the following output:

```
custid      companyname
----------- ----------------
32          Customer YSIQX
36          Customer LVJSO
43          Customer UISOJ
45          Customer QXPPT
48          Customer DVFMB
55          Customer KZQZT
65          Customer NYUHS
71          Customer LCOUJ
75          Customer XOJYP
77          Customer LCYBZ
78          Customer NLTYP
82          Customer EYHKM
89          Customer YBQTI
```

With all types of table expressions, a query must meet three requirements to be a valid inner query in a table-expression definition:

- **Order is not guaranteed.** A table expression is supposed to represent a table, and the rows in a table have no guaranteed order. Recall that this aspect of a relation stems from set theory. For this reason, standard SQL disallows an ORDER BY clause in queries that are used to define table expressions, unless the ORDER BY serves a purpose other than presentation. An example for such an exception is when the query uses the OFFSET-FETCH filter. T-SQL enforces similar restrictions, with similar exceptions—when TOP or OFFSET-FETCH is also specified. In the context of a query with the TOP or OFFSET-FETCH filter, the ORDER BY clause serves as part of the specification of the filter. If you use a query with TOP or OFFSET-FETCH and ORDER BY to define a table expression, ORDER BY is guaranteed to serve only the filtering-related purpose and not the usual presentation purpose. If the outer query against the table expression does not have a presentation ORDER BY, the output is not guaranteed to be returned in any particular order. See the "Views and the ORDER BY clause" section later in this chapter for more detail on this item (which applies to all types of named table expressions).

- **All columns must have names.** All columns in a table must have names; therefore, you must assign column aliases to all expressions in the *SELECT* list of the query that is used to define a table expression. Sometimes T-SQL will allow an anonymous result column in a query, but not when it's used as the inner query of a named table expression.

- **All column names must be unique.** All column names in a table must be unique; therefore, a table expression that has multiple columns with the same name is invalid. Having multiple columns with the same name might happen when the query defining the table expression joins two tables that have a column with the same name. If you need to incorporate both columns in your table expression, they must have different column names. You can resolve this issue by assigning different column aliases to the two columns.

All three requirements are related to the fact that the table expression is supposed to represent a table—SQL's counterpart to a relation. All relation attributes must have names; all attribute names must be unique; and, because the relation's body is a set of tuples, there's no order.

Assigning column aliases

One of the benefits of using table expressions is that, in any clause of the outer query, you can refer to column aliases that were assigned in the *SELECT* clause of the inner query. This behavior helps you get around the fact that you can't refer to column aliases assigned in the *SELECT* clause in query clauses that are logically processed prior to the *SELECT* clause (for example, *WHERE* or *GROUP BY*).

For example, suppose you need to write a query against the *Sales.Orders* table and return the number of distinct customers handled in each order year. The following attempt is invalid because the *GROUP BY* clause refers to a column alias that was assigned in the *SELECT* clause, and the *GROUP BY* clause is logically processed prior to the *SELECT* clause:

```
SELECT
  YEAR(orderdate) AS orderyear,
  COUNT(DISTINCT custid) AS numcusts
FROM Sales.Orders
GROUP BY orderyear;
```

If you try running this query, you get the following error:

```
Msg 207, Level 16, State 1, Line 28
Invalid column name 'orderyear'.
```

You can solve the problem by referring to the expression *YEAR(orderdate)* in both the *GROUP BY* and *SELECT* clauses, but this is an example with a short expression. What if the expression is much longer and you want to avoid the repetition of the code? You can achieve this with a table expression like the one shown in Listing 5-1.

LISTING 5-1 Query with a derived table using inline aliasing form

```
SELECT orderyear, COUNT(DISTINCT custid) AS numcusts
FROM (SELECT YEAR(orderdate) AS orderyear, custid
      FROM Sales.Orders) AS D
GROUP BY orderyear;
```

This query returns the following output:

```
orderyear   numcusts
----------- -----------
2020        67
2021        86
2022        81
```

This code defines a derived table called *D* based on a query against the *Orders* table that returns the order year and customer ID from all rows. The *SELECT* list of the inner query uses the inline aliasing form to assign the alias *orderyear* to the expression *YEAR(orderdate)*. The outer query can refer to the *orderyear* column alias in both the *GROUP BY* and *SELECT* clauses, because as far as the outer query is concerned, it queries a table called *D* with columns called *orderyear* and *custid*.

As I mentioned earlier, Microsoft SQL Server expands the definition of the table expression and accesses the underlying objects directly. After expansion, the query in Listing 5-1 looks like the following:

```
SELECT YEAR(orderdate) AS orderyear, COUNT(DISTINCT custid) AS numcusts
FROM Sales.Orders
GROUP BY YEAR(orderdate);
```

I present this example just to emphasize that you usually use table expressions for logical (not performance-related) reasons. Generally speaking, table expressions have neither a positive nor a negative impact on performance when compared to the expanded query without the table expression.

Listing 5-1 uses the inline aliasing form to assign column aliases to expressions. The syntax for inline aliasing is *<expression> [AS] <alias>*. Note that the word *AS* is optional in the syntax for inline aliasing; however, I find that it helps the readability of the code and recommend using it.

In some cases, you might prefer to use a second aliasing form, which you can think of as external aliasing. With this form, you do not assign column aliases following the expressions in the *SELECT* list—you specify all target column names (not only the aliased ones) in parentheses following the table expression's name, like so:

```
SELECT orderyear, COUNT(DISTINCT custid) AS numcusts
FROM (SELECT YEAR(orderdate), custid
      FROM Sales.Orders) AS D(orderyear, custid)
GROUP BY orderyear;
```

Each form has its advantages. I'll start with the advantages of inline aliasing. If you need to debug the code when using the inline form, when you highlight the query defining the table expression and run it, the columns in the result appear with the aliases you assigned. With the external form, you cannot include the target column names when you highlight the table expression query, so the result appears with no column names in the case of the unnamed expressions. Also, when the table expression query is lengthy, using the external form can make it quite difficult to figure out which column alias belongs to which expression.

Then again, the external aliasing form has its advantages—for example, when the query defining the table expression won't undergo any further revisions and you want to treat it like a "black box." You want to focus your attention on the table-expression name followed by the target-column list when you look at the outer query. To use terminology from traditional programming, you can use external aliasing to specify a contract interface between the outer query and the table expression.

Using arguments

In the query that defines a derived table, you can refer to arguments. The arguments can be local variables and input parameters to a routine, such as a stored procedure or function. For example, the following code declares and initializes a variable called @empid, and the query in the derived table D refers to that variable in the WHERE clause:

```
DECLARE @empid AS INT = 3;

SELECT orderyear, COUNT(DISTINCT custid) AS numcusts
FROM (SELECT YEAR(orderdate) AS orderyear, custid
      FROM Sales.Orders
      WHERE empid = @empid) AS D
GROUP BY orderyear;
```

This query returns the number of distinct customers per year whose orders were handled by the input employee (the employee whose ID is stored in the variable @empid, in this case employee ID 3). Here's the output of this query:

```
orderyear   numcusts
----------- -----------
2020        16
2021        46
2022        30
```

Nesting

If you need to define a derived table based on a query that itself is based on a derived table, you can nest those. Nesting tends to complicate the code and reduces its readability.

As an example, Listing 5-2 returns order years and the number of customers handled in each year only for years in which more than 70 customers were handled.

LISTING 5-2 Query with nested derived tables

```
SELECT orderyear, numcusts
FROM (SELECT orderyear, COUNT(DISTINCT custid) AS numcusts
      FROM (SELECT YEAR(orderdate) AS orderyear, custid
            FROM Sales.Orders) AS D1
      GROUP BY orderyear) AS D2
WHERE numcusts > 70;
```

This code returns the following output:

```
orderyear   numcusts
----------- -----------
2021        86
2022        81
```

The purpose of the innermost derived table, *D1*, is to assign the column alias *orderyear* to the expression *YEAR(orderdate)*. The query against *D1* refers to *orderyear* in both the *GROUP BY* and *SELECT* clauses and assigns the column alias *numcusts* to the expression *COUNT(DISTINCT custid)*. The query against *D1* is used to define the derived table *D2*. The query against *D2* refers to *numcusts* in the *WHERE* clause to filter order years in which more than 70 customers were handled.

The whole purpose of using table expressions here is to simplify the code by reusing column aliases. However, with the complexity added by the nesting, I'm not sure this solution is really simpler than the alternative without table expressions:

```
SELECT YEAR(orderdate) AS orderyear, COUNT(DISTINCT custid) AS numcusts
FROM Sales.Orders
GROUP BY YEAR(orderdate)
HAVING COUNT(DISTINCT custid) > 70;
```

Multiple references

Another problematic aspect of derived tables is related to cases where you need to join multiple instances of the same one. A join treats its two inputs as a set, and as you know, a set has no order to its elements. This means that if you define a derived table and alias it as one input of the join, you can't refer to the same alias in the other input of the join. The query in Listing 5-3 illustrates this point.

LISTING 5-3 Multiple derived tables based on the same query

```
SELECT Cur.orderyear,
   Cur.numcusts AS curnumcusts, Prv.numcusts AS prvnumcusts,
   Cur.numcusts - Prv.numcusts AS growth
FROM (SELECT YEAR(orderdate) AS orderyear,
         COUNT(DISTINCT custid) AS numcusts
      FROM Sales.Orders
      GROUP BY YEAR(orderdate)) AS Cur
   LEFT OUTER JOIN
      (SELECT YEAR(orderdate) AS orderyear,
         COUNT(DISTINCT custid) AS numcusts
      FROM Sales.Orders
      GROUP BY YEAR(orderdate)) AS Prv
   ON Cur.orderyear = Prv.orderyear + 1;
```

This query joins two derived tables that are based on the same query. The first derived table, *Cur*, represents current years, and the second derived table, *Prv*, represents previous years. The join condition *Cur.orderyear = Prv.orderyear + 1* ensures that each year from the first derived table matches the previous year of the second. Because the code uses a left outer join, all left years are preserved, including the first, which has no previous year. The *SELECT* clause of the outer query calculates the difference between the number of customers handled in the current and previous years.

Listing 5-3 produces the following output:

```
orderyear   curnumcusts prvnumcusts growth
----------- ----------- ----------- -----------
2020        67          NULL        NULL
2021        86          67          19
2022        81          86          5
```

The fact that you cannot refer to multiple instances of the same derived table in the same join forces you to maintain multiple copies of the same query definition. This leads to lengthy code that is hard to maintain and prone to errors.

Common table expressions

Common table expressions (CTEs) are another standard form of table expression similar to derived tables, yet with a couple of important advantages.

CTEs are defined by using a *WITH* statement and have the following general form:

```
WITH <CTE_Name>[(<target_column_list>)]
AS
(
  <inner_query_defining_CTE>
)
<outer_query_against_CTE>;
```

The inner query defining the CTE must follow all requirements mentioned earlier to be valid to define a table expression. As a simple example, the following code defines a CTE called *USACusts* based on a query that returns all customers from the United States, and the outer query selects all rows from the CTE:

```
WITH USACusts AS
(
  SELECT custid, companyname
  FROM Sales.Customers
  WHERE country = N'USA'
)
SELECT * FROM USACusts;
```

As with derived tables, as soon as the outer query finishes, the CTE goes out of scope.

> **Note** The *WITH* clause is used in T-SQL for several purposes. For example, it's used to define a table hint in a query to force a certain optimization option or isolation level. To avoid ambiguity, when the *WITH* clause is used to define a CTE, the preceding statement in the same batch—if one exists—must be terminated with a semicolon. And oddly enough, the semicolon for the entire CTE is not required, though I still recommend specifying it—as I do to terminate all T-SQL statements.

Assigning column aliases in CTEs

CTEs also support two forms of column aliasing: inline and external. For the inline form, specify *<expression> AS <column_alias>*; for the external form, specify the target column list in parentheses immediately after the CTE name.

Here's an example of the inline form:

```
WITH C AS
(
  SELECT YEAR(orderdate) AS orderyear, custid
  FROM Sales.Orders
)
SELECT orderyear, COUNT(DISTINCT custid) AS numcusts
FROM C
GROUP BY orderyear;
```

And here's an example of the external form:

```
WITH C(orderyear, custid) AS
(
  SELECT YEAR(orderdate), custid
  FROM Sales.Orders
)
SELECT orderyear, COUNT(DISTINCT custid) AS numcusts
FROM C
GROUP BY orderyear;
```

The motivations for using one form or the other are similar to those described for derived tables.

Using arguments in CTEs

As with derived tables, you also can use arguments in the inner query used to define a CTE. Here's an example:

```
DECLARE @empid AS INT = 3;

WITH C AS
(
  SELECT YEAR(orderdate) AS orderyear, custid
  FROM Sales.Orders
  WHERE empid = @empid
)
SELECT orderyear, COUNT(DISTINCT custid) AS numcusts
FROM C
GROUP BY orderyear;
```

Defining multiple CTEs

On the surface, the difference between derived tables and CTEs might seem to be merely semantic. However, the fact that you first name and define a CTE and then use it gives it several important advantages over derived tables. One advantage is that if you need to refer to one CTE from another, you don't nest them; rather, you separate them by commas. Each CTE can refer to all previously defined CTEs, and the outer query can refer to all CTEs. For example, the following code is the CTE alternative to the nested derived tables approach in Listing 5-2:

```
WITH C1 AS
(
  SELECT YEAR(orderdate) AS orderyear, custid
  FROM Sales.Orders
),
C2 AS
(
  SELECT orderyear, COUNT(DISTINCT custid) AS numcusts
  FROM C1
  GROUP BY orderyear
)
SELECT orderyear, numcusts
FROM C2
WHERE numcusts > 70;
```

This modular approach substantially improves the readability and maintainability of the code compared to the nested derived-table approach.

Note that even if you want to, you cannot nest CTEs in T-SQL, nor can you define a CTE within the parentheses of a derived table. I think of this restriction as a good thing.

Multiple references in CTEs

The fact that a CTE is named and defined first and then queried has another advantage: as far as the *FROM* clause of the outer query is concerned, the CTE already exists; therefore, you can refer to multiple instances of the same CTE in table operators like joins. That's probably the source for the term *common* in common table expression. The table expression's name is common to the outer query. For example, the following code is the CTE alternative to the solution shown earlier in Listing 5-3 with derived tables:

```
WITH YearlyCount AS
(
  SELECT YEAR(orderdate) AS orderyear,
    COUNT(DISTINCT custid) AS numcusts
  FROM Sales.Orders
  GROUP BY YEAR(orderdate)
)
SELECT Cur.orderyear,
  Cur.numcusts AS curnumcusts, Prv.numcusts AS prvnumcusts,
  Cur.numcusts - Prv.numcusts AS growth
FROM YearlyCount AS Cur
  LEFT OUTER JOIN YearlyCount AS Prv
    ON Cur.orderyear = Prv.orderyear + 1;
```

As you can see, the CTE *YearlyCount* is defined only once and accessed twice in the *FROM* clause of the outer query—once as *Cur* and once as *Prv*. You need to maintain only one copy of the inner query (the code inside the CTE). The solution is clearer and less prone to errors.

If you're curious about performance, recall that earlier I mentioned that table expressions typically have no impact on performance because they're not physically materialized anywhere. Both references to the CTE in the previous query are going to be expanded. Internally, this query has a self join between two instances of the *Orders* table, each of which involves scanning the table data and aggregating it before the join—the same physical processing that takes place with the derived-table approach. If you want to avoid the repetition of the work done here, you should persist the inner query's result in a temporary table or a table variable. I discuss temporary objects in Chapter 12. My focus in this discussion is on coding aspects and not performance, and clearly the ability to specify the inner query only once is a great benefit.

Recursive CTEs

CTEs are unique among table expressions in the sense that they support recursion. Recursive CTEs, like nonrecursive ones, are defined by the SQL standard. A recursive CTE is defined by at least two queries (more are possible)—at least one query known as the anchor member and at least one query known as the recursive member. The general form of a basic recursive CTE looks like the following:

```
WITH <CTE_Name>[(<target_column_list>)]
AS
(
  <anchor_member>
  UNION ALL
  <recursive_member>
)
<outer_query_against_CTE>;
```

The anchor member is a query that returns a valid relational result table—like a query that is used to define a nonrecursive table expression. The anchor member query is invoked only once.

The recursive member is a query that has a reference to the CTE name and is invoked repeatedly until it returns an empty set. The reference to the CTE name represents the previous result set. The first time that the recursive member is invoked, the previous result set represents whatever the anchor member returned. In each subsequent invocation of the recursive member, the reference to the CTE name represents the result set returned by the previous invocation of the recursive member. Both queries must be compatible in terms of the number of columns they return and the data types of the corresponding columns. The reference to the CTE name in the outer query represents the unified result sets of the invocation of the anchor member and all invocations of the recursive member.

If this is your first encounter with recursive CTEs, you might find this explanation hard to understand. They are best explained with an example. The following code demonstrates how to return information about an employee (Don Funk, employee ID 2) and all the employee's subordinates at all levels (direct or indirect):

```
WITH EmpsCTE AS
(
    SELECT empid, mgrid, firstname, lastname
    FROM HR.Employees
    WHERE empid = 2

    UNION ALL

    SELECT C.empid, C.mgrid, C.firstname, C.lastname
    FROM EmpsCTE AS P
        INNER JOIN HR.Employees AS C
            ON C.mgrid = P.empid
)
SELECT empid, mgrid, firstname, lastname
FROM EmpsCTE;
```

The anchor member queries the *HR.Employees* table and simply returns the row for employee 2:

```
SELECT empid, mgrid, firstname, lastname
FROM HR.Employees
WHERE empid = 2
```

The recursive member joins the CTE—representing the previous result set—with the *Employees* table to return the direct subordinates of the employees returned in the previous result set:

```
SELECT C.empid, C.mgrid, C.firstname, C.lastname
FROM EmpsCTE AS P
    INNER JOIN HR.Employees AS C
        ON C.mgrid = P.empid
```

In other words, the recursive member is invoked repeatedly, and in each invocation it returns the next level of subordinates. The first time the recursive member is invoked, it returns the direct subordinates of employee 2—employees 3 and 5. The second time the recursive member is invoked, it returns the direct subordinates of employees 3 and 5—employees 4, 6, 7, 8, and 9. The third time the recursive member is invoked, there are no more subordinates; the recursive member returns an empty set, and therefore recursion stops.

The reference to the CTE name in the outer query represents the unified result sets—in other words, employee 2 and all the employee's subordinates.

Here's the output of this code:

```
empid        mgrid        firstname  lastname
-----------  -----------  ---------- --------------------
2            1            Don        Funk
3            2            Judy       Lew
5            2            Sven       Mortensen
6            5            Paul       Suurs
7            5            Russell    King
9            5            Patricia   Doyle
4            3            Yael       Peled
8            3            Maria      Cameron
```

In the event of a logical error in the join predicate in the recursive member, or if there are problems with the data that result in cycles, the recursive member potentially can be invoked an infinite number of times. As a safety measure, SQL Server restricts the number of times the recursive member can be invoked to 100 by default. The code will fail if the recursive member is invoked more than 100 times. You can change the default maximum recursion limit (that is, the number of times the recursive member can be invoked) by specifying the hint *OPTION(MAXRECURSION n)* at the end of the outer query, where *n* is an integer in the range 0 through 32,767. If you want to remove the restriction altogether, specify *MAXRECURSION 0*. Note that SQL Server stores the intermediate result sets returned by the anchor and recursive members in a work table in *tempdb*; if you remove the restriction and have a runaway query, the work table will quickly get very large, and the query will never finish.

Views

Derived tables and CTEs have a single-statement scope, which means they are not reusable. Views and inline table-valued functions (inline TVFs) are two types of table expressions whose definitions are stored as permanent objects in the database, making them reusable. In most other respects, views and inline TVFs are treated like derived tables and CTEs. For example, when querying a view or an inline TVF, SQL Server expands the definition of the table expression and queries the underlying objects directly, as with derived tables and CTEs. In this section, I describe views; in the next section, I describe inline TVFs.

Note Before running code samples that are supposed to create objects in the sample database *TSQLV6*, make sure you are connected to this database.

As an example, the following code creates a view called *USACusts* in the *Sales* schema in the *TSQLV6* database, representing all customers from the United States:

```
CREATE OR ALTER VIEW Sales.USACusts
AS

SELECT
  custid, companyname, contactname, contacttitle, address,
  city, region, postalcode, country, phone, fax
FROM Sales.Customers
WHERE country = N'USA';
GO
```

> **Note** The *GO* command is used here to terminate what's called a batch in T-SQL. I explain the *GO* command and what batches are in detail in Chapter 12.

The *CREATE OR ALTER* syntax creates the object if it doesn't exist or alters its definition to the new one if it does. If you use the *CREATE VIEW* command instead, and the object already exists, you get an error.

Just as with derived tables and CTEs, instead of using inline column aliasing as shown in the preceding code, you can use external column aliasing by specifying the target column names in parentheses immediately after the view name.

After you create this view, you can query it much like you query other tables in the database:

```
SELECT custid, companyname
FROM Sales.USACusts;
```

Because a view is an object in the database, you can manage access permissions similar to the way you do for tables. (These permissions include *SELECT, INSERT, UPDATE,* and *DELETE.*) You can even deny direct access to the underlying objects while granting access to the view. I provide details on modifications through table expressions in Chapter 8.

Note that the general recommendation to avoid using *SELECT ** has specific relevance in the context of views. The columns are enumerated in the compiled form of the view, and new table columns will not be automatically added to the view. For example, suppose you define a view based on the query *SELECT * FROM dbo.T1,* and at the view creation time the table *T1* has the columns *col1* and *col2.* SQL Server stores information only on those two columns in the view's metadata. If you alter the definition of the table to add new columns, those new columns will not be added to the view. You can refresh the view's metadata by using the stored procedure *sp_refreshview* or *sp_refreshsqlmodule,* but to avoid confusion, the best practice is to explicitly list the column names you need in the definition of the view. If columns are added to the underlying tables and you need them in the view, use the *CREATE OR ALTER VIEW* statement or the *ALTER VIEW* statement to revise the view definition accordingly.

Views and the *ORDER BY* clause

The query you use to define a view must meet all requirements mentioned earlier with respect to the inner query in the other types of table expressions. The view should not guarantee any order to the rows, all view columns must have names, and all column names must be unique. In this section, I elaborate a bit about the ordering issue, which is a fundamental point that is crucial to understand.

Remember that a presentation *ORDER BY* clause is not allowed in the query defining a table expression because a relation isn't ordered. If you need to return rows from a view sorted for presentation purposes, you should specify a presentation *ORDER BY* clause in the outer query against the view, like this:

```
SELECT custid, companyname, region
FROM Sales.USACusts
ORDER BY region;
```

Try running the following code to create a view with a presentation *ORDER BY* clause:

```
CREATE OR ALTER VIEW Sales.USACusts
AS

SELECT
  custid, companyname, contactname, contacttitle, address,
  city, region, postalcode, country, phone, fax
FROM Sales.Customers
WHERE country = N'USA'
ORDER BY region;
GO
```

This attempt fails, and you get the following error:

```
Msg 1033, Level 15, State 1, Procedure USACusts, Line 9 [Batch Start Line 239]
The ORDER BY clause is invalid in views, inline functions, derived tables, subqueries, and
common table expressions, unless TOP, OFFSET or FOR XML is also specified.
```

The error message indicates that T-SQL allows the *ORDER BY* clause only in exceptional cases—when the *TOP, OFFSET-FETCH,* or *FOR XML* option is used. In those cases, the *ORDER BY* clause serves a purpose other than its usual presentation purpose. Even standard SQL has a similar restriction, with a similar exception when the *OFFSET-FETCH* option is used.

Because T-SQL allows an *ORDER BY* clause in a view when *TOP* or *OFFSET-FETCH* is also specified, some people think they can create "ordered views." One of the ways people try to achieve this is by using *TOP (100) PERCENT*, like the following:

```
CREATE OR ALTER VIEW Sales.USACusts
AS

SELECT TOP (100) PERCENT
  custid, companyname, contactname, contacttitle, address,
  city, region, postalcode, country, phone, fax
FROM Sales.Customers
WHERE country = N'USA'
ORDER BY region;
GO
```

Even though the code is technically valid and the view is created, you should be aware that if an outer query against the view doesn't have an *ORDER BY* clause, presentation order is not guaranteed. For example, run the following query against the view:

```
SELECT custid, companyname, region
FROM Sales.USACusts;
```

Here's the output from one of my executions, showing that the rows are not sorted by region:

```
custid       companyname              region
-----------  -----------------------  ---------------
32           Customer YSIQX           OR
36           Customer LVJSO           OR
43           Customer UISOJ           WA
45           Customer QXPPT           CA
48           Customer DVFMB           OR
55           Customer KZQZT           AK
65           Customer NYUHS           NM
71           Customer LCOUJ           ID
75           Customer XOJYP           WY
77           Customer LCYBZ           OR
78           Customer NLTYP           MT
82           Customer EYHKM           WA
89           Customer YBQTI           WA
```

If the outer query doesn't have an *ORDER BY* clause but the result seems to be ordered, it could be because of certain physical conditions and optimization choices, but those things are not guaranteed to be repeatable. The only way to guarantee presentation order is to have an *ORDER BY* clause in the outer query. Nothing else counts.

In old versions of SQL Server, when the inner query had the combination of *TOP (100) PERCENT* and *ORDER BY* and the outer query didn't have an *ORDER BY* clause, you got the rows ordered. It wasn't a guaranteed behavior, but it happened to be the result of the way the optimizer handled things. At some point, Microsoft added smarter optimization that optimizes out this meaningless combination. Unfortunately, the optimizer doesn't yet optimize out the combination when the inner query uses the *OFFSET* clause with *0 ROWS*, and without a *FETCH* clause, like the following:

```
CREATE OR ALTER VIEW Sales.USACusts
AS

SELECT
  custid, companyname, contactname, contacttitle, address,
  city, region, postalcode, country, phone, fax
FROM Sales.Customers
WHERE country = N'USA'
ORDER BY region
OFFSET 0 ROWS;
GO
```

At the moment, when I query the view and don't indicate an *ORDER BY* clause in the outer query, the result rows happen to be sorted by region. But I stress—*do not* assume that's guaranteed.

It happens to be the case because of the current optimization. If you need a guarantee that the rows will be returned sorted, you need an *ORDER BY* clause in the outer query.

Do not confuse the behavior of a query that is used to define a table expression with an outer query. An outer query with an *ORDER BY* clause and a *TOP* or *OFFSET-FETCH* option does guarantee presentation order. The simple rule is that if the outer query has an *ORDER BY* clause, you have a presentation ordering guarantee, regardless of whether that *ORDER BY* clause also serves another purpose.

View options

When you create or alter a view, you can specify view attributes and options as part of the view definition. In the header of the view, under the *WITH* clause, you can specify attributes such as *ENCRYPTION* and *SCHEMABINDING*, and at the end of the query you can specify *WITH CHECK OPTION*. The following sections describe the purpose of these options.

The *ENCRYPTION* option

The *ENCRYPTION* option is available when you create or alter views, stored procedures, triggers, and user-defined functions (UDFs). The *ENCRYPTION* option indicates that SQL Server will internally store the text with the definition of the object in an obfuscated format. The obfuscated text is not directly visible to users through any of the catalog objects—only to privileged users through special means.

Before you look at the *ENCRYPTION* option, run the following code to alter the definition of the *USACusts* view to its original version:

```
CREATE OR ALTER VIEW Sales.USACusts
AS

SELECT
  custid, companyname, contactname, contacttitle, address,
  city, region, postalcode, country, phone, fax
FROM Sales.Customers
WHERE country = N'USA';
GO
```

To get the definition of the view, invoke the *OBJECT_DEFINITION* function, like this:

```
SELECT OBJECT_DEFINITION(OBJECT_ID('Sales.USACusts'));
```

The text with the definition of the view is available because the view was created without the *ENCRYPTION* option. You get the following output:

```
CREATE    VIEW Sales.USACusts
AS

SELECT
  custid, companyname, contactname, contacttitle, address,
  city, region, postalcode, country, phone, fax
FROM Sales.Customers
WHERE country = N'USA';
```

Next, alter the view definition—only this time, include the *ENCRYPTION* option:

```
CREATE OR ALTER VIEW Sales.USACusts WITH ENCRYPTION
AS

SELECT
  custid, companyname, contactname, contacttitle, address,
  city, region, postalcode, country, phone, fax
FROM Sales.Customers
WHERE country = N'USA';
GO
```

> **Note** When you alter a view, if you want to keep options you specified when you created it, you need to repeat those as part of the *CREATE OR ALTER VIEW* command or as part of the *ALTER VIEW* command; otherwise, the view will be created without them. Altering a view does retain existing permissions, so you do not need to reassign those.

Try again to get the text with the definition of the view:

```
SELECT OBJECT_DEFINITION(OBJECT_ID('Sales.USACusts'));
```

This time you get a *NULL* back.

As an alternative to the *OBJECT_DEFINITION* function, you can use the *sp_helptext* stored procedure to get object definitions. For example, the following code requests the object definition of the *USACusts* view:

```
EXEC sp_helptext 'Sales.USACusts';
```

Because in our case the view was created with the *ENCRYPTION* option, you will not get the object definition back; instead, you'll get the following message:

```
The text for object 'Sales.USACusts' is encrypted.
```

The *SCHEMABINDING* option

The *SCHEMABINDING* option is available to views, UDFs, and natively compiled modules; it binds the schema of referenced objects and columns to the schema of the referencing object. It indicates that referenced objects cannot be dropped and that referenced columns cannot be dropped or altered.

For example, alter the *USACusts* view with the *SCHEMABINDING* option:

```
CREATE OR ALTER VIEW Sales.USACusts WITH SCHEMABINDING
AS

SELECT
  custid, companyname, contactname, contacttitle, address,
  city, region, postalcode, country, phone, fax
FROM Sales.Customers
WHERE country = N'USA';
GO
```

Now try to drop the *address* column from the *Customers* table:

```
ALTER TABLE Sales.Customers DROP COLUMN address;
```

You get the following error:

```
Msg 5074, Level 16, State 1, Line 345
The object 'USACusts' is dependent on column 'address'.
Msg 4922, Level 16, State 9, Line 345
ALTER TABLE DROP COLUMN address failed because one or more objects access this column.
```

Without the *SCHEMABINDING* option, you would have been allowed to make such a schema change, as well as drop the *Customers* table altogether. This can lead to errors at run time when you try to query the view and referenced objects or columns do not exist. If you create the view with the *SCHEMABINDING* option, you can avoid these errors.

To support the *SCHEMABINDING* option, the object definition must meet a couple of requirements. The query is not allowed to use * in the *SELECT* clause; instead, you have to explicitly list column names. Also, you must use schema-qualified two-part names when referring to objects. Both requirements are actually good practices in general.

As you can imagine, creating your objects with the *SCHEMABINDING* option is generally considered a good practice. However, it could complicate application upgrades that involve structural object changes and make them longer due to the dependencies that are created.

The *CHECK OPTION* option

The purpose of *CHECK OPTION* is to prevent modifications through the view that conflict with the view's inner query filter.

The query defining the view *USACusts* filters customers from the United States. The view is currently defined without *CHECK OPTION*. This means you can currently insert through the view customers from other countries, and you can update the country of existing customers through the view to one other than the United States. For example, the following code successfully inserts a customer from the United Kingdom through the view:

```
INSERT INTO Sales.USACusts(
  companyname, contactname, contacttitle, address,
  city, region, postalcode, country, phone, fax)
VALUES(
  N'Customer ABCDE', N'Contact ABCDE', N'Title ABCDE', N'Address ABCDE',
  N'London', NULL, N'12345', N'UK', N'012-3456789', N'012-3456789');
```

The row was inserted through the view into the *Customers* table. However, because the view filters only customers from the United States, if you query the view looking for the new customer, you get an empty set back:

```
SELECT custid, companyname, country
FROM Sales.USACusts
WHERE companyname = N'Customer ABCDE';
```

Query the *Customers* table directly to look for the new customer:

```
SELECT custid, companyname, country
FROM Sales.Customers
WHERE companyname = N'Customer ABCDE';
```

You get the customer in the output, because the new row made it to the *Customers* table:

```
custid      companyname         country
----------- ------------------- ---------------
92          Customer ABCDE      UK
```

Similarly, if you update a customer row through the view, changing the country attribute to a country other than the United States, the update succeeds. But that customer information doesn't show up anymore in the view because it doesn't satisfy the view's query filter.

If you want to prevent modifications that conflict with the view's filter, add *WITH CHECK OPTION* at the end of the query defining the view:

```
CREATE OR ALTER VIEW Sales.USACusts WITH SCHEMABINDING
AS

SELECT
  custid, companyname, contactname, contacttitle, address,
  city, region, postalcode, country, phone, fax
FROM Sales.Customers
WHERE country = N'USA'
WITH CHECK OPTION;
GO
```

Now try to insert a row that conflicts with the view's filter:

```
INSERT INTO Sales.USACusts(
  companyname, contactname, contacttitle, address,
  city, region, postalcode, country, phone, fax)
 VALUES(
  N'Customer FGHIJ', N'Contact FGHIJ', N'Title FGHIJ', N'Address FGHIJ',
  N'London', NULL, N'12345', N'UK', N'012-3456789', N'012-3456789');
```

You get the following error:

```
Msg 550, Level 16, State 1, Line 386
The attempted insert or update failed because the target view either specifies WITH CHECK
OPTION or spans a view that specifies WITH CHECK OPTION and one or more rows resulting from the
operation did not qualify under the CHECK OPTION constraint.
The statement has been terminated.
```

When you're done, run the following code for cleanup:

```
DELETE FROM Sales.Customers
WHERE custid > 91;

DROP VIEW IF EXISTS Sales.USACusts;
```

Inline table-valued functions

Inline TVFs are reusable table expressions that support input parameters. In most respects, except for the support for input parameters, inline TVFs are similar to views. For this reason, I like to think of inline TVFs as parameterized views, even though they are not formally referred to this way.

T-SQL supports another type of table function called multi-statement TVF, which populates and returns a table variable. This type isn't considered a table expression, because it's not based on a query.

For example, the following code creates an inline TVF called *GetCustOrders* in the *TSQLV6* database:

```
USE TSQLV6;
GO
CREATE OR ALTER FUNCTION dbo.GetCustOrders
  (@cid AS INT) RETURNS TABLE
AS
RETURN
  SELECT orderid, custid, empid, orderdate, requireddate,
    shippeddate, shipperid, freight, shipname, shipaddress, shipcity,
    shipregion, shippostalcode, shipcountry
  FROM Sales.Orders
  WHERE custid = @cid;
GO
```

You can see a couple of differences in the syntax for creating an inline TVF compared to creating a view. The inline TVF's header has a mandatory *RETURNS TABLE* clause, meaning that conceptually the function returns a table result. The inline TVF also has a mandatory *RETURN* clause before the inner query, which a view definition doesn't have.

This inline TVF accepts an input parameter called *@cid*, representing a customer ID, and returns all orders placed by the input customer. You query inline TVFs by using DML statements, which is the same way you query other tables. If the function accepts input parameters, you specify those in parentheses following the function's name when you query it. Also, make sure you provide an alias for the table expression. Providing a table expression with an alias is not always a requirement, but it is a good practice because it makes your code more readable and less prone to errors. For example, the following code queries the function to request all orders that were placed by customer 1:

```
SELECT orderid, custid
FROM dbo.GetCustOrders(1) AS O;
```

This code returns the following output:

```
orderid      custid
-----------  -----------
10643        1
10692        1
10702        1
10835        1
10952        1
11011        1
```

As with tables, you can refer to an inline TVF as part of a join. For example, the following query joins the inline TVF returning customer 1's orders with the *Sales.OrderDetails* table, matching the orders with their respective order lines:

```
SELECT O.orderid, O.custid, OD.productid, OD.qty
FROM dbo.GetCustOrders(1) AS O
  INNER JOIN Sales.OrderDetails AS OD
    ON O.orderid = OD.orderid;
```

This code returns the following output:

orderid	custid	productid	qty
10643	1	28	15
10643	1	39	21
10643	1	46	2
10692	1	63	20
10702	1	3	6
10702	1	76	15
10835	1	59	15
10835	1	77	2
10952	1	6	16
10952	1	28	2
11011	1	58	40
11011	1	71	20

When you're done, run the following code for cleanup:

```
DROP FUNCTION IF EXISTS dbo.GetCustOrders;
```

The *APPLY* operator

The *APPLY* operator is a powerful table operator. Like all table operators, *APPLY* is used in the *FROM* clause of a query. There are two supported types of *APPLY*: *CROSS APPLY* and *OUTER APPLY*. Like the *JOIN* table operator, *APPLY* performs its work in logical-query phases. *CROSS APPLY* implements only one logical-query processing phase, whereas *OUTER APPLY* implements two.

> **Note** *APPLY* isn't standard; the standard counterpart is called *LATERAL*, but the standard form wasn't implemented in SQL Server.

The *APPLY* operator operates on two input tables; I'll refer to them as the "left" and "right" tables. The right table is typically a derived table or a TVF. The *CROSS APPLY* operator implements one logical-query processing phase—it applies the right table to each row from the left table and produces a result table with the unified result sets.

It might sound like the *CROSS APPLY* operator is similar to a cross join, and in a sense that's true. For example, the following two queries return the same result sets:

```
SELECT S.shipperid, E.empid
FROM Sales.Shippers AS S
  CROSS JOIN HR.Employees AS E;

SELECT S.shipperid, E.empid
FROM Sales.Shippers AS S
  CROSS APPLY HR.Employees AS E;
```

Remember that a join treats its two inputs as a set, and therefore there's no order between them. This means you cannot refer on one side to elements from the other. With *APPLY*, the left side is evaluated first, and the right side is evaluated per row from the left. So the right side can have references to elements from the left. Those references are essentially correlations. In other words, you can think of *APPLY* as a correlated join. For example, the following code uses the *CROSS APPLY* operator to return the three most recent orders for each customer:

```
SELECT C.custid, A.orderid, A.orderdate
FROM Sales.Customers AS C
  CROSS APPLY
    (SELECT TOP (3) orderid, empid, orderdate, requireddate
     FROM Sales.Orders AS O
     WHERE O.custid = C.custid
     ORDER BY orderdate DESC, orderid DESC) AS A;
```

You can think of the table expression *A* as a correlated derived table. In terms of logical-query processing, the right table expression (a derived table, in this case) is applied to each row from the *Customers* table. Notice in the inner query's filter the reference to the attribute *C.custid* from the left table. The derived table returns the three most recent orders for the current customer from the left row. Because the derived table is applied to each left row, the *CROSS APPLY* operator returns the three most recent orders for each customer.

Here's the output of this query, shown in abbreviated form:

```
custid       orderid      orderdate
-----------  -----------  -----------
1            11011        2022-04-09
1            10952        2022-03-16
1            10835        2022-01-15
2            10926        2022-03-04
2            10759        2021-11-28
2            10625        2021-08-08
3            10856        2022-01-28
3            10682        2021-09-25
3            10677        2021-09-22
...

(263 rows affected)
```

Remember that you can use the standard *OFFSET-FETCH* option instead of *TOP*, like this:

```
SELECT C.custid, A.orderid, A.orderdate
FROM Sales.Customers AS C
  CROSS APPLY
    (SELECT orderid, empid, orderdate, requireddate
     FROM Sales.Orders AS O
     WHERE O.custid = C.custid
     ORDER BY orderdate DESC, orderid DESC
     OFFSET 0 ROWS FETCH NEXT 3 ROWS ONLY) AS A;
```

If the right table expression returns an empty set, the *CROSS APPLY* operator does not return the corresponding left row. For example, customers 22 and 57 did not place orders. In both cases, the derived table is an empty set; therefore, those customers are not returned in the output. If you want to return rows from the left side even if there are no matches on the right side, use *OUTER APPLY*. This operator has a second logical phase that preserves all left rows. It keeps the rows from the left side for which there are no matches on the right side, and it uses *NULLs* as placeholders on the right side. You probably noticed that, in the sense that *OUTER APPLY* preserves all left rows, it's similar to a *LEFT OUTER JOIN*. Because of the way *APPLY* works, there's no *APPLY* equivalent of a *RIGHT OUTER JOIN*.

For example, run the following code to return the three most recent orders for each customer and include in the output customers who did not place orders:

```
SELECT C.custid, A.orderid, A.orderdate
FROM Sales.Customers AS C
  OUTER APPLY
    (SELECT TOP (3) orderid, empid, orderdate, requireddate
     FROM Sales.Orders AS O
     WHERE O.custid = C.custid
     ORDER BY orderdate DESC, orderid DESC) AS A;
```

This time, customers 22 and 57 are included in the output, which is shown here in abbreviated form:

```
custid       orderid       orderdate
-----------  -----------   -----------
1            11011         2022-04-09
1            10952         2022-03-16
1            10835         2022-01-15
2            10926         2022-03-04
2            10759         2021-11-28
2            10625         2021-08-08
3            10856         2022-01-28
3            10682         2021-09-25
3            10677         2021-09-22
...
22           NULL          NULL
...
57           NULL          NULL
...

(265 rows affected)
```

You might find it more convenient to work with inline TVFs instead of derived tables. This way, your code will be simpler to follow and maintain. For example, the following code creates an inline TVF called *TopOrders* that accepts as inputs a customer ID (*@custid*) and a number (*@n*), and returns the *@n* most recent orders for customer *@custid*:

```
CREATE OR ALTER FUNCTION dbo.TopOrders
  (@custid AS INT, @n AS INT)
  RETURNS TABLE
AS
RETURN
  SELECT TOP (@n) orderid, empid, orderdate, requireddate
  FROM Sales.Orders
  WHERE custid = @custid
  ORDER BY orderdate DESC, orderid DESC;
GO
```

You can now substitute the use of the derived table from the previous examples with the new function:

```
SELECT
  C.custid, C.companyname,
  A.orderid, A.empid, A.orderdate, A.requireddate
FROM Sales.Customers AS C
  CROSS APPLY dbo.TopOrders(C.custid, 3) AS A;
```

In terms of physical processing, nothing really changed, because, as I stated earlier, the definition of table expressions is expanded, or inlined, and SQL Server will in any case end up querying the underlying objects directly.

Conclusion

Table expressions can help you simplify your code, improve its maintainability, and encapsulate querying logic. When you need to use table expressions and are not planning to reuse their definitions, use derived tables or CTEs. CTEs have a couple of advantages over derived tables; they are easier to maintain because you do not nest them like you do derived tables. Also, you can refer to multiple instances of the same CTE, which you cannot do with derived tables.

When you need to define reusable table expressions, use views or inline TVFs. When you do not need to support input parameters, use views; otherwise, use inline TVFs.

Use the *APPLY* operator when you want to apply a correlated table expression to each row from a source table and unify all result sets into one result table.

> **See Also** The information provided in this chapter about table expressions should be
> sufficient as the background that is required for the remainder of this book. However, if
> you find this topic interesting and would like to delve into it more deeply, including optimi-
> zation considerations, you can find more info in two article series in my column here:
> *https://sqlperformance.com/author/itzikbengan*. One series is about table expressions,
> starting with this article: *https://sqlperformance.com/2020/04/t-sql-queries/*
> *table-expressions-part-1*. Another series is about a number series generator challenge
> and solutions, which involve extensive use of table expressions, starting with this article:
> *https://sqlperformance.com/2020/12/t-sql-queries/number-series-challenge*.

Exercises

This section provides exercises to help you familiarize yourself with the subjects discussed in this chapter. All the exercises in this chapter require your session to be connected to the *TSQLV6* database.

Exercise 1

The following query attempts to filter orders that were not placed on the last day of the year. It's supposed to return the order ID, order date, customer ID, employee ID, and respective end-of-year date
for each order.

```
SELECT orderid, orderdate, custid, empid,
  DATEFROMPARTS(YEAR(orderdate), 12, 31) AS endofyear
FROM Sales.Orders
WHERE orderdate <> endofyear;
```

When you try to run this query, you get the following error:

```
Msg 207, Level 16, State 1, Line 17
Invalid column name 'endofyear'.
```

Explain what the problem is, and suggest a valid solution.

Exercise 2-1

Write a query that returns the maximum value in the *orderdate* column for each employee:

- Table involved: *TSQLV6* database, *Sales.Orders* table

- Desired output:

```
empid        maxorderdate
-----------  -------------
3            2022-04-30
6            2022-04-23
```

```
9              2022-04-29
7              2022-05-06
1              2022-05-06
4              2022-05-06
2              2022-05-05
5              2022-04-22
8              2022-05-06

(9 rows affected)
```

Exercise 2-2

Encapsulate the query from Exercise 2-1 in a derived table. Write a join query between the derived table and the *Orders* table to return the orders with the maximum order date for each employee:

- Table involved: *Sales.Orders*

- Desired output:

```
empid        orderdate    orderid      custid
-----------  -----------  -----------  -----------
9            2022-04-29   11058        6
8            2022-05-06   11075        68
7            2022-05-06   11074        73
6            2022-04-23   11045        10
5            2022-04-22   11043        74
4            2022-05-06   11076        9
3            2022-04-30   11063        37
2            2022-05-05   11073        58
2            2022-05-05   11070        44
1            2022-05-06   11077        65

(10 rows affected)
```

Exercise 3-1

Write a query that calculates a row number for each order based on *orderdate, orderid* ordering:

- Table involved: *Sales.Orders*

- Desired output (abbreviated):

```
orderid      orderdate    custid       empid        rownum
-----------  -----------  -----------  -----------  -------
10248        2020-07-04   85           5            1
10249        2020-07-05   79           6            2
10250        2020-07-08   34           4            3
10251        2020-07-08   84           3            4
10252        2020-07-09   76           4            5
10253        2020-07-10   34           3            6
10254        2020-07-11   14           5            7
10255        2020-07-12   68           9            8
10256        2020-07-15   88           3            9
10257        2020-07-16   35           4            10
...

(830 rows affected)
```

Exercise 3-2

Write a query that returns rows with row numbers 11 through 20 based on the row-number definition in Exercise 3-1. Use a CTE to encapsulate the code from Exercise 3-1:

- Table involved: *Sales.Orders*

- Desired output:

```
orderid      orderdate   custid    empid      rownum
-----------  ----------- ----------- ---------  -------
10258        2020-07-17  20        1          11
10259        2020-07-18  13        4          12
10260        2020-07-19  56        4          13
10261        2020-07-19  61        4          14
10262        2020-07-22  65        8          15
10263        2020-07-23  20        9          16
10264        2020-07-24  24        6          17
10265        2020-07-25  7         2          18
10266        2020-07-26  87        3          19
10267        2020-07-29  25        4          20

(10 rows affected)
```

Exercise 4

Write a solution using a recursive CTE that returns the management chain leading to Patricia Doyle (employee ID 9):

- Table involved: *HR.Employees*

- Desired output:

```
empid        mgrid       firstname   lastname
-----------  ----------- ----------- ----------------------
9            5           Patricia    Doyle
5            2           Sven        Mortensen
2            1           Don         Funk
1            NULL        Sara        Davis

(4 rows affected)
```

Exercise 5-1

Create a view that returns the total quantity for each employee and year:

- Tables involved: *Sales.Orders* and *Sales.OrderDetails*

- When running the following code:

```
SELECT * FROM Sales.VEmpOrders ORDER BY empid, orderyear;
```

- Desired output:

```
empid        orderyear     qty
-----------  -----------   -----------
1            2020          1620
1            2021          3877
1            2022          2315
2            2020          1085
2            2021          2604
2            2022          2366
3            2020          940
3            2021          4436
3            2022          2476
4            2020          2212
4            2021          5273
4            2022          2313
5            2020          778
5            2021          1471
5            2022          787
6            2020          963
6            2021          1738
6            2022          826
7            2020          485
7            2021          2292
7            2022          1877
8            2020          923
8            2021          2843
8            2022          2147
9            2020          575
9            2021          955
9            2022          1140

(27 rows affected)
```

Exercise 5-2

Write a query against *Sales.VEmpOrders* that returns the running total quantity for each employee and year:

- Table involved: *Sales.VEmpOrders* view

- Desired output:

```
empid        orderyear     qty           runqty
-----------  -----------   -----------   -----------
1            2020          1620          1620
1            2021          3877          5497
1            2022          2315          7812
2            2020          1085          1085
2            2021          2604          3689
2            2022          2366          6055
3            2020          940           940
3            2021          4436          5376
3            2022          2476          7852
4            2020          2212          2212
4            2021          5273          7485
4            2022          2313          9798
5            2020          778           778
5            2021          1471          2249
5            2022          787           3036
```

```
6       2020        963         963
6       2021        1738        2701
6       2022        826         3527
7       2020        485         485
7       2021        2292        2777
7       2022        1877        4654
8       2020        923         923
8       2021        2843        3766
8       2022        2147        5913
9       2020        575         575
9       2021        955         1530
9       2022        1140        2670

(27 rows affected)
```

Exercise 6-1

Create an inline TVF that accepts as inputs a supplier ID (*@supid AS INT*) and a requested number of products (*@n AS INT*). The function should return *@n* products with the highest unit prices that are supplied by the specified supplier ID:

- Table involved: *Production.Products*

- When issuing the following query:

```
SELECT * FROM Production.TopProducts(5, 2);
```

- Desired output:

```
productid    productname           unitprice
-----------  --------------------  -----------
12           Product OSFNS         38.00
11           Product QMVUN         21.00

(2 rows affected)
```

Exercise 6-2

Using the *CROSS APPLY* operator and the function you created in Exercise 6-1, return the two most expensive products for each supplier:

- Table involved: *Production.Suppliers*

- Desired output (shown here in abbreviated form):

```
supplierid   companyname       productid    productname       unitprice
-----------  ----------------  -----------  ----------------  ----------
8            Supplier BWGYE    20           Product QHFFP     81.00
8            Supplier BWGYE    68           Product TBTBL     12.50
20           Supplier CIYNM    43           Product ZZZHR     46.00
20           Supplier CIYNM    44           Product VJIEO     19.45
23           Supplier ELCRN    49           Product FPYPN     20.00
23           Supplier ELCRN    76           Product JYGFE     18.00
5            Supplier EQPNC    12           Product OSFNS     38.00
5            Supplier EQPNC    11           Product QMVUN     21.00
...

(55 rows affected)
```

- When you're done, run the following code for cleanup:

```
DROP VIEW IF EXISTS Sales.VEmpOrders;
DROP FUNCTION IF EXISTS Production.TopProducts;
```

Solutions

This section provides solutions to the exercises in the preceding section.

Exercise 1

The problem is that in terms of logical-query processing, the *SELECT* clause is evaluated after the *WHERE* clause. This means you're not allowed to refer to an alias you create in the *SELECT* clause within the *WHERE* clause. One solution that doesn't require you to repeat lengthy expressions is to define a table expression such as a CTE based on a query that defines the alias, and then refer to the alias multiple times in the outer query. In our case, the solution looks like this:

```
WITH C AS
(
  SELECT *,
    DATEFROMPARTS(YEAR(orderdate), 12, 31) AS endofyear
  FROM Sales.Orders
)
SELECT orderid, orderdate, custid, empid, endofyear
FROM C
WHERE orderdate <> endofyear;
```

Exercise 2-1

This exercise is just a preliminary step required for the next exercise. This step involves writing a query that returns the maximum order date for each employee:

```
USE TSQLV6;

SELECT empid, MAX(orderdate) AS maxorderdate
FROM Sales.Orders
GROUP BY empid;
```

Exercise 2-2

This exercise requires you to use the query from the previous step to define a derived table and join this derived table with the *Orders* table to return the orders with the maximum order date for each employee, like the following:

```
SELECT O.empid, O.orderdate, O.orderid, O.custid
FROM Sales.Orders AS O
  INNER JOIN (SELECT empid, MAX(orderdate) AS maxorderdate
              FROM Sales.Orders
              GROUP BY empid) AS D
    ON O.empid = D.empid
    AND O.orderdate = D.maxorderdate;
```

Exercise 3-1

This exercise is a preliminary step for the next exercise. It requires you to query the *Orders* table and calculate row numbers based on *orderdate, orderid* ordering, like the following:

```
SELECT orderid, orderdate, custid, empid,
  ROW_NUMBER() OVER(ORDER BY orderdate, orderid) AS rownum
FROM Sales.Orders;
```

Exercise 3-2

This exercise requires you to define a CTE based on the query from the previous step and filter only rows with row numbers in the range 11 through 20 from the CTE, like the following:

```
WITH OrdersRN AS
(
  SELECT orderid, orderdate, custid, empid,
    ROW_NUMBER() OVER(ORDER BY orderdate, orderid) AS rownum
  FROM Sales.Orders
)
SELECT * FROM OrdersRN WHERE rownum BETWEEN 11 AND 20;
```

You might wonder why you need a table expression here. Window functions (such as the *ROW_NUMBER* function) are allowed only in the *SELECT* and *ORDER BY* clauses of a query, and not directly in the *WHERE* clause. By using a table expression, you can invoke the *ROW_NUMBER* function in the *SELECT* clause, assign an alias to the result column, and refer to that alias in the *WHERE* clause of the outer query.

Exercise 4

You can think of this exercise as the inverse of the request to return an employee and all subordinates in all levels. Here, the anchor member is a query that returns the row for employee 9. The recursive member joins the CTE (call it C)—representing the subordinate/child from the previous level—with the *Employees* table (call it P)—representing the manager/parent in the next level. This way, each invocation of the recursive member returns the manager from the next level, until no next-level manager is found (in the case of the CEO).

Here's the complete solution query:

```
WITH EmpsCTE AS
(
  SELECT empid, mgrid, firstname, lastname
  FROM HR.Employees
  WHERE empid = 9

  UNION ALL

  SELECT P.empid, P.mgrid, P.firstname, P.lastname
  FROM EmpsCTE AS C
    INNER JOIN HR.Employees AS P
```

```
        ON C.mgrid = P.empid
)
SELECT empid, mgrid, firstname, lastname
FROM EmpsCTE;
```

Exercise 5-1

This exercise is a preliminary step for the next exercise. Here you are required to define a view based on a query that joins the *Orders* and *OrderDetails* tables, group the rows by employee ID and order year, and return the total quantity for each group. The view definition should look like the following:

```
USE TSQLV6;
GO
CREATE OR ALTER VIEW  Sales.VEmpOrders
AS

SELECT
  empid,
  YEAR(orderdate) AS orderyear,
  SUM(qty) AS qty
FROM Sales.Orders AS O
  INNER JOIN Sales.OrderDetails AS OD
    ON O.orderid = OD.orderid
GROUP BY
  empid,
  YEAR(orderdate);
GO
```

Exercise 5-2

In this exercise, you query the *VEmpOrders* view and return the running total quantity for each employee and order year. To achieve this, you can write a query against the *VEmpOrders* view (calling it *V1*) that returns from each row the employee ID, order year, and quantity. In the *SELECT* list, you can incorporate a subquery against a second instance of *VEmpOrders* (calling it *V2*), that returns the sum of all quantities from the rows where the employee ID is equal to the one in *V1*, and the order year is smaller than or equal to the one in *V1*. The complete solution query looks like the following:

```
SELECT empid, orderyear, qty,
  (SELECT SUM(V2.qty)
   FROM  Sales.VEmpOrders AS V2
   WHERE V2.empid = V1.empid
     AND V2.orderyear <= V1.orderyear) AS runqty
FROM  Sales.VEmpOrders AS V1
ORDER BY empid, orderyear;
```

Note that in Chapter 7, "T-SQL for data analysis," you'll learn techniques to compute running totals by using window functions, resulting in simpler and more optimal solutions than ones that use subqueries or joins.

Exercise 6-1

This exercise requires you to define an inline TVF called *TopProducts* that accepts a supplier ID (*@supid*) and a number (*@n*) and is supposed to return the *@n* most expensive products supplied by the input supplier ID. Here's how the function definition should look:

```
USE TSQLV6;
GO
CREATE OR ALTER FUNCTION Production.TopProducts
  (@supid AS INT, @n AS INT)
  RETURNS TABLE
AS
RETURN
  SELECT TOP (@n) productid, productname, unitprice
  FROM Production.Products
  WHERE supplierid = @supid
  ORDER BY unitprice DESC;
GO
```

Alternatively, you can use the *OFFSET-FETCH* filter. You replace the inner query in the function with the following one:

```
SELECT productid, productname, unitprice
FROM Production.Products
WHERE supplierid = @supid
ORDER BY unitprice DESC
OFFSET 0 ROWS FETCH NEXT @n ROWS ONLY;
```

Exercise 6-2

In this exercise, you write a query against the *Production.Suppliers* table and use the *CROSS APPLY* operator to apply the function you defined in the previous step to each supplier. Your query is supposed to return the two most expensive products for each supplier. Here's the solution query:

```
SELECT S.supplierid, S.companyname, P.productid, P.productname, P.unitprice
FROM Production.Suppliers AS S
  CROSS APPLY Production.TopProducts(S.supplierid, 2) AS P;
```

CHAPTER 6

Set operators

S et operators are operators that combine rows from two query result sets (or multisets). Some of the operators remove duplicates from the result, and hence return a set, whereas others don't, and hence return a multiset. T-SQL supports the following operators: *UNION*, *UNION ALL*, *INTERSECT*, and *EXCEPT*. In this chapter, I first introduce the general form and requirements of these operators, and then I describe each operator in detail.

The general form of a query with a set operator is as follows:

```
Input Query1
<set_operator>
Input Query2
[ORDER BY ...];
```

A set operator compares complete rows between the results of the two input queries involved. Whether a row will be returned in the result of the operator depends on the outcome of the comparison and the operator used. Because a set operator expects multisets as inputs, the two queries involved cannot have *ORDER BY* clauses. Remember that a query with an *ORDER BY* clause does not return a multiset—it returns an ordered result. However, although the queries involved cannot have *ORDER BY* clauses, you can optionally add an *ORDER BY* clause to the result of the operator. If you're wondering how you apply a set operator to queries with *TOP* and *OFFSET-FETCH* filters, I'll get to this later in the chapter, in the section "Circumventing unsupported logical phases."

In terms of logical-query processing, each of the individual queries can have all logical-query processing phases except for a presentation *ORDER BY*, as I just explained. The operator is applied to the results of the two queries, and the outer *ORDER BY* clause (if one exists) is applied to the result of the operator.

The two input queries must produce results with the same number of columns, and corresponding columns must have compatible data types. By *compatible data types*, I mean that the data type that is lower in terms of data-type precedence must be implicitly convertible to the higher data type. Of course, you also can explicitly convert the data type of a column in one query to the data type of the corresponding column in the other query using the *CAST* or *CONVERT* function.

The names of the columns in the result are determined by the first query; therefore, if you need to assign aliases to result columns, you should assign those in the first query. Still, it's considered a best practice to make sure that all columns have names in both queries, and that the names of the corresponding columns are the same.

Interestingly, when a set operator compares rows between the two inputs, it doesn't use an equality-based comparison; rather, it uses a distinctness-based comparison. The semantics of distinctness-based comparisons are the same as the ones used by a standard predicate called the *distinct predicate*. This predicate treats *NULLs* just like non-*NULL* values for comparison purposes. Just like the value 5 is not distinct from the value 5, one *NULL* is not distinct from another *NULL*. And just like the value 5 is distinct from the value 13, a *NULL* is distinct from 13. I'll demonstrate the importance of this point later in the chapter.

The SQL standard supports two "flavors" of each operator—*DISTINCT* (the default) and *ALL*. The *DISTINCT* flavor eliminates duplicates and returns a set. *ALL* doesn't attempt to remove duplicates and therefore returns a multiset. All three operators in T-SQL support an implicit distinct version, but only the *UNION* operator supports the *ALL* version. In terms of syntax, T-SQL doesn't allow you to specify the *DISTINCT* clause explicitly. Instead, it's implied when you don't specify *ALL*. I'll provide alternatives to the missing *INTERSECT ALL* and *EXCEPT ALL* operators in the "The *INTERSECT ALL* operator" and "The *EXCEPT ALL* operator" sections later in this chapter.

The *UNION* operator

The *UNION* operator unifies the results of two input queries. If a row appears in any of the input sets, it will appear in the result of the *UNION* operator. T-SQL supports both the *UNION ALL* and *UNION* (implicit *DISTINCT*) flavors of the *UNION* operator.

Figure 6-1 illustrates the *UNION* operator. The shaded area represents the result of the operator. The nonshaded areas reflect the fact that the inputs—and hence the result—don't have to include all columns of the original tables (in relational terms, all attributes of the original relations).

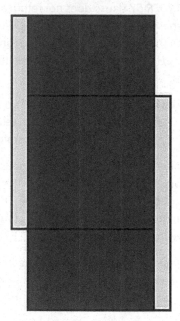

FIGURE 6-1 The *UNION* operator

The *UNION ALL* operator

The *UNION ALL* operator unifies the two input query results without attempting to remove duplicates from the result. Assuming that *Query1* returns *m* rows and *Query2* returns *n* rows, *Query1 UNION ALL Query2* returns *m* + *n* rows.

For example, the following code uses the *UNION ALL* operator to unify employee locations and customer locations:

```
USE TSQLV6;

SELECT country, region, city FROM HR.Employees
UNION ALL
SELECT country, region, city FROM Sales.Customers;
```

The result has 100 rows—9 from the *Employees* table and 91 from the *Customers* table—and is shown here in abbreviated form:

```
country            region             city
---------------    ---------------    ---------------
USA                WA                 Seattle
USA                WA                 Tacoma
USA                WA                 Kirkland
USA                WA                 Redmond
UK                 NULL               London
UK                 NULL               London
UK                 NULL               London
...
Finland            NULL               Oulu
Brazil             SP                 Resende
USA                WA                 Seattle
Finland            NULL               Helsinki
Poland             NULL               Warszawa

(100 rows affected)
```

Because *UNION ALL* doesn't eliminate duplicates, the result is a multiset and not a set. The same row can appear multiple times in the result, as is the case with *(UK, NULL, London)* in the result of this query.

The *UNION (DISTINCT)* operator

The *UNION* (implicit *DISTINCT*) operator unifies the results of the two queries and eliminates duplicates. Note that if a row appears in both input sets, it will appear only once in the result; in other words, the result is a set and not a multiset.

For example, the following code returns distinct locations that are either employee locations or customer locations:

```
SELECT country, region, city FROM HR.Employees
UNION
SELECT country, region, city FROM Sales.Customers;
```

This code returns 71 distinct rows (unlike the 100 rows in the result with the duplicates), as shown here in abbreviated form:

```
country          region           city
---------------  ---------------  ---------------
Argentina        NULL             Buenos Aires
Austria          NULL             Graz
Austria          NULL             Salzburg
Belgium          NULL             Bruxelles
Belgium          NULL             Charleroi
...
USA              WY               Lander
Venezuela        DF               Caracas
Venezuela        Lara             Barquisimeto
Venezuela        Nueva Esparta    I. de Margarita
Venezuela        Táchira          San Cristóbal

(71 rows affected)
```

So when should you use *UNION ALL* and when should you use *UNION*? If duplicates are possible in the unified result and you do not need to return them, use *UNION*. Otherwise, use *UNION ALL*. If duplicates cannot exist when unifying the inputs, *UNION* and *UNION ALL* will return the same result. However, in such a case I recommend you use *UNION ALL* so that you don't pay the unnecessary performance penalty related to checking for duplicates.

The *INTERSECT* operator

The *INTERSECT* operator returns only the rows that are common to the results of the two input queries. Figure 6-2 illustrates this operator.

FIGURE 6-2 The *INTERSECT* operator

The *INTERSECT* (*DISTINCT*) operator

The *INTERSECT* operator (implied *DISTINCT*) returns only distinct rows that appear in both input query results. As long as a row appears at least once in both query results, it's returned only once in the operator's result.

For example, the following code returns distinct locations that are both employee locations and customer locations:

```
SELECT country, region, city FROM HR.Employees
INTERSECT
SELECT country, region, city FROM Sales.Customers;
```

This query returns the following output:

```
country          region           city
---------------  ---------------  ----------------
UK               NULL             London
USA              WA               Kirkland
USA              WA               Seattle
```

I mentioned earlier that when these operators compare rows, they use distinctness-based comparison semantics (implicitly using what the SQL standard calls the distinct predicate). For example, observe that the location *(UK, NULL, London)* appears in the result of the intersection. If instead of using the *INTERSECT* operator you use an alternative tool like an inner join or a correlated subquery, you need to add special treatment for *NULLs*—for example, assuming the alias *E* for *Employees* and *C* for *Customers*, using the predicate *E.region = C.region OR (E.region IS NULL AND C.region IS NULL)*. Note that if you're using SQL Server 2022 or later, instead of adding special *NULL* treatment, you can explicitly use the distinct predicate, which I described in Chapter 2. Either way, using the *INTERSECT* operator, the solution is much simpler—you don't need to explicitly compare corresponding attributes, and you don't need to add special treatment for *NULLs*.

The *INTERSECT ALL* operator

The SQL standard supports an *ALL* flavor of the *INTERSECT* operator, but this flavor has not been implemented in T-SQL. However, you can write your own logical equivalent with T-SQL.

Remember the meaning of the *ALL* keyword in the *UNION ALL* operator: it returns all duplicate rows. Similarly, the keyword *ALL* in the *INTERSECT ALL* operator means that duplicate intersections will not be removed. *INTERSECT ALL* returns the number of duplicate rows matching the lower of the counts in both input multisets. It's as if this operator looks for matches for each occurrence of each row. If there are x occurrences of a row R in the first input multiset and y occurrences of R in the second, R appears *minimum(x, y)* times in the result. For example, the location *(UK, NULL, London)* appears four times in *Employees* and six times in *Customers*; hence, *INTERSECT ALL* returns four occurrences in the output.

Even though T-SQL does not support a built-in *INTERSECT ALL* operator, you can write your own alternative solution that produces the same result. You can use the *ROW_NUMBER* function to number the occurrences of each row in each input query. To achieve this, specify all participating attributes in the *PARTITION BY* clause of the function, and use *(SELECT <any constant>)* in the *ORDER BY* clause of the function. You do this since *ORDER BY* is mandatory in the *ROW_NUMBER* function's *OVER* clause and you want to indicate that order doesn't matter. Window functions, including the *ROW_NUMBER* function, are covered in Chapter 7, "T-SQL for data analysis."

> **Tip** A window order clause is mandatory in window ranking functions like *ROW_NUMBER*. As a trick, when you don't care about ordering, use *ORDER BY (SELECT <constant>)* as the window order clause. Microsoft SQL Server realizes in such a case that order doesn't matter.

Then apply the *INTERSECT* operator between the two queries with the *ROW_NUMBER* function. Because the occurrences of the rows are numbered, the intersection is based on the row numbers in addition to the original attributes. For example, in the *Employees* table the four occurrences of the location *(UK, NULL, London)* are numbered 1 through 4. In the *Customers* table the six occurrences of the same row are numbered 1 through 6. Occurrences 1 through 4 intersect between the two.

Here's the complete solution code:

```
SELECT
  ROW_NUMBER()
    OVER(PARTITION BY country, region, city
         ORDER     BY (SELECT 0)) AS rownum,
  country, region, city
FROM HR.Employees

INTERSECT

SELECT
  ROW_NUMBER()
    OVER(PARTITION BY country, region, city
         ORDER     BY (SELECT 0)),
  country, region, city
FROM Sales.Customers;
```

This code produces the following output.

rownum	country	region	city
1	UK	NULL	London
1	USA	WA	Kirkland
1	USA	WA	Seattle
2	UK	NULL	London
3	UK	NULL	London
4	UK	NULL	London

The standard *INTERSECT ALL* operator is not supposed to return any row numbers. To exclude those from the output, define a named table expression based on this query, and in the outer query select only the attributes you want to return. Here's the complete solution code:

```
WITH INTERSECT_ALL
AS
(
  SELECT
    ROW_NUMBER()
      OVER(PARTITION BY country, region, city
           ORDER    BY (SELECT 0)) AS rownum,
    country, region, city
  FROM HR.Employees

  INTERSECT

  SELECT
    ROW_NUMBER()
      OVER(PARTITION BY country, region, city
           ORDER    BY (SELECT 0)),
    country, region, city
  FROM Sales.Customers
)
SELECT country, region, city
FROM INTERSECT_ALL;
```

This code generates the following output:

```
country            region             city
-----------------  -----------------  ---------
UK                 NULL               London
USA                WA                 Kirkland
USA                WA                 Seattle
UK                 NULL               London
UK                 NULL               London
UK                 NULL               London
```

The *EXCEPT* operator

The *EXCEPT* operator implements a minus, or a set difference, operation. It operates on the results of two input queries and returns rows that appear in the first input but not the second. Figure 6-3 illustrates this operator.

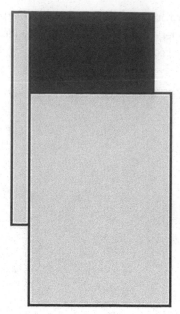

FIGURE 6-3 The *EXCEPT* operator

The *EXCEPT* (*DISTINCT*) operator

The *EXCEPT* operator (implied *DISTINCT*) returns only distinct rows that appear in the first set but not the second. In other words, a row is returned once in the output as long as it appears at least once in the first input multiset and zero times in the second. Note that unlike *UNION* and *INTERSECT*, *EXCEPT* is noncommutative; that is, the order in which you specify the two input queries matters.

For example, the following code returns distinct locations that are employee locations but not customer locations:

```
SELECT country, region, city FROM HR.Employees
EXCEPT
SELECT country, region, city FROM Sales.Customers;
```

This query returns the following two locations:

```
country          region           city
---------------  ---------------  ---------------
USA              WA               Redmond
USA              WA               Tacoma
```

The following query returns distinct locations that are customer locations but not employee locations:

```
SELECT country, region, city FROM Sales.Customers
EXCEPT
SELECT country, region, city FROM HR.Employees;
```

This query returns 66 locations, shown here in abbreviated form:

```
country           region            city
---------------   ---------------   ---------------
Argentina         NULL              Buenos Aires
Austria           NULL              Graz
Austria           NULL              Salzburg
Belgium           NULL              Bruxelles
Belgium           NULL              Charleroi
...
USA               WY                Lander
Venezuela         DF                Caracas
Venezuela         Lara              Barquisimeto
Venezuela         Nueva Esparta     I. de Margarita
Venezuela         Táchira           San Cristóbal

(66 rows affected)
```

Naturally, there are alternatives to the *EXCEPT* operator. One is an outer join that filters only outer rows, and another is to use the *NOT EXISTS* predicate. However, recall that set operators use distinctness-based comparison semantics, and the comparison between corresponding columns is implied. With joins and subqueries, you need to be explicit about comparisons and you also need to explicitly add special treatment for *NULLs*. Again, if you're using SQL Server 2022 or later, when using joins or subqueries, you can use the explicit distinct predicate, which I described in Chapter 2, to avoid special *NULL* treatment. Either way, using the *EXCEPT* operator avoids the need for explicit comparisons.

The *EXCEPT ALL* operator

The *EXCEPT ALL* operator is similar to the *EXCEPT* operator, but it also takes into account the number of occurrences of each row. If a row R appears x times in the first multiset and y times in the second, and $x > y$, R will appear $x - y$ times in *Query1 EXCEPT ALL Query2*. In other words, *EXCEPT ALL* returns only occurrences of a row from the first multiset that do not have a corresponding occurrence in the second.

T-SQL does not provide a built-in *EXCEPT ALL* operator, but you can provide an alternative of your own similar to how you handled *INTERSECT ALL*. Namely, add a *ROW_NUMBER* calculation to each of the input queries to number the occurrences of the rows, and use the *EXCEPT* operator between the two input queries. Only occurrences that don't have matches will be returned.

The following code returns occurrences of employee locations that have no corresponding occurrences of customer locations:

```
WITH EXCEPT_ALL
AS
(
  SELECT
    ROW_NUMBER()
      OVER(PARTITION BY country, region, city
           ORDER     BY (SELECT 0)) AS rownum,
    country, region, city
  FROM HR.Employees

  EXCEPT
```

```
SELECT
  ROW_NUMBER()
    OVER(PARTITION BY country, region, city
         ORDER     BY (SELECT 0)),
    country, region, city
  FROM Sales.Customers
)
SELECT country, region, city
FROM EXCEPT_ALL;
```

This query returns the following output:

```
country          region           city
---------------  ---------------  ---------------
USA              WA               Redmond
USA              WA               Tacoma
USA              WA               Seattle
```

Precedence

SQL defines precedence among set operators. The *INTERSECT* operator precedes *UNION* and *EXCEPT*, and *UNION* and *EXCEPT* are evaluated in order of appearance. Using the *ALL* variant doesn't change the precedence. In a query that contains multiple set operators, first *INTERSECT* operators are evaluated, and then operators with the same precedence are evaluated based on their order of appearance.

Consider the following code:

```
SELECT country, region, city FROM Production.Suppliers
EXCEPT
SELECT country, region, city FROM HR.Employees
INTERSECT
SELECT country, region, city FROM Sales.Customers;
```

Because *INTERSECT* precedes *EXCEPT*, the *INTERSECT* operator is evaluated first, even though it appears second in the code. The meaning of this query is "locations that are supplier locations, but not (locations that are both employee and customer locations)."

This query returns the following output:

```
country          region           city
---------------  ---------------  ---------------
Australia        NSW              Sydney
Australia        Victoria         Melbourne
Brazil           NULL             Sao Paulo
Canada           Québec           Montréal
Canada           Québec           Ste-Hyacinthe
Denmark          NULL             Lyngby
Finland          NULL             Lappeenranta
France           NULL             Annecy
France           NULL             Montceau
France           NULL             Paris
Germany          NULL             Berlin
```

Germany	NULL	Cuxhaven
Germany	NULL	Frankfurt
Italy	NULL	Ravenna
Italy	NULL	Salerno
Japan	NULL	Osaka
Japan	NULL	Tokyo
Netherlands	NULL	Zaandam
Norway	NULL	Sandvika
Singapore	NULL	Singapore
Spain	Asturias	Oviedo
Sweden	NULL	Göteborg
Sweden	NULL	Stockholm
UK	NULL	Manchester
USA	LA	New Orleans
USA	MA	Boston
USA	MI	Ann Arbor
USA	OR	Bend

(28 rows affected)

To control the order of evaluation of set operators, use parentheses, because they have the highest precedence. Also, using parentheses increases the readability, thus reducing the chance for errors. For example, if you want to return "(locations that are supplier locations but not employee locations) and that are also customer locations," use the following code:

```
(SELECT country, region, city FROM Production.Suppliers
  EXCEPT
  SELECT country, region, city FROM HR.Employees)
INTERSECT
SELECT country, region, city FROM Sales.Customers;
```

This query returns the following output:

country	region	city
Canada	Québec	Montréal
France	NULL	Paris
Germany	NULL	Berlin

Circumventing unsupported logical phases

The individual queries that are used as inputs to a set operator support all logical-query processing phases (such as table operators, *WHERE*, *GROUP BY*, and *HAVING*) except for *ORDER BY*. However, only the *ORDER BY* phase is allowed on the result of the operator.

What if you need to apply other logical phases besides *ORDER BY* to the result of the operator? This is not supported directly as part of the query that applies the operator, but you can easily circumvent this restriction by using table expressions. Define a named table expression based on a query with a set operator, and apply any logical-query processing phases you want in the outer query. For example, the following query returns the number of distinct locations that are either employee or customer locations in each country:

```
SELECT country, COUNT(*) AS numlocations
FROM (SELECT country, region, city FROM HR.Employees
      UNION
      SELECT country, region, city FROM Sales.Customers) AS U
GROUP BY country;
```

This query returns the following output:

```
country          numlocations
---------------  ------------
Argentina        1
Austria          2
Belgium          2
Brazil           4
Canada           3
Denmark          2
Finland          2
France           9
Germany          11
Ireland          1
Italy            3
Mexico           1
Norway           1
Poland           1
Portugal         1
Spain            3
Sweden           2
Switzerland      2
UK               2
USA              14
Venezuela        4
```

```
(21 rows affected)
```

This query demonstrates how to group the result of a *UNION* operator; similarly, you can, of course, apply other logical-query phases in the outer query.

Remember that the *ORDER BY* clause is not allowed in the input queries. What if you need to restrict the number of rows in those queries with the *TOP* or *OFFSET-FETCH* filter? Again, you can resolve this problem with table expressions. Recall that an *ORDER BY* clause is allowed in an inner query with *TOP* or *OFFSET-FETCH*. In such a case, the *ORDER BY* clause serves only the filtering-related purpose and has no presentation meaning. For example, the following code uses *TOP* queries to return the two most recent orders for employees 3 and 5:

```
SELECT empid, orderid, orderdate
FROM (SELECT TOP (2) empid, orderid, orderdate
      FROM Sales.Orders
      WHERE empid = 3
      ORDER BY orderdate DESC, orderid DESC) AS D1
```

```
UNION ALL

SELECT empid, orderid, orderdate
FROM (SELECT TOP (2) empid, orderid, orderdate
      FROM Sales.Orders
      WHERE empid = 5
      ORDER BY orderdate DESC, orderid DESC) AS D2;
```

This query returns the following output:

```
empid       orderid     orderdate
----------- ----------- -----------
3           11063       2022-04-30
3           11057       2022-04-29
5           11043       2022-04-22
5           10954       2022-03-17
```

Conclusion

In this chapter, I covered the operators UNION, UNION ALL, EXCEPT, and INTERSECT. I explained that the SQL standard also supports operators called INTERSECT ALL and EXCEPT ALL and explained how to achieve similar functionality in T-SQL. Finally, I introduced precedence among set operators, and I explained how to circumvent unsupported logical-query processing phases by using table expressions.

Exercises

This section provides exercises to help you familiarize yourself with the subjects discussed in Chapter 6. All exercises require you to be connected to the sample database TSQLV6.

Exercise 1

Explain the difference between the UNION ALL and UNION operators. In what cases are the two equivalent? When they are equivalent, which one should you use?

Exercise 2

Write a query that generates a virtual auxiliary table of 10 numbers in the range 1 through 10 without using a looping construct or the GENERATE_SERIES function. You do not need to guarantee any presentation order of the rows in the output of your solution.

- Tables involved: None

- Desired output:

```
n
-----------
1
2
```

```
3
4
5
6
7
8
9
10

(10 rows affected)
```

Exercise 3

Write a query that returns customer and employee pairs that had order activity in January 2022 but not in February 2022.

- Table involved: *Sales.Orders* table

- Desired output:

```
custid      empid
----------- -----------
1           1
3           3
5           8
5           9
6           9
7           6
9           1
12          2
16          7
17          1
20          7
24          8
25          1
26          3
32          4
38          9
39          3
40          2
41          2
42          2
44          8
47          3
47          4
47          8
49          7
55          2
55          3
56          6
59          8
63          8
64          9
65          3
65          8
66          5
67          5
70          3
```

```
71          2
75          1
76          2
76          5
80          1
81          1
81          3
81          4
82          6
84          1
84          3
84          4
88          7
89          4
```

```
(50 rows affected)
```

Exercise 4

Write a query that returns customer and employee pairs that had order activity in both January 2022 and February 2022.

- Table involved: *Sales.Orders*

- Desired output:

```
custid      empid
----------- -----------
20          3
39          9
46          5
67          1
71          4
```

```
(5 rows affected)
```

Exercise 5

Write a query that returns customer and employee pairs that had order activity in both January 2022 and February 2022 but not in 2021.

- Table involved: *Sales.Orders*

- Desired output:

```
custid      empid
----------- -----------
67          1
46          5
```

```
(2 rows affected)
```

Exercise 6

You are given the following query:

```
SELECT country, region, city
FROM HR.Employees

UNION ALL

SELECT country, region, city
FROM Production.Suppliers;
```

You are asked to add logic to the query so that it guarantees that the rows from *Employees* are returned in the output before the rows from *Suppliers*. Also, within each segment, the rows should be sorted by country, region, and city.

- Tables involved: *HR.Employees* and *Production.Suppliers*

- Desired output:

```
country           region            city
----------------  ----------------  ----------------
UK                NULL              London
UK                NULL              London
UK                NULL              London
UK                NULL              London
USA               WA                Kirkland
USA               WA                Redmond
USA               WA                Seattle
USA               WA                Seattle
USA               WA                Tacoma
Australia         NSW               Sydney
Australia         Victoria          Melbourne
Brazil            NULL              Sao Paulo
Canada            Québec            Montréal
Canada            Québec            Ste-Hyacinthe
Denmark           NULL              Lyngby
Finland           NULL              Lappeenranta
France            NULL              Annecy
France            NULL              Montceau
France            NULL              Paris
Germany           NULL              Berlin
Germany           NULL              Cuxhaven
Germany           NULL              Frankfurt
Italy             NULL              Ravenna
Italy             NULL              Salerno
Japan             NULL              Osaka
Japan             NULL              Tokyo
Netherlands       NULL              Zaandam
Norway            NULL              Sandvika
Singapore         NULL              Singapore
Spain             Asturias          Oviedo
Sweden            NULL              Göteborg
Sweden            NULL              Stockholm
UK                NULL              London
UK                NULL              Manchester
USA               LA                New Orleans
USA               MA                Boston
USA               MI                Ann Arbor
USA               OR                Bend
```

(38 rows affected)

Solutions

This section provides solutions to the Chapter 6 exercises.

Exercise 1

The *UNION ALL* operator unifies the two input query result sets and doesn't remove duplicates from the result. The *UNION* operator (implied *DISTINCT*) also unifies the two input query result sets, but it does remove duplicates from the result.

The two have different meanings when the result can potentially have duplicates. They have an equivalent meaning when the result can't have duplicates, such as when you're unifying disjoint sets (for example, sales 2021 with sales 2022).

When they do have the same meaning, you need to use *UNION ALL* by default. That's to avoid paying unnecessary performance penalties for the work involved in removing duplicates when they don't exist.

Exercise 2

T-SQL supports a *SELECT* statement based on constants with no *FROM* clause. Such a *SELECT* statement returns a table with a single row. For example, the following statement returns a row with a single column called *n* with the value *1*:

SELECT 1 AS n;

Here's the output of this statement:

```
n
-----------
1

(1 row affected)
```

By using the *UNION ALL* operator, you can unify the result sets of multiple statements like the one just mentioned, each returning a row with a different number in the range 1 through 10, like the following:

```
SELECT 1 AS n
UNION ALL SELECT 2
UNION ALL SELECT 3
UNION ALL SELECT 4
UNION ALL SELECT 5
UNION ALL SELECT 6
UNION ALL SELECT 7
UNION ALL SELECT 8
UNION ALL SELECT 9
UNION ALL SELECT 10;
```

> **Tip** T-SQL supports a standard feature called *table value constructor*, which employs an enhanced version of the *VALUES* clause, which you might be familiar with in the context of the *INSERT* statement. The *VALUES* clause is not restricted to representing a single row; it can represent multiple rows. Also, the *VALUES* clause is not restricted to *INSERT* statements but can be used to define a table expression with rows based on self-contained expressions.
>
> As an example, here's how you can use a table value constructor to provide a solution to this exercise instead of using the *UNION ALL* operator:
>
> ```
> SELECT n
> FROM (VALUES(1),(2),(3),(4),(5),(6),(7),(8),(9),(10)) AS Nums(n);
> ```
>
> I provide details about the *VALUES* clause and the table value constructor in Chapter 8, "Data modification," as part of the discussion of the *INSERT* statement.

Exercise 3

You can solve this exercise by using the *EXCEPT* set operator. The first input is a query that returns customer and employee pairs that had order activity in January 2022. The second input is a query that returns customer and employee pairs that had order activity in February 2022. Here's the solution query:

```
USE TSQLV6;

SELECT custid, empid
FROM Sales.Orders
WHERE orderdate >= '20220101' AND orderdate < '20220201'

EXCEPT

SELECT custid, empid
FROM Sales.Orders
WHERE orderdate >= '20220201' AND orderdate < '20220301';
```

Exercise 4

Whereas Exercise 3 requested customer and employee pairs that had activity in one period but not another, this exercise concerns customer and employee pairs that had activity in both periods. So this time, instead of using the *EXCEPT* operator, you need to use the *INTERSECT* operator, like this:

```
SELECT custid, empid
FROM Sales.Orders
WHERE orderdate >= '20220101' AND orderdate < '20220201'
```

```
INTERSECT

SELECT custid, empid
FROM Sales.Orders
WHERE orderdate >= '20220201' AND orderdate < '20220301';
```

Exercise 5

This exercise requires you to combine set operators. To return customer and employee pairs that had order activity in both January 2022 and February 2022, you need to use the *INTERSECT* operator, as in Exercise 4. To exclude customer and employee pairs that had order activity in 2021 from the result, you need to use the *EXCEPT* operator between the result and a third query. The solution query looks like this:

```
SELECT custid, empid
FROM Sales.Orders
WHERE orderdate >= '20220101' AND orderdate < '20220201'

INTERSECT

SELECT custid, empid
FROM Sales.Orders
WHERE orderdate >= '20220201' AND orderdate < '20220301'

EXCEPT

SELECT custid, empid
FROM Sales.Orders
WHERE orderdate >= '20210101' AND orderdate < '20220101';
```

Keep in mind that the *INTERSECT* operator precedes *EXCEPT*. In this case, the default precedence is also the precedence you want, so you don't need to intervene by using parentheses. But you might prefer to add them for clarity, as shown here:

```
(SELECT custid, empid
 FROM Sales.Orders
 WHERE orderdate >= '20220101' AND orderdate < '20220201'

 INTERSECT

 SELECT custid, empid
 FROM Sales.Orders
 WHERE orderdate >= '20220201' AND orderdate < '20220301')

EXCEPT

SELECT custid, empid
FROM Sales.Orders
WHERE orderdate >= '20210101' AND orderdate < '20220101';
```

Exercise 6

The problem here is that the individual queries are not allowed to have *ORDER BY* clauses, and for a good reason. You can solve the problem by adding a result column based on a constant to each of the queries involved in the operator (call it *sortcol*). In the query against *Employees*, specify a smaller constant value than the one you specify in the query against *Suppliers*. Define a table expression based on the query with the operator, and in the *ORDER BY* clause of the outer query, specify *sortcol* as the first sort column, followed by *country, region*, and *city*. Here's the complete solution query:

```
SELECT country, region, city
FROM (SELECT 1 AS sortcol, country, region, city
      FROM HR.Employees

      UNION ALL

      SELECT 2, country, region, city
      FROM Production.Suppliers) AS D
ORDER BY sortcol, country, region, city;
```

CHAPTER 7

T-SQL for data analysis

This chapter focuses on using T-SQL for data analysis needs. It starts with the powerful window functions, which you can use to apply data-analysis calculations in a flexible and efficient manner. It then covers techniques for pivoting and unpivoting data. Pivoting rotates data from a state of rows to columns, and unpivoting rotates data from columns to rows, similar to pivot tables in Excel. The chapter then continues with a discussion about *grouping sets*, which are the sets of expressions that you group the data by. It covers techniques for defining multiple grouping sets in the same query. The chapter finishes with coverage of handling of time series data.

Window functions

A *window function* is a function that, for each row, computes a scalar result value based on a calculation against a subset of the rows from the underlying query. The subset of rows is known as a *window* and is based on a window descriptor that relates to the current row. The syntax for window functions uses a clause called *OVER*, in which you provide the window specification.

If this sounds too technical, simply think of the need to perform a calculation against a set and return a single value. A classic example is aggregate calculations—such as *SUM*, *COUNT*, and *AVG*—but there are others as well, such as ranking and offset functions. You're familiar already with a couple of ways to apply aggregate calculations—one is by using grouped queries, and another is by using sub-queries. However, both options have shortcomings that window functions elegantly resolve.

> **Note** If the upcoming explanations about the design of window functions seem a bit overwhelming, bear with me until I show code samples, which should help clarify things. After you see a couple of code samples, you might want to reread the next several paragraphs.

Grouped queries do provide insights into new information in the form of aggregates, but they also cause you to lose something—the detail. After you group the rows, all computations in the query have to be done in the context of the defined groups. Often, you need to perform calculations that involve both detail and aggregate elements. Window functions are not limited in the same way. A window function is evaluated per detailed row, and it's applied to a subset of rows that is derived from the underlying query result set. The result of the window function is a scalar value, which is added as another column to the query result. In other words, unlike grouped functions, window functions don't cause you to lose the detail. For example, suppose you want to query order values and return the current order value and the percent it constitutes out of the customer total. If you group by the customer, you can get only the customer total. With a window function, you can return the customer total in addition to the detail order value, and you can even compute the percent of the current order value out of the customer total. I'll demonstrate the code to achieve this later in the chapter.

As for subqueries, you can use them to apply a scalar aggregate calculation against a set, but their starting point is a fresh view of the data rather than the underlying query result set. Suppose the underlying query has table operators, filters, and other query elements; those do not affect what a subquery sees as its starting point. If you need the subquery to apply to the underlying query result set as its starting point, you need to repeat all the underlying query logic in the subquery. In contrast, a window function is applied to a subset of rows from the underlying query's result set—not a fresh view of the data. Therefore, anything you add to the underlying query is automatically applicable to all window functions used in the query. If you want, you can further restrict the window.

Another benefit of using window functions is that you gain the ability to define order, when applicable, as part of the specification of the calculation. This does not conflict with relational aspects of the result. That is, order is defined for the calculation and not confused with presentation ordering. The ordering specification for the window function, if applicable, is different from the ordering specification for presentation. If you don't include a presentation ORDER BY clause, you have no assurances that the result will be returned in a particular order. If you do decide to force a certain presentation ordering, the resulting ordering can be different than the ordering for the window function.

Following is an example of a query against the *Sales.EmpOrders* view in the *TSQLV6* database that uses a window aggregate function to compute the running-total values for each employee and month:

```
USE TSQLV6;

SELECT empid, ordermonth, val,
    SUM(val) OVER(PARTITION BY empid
                  ORDER BY ordermonth
                  ROWS BETWEEN UNBOUNDED PRECEDING
                         AND CURRENT ROW) AS runval
FROM Sales.EmpOrders;
```

Here's the output of this query, shown in abbreviated form:

```
empid  ordermonth   val       runval
------ -----------  --------  ----------
1      2020-07-01   1614.88   1614.88
1      2020-08-01   5555.90   7170.78
1      2020-09-01   6651.00   13821.78
1      2020-10-01   3933.18   17754.96
1      2020-11-01   9562.65   27317.61
...
2      2020-07-01   1176.00   1176.00
2      2020-08-01   1814.00   2990.00
2      2020-09-01   2950.80   5940.80
```

```
2       2020-10-01    5164.00    11104.80
2       2020-11-01    4614.58    15719.38
...
```

```
(192 rows affected)
```

There are up to three parts in the definition of a window function, which you specify in a clause called *OVER*: the window-partition clause, window-order clause, and window-frame clause. An empty *OVER()* clause represents the entire underlying query's result set. Then anything you add to the window specification essentially restricts the window.

The window-partition clause (*PARTITION BY*) restricts the window to the subset of rows that have the same values in the partitioning columns as in the current row. In the last query, the window is partitioned by *empid*. For an underlying row with employee ID 1, the window exposed to the function filters only the rows where the employee ID is 1.

The window-order clause (*ORDER BY*) defines ordering, but don't confuse this with presentation ordering. In a window aggregate function, window ordering supports a frame specification. In a window ranking function, window ordering gives meaning to the rank. In our example, the window ordering is based on *ordermonth*.

A window-frame clause (*ROWS BETWEEN <top delimiter> AND <bottom delimiter>*) filters a frame, or a subset, of rows from the window partition between the two specified delimiters. In this example, the frame is defined with no low boundary point (*UNBOUNDED PRECEDING*) and extends until the current row (*CURRENT ROW*). In addition to the window-frame unit *ROWS*, there's a unit called *RANGE*, but it's implemented in T-SQL in a limited capacity.

Putting all these together, you get the running-total values for each employee and month from the function in the example.

Note that because the starting point of a window function is the underlying query's result set, and the underlying query's result set is generated only when you reach the *SELECT* phase, window functions are allowed only in the *SELECT* and *ORDER BY* clauses of a query. Mostly, you'll use window functions in the *SELECT* clause. If you need to refer to a window function in an earlier logical-query processing phase (such as *WHERE*), you need to use a table expression. You specify the window function in the *SELECT* list of the inner query and assign it with an alias. Then, in the outer query, you can refer to that alias anywhere you like.

The windowing concept can take some getting used to, but when you're comfortable with it, you'll realize it's immensely powerful. Beyond being used for the obvious data-analysis calculations, window functions can be used to perform a variety of tasks, typically more elegantly and more efficiently than with alternative methods.

The following sections cover ranking, offset, and aggregate window functions. Because this book is about fundamentals, I will not get into certain topics here. Those topics include the optimization of window functions, distribution functions, and the *RANGE* window-frame unit. For details about those items, see my book on the topic, *T-SQL Window Functions, 2nd Ed* (Microsoft Press, 2019, ISBN: 978-0135861448).

Ranking window functions

You use ranking window functions to rank each row with respect to others in the window. T-SQL supports four ranking functions: *ROW_NUMBER*, *RANK*, *DENSE_RANK*, and *NTILE*. The following query demonstrates the use of these functions:

```
SELECT orderid, custid, val,
  ROW_NUMBER() OVER(ORDER BY val) AS rownum,
  RANK()       OVER(ORDER BY val) AS rank,
  DENSE_RANK() OVER(ORDER BY val) AS dense_rank,
  NTILE(10)    OVER(ORDER BY val) AS ntile
FROM Sales.OrderValues
ORDER BY val;
```

This query generates the following output, shown here in abbreviated form:

orderid	custid	val	rownum	rank	dense_rank	ntile
10782	12	12.50	1	1	1	1
10807	27	18.40	2	2	2	1
10586	66	23.80	3	3	3	1
10767	76	28.00	4	4	4	1
10898	54	30.00	5	5	5	1
10900	88	33.75	6	6	6	1
10883	48	36.00	7	7	7	1
11051	41	36.00	8	7	7	1
10815	71	40.00	9	9	8	1
10674	38	45.00	10	10	9	1
...						
10691	63	10164.80	821	821	786	10
10540	63	10191.70	822	822	787	10
10479	65	10495.60	823	823	788	10
10897	37	10835.24	824	824	789	10
10817	39	10952.85	825	825	790	10
10417	73	11188.40	826	826	791	10
10889	65	11380.00	827	827	792	10
11030	71	12615.05	828	828	793	10
10981	34	15810.00	829	829	794	10
10865	63	16387.50	830	830	795	10

```
(830 rows affected)
```

The *ROW_NUMBER* function assigns incremental sequential integers to the rows in the query result based on the mandatory window ordering. In the sample query, the ordering is based on the *val* column; therefore, you can see in the output that when the value increases, the row number increases as well. However, even when the ordering value doesn't increase, the row number still must increase. Therefore, if the *ROW_NUMBER* function's *ORDER BY* list is not unique, as in the preceding example, the query is nondeterministic—that is, more than one correct result is possible. For example, observe that two rows with the value 36.00 got the row numbers 7 and 8. Any arrangement of these row numbers would be considered correct. If you want to make a row number calculation deterministic, you need to add a tiebreaker to the *ORDER BY* list to make it unique. For example, you can add the *orderid* column.

As mentioned, the *ROW_NUMBER* function must produce unique values even when there are ties in the ordering values, making it nondeterministic when there are ties. If you want to produce the same rank value given the same ordering value, use the *RANK* or *DENSE_RANK* function instead. The difference between the two is that *RANK* reflects the count of rows that have a lower ordering value than the current row (plus 1), whereas *DENSE_RANK* reflects the count of distinct ordering values that are lower than the current row (plus 1). For example, in the sample query, a rank of 9 indicates eight rows have lower values. In the same row, a dense rank of 8 indicates seven rows that have distinct lower values.

You use the *NTILE* function to associate the rows in the result with tiles (equally sized groups of rows) by assigning a tile number to each row. You specify the number of tiles you are after and window ordering. The sample query has 830 rows and the request was for 10 tiles; therefore, the tile size is 83 (830 divided by 10). Window ordering is based on the *val* column. This means that the 83 rows with the lowest values are assigned tile number 1, the next 83 are assigned tile number 2, the next 83 are assigned tile number 3, and so on. If the number of rows can't be evenly divided by the number of tiles, an extra row is added to each of the first tiles from the remainder. For example, if 102 rows and five tiles were requested, the first two tiles would have 21 rows instead of 20.

Like all window functions, ranking functions support a window partition clause. Remember that window partitioning restricts the window to only those rows that have the same values in the partitioning attributes as in the current row. For example, the expression *ROW_NUMBER() OVER(PARTITION BY custid ORDER BY val)* assigns row numbers independently for each customer. Here's the expression in a query:

```
SELECT orderid, custid, val,
  ROW_NUMBER() OVER(PARTITION BY custid
                    ORDER BY val) AS rownum
FROM Sales.OrderValues
ORDER BY custid, val;
```

This query generates the following output, shown here in abbreviated form:

```
orderid     custid       val           rownum
----------- ------------ ------------- --------
10702       1            330.00        1
10952       1            471.20        2
10643       1            814.50        3
10835       1            845.80        4
10692       1            878.00        5
11011       1            933.50        6
10308       2            88.80         1
10759       2            320.00        2
10625       2            479.75        3
10926       2            514.40        4
10682       3            375.50        1
...

(830 rows affected)
```

Remember that window ordering has nothing to do with presentation ordering and does not change the nature of the result from being relational. If you need to guarantee presentation ordering, you have to add a presentation *ORDER BY* clause, as I did in the last two queries.

Window functions are logically evaluated as part of the *SELECT* list, before the *DISTINCT* clause is evaluated. If you're wondering why it matters, I'll explain this with an example. Currently, the *OrderValues* view has 830 rows with 795 distinct values in the *val* column. Consider the following query and its output, shown here in abbreviated form:

```
SELECT DISTINCT val, ROW_NUMBER() OVER(ORDER BY val) AS rownum
FROM Sales.OrderValues;
```

```
val         rownum
----------  -------
12.50       1
18.40       2
23.80       3
28.00       4
30.00       5
33.75       6
36.00       7
36.00       8
40.00       9
45.00       10
...
12615.05    828
15810.00    829
16387.50    830

(830 rows affected)
```

The *ROW_NUMBER* function is processed before the *DISTINCT* clause. First, unique row numbers are assigned to the 830 rows from the *OrderValues* view. Then the *DISTINCT* clause is processed—but there are no duplicate rows to remove. The *DISTINCT* clause has no effect here. If you want to assign row numbers to the 795 unique values, you need to come up with a different solution. For example, because the *GROUP BY* phase is processed before the *SELECT* phase, you can use the following query:

```
SELECT val, ROW_NUMBER() OVER(ORDER BY val) AS rownum
FROM Sales.OrderValues
GROUP BY val;
```

This query generates the following output, shown here in abbreviated form:

```
val         rownum
----------  -------
12.50       1
18.40       2
23.80       3
28.00       4
30.00       5
33.75       6
36.00       7
40.00       8
```

```
45.00      9
48.00     10
...
12615.05  793
15810.00  794
16387.50  795

(795 rows affected)
```

Here, the *GROUP BY* phase produces 795 groups for the 795 distinct values, and then the *SELECT* phase produces a row for each group, with *val* and a row number based on *val* order. You'll get to work on an alternative solution in this chapter's exercises.

Offset window functions

You use offset window functions to return an element from a row that is at a certain offset from the current row or at the beginning or end of a window frame. T-SQL supports two pairs of offset functions: *LAG* and *LEAD*, and *FIRST_VALUE* and *LAST_VALUE*.

The *LAG* and *LEAD* functions support window partitions and window-order clauses. There's no relevance to window framing here. You use these functions to obtain an element from a row that is at a certain offset from the current row within the partition, based on the indicated ordering. The *LAG* function looks before the current row, and the *LEAD* function looks ahead. The first argument to the functions (which is mandatory) is the element you want to return; the second argument (optional) is the offset (1 if not specified); the third argument (optional) is the default value to return if there is no row at the requested offset (which is *NULL* if not specified otherwise).

As an example, the following query returns order information from the *OrderValues* view. For each customer order, the query uses the *LAG* function to return the value of the previous customer's order and the *LEAD* function to return the value of the next customer's order:

```
SELECT custid, orderid, val,
  LAG(val)  OVER(PARTITION BY custid
                 ORDER BY orderdate, orderid) AS prevval,
  LEAD(val) OVER(PARTITION BY custid
                 ORDER BY orderdate, orderid) AS nextval
FROM Sales.OrderValues
ORDER BY custid, orderdate, orderid;
```

Here's the output of this query in abbreviated form:

```
custid  orderid  val       prevval   nextval
-------  -------  --------  --------  --------
1        10643    814.50    NULL      878.00
1        10692    878.00    814.50    330.00
1        10702    330.00    878.00    845.80
1        10835    845.80    330.00    471.20
1        10952    471.20    845.80    933.50
1        11011    933.50    471.20    NULL
2        10308    88.80     NULL      479.75
2        10625    479.75    88.80     320.00
```

2	10759	320.00	479.75	514.40
2	10926	514.40	320.00	NULL
3	10365	403.20	NULL	749.06
3	10507	749.06	403.20	1940.85
3	10535	1940.85	749.06	2082.00
3	10573	2082.00	1940.85	813.37
3	10677	813.37	2082.00	375.50
3	10682	375.50	813.37	660.00
3	10856	660.00	375.50	NULL

...

```
(830 rows affected)
```

Because you didn't indicate the offset, the functions assumed *1* by default. *LAG* obtained the value of the immediately previous customer's order, and *LEAD* obtained it from the next order. Also, because you didn't specify a third argument, *NULL* was assumed by default when there was no previous or next row. The expression *LAG(val, 3, 0)* obtains the value from three rows back and returns 0 if a row wasn't found.

In this example, I just returned the values from the previous and next orders, but normally you compute something based on the returned values. For example, you can compute the difference between the values of the current and previous customers' orders using *val – LAG(val) OVER(...)*. Or you can compute the difference between the current and next customers' orders using *val – LEAD(val) OVER(...)*.

You use the *FIRST_VALUE* and *LAST_VALUE* functions to return an element from the first and last rows in the window frame, respectively. Therefore, these functions support window-partition, window-order, and window-frame clauses. If you want the element from the first row in the window partition, use *FIRST_VALUE* with the window-frame extent *ROWS BETWEEN UNBOUNDED PRECEDING AND CURRENT ROW*. If you want the element from the last row in the window partition, use *LAST_VALUE* with the window-frame extent *ROWS BETWEEN CURRENT ROW AND UNBOUNDED FOLLOWING*. Note that if you specify *ORDER BY* without a window-frame unit (such as *ROWS*), the bottom delimiter will by default be *CURRENT ROW*, and clearly that's not what you want with *LAST_VALUE*. Also, for performance-related reasons that are beyond the scope of this book, you should be explicit about the window-frame extent even for *FIRST_VALUE*.

As an example, the following query uses the *FIRST_VALUE* function to return the value of the first customer's order and the *LAST_VALUE* function to return the value of the last customer's order:

```
SELECT custid, orderid, val,
  FIRST_VALUE(val) OVER(PARTITION BY custid
                        ORDER BY orderdate, orderid
                        ROWS BETWEEN UNBOUNDED PRECEDING
                                AND CURRENT ROW) AS firstval,
  LAST_VALUE(val)  OVER(PARTITION BY custid
                        ORDER BY orderdate, orderid
                        ROWS BETWEEN CURRENT ROW
                                AND UNBOUNDED FOLLOWING) AS lastval
FROM Sales.OrderValues
ORDER BY custid, orderdate, orderid;
```

This query generates the following output, shown here in abbreviated form:

```
custid  orderid  val      firstval  lastval
------- -------- -------- --------- --------
1       10643    814.50   814.50    933.50
1       10692    878.00   814.50    933.50
1       10702    330.00   814.50    933.50
1       10835    845.80   814.50    933.50
1       10952    471.20   814.50    933.50
1       11011    933.50   814.50    933.50
2       10308    88.80    88.80     514.40
2       10625    479.75   88.80     514.40
2       10759    320.00   88.80     514.40
2       10926    514.40   88.80     514.40
3       10365    403.20   403.20    660.00
3       10507    749.06   403.20    660.00
3       10535    1940.85  403.20    660.00
3       10573    2082.00  403.20    660.00
3       10677    813.37   403.20    660.00
3       10682    375.50   403.20    660.00
3       10856    660.00   403.20    660.00
...

(830 rows affected)
```

As with *LAG* and *LEAD*, normally you compute something based on the returned values. For example, you can compute the difference between the current and the first customer's order values: *val – FIRST_VALUE(val) OVER(…)*. Or you can compute the difference between the current and last customer's order values: *val – LAST_VALUE(val) OVER(…)*.

SQL Server 2022 introduces support for the standard *NULL treatment clause* with offset window functions. The syntax for this clause is as follows:

```
<function>( <expression> ) [ IGNORE NULLS | RESPECT NULLS ] OVER( <specification> )
```

This clause allows you to indicate whether to ignore or respect *NULLs* returned by the input expression. The *RESPECT NULLS* option, which is the default, essentially treats *NULLs* just like normal values. So even if the input expression evaluates to *NULL*, the function will return it. The *IGNORE NULLS* option means that if the input expression is *NULL*, you want the function to keep going in the applicable ordering direction until it finds a non-*NULL* value, if one exists. If none exists, the function returns a *NULL*.

Consider the following query, which returns shipped dates for orders placed by customers 9, 20, 32, and 73 in or after 2022:

```
SELECT orderid, custid, orderdate, shippeddate
FROM Sales.Orders
WHERE custid IN (9, 20, 32, 73)
  AND orderdate >= '20220101'
ORDER BY custid, orderdate, orderid;
```

This query generates the following output:

```
orderid     custid      orderdate  shippeddate
----------- ----------- ---------- -----------
10827       9           2022-01-12 2022-02-06
10871       9           2022-02-05 2022-02-10
10876       9           2022-02-09 2022-02-12
10932       9           2022-03-06 2022-03-24
10940       9           2022-03-11 2022-03-23
11076       9           2022-05-06 NULL
10836       20          2022-01-16 2022-01-21
10854       20          2022-01-27 2022-02-05
10895       20          2022-02-18 2022-02-23
10968       20          2022-03-23 2022-04-01
10979       20          2022-03-26 2022-03-31
10990       20          2022-04-01 2022-04-07
11008       20          2022-04-08 NULL
11017       20          2022-04-13 2022-04-20
11072       20          2022-05-05 NULL
10816       32          2022-01-06 2022-02-04
10936       32          2022-03-09 2022-03-18
11006       32          2022-04-07 2022-04-15
11040       32          2022-04-22 NULL
11061       32          2022-04-30 NULL
11074       73          2022-05-06 NULL
```

Observe that orders that have not been shipped yet have a *NULL* shipped date. Suppose that you want to add a result column that shows the last known shipped date at that point for orders placed by the same customer in or after 2022, based on order date ordering, with order ID as a tiebreaker. Note that the last known shipped date at that point (from the last row where the shipped date is not *NULL*) is not necessarily the maximum shipped date at that point. For instance, consider the order by customer 9 with ID 11076. The last known shipped date at that point is March 23, 2022, whereas the maximum shipped date known at that point is March 24, 2022. You need to return the former. To achieve this, you use the *LAST_VALUE* function with the *IGNORE NULLS* option, like so:

```
SELECT orderid, custid, orderdate, shippeddate,
  LAST_VALUE(shippeddate) IGNORE NULLS
    OVER(PARTITION BY custid
         ORDER BY orderdate, orderid
         ROWS UNBOUNDED PRECEDING) AS lastknownshippeddate
FROM Sales.Orders
WHERE custid IN (9, 20, 32, 73)
  AND orderdate >= '20220101'
ORDER BY custid, orderdate, orderid;
```

This code generates the following output:

```
orderid     custid      orderdate  shippeddate lastknownshippeddate
----------- ----------- ---------- ----------- --------------------
10827       9           2022-01-12 2022-02-06  2022-02-06
10871       9           2022-02-05 2022-02-10  2022-02-10
10876       9           2022-02-09 2022-02-12  2022-02-12
10932       9           2022-03-06 2022-03-24  2022-03-24
10940       9           2022-03-11 2022-03-23  2022-03-23
11076       9           2022-05-06 NULL        2022-03-23
```

10836	20	2022-01-16 2022-01-21	2022-01-21
10854	20	2022-01-27 2022-02-05	2022-02-05
10895	20	2022-02-18 2022-02-23	2022-02-23
10968	20	2022-03-23 2022-04-01	2022-04-01
10979	20	2022-03-26 2022-03-31	2022-03-31
10990	20	2022-04-01 2022-04-07	2022-04-07
11008	20	2022-04-08 NULL	2022-04-07
11017	20	2022-04-13 2022-04-20	2022-04-20
11072	20	2022-05-05 NULL	2022-04-20
10816	32	2022-01-06 2022-02-04	2022-02-04
10936	32	2022-03-09 2022-03-18	2022-03-18
11006	32	2022-04-07 2022-04-15	2022-04-15
11040	32	2022-04-22 NULL	2022-04-15
11061	32	2022-04-30 NULL	2022-04-15
11074	73	2022-05-06 NULL	NULL

Notice that order 11074 by customer 73 gets a *NULL* as the last known shipped date in 2022 since that's the only order placed by customer 73 in or after 2022, and it hasn't been shipped yet.

In a similar way, if you want to return the previously known shipped date for the customer, you use the *LAG* function with the *IGNORE NULLS* option, like so:

```
SELECT orderid, custid, orderdate, shippeddate,
  LAG(shippeddate) IGNORE NULLS
    OVER(PARTITION BY custid
        ORDER BY orderdate, orderid) AS prevknownshippeddate
FROM Sales.Orders
WHERE custid IN (9, 20, 32, 73)
  AND orderdate >= '20220101'
ORDER BY custid, orderdate, orderid;
```

This code generates the following output:

orderid	custid	orderdate	shippeddate	prevknownshippeddate
10827	9	2022-01-12	2022-02-06	NULL
10871	9	2022-02-05	2022-02-10	2022-02-06
10876	9	2022-02-09	2022-02-12	2022-02-10
10932	9	2022-03-06	2022-03-24	2022-02-12
10940	9	2022-03-11	2022-03-23	2022-03-24
11076	9	2022-05-06	NULL	2022-03-23
10836	20	2022-01-16	2022-01-21	NULL
10854	20	2022-01-27	2022-02-05	2022-01-21
10895	20	2022-02-18	2022-02-23	2022-02-05
10968	20	2022-03-23	2022-04-01	2022-02-23
10979	20	2022-03-26	2022-03-31	2022-04-01
10990	20	2022-04-01	2022-04-07	2022-03-31
11008	20	2022-04-08	NULL	2022-04-07
11017	20	2022-04-13	2022-04-20	2022-04-07
11072	20	2022-05-05	NULL	2022-04-20
10816	32	2022-01-06	2022-02-04	NULL
10936	32	2022-03-09	2022-03-18	2022-02-04
11006	32	2022-04-07	2022-04-15	2022-03-18
11040	32	2022-04-22	NULL	2022-04-15
11061	32	2022-04-30	NULL	2022-04-15
11074	73	2022-05-06	NULL	NULL

Observe, for example, that with order 11017 you get April 7, 2022, as the previously known shipped date for customer 20 instead of a *NULL* thanks to the *IGNORE NULLS* option.

Aggregate window functions

You use aggregate window functions to aggregate the rows in the defined window. They support window-partition, window-order, and window-frame clauses.

I'll start with an example that doesn't involve ordering and framing. Recall that using an *OVER* clause with empty parentheses exposes a window of all rows from the underlying query's result set to the function. For example, *SUM(val) OVER()* returns the grand total of all values. If you do add a window-partition clause, you expose a restricted window to the function, with only those rows from the underlying query's result set that share the same values in the partitioning elements as in the current row. For example, *SUM(val) OVER(PARTITION BY custid)* returns the total values for the current customer.

Here's a query against *OrderValues* that returns, along with each order, the grand total of all order values, as well as the customer total:

```
SELECT orderid, custid, val,
  SUM(val) OVER() AS totalvalue,
  SUM(val) OVER(PARTITION BY custid) AS custtotalvalue
FROM Sales.OrderValues;
```

This query returns the following output, shown here in abbreviated form:

```
orderid      custid       val          totalvalue        custtotalvalue
-----------  -----------  -----------  ----------------  ---------------
10643        1            814.50       1265793.22        4273.00
10692        1            878.00       1265793.22        4273.00
10702        1            330.00       1265793.22        4273.00
10835        1            845.80       1265793.22        4273.00
10952        1            471.20       1265793.22        4273.00
11011        1            933.50       1265793.22        4273.00
10926        2            514.40       1265793.22        1402.95
10759        2            320.00       1265793.22        1402.95
10625        2            479.75       1265793.22        1402.95
10308        2            88.80        1265793.22        1402.95
10365        3            403.20       1265793.22        7023.98
...

(830 rows affected)
```

The *totalvalue* column shows, for each row, the grand total of all values. The column *custtotalvalue* has the total values for the current customer.

Important As mentioned at the beginning of the chapter, one of the great advantages of window functions is that they don't hide the detail. This means you can write expressions that mix detail and aggregates. The next example demonstrates this.

As an example of mixing detail and aggregates, the following query calculates for each row the percentage of the current value out of the grand total, as well as out of the customer total:

```
SELECT orderid, custid, val,
  100. * val / SUM(val) OVER() AS pctall,
  100. * val / SUM(val) OVER(PARTITION BY custid) AS pctcust
FROM Sales.OrderValues;
```

This query returns the following output, shown here in abbreviated form:

orderid	custid	val	pctall	pctcust
10643	1	814.50	0.0643470029014691672941	19.0615492628130119354083
10692	1	878.00	0.0693636200705830925528	20.5476246197051252047741
10702	1	330.00	0.0260706089103558320528	7.7229113035338169904048
10835	1	845.80	0.0668197606556938265161	19.7940556985724315469225
10952	1	471.20	0.0372256694501808123130	11.0273812309852562602387
11011	1	933.50	0.0737482224782338461253	21.8464778843903580622513
10926	2	514.40	0.0406385491620819394181	36.6655974910011048148544
10759	2	320.00	0.0252805904585268674452	22.8090808653195053280587
10625	2	479.75	0.0379011352264945770526	34.1958017035532271285505
10308	2	88.80	0.0070153638522412057160	6.3295199401261627285362
10365	3	403.20	0.0318535439777438529809	5.7403352515240647040566

...

```
(830 rows affected)
```

Aggregate window functions also support a window frame. The frame allows for more sophisticated calculations, such as running and moving aggregates, YTD and MTD calculations, and others. Let's re-examine the query I used in the introduction to the section about window functions:

```
SELECT empid, ordermonth, val,
  SUM(val) OVER(PARTITION BY empid
               ORDER BY ordermonth
               ROWS BETWEEN UNBOUNDED PRECEDING
                   AND CURRENT ROW) AS runval
FROM Sales.EmpOrders;
```

This query generates the following output (abbreviated).

empid	ordermonth	val	runval
1	2020-07-01	1614.88	1614.88
1	2020-08-01	5555.90	7170.78
1	2020-09-01	6651.00	13821.78
1	2020-10-01	3933.18	17754.96
1	2020-11-01	9562.65	27317.61
...			
2	2020-07-01	1176.00	1176.00
2	2020-08-01	1814.00	2990.00
2	2020-09-01	2950.80	5940.80
2	2020-10-01	5164.00	11104.80
2	2020-11-01	4614.58	15719.38

...

```
(192 rows affected)
```

Each row in the *EmpOrders* view holds information about the order activity for an employee and month. The query returns for each employee and month the monthly value, plus the running-total values from the beginning of the employee's activity until the current month. To apply the calculation to each employee independently, you partition the window by *empid*. Then you define ordering based on *ordermonth*, giving meaning to the window frame: *ROWS BETWEEN UNBOUNDED PRECEDING AND CURRENT ROW*. This frame means "all activity from the beginning of the partition until the current month."

T-SQL supports other delimiters for the *ROWS* window-frame unit. You can indicate an offset back from the current row as well as an offset forward. For example, to capture all rows from two rows before the current row until one row ahead, you use *ROWS BETWEEN 2 PRECEDING AND 1 FOLLOWING*. Also, if you do not want an upper bound, you can use *UNBOUNDED FOLLOWING*.

Because window functions are so profound and have so many practical uses, I urge you to invest the time and effort to get to know the concept well.

The *WINDOW* clause

The *WINDOW* clause allows you to name an entire window specification or part of it in a query, and then use the window name in the *OVER* clause of window functions in that query. Its main purpose is to shorten the length of your query string when you have repetitive window specifications. This clause is available in SQL Server 2022 and higher, as well as in Azure SQL Database, provided that the database compatibility level is set to 160 or higher. If you're not sure what the compatibility level of your database is, you can use the following code to query it:

```
SELECT DATABASEPROPERTYEX(N'TSQLV6', N'CompatibilityLevel');
```

When considering all major query clauses (*SELECT, FROM, WHERE, GROUP BY, HAVING, ORDER BY*), you place the *WINDOW* clause between the *HAVING* and *ORDER BY* clauses of the query.

Consider the following query as an example:

```
SELECT empid, ordermonth, val,
  SUM(val) OVER(PARTITION BY empid
               ORDER BY ordermonth
               ROWS BETWEEN UNBOUNDED PRECEDING
                       AND CURRENT ROW) AS runsum,
  MIN(val) OVER(PARTITION BY empid
               ORDER BY ordermonth
               ROWS BETWEEN UNBOUNDED PRECEDING
                       AND CURRENT ROW) AS runmin,
  MAX(val) OVER(PARTITION BY empid
               ORDER BY ordermonth
               ROWS BETWEEN UNBOUNDED PRECEDING
                       AND CURRENT ROW) AS runmax,
  AVG(val) OVER(PARTITION BY empid
               ORDER BY ordermonth
               ROWS BETWEEN UNBOUNDED PRECEDING
                       AND CURRENT ROW) AS runavg
FROM Sales.EmpOrders;
```

Here you have four window functions with identical window specifications. Using the *WINDOW* clause, you can shorten the query string like so:

```
SELECT empid, ordermonth, val,
  SUM(val) OVER W AS runsum,
  MIN(val) OVER W AS runmin,
  MAX(val) OVER W AS runmax,
  AVG(val) OVER W AS runavg
FROM Sales.EmpOrders
WINDOW W AS (PARTITION BY empid
             ORDER BY ordermonth
             ROWS BETWEEN UNBOUNDED PRECEDING
                   AND CURRENT ROW);
```

Observe that when a window name represents an entire window specification, like *W* in this example, you specify it right after the *OVER* clause without parentheses.

As mentioned, you can use the *WINDOW* clause to name part of a window specification. In such a case, when using the window name in an *OVER* clause you specify it in parentheses at the beginning, before the remaining windowing elements. Here's an example demonstrating this:

```
SELECT custid, orderid, val,
  FIRST_VALUE(val) OVER(PO
                        ROWS BETWEEN UNBOUNDED PRECEDING
                              AND CURRENT ROW) AS firstval,
  LAST_VALUE(val)  OVER(PO
                        ROWS BETWEEN CURRENT ROW
                              AND UNBOUNDED FOLLOWING) AS lastval
FROM Sales.OrderValues
WINDOW PO AS (PARTITION BY custid
              ORDER BY orderdate, orderid)
ORDER BY custid, orderdate, orderid;
```

In this example both *FIRST_VALUE* and *LAST_VALUE* functions have the same window partitioning and ordering specifications, but different window-frame specifications. So you assign the name *PO* to the combination of partitioning and ordering specifications, and use this name as part of the window specifications of both functions. Since here the window name is just part of the specifications of both window functions, you do have parentheses right after the *OVER* clause, and within the parentheses you start with the window name *PO*, followed by the explicit window-frame specification.

In a similar way you can define multiple window names, and recursively reuse one window name within another. Here's an example demonstrating this:

```
SELECT orderid, custid, orderdate, qty, val,
  ROW_NUMBER() OVER PO AS ordernum,
  MAX(orderdate) OVER P AS maxorderdate,
  SUM(qty) OVER POF AS runsumqty,
  SUM(val) OVER POF AS runsumval
FROM Sales.OrderValues
WINDOW P AS ( PARTITION BY custid ),
       PO AS ( P ORDER BY orderdate, orderid ),
       POF AS ( PO ROWS UNBOUNDED PRECEDING )
ORDER BY custid, orderdate, orderid;
```

Here you assign the name *P* to some window partitioning specification. You then assign the name *PO* to a window specification with *P* as well as some window ordering specification. You then assign the name *POF* to a window specification with *PO* as well as some window-frame specification. Then in the *SELECT* list you use all assigned window names in various window functions. Note that the definition order of the window names in the *WINDOW* clause is insignificant.

If you want to practice the window functions topic, you can work on exercises 1, 2, and 3.

Pivoting data

Pivoting data involves rotating data from a state of rows to a state of columns, possibly aggregating values along the way. In many cases, the pivoting of data is handled by the presentation layer for purposes such as reporting. This section teaches you how to handle pivoting with T-SQL for cases you do decide to handle in the database.

For the rest of the topics in this chapter, I use a sample table called *dbo.Orders* that you create and populate in the *TSQLV6* database by running Listing 7-1.

LISTING 7-1 Code to create and populate the *dbo.Orders* table

```
USE TSQLV6;

DROP TABLE IF EXISTS dbo.Orders;

CREATE TABLE dbo.Orders
(
  orderid   INT       NOT NULL
    CONSTRAINT PK_Orders PRIMARY KEY,
  orderdate DATE      NOT NULL,
  empid     INT       NOT NULL,
  custid    VARCHAR(5) NOT NULL,
  qty       INT       NOT NULL
);

INSERT INTO dbo.Orders(orderid, orderdate, empid, custid, qty)
VALUES
  (30001, '20200802', 3, 'A', 10),
  (10001, '20201224', 2, 'A', 12),
  (10005, '20201224', 1, 'B', 20),
  (40001, '20210109', 2, 'A', 40),
  (10006, '20210118', 1, 'C', 14),
  (20001, '20210212', 2, 'B', 12),
  (40005, '20220212', 3, 'A', 10),
  (20002, '20220216', 1, 'C', 20),
  (30003, '20220418', 2, 'B', 15),
  (30004, '20200418', 3, 'C', 22),
  (30007, '20220907', 3, 'D', 30);

SELECT * FROM dbo.Orders;
```

The query at the end of Listing 7-1 produces the following output:

```
orderid     orderdate   empid           custid   qty
----------- ----------- --------------- -------- -----------
10001       2020-12-24  2               A        12
10005       2020-12-24  1               B        20
10006       2021-01-18  1               C        14
20001       2021-02-12  2               B        12
20002       2022-02-16  1               C        20
30001       2020-08-02  3               A        10
30003       2022-04-18  2               B        15
30004       2020-04-18  3               C        22
30007       2022-09-07  3               D        30
40001       2021-01-09  2               A        40
40005       2022-02-12  3               A        10
```

Suppose you need to query this table and return the total order quantity for each employee and customer. The following grouped query achieves this task:

```
SELECT empid, custid, SUM(qty) AS sumqty
FROM dbo.Orders
GROUP BY empid, custid;
```

This query generates the following output:

```
empid       custid    sumqty
----------- --------- -----------
2           A         52
3           A         20
1           B         20
2           B         27
1           C         34
3           C         22
3           D         30
```

Suppose, however, you have a requirement to produce the output in the form shown in Table 7-1.

TABLE 7-1 Pivoted view of total quantity per employee (on rows) and customer (on columns)

empid	A	B	C	D
1	NULL	20	34	NULL
2	52	27	NULL	NULL
3	20	NULL	22	30

What you see in Table 7-1 is an aggregated and pivoted view of the data; the technique for generating this view is called *pivoting*.

Every pivoting request involves three logical processing phases, each with associated elements:

1. A grouping phase with an associated grouping or *on rows* element

2. A spreading phase with an associated spreading or *on cols* element

3. An aggregation phase with an associated aggregation element and aggregate function

Let's observe these three phases in this example. First you need to produce a single row in the result for each unique employee ID. This means the rows from the *dbo.Orders* table need to be grouped by the *empid* attribute (the grouping element).

The *dbo.Orders* table has a single column that holds all customer ID values and a single column that holds their ordered quantities. The pivoting task requires you to produce a different result column for each unique customer ID, holding the aggregated quantities for that customer. You can think of this process as "spreading" the quantities by customer ID. The spreading element in this case is the *custid* attribute.

Finally, because pivoting involves grouping, you need to aggregate data to produce the result values in the "intersection" of the grouping (employee) and spreading (customer) elements. You need to identify the aggregate function (*SUM,* in this case) and the aggregation element (the *qty* attribute, in this case).

To recap, pivoting involves grouping, spreading, and aggregating. In this example, you group by *empid*, spread (quantities) by *custid*, and aggregate with *SUM(qty)*. After you identify the elements involved in pivoting, the rest is just a matter of incorporating those elements in the right places in a generic query template for pivoting.

This chapter presents two solutions for pivoting—one based on an explicit grouped query and another with a table operator called *PIVOT*.

Pivoting with a grouped query

The solution using a grouped query handles all three phases in an explicit and straightforward manner.

The grouping phase is achieved with a *GROUP BY* clause—in this case, *GROUP BY empid*.

The spreading phase is achieved in the *SELECT* clause with a *CASE* expression for each target column. You need to know the spreading element values ahead of time and specify a separate expression for each. Because in this case you need to "spread" the quantities of four customers (A, B, C, and D), there are four *CASE* expressions. For example, here's the *CASE* expression for customer A:

```
CASE WHEN custid = 'A' THEN qty END
```

This expression returns the quantity from the current row only when the current row represents an order for customer A; otherwise, the expression returns a *NULL*. Remember that if an *ELSE* clause is not specified in a *CASE* expression, the implied default is *ELSE NULL*. This means that in the target column for customer A, only quantities associated with customer A appear as column values, and in all other cases the column values are *NULL*.

If you don't know the spreading values ahead of time (the distinct customer IDs in this case), you need to query them from the data, construct the query string yourself by using an aggregate string concatenation method, and use dynamic SQL to execute it. I'll demonstrate how to achieve this in Chapter 12, "Programmable objects."

Finally, the aggregation phase is achieved by applying the relevant aggregate function (*SUM,* in this case) to the result of each *CASE* expression. For example, here's the expression that produces the result column for customer A:

```
SUM(CASE WHEN custid = 'A' THEN qty END) AS A
```

Of course, depending on the request, you might need to use another aggregate function (such as *MAX, MIN,* or *COUNT*).

Here's the complete solution query that pivots order data, returning the total quantity for each employee (on rows) and customer (on columns):

```
SELECT empid,
  SUM(CASE WHEN custid = 'A' THEN qty END) AS A,
  SUM(CASE WHEN custid = 'B' THEN qty END) AS B,
  SUM(CASE WHEN custid = 'C' THEN qty END) AS C,
  SUM(CASE WHEN custid = 'D' THEN qty END) AS D
FROM dbo.Orders
GROUP BY empid;
```

This query produces the output shown in Table 7-1. SQL Server also generates the following warning in the Messages pane of SSMS:

```
Warning: Null value is eliminated by an aggregate or other SET operation.
```

The warning notifies you that *NULLs* are ignored by an aggregate function, as we discussed earlier.

Pivoting with the *PIVOT* operator

The solution for pivoting based on an explicit grouped query is standard. T-SQL also supports a proprietary table operator called *PIVOT* that you can use to achieve pivoting in a more concise manner. As a table operator, *PIVOT* operates in the context of the *FROM* clause like any other table operator (for example, *JOIN*). It operates on the source table or table expression provided to it as its left input, pivots the data, and returns a result table. The *PIVOT* operator involves the same logical processing phases as described earlier (grouping, spreading, and aggregating), only it requires less code than the previous solution.

The general form of a query with the *PIVOT* operator is shown here:

```
SELECT ...
FROM <input_table>
  PIVOT(<agg_function>(<aggregation_element>)
        FOR <spreading_element> IN (<list_of_target_columns>)) AS <result_table_alias>
WHERE ...;
```

In the parentheses of the *PIVOT* operator, you specify the aggregate function (*SUM,* in this example), aggregation element (*qty*), spreading element (*custid*), and the list of target column names (*A, B, C, D*). Following the parentheses of the *PIVOT* operator, you specify an alias for the result table.

Note that with the *PIVOT* operator, you do not explicitly specify the grouping elements, removing the need for *GROUP BY* in the query. The *PIVOT* operator figures out the grouping elements implicitly by elimination. The grouping elements are all attributes from the source table that were not specified as either the spreading element or the aggregation element. You must ensure that the source table for the *PIVOT* operator has no attributes other than the grouping, spreading, and aggregation elements so that the implied selection of the grouping elements will be what you want. You achieve this by using a table expression that includes only the attributes you need as the input of the operator. For example, here's the solution query to the original pivoting request, using the *PIVOT* operator:

```
SELECT empid, A, B, C, D
FROM (SELECT empid, custid, qty
      FROM dbo.Orders) AS D
  PIVOT(SUM(qty) FOR custid IN(A, B, C, D)) AS P;
```

Instead of operating directly on the *dbo.Orders* table, the *PIVOT* operator operates on a derived table called *D* that includes only the pivoting elements *empid*, *custid*, and *qty*. When you account for the spreading element, which is *custid*, and the aggregation element, which is *qty*, what's left is the implied grouping element *empid*.

This query returns the output shown in Table 7-1.

To understand why you're required to use a table expression here, consider the following query, which applies the *PIVOT* operator directly to the *dbo.Orders* table:

```
SELECT empid, A, B, C, D
FROM dbo.Orders
  PIVOT(SUM(qty) FOR custid IN(A, B, C, D)) AS P;
```

The *dbo.Orders* table contains the attributes *orderid*, *orderdate*, *empid*, *custid*, and *qty*. Because the query specifies *custid* as the spreading element and *qty* as the aggregation element, the remaining attributes (*orderid*, *orderdate*, and *empid*) are all considered the grouping elements. This query, therefore, returns the following output:

empid	A	B	C	D
2	12	NULL	NULL	NULL
1	NULL	20	NULL	NULL
1	NULL	NULL	14	NULL
2	NULL	12	NULL	NULL
1	NULL	NULL	20	NULL
3	10	NULL	NULL	NULL
2	NULL	15	NULL	NULL
3	NULL	NULL	22	NULL
3	NULL	NULL	NULL	30
2	40	NULL	NULL	NULL
3	10	NULL	NULL	NULL

```
(11 rows affected)
```

Because *orderid* is part of the grouping elements, you get a row for each order instead of a row for each employee. The logical equivalent of this query that uses the standard solution for pivoting has *orderid*, *orderdate*, and *empid* listed in the *GROUP BY* list as follows:

```
SELECT empid,
  SUM(CASE WHEN custid = 'A' THEN qty END) AS A,
  SUM(CASE WHEN custid = 'B' THEN qty END) AS B,
  SUM(CASE WHEN custid = 'C' THEN qty END) AS C,
  SUM(CASE WHEN custid = 'D' THEN qty END) AS D
FROM dbo.Orders
GROUP BY orderid, orderdate, empid;
```

As a best practice with the *PIVOT* operator, you should always work with a table expression and not query the underlying table directly. Even if currently the table contains only the columns that are supposed to take part in pivoting, you might add columns to the table in the future, rendering your queries incorrect. It is also important to enumerate the columns both in the table expression's inner query and in the outer query.

As another example of a pivoting request, suppose that instead of returning employees on rows and customers on columns, you want it the other way around: the grouping element is *custid*, the spreading element is *empid*, and the aggregation element and aggregate function remain *SUM(qty)*. After you learn the "template" for a pivoting solution (with the grouped query or with the *PIVOT* operator), it's just a matter of fitting those elements in the right places. The following solution query uses the *PIVOT* operator to achieve the result:

```
SELECT custid, [1], [2], [3]
FROM (SELECT empid, custid, qty
      FROM dbo.Orders) AS D
  PIVOT(SUM(qty) FOR empid IN([1], [2], [3])) AS P;
```

The employee IDs 1, 2, and 3 are values in the *empid* column in the source table, but in terms of the result, these values become target column names. You must refer to them as identifiers in the *IN* clause. When identifiers are irregular (for example, when they start with a digit), you need to delimit them—hence, the use of square brackets.

This query returns the following output:

```
custid    1             2             3
--------- ------------- ------------- ------------
A         NULL          52            20
B         20            27            NULL
C         34            NULL          22
D         NULL          NULL          30
```

Unpivoting data

Unpivoting is a technique that rotates data from a state of columns to a state of rows. Usually, it involves querying a pivoted state of the data and producing from each source row multiple result rows, each with a different source column value. A common use case is to unpivot data you imported from a spreadsheet into the database for easier manipulation.

Run the following code to create and populate a table called *EmpCustOrders* in the *TSQLV6* sample database. Don't worry if you're not familiar with the *INSERT* statement syntax yet; it's covered later in the book, in Chapter 8. I'll use this table to demonstrate unpivoting techniques:

```
USE TSQLV6;

DROP TABLE IF EXISTS dbo.EmpCustOrders;

CREATE TABLE dbo.EmpCustOrders
(
  empid INT NOT NULL
    CONSTRAINT PK_EmpCustOrders PRIMARY KEY,
  A VARCHAR(5) NULL,
  B VARCHAR(5) NULL,
  C VARCHAR(5) NULL,
  D VARCHAR(5) NULL
);

INSERT INTO dbo.EmpCustOrders(empid, A, B, C, D)
  SELECT empid, A, B, C, D
  FROM (SELECT empid, custid, qty
        FROM dbo.Orders) AS D
    PIVOT(SUM(qty) FOR custid IN(A, B, C, D)) AS P;

SELECT * FROM dbo.EmpCustOrders;
```

Here's the output of the query against *EmpCustOrders* showing its contents:

empid	A	B	C	D
1	NULL	20	34	NULL
2	52	27	NULL	NULL
3	20	NULL	22	30

The table has a row for each employee; a column for each of the four customers A, B, C, and D; and the order quantity for each employee and customer. Notice that irrelevant intersections (employee-customer combinations that had no intersecting order activity) are represented by *NULLs*. Suppose you get a request to unpivot the data, requiring you to return a row for each employee and customer, along with the order quantity, if such exists. The result should look like this:

empid	custid	qty
1	B	20
1	C	34
2	A	52
2	B	27
3	A	20
3	C	22
3	D	30

In the following sections, I'll discuss two techniques for solving this problem—one using the *APPLY* operator and another using the *UNPIVOT* operator.

Unpivoting with the *APPLY* operator

Unpivoting involves three logical processing phases:

1. Producing copies

2. Extracting values

3. Eliminating irrelevant rows

The first step in the solution involves producing multiple copies of each source row—one for each column you need to unpivot. In this case, you need to produce a copy for each of the columns A, B, C, and D, which represent customer IDs. You can achieve this step by applying a cross join between the *EmpCustOrders* table and a table that has a row for each customer.

If you already have a table of customers in your database, you can use that table in the cross join. If you don't have a table of customers, you can build a virtual one on the fly using a table-value constructor based on the *VALUES* clause. Here's the code that implements this step:

```
SELECT *
FROM dbo.EmpCustOrders
  CROSS JOIN (VALUES('A'),('B'),('C'),('D')) AS C(custid);
```

The *VALUES* clause defines a set of four rows, each with a single customer ID value. The code defines a derived table called *C* based on this clause and names the only column in it *custid*. The code then applies a cross join between *EmpCustOrders* and C.

> **Note** If you're not familiar yet with the *VALUES* clause, it's described in detail in Chapter 8, "Data modification."

In this example, the query that implements the first step in the solution returns the following output:

empid	A	B	C	D	custid
1	NULL	20	34	NULL	A
1	NULL	20	34	NULL	B
1	NULL	20	34	NULL	C
1	NULL	20	34	NULL	D
2	52	27	NULL	NULL	A
2	52	27	NULL	NULL	B
2	52	27	NULL	NULL	C
2	52	27	NULL	NULL	D
3	20	NULL	22	30	A
3	20	NULL	22	30	B
3	20	NULL	22	30	C
3	20	NULL	22	30	D

As you can see, four copies were produced for each source row—one each for customers A, B, C, and D.

The second step in the solution is to extract a value from one of the original customer quantity columns (*A*, *B*, *C*, or *D*) to return a single value column (call it *qty* in our case). You need to extract the value from the column that corresponds to the current *custid* value. If *custid* is 'A', the *qty* column should return the value from column *A*, if *custid* is 'B', *qty* should return the value from column *B*, and so on. To achieve this step, you might think you can simply add the *qty* column as a second column to each row in the table value constructor (the *VALUES* clause), like this:

```
SELECT empid, custid, qty
FROM dbo.EmpCustOrders
  CROSS JOIN (VALUES('A', A),('B', B),('C', C),('D', D)) AS C(custid, qty);
```

However, remember that a join treats its two inputs as a set; hence, there's no order between those inputs. You can't refer to the elements of either of the inputs when constructing the other. In our case, the table-value constructor on the right side of the join has references to the columns *A*, *B*, *C*, and *D* from the left side of the join (*EmpCustOrders*). Consequently, when you try to run this code, you get the following errors:

```
Msg 207, Level 16, State 1, Line 222
Invalid column name 'A'.
Msg 207, Level 16, State 1, Line 222
Invalid column name 'B'.
Msg 207, Level 16, State 1, Line 222
Invalid column name 'C'.
Msg 207, Level 16, State 1, Line 222
Invalid column name 'D'.
```

The solution is to use the *CROSS APPLY* operator instead of the *CROSS JOIN* operator. They are similar, but the former evaluates the left side first and then applies the right side to each left row, making the left side's elements accessible to the right side. Here's the code implementing this step with the *CROSS APPLY* operator:

```
SELECT empid, custid, qty
FROM dbo.EmpCustOrders
  CROSS APPLY (VALUES('A', A),('B', B),('C', C),('D', D)) AS C(custid, qty);
```

This query runs successfully, returning the following output:

```
empid       custid      qty
----------- ----------- -----------
1           A           NULL
1           B           20
1           C           34
1           D           NULL
2           A           52
2           B           27
2           C           NULL
2           D           NULL
3           A           20
3           B           NULL
3           C           22
3           D           30
```

As for the third step, recall that in the original table *NULLs* represent irrelevant intersections. In the result, there's typically no reason to keep irrelevant rows where *qty* is *NULL*. The nice thing in our case is that the *CROSS APPLY* operator, which created the column *qty*, was processed in the *FROM* clause, and the *FROM* clause is evaluated before the *WHERE* clause. This means that the *qty* column is accessible to expressions in the *WHERE* clause. To remove irrelevant rows, add a filter in the *WHERE* clause that discards rows with a *NULL* in the *qty* column, like this:

```
SELECT empid, custid, qty
FROM dbo.EmpCustOrders
  CROSS APPLY (VALUES('A', A),('B', B),('C', C),('D', D)) AS C(custid, qty)
WHERE qty IS NOT NULL;
```

This query returns the following output:

```
empid       custid     qty
----------- ---------- -----------
1           B          20
1           C          34
2           A          52
2           B          27
3           A          20
3           C          22
3           D          30
```

Unpivoting with the *UNPIVOT* operator

Unpivoting data involves producing two result columns from any number of source columns—one to hold the source column names as strings and another to hold the source column values. In this example, you need to unpivot the source columns *A*, *B*, *C*, and *D*, producing the result names column *custid* and values column *qty*. Similar to the *PIVOT* operator, T-SQL also supports the *UNPIVOT* operator to enable you to unpivot data. The general form of a query with the *UNPIVOT* operator is as follows:

```
SELECT ...
FROM <input_table>
  UNPIVOT(<values_column> FOR <names_column> IN(<source_columns>)) AS <result table_alias>
WHERE ...;
```

Like the *PIVOT* operator, *UNPIVOT* was also implemented as a table operator in the context of the *FROM* clause. It operates on a source table or table expression (*EmpCustOrders* in this case). Within the parentheses of the *UNPIVOT* operator, you specify the name you want to assign to the column that will hold the source column values (*qty* here), the name you want to assign to the column that will hold the source column names (*custid*), and the list of source column names (*A*, *B*, *C*, and *D*). Following the parentheses, you provide an alias to the table resulting from the table operator.

Here's the query that uses the *UNPIVOT* operator to handle our unpivoting task:

```
SELECT empid, custid, qty
FROM dbo.EmpCustOrders
  UNPIVOT(qty FOR custid IN(A, B, C, D)) AS U;
```

Note that the *UNPIVOT* operator implements the same logical-processing phases described earlier—generating copies, extracting elements, and eliminating *NULL* intersections. However, the last phase is not optional as in the solution with the *APPLY* operator. When you need to apply the third phase, it's convenient to use the solution with the *UNPIVOT* operator because it's more concise. When you need to keep the rows with the *NULLs*, use the solution with the *APPLY* operator.

When you're done, run the following code for cleanup:

```
DROP TABLE IF EXISTS dbo.EmpCustOrders;
```

If you want to practice the pivoting and unpivoting topics, you can work on exercises 4 and 5.

Grouping sets

This section describes what a grouping set is and the features in T-SQL that support grouping sets.

A *grouping set* is a set of expressions you group the data by in a grouped query (a query with a *GROUP BY* clause). The reason for using the term "set" here is that there's no significance to the order in which you specify the expressions in the *GROUP BY* clause. Traditionally in SQL, a single grouped query defines a single grouping set. For example, each of the following four queries defines a different single grouping set:

```
SELECT empid, custid, SUM(qty) AS sumqty
FROM dbo.Orders
GROUP BY empid, custid;

SELECT empid, SUM(qty) AS sumqty
FROM dbo.Orders
GROUP BY empid;

SELECT custid, SUM(qty) AS sumqty
FROM dbo.Orders
GROUP BY custid;

SELECT SUM(qty) AS sumqty
FROM dbo.Orders;
```

The first query defines the grouping set *(empid, custid)*; the second *(empid)*, the third *(custid)*, and the last query define what's known as the empty grouping set, *()*. This code returns four result sets—one for each of the four queries.

Suppose, for reporting purposes, that instead of wanting four separate result sets returned, you want a single unified result set. You can achieve this by using the *UNION ALL* operator between the queries, after planting *NULLs* as placeholders for columns that appear in one query but not others. Here's what the code looks like:

```
SELECT empid, custid, SUM(qty) AS sumqty
FROM dbo.Orders
GROUP BY empid, custid
```

```
UNION ALL

SELECT empid, NULL, SUM(qty) AS sumqty
FROM dbo.Orders
GROUP BY empid

UNION ALL

SELECT NULL, custid, SUM(qty) AS sumqty
FROM dbo.Orders
GROUP BY custid

UNION ALL

SELECT NULL, NULL, SUM(qty) AS sumqty
FROM dbo.Orders;
```

This code generates a single result set with the aggregates for all four groupings:

```
empid       custid    sumqty
----------- --------- -----------
2           A         52
3           A         20
1           B         20
2           B         27
1           C         34
3           C         22
3           D         30
1           NULL      54
2           NULL      79
3           NULL      72
NULL        A         72
NULL        B         47
NULL        C         56
NULL        D         30
NULL        NULL      205

(15 rows affected)
```

Even though you managed to get what you were after, this solution has two main problems—the length of the code and performance. It's long because you have a separate query for each grouping set. Also, SQL Server needs to apply a separate scanning of the data for each query.

T-SQL supports standard features you can use to define multiple grouping sets in the same query. Those are the *GROUPING SETS, CUBE,* and *ROLLUP* subclauses of the *GROUP BY* clause, and the *GROUPING* and *GROUPING_ID* functions. The main use cases are reporting and data analysis. These features usually need the presentation layer to use more sophisticated GUI controls to display the data than does the typical grid control with its columns and rows. But we will not get into this here, as this book's focus is the T-SQL code in the database and not the presentation layer.

The *GROUPING SETS* subclause

The *GROUPING SETS* subclause is a powerful enhancement to the *GROUP BY* clause. You can use it to define multiple grouping sets in the same query. Simply list the grouping sets you want, separated by commas within the parentheses of the *GROUPING SETS* subclause, and for each grouping set list the members, separated by commas, within parentheses. For example, the following query defines four grouping sets: *(empid, custid)*, *(empid)*, *(custid)*, and *()*:

```
SELECT empid, custid, SUM(qty) AS sumqty
FROM dbo.Orders
GROUP BY
  GROUPING SETS
  (
    (empid, custid),
    (empid),
    (custid),
    ()
  );
```

The last grouping set is the empty grouping set representing the grand total. This query is a logical equivalent of the previous solution that unified the result sets of four aggregate queries. Only this one is much shorter, plus it gets optimized better. SQL Server typically needs fewer scans of the data than the number of grouping sets because it can roll up aggregates internally.

The *CUBE* subclause

The *CUBE* subclause of the *GROUP BY* clause provides an abbreviated way to define multiple grouping sets. In the parentheses of the *CUBE* subclause, you provide a set of members separated by commas, and you get all possible grouping sets that can be defined based on the input members. For example, *CUBE(a, b, c)* is equivalent to *GROUPING SETS((a, b, c), (a, b), (a, c), (b, c), (a), (b), (c), ())*. In set theory, the set of all subsets of elements that can be produced from a particular set is called the *power set*. You can think of the *CUBE* subclause as producing the power set of grouping sets that can be formed from the given set of elements.

Instead of using the *GROUPING SETS* subclause in the previous query to define the four grouping sets *(empid, custid)*, *(empid)*, *(custid)*, and *()*, you can simply use *CUBE(empid, custid)*. Here's the complete query:

```
SELECT empid, custid, SUM(qty) AS sumqty
FROM dbo.Orders
GROUP BY CUBE(empid, custid);
```

The *ROLLUP* subclause

The *ROLLUP* subclause of the *GROUP BY* clause also provides an abbreviated way to define multiple grouping sets. However, unlike the *CUBE* subclause, *ROLLUP* doesn't produce all possible grouping sets. *ROLLUP* assumes a hierarchy among the input members and produces only grouping sets that form leading combinations of the input members. For example, whereas *CUBE(a, b, c)* produces all eight possible grouping sets, *ROLLUP(a, b, c)* produces only four based on the hierarchy a>b>c. It is the equivalent of specifying *GROUPING SETS((a, b, c), (a, b), (a), ())*.

For example, suppose you want to return total quantities for all grouping sets that can be defined based on the time hierarchy of *order year, order month, order day*. You can use the *GROUPING SETS* subclause and explicitly list all four possible grouping sets:

```
GROUPING SETS(
  (YEAR(orderdate), MONTH(orderdate), DAY(orderdate)),
  (YEAR(orderdate), MONTH(orderdate)),
  (YEAR(orderdate)),
  () )
```

The logical equivalent that uses the *ROLLUP* subclause is much more concise:

```
ROLLUP(YEAR(orderdate), MONTH(orderdate), DAY(orderdate))
```

Here's the complete query you need to run:

```
SELECT
  YEAR(orderdate) AS orderyear,
  MONTH(orderdate) AS ordermonth,
  DAY(orderdate) AS orderday,
  SUM(qty) AS sumqty
FROM dbo.Orders
GROUP BY ROLLUP(YEAR(orderdate), MONTH(orderdate), DAY(orderdate));
```

This query produces the following output:

```
orderyear    ordermonth       orderday      sumqty
-----------  ---------------  -----------   -----------
2020         4                18            22
2020         4                NULL          22
2020         8                2             10
2020         8                NULL          10
2020         12               24            32
2020         12               NULL          32
2020         NULL             NULL          64
2021         1                9             40
2021         1                18            14
2021         1                NULL          54
2021         2                12            12
2021         2                NULL          12
2021         NULL             NULL          66
2022         2                12            10
2022         2                16            20
2022         2                NULL          30
2022         4                18            15
2022         4                NULL          15
2022         9                7             30
2022         9                NULL          30
2022         NULL             NULL          75
NULL         NULL             NULL          205
```

The *GROUPING* and *GROUPING_ID* functions

When you have a single query that defines multiple grouping sets, you might need to associate result rows and grouping sets. As long as all grouping elements are defined as *NOT NULL*, this is easy. For example, consider the following query:

```
SELECT empid, custid, SUM(qty) AS sumqty
FROM dbo.Orders
GROUP BY CUBE(empid, custid);
```

This query produces the following output:

```
empid       custid    sumqty
----------- --------- -----------
2           A         52
3           A         20
NULL        A         72
1           B         20
2           B         27
NULL        B         47
1           C         34
3           C         22
NULL        C         56
3           D         30
NULL        D         30
NULL        NULL      205
1           NULL      54
2           NULL      79
3           NULL      72
```

Because both the *empid* and *custid* columns were defined in the *dbo.Orders* table as *NOT NULL*, a *NULL* in those columns can only represent a placeholder, indicating that the column did not participate in the current grouping set. For example, all rows in which *empid* is not *NULL* and *custid* is not *NULL* are associated with the grouping set *(empid, custid)*. All rows in which *empid* is not *NULL* and *custid* is *NULL* are associated with the grouping set *(empid)*, and so on.

However, if a grouping column allows *NULLs* in the table, you cannot tell for sure whether a *NULL* in the result set originated from the data or is a placeholder for a nonparticipating member in a grouping set. One way to solve this problem is to use the *GROUPING* function. This function accepts a name of a column and returns *0* if it is a member of the current grouping set (a detail element) and *1* otherwise (an aggregate element).

> **Note** I find it counterintuitive that the *GROUPING* function returns *1* when the element isn't part of the grouping set and *0* when it is. To me, it would make more sense to return *1* when the element is part of the grouping set and *0* otherwise. The current perspective is to use *1* to indicate the element is an aggregate element and *0* when it's a detail element. You just need to make sure you realize this fact.

For example, the following query invokes the *GROUPING* function for each of the grouping elements:

```
SELECT
  GROUPING(empid) AS grpemp,
  GROUPING(custid) AS grpcust,
  empid, custid, SUM(qty) AS sumqty
FROM dbo.Orders
GROUP BY CUBE(empid, custid);
```

This query returns the following output:

grpemp	grpcust	empid	custid	sumqty
0	0	2	A	52
0	0	3	A	20
1	0	NULL	A	72
0	0	1	B	20
0	0	2	B	27
1	0	NULL	B	47
0	0	1	C	34
0	0	3	C	22
1	0	NULL	C	56
0	0	3	D	30
1	0	NULL	D	30
1	1	NULL	NULL	205
0	1	1	NULL	54
0	1	2	NULL	79
0	1	3	NULL	72

```
(15 rows affected)
```

Now you don't need to rely on the *NULLs* anymore to figure out the association between result rows and grouping sets. For example, all rows in which *grpemp* is *0* and *grpcust* is *0* are associated with the grouping set *(empid, custid)*. All rows in which *grpemp* is *0* and *grpcust* is *1* are associated with the grouping set *(empid)*, and so on.

T-SQL supports another function, called *GROUPING_ID*, that can further simplify the process of associating result rows and grouping sets. You provide the function with all elements that participate in any grouping set as inputs—for example, *GROUPING_ID(a, b, c, d)*—and the function returns an integer bitmap in which each bit represents a different input element—the rightmost element represented by the rightmost bit. For details on binary representation of numbers, see *https://en.wikipedia.org/wiki/Binary_number#Representation*. For example, based on the positions of the inputs provided to the *GROUPING_ID* function above, the grouping set *(a, b, c, d)* is represented by the Integer 0 ($0\times8 + 0\times4 + 0\times2 + 0\times1$). The grouping set *(a, c)* is represented by the integer 5 ($0\times8 + 1\times4 + 0\times2 + 1\times1$), and so on.

Instead of calling the *GROUPING* function for each grouping element as in the previous query, you can call the *GROUPING_ID* function once and provide it with all grouping elements as input, as shown here:

```
SELECT
  GROUPING_ID(empid, custid) AS groupingset,
  empid, custid, SUM(qty) AS sumqty
FROM dbo.Orders
GROUP BY CUBE(empid, custid);
```

This query produces the following output:

```
groupingset    empid        custid    sumqty
-------------- ------------ --------- -----------
0              2            A         52
0              3            A         20
2              NULL         A         72
0              1            B         20
0              2            B         27
2              NULL         B         47
0              1            C         34
0              3            C         22
2              NULL         C         56
0              3            D         30
2              NULL         D         30
3              NULL         NULL      205
1              1            NULL      54
1              2            NULL      79
1              3            NULL      72
```

Now you can easily figure out which grouping set each row is associated with. The integer *0* (binary 00) represents the grouping set *(empid, custid)*; the integer *1* (binary 01) represents *(empid)*; the integer *2* (binary 10) represents *(custid)*; and the integer *3* (binary 11) represents *()*.

If you want to practice the grouping sets topic, you can work on exercise 6.

Time series

Time series data is data representing a series of events, or measurements, typically taken at regular time intervals. One example of time series data could be temperature and humidity readings taken every four hours by sensors installed at various locations. Another could be sales quantities and values recorded daily per sales person. Time series data analysis usually involves organizing the data in groups, also known as buckets, and then aggregating some measures per bucket. For example, suppose that you need to organize your sensor readings in 12-hour buckets per sensor, and compute minimum, maximum, and average temperatures per sensor and 12-hour bucket.

Analyzing time series data can sometimes be very simple. For instance, if you want to compute daily extreme and average temperatures per sensor, you can simply group the data by sensor and reading date and apply the relevant aggregates. However, sometimes the analysis can be much trickier. For example, suppose that you want to analyze the data in 12-hour buckets, one starting at 00:05 AM and another starting at 12:05 PM every day. What exactly do you group the data by? Also, what if sensors can sometimes be offline, and you want to apply gap-filling logic to include buckets with no activity in your analysis?

In this section I explain how to handle such more sophisticated needs. I start by describing how to bucketize the data using a function called *DATE_BUCKET*. I then explain how to bucketize the data with a more custom method in case you're using a platform that doesn't support the function. Lastly, I provide a solution for gap filling that relies on either the *GENERATE_SERIES* system-supplied function or the *dbo.GetNums* user-defined function, which I provide as part of the sample database *TSQLV6*.

Sample data

I'll use sensor temperature and humidity readings as my sample data for time series analysis. The data is stored in two tables. One table called *Sensors,* holding data about sensors, and another called *SensorMeasurements,* holding sensor readings.

Run the following code to create the *Sensors* and *SensorMeasurements* tables and to populate them with fictitious sample data:

```
USE TSQLV6;

DROP TABLE IF EXISTS dbo.SensorMeasurements, dbo.Sensors;

CREATE TABLE dbo.Sensors
(
  sensorid    INT        NOT NULL
    CONSTRAINT PK_Sensors PRIMARY KEY,
  description VARCHAR(50) NOT NULL
);

INSERT INTO dbo.Sensors(sensorid, description)
VALUES
  (1, 'Restaurant Fancy Schmancy beer fridge'),
  (2, 'Restaurant Fancy Schmancy wine cellar');

CREATE TABLE dbo.SensorMeasurements
(
  sensorid    INT NOT NULL
    CONSTRAINT FK_SensorMeasurements_Sensors REFERENCES dbo.Sensors,
  ts          DATETIME2(0)  NOT NULL,
  temperature NUMERIC(5, 2) NOT NULL, -- Fahrenheit
  humidity    NUMERIC(5, 2) NOT NULL, -- percent
  CONSTRAINT PK_SensorMeasurements PRIMARY KEY(sensorid, ts)
);

INSERT INTO dbo.SensorMeasurements(sensorid, ts, temperature, humidity)
VALUES
  (1, '20220609 06:00:03', 39.16, 86.28),
  (1, '20220609 09:59:57', 39.72, 83.44),
  (1, '20220609 13:59:59', 38.93, 84.33),
  (1, '20220609 18:00:00', 39.42, 79.66),
```

```
(1, '20220609 22:00:01', 40.08, 94.44),
(1, '20220610 01:59:57', 41.26, 90.42),
(1, '20220610 05:59:59', 40.89, 72.94),
(1, '20220610 09:59:58', 40.03, 84.48),
(1, '20220610 14:00:03', 41.23, 93.47),
(1, '20220610 17:59:59', 39.32, 88.09),
(1, '20220610 21:59:57', 41.19, 92.89),
(1, '20220611 01:59:58', 40.88, 89.23),
(1, '20220611 06:00:03', 41.14, 82.27),
(1, '20220611 10:00:00', 39.20, 86.00),
(1, '20220611 14:00:02', 39.41, 74.92),
(1, '20220611 18:00:02', 41.12, 87.37),
(1, '20220611 21:59:59', 40.67, 84.63),
(1, '20220612 02:00:02', 41.15, 86.16),
(1, '20220612 06:00:02', 39.23, 74.59),
(1, '20220612 10:00:00', 41.40, 86.80),
(1, '20220612 14:00:00', 41.20, 79.97),
(1, '20220612 18:00:03', 40.11, 92.84),
(1, '20220612 22:00:03', 40.87, 94.23),
(1, '20220613 02:00:00', 39.03, 92.44),
(1, '20220613 05:59:57', 40.19, 94.72),
(1, '20220613 10:00:02', 39.55, 87.77),
(1, '20220613 14:00:02', 38.94, 89.06),
(1, '20220613 18:00:03', 40.88, 73.81),
(1, '20220613 21:59:57', 41.24, 86.56),
(1, '20220614 02:00:00', 40.25, 76.64),
(1, '20220614 06:00:01', 40.73, 90.66),
(1, '20220614 10:00:03', 40.82, 92.76),
(1, '20220614 13:59:58', 39.70, 73.74),
(1, '20220614 17:59:57', 39.65, 89.38),
(1, '20220614 22:00:02', 39.47, 73.36),
(1, '20220615 02:00:03', 39.14, 77.89),
(1, '20220615 06:00:00', 40.82, 86.84),
(1, '20220615 09:59:57', 39.91, 90.09),
(1, '20220615 13:59:57', 41.34, 82.88),
(1, '20220615 18:00:01', 40.51, 86.58),
(1, '20220615 22:00:00', 41.23, 83.85),
(2, '20220609 06:00:01', 54.95, 75.39),
(2, '20220609 10:00:03', 56.94, 71.34),
(2, '20220609 13:59:59', 54.07, 68.09),
(2, '20220609 18:00:02', 54.05, 65.50),
(2, '20220609 22:00:00', 53.37, 66.28),
(2, '20220610 01:59:58', 56.33, 79.90),
(2, '20220610 05:59:58', 57.00, 65.88),
(2, '20220610 10:00:02', 54.64, 61.10),
(2, '20220610 14:00:01', 53.48, 69.76),
(2, '20220610 17:59:57', 55.15, 65.85),
(2, '20220610 22:00:02', 54.48, 75.90),
(2, '20220611 02:00:00', 54.55, 62.28),
(2, '20220611 06:00:01', 54.56, 66.36),
(2, '20220611 09:59:58', 55.92, 77.53),
(2, '20220611 14:00:02', 55.89, 68.57),
(2, '20220611 18:00:01', 54.82, 62.04),
(2, '20220611 22:00:01', 55.58, 76.20),
(2, '20220613 01:59:58', 56.29, 62.33),
(2, '20220615 10:00:03', 53.24, 70.67),
(2, '20220615 13:59:59', 55.93, 77.60),
```

```
    (2, '20220615 18:00:01', 54.05, 66.56),
    (2, '20220615 21:59:58', 54.66, 61.13);

SELECT * FROM dbo.Sensors;

SELECT * FROM dbo.SensorMeasurements;
```

The last two queries in the above code return the following output with the contents of both tables:

```
sensorid   description
---------  ------------------------------------
1          Restaurant Fancy Schmancy beer fridge
2          Restaurant Fancy Schmancy wine cellar

(2 rows affected)

sensorid   ts                   temperature humidity
---------  -------------------- ----------- ---------
1          2022-06-09 06:00:03  39.16       86.28
1          2022-06-09 09:59:57  39.72       83.44
1          2022-06-09 13:59:59  38.93       84.33
1          2022-06-09 18:00:00  39.42       79.66
1          2022-06-09 22:00:01  40.08       94.44
1          2022-06-10 01:59:57  41.26       90.42
1          2022-06-10 05:59:59  40.89       72.94
1          2022-06-10 09:59:58  40.03       84.48
1          2022-06-10 14:00:03  41.23       93.47
1          2022-06-10 17:59:59  39.32       88.09
1          2022-06-10 21:59:57  41.19       92.89
1          2022-06-11 01:59:58  40.88       89.23
1          2022-06-11 06:00:03  41.14       82.27
1          2022-06-11 10:00:00  39.20       86.00
1          2022-06-11 14:00:02  39.41       74.92
1          2022-06-11 18:00:02  41.12       87.37
1          2022-06-11 21:59:59  40.67       84.63
1          2022-06-12 02:00:02  41.15       86.16
1          2022-06-12 06:00:02  39.23       74.59
1          2022-06-12 10:00:00  41.40       86.80
1          2022-06-12 14:00:00  41.20       79.97
1          2022-06-12 18:00:03  40.11       92.84
1          2022-06-12 22:00:03  40.87       94.23
1          2022-06-13 02:00:00  39.03       92.44
1          2022-06-13 05:59:57  40.19       94.72
1          2022-06-13 10:00:02  39.55       87.77
1          2022-06-13 14:00:02  38.94       89.06
1          2022-06-13 18:00:03  40.88       73.81
1          2022-06-13 21:59:57  41.24       86.56
1          2022-06-14 02:00:00  40.25       76.64
1          2022-06-14 06:00:01  40.73       90.66
1          2022-06-14 10:00:03  40.82       92.76
1          2022-06-14 13:59:58  39.70       73.74
1          2022-06-14 17:59:57  39.65       89.38
1          2022-06-14 22:00:02  39.47       73.36
1          2022-06-15 02:00:03  39.14       77.89
1          2022-06-15 06:00:00  40.82       86.84
1          2022-06-15 09:59:57  39.91       90.09
```

```
1        2022-06-15 13:59:57    41.34      82.88
1        2022-06-15 18:00:01    40.51      86.58
1        2022-06-15 22:00:00    41.23      83.85
2        2022-06-09 06:00:01    54.95      75.39
2        2022-06-09 10:00:03    56.94      71.34
2        2022-06-09 13:59:59    54.07      68.09
2        2022-06-09 18:00:02    54.05      65.50
2        2022-06-09 22:00:00    53.37      66.28
2        2022-06-10 01:59:58    56.33      79.90
2        2022-06-10 05:59:58    57.00      65.88
2        2022-06-10 10:00:02    54.64      61.10
2        2022-06-10 14:00:01    53.48      69.76
2        2022-06-10 17:59:57    55.15      65.85
2        2022-06-10 22:00:02    54.48      75.90
2        2022-06-11 02:00:00    54.55      62.28
2        2022-06-11 06:00:01    54.56      66.36
2        2022-06-11 09:59:58    55.92      77.53
2        2022-06-11 14:00:02    55.89      68.57
2        2022-06-11 18:00:01    54.82      62.04
2        2022-06-11 22:00:01    55.58      76.20
2        2022-06-13 01:59:58    56.29      62.33
2        2022-06-15 10:00:03    53.24      70.67
2        2022-06-15 13:59:59    55.93      77.60
2        2022-06-15 18:00:01    54.05      66.56
2        2022-06-15 21:59:58    54.66      61.13

(63 rows affected)
```

As you can see, the sensors take readings about every four hours. Also notice that sensor 2 was offline during a few periods between June 12 and June 15, 2022, and while it was offline no reading was recorded.

The *DATE_BUCKET* function

The *DATE_BUCKET* function was initially introduced in Azure SQL Edge, which is Microsoft's optimized relational database engine for IoT and IoT Edge deployments. Later on, Microsoft added the function to SQL Server 2022 and Azure SQL Database. I'll start by explaining how to use the function in case you do have access to it, but also how to achieve the same functionality with a custom method in case you don't.

The purpose of the *DATE_BUCKET* function is to return the starting point of the time bucket that contains the input timestamp. You might find it odd, then, that the choice for the function's name was *DATE*_BUCKET and not *TIME*_BUCKET, but that ship has sailed already. The function's result can be used as the identifier of the containing bucket, and as such as a grouping element in a query.

Syntax

DATE_BUCKET (*datepart*, *bucketwidth*, *ts*[, *origin*])

In order to identify the containing time bucket for some input timestamp (*ts* in short), you first need to think of the arrow of time as being divided into time buckets. Naturally, you need some starting point for the buckets. That's what you define with the input *origin*. This input can be of any date and time data type. It is optional. If unspecified, the default is 1900-01-01 00:00:00.000. With the *datepart* input you specify the date and time part you want to use, such as *year, month, day, hour, minute, second,* and so on. With the *bucketwidth* input you specify the bucket width in terms of the specified part. For example, if you specify *hour* as *datepart* and 12 as *bucketwidth* you define 12-hour buckets. The input *ts* represents the input timestamp for which you want to return the containing bucket's start time. This input can be of any date and time type, and should match the type of the input *origin*. The function's return type is the same as the type of the input *ts*.

Later I'll demonstrate how to use the function in a query against the *SensorMeasurements* table, but first I want to show an example using local variables as inputs. Variables and parameters are covered later in the book, in Chapter 12. Consider the following code:

```
DECLARE
  @ts            AS DATETIME2(0) = '20220102 12:00:03',
  @bucketwidth AS INT = 12,
  @origin        AS DATETIME2(0) = '20220101 00:05:00';

SELECT DATE_BUCKET(hour, @bucketwidth, @ts, @origin);
```

Here you define 12-hour buckets, starting with 2022-01-01 00:05:00 as the origin point, and request the starting point of the bucket containing the timestamp 2022-01-02 12:00:03.

This code generates the following output:

```
---------------------------
2022-01-02 00:05:00
```

Figure 7-1 can help you understand visually how the function works and the logic leading to the function's result.

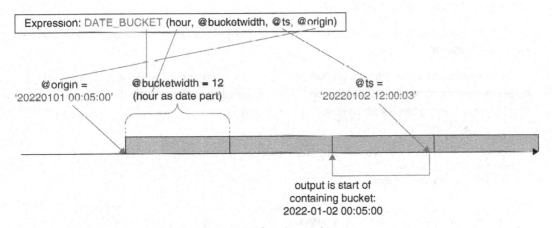

FIGURE 7-1 Understanding how the *DATE_BUCKET* function works

The first four 12-hour buckets to the right of the origin point 2022-01-01 00:05:00 have the following start times:

1. 2022-01-01 00:05:00

2. 2022-01-01 12:05:00

3. 2022-01-02 00:05:00

4. 2022-01-02 12:05:00

The input timestamp 2022-01-02 12:00:03 belongs to the third bucket, and hence the function returns the value 2022-01-02 00:05:00, which is the start of the containing bucket.

Custom computation of start of containing bucket

In this section I describe a custom computation of the start of the containing bucket for given *datepart*, *@bucketwidth*, *@ts*, and *@origin*. At a high level, you need to add to *@origin* as many units of *datepart* as appear in the whole buckets that exist between *@origin* and *@ts*. Consider the sample inputs that I used earlier in the example with the *DATE_BUCKET* function:

```
DECLARE
  @ts          AS DATETIME2(0) = '20220102 12:00:03',
  @bucketwidth AS INT = 12,
  @origin      AS DATETIME2(0) = '20220101 00:05:00';
```

Make sure that you identify both the inputs and the desired output in the illustration in Figure 7-1. There are two whole 12-hour buckets that exist between *@origin* (2022-01-01 00:05:00) and *@ts* (2022-01-02 12:00:03). Since each whole bucket contains 12 units of an hour, those two whole buckets contain 24 hours. Add those 24 hours to *@origin*, and you get the desired result, 2022-01-02 00:05:00, which is the start of the bucket that contains *@ts*.

Hopefully the logic behind the computation is clear. Now you need to translate this to T-SQL code. I'll build the solution in steps.

Before you can compute how many whole buckets exist between *@origin* and *@ts*, you need to compute how many whole units of *datepart* (hour in our case) exist between the two. An obvious attempt at achieving this is with the *DATEDIFF* function, like so:

```
DECLARE
  @ts          AS DATETIME2(0) = '20220102 12:00:03',
  @bucketwidth AS INT = 12,
  @origin      AS DATETIME2(0) = '20220101 00:05:00';
SELECT
  DATEDIFF(hour, @origin, @ts) AS grosshourdiff;
```

Let's call the result of this step's computation *grosshourdiff*. There is a tricky situation with the *DATEDIFF* function, though. When you use it to get the difference in terms of hours, it only cares about the hour part of the inputs and above (day, month, and year), ignoring the parts below the hour (minutes, seconds, and so on). So if the point within the hour in *@origin* (05:00) is greater than the point within the hour in *@ts* (00:03), which it is in this example, the difference will be greater than the actual by 1. In this example, the *DATEDIFF* function reports that there are 36 hours between the inputs, even though there are actually only 35 whole hours between the two.

To check whether you need to correct *grosshourdiff*, add *grosshourdiff* hours to *@origin*. If the result is greater than *@ts*, you need to subtract 1; otherwise, you don't. You can handle the correction logic with a *CASE* expression, like so:

```
DECLARE
  @ts          AS DATETIME2(0) = '20220102 12:00:03',
  @bucketwidth AS INT = 12,
  @origin      AS DATETIME2(0) = '20220101 00:05:00';

SELECT
  DATEDIFF(hour, @origin, @ts)
    - CASE
        WHEN DATEADD(hour, DATEDIFF(hour, @origin, @ts), @origin)
               > @ts THEN 1
        ELSE 0
      END AS nethourdiff;
```

Let's call the result of this computation *nethourdiff*. In our case, this step's result is 35, meaning that there are 35 whole hours between *@origin* and *@ts*.

Next, you need to identify how many units of *datepart* appear in the whole buckets that exist between *@origin* and *@ts*. To achieve this, you first divide *nethourdiff* by *@bucketwidth*, using integer division. This gives you the number of whole buckets. Then you multiply the result by *@bucketwidth* to get the number of units of *datepart* (hour in our case) in those whole buckets. This step is achieved with the following code:

```
DECLARE
  @ts          AS DATETIME2(0) = '20220102 12:00:03',
  @bucketwidth AS INT = 12,
  @origin      AS DATETIME2(0) = '20220101 00:05:00';

SELECT
  (DATEDIFF(hour, @origin, @ts)
    - CASE
        WHEN DATEADD(hour, DATEDIFF(hour, @origin, @ts), @origin)
               > @ts THEN 1
        ELSE 0
      END) / @bucketwidth * @bucketwidth AS hoursinwholebuckets;
```

As explained in Chapter 2, in the section about predicates and operators, when using the division operator / with integer operands, you get integer division. Let's call the output of this step *hoursin-wholebuckets*. In our case, this step's result is 24. Indeed, there are 24 hours in the two whole 12-hour buckets that exist between *@origin* and *@ts*.

The last step is to add *hoursinwholebuckets* hours to *@origin* to get the start of the bucket that contains *@ts*. This is achieved with the following code, holding the complete solution expression:

```
DECLARE
  @ts          AS DATETIME2(0) = '20220102 12:00:03',
  @bucketwidth AS INT = 12,
  @origin      AS DATETIME2(0) = '20220101 00:05:00';

SELECT
  DATEADD(
    hour,
    (DATEDIFF(hour, @origin, @ts)
      - CASE
          WHEN DATEADD(hour, DATEDIFF(hour, @origin, @ts), @origin)
                 > @ts THEN 1
          ELSE 0
        END) / @bucketwidth * @bucketwidth,
    @origin) AS bucketstart;
```

This code generates the following output:

```
bucketstart
---------------------------
2022-01-02 00:05:00
```

This value is indeed the start of the 12-hour bucket that contains *@ts*.

Applying bucket logic to sample data

In real life you will typically want to bucketize time series data stored in a table, like in our *SensorMeasurements* table. As an example, suppose that you need to query this table and, for each reading, compute the respective start of the bucket. For this purpose, you need to define 12-hour buckets starting at midnight, so you can use midnight of any date as the origin. Here's a query using the *DATE_BUCKET* function that achieves this task:

```
DECLARE
  @bucketwidth AS INT = 12,
  @origin      AS DATETIME2(0) = '19000101 00:00:00';

SELECT sensorid, ts,
  DATE_BUCKET(hour, @bucketwidth, ts, @origin) AS bucketstart
FROM dbo.SensorMeasurements;
```

Recall that the base date at midnight happens to be the default value of the input *origin*, so in this example it would be safe to omit this input if you like. Observe that this time the input timestamp value to the function is the column *ts* from the table.

To achieve the same task without the *DATE_BUCKET* function, replace the function call with our custom computation, like so:

```
DECLARE
  @bucketwidth AS INT = 12,
  @origin      AS DATETIME2(0) = '19000101 00:00:00';

SELECT sensorid, ts,
  DATEADD(
    hour,
    (DATEDIFF(hour, @origin, ts)
      - CASE
          WHEN DATEADD(hour, DATEDIFF(hour, @origin, ts), @origin)
                 > ts THEN 1
          ELSE 0
        END) / @bucketwidth * @bucketwidth,
    @origin) AS bucketstart
FROM dbo.SensorMeasurements;
```

Both queries generate the following output:

```
sensorid  ts                   bucketstart
--------- -------------------- --------------------
1         2022-06-09 06:00:03  2022-06-09 00:00:00
1         2022-06-09 09:59:57  2022-06-09 00:00:00
1         2022-06-09 13:59:59  2022-06-09 12:00:00
1         2022-06-09 18:00:00  2022-06-09 12:00:00
1         2022-06-09 22:00:01  2022-06-09 12:00:00
1         2022-06-10 01:59:57  2022-06-10 00:00:00
1         2022-06-10 05:59:59  2022-06-10 00:00:00
1         2022-06-10 09:59:58  2022-06-10 00:00:00
1         2022-06-10 14:00:03  2022-06-10 12:00:00
1         2022-06-10 17:59:59  2022-06-10 12:00:00
1         2022-06-10 21:59:57  2022-06-10 12:00:00
1         2022-06-11 01:59:58  2022-06-11 00:00:00
1         2022-06-11 06:00:03  2022-06-11 00:00:00
1         2022-06-11 10:00:00  2022-06-11 00:00:00
1         2022-06-11 14:00:02  2022-06-11 12:00:00
1         2022-06-11 18:00:02  2022-06-11 12:00:00
1         2022-06-11 21:59:59  2022-06-11 12:00:00
1         2022-06-12 02:00:02  2022-06-12 00:00:00
1         2022-06-12 06:00:02  2022-06-12 00:00:00
1         2022-06-12 10:00:00  2022-06-12 00:00:00
1         2022-06-12 14:00:00  2022-06-12 12:00:00
1         2022-06-12 18:00:03  2022-06-12 12:00:00
1         2022-06-12 22:00:03  2022-06-12 12:00:00
1         2022-06-13 02:00:00  2022-06-13 00:00:00
1         2022-06-13 05:59:57  2022-06-13 00:00:00
1         2022-06-13 10:00:02  2022-06-13 00:00:00
1         2022-06-13 14:00:02  2022-06-13 12:00:00
1         2022-06-13 18:00:03  2022-06-13 12:00:00
1         2022-06-13 21:59:57  2022-06-13 12:00:00
1         2022-06-14 02:00:00  2022-06-14 00:00:00
```

```
1          2022-06-14 06:00:01  2022-06-14 00:00:00
1          2022-06-14 10:00:03  2022-06-14 00:00:00
1          2022-06-14 13:59:58  2022-06-14 12:00:00
1          2022-06-14 17:59:57  2022-06-14 12:00:00
1          2022-06-14 22:00:02  2022-06-14 12:00:00
1          2022-06-15 02:00:03  2022-06-15 00:00:00
1          2022-06-15 06:00:00  2022-06-15 00:00:00
1          2022-06-15 09:59:57  2022-06-15 00:00:00
1          2022-06-15 13:59:57  2022-06-15 12:00:00
1          2022-06-15 18:00:01  2022-06-15 12:00:00
1          2022-06-15 22:00:00  2022-06-15 12:00:00
2          2022-06-09 06:00:01  2022-06-09 00:00:00
2          2022-06-09 10:00:03  2022-06-09 00:00:00
2          2022-06-09 13:59:59  2022-06-09 12:00:00
2          2022-06-09 18:00:02  2022-06-09 12:00:00
2          2022-06-09 22:00:00  2022-06-09 12:00:00
2          2022-06-10 01:59:58  2022-06-10 00:00:00
2          2022-06-10 05:59:58  2022-06-10 00:00:00
2          2022-06-10 10:00:02  2022-06-10 00:00:00
2          2022-06-10 14:00:01  2022-06-10 12:00:00
2          2022-06-10 17:59:57  2022-06-10 12:00:00
2          2022-06-10 22:00:02  2022-06-10 12:00:00
2          2022-06-11 02:00:00  2022-06-11 00:00:00
2          2022-06-11 06:00:01  2022-06-11 00:00:00
2          2022-06-11 09:59:58  2022-06-11 00:00:00
2          2022-06-11 14:00:02  2022-06-11 12:00:00
2          2022-06-11 18:00:01  2022-06-11 12:00:00
2          2022-06-11 22:00:01  2022-06-11 12:00:00
2          2022-06-13 01:59:58  2022-06-13 00:00:00
2          2022-06-15 10:00:03  2022-06-15 00:00:00
2          2022-06-15 13:59:59  2022-06-15 12:00:00
2          2022-06-15 18:00:01  2022-06-15 12:00:00
2          2022-06-15 21:59:58  2022-06-15 12:00:00

(63 rows affected)
```

Typically, time series analysis obviously doesn't end with the computation of the start of bucket per reading. Usually, you will want to group the data by the start of bucket, and then compute aggregates like the minimum, maximum, and average temperatures per bucket. You could define a named table expression like a CTE based on the query that computes the *bucketstart* column. This will allow the outer query to interact with this column name with multiple references. Then have the outer query group the data from the CTE by the *sensorid* and *bucketstart* columns, and return the *bucketstart* column along with the desired aggregates per group. You can also compute the exclusive end of each bucket by adding *@bucketwidth* units of *datepart* to *bucketstart*.

Here's the code that achieves this using the *DATE_BUCKET* function:

```
DECLARE
  @bucketwidth AS INT = 12,
  @origin      AS DATETIME2(0) = '19000101 00:00:00';

WITH C AS
(
```

```
  SELECT sensorid, ts, temperature,
    DATE_BUCKET(hour, @bucketwidth, ts, @origin) AS bucketstart
  FROM dbo.SensorMeasurements
)
SELECT sensorid, bucketstart,
  DATEADD(hour, @bucketwidth, bucketstart) AS bucketend,
  MIN(temperature) AS mintemp,
  MAX(temperature) AS maxtemp,
  AVG(temperature) AS avgtemp
FROM C
GROUP BY sensorid, bucketstart
ORDER BY sensorid, bucketstart;
```

And here's the code that achieves this without the *DATE_BUCKET* function:

```
DECLARE
  @bucketwidth AS INT = 12,
  @origin      AS DATETIME2(0) = '19000101 00:00:00';

WITH C AS
(
  SELECT sensorid, ts, temperature,
    DATEADD(
      hour,
      (DATEDIFF(hour, @origin, ts)
        - CASE
            WHEN DATEADD(hour, DATEDIFF(hour, @origin, ts), @origin)
                    > ts THEN 1
            ELSE 0
          END) / @bucketwidth * @bucketwidth,
      @origin) AS bucketstart
  FROM dbo.SensorMeasurements
)
SELECT sensorid, bucketstart,
  DATEADD(hour, @bucketwidth, bucketstart) AS bucketend,
  MIN(temperature) AS mintemp,
  MAX(temperature) AS maxtemp,
  AVG(temperature) AS avgtemp
FROM C
GROUP BY sensorid, bucketstart
ORDER BY sensorid, bucketstart;
```

Both queries return the following output:

```
sensorid  bucketstart          bucketend            mintemp   maxtemp   avgtemp
--------  -------------------  -------------------  --------  --------  ----------
1         2022-06-09 00:00:00  2022-06-09 12:00:00  39.16     39.72     39.440000
1         2022-06-09 12:00:00  2022-06-10 00:00:00  38.93     40.08     39.476666
1         2022-06-10 00:00:00  2022-06-10 12:00:00  40.03     41.26     40.726666
1         2022-06-10 12:00:00  2022-06-11 00:00:00  39.32     41.23     40.580000
1         2022-06-11 00:00:00  2022-06-11 12:00:00  39.20     41.14     40.406666
1         2022-06-11 12:00:00  2022-06-12 00:00:00  39.41     41.12     40.400000
1         2022-06-12 00:00:00  2022-06-12 12:00:00  39.23     41.40     40.593333
1         2022-06-12 12:00:00  2022-06-13 00:00:00  40.11     41.20     40.726666
```

```
1          2022-06-13 00:00:00  2022-06-13 12:00:00  39.03   40.19   39.590000
1          2022-06-13 12:00:00  2022-06-14 00:00:00  38.94   41.24   40.353333
1          2022-06-14 00:00:00  2022-06-14 12:00:00  40.25   40.82   40.600000
1          2022-06-14 12:00:00  2022-06-15 00:00:00  39.47   39.70   39.606666
1          2022-06-15 00:00:00  2022-06-15 12:00:00  39.14   40.82   39.956666
1          2022-06-15 12:00:00  2022-06-16 00:00:00  40.51   41.34   41.026666
2          2022-06-09 00:00:00  2022-06-09 12:00:00  54.95   56.94   55.945000
2          2022-06-09 12:00:00  2022-06-10 00:00:00  53.37   54.07   53.830000
2          2022-06-10 00:00:00  2022-06-10 12:00:00  54.64   57.00   55.990000
2          2022-06-10 12:00:00  2022-06-11 00:00:00  53.48   55.15   54.370000
2          2022-06-11 00:00:00  2022-06-11 12:00:00  54.55   55.92   55.010000
2          2022-06-11 12:00:00  2022-06-12 00:00:00  54.82   55.89   55.430000
2          2022-06-13 00:00:00  2022-06-13 12:00:00  56.29   56.29   56.290000
2          2022-06-15 00:00:00  2022-06-15 12:00:00  53.24   53.24   53.240000
2          2022-06-15 12:00:00  2022-06-16 00:00:00  54.05   55.93   54.880000

(23 rows affected)
```

From here on I'll compute the bucket start using the longer, custom method. If you have access to the *DATE_BUCKET* function, you can use it instead.

As the next example, suppose that you want to aggregate temperatures using 7-day buckets, with Monday as the start of week. To achieve this, you will want to use any date that is a Monday as the origin point. For example, January 1, 1900, happens to be a Monday. You will also want to use *DATE* as the type for the input *@origin*, the date part *day* in all *DATEDIFF* and *DATEADD* computations, and 7 as the bucket width. Here's the complete solution's code:

```
DECLARE
  @bucketwidth AS INT = 7,
  @origin      AS DATE = '19000101';

WITH C AS
(
  SELECT sensorid, ts, temperature,
    DATEADD(
      day,
      (DATEDIFF(day, @origin, ts)
        - CASE
            WHEN DATEADD(day, DATEDIFF(day, @origin, ts), @origin)
                   > ts THEN 1
            ELSE 0
          END) / @bucketwidth * @bucketwidth,
      @origin) AS bucketstart
  FROM dbo.SensorMeasurements
)
SELECT sensorid, bucketstart,
  DATEADD(day, @bucketwidth, bucketstart) AS bucketend,
  MIN(temperature) AS mintemp,
  MAX(temperature) AS maxtemp,
  AVG(temperature) AS avgtemp
FROM C
GROUP BY sensorid, bucketstart
ORDER BY sensorid, bucketstart;
```

This code generates the following output:

```
sensorid  bucketstart bucketend   mintemp  maxtemp   avgtemp
--------- ----------- ----------- -------- -------- ----------
1         2022-06-06  2022-06-13  38.93    41.40    40.330869
1         2022-06-13  2022-06-20  38.94    41.34    40.188888
2         2022-06-06  2022-06-13  53.37    57.00    55.045882
2         2022-06-13  2022-06-20  53.24    56.29    54.834000

(4 rows affected)
```

Alternatively, you can use 1 as the bucket width and *week* as the date part.

```
DECLARE
  @bucketwidth AS INT = 1,
  @origin      AS DATE = '19000101';

WITH C AS
(
  SELECT sensorid, ts, temperature,
    DATEADD(
      week,
      (DATEDIFF(week, @origin, ts)
        - CASE
            WHEN DATEADD(week, DATEDIFF(week, @origin, ts), @origin)
                   > ts THEN 1
            ELSE 0
          END) / @bucketwidth * @bucketwidth,
      @origin) AS bucketstart
  FROM dbo.SensorMeasurements
)
SELECT sensorid, bucketstart,
  DATEADD(week, @bucketwidth, bucketstart) AS bucketend,
  MIN(temperature) AS mintemp,
  MAX(temperature) AS maxtemp,
  AVG(temperature) AS avgtemp
FROM C
GROUP BY sensorid, bucketstart
ORDER BY sensorid, bucketstart;
```

Feel free to try various origins, date parts, and bucket sizes to see how your choices affect the result.

Gap filling

A common challenge with time series handling is that sometimes entire buckets are missing, yet you still want them represented in the analysis's result. This happens when the source data doesn't even have a single measurement in the bucket in question. For example, suppose that you want to analyze temperature data during the week starting on June 9, 2022, and ending on June 15, 2022, in 12-hour buckets starting at midnight. You want a result row with aggregated temperatures (min, max, and average) per sensor and bucket during this week. Recall that in our sample data, sensor 2 was offline during a couple of periods between June 12, 2022, and June 15, 2022. Perhaps the sensor's battery was depleted or it had some malfunction. You need to come up with some gap-filling method that will add the missing buckets to the result. Naturally, since there were no relevant measurements during the empty buckets, the result of the aggregates for those buckets should be *NULL*.

Gap-filling is typically handled by arranging a table holding all possible points in the range of interest. In our case, this would mean all possible bucket start times in the week in question. You then apply a left outer join between that table and the bucketized data with the missing buckets. This way, you get all bucket information, including missing buckets, from the left side of the join, and all aggregated measures for existing buckets from the right side.

Regarding the table with all possible bucket start times, it could be an actual base table that you create in the database and fill with the relevant data. It could also be a table expression created by a query. Either way, if you're using SQL Server 2022 or higher, or Azure SQL Database, you can use the *GENERATE_SERIES* function to help you generate the desired sequence of date and time values. If you need a reminder of how to use this function, see Chapter 2. Recall that this function accepts two numeric inputs for the range start and stop values and returns a result set with a column called *value* with the sequence of numbers in the desired range. You can use this function with inputs 0 as the start value and 13 as the stop value (13 is the number of 12-hour buckets in a week minus 1). For these inputs, the function will return 14 rows with the values 0 through 13 in the column *value*. Using the *DATEADD* function, you can add *value* times 12 hours to the start of the period of interest (2022-06-09 00:00:00, in our case), and this way get all possible bucket start times in the period of interest.

Of course, all of this logic can be easily parameterized. Suppose that you get the delimiters of the period of interest as parameters called *@startperiod* and *@endperiod*. You also get the hourly bucket width as a parameter called *@bucketwidth*. The computation of the input stop value for the *GENERATE_SERIES* function is DATEDIFF(hour, @startperiod, @endperiod) / @bucketwidth. The computation of the result start of bucket is DATEADD(hour, value * @bucketwidth, @startperiod).

Here's the complete query generating all possible 12-hour bucket start times during the week of interest, using local variables representing the parameters:

```
DECLARE
  @bucketwidth AS INT = 12,
  @startperiod AS DATETIME2(0) = '20220609 00:00:00',
  @endperiod   AS DATETIME2(0) = '20220615 12:00:00';

SELECT DATEADD(hour, value * @bucketwidth, @startperiod) AS ts
FROM GENERATE_SERIES(0, DATEDIFF(hour, @startperiod, @endperiod) / @bucketwidth) AS N;
```

This code generates the following output:

```
ts
---------------------------
2022-06-09 00:00:00
2022-06-09 12:00:00
2022-06-10 00:00:00
2022-06-10 12:00:00
2022-06-11 00:00:00
2022-06-11 12:00:00
2022-06-12 00:00:00
```

```
2022-06-12 12:00:00
2022-06-13 00:00:00
2022-06-13 12:00:00
2022-06-14 00:00:00
2022-06-14 12:00:00
2022-06-15 00:00:00
2022-06-15 12:00:00

(14 rows affected)
```

You're now ready to use the above query in our gap-filling solution for the task at hand. You can use a multi-CTE solution, with a CTE for each step.

Define a CTE called *TS* (short for timestamps) based on the above query. This CTE represents all possible bucket start times in the period of interest. Define another CTE called *C1* that computes bucket start times for the measurements in the *SensorMeasurements* table, and a CTE called *C2* that groups and aggregates the data from *C1* for existing buckets. You're now ready for the final step with the outer query. In this step you apply a cross join between the table *Sensors* and the CTE called *TS* to get a row for every possible pair of sensor and bucket start time. You then apply a left outer join between the result and *C2*, matching sensor IDs and time stamps from both sides, and return bucket information from the left side of the join, and measure information from the right side.

Here's the complete code implementing this logic using the *DATE_BUCKET* function:

```
DECLARE
  @bucketwidth AS INT = 12,
  @startperiod AS DATETIME2(0) = '20220609 00:00:00',
  @endperiod   AS DATETIME2(0) = '20220615 12:00:00';

WITH TS AS
(
  SELECT DATEADD(hour, value * @bucketwidth, @startperiod) AS ts
  FROM GENERATE_SERIES(0, DATEDIFF(hour, @startperiod, @endperiod) / @bucketwidth) AS N
),
C1 AS
(
  SELECT sensorid, ts, temperature,
    DATE_BUCKET(hour, @bucketwidth, ts, @startperiod) AS bucketstart
  FROM dbo.SensorMeasurements
),
C2 AS
(
  SELECT sensorid, bucketstart,
    MIN(temperature) AS mintemp,
    MAX(temperature) AS maxtemp,
    AVG(temperature) AS avgtemp
  FROM C1
  GROUP BY sensorid, bucketstart
)
SELECT S.sensorid, TS.ts AS bucketstart,
  DATEADD(hour, @bucketwidth, TS.ts) AS bucketend,
  mintemp, maxtemp, avgtemp
FROM dbo.Sensors AS S
  CROSS JOIN TS
```

```
    LEFT OUTER JOIN C2
      ON S.sensorid = C2.sensorid
      AND TS.ts = C2.bucketstart
ORDER BY sensorid, bucketstart;
```

This code generates the following desired output:

sensorid	bucketstart	bucketend	mintemp	maxtemp	avgtemp
1	2022-06-09 00:00:00	2022-06-09 12:00:00	39.16	39.72	39.440000
1	2022-06-09 12:00:00	2022-06-10 00:00:00	38.93	40.08	39.476666
1	2022-06-10 00:00:00	2022-06-10 12:00:00	40.03	41.26	40.726666
1	2022-06-10 12:00:00	2022-06-11 00:00:00	39.32	41.23	40.580000
1	2022-06-11 00:00:00	2022-06-11 12:00:00	39.20	41.14	40.406666
1	2022-06-11 12:00:00	2022-06-12 00:00:00	39.41	41.12	40.400000
1	2022-06-12 00:00:00	2022-06-12 12:00:00	39.23	41.40	40.593333
1	2022-06-12 12:00:00	2022-06-13 00:00:00	40.11	41.20	40.726666
1	2022-06-13 00:00:00	2022-06-13 12:00:00	39.03	40.19	39.590000
1	2022-06-13 12:00:00	2022-06-14 00:00:00	38.94	41.24	40.353333
1	2022-06-14 00:00:00	2022-06-14 12:00:00	40.25	40.82	40.600000
1	2022-06-14 12:00:00	2022-06-15 00:00:00	39.47	39.70	39.606666
1	2022-06-15 00:00:00	2022-06-15 12:00:00	39.14	40.82	39.956666
1	2022-06-15 12:00:00	2022-06-16 00:00:00	40.51	41.34	41.026666
2	2022-06-09 00:00:00	2022-06-09 12:00:00	54.95	56.94	55.945000
2	2022-06-09 12:00:00	2022-06-10 00:00:00	53.37	54.07	53.830000
2	2022-06-10 00:00:00	2022-06-10 12:00:00	54.64	57.00	55.990000
2	2022-06-10 12:00:00	2022-06-11 00:00:00	53.48	55.15	54.370000
2	2022-06-11 00:00:00	2022-06-11 12:00:00	54.55	55.92	55.010000
2	2022-06-11 12:00:00	2022-06-12 00:00:00	54.82	55.89	55.430000
2	2022-06-12 00:00:00	2022-06-12 12:00:00	NULL	NULL	NULL
2	2022-06-12 12:00:00	2022-06-13 00:00:00	NULL	NULL	NULL
2	2022-06-13 00:00:00	2022-06-13 12:00:00	56.29	56.29	56.290000
2	2022-06-13 12:00:00	2022-06-14 00:00:00	NULL	NULL	NULL
2	2022-06-14 00:00:00	2022-06-14 12:00:00	NULL	NULL	NULL
2	2022-06-14 12:00:00	2022-06-15 00:00:00	NULL	NULL	NULL
2	2022-06-15 00:00:00	2022-06-15 12:00:00	53.24	53.24	53.240000
2	2022-06-15 12:00:00	2022-06-16 00:00:00	54.05	55.93	54.880000

```
(28 rows affected)
```

Observe that empty buckets are included, showing *NULLs* in the aggregated measures.

If you're using a version of SQL Server earlier than 2022, you don't have access to the *GENERATE_SERIES* function. However, I provide a user-defined function called *dbo.GetNums* in the *TSQLV6* database, with similar functionality. This function accepts two integer inputs called @*low* and @*high* and returns a result set with a column called *n* with the sequence of integers in the desired range. You can use *dbo.GetNums* just like you used *GENERATE_SERIES* before to generate the desired sequence of date and time values, like so:

```
DECLARE
  @bucketwidth AS INT = 12,
  @startperiod AS DATETIME2(0) = '20220609 00:00:00',
  @endperiod   AS DATETIME2(0) = '20220615 12:00:00';

SELECT DATEADD(hour, n * @bucketwidth, @startperiod) AS ts
FROM dbo.GetNums(0, DATEDIFF(hour, @startperiod, @endperiod) / @bucketwidth) AS N;
```

As for the complete solution's code, you then combine the above technique with the custom method to compute bucket start times, like so:

```
DECLARE
  @bucketwidth AS INT = 12,
  @startperiod AS DATETIME2(0) = '20220609 00:00:00',
  @endperiod   AS DATETIME2(0) = '20220615 12:00:00';

WITH TS AS
(
  SELECT DATEADD(hour, n * @bucketwidth, @startperiod) AS ts
  FROM dbo.GetNums(0, DATEDIFF(hour, @startperiod, @endperiod) / @bucketwidth) AS N
),
C1 AS
(
  SELECT sensorid, ts, temperature,
    DATEADD(
      hour,
      (DATEDIFF(hour, @startperiod, ts)
        - CASE
            WHEN DATEADD(hour, DATEDIFF(hour, @startperiod, ts), @startperiod)
                  > ts THEN 1
            ELSE 0
          END) / @bucketwidth * @bucketwidth,
      @startperiod) AS bucketstart
  FROM dbo.SensorMeasurements
),
C2 AS
(
  SELECT sensorid, bucketstart,
    MIN(temperature) AS mintemp,
    MAX(temperature) AS maxtemp,
    AVG(temperature) AS avgtemp
  FROM C1
  GROUP BY sensorid, bucketstart
)
SELECT S.sensorid, TS.ts AS bucketstart,
  DATEADD(hour, @bucketwidth, TS.ts) AS bucketend,
  mintemp, maxtemp, avgtemp
FROM dbo.Sensors AS S
  CROSS JOIN TS
  LEFT OUTER JOIN C2
    ON S.sensorid = C2.sensorid
    AND TS.ts = C2.bucketstart
ORDER BY sensorid, bucketstart;
```

If you want to practice the time series topic, you can work on exercises 7 and 8.

Conclusion

This chapter covered window functions, pivoting and unpivoting data, features related to grouping sets, and handling time series.

You use window functions to perform data analysis calculations in a more flexible and efficient manner than you can when using alternative methods. Window functions have numerous practical uses, so it's worth your time to get to know them well.

Using the *NULL treatment clause* with offset window functions that support it, you can indicate that you want to ignore *NULLs* when looking for a value in the requested offset. For example, you can request the last non-*NULL* value with the *LAST_VALUE* function and the *IGNORE NULLS* option.

I covered two techniques to handle pivoting: one using a standard grouped query and another using the more concise yet proprietary *PIVOT* operator. I also covered two methods to handle unpivoting: one using the *APPLY* operator, which allows you to control whether to remove rows with *NULLs*, and another using the *UNPIVOT* operator, which is more concise but removes rows with *NULLs* as a mandatory step.

T-SQL supports features that make the handling of grouping sets flexible and efficient: the *GROUPING SETS*, *CUBE*, and *ROLLUP* subclauses and the *GROUPING* and *GROUPING_ID* functions.

To handle time series data, you usually need to organize the data in time buckets and group and aggregate it by bucket. I showed both a built-in method to achieve this using the *DATE_BUCKET* function as well as a custom method. The former is much simpler and therefore the preferred method in case you're using a platform that supports the function. But it's good to have the custom method in case you're using a platform that doesn't support the function. I also covered a technique to apply gap-filling in case there are missing buckets. For this purpose it's handy to have a table function like the *GetNums* function, which I provide as part of the *TSQLV6* sample database.

Exercises

This section provides exercises to help you familiarize yourself with the subjects discussed in Chapter 7. All exercises for this chapter involve querying the *dbo.Orders* table in the *TSQLV6* database that you created and populated earlier in this chapter by running the code in Listing 7-1.

Exercise 1

Write a query against the *dbo.Orders* table that computes both a rank and a dense rank for each customer order, partitioned by *custid* and ordered by *qty*:

- Table involved: *TSQLV6* database, *dbo.Orders* table

- Desired output:

custid	orderid	qty	rnk	drnk
A	30001	10	1	1
A	40005	10	1	1
A	10001	12	3	2
A	40001	40	4	3
B	20001	12	1	1
B	30003	15	2	2
B	10005	20	3	3
C	10006	14	1	1
C	20002	20	2	2
C	30004	22	3	3
D	30007	30	1	1

Exercise 2

Earlier in the chapter, in the section "Ranking window functions," I provided the following query against the *Sales.OrderValues* view to return distinct values and their associated row numbers:

```
SELECT val, ROW_NUMBER() OVER(ORDER BY val) AS rownum
FROM Sales.OrderValues
GROUP BY val;
```

Can you think of an alternative way to achieve the same task?

- Table involved: *TSQLV6* database, *Sales.OrderValues* view

- Desired output:

```
val        rownum
---------  -------
12.50      1
18.40      2
23.80      3
28.00      4
30.00      5
33.75      6
36.00      7
40.00      8
45.00      9
48.00      10
...
12615.05   793
15810.00   794
16387.50   795

(795 rows affected)
```

Exercise 3

Write a query against the *dbo.Orders* table that computes for each customer order both the difference between the current order quantity and the customer's previous order quantity *and* the difference between the current order quantity and the customer's next order quantity:

- Table involved: *TSQLV6* database, *dbo.Orders* table

- Desired output:

```
custid orderid     qty          diffprev    diffnext
------ ----------- ------------ ----------- -----------
A      30001       10           NULL        -2
A      10001       12           2           -28
A      40001       40           28          30
A      40005       10           -30         NULL
B      10005       20           NULL        8
B      20001       12           -8          -3
B      30003       15           3           NULL
C      30004       22           NULL        8
C      10006       14           -8          -6
C      20002       20           6           NULL
D      30007       30           NULL        NULL
```

Exercise 4

Write a query against the *dbo.Orders* table that returns a row for each employee, a column for each order year, and the count of orders for each employee and order year:

- Table involved: *TSQLV6* database, *dbo.Orders* table

- Desired output:

```
empid       cnt2020     cnt2021     cnt2022
----------- ----------- ----------- -----------
1           1           1           1
2           1           2           1
3           2           0           2
```

Exercise 5

Run the following code to create and populate the *EmpYearOrders* table:

```
USE TSQLV6;

DROP TABLE IF EXISTS dbo.EmpYearOrders;

CREATE TABLE dbo.EmpYearOrders
(
  empid INT NOT NULL
    CONSTRAINT PK_EmpYearOrders PRIMARY KEY,
  cnt2020 INT NULL,
  cnt2021 INT NULL,
  cnt2022 INT NULL
);
```

```
INSERT INTO dbo.EmpYearOrders(empid, cnt2020, cnt2021, cnt2022)
  SELECT empid, [2020] AS cnt2020, [2021] AS cnt2021, [2022] AS cnt2022
  FROM (SELECT empid, YEAR(orderdate) AS orderyear
        FROM dbo.Orders) AS D
    PIVOT(COUNT(orderyear)
          FOR orderyear IN([2020], [2021], [2022])) AS P;

SELECT * FROM dbo.EmpYearOrders;
```

Here's the output for the query:

```
empid       cnt2020      cnt2021      cnt2022
----------- ------------ ------------ -----------
1           1            1            1
2           1            2            1
3           2            0            2
```

Write a query against the *EmpYearOrders* table that unpivots the data, returning a row for each employee and order year with the number of orders. Exclude rows in which the number of orders is 0 (in this example, employee 3 in the year 2021).

- Desired output:

```
empid       orderyear    numorders
----------- ------------ -----------
1           2020         1
1           2021         1
1           2022         1
2           2020         1
2           2021         2
2           2022         1
3           2020         2
3           2022         2
```

Exercise 6

Write a query against the *dbo.Orders* table that returns the total quantities for each of the following: (employee, customer, and order year), (employee and order year), and (customer and order year). Include a result column in the output that uniquely identifies the grouping set with which the current row is associated:

- Table involved: *TSQLV6* database, *dbo.Orders* table

- Desired output:

```
groupingset    empid        custid    orderyear    sumqty
-------------- ------------ --------- ------------ -----------
0              2            A         2020         12
0              3            A         2020         10
4              NULL         A         2020         ??
0              2            A         2021         40
4              NULL         A         2021         40
0              3            A         2022         10
4              NULL         A         2022         10
0              1            B         2020         20
4              NULL         B         2020         20
```

0	2	B	2021	12
4	NULL	B	2021	12
0	2	B	2022	15
4	NULL	B	2022	15
0	3	C	2020	22
4	NIII I	C	2020	22
0	1	C	2021	14
4	NULL	C	2021	14
0	1	C	2022	20
4	NULL	C	2022	20
0	3	D	2022	30
4	NULL	D	2022	30
2	1	NULL	2020	20
2	2	NULL	2020	12
2	3	NULL	2020	32
2	1	NULL	2021	14
2	2	NULL	2021	52
2	1	NULL	2022	20
2	2	NULL	2022	15
2	3	NULL	2022	40

```
(29 rows affected)
```

Exercise 7

Write a query against the *Sales.Orders* table that returns a row for each week, assuming the week starts on a Sunday, with result columns showing when the week started, when the week ended, and the week's order count:

- Table involved: *TSQLV6* database, *Sales.Orders* table

- Desired output, shown here in abbreviated form:

```
startofweek   endofweek    numorders
-----------   ----------   -----------
2020-06-28    2020-07-04   1
2020-07-05    2020-07-11   6
2020-07-12    2020-07-18   5
2020-07-19    2020-07-25   6
2020-07-26    2020-08-01   6
2020-08-02    2020-08-08   5
2020-08-09    2020-08-15   6
2020-08-16    2020-08-22   5
2020-08-23    2020-08-29   6
2020-08-30    2020-09-05   5
...
2022-02-27    2022-03-05   16
2022-03-06    2022-03-12   17
2022-03-13    2022-03-19   17
2022-03-20    2022-03-26   16
2022-03-27    2022-04-02   17
2022-04-03    2022-04-09   17
2022-04-10    2022-04-16   16
2022-04-17    2022-04-23   17
2022-04-24    2022-04-30   17
2022-05-01    2022-05-07   14

(97 rows affected)
```

Exercise 8

Suppose that your organization's fiscal year runs from July 1 to June 30. Write a query against the *Sales. OrderValues* view that returns the total quantities and values per shipper and fiscal year of the order date. The result should have columns for the shipper ID, start date of fiscal year, end date of fiscal year, total quantity, and total value:

- Table involved: *TSQLV6* database, *Sales.OrderValues* view

- Desired output:

```
shipperid   startofyear endofyear   totalqty    totalval
----------- ----------- ----------- ----------- ----------
1           2020-07-01  2021-06-30  6141        123376.50
1           2021-07-01  2022-06-30  9778        225463.50
2           2020-07-01  2021-06-30  8284        190603.18
2           2021-07-01  2022-06-30  11661       342944.51
3           2020-07-01  2021-06-30  7170        175570.33
3           2021-07-01  2022-06-30  8283        207835.20

(6 rows affected)
```

Solutions

This section provides solutions to the Chapter 7 exercises.

Exercise 1

This exercise is pretty basic. Figuring it out is just a matter of being familiar with the syntax for window-ranking functions. Here's the solution query, returning for each order both the rank and the dense rank, partitioned by *custid* and ordered by *qty*:

```
SELECT custid, orderid, qty,
  RANK() OVER(PARTITION BY custid ORDER BY qty) AS rnk,
  DENSE_RANK() OVER(PARTITION BY custid ORDER BY qty) AS drnk
FROM dbo.Orders;
```

You can shorten the query string a bit by using the *WINDOW* clause, like so:

```
SELECT custid, orderid, qty,
  RANK() OVER W AS rnk,
  DENSE_RANK() OVER W AS drnk
FROM dbo.Orders
WINDOW W AS (PARTITION BY custid ORDER BY qty);
```

Exercise 2

Another way to handle this task is to write a query that returns distinct values without a row number computation, define a table expression based on this query, and then compute row numbers in the outer query against the table expression. Here's the solution query:

```
WITH C AS
(
  SELECT DISTINCT val
  FROM Sales.OrderValues
)
SELECT val, ROW_NUMBER() OVER(ORDER BY val) AS rownum
FROM C;
```

Exercise 3

You use the window offset functions *LAG* and *LEAD* to return an element from the previous row and the next row, respectively, based on the indicated partitioning and ordering specification. In this exercise, you need to perform the calculations within each customer's orders; hence, the window partitioning should be based on *custid*. As for ordering, use *orderdate* as the first ordering column and *orderid* as the tiebreaker. Here's the complete solution query:

```
SELECT custid, orderid, qty,
  qty - LAG(qty) OVER(PARTITION BY custid
                      ORDER BY orderdate, orderid) AS diffprev,
  qty - LEAD(qty) OVER(PARTITION BY custid
                       ORDER BY orderdate, orderid) AS diffnext
FROM dbo.Orders;
```

Again, you can shorten the query string a bit by using the *WINDOW* clause, like so:

```
SELECT custid, orderid, qty,
  qty - LAG(qty) OVER W AS diffprev,
  qty - LEAD(qty) OVER W AS diffnext
FROM dbo.Orders
WINDOW W AS (PARTITION BY custid
             ORDER BY orderdate, orderid);
```

This query is a good example that shows you can mix detail elements from the row with window functions in the same expression.

Exercise 4

Solving a pivoting problem is all about identifying the elements involved: the grouping element, spreading element, aggregation element, and aggregate function. After you identify those, you simply fit them into the "template" query for pivoting—whether it's the solution with the grouped query or the solution using the *PIVOT* operator.

In this exercise, the grouping element is the employee (*empid*), the spreading element is order year (*YEAR(orderdate)*), and the aggregate function is *COUNT*; however, identifying the aggregation element is not that straightforward. You want the *COUNT* aggregate function to count matching rows—you don't really care which attribute it counts. In other words, you can use any attribute you want, as long as the attribute does not allow *NULLs*, because aggregate functions ignore *NULLs*.

If it doesn't really matter which attribute you use as the input to the *COUNT* aggregate, why not use the same attribute you already use as the spreading element? In this case, you can use the order year as both the spreading element and aggregation element.

Now that you've identified all pivoting elements, you're ready to write the complete solution. Here's the solution query without using the *PIVOT* operator:

```
USE TSQLV6;

SELECT empid,
  COUNT(CASE WHEN orderyear = 2020 THEN orderyear END) AS cnt2020,
  COUNT(CASE WHEN orderyear = 2021 THEN orderyear END) AS cnt2021,
  COUNT(CASE WHEN orderyear = 2022 THEN orderyear END) AS cnt2022
FROM (SELECT empid, YEAR(orderdate) AS orderyear
      FROM dbo.Orders) AS D
GROUP BY empid;
```

Recall that if you do not specify an *ELSE* clause in a *CASE* expression, an implicit *ELSE NULL* is assumed. Thus, the *CASE* expression produces non-*NULLs* only for matching orders (orders placed by the current employee in the current order year), and only those matching orders are taken into consideration by the *COUNT* aggregate.

Notice that even though this solution does not require you to use a table expression, I used one here to alias the *YEAR(orderdate)* expression as *orderyear* to avoid repeating the expression.

Here's the solution query that uses the *PIVOT* operator:

```
SELECT empid, [2020] AS cnt2020, [2021] AS cnt2021, [2022] AS cnt2022
FROM (SELECT empid, YEAR(orderdate) AS orderyear
      FROM dbo.Orders) AS D
  PIVOT(COUNT(orderyear)
        FOR orderyear IN([2020], [2021], [2022])) AS P;
```

As you can see, it's just a matter of fitting the pivoting elements in the right places.

If you prefer to use your own target column names and not the ones based on the actual data, you can provide your own aliases in the *SELECT* list. In this query, I aliased the result columns *[2020]*, *[2021]*, and *[2022]* as *cnt2020*, *cnt2021*, and *cnt2022*, respectively.

Exercise 5

This exercise involves a request to unpivot the source columns *cnt2020*, *cnt2021*, and *cnt2022* to two target columns—*orderyear* to hold the year that the source column name represents and *numorders* to hold the source column value. You can use the solutions I showed in the chapter as the basis for solving this exercise with a couple of small revisions.

In the examples I used in the chapter, *NULLs* in the table represented irrelevant column values. The unpivoting solutions I presented filtered out rows with *NULLs*. The *EmpYearOrders* table has no *NULLs*, but it does have zeros in some cases, and the request is to filter out rows with 0 number of orders. With the solution that is based on the *APPLY* operator, simply use the predicate *numorders* <> 0 instead of using *IS NOT NULL*, like this:

```
SELECT empid, orderyear, numorders
FROM dbo.EmpYearOrders
  CROSS APPLY (VALUES(2020, cnt2020),
                     (2021, cnt2021),
                     (2022, cnt2022)) AS A(orderyear, numorders)
WHERE numorders <> 0;
```

As for the solution that uses the *UNPIVOT* operator, remember that it eliminates *NULLs* as an integral part of its logic. However, it does not eliminate zeros—you have to take care of eliminating zeros yourself by adding a *WHERE* clause, like this:

```
SELECT empid, CAST(RIGHT(orderyear, 4) AS INT) AS orderyear, numorders
FROM dbo.EmpYearOrders
  UNPIVOT(numorders FOR orderyear IN(cnt2020, cnt2021, cnt2022)) AS U
WHERE numorders <> 0;
```

Notice the expression used in the *SELECT* list to produce the *orderyear* result column: *CAST(RIGHT(orderyear, 4) AS INT)*. The original column names that the query unpivots are *cnt2020*, *cnt2021*, and *cnt2022*. These column names become the values '*cnt2020*', '*cnt2021*', and '*cnt2022*', respectively, in the *orderyear* column in the result of the *UNPIVOT* operator. The purpose of this expression is to extract the four rightmost characters representing the order year and convert the value to an integer. This manipulation was not required in the standard solution, because the constants used to construct the table expression *A* were specified explicitly.

Exercise 6

You can use the *GROUPING SETS* subclause to list the requested grouping sets and the *GROUPING_ID* function to produce a unique identifier for the grouping sets. Here's the complete solution query:

```
SELECT
  GROUPING_ID(empid, custid, YEAR(Orderdate)) AS groupingset,
  empid, custid, YEAR(Orderdate) AS orderyear, SUM(qty) AS sumqty
FROM dbo.Orders
GROUP BY
  GROUPING SETS
  (
    (empid, custid, YEAR(orderdate)),
    (empid, YEAR(orderdate)),
    (custid, YEAR(orderdate))
  );
```

The requested grouping sets are neither a power set nor a rollup of some set of attributes. Therefore, you cannot use either the *CUBE* or *ROLLUP* subclause to further abbreviate the code.

Exercise 7

To handle this task you can first compute the start of week date that corresponds to the *orderdate* value, and then group the data by the start of week date and compute the order count per group. You can compute the start of week date either using the *DATE_BUCKET* function or with the alternative custom method.

Using the *DATE_BUCKET*, you compute the start of week date with the following expression:

```
DATE_BUCKET(week, 1, orderdate, CAST('19000107' AS DATE))
```

As the date part and width elements you can either use *week* and 1 or *day* and 7. I used the former in this example. The input date and time value is of course the *orderdate* column. As for the origin point, since the exercise instructed you to assume the week starts on a Sunday, it's important to choose a date that falls on a Sunday. I chose January 7, 1900, but you can choose a different date so long as it falls on a Sunday. Notice that since the literal '19000107' is normally considered a character string literal, the code explicitly casts the type of the literal to a *DATE*-typed one.

You're now ready to write the complete solution code. Define a CTE based on a query against *Sales. Orders* that computes the week start date using the above expression, naming the result column *startofweek*. Then, in the query against the CTE, group the rows by *startofweek*. Compute the end of week by adding 6 days to *startofweek*, and the order count with the *COUNT(*)* aggregate. Here's the complete solution code:

```
WITH C AS
(
  SELECT
    DATE_BUCKET(week, 1, orderdate, CAST('19000107' AS DATE)) AS startofweek
  FROM Sales.Orders
)
SELECT
  startofweek, DATEADD(day, 6, startofweek) AS endofweek,
  COUNT(*) AS numorders
FROM C
GROUP BY startofweek
ORDER BY startofweek;
```

If you're using a version of SQL Server earlier than 2022, you can use the alternative custom method for computing the start of bucket, like so:

```
WITH C AS
(
  SELECT
    DATEADD(
      week,
      (DATEDIFF(week, '19000107', orderdate)
        - CASE
            WHEN DATEADD(week, DATEDIFF(week, '19000107', orderdate), '19000107')
                   > orderdate THEN 1
            ELSE 0
          END),
      CAST('19000107' AS DATE)) AS startofweek
```

```
  FROM Sales.Orders
)
SELECT
  startofweek, DATEADD(day, 6, startofweek) AS endofweek,
  COUNT(*) AS numorders
FROM C
GROUP BY startofweek
ORDER BY startofweek;
```

Notice that in the last input of the outer *DATEADD* function, the code casts the literal '19000107' to *DATE* to ensure that the result value's type is *DATE*; otherwise, it would have been implicitly cast to *DATETIME* by default. Also, I didn't include the part of the expression that divides and multiplies by the bucket width, since in this example the bucket width is 1.

Exercise 8

You can use the techniques described in the time series section in this chapter to bucketize the order data by fiscal year. The bucket start point is the start of the fiscal year. Use July 1 of any year as the origin point, the *year* part as the date part, and 1 as the bucket width. Here's the complete solution query using the *DATE_BUCKET* function in case you're using a platform that supports it:

```
DECLARE
  @bucketwidth AS INT = 1,
  @origin      AS DATE = '19000701';

WITH C AS
(
  SELECT shipperid, qty, val,
    DATE_BUCKET(year, @bucketwidth, orderdate, @origin) AS startofyear
  FROM Sales.OrderValues
)
SELECT shipperid, startofyear,
  DATEADD(day, -1, DATEADD(year, @bucketwidth, startofyear)) AS endofyear,
  SUM(qty) AS totalqty,
  SUM(val) AS totalval
FROM C
GROUP BY shipperid, startofyear
ORDER BY shipperid, startofyear;
```

As mentioned, the start of the fiscal year is the start of the bucket. You group the data by the shipper ID and the start of the fiscal year, returning the grouping elements and the aggregated quantities and values. To compute an inclusive end of the fiscal year, you add a year to the bucket start point and subtract a day.

If you're using a platform that does not support the *DATE_BUCKET* function, you can always use the alternative custom method, like so:

```
DECLARE
  @bucketwidth AS INT = 1,
  @origin      AS DATE = '19000701';
```

```
WITH C AS
(
  SELECT shipperid, qty, val,
    DATEADD(
      year,
      (DATEDIFF(year, @origin, orderdate)
        - CASE
            WHEN DATEADD(year, DATEDIFF(year, @origin, orderdate), @origin)
                   > orderdate THEN 1
            ELSE 0
          END) / @bucketwidth * @bucketwidth,
      @origin) AS startofyear
  FROM Sales.OrderValues
)
SELECT shipperid, startofyear,
  DATEADD(day, -1, DATEADD(year, @bucketwidth, startofyear)) AS endofyear,
  SUM(qty) AS totalqty,
  SUM(val) AS totalval
FROM C
GROUP BY shipperid, startofyear
ORDER BY shipperid, startofyear;
```

Note that since the bucket width is 1 here, you could remove the / @bucketwidth * @bucketwidth part from the computation of the start of bucket, but here I wanted to show the more generalized form of the calculation.

When you're done with the exercises in this chapter, run the following code for cleanup:

```
DROP TABLE IF EXISTS
  dbo.Orders,
  dbo.EmpYearOrders,
  dbo.EmpCustOrders,
  dbo.SensorMeasurements,
  dbo.Sensors;
```

CHAPTER 8

Data modification

SQL has a set of statements known as Data Manipulation Language (DML) that deals with data manipulation. Some people think that DML involves only data modification, but it also involves data retrieval. DML includes the statements *SELECT, INSERT, UPDATE, DELETE, TRUNCATE*, and *MERGE*. So far I've focused on the *SELECT* statement. This chapter focuses on data modification statements. In addition to covering standard aspects of data modification, I'll also cover aspects specific to T-SQL.

To avoid changing existing data in your sample database, most of the examples in this chapter create and populate new tables in the *dbo* schema in the *TSQLV6* database.

Inserting data

T-SQL provides several statements for inserting data into tables: *INSERT VALUES, INSERT SELECT, INSERT EXEC, SELECT INTO*, and *BULK INSERT*. I'll first describe those statements, and then I'll talk about tools for generating keys, such as the identity property and the sequence object.

The *INSERT VALUES* statement

You use the standard *INSERT VALUES* statement to insert rows into a table based on specified values. To practice using this statement and others, you will work with a table called *Orders* in the *dbo* schema in the *TSQLV6* database. Run the following code to create the *Orders* table:

```
USE TSQLV6;

DROP TABLE IF EXISTS dbo.Orders;

CREATE TABLE dbo.Orders
(
  orderid   INT         NOT NULL
    CONSTRAINT PK_Orders PRIMARY KEY,
  orderdate DATE        NOT NULL
    CONSTRAINT DFT_orderdate DEFAULT(SYSDATETIME()),
  empid     INT         NOT NULL,
  custid    VARCHAR(10) NOT NULL
);
```

The following example demonstrates how to use the *INSERT VALUES* statement to insert a single row into the *Orders* table:

```
INSERT INTO dbo.Orders(orderid, orderdate, empid, custid)
  VALUES(10001, '20220212', 3, 'A');
```

Specifying the target column names right after the table name is optional, but by doing so, you control the value-column associations instead of relying on the order of the columns in the *CREATE TABLE* statement. In T-SQL, specifying the *INTO* clause is optional.

If you don't specify a value for a column, Microsoft SQL Server will use a default value if one was defined for the column. If a default value isn't defined and the column allows *NULLs*, a *NULL* will be used. If no default is defined and the column does not allow *NULLs* and does not somehow get its value automatically, your *INSERT* statement will fail. The following statement doesn't specify a value for the *orderdate* column; rather, it relies on its default (*SYSDATETIME*):

```
INSERT INTO dbo.Orders(orderid, empid, custid)
  VALUES(10002, 5, 'B');
```

When you try to insert or update data in a table and the modification attempts to write a value of a character string or binary type that is longer than the maximum size of the target column, by default SQL Server generates an error and fails the attempted modification. Prior to SQL Server 2019 it was especially tricky to troubleshoot such a situation, since the error message didn't indicate which table, column, and value caused the error. It was the generalized error message 8152: "String or binary data would be truncated." Starting with SQL Server 2019, assuming your database is set to database compatibility level 150 or higher, the error message is a more specific one. It's error message 2628, indicating the table, column, and value that caused the error: "String or binary data would be truncated in table '<table name goes here>', column '<column name goes here>. Truncated value: '<truncated value goes here>'."

For example, try executing the following statement either on a version of SQL Server prior to SQL Server 2019 or with the database compatibility level set to a lower compatibility than 150:

```
-- To change compatibility level use: ALTER DATABASE CURRENT SET COMPATIBILITY_LEVEL = <level>
INSERT INTO dbo.Orders(orderid, orderdate, empid, custid)
  VALUES(20001, '20220212', 1, 'TooLongCustID');
```

Recall that the *custid* column is defined with the type *VARCHAR(10)*, yet the value 'TooLongCustID' that is specified for this column has 13 characters. The statement fails with the following generalized error:

```
Msg 8152, Level 16, State 30, Line 39
String or binary data would be truncated.
The statement has been terminated.
```

Try executing the same statement on SQL Server 2019 or higher, or on Azure SQL Database, with the database compatibility level set to 150 or higher, and this time you get a more specific error:

```
Msg 2628, Level 16, State 1, Line 39
String or binary data would be truncated in table 'TSQLV6.dbo.Orders', column 'custid'.
Truncated value: 'TooLongCus'.
The statement has been terminated.
```

T-SQL supports an enhanced standard *VALUES* clause you can use to specify multiple rows separated by commas. For example, the following statement inserts four rows into the *Orders* table:

```
INSERT INTO dbo.Orders
   (orderid, orderdate, empid, custid)
VALUES
   (10003, '20220213', 4, 'B'),
   (10004, '20220214', 1, 'A'),
   (10005, '20220213', 1, 'C'),
   (10006, '20220215', 3, 'C');
```

This statement is processed as a transaction, meaning that if any row fails to enter the table, none of the rows in the statement enters the table. There's extensive coverage of transactions later in the book, in Chapter 10, "Transaction and concurrency."

There's more to this enhanced *VALUES* clause. You can use it as a table-value constructor to construct a derived table. Here's an example:

```
SELECT *
FROM ( VALUES
          (10003, '20220213', 4, 'B'),
          (10004, '20220214', 1, 'A'),
          (10005, '20220213', 1, 'C'),
          (10006, '20220215', 3, 'C') )
     AS O(orderid, orderdate, empid, custid);
```

Following the parentheses that contain the table value constructor, you assign an alias to the table (*O* in this case), and following the table alias, you assign aliases to the target columns in parentheses. This query generates the following output:

```
orderid     orderdate   empid       custid
----------- ----------- ----------- ------
10003       20220213    4           B
10004       20220214    1           A
10005       20220213    1           C
10006       20220215    3           C
```

The *INSERT SELECT* statement

The standard *INSERT SELECT* statement inserts a set of rows returned by a *SELECT* query into a target table. The syntax is similar to that of an *INSERT VALUES* statement, but instead of using the *VALUES* clause, you specify a *SELECT* query. For example, the following code inserts into the *dbo.Orders* table the result of a query against the *Sales.Orders* table and returns orders that were shipped to the United Kingdom:

```
INSERT INTO dbo.Orders(orderid, orderdate, empid, custid)
   SELECT orderid, orderdate, empid, custid
   FROM Sales.Orders
   WHERE shipcountry = N'UK';
```

You can also use the *INSERT SELECT* statement to specify the target column names, and the recommendation I gave earlier regarding specifying those names remains the same. The behavior in terms of relying on a default constraint or column nullability is also the same as with the *INSERT VALUES* statement. The *INSERT SELECT* statement is performed as a transaction, so if any row fails to enter the target table, none of the rows enters the table.

> **Note** If you include a system function such as *SYSDATETIME* in the inserted query, the function gets invoked only once for the entire query and not once per row. The exception to this rule is if you generate globally unique identifiers (GUIDs) using the *NEWID* function, which gets invoked per row.

The *INSERT EXEC* statement

You use the *INSERT EXEC* statement to insert a result set returned from a stored procedure or a dynamic SQL batch into a target table. You'll find information about stored procedures, batches, and dynamic SQL in Chapter 12, "Programmable objects." The *INSERT EXEC* statement is similar in syntax and concept to the *INSERT SELECT* statement, but instead of using a *SELECT* statement, you specify an *EXEC* statement.

For example, the following code creates a stored procedure called *Sales.GetOrders*, and it returns orders that were shipped to a specified input country (with the *@country* parameter):

```
CREATE OR ALTER PROC Sales.GetOrders
  @country AS NVARCHAR(40)
AS

SELECT orderid, orderdate, empid, custid
FROM Sales.Orders
WHERE shipcountry = @country;
GO
```

To test the stored procedure, execute it with the input country *France*:

```
EXEC Sales.GetOrders @country = N'France';
```

You get the following output, shown here in abbreviated form:

```
orderid      orderdate    empid        custid
-----------  -----------  -----------  -----------
10248        2020-07-04   5            85
10251        2020-07-08   3            84
10265        2020-07-25   2            7
10274        2020-08-06   6            85
10295        2020-09-02   2            85
10297        2020-09-04   5            7
10311        2020-09-20   1            18
10331        2020-10-16   9            9
10334        2020-10-21   8            84
```

```
10340       2020-10-29  1           9
...
```

```
(77 rows affected)
```

By using an *INSERT EXEC* statement, you can insert the result set returned from the procedure into the *dbo.Orders* table:

```
INSERT INTO dbo.Orders(orderid, orderdate, empid, custid)
  EXEC Sales.GetOrders @country = N'France';
```

The *SELECT INTO* statement

The *SELECT INTO* statement is a nonstandard T-SQL statement that creates a target table and populates it with the result set of a query. By "nonstandard," I mean that it's not part of the ISO and ANSI SQL standards. You cannot use this statement to insert data into an existing table. In terms of syntax, simply add *INTO <target_table_name>* right before the *FROM* clause of the *SELECT* query you want to use to produce the result set. For example, the following code creates a table called *dbo.Orders* and populates it with all rows from the *Sales.Orders* table:

```
DROP TABLE IF EXISTS dbo.Orders;

SELECT orderid, orderdate, empid, custid
INTO dbo.Orders
FROM Sales.Orders;
```

The target table's structure and data are based on the source table. The *SELECT INTO* statement copies from the source the base structure (such as column names, types, nullability, and identity property) and the data. It does not copy from the source constraints, indexes, triggers, column properties, and permissions. If you need those in the target, you'll need to create them yourself.

One of the benefits of the *SELECT INTO* statement is its efficiency. As long as a database property called *Recovery Model* is not set to *FULL*, this statement uses an optimized mode that applies minimal logging. This translates to a very fast operation compared to a fully logged one. Note that the *INSERT SELECT* statement also can benefit from minimal logging, but the list of requirements it needs to meet is longer. For details, see "Prerequisites for Minimal Logging in Bulk Import" in the product documentation at the following URL: *https://learn.microsoft.com/en-us/sql/relational-databases/import-export/prerequisites-for-minimal-logging-in-bulk-import*.

If you need to use a *SELECT INTO* statement with set operations, you specify the *INTO* clause right in front of the *FROM* clause of the first query. For example, the following *SELECT INTO* statement creates a table called *Locations* and populates it with the result of an *EXCEPT* set operation, returning locations that are customer locations but not employee locations:

```
DROP TABLE IF EXISTS dbo.Locations;

SELECT country, region, city
INTO dbo.Locations
FROM Sales.Customers
```

EXCEPT

```
SELECT country, region, city
FROM HR.Employees;
```

The *BULK INSERT* statement

You use the *BULK INSERT* statement to insert into an existing table data originating from a file. In the statement, you specify the target table, the source file, and options. You can specify many options, including the data file type (for example, *char* or *native*), the field terminator, the row terminator, and others—all of which are fully documented.

For example, the following code bulk inserts the contents of the file *c:\temp\orders.txt* into the table *dbo.Orders*, specifying that the data file type is *char*, the field terminator is a comma, and the row terminator is the newline character:

```
BULK INSERT dbo.Orders FROM 'c:\temp\orders.txt'
  WITH
    (
        DATAFILETYPE    = 'char',
        FIELDTERMINATOR = ',',
        ROWTERMINATOR   = '\n'
    );
```

Note that if you want to actually run this statement, you need to place the *orders.txt* file provided along with the source code for this book into the c:\temp folder.

You can run the *BULK INSERT* statement in a fast, minimally logged mode in certain scenarios as long as certain requirements are met. For details, see "Prerequisites for Minimal Logging in Bulk Import" in the product documentation.

The identity property and the sequence object

SQL Server supports two built-in solutions to automatically generate numeric keys: the identity column property and the sequence object. The identity property works well for some scenarios, but it also has many limitations. The sequence object resolves many of the identity property's limitations. I'll start with identity.

Identity

Identity is a standard column property. You can define this property for a column with any numeric type with a scale of zero (no fraction). When defining the property, you can optionally specify a seed (the first value) and an increment (a step value). If you don't provide those, the default is *1* for both. You typically use this property to generate *surrogate keys*, which are keys that are produced by the system and are not derived from the application data.

For example, the following code creates a table called *dbo.T1*:

```
DROP TABLE IF EXISTS dbo.T1;

CREATE TABLE dbo.T1
(
  keycol  INT           NOT NULL IDENTITY(1, 1)
    CONSTRAINT PK_T1 PRIMARY KEY,
  datacol VARCHAR(10) NOT NULL
    CONSTRAINT CHK_T1_datacol CHECK(datacol LIKE '[ABCDEFGHIJKLMNOPQRSTUVWXYZ]%')
);
```

The table contains a column called *keycol* that is defined with an identity property using *1* as the seed and *1* as the increment. The table also contains a character string column called *datacol*, whose data is restricted with a *CHECK* constraint to strings starting with an alphabetical character.

In your *INSERT* statements, you must completely ignore the identity column. For example, the following code inserts three rows into the table, specifying values only for the column *datacol*:

```
INSERT INTO dbo.T1(datacol) VALUES('AAAAA'),('CCCCC'),('BBBBB');
```

SQL Server produced the values for *keycol* automatically. Query the table to see the values that were generated:

```
SELECT * FROM dbo.T1;
```

You get the following output:

```
keycol      datacol
----------- ----------
1           AAAAA
2           CCCCC
3           BBBBB
```

When you query the table, naturally you can refer to the identity column by its name (*keycol*, in this case). SQL Server also provides a way to refer to the identity column by using the more generic form *$identity*.

For example, the following query selects the identity column from *T1* by using the generic form:

```
SELECT $identity FROM dbo.T1;
```

This query returns the following output:

```
keycol
-----------
1
2
3
```

When you insert a new row into the table, SQL Server generates a new identity value based on the current identity value in the table and the increment. If you need to obtain the newly generated identity value—for example, to insert child rows into a referencing table—you query one of two functions, called *@@identity* and *SCOPE_IDENTITY*.

The @@*identity* function returns the last identity value generated by the session, regardless of scope (for example, a procedure issuing an *INSERT* statement, and a trigger fired by that statement are in different scopes). *SCOPE_IDENTITY* returns the last identity value generated by the current scope (for example, the same procedure). Except in the rare cases when you don't really care about scope, you should use the *SCOPE_IDENTITY* function.

For example, the following code inserts a new row into the table *T1*, obtains the newly generated identity value, places it into a variable by querying the *SCOPE_IDENTITY* function, and then queries the variable:

```
DECLARE @new_key AS INT;

INSERT INTO dbo.T1(datacol) VALUES('AAAAA');

SET @new_key = SCOPE_IDENTITY();

SELECT @new_key AS new_key;
```

If you ran all previous code samples provided in this section, this code returns the following output:

```
new_key
-----------
4
```

Remember that both @@*identity* and *SCOPE_IDENTITY* return the last identity value produced by the current session. Neither is affected by inserts issued by other sessions. However, if you want to know the current identity value in a table (the last value produced) regardless of session, you should use the *IDENT_CURRENT* function and provide the table name as input. For example, run the following code from a new session (not the one from which you ran the previous *INSERT* statements):

```
SELECT
  SCOPE_IDENTITY() AS [SCOPE_IDENTITY],
  @@identity AS [@@identity],
  IDENT_CURRENT(N'dbo.T1') AS [IDENT_CURRENT];
```

You get the following output:

```
SCOPE_IDENTITY    @@identity    IDENT_CURRENT
----------------  ------------  -------------
NULL              NULL          4
```

Both @@*identity* and *SCOPE_IDENTITY* returned *NULLs* because no identity values were created in the session in which this query ran. *IDENT_CURRENT* returned the value 4 because it returns the current identity value in the table, regardless of the session in which it was produced.

There's a certain part of the design of the identity property that comes as a surprise to some. The change to the current identity value in a table is not undone if the *INSERT* that generated the change fails or the transaction in which the statement runs is rolled back. For example, run the following *INSERT* statement, which conflicts with the *CHECK* constraint defined in the table:

```
INSERT INTO dbo.T1(datacol) VALUES('12345');
```

The insert fails, and you get the following error:

```
Msg 547, Level 16, State 0, Line 159
The INSERT statement conflicted with the CHECK constraint "CHK_T1_datacol". The conflict
occurred in database "TSQLV6", table "dbo.T1", column 'datacol'.
The statement has been terminated.
```

Even though the insert failed, the current identity value in the table changed from 4 to 5, and this change was not undone because of the failure. This means that the next insert will produce the value 6:

```
INSERT INTO dbo.T1(datacol) VALUES('EEEEE');
```

Query the table:

```
SELECT * FROM dbo.T1;
```

Notice a gap between the values 4 and 6 in the output:

```
keycol        datacol
-----------   ----------
1             AAAAA
2             CCCCC
3             BBBBB
4             AAAAA
6             EEEEE
```

Also, SQL Server uses a performance cache feature for the identity property, which can result in gaps between the keys when there's an unclean termination of the SQL Server process—for example, because of a power failure. As you might realize, you should use the identity property only if you can allow gaps between the keys. Otherwise, you should implement your own mechanism to generate keys.

One of the shortcomings of the identity property is that you cannot add it to an existing column or remove it from an existing column. If you need to make such a change, it's an expensive and cumbersome offline operation.

With SQL Server, you can specify your own explicit values for the identity column when you insert rows, as long as you enable a session option called *IDENTITY_INSERT* against the table involved. There's no option you can use to update an identity column, though.

For example, the following code demonstrates how to insert a row into *T1* with the explicit value 5 in *keycol*:

```
SET IDENTITY_INSERT dbo.T1 ON;
INSERT INTO dbo.T1(keycol, datacol) VALUES(5, 'FFFFF');
SET IDENTITY_INSERT dbo.T1 OFF;
```

Interestingly, when you turn off the *IDENTITY_INSERT* option, SQL Server changes the current identity value in the table only if the explicit value you provided is greater than the current identity value. Because the current identity value in the table prior to running the preceding code was 6, and the *INSERT* statement in this code used the lower explicit value 5, the current identity value in the table did not change. So if at this point you query the *IDENT_CURRENT* function for this table, you will get 6 and not 5. This way, the next *INSERT* statement against the table will produce the value 7:

```
INSERT INTO dbo.T1(datacol) VALUES('GGGGG');
```

Query the current contents of the table *T1*:

```
SELECT * FROM dbo.T1;
```

You get the following output:

```
keycol       datacol
-----------  ----------
1            AAAAA
2            CCCCC
3            BBBBB
4            AAAAA
5            FFFFF
6            EEEEE
7            GGGGG
```

You need to understand that the identity property itself does not enforce uniqueness in the column. I already explained that you can provide your own explicit values after setting the *IDENTITY_INSERT* option to *ON*, and those values can be ones that already exist in rows in the table. Also, you can reseed the current identity value in the table by using the *DBCC CHECKIDENT* command—for syntax, see "DBCC CHECKIDENT (Transact-SQL)" in the product documentation at the following URL: *https://learn. microsoft.com/en-us/sql/t-sql/database-console-commands/dbcc-checkident-transact-sql*. If you need to guarantee uniqueness in an identity column, make sure you also define a primary key or a unique constraint on that column.

Sequence

T-SQL supports the standard sequence object as an alternative key-generating mechanism for identity. The sequence object is more flexible than identity in many ways, making it the preferred choice in many cases.

One of the advantages of the sequence object is that, unlike identity, it's not tied to a particular column in a particular table; rather, it's an independent object in the database. Whenever you need to generate a new value, you invoke a function against the object and use the returned value wherever you like. For example, if you have such a use case, you can use one sequence object that will help you maintain keys that will not conflict across multiple tables.

To create a sequence object, use the *CREATE SEQUENCE* command. The minimum required information is just the sequence name, but note that the defaults for the various properties in such a case might not be what you want. If you don't indicate the data type, SQL Server will use *BIGINT* by default. If you want a different type, indicate *AS <type>*. The type can be any numeric type with a scale of zero. For example, if you need your sequence to be of an *INT* type, indicate *AS INT*.

Unlike the identity property, the sequence object supports the specification of a minimum value (*MINVALUE <val>*) and a maximum value (*MAXVALUE <val>*) within the type. If you don't indicate what the minimum and maximum values are, the sequence object will assume the minimum and maximum values supported by the type. For example, for an *INT* type, those would be –2,147,483,648 and 2,147,483,647, respectively.

Also, unlike identity, the sequence object supports cycling. Cycling means that after it reaches the maximum value, it proceeds next to the minimum value. Note, though, that the default is *NO CYCLE*. If you want the sequence object to cycle, you need to be explicit about it by using the *CYCLE* option.

Like identity, the sequence object allows you to specify the starting value (*START WITH <val>*) and the increment (*INCREMENT BY <val>*). If you don't indicate the starting value, the default will be the same as the minimum value (*MINVALUE*). If you don't indicate the increment value, it will be *1* by default.

For example, suppose you want to create a sequence that will help you generate order IDs. You want it to be of an *INT* type, have a minimum value of *1* and a maximum value that is the maximum supported by the type, start with *1*, increment by *1*, and allow cycling. Here's the *CREATE SEQUENCE* command you would use to create such a sequence:

```
CREATE SEQUENCE dbo.SeqOrderIDs AS INT
  MINVALUE 1
  CYCLE;
```

You had to be explicit about the type, minimum value, and cycling option because they are different than the defaults. You didn't need to indicate the maximum, start with, and increment values, because you wanted the defaults.

The sequence object also supports a caching option (*CACHE <val> | NO CACHE*) that tells SQL Server how often to write the recoverable value to disk. For example, if you specify a cache value of 10,000, SQL Server will write to disk every 10,000 requests, and in between disk writes, it will maintain the current value and how many values are left in memory. If you write less frequently to disk, you'll get better performance when generating a value (on average), but you'll risk losing more values in case of an unexpected termination of the SQL Server process, such as in a power failure. SQL Server has a default cache value of 50, although this number is not officially documented because Microsoft wants to be able to change it.

You can change any of the sequence properties except the data type with the *ALTER SEQUENCE* command (*MINVAL <val>, MAXVAL <val>, RESTART WITH <val>, INCREMENT BY <val>, CYCLE | NO CYCLE, or CACHE <val> | NO CACHE*). For example, suppose you want to prevent the sequence *dbo. SeqOrderIDs* from cycling. You can change the current sequence definition with the following *ALTER SEQUENCE* command:

```
ALTER SEQUENCE dbo.SeqOrderIDs
  NO CYCLE;
```

To generate a new sequence value, you need to invoke the standard function *NEXT VALUE FOR <sequence name>*. Here's an example of invoking the function:

```
SELECT NEXT VALUE FOR dbo.SeqOrderIDs;
```

This code generates the following output:

```
-----------
1
```

Notice that, unlike with identity, you didn't need to insert a row into a table in order to generate a new value. Some applications need to generate the new value before using it. With sequences, you can store the result of the function in a variable and use it later in the code. To demonstrate this, first create a table called *T1* with the following code:

```
DROP TABLE IF EXISTS dbo.T1;

CREATE TABLE dbo.T1
(
  keycol  INT          NOT NULL
    CONSTRAINT PK_T1 PRIMARY KEY,
  datacol VARCHAR(10) NOT NULL
);
```

The following code generates a new sequence value, stores it in a variable, and then uses the variable in an *INSERT* statement to insert a row into the table:

```
DECLARE @neworderid AS INT = NEXT VALUE FOR dbo.SeqOrderIDs;
INSERT INTO dbo.T1(keycol, datacol) VALUES(@neworderid, 'a');

SELECT * FROM dbo.T1;
```

This code returns the following output:

```
keycol      datacol
----------- ----------
2           a
```

If you need to use the new key in related rows that you add to another table, you can use the variable when you insert those rows.

If you don't need to generate the new sequence value before using it, you can specify the *NEXT VALUE FOR* function directly as part of your *INSERT* statement, like this:

```
INSERT INTO dbo.T1(keycol, datacol)
  VALUES(NEXT VALUE FOR dbo.SeqOrderIDs, 'b');

SELECT * FROM dbo.T1;
```

This code returns the following output:

```
keycol      datacol
----------- ----------
2           a
3           b
```

Unlike with identity, you can generate new sequence values in an *UPDATE* statement, like this:

```
UPDATE dbo.T1
  SET keycol = NEXT VALUE FOR dbo.SeqOrderIDs;

SELECT * FROM dbo.T1;
```

This code returns the following output:

```
keycol       datacol
-----------  ----------
4            a
5            b
```

To get information about your sequences, query a view called *sys.sequences*. For example, to find the current sequence value in the *SeqOrderIDs* sequence, you use the following code:

```
SELECT current_value
FROM sys.sequences
WHERE OBJECT_ID = OBJECT_ID(N'dbo.SeqOrderIDs');
```

This code generates the following output:

```
current_value
--------------
5
```

SQL Server extends its support for the sequence option with capabilities beyond what the competitors and the standard currently support. One of the extensions enables you to control the order of the assigned sequence values in a multirow insert by using an *OVER* clause. Here's an example:

```
INSERT INTO dbo.T1(keycol, datacol)
  SELECT
    NEXT VALUE FOR dbo.SeqOrderIDs OVER(ORDER BY hiredate),
    LEFT(firstname, 1) + LEFT(lastname, 1)
  FROM HR.Employees;

SELECT * FROM dbo.T1;
```

This code returns the following output:

```
keycol       datacol
-----------  ----------
4            a
5            b
6            JL
7            SD
8            DF
9            YP
10           SM
11           PS
12           RK
13           MC
14           PD
```

Another extension to the standard allows the use of the *NEXT VALUE FOR* function in a default constraint. Here's an example:

```
ALTER TABLE dbo.T1
  ADD CONSTRAINT DFT_T1_keycol
    DEFAULT (NEXT VALUE FOR dbo.SeqOrderIDs)
    FOR keycol;
```

Now when you insert rows into the table, you don't have to indicate a value for *keycol*:

```
INSERT INTO dbo.T1(datacol) VALUES('c');

SELECT * FROM dbo.T1;
```

This code returns the following output:

```
keycol       datacol
-----------  ----------
4            a
5            b
6            JL
7            SD
8            DF
9            YP
10           SM
11           PS
12           RK
13           MC
14           PD
15           c
```

Unlike with identity, which you cannot add to or remove from an existing column, you can add or remove a default constraint. The preceding example showed how to add a default constraint to a table and associate it with a column. To remove a constraint, use the syntax *ALTER TABLE <table_name> DROP CONSTRAINT <constraint_name>*.

There's another extension to the standard you can use to allocate a whole range of sequence values at once by using a stored procedure called *sp_sequence_get_range*. The idea is that if the application needs to assign a range of sequence values, it's efficient to update the sequence only once, incrementing it by the size of the range. You call the procedure, indicate the size of the range you want, and collect the first value in the range, as well as other information, by using output parameters. Here's an example of calling the procedure and asking for a range of 1,000,000 sequence values:

```
DECLARE @first AS SQL_VARIANT;

EXEC sys.sp_sequence_get_range
  @sequence_name     = N'dbo.SeqOrderIDs',
  @range_size        = 1000000,
  @range_first_value = @first OUTPUT ;

SELECT @first;
```

> **Note** *SQL_VARIANT* is a generic data type that can hold within it various base data types. The *sp_sequence_get_range* procedure uses this type for several of its parameters, including the output parameter *@range_first_value*. For details about this data type, see the product documentation at the following URL: *https://learn.microsoft.com/en-us/sql/t-sql/data-types/sql-variant-transact-sql*.

If you run the code twice, you will find that the returned first value in the second call is greater than the first by 1,000,000.

Note that as with identity, the sequence object does not guarantee you will have no gaps. If a new sequence value was generated by a transaction that failed or intentionally rolled back, the sequence change is not undone. Also, as mentioned earlier with identity, sequence objects support a performance cache feature, which can result in gaps when there's an unclean termination of the SQL Server process.

When you're done, run the following code for cleanup:

```
DROP TABLE IF EXISTS dbo.T1;
DROP SEQUENCE IF EXISTS dbo.SeqOrderIDs;
```

Deleting data

T-SQL provides two statements for deleting rows from a table: *DELETE* and *TRUNCATE*. This section describes those statements. The examples I provide in this section are applied against copies of the *Customers* and *Orders* tables from the *Sales* schema created in the *dbo* schema. Run the following code to create and populate those tables:

```
DROP TABLE IF EXISTS dbo.Orders, dbo.Customers;

CREATE TABLE dbo.Customers
(
  custid       INT          NOT NULL,
  companyname  NVARCHAR(40) NOT NULL,
  contactname  NVARCHAR(30) NOT NULL,
  contacttitle NVARCHAR(30) NOT NULL,
  address      NVARCHAR(60) NOT NULL,
  city         NVARCHAR(15) NOT NULL,
  region       NVARCHAR(15) NULL,
  postalcode   NVARCHAR(10) NULL,
  country      NVARCHAR(15) NOT NULL,
  phone        NVARCHAR(24) NOT NULL,
  fax          NVARCHAR(24) NULL,
  CONSTRAINT PK_Customers PRIMARY KEY(custid)
);
```

```
CREATE TABLE dbo.Orders
(
  orderid         INT           NOT NULL,
  custid          INT           NULL,
  empid           INT           NOT NULL,
  orderdate       DATE          NOT NULL,
  requireddate    DATE          NOT NULL,
  shippeddate     DATE          NULL,
  shipperid       INT           NOT NULL,
  freight         MONEY         NOT NULL
    CONSTRAINT DFT_Orders_freight DEFAULT(0),
  shipname        NVARCHAR(40)  NOT NULL,
  shipaddress     NVARCHAR(60)  NOT NULL,
  shipcity        NVARCHAR(15)  NOT NULL,
  shipregion      NVARCHAR(15)  NULL,
  shippostalcode  NVARCHAR(10)  NULL,
  shipcountry     NVARCHAR(15)  NOT NULL,
  CONSTRAINT PK_Orders PRIMARY KEY(orderid),
  CONSTRAINT FK_Orders_Customers FOREIGN KEY(custid)
    REFERENCES dbo.Customers(custid)
);
GO

INSERT INTO dbo.Customers SELECT * FROM Sales.Customers;
INSERT INTO dbo.Orders SELECT * FROM Sales.Orders;
```

The *DELETE* statement

The *DELETE* statement is a standard statement used to delete data from a table based on an optional filter predicate. The standard statement has only two clauses—the *FROM* clause, in which you specify the target table name, and a *WHERE* clause, in which you specify a predicate. Only the subset of rows for which the predicate evaluates to *TRUE* will be deleted.

For example, the following statement deletes, from the *dbo.Orders* table, all orders that were placed prior to 2021:

```
DELETE FROM dbo.Orders
WHERE orderdate < '20210101';
```

Run this statement. SQL Server will report that it deleted 152 rows:

```
(152 rows affected)
```

Note that you can suppress returning the message that indicates the number of rows affected by turning on the session option *NOCOUNT*. As you probably noticed, this option is off by default.

The *DELETE* statement tends to be expensive when you delete a large number of rows, mainly because it's a fully logged operation.

The *TRUNCATE* statement

The standard *TRUNCATE* statement deletes all rows from a table. Unlike the *DELETE* statement, *TRUNCATE* has no filter. For example, to delete all rows from a table called *dbo.T1*, you run the following code:

```
TRUNCATE TABLE dbo.T1;
```

Note that the chapter's companion source code file has the code to create the table in case you want to actually test the code in this section.

The advantage that *TRUNCATE* has over *DELETE* is that the former is minimally logged, whereas the latter is fully logged, resulting in significant performance differences. For example, if you use the *TRUNCATE* statement to delete all rows from a table with millions of rows, the operation will finish in a matter of seconds. If you use the *DELETE* statement, the operation can take many minutes. Note that I said *TRUNCATE* is *minimally* logged, as opposed to not being logged at all. SQL Server records which blocks of data were deallocated by the operation so that it can reclaim those in case the transaction needs to be undone. Both *DELETE* and *TRUNCATE* are transactional.

TRUNCATE and *DELETE* also have a functional difference when the table has an identity column. *TRUNCATE* resets the identity value back to the original seed, but *DELETE* doesn't—even when used without a filter. Interestingly, the standard defines an *identity column restart option* for the *TRUNCATE* statement, which you use to control whether to restart or continue the identity value, but unfortunately T-SQL doesn't support this option.

The *TRUNCATE* statement is not allowed when the target table is referenced by a foreign-key constraint, even if the referencing table is empty and even if the foreign key is disabled. The only way to allow a *TRUNCATE* statement is to drop all foreign keys referencing the table with the *ALTER TABLE DROP CONSTRAINT* command. You can then re-create the foreign keys after truncating the table with the *ALTER TABLE ADD CONSTRAINT* command. As a reminder, the syntax for these commands is covered in Chapter 1.

Accidents such as truncating or dropping the incorrect table can happen. For example, let's say you have connections open against both the production and the development environments, and you submit your code in the wrong connection. Both the *TRUNCATE* and *DROP* statements are so fast that the transaction is committed before you realize your mistake. To prevent such accidents, you can protect a production table by simply creating a dummy table with a foreign key pointing to that table. You can even disable the foreign key so that it won't have any impact on performance. As I mentioned earlier, even when disabled, this foreign key prevents you from truncating or dropping the referenced table.

In case you have partitioned tables in your database, starting with SQL Server 2016 you can use the *TRUNCATE* statement to truncate individual partitions. You can specify a list of partitions and partition ranges (with the keyword *TO* between the range delimiters). As an example, suppose you had a partitioned table called *T1* and you wanted to truncate partitions 1, 3, 5, and 7 through 10. You would use the following code to achieve this:

```
TRUNCATE TABLE dbo.T1 WITH ( PARTITIONS(1, 3, 5, 7 TO 10) );
```

Note Table partitioning is about dividing your table into multiple units called *partitions*, mainly for manageability purposes. This allows handling processes like importing data into the table and purging historic data to be handled more efficiently. You can find details on the topic in the product documentation at the following URL: *https://learn.microsoft.com/en-us/sql/relational-databases/partitions/partitioned-tables-and-indexes*.

DELETE based on a join

T-SQL supports a nonstandard *DELETE* syntax based on joins. The join serves a filtering purpose and also gives you access to the attributes of the related rows from the joined tables. This means you can delete rows from one table based on a filter against attributes in related rows from another table.

For example, the following statement deletes orders placed by customers from the United States:

```
DELETE FROM O
FROM dbo.Orders AS O
  INNER JOIN dbo.Customers AS C
    ON O.custid = C.custid
WHERE C.country = N'USA';
```

Much like in a *SELECT* statement, the first clause that is logically processed in a *DELETE* statement is the *FROM* clause (the second one that appears in this statement). Then the *WHERE* clause is processed, and finally the *DELETE* clause. In our case, the statement first joins the *Orders* table (aliased as *O*) with the *Customers* table (aliased as *C*) based on a match between the order's customer ID and the customer's customer ID. It then filters only orders placed by customers from the United States. Finally, the statement deletes all qualifying rows from *O* (the alias representing the *Orders* table).

The two *FROM* clauses in a *DELETE* statement based on a join might be confusing. But when you develop the code, develop it as if it were a *SELECT* statement with a join. That is, start with the *FROM* clause with the joins, move on to the *WHERE* clause, and finally—instead of specifying a *SELECT* clause—specify a *DELETE* clause with the alias of the side of the join that is supposed to be the target for the deletion. Note that the first *FROM* clause is optional. In our example, you can specify *DELETE O* instead of *DELETE FROM O*.

As I mentioned earlier, a *DELETE* statement based on a join is nonstandard. If you want to stick to standard code, you can use subqueries instead of joins. For example, the following *DELETE* statement uses a subquery to achieve the same task:

```
DELETE FROM dbo.Orders
WHERE EXISTS
  (SELECT *
   FROM dbo.Customers AS C
   WHERE Orders.custid = C.custid
     AND C.country = N'USA');
```

This code deletes all rows from the *Orders* table for which a related customer from the United States exists in the *Customers* table.

SQL Server processes the two queries the same way, using the same query execution plan; therefore, you shouldn't expect any performance difference between them. I usually recommend sticking to the standard as much as possible unless you have a compelling reason to do otherwise—for example, in the case of a performance difference.

> **NOTE** SQL Server creates an execution plan as an outcome of a query optimization process. The plan contains the physical instructions and algorithms that are needed to physically process the query. Query optimization is outside the scope of this book, but you should be aware that after you learn about T-SQL fundamentals and become more comfortable with the material, the natural next step is to proceed to query optimization. You can find more information about query execution plans in the product documentation here: *https://learn. microsoft.com/en-us/sql/relational-databases/performance/execution-plans*.

When you're done, run the following code for cleanup:

```
DROP TABLE IF EXISTS dbo.Orders, dbo.Customers;
```

Updating data

T-SQL supports a standard *UPDATE* statement you can use to update rows in a table. T-SQL also supports nonstandard forms of the *UPDATE* statement with joins and with variables. This section describes the different forms of the statement.

Some of the examples I provide in this section are against copies of the *Orders* and *OrderDetails* tables from the *Sales* schema created in the *dbo* schema. Run the following code to create and populate those tables:

```
DROP TABLE IF EXISTS dbo.OrderDetails, dbo.Orders;

CREATE TABLE dbo.Orders
(
  orderid         INT          NOT NULL,
  custid          INT          NULL,
  empid           INT          NOT NULL,
  orderdate       DATE         NOT NULL,
  requireddate    DATE         NOT NULL,
  shippeddate     DATE         NULL,
  shipperid       INT          NOT NULL,
  freight         MONEY        NOT NULL
    CONSTRAINT DFT_Orders_freight DEFAULT(0),
  shipname        NVARCHAR(40) NOT NULL,
  shipaddress     NVARCHAR(60) NOT NULL,
  shipcity        NVARCHAR(15) NOT NULL,
  shipregion      NVARCHAR(15) NULL,
  shippostalcode  NVARCHAR(10) NULL,
  shipcountry     NVARCHAR(15) NOT NULL,
  CONSTRAINT PK_Orders PRIMARY KEY(orderid)
);
```

```
CREATE TABLE dbo.OrderDetails
(
  orderid   INT          NOT NULL,
  productid INT          NOT NULL,
  unitprice MONEY        NOT NULL
    CONSTRAINT DFT_OrderDetails_unitprice DEFAULT(0),
  qty       SMALLINT     NOT NULL
    CONSTRAINT DFT_OrderDetails_qty DEFAULT(1),
  discount  NUMERIC(4, 3) NOT NULL
    CONSTRAINT DFT_OrderDetails_discount DEFAULT(0),
  CONSTRAINT PK_OrderDetails PRIMARY KEY(orderid, productid),
  CONSTRAINT FK_OrderDetails_Orders FOREIGN KEY(orderid)
    REFERENCES dbo.Orders(orderid),
  CONSTRAINT CHK_discount  CHECK (discount BETWEEN 0 AND 1),
  CONSTRAINT CHK_qty  CHECK (qty > 0),
  CONSTRAINT CHK_unitprice CHECK (unitprice >= 0)
);
GO

INSERT INTO dbo.Orders SELECT * FROM Sales.Orders;
INSERT INTO dbo.OrderDetails SELECT * FROM Sales.OrderDetails;
```

Other examples in this section are against tables called *dbo.T1* and *dbo.T2*. Run the following code to create and populate those tables:

```
DROP TABLE IF EXISTS dbo.T1, dbo.T2;

CREATE TABLE dbo.T1
(
  keycol INT NOT NULL
    CONSTRAINT PK_T1 PRIMARY KEY,
  col1 INT NOT NULL,
  col2 INT NOT NULL,
  col3 INT NOT NULL,
  col4 VARCHAR(10) NOT NULL
);

CREATE TABLE dbo.T2
(
  keycol INT NOT NULL
    CONSTRAINT PK_T2 PRIMARY KEY,
  col1 INT NOT NULL,
  col2 INT NOT NULL,
  col3 INT NOT NULL,
  col4 VARCHAR(10) NOT NULL
);
GO

INSERT INTO dbo.T1(keycol, col1, col2, col3, col4)
  VALUES(2, 10, 5, 30, 'D'),
        (3, 40, 15, 20, 'A'),
        (5, 17, 60, 12, 'B');

INSERT INTO dbo.T2(keycol, col1, col2, col3, col4)
  VALUES(3, 200, 32, 11, 'ABC'),
        (5, 400, 43, 10, 'ABC'),
        (7, 600, 54, 90, 'XYZ');
```

The *UPDATE* statement

The *UPDATE* statement is a standard statement you can use to update a subset of rows in a table. To identify the subset of rows you need to update, you specify a predicate in a *WHERE* clause. You specify the assignment of values to columns in a *SET* clause, separated by commas.

For example, the following *UPDATE* statement increases the discount of all order details for product 51 by 5 percent:

```
UPDATE dbo.OrderDetails
  SET discount = discount + 0.05
WHERE productid = 51;
```

Of course, you can run a *SELECT* statement with the same filter before and after the update to see the changes. Later in this chapter, I'll show you another way to see the changes, by using a clause called *OUTPUT* that you can add to modification statements.

T-SQL supports compound assignment operators: += (plus equal), −= (minus equal), *= (multiplication equal), /= (division equal), %= (modulo equal), and others. You can use these operators to shorten assignment expressions such as the one in the preceding query. Instead of the expression *discount = discount + 0.05*, you can use this expression: *discount += 0.05*. The full *UPDATE* statement looks like this:

```
UPDATE dbo.OrderDetails
  SET discount += 0.05
WHERE productid = 51;
```

All-at-once operations are an important aspect of SQL you should keep in mind when writing *UPDATE* statements. I explained the concept in Chapter 2, "Single-table queries," in the context of *SELECT* statements, but it's just as applicable with *UPDATE* statements. Remember that all expressions that appear in the same logical phase are evaluated as a set, logically at the same point in time. Consider the following *UPDATE* statement:

```
UPDATE dbo.T1
  SET col1 = col1 + 10, col2 = col1 + 10;
```

Suppose one row in the table has the value 100 in *col1* prior to the update. Can you determine the values of *col1* and *col2* in that row after the update?

If you do not consider the all-at-once concept, you would think that *col1* will be set to 110 and *col2* to 120, as if the assignments were performed from left to right. However, the assignments take place all at once, meaning that both assignments use the same value of *col1*—the value before the update. The result of this update is that both *col1* and *col2* will end up with the value 110.

With the concept of all-at-once in mind, can you figure out how to write an *UPDATE* statement that swaps the values in the columns *col1* and *col2*? In most programming languages where expressions and assignments are evaluated in some order (typically left to right), you need a temporary variable.

However, because in SQL all assignments take place as if they happen at the same point in time, the solution is simple:

```
UPDATE dbo.T1
  SET col1 = col2, col2 = col1;
```

In both assignments, the source column values used are those prior to the update, so you don't need a temporary variable.

UPDATE based on a join

Similar to the *DELETE* statement, the *UPDATE* statement also supports a nonstandard form based on joins. As with *DELETE* statements, the join serves a filtering purpose as well as giving you access to attributes from the joined tables.

The syntax is similar to a *SELECT* statement based on a join; that is, the *FROM* and *WHERE* clauses are the same, but instead of the *SELECT* clause, you specify an *UPDATE* clause. The *UPDATE* keyword is followed by the alias of the table that is the target of the update (you can't update more than one table in the same statement), followed by the *SET* clause with the column assignments.

For example, the *UPDATE* statement in Listing 8-1 increases the discount of all order details of orders placed by customer 1 by 5 percent.

LISTING 8-1 *UPDATE* based on a join

```
UPDATE OD
  SET discount += 0.05
FROM dbo.OrderDetails AS OD
  INNER JOIN dbo.Orders AS O
    ON OD.orderid = O.orderid
WHERE O.custid = 1;
```

In terms of logical processing, you start with the *FROM* clause, move on to the *WHERE* clause, and finally go to the *UPDATE* clause. The query joins the *OrderDetails* table (aliased as *OD*) with the *Orders* table (aliased as *O*) based on a match between the order detail's order ID and the order's order ID. The query then filters only the rows where the order's customer ID is *1*. Next, the query specifies in the *UPDATE* clause that *OD* (the alias of the *OrderDetails* table) is the target of the update, and it increases the discount by 5 percent. You can also specify the full table name in the *UPDATE* clause if you like.

If you want to achieve the same task by using standard code, you can use a subquery instead of a join, like this:

```
UPDATE dbo.OrderDetails
  SET discount += 0.05
WHERE EXISTS
  (SELECT * FROM dbo.Orders AS O
   WHERE O.orderid = OrderDetails.orderid
     AND O.custid = 1);
```

The query's *WHERE* clause filters only order details in which a related order is placed by customer 1. With this particular task, SQL Server processes both versions the same way (using the same query plan); therefore, you shouldn't expect performance differences between the two. As I mentioned earlier, I recommend sticking to standard code unless you have a compelling reason to do otherwise.

There are cases where the join version has advantages. In addition to filtering, the join also gives you access to attributes from other tables you can use in the column assignments in the *SET* clause. The same access to the joined table is used for both filtering and assignment purposes. However, with the subquery approach, you need separate subqueries for filtering and assignments; plus, you need a separate subquery for each assignment. In SQL Server, each subquery involves separate access to the other table.

For example, consider the following nonstandard *UPDATE* statement based on a join:

```
UPDATE T1
  SET col1 = T2.col1,
      col2 = T2.col2,
      col3 = T2.col3
FROM dbo.T1 JOIN dbo.T2
  ON T2.keycol = T1.keycol
WHERE T2.col4 = 'ABC';
```

This statement joins the tables *T1* and *T2* based on a match between *T1.keycol* and *T2.keycol*. The *WHERE* clause filters only rows where *T2.col4* is equal to 'ABC'. The *UPDATE* statement marks the *T1* table as the target for the *UPDATE*, and the *SET* clause sets the values of the columns *col1*, *col2*, and *col3* in *T1* to the values of the corresponding columns from *T2*.

An attempt to express this task by using standard code with subqueries yields the following lengthy query:

```
UPDATE dbo.T1
  SET col1 = (SELECT col1
                FROM dbo.T2
                WHERE T2.keycol = T1.keycol),

      col2 = (SELECT col2
                FROM dbo.T2
                WHERE T2.keycol = T1.keycol),

      col3 = (SELECT col3
                FROM dbo.T2
                WHERE T2.keycol = T1.keycol)
WHERE EXISTS
  (SELECT *
   FROM dbo.T2
   WHERE T2.keycol = T1.keycol
     AND T2.col4 = 'ABC');
```

Not only is this version convoluted, but each subquery involves separate access to table *T2*. So this version is less efficient than the join version.

Standard SQL has support for *row constructors* (also known as *vector expressions*) that were only implemented partially in T-SQL. At the time of this writing, many aspects of row constructors have not yet been implemented, including the ability to use them in the *SET* clause of an *UPDATE* statement, like this:

```
UPDATE dbo.T1

  SET (col1, col2, col3) =

      (SELECT col1, col2, col3
       FROM dbo.T2
       WHERE T2.keycol = T1.keycol)

WHERE EXISTS
  (SELECT *
   FROM dbo.T2
   WHERE T2.keycol = T1.keycol
     AND T2.col4 = 'ABC');
```

But as you can see, this version would still be more complicated than the join version, because it requires separate subqueries for the filtering part and for obtaining the attributes from the other table for the assignments.

When you're done, run the following code for cleanup:

```
DROP TABLE IF EXISTS dbo.T1, dbo.T2;
```

Assignment *UPDATE*

T-SQL supports a proprietary *UPDATE* syntax that both updates data in a table and assigns values to variables at the same time. This syntax saves you the need to use separate *UPDATE* and *SELECT* statements to achieve the same task.

One of the common cases for which you can use this syntax is in maintaining a custom sequence/ autonumbering mechanism when the identity column property and the sequence object don't work for you. One example is when you need to guarantee that there are no gaps between the values. To achieve this, you keep the last-used value in a table, and whenever you need a new value, you use the special *UPDATE* syntax to both increment the value in the table and assign it to a variable.

Run the following code to first create the *MySequences* table with the column *val*, and then populate it with a single row with the value 0—one less than the first value you want to use:

```
DROP TABLE IF EXISTS dbo.MySequences;

CREATE TABLE dbo.MySequences
(
  id VARCHAR(10) NOT NULL
    CONSTRAINT PK_MySequences PRIMARY KEY(id),
  val INT NOT NULL
);
INSERT INTO dbo.MySequences VALUES('SEQ1', 0);
```

Now, whenever you need to obtain a new sequence value, use the following code:

```
DECLARE @nextval AS INT;

UPDATE dbo.MySequences
  SET @nextval = val += 1
WHERE id = 'SEQ1';

SELECT @nextval;
```

The code declares a local variable called *@nextval*. Then it uses the special *UPDATE* syntax to increment the column value by 1 and assigns the new value to a variable. The code then presents the value in the variable. First *val* is set to *val* + 1, and then the result (*val* + 1) is set to the variable *@nextval*.

The specialized *UPDATE* syntax is run as a transaction, and it's more efficient than using separate *UPDATE* and *SELECT* statements because it accesses the data only once. Note that variable assignment isn't transactional, though. This means that if you assign a value to a variable within a transaction, and the transaction fails after the assignment, the variable assignment is not undone.

When you're done, run the following code for cleanup:

```
DROP TABLE IF EXISTS dbo.MySequences;
```

Merging data

T-SQL supports a statement called *MERGE* you can use to merge data from a source into a target, applying different actions (*INSERT, UPDATE,* and *DELETE*) based on conditional logic. The *MERGE* statement is part of the SQL standard, although the T-SQL version adds a few nonstandard extensions.

A task achieved by a single *MERGE* statement typically translates to a combination of several other DML statements (*INSERT, UPDATE,* and *DELETE*) without *MERGE*.

To demonstrate the *MERGE* statement, I'll use tables called *dbo.Customers* and *dbo.CustomersStage*. Run Listing 8-2 to create those tables and populate them with sample data.

LISTING 8-2 Code that creates and populates *Customers* and *CustomersStage*

```
DROP TABLE IF EXISTS dbo.Customers, dbo.CustomersStage;
GO

CREATE TABLE dbo.Customers
(
  custid      INT          NOT NULL,
  companyname VARCHAR(25) NOT NULL,
  phone       VARCHAR(20) NOT NULL,
  address     VARCHAR(50) NOT NULL,
  CONSTRAINT PK_Customers PRIMARY KEY(custid)
);
```

```
INSERT INTO dbo.Customers(custid, companyname, phone, address)
VALUES
  (1, 'cust 1', '(111) 111-1111', 'address 1'),
  (2, 'cust 2', '(222) 222-2222', 'address 2'),
  (3, 'cust 3', '(333) 333-3333', 'address 3'),
  (4, 'cust 4', '(444) 444-4444', 'address 4'),
  (5, 'cust 5', '(555) 555-5555', 'address 5');

CREATE TABLE dbo.CustomersStage
(
  custid       INT         NOT NULL,
  companyname  VARCHAR(25) NOT NULL,
  phone        VARCHAR(20) NOT NULL,
  address      VARCHAR(50) NOT NULL,
  CONSTRAINT PK_CustomersStage PRIMARY KEY(custid)
);

INSERT INTO dbo.CustomersStage(custid, companyname, phone, address)
VALUES
  (2, 'AAAAA', '(222) 222-2222', 'address 2'),
  (3, 'cust 3', '(333) 333-3333', 'address 3'),
  (5, 'BBBBB', 'CCCCC', 'DDDDD'),
  (6, 'cust 6 (new)', '(666) 666-6666', 'address 6'),
  (7, 'cust 7 (new)', '(777) 777-7777', 'address 7');
```

Run the following query to examine the contents of the *Customers* table:

```
SELECT * FROM dbo.Customers;
```

This query returns the following output:

```
custid       companyname       phone                  address
-----------  ----------------  --------------------- ------------
1            cust 1            (111) 111-1111         address 1
2            cust 2            (222) 222-2222         address 2
3            cust 3            (333) 333-3333         address 3
4            cust 4            (444) 444-4444         address 4
5            cust 5            (555) 555-5555         address 5
```

Run the following query to examine the contents of the *CustomersStage* table:

```
SELECT * FROM dbo.CustomersStage;
```

This query returns the following output:

```
custid       companyname       phone                  address
-----------  ----------------  --------------------- ------------
2            AAAAA             (222) 222-2222         address 2
3            cust 3            (333) 333-3333         address 3
5            BBBBB             CCCCC                  DDDDD
6            cust 6 (new)      (666) 666-6666         address 6
7            cust 7 (new)      (777) 777-7777         address 7
```

Suppose you need to merge the contents of the *CustomersStage* table (the source) into the *Customers* table (the target). More specifically, you need to add customers that do not exist and update the customers that do exist.

If you already feel comfortable with deletions and updates based on joins, you should feel quite comfortable with *MERGE* because it's based on join semantics. You specify the target table name in the *MERGE* clause and the source table name in the *USING* clause. You define a merge condition by specifying a predicate in the *ON* clause. The merge condition defines which rows in the source table have matches in the target and which don't. You define the action to take when a match is found in a clause called *WHEN MATCHED THEN*, and the action to take when a match is not found in the *WHEN NOT MATCHED THEN* clause.

Here's the first example for the *MERGE* statement. It adds nonexistent customers and updates existing ones:

```
MERGE INTO dbo.Customers AS TGT
USING dbo.CustomersStage AS SRC
  ON TGT.custid = SRC.custid
WHEN MATCHED THEN
  UPDATE SET
    TGT.companyname = SRC.companyname,
    TGT.phone = SRC.phone,
    TGT.address = SRC.address
WHEN NOT MATCHED THEN
  INSERT (custid, companyname, phone, address)
  VALUES (SRC.custid, SRC.companyname, SRC.phone, SRC.address);
```

> **Note** It's mandatory to terminate the *MERGE* statement with a semicolon, whereas in most other statements in T-SQL, this is optional. As mentioned, it's a best practice to terminate all statements even when you're not required to.

This *MERGE* statement defines the *Customers* table as the target (in the *MERGE* clause) and the *CustomersStage* table as the source (in the *USING* clause). Notice that you can assign aliases to the target and source tables for brevity (TGT and SRC in this case). The predicate *TGT.custid = SRC.custid* is used to define what is considered a match and what is considered a nonmatch. In this case, if a customer ID that exists in the source also exists in the target, that's a match. If a customer ID in the source does not exist in the target, that's a nonmatch.

This *MERGE* statement defines an *UPDATE* action when a match is found, setting the target *companyname*, *phone*, and *address* values to those of the corresponding row from the source. Notice that the syntax of the *UPDATE* action is similar to a normal *UPDATE* statement, except that you don't need to provide the name of the table that is the target of the update, because it was already defined in the *MERGE INTO* clause.

This *MERGE* statement defines an *INSERT* action when a match is not found, inserting the row from the source to the target. Again, the syntax of the *INSERT* action is similar to a normal *INSERT* statement, except that you don't need to provide the name of the target table, because it was already defined in the *MERGE INTO* clause.

The *MERGE* statement reports that five rows were modified:

```
(5 rows affected)
```

This includes three rows that were updated (customers 2, 3, and 5) and two that were inserted (customers 6 and 7). Query the *Customers* table to get the new contents:

```
SELECT * FROM dbo.Customers;
```

This query returns the following output:

```
custid      companyname          phone                address
----------- -------------------- -------------------- ----------
1           cust 1               (111) 111-1111       address 1
2           AAAAA                (222) 222-2222       address 2
3           cust 3               (333) 333-3333       address 3
4           cust 4               (444) 444-4444       address 4
5           BBBBB                CCCCC                DDDDD
6           cust 6 (new)         (666) 666-6666       address 6
7           cust 7 (new)         (777) 777-7777       address 7
```

The *WHEN MATCHED* clause defines what action to take against the target when a source row is matched by a target row. The *WHEN NOT MATCHED* clause defines what action to take against the target when a source row is not matched by a target row. T-SQL also supports a third clause that defines what action to take when a target row is not matched by a source row; this clause is called *WHEN NOT MATCHED BY SOURCE*. For example, suppose you want to add logic to the *MERGE* example to delete rows from the target when there's no matching source row. To achieve this, add the *WHEN NOT MATCHED BY SOURCE* clause with a *DELETE* action, like this:

```
MERGE dbo.Customers AS TGT
USING dbo.CustomersStage AS SRC
  ON TGT.custid = SRC.custid
WHEN MATCHED THEN
  UPDATE SET
    TGT.companyname = SRC.companyname,
    TGT.phone = SRC.phone,
    TGT.address = SRC.address
WHEN NOT MATCHED THEN
  INSERT (custid, companyname, phone, address)
  VALUES (SRC.custid, SRC.companyname, SRC.phone, SRC.address)
WHEN NOT MATCHED BY SOURCE THEN
  DELETE;
```

Query the *Customers* table to see the result of this *MERGE* statement:

```
SELECT * FROM dbo.Customers;
```

This query returns the following output, showing that customers 1 and 4 were deleted:

```
custid        companyname            phone                  address
-----------   --------------------   --------------------   ----------
2             AAAAA                  (222) 222-2222         address 2
3             cust 3                 (333) 333-3333         address 3
5             BBBBB                  CCCCC                  DDDDD
6             cust 6 (new)           (666) 666-6666         address 6
7             cust 7 (new)           (777) 777-7777         address 7
```

Going back to the first *MERGE* example, which updates existing customers and adds nonexistent ones, you can see that it doesn't check whether column values are actually different before applying an update. This means that a customer row is modified even when the source and target rows are identical. If you want to apply the update only if at least one column value is different, there is a way to achieve this.

The *MERGE* statement supports adding a predicate to the different action clauses by using the *AND* option; the action will take place only if the additional predicate evaluates to *TRUE*. In this case, you need to add a predicate under the *WHEN MATCHED AND* clause that checks that at least one of the column values is different to justify the *UPDATE* action. The complete *MERGE* statement looks like this:

```
MERGE dbo.Customers AS TGT
USING dbo.CustomersStage AS SRC
  ON TGT.custid = SRC.custid
WHEN MATCHED AND
        (   TGT.companyname <> SRC.companyname
        OR TGT.phone        <> SRC.phone
        OR TGT.address      <> SRC.address) THEN
  UPDATE SET
    TGT.companyname = SRC.companyname,
    TGT.phone = SRC.phone,
    TGT.address = SRC.address
WHEN NOT MATCHED THEN
  INSERT (custid, companyname, phone, address)
  VALUES (SRC.custid, SRC.companyname, SRC.phone, SRC.address);
```

As you can see, the *MERGE* statement is powerful, allowing you to express complex modification logic in a single statement.

Modifying data through table expressions

T-SQL doesn't limit the actions against table expressions to *SELECT* only; it also allows other DML statements (*INSERT, UPDATE, DELETE,* and *MERGE*) against those. Think about it: as explained in Chapter 5, a table expression doesn't really contain data—it's a reflection of data in underlying tables. With this in mind, think of a modification against a table expression as modifying the data in the underlying tables through the table expression. Just as with a *SELECT* statement against a table expression, a modification statement against a table expression also gets expanded, so in practice the activity is done against the underlying tables.

Modifying data through table expressions has a few restrictions:

- If the query defining the table expression joins tables, you're allowed to affect only one of the sides of the join, not both, in the same modification statement.

- You cannot update a column that is a result of a calculation; SQL Server doesn't try to reverse-engineer the values.

- *INSERT* statements must specify values for any columns in the underlying table that do not get their values implicitly. Examples for cases where a column can get a value implicitly include a column that allows *NULLs*, has a default value, has an identity property, or is typed as *ROWVERSION*.

You can find other requirements in the product documentation.

One use case for modifying data through table expressions is for better debugging and troubleshooting capabilities. For example, Listing 8-1 contained the following *UPDATE* statement:

```
UPDATE OD
  SET discount += 0.05
FROM dbo.OrderDetails AS OD
  INNER JOIN dbo.Orders AS O
    ON OD.orderid = O.orderid
WHERE O.custid = 1;
```

Suppose, for troubleshooting purposes, you first want to see which rows would be modified by this statement without actually modifying them. One option is to revise the code to a *SELECT* statement, and after troubleshooting the code, change it back to an *UPDATE* statement. But instead of needing to make such revisions, you define a table expression based on a *SELECT* statement with the join query and issue an *UPDATE* statement against the table expression. The following example uses a CTE:

```
WITH C AS
(
  SELECT custid, OD.orderid,
    productid, discount, discount + 0.05 AS newdiscount
  FROM dbo.OrderDetails AS OD
    INNER JOIN dbo.Orders AS O
      ON OD.orderid = O.orderid
  WHERE O.custid = 1
)
UPDATE C
  SET discount = newdiscount;
```

And here's an example using a derived table:

```
UPDATE D
  SET discount = newdiscount
FROM ( SELECT custid, OD.orderid,
         productid, discount, discount + 0.05 AS newdiscount
       FROM dbo.OrderDetails AS OD
         INNER JOIN dbo.Orders AS O
           ON OD.orderid = O.orderid
       WHERE O.custid = 1 ) AS D;
```

With the table expression, troubleshooting is simpler because you can always highlight just the inner *SELECT* statement and run it without making any data changes. With this example, the use of table expressions is for convenience. However, in some cases using a table expression is the only option. To demonstrate such a case, I'll use a table called *T1* that you create and populate by running the following code:

```
DROP TABLE IF EXISTS dbo.T1;
CREATE TABLE dbo.T1(col1 INT, col2 INT);
GO

INSERT INTO dbo.T1(col1) VALUES(20),(10),(30);

SELECT * FROM dbo.T1;
```

This code generates the following output:

```
col1        col2
----------- -----------
20          NULL
10          NULL
30          NULL
```

Suppose you want to update the table, setting *col2* to the result of an expression with the *ROW_NUMBER* function. The problem is that the *ROW_NUMBER* function is not allowed in the *SET* clause of an *UPDATE* statement. Try running the following code:

```
UPDATE dbo.T1
  SET col2 = ROW_NUMBER() OVER(ORDER BY col1);
```

You get the following error:

```
Msg 4108, Level 15, State 1, Line 672
Windowed functions can only appear in the SELECT or ORDER BY clauses.
```

To get around this problem, define a table expression that returns both the column you need to update (*col2*) and a result column based on an expression with the *ROW_NUMBER* function (call it *rownum*). Use an *UPDATE* statement against the table expression to set *col2* to *rownum*. Here's how the code looks when using a CTE:

```
WITH C AS
(
  SELECT col1, col2, ROW_NUMBER() OVER(ORDER BY col1) AS rownum
  FROM dbo.T1
)
UPDATE C
  SET col2 = rownum;
```

Query the table to see the result of the update:

```
SELECT * FROM dbo.T1;
```

You get the following output:

```
col1         col2
-----------  -----------
20           2
10           1
30           3
```

Modifications with *TOP* and *OFFSET-FETCH*

T-SQL supports using the *TOP* option directly in *INSERT*, *UPDATE*, *DELETE*, and *MERGE* statements. When you use the *TOP* option with such statements, SQL Server stops processing the modification as soon as the specified number or percentage of rows is processed. Unfortunately, unlike with the *SELECT* statement, you cannot specify an *ORDER BY* clause for the *TOP* filter in modification statements. Essentially, whichever rows SQL Server happens to access first will be modified.

The *OFFSET-FETCH* filter is not allowed directly in modifications because this filter requires an *ORDER BY* clause and modification statements don't support one.

An example for a typical usage scenario for modifications with *TOP* is when you have a large modification, such as a large deletion operation, and you want to split it into multiple smaller chunks.

I'll demonstrate modifications with *TOP* by using a table called *dbo.Orders* that you create and populate by running the following code:

```
DROP TABLE IF EXISTS dbo.OrderDetails, dbo.Orders;

CREATE TABLE dbo.Orders
(
  orderid           INT           NOT NULL,
  custid            INT           NULL,
  empid             INT           NOT NULL,
  orderdate         DATE          NOT NULL,
  requireddate      DATE          NOT NULL,
  shippeddate       DATE          NULL,
  shipperid         INT           NOT NULL,
  freight           MONEY         NOT NULL
    CONSTRAINT DFT_Orders_freight DEFAULT(0),
  shipname          NVARCHAR(40) NOT NULL,
  shipaddress       NVARCHAR(60) NOT NULL,
  shipcity          NVARCHAR(15) NOT NULL,
  shipregion        NVARCHAR(15) NULL,
  shippostalcode NVARCHAR(10) NULL,
  shipcountry       NVARCHAR(15) NOT NULL,
  CONSTRAINT PK_Orders PRIMARY KEY(orderid)
);
GO

INSERT INTO dbo.Orders SELECT * FROM Sales.Orders;
```

The following example demonstrates the use of a *DELETE* statement with the *TOP* option to delete 50 rows from the *Orders* table:

```
DELETE TOP (50) FROM dbo.Orders;
```

Because the statement doesn't have an *ORDER BY* clause, it deletes whichever 50 rows it stumbles into first. Which rows get chosen is a result of physical data layout and optimization choices.

Similarly, you can use the *TOP* option with *UPDATE* and *INSERT* statements, but again, an *ORDER BY* is not allowed. As an example of an *UPDATE* statement with *TOP*, the following code updates 50 rows from the *Orders* table, increasing their *freight* values by 10:

```
UPDATE TOP (50) dbo.Orders
  SET freight += 10.00;
```

Again, you cannot control which 50 rows will be updated; they are the 50 rows that SQL Server happens to access first.

In practice, you typically do care which rows are affected. To control this, you can rely on the ability to modify data through table expressions. You define a table expression based on a *SELECT* query with the *TOP* filter and an *ORDER BY* clause. You then issue the modification statement against the table expression.

For example, the following code deletes the 50 orders with the lowest order ID values:

```
WITH C AS
(
  SELECT TOP (50) *
  FROM dbo.Orders
  ORDER BY orderid
)
DELETE FROM C;
```

Similarly, the following code updates the 50 orders with the highest order ID values, increasing their *freight* values by 10:

```
WITH C AS
(
  SELECT TOP (50) *
  FROM dbo.Orders
  ORDER BY orderid DESC
)
UPDATE C
  SET freight += 10.00;
```

Alternatively, you can use the *OFFSET-FETCH* option instead of *TOP*, like this:

```
WITH C AS
(
  SELECT *
  FROM dbo.Orders
  ORDER BY orderid
  OFFSET 0 ROWS FETCH NEXT 50 ROWS ONLY
)
DELETE FROM C;
```

And here's the revised *UPDATE* example:

```
WITH C AS
(
  SELECT *
  FROM dbo.Orders
  ORDER BY orderid DESC
  OFFSET 0 ROWS FETCH NEXT 50 ROWS ONLY
)
UPDATE C
  SET freight += 10.00;
```

The *OUTPUT* clause

Normally, a modification statement just modifies data. However, sometimes you might find it useful to return information from the modified rows for troubleshooting, auditing, and archiving. T-SQL supports this capability via a clause called *OUTPUT* that you add to the modification statement. In this clause, you specify attributes you want to return from the modified rows.

The *OUTPUT* clause is designed similarly to the *SELECT* clause, only you need to prefix the attributes with either the *inserted* or *deleted* keyword. In an *INSERT* statement, you refer to *inserted*; in a *DELETE* statement, you refer to *deleted*; and in an *UPDATE* statement, you refer to *deleted* for the old state of the row and to *inserted* for the new state.

The *OUTPUT* clause returns a result set, much like a *SELECT* statement does. If you want to direct the result set to a table, add an *INTO* clause with the target table name. If you want to return modified rows back to the caller and also direct a copy to a table, specify two *OUTPUT* clauses: one with the *INTO* clause and one without it.

The following sections provide examples of using the *OUTPUT* clause with the different modification statements.

INSERT with *OUTPUT*

An example for a use case of the *OUTPUT* clause with an *INSERT* statement is when you need to insert a row set into a table with an identity column and get back all identity values that were generated. The *SCOPE_IDENTITY* function returns only the very last identity value that was generated—not all those generated by the statement. The *OUTPUT* clause makes the task simple. I'll use a table called *T1* to demonstrate the technique. Run the following code to create the table *T1* with an identity column called *keycol* and another column called *datacol*:

```
DROP TABLE IF EXISTS dbo.T1;

CREATE TABLE dbo.T1
(
  keycol  INT          NOT NULL IDENTITY(1, 1) CONSTRAINT PK_T1 PRIMARY KEY,
  datacol NVARCHAR(40) NOT NULL
);
```

Suppose you want to insert into *T1* the result of a query against the *HR.Employees* table and return all newly generated identity values. To achieve this, add the *OUTPUT* clause to the *INSERT* statement and specify the attributes you want to return:

```
INSERT INTO dbo.T1(datacol)
  OUTPUT inserted.keycol, inserted.datacol
    SELECT lastname
    FROM HR.Employees
    WHERE country = N'USA';
```

This statement returns the following result set:

```
keycol      datacol
----------- ---------
1           Davis
2           Funk
3           Lew
4           Peled
5           Cameron

(5 rows affected)
```

As you can guess, you can use a similar technique to return sequence values generated for an *INSERT* statement by the *NEXT VALUE FOR* function (either directly or in a default constraint).

As mentioned, you can also direct the result set into a table. The table can be a permanent table, a temporary table, or a table variable. You can find details about temporary tables and table variables in Chapter 12. When the result set is stored in the target table, you can manipulate the data by querying that table. For example, the following code declares a table variable called *@NewRows*, inserts another result set into *T1*, and directs the result set returned by the *OUTPUT* clause into the table variable. The code then queries the table variable just to show the data that was stored in it:

```
DECLARE @NewRows TABLE(keycol INT, datacol NVARCHAR(40));

INSERT INTO dbo.T1(datacol)
  OUTPUT inserted.keycol, inserted.datacol
  INTO @NewRows(keycol, datacol)
    SELECT lastname
    FROM HR.Employees
    WHERE country = N'UK';

SELECT * FROM @NewRows;
```

This code returns the following output showing the contents of the table variable:

```
keycol      datacol
----------- -------------
6           Mortensen
7           Suurs
8           King
9           Doyle

(4 rows affected)
```

DELETE with OUTPUT

The next example demonstrates the use of the *OUTPUT* clause with a *DELETE* statement. First, run the following code to create a copy of the *Orders* table from the *Sales* schema in the *dbo* schema:

```
DROP TABLE IF EXISTS dbo.Orders;

CREATE TABLE dbo.Orders
(
  orderid         INT           NOT NULL,
  custid          INT           NULL,
  empid           INT           NOT NULL,
  orderdate       DATE          NOT NULL,
  requireddate    DATE          NOT NULL,
  shippeddate     DATE          NULL,
  shipperid       INT           NOT NULL,
  freight         MONEY         NOT NULL
    CONSTRAINT DFT_Orders_freight DEFAULT(0),
  shipname        NVARCHAR(40) NOT NULL,
  shipaddress     NVARCHAR(60) NOT NULL,
  shipcity        NVARCHAR(15) NOT NULL,
  shipregion      NVARCHAR(15) NULL,
  shippostalcode  NVARCHAR(10) NULL,
  shipcountry     NVARCHAR(15) NOT NULL,
  CONSTRAINT PK_Orders PRIMARY KEY(orderid)
);
GO

INSERT INTO dbo.Orders SELECT * FROM Sales.Orders;
```

The following code deletes all orders that were placed prior to 2022 and, using the *OUTPUT* clause, returns attributes from the deleted rows:

```
DELETE FROM dbo.Orders
  OUTPUT
    deleted.orderid,
    deleted.orderdate,
    deleted.empid,
    deleted.custid
WHERE orderdate < '20220101';
```

This *DELETE* statement returns the following result set, shown here in abbreviated form:

```
orderid      orderdate  empid        custid
-----------  ---------- -----------  -----------
10248        2020-07-04 5            85
10249        2020-07-05 6            79
10250        2020-07-08 4            34
10251        2020-07-08 3            84
...
10803        2021-12-30 4            88
10804        2021-12-30 6            72
10805        2021-12-30 2            77
10806        2021-12-31 3            84
10807        2021-12-31 4            27

(560 rows affected)
```

If you want to archive the rows that are deleted, add an *INTO* clause and specify the archive table name as the target.

UPDATE with OUTPUT

By using the *OUTPUT* clause with an *UPDATE* statement, you can refer both to the state of the modified row before the change (by prefixing the attribute names with the *deleted* keyword) and to the state after the change (by prefixing the attribute names with the *inserted* keyword). This way, you can return both old and new states of the updated attributes.

Before I demonstrate how to use the *OUTPUT* clause in an *UPDATE* statement, you should first run the following code to create a copy of the *Sales.OrderDetails* table from the *Sales* schema in the *dbo* schema:

```
DROP TABLE IF EXISTS dbo.OrderDetails;

CREATE TABLE dbo.OrderDetails
(
  orderid   INT          NOT NULL,
  productid INT          NOT NULL,
  unitprice MONEY        NOT NULL
    CONSTRAINT DFT_OrderDetails_unitprice DEFAULT(0),
  qty       SMALLINT     NOT NULL
    CONSTRAINT DFT_OrderDetails_qty DEFAULT(1),
  discount  NUMERIC(4, 3) NOT NULL
    CONSTRAINT DFT_OrderDetails_discount DEFAULT(0),
  CONSTRAINT PK_OrderDetails PRIMARY KEY(orderid, productid),
  CONSTRAINT CHK_discount  CHECK (discount BETWEEN 0 AND 1),
  CONSTRAINT CHK_qty  CHECK (qty > 0),
  CONSTRAINT CHK_unitprice CHECK (unitprice >= 0)
);
GO

INSERT INTO dbo.OrderDetails SELECT * FROM Sales.OrderDetails;
```

The following *UPDATE* statement increases the discount of all order details for product 51 by 5 percent and uses the *OUTPUT* clause to return the product ID, old discount, and new discount from the modified rows:

```
UPDATE dbo.OrderDetails
  SET discount += 0.05
OUTPUT
  inserted.orderid,
  inserted.productid,
  deleted.discount AS olddiscount,
  inserted.discount AS newdiscount
WHERE productid = 51;
```

This statement returns the following output, shown here in abbreviated form:

```
orderid      productid    olddiscount   newdiscount
-----------  -----------  ------------  ------------
10249        51           0.000         0.050
10250        51           0.150         0.200
10291        51           0.100         0.150
10335        51           0.200         0.250
10362        51           0.000         0.050
10397        51           0.150         0.200
10472        51           0.000         0.050
10484        51           0.000         0.050
10486        51           0.000         0.050
10537        51           0.000         0.050
...

(39 rows affected)
```

MERGE with OUTPUT

You can also use the OUTPUT clause with the MERGE statement, but remember that a single MERGE statement can invoke multiple different DML actions. To identify which DML action produced each output row, you can invoke a function called $action in the OUTPUT clause, which will return a string representing the action (INSERT, UPDATE, or DELETE).

To demonstrate MERGE with OUTPUT, I'll use the tables you created earlier, in the section "Merging data," by running Listing 8-2. (Rerun that code listing to follow the example.) The following code merges the contents of CustomersStage into Customers, updating the attributes of customers who already exist in the target, adding customers who don't, and deleting customers who exist in the target but not in the source:

```
MERGE INTO dbo.Customers AS TGT
USING dbo.CustomersStage AS SRC
  ON TGT.custid = SRC.custid
WHEN MATCHED THEN
  UPDATE SET
    TGT.companyname = SRC.companyname,
    TGT.phone = SRC.phone,
    TGT.address = SRC.address
WHEN NOT MATCHED THEN
  INSERT (custid, companyname, phone, address)
  VALUES (SRC.custid, SRC.companyname, SRC.phone, SRC.address)
WHEN NOT MATCHED BY SOURCE THEN
  DELETE
OUTPUT $action AS theaction, inserted.custid,
  deleted.companyname AS oldcompanyname,
  inserted.companyname AS newcompanyname,
  deleted.phone AS oldphone,
  inserted.phone AS newphone,
  deleted.address AS oldaddress,
  inserted.address AS newaddress;
```

This *MERGE* statement uses the *OUTPUT* clause to return the old and new values of the modified rows. Of course, with *INSERT* actions, there are no old values, so all references to deleted attributes return *NULLs*. With *DELETE* actions, there are no new values, so all references to inserted attributes return *NULLs*. The *$action* function tells you whether an *UPDATE* action, a *DELETE* action, or an *INSERT* action produced the output row. Here's the output of this *MERGE* statement:

```
theaction   custid  oldcompanyname  newcompanyname
----------  ------- --------------- ---------------
DELETE      NULL    cust 1          NULL
UPDATE      2       cust 2          AAAAA
UPDATE      3       cust 3          cust 3
DELETE      NULL    cust 4          NULL
UPDATE      5       cust 5          BBBBB
INSERT      6       NULL            cust 6 (new)
INSERT      7       NULL            cust 7 (new)


theaction   custid  oldphone          newphone          oldaddress   newaddress
----------  ------- ----------------- ----------------- ------------ -----------
DELETE      NULL    (111) 111-1111    NULL              address 1    NULL
UPDATE      2       (222) 222-2222    (222) 222-2222    address 2    address 2
UPDATE      3       (333) 333-3333    (333) 333-3333    address 3    address 3
DELETE      NULL    (444) 444-4444    NULL              address 4    NULL
UPDATE      5       (555) 555-5555    CCCCC             address 5    DDDDD
INSERT      6       NULL              (666) 666-6666    NULL         address 6
INSERT      7       NULL              (777) 777-7777    NULL         address 7

(7 rows affected)
```

Nested DML

The *OUTPUT* clause returns an output row for every modified row. But what if you need to direct only a subset of the modified rows to a table, perhaps for auditing purposes? T-SQL supports a feature called *nested DML* you can use to directly insert into the final target table only the subset of rows you need from the full set of modified rows.

To demonstrate this capability, first create a copy of the *Products* table from the *Production* schema in the *dbo* schema, as well as the *dbo.ProductsAudit* table, by running the following code:

```
DROP TABLE IF EXISTS dbo.ProductsAudit, dbo.Products;

CREATE TABLE dbo.Products
(
  productid    INT          NOT NULL,
  productname  NVARCHAR(40) NOT NULL,
  supplierid   INT          NOT NULL,
  categoryid   INT          NOT NULL,
  unitprice    MONEY        NOT NULL
    CONSTRAINT DFT_Products_unitprice DEFAULT(0),
  discontinued BIT          NOT NULL
    CONSTRAINT DFT_Products_discontinued DEFAULT(0),
  CONSTRAINT PK_Products PRIMARY KEY(productid),
  CONSTRAINT CHK_Products_unitprice CHECK(unitprice >= 0)
);
```

```
INSERT INTO dbo.Products SELECT * FROM Production.Products;

CREATE TABLE dbo.ProductsAudit
(
  LSN INT NOT NULL IDENTITY PRIMARY KEY,
  TS DATETIME2 NOT NULL DEFAULT(SYSDATETIME()),
  productid INT NOT NULL,
  colname SYSNAME NOT NULL,
  oldval SQL_VARIANT NOT NULL,
  newval SQL_VARIANT NOT NULL
);
```

Suppose you now need to update all products supplied by supplier 1, increasing their price by 15 percent. You also need to audit the old and new values of updated products, but only those with an old price that was less than 20 and a new price that is greater than or equal to 20.

You can achieve this by using nested DML. You write an *UPDATE* statement with an *OUTPUT* clause and define a derived table based on the *UPDATE* statement. You write an *INSERT SELECT* statement that queries the derived table, filtering only the subset of rows that is needed. Here's the complete solution code:

```
INSERT INTO dbo.ProductsAudit(productid, colname, oldval, newval)
  SELECT productid, N'unitprice', oldval, newval
  FROM (UPDATE dbo.Products
          SET unitprice *= 1.15
        OUTPUT
          inserted.productid,
          deleted.unitprice AS oldval,
          inserted.unitprice AS newval
        WHERE supplierid = 1) AS D
  WHERE oldval < 20.0 AND newval >= 20.0;
```

Recall earlier discussions in the book about table expressions—the result of one query can be used as input to another. Here, the result of the statement with the *OUTPUT* clause is used as the input for the outer *INSERT SELECT* statement.

Run the following code to query the *ProductsAudit* table:

```
SELECT * FROM dbo.ProductsAudit;
```

You get the following output:

```
LSN TS                       ProductID   ColName     OldVal   NewVal
--- ------------------------ ----------- ----------- -------- ------
1   2022-02-12 18:56:04.793  1           unitprice   18.00    20.70
2   2022-02-12 18:56:04.793  2           unitprice   19.00    21.85
```

Three products were updated, but only two were filtered by the outer query; therefore, only those two were written to the audit table.

When you're done, run the following code for cleanup:

```
DROP TABLE IF EXISTS dbo.OrderDetails, dbo.ProductsAudit, dbo.Products,
  dbo.Orders, dbo.Customers, dbo.T1, dbo.T2, dbo.MySequences, dbo.CustomersStage;
```

Conclusion

In this chapter, I covered various aspects of data modification. I described inserting, updating, deleting, and merging data. I also discussed identity and sequence, modifying data through table expressions, using *TOP* (and indirectly *OFFSET-FETCH*) with modification statements, and returning information from modified rows using the *OUTPUT* clause.

Exercises

This section provides exercises so that you can practice the subjects discussed in this chapter. The database assumed in the exercise is *TSQLV6*.

Exercise 1

Run the following code to create the *dbo.Customers* table in the *TSQLV6* database:

```
USE TSQLV6;

DROP TABLE IF EXISTS dbo.Customers;

CREATE TABLE dbo.Customers
(
  custid      INT          NOT NULL PRIMARY KEY,
  companyname NVARCHAR(40) NOT NULL,
  country     NVARCHAR(15) NOT NULL,
  region      NVARCHAR(15) NULL,
  city        NVARCHAR(15) NOT NULL
);
```

Exercise 1-1

Insert into the *dbo.Customers* table a row with the following information:

- *custid*: 100

- *companyname*: Coho Winery

- *country*: USA

- *region*: WA

- *city*: Redmond

Exercise 1-2

Insert into the *dbo.Customers* table all customers from *Sales.Customers* who placed orders.

Exercise 1-3

Use a *SELECT INTO* statement to create and populate the *dbo.Orders* table with orders from the *Sales.Orders* table that were placed in the years 2020 through 2022.

Exercise 2

Delete from the *dbo.Orders* table orders that were placed before August 2020. Use the *OUTPUT* clause to return the *orderid* and *orderdate* values of the deleted orders:

- Desired output:

```
orderid     orderdate
----------- -----------
10248       2020-07-04
10249       2020-07-05
10250       2020-07-08
10251       2020-07-08
10252       2020-07-09
10253       2020-07-10
10254       2020-07-11
10255       2020-07-12
10256       2020-07-15
10257       2020-07-16
10258       2020-07-17
10259       2020-07-18
10260       2020-07-19
10261       2020-07-19
10262       2020-07-22
10263       2020-07-23
10264       2020-07-24
10265       2020-07-25
10266       2020-07-26
10267       2020-07-29
10268       2020-07-30
10269       2020-07-31

(22 rows affected)
```

Exercise 3

Delete from the *dbo.Orders* table orders placed by customers from Brazil.

Exercise 4

Run the following query against *dbo.Customers*, and notice that some rows have a *NULL* in the region column:

```
SELECT * FROM dbo.Customers;
```

The output from this query is as follows:

```
custid       companyname      country           region       city
-----------  ---------------  ----------------  -----------  ----------------
1            Customer NRZBB   Germany           NULL         Berlin
2            Customer MLTDN   Mexico            NULL         México D.F.
3            Customer KBUDE   Mexico            NULL         México D.F.
4            Customer HFBZG   UK                NULL         London
5            Customer HGVLZ   Sweden            NULL         Luleå
6            Customer XHXJV   Germany           NULL         Mannheim
7            Customer QXVLA   France            NULL         Strasbourg
8            Customer QUHWH   Spain             NULL         Madrid
9            Customer RTXGC   France            NULL         Marseille
10           Customer EEALV   Canada            BC           Tsawassen
...

(90 rows affected)
```

Update the *dbo.Customers* table, and change all *NULL* region values to *<None>*. Use the *OUTPUT* clause to show the *custid, oldregion,* and *newregion*:

- Desired output:

```
custid       oldregion        newregion
-----------  ---------------  ----------------
1            NULL             <None>
2            NULL             <None>
3            NULL             <None>
4            NULL             <None>
5            NULL             <None>
6            NULL             <None>
7            NULL             <None>
8            NULL             <None>
9            NULL             <None>
11           NULL             <None>
12           NULL             <None>
13           NULL             <None>
14           NULL             <None>
16           NULL             <None>
17           NULL             <None>
18           NULL             <None>
19           NULL             <None>
20           NULL             <None>
23           NULL             <None>
24           NULL             <None>
25           NULL             <None>
26           NULL             <None>
27           NULL             <None>
28           NULL             <None>
29           NULL             <None>
30           NULL             <None>
39           NULL             <None>
40           NULL             <None>
41           NULL             <None>
44           NULL             <None>
49           NULL             <None>
50           NULL             <None>
52           NULL             <None>
53           NULL             <None>
54           NULL             <None>
56           NULL             <None>
58           NULL             <None>
```

59	NULL	<None>
60	NULL	<None>
63	NULL	<None>
64	NULL	<None>
66	NULL	<None>
68	NULL	<None>
69	NULL	<None>
70	NULL	<None>
72	NULL	<None>
73	NULL	<None>
74	NULL	<None>
76	NULL	<None>
79	NULL	<None>
80	NULL	<None>
83	NULL	<None>
84	NULL	<None>
85	NULL	<None>
86	NULL	<None>
87	NULL	<None>
90	NULL	<None>
91	NULL	<None>

```
(58 rows affected)
```

Exercise 5

Update all orders in the *dbo.Orders* table that were placed by United Kingdom customers, and set their *shipcountry*, *shipregion*, and *shipcity* values to the *country*, *region*, and *city* values of the corresponding customers.

Exercise 6

Run the following code to create the tables *dbo.Orders* and *dbo.OrderDetails* and populate them with data:

```
USE TSQLV6;

DROP TABLE IF EXISTS dbo.OrderDetails, dbo.Orders;

CREATE TABLE dbo.Orders
(
  orderid        INT         NOT NULL,
  custid         INT         NULL,
  empid          INT         NOT NULL,
  orderdate      DATE        NOT NULL,
  requireddate   DATE        NOT NULL,
  shippeddate    DATE        NULL,
  shipperid      INT         NOT NULL,
  freight        MONEY       NOT NULL
    CONSTRAINT DFT_Orders_freight DEFAULT(0),
  shipname       NVARCHAR(40) NOT NULL,
  shipaddress    NVARCHAR(60) NOT NULL,
  shipcity       NVARCHAR(15) NOT NULL,
  shipregion     NVARCHAR(15) NULL,
  shippostalcode NVARCHAR(10) NULL,
```

```
  shipcountry      NVARCHAR(15) NOT NULL,
  CONSTRAINT PK_Orders PRIMARY KEY(orderid)
);

CREATE TABLE dbo.OrderDetails
(
  orderid   INT              NOT NULL,
  productid INT              NOT NULL,
  unitprice MONEY            NOT NULL
    CONSTRAINT DFT_OrderDetails_unitprice DEFAULT(0),
  qty       SMALLINT         NOT NULL
    CONSTRAINT DFT_OrderDetails_qty DEFAULT(1),
  discount  NUMERIC(4, 3) NOT NULL
    CONSTRAINT DFT_OrderDetails_discount DEFAULT(0),
  CONSTRAINT PK_OrderDetails PRIMARY KEY(orderid, productid),
  CONSTRAINT FK_OrderDetails_Orders FOREIGN KEY(orderid)
    REFERENCES dbo.Orders(orderid),
  CONSTRAINT CHK_discount  CHECK (discount BETWEEN 0 AND 1),
  CONSTRAINT CHK_qty  CHECK (qty > 0),
  CONSTRAINT CHK_unitprice CHECK (unitprice >= 0)
);
GO

INSERT INTO dbo.Orders SELECT * FROM Sales.Orders;
INSERT INTO dbo.OrderDetails SELECT * FROM Sales.OrderDetails;
```

Write and test the T-SQL code that is required to truncate both tables, and make sure your code runs successfully.

When you're done, run the following code for cleanup:

```
DROP TABLE IF EXISTS dbo.OrderDetails, dbo.Orders, dbo.Customers;
```

Solutions

This section provides solutions to the preceding exercises.

Exercise 1

This exercise is split into three parts. The following sections provide the solutions to those parts.

Exercise 1-1

Make sure you are connected to the *TSQLV6* database:

```
USE TSQLV6;
```

Use the following *INSERT VALUES* statement to insert a row into the *Customers* table with the values provided in the exercise:

```
INSERT INTO dbo.Customers(custid, companyname, country, region, city)
  VALUES(100, N'Coho Winery', N'USA', N'WA', N'Redmond');
```

Exercise 1-2

One way to identify customers who placed orders is to use the *EXISTS* predicate, as the following query shows:

```
SELECT custid, companyname, country, region, city
FROM Sales.Customers AS C
WHERE EXISTS
  (SELECT * FROM Sales.Orders AS O
   WHERE O.custid = C.custid);
```

To insert the rows returned from this query into the *dbo.Customers* table, you can use an *INSERT SELECT* statement as follows:

```
INSERT INTO dbo.Customers(custid, companyname, country, region, city)
  SELECT custid, companyname, country, region, city
  FROM Sales.Customers AS C
  WHERE EXISTS
    (SELECT * FROM Sales.Orders AS O
     WHERE O.custid = C.custid);
```

Exercise 1-3

The following code first ensures that the session is connected to the *TSQLV6* database, and then it drops the *dbo.Orders* table if it already exists. Finally, it uses the *SELECT INTO* statement to create a new *dbo.Orders* table and populate it with orders from the *Sales.Orders* table placed in the years 2020 through 2022:

```
USE TSQLV6;

DROP TABLE IF EXISTS dbo.Orders;

SELECT *
INTO dbo.Orders
FROM Sales.Orders
WHERE orderdate >= '20200101'
  AND orderdate < '20230101';
```

Exercise 2

To delete orders placed before August 2020, you need a *DELETE* statement with a filter based on the predicate *orderdate < '20200801'*. As requested, use the *OUTPUT* clause to return attributes from the deleted rows:

```
DELETE FROM dbo.Orders
  OUTPUT deleted.orderid, deleted.orderdate
WHERE orderdate < '20200801';
```

Exercise 3

This exercise requires you to write a *DELETE* statement that deletes rows from one table (*dbo.Orders*) based on the existence of a matching row in another table (*dbo.Customers*). One way to handle the task is to use a standard *DELETE* statement with an *EXISTS* predicate in the *WHERE* clause, like this:

```
DELETE FROM dbo.Orders
WHERE EXISTS
  (SELECT *
   FROM dbo.Customers AS C
   WHERE Orders.custid = C.custid
     AND C.country = N'Brazil');
```

This *DELETE* statement deletes the rows from the *dbo.Orders* table for which a related row exists in the *dbo.Customers* table with the same customer ID as the order's customer ID and the customer's country is Brazil.

Another way to handle this task is to use the T-SQL-specific *DELETE* syntax based on a join, like this:

```
DELETE FROM O
FROM dbo.Orders AS O
  INNER JOIN dbo.Customers AS C
    ON O.custid = C.custid
WHERE country = N'Brazil';
```

The join between the *dbo.Orders* and *dbo.Customers* tables serves a filtering purpose. The join matches each order with the customer who placed the order. The *WHERE* clause filters only rows for which the customer's country is Brazil. The *DELETE FROM* clause refers to the alias *O* representing the table *Orders*, indicating that *Orders* is the target of the *DELETE* operation.

As a standard alternative, you can use the *MERGE* statement to handle this task. Even though you normally think of using *MERGE* when you need to apply different actions based on conditional logic, you also can use it when you need to apply only one action. In our case, you can use the *MERGE* statement with the *WHEN MATCHED* clause alone; you don't need to have a *WHEN NOT MATCHED* clause as well. The following *MERGE* statement handles the request in the exercise:

```
MERGE INTO dbo.Orders AS O
USING (SELECT * FROM dbo.Customers WHERE country = N'Brazil') AS C
  ON O.custid = C.custid
WHEN MATCHED THEN DELETE;
```

This *MERGE* statement defines the *dbo.Orders* table as the target. It defines a table expression with customers from the *dbo.Customers* table that are from Brazil as the source. An order is deleted from the target (*dbo.Orders*) when a matching row is found in the source (*dbo.Customers*) with the same customer ID.

Exercise 4

This exercise involves writing an *UPDATE* statement that filters only rows for which the region attribute is *NULL*. Make sure you use the *IS NULL* predicate and not an equality operator when looking for *NULLs*. Use the *OUTPUT* clause to return the requested information. Here's the complete *UPDATE* statement:

```
UPDATE dbo.Customers
  SET region = '<None>'
OUTPUT
  deleted.custid,
  deleted.region AS oldregion,
  inserted.region AS newregion
WHERE region IS NULL;
```

Exercise 5

One way to solve this exercise is to use the T-SQL-specific *UPDATE* syntax based on a join. You can join *dbo.Orders* and *dbo.Customers* based on a match between the order's customer ID and the customer's customer ID. In the *WHERE* clause, you can filter only the rows where the customer's country is the United Kingdom. In the *UPDATE* clause, specify the alias you assigned to the *dbo.Orders* table to indicate that it's the target of the modification. In the *SET* clause, assign the values of the shipping location attributes of the order to the location attributes of the corresponding customer. Here's the complete *UPDATE* statement:

```
UPDATE O
  SET shipcountry = C.country,
      shipregion = C.region,
      shipcity = C.city
FROM dbo.Orders AS O
  INNER JOIN dbo.Customers AS C
    ON O.custid = C.custid
WHERE C.country = N'UK';
```

Another solution is to define a CTE based on a *SELECT* query that joins *dbo.Orders* and *dbo.Customers* and returns both the target location attributes from *dbo.Orders* and the source location attributes from *dbo.Customers*. The outer query would then be an *UPDATE* statement modifying the target attributes with the values of the source attributes. Here's the complete solution statement:

```
WITH CTE_UPD AS
(
  SELECT
    O.shipcountry AS ocountry, C.country AS ccountry,
    O.shipregion  AS oregion,  C.region  AS cregion,
    O.shipcity    AS ocity,    C.city    AS ccity
  FROM dbo.Orders AS O
    INNER JOIN dbo.Customers AS C
      ON O.custid = C.custid
  WHERE C.country = N'UK'
)
UPDATE CTE_UPD
  SET ocountry = ccountry, oregion = cregion, ocity = ccity;
```

You can also use the *MERGE* statement to achieve this task. As explained earlier, even though in a *MERGE* statement you usually want to specify both the *WHEN MATCHED* and *WHEN NOT MATCHED* clauses, the statement supports specifying only one of the clauses. Using only a *WHEN MATCHED* clause with an *UPDATE* action, you can write a solution that is logically equivalent to the last two solutions. Here's the complete solution statement:

```
MERGE INTO dbo.Orders AS O
USING (SELECT * FROM dbo.Customers WHERE country = N'UK') AS C
  ON O.custid = C.custid
WHEN MATCHED THEN
  UPDATE SET shipcountry = C.country,
             shipregion = C.region,
             shipcity = C.city;
```

Exercise 6

There's a foreign-key relationship between *OrderDetails* and *Orders*. In such a case, you're allowed to truncate the referencing table, but not the referenced table, even if there are no related rows in the referencing table. You will need to drop the foreign-key constraint, truncate the tables, and then re-create the constraint, like this:

```
ALTER TABLE dbo.OrderDetails DROP CONSTRAINT FK_OrderDetails_Orders;

TRUNCATE TABLE dbo.OrderDetails;
TRUNCATE TABLE dbo.Orders;

ALTER TABLE dbo.OrderDetails ADD CONSTRAINT FK_OrderDetails_Orders
  FOREIGN KEY(orderid) REFERENCES dbo.Orders(orderid);
```

When you're done, run the following code for cleanup:

```
DROP TABLE IF EXISTS dbo.OrderDetails, dbo.Orders, dbo.Customers;
```

CHAPTER 9

Temporal tables

When you modify data in tables, normally you lose any trace of the premodified state of the rows. You can access only the current state. What if you need to be able to access historical states of the data? Perhaps you need these states for auditing, point-in-time analysis, comparing current states with older states, slowly changing dimensions (details of which you can find in the Wikipedia article at *https://en.wikipedia.org/wiki/Slowly_changing_dimension*), restoring an older state of rows because of accidental deletion or updating, and so on. You could roll your own customized solution based on triggers. Better yet, starting with Microsoft SQL Server 2016, you can use a built-in feature called *system-versioned temporal tables*. This built-in feature provides a solution that is both simpler and more efficient than a customized one can be.

A system-versioned temporal table has two columns representing the validity period of the row, plus a linked history table with a mirrored schema holding older states of modified rows. When you need to modify data, you interact with the current table, issuing normal data-modification statements. SQL Server automatically updates the period columns and moves older versions of rows to the history table. When you need to query data, if you want the current state, you simply query the current table as usual. If you need access to older states, you still query the current table, but you add a clause indicating that you want to see an older state or period of time. SQL Server queries the current and history tables behind the scenes as needed.

The SQL standard supports three types of temporal tables:

- System-versioned temporal tables rely on the system transaction time to define the validity period of a row.

- Application-time period tables rely on the application's definition of the validity period of a row. This means you can define a validity period that will become effective in the future.

- Bitemporal combines the two types just mentioned (transaction and valid time).

SQL Server 2022 supports only system-versioned temporal tables. I hope Microsoft will add support for application-time period tables and bitemporal tables to future versions of SQL Server.

This chapter covers system-versioned temporal tables in three sections: creating tables, modifying data, and querying data.

Creating tables

When you create a system-versioned temporal table, you need to make sure the table definition has all the following elements:

- A primary key

- Two columns defined as *DATETIME2* with any precision, which are non-nullable and represent the start and end of the row's validity period in the UTC time zone

  - A start column that should be marked with the option *GENERATED ALWAYS AS ROW START*
  - An end column that should be marked with the option *GENERATED ALWAYS AS ROW END*

- A designation of the period columns with the option *PERIOD FOR SYSTEM_TIME (<startcol>, <endcol>)*

- The table option *SYSTEM_VERSIONING*, which should be set to ON

- A linked history table (which SQL Server can create for you) to hold the past states of modified rows

Optionally, you can mark the period columns as hidden so that when you're querying the table with *SELECT* * they won't be returned and when you're inserting data they'll be ignored.

Also, starting with SQL Server 2017, you can optionally define a history retention policy using the *HISTORY_RETENTION_PERIOD* subclause of the *SYSTEM_VERSIONING* clause. You can set the retention period using the units *DAYS*, *WEEKS*, *MONTHS*, *YEARS*, and *INFINITE*. If you omit this clause, *INFINITE* retention is assumed by default. If you set a finite retention policy, SQL Server regularly deletes data that ages beyond the defined period (with respect to the period end column) in chunks. It does so using an automated background task.

Run the following code to create a system-versioned temporal table called *Employees* and a linked history table called *EmployeesHistory*:

```
USE TSQLV6;

CREATE TABLE dbo.Employees
(
  empid       INT                        NOT NULL
    CONSTRAINT PK_Employees PRIMARY KEY,
  empname     VARCHAR(25)                NOT NULL,
  department  VARCHAR(50)                NOT NULL,
  salary      NUMERIC(10, 2)             NOT NULL,
  validfrom   DATETIME2(0)
    GENERATED ALWAYS AS ROW START HIDDEN NOT NULL,
  validto     DATETIME2(0)
    GENERATED ALWAYS AS ROW END   HIDDEN NOT NULL,
  PERIOD FOR SYSTEM_TIME (validfrom, validto)
)
```

```
WITH ( SYSTEM_VERSIONING = ON
      ( HISTORY_TABLE = dbo.EmployeesHistory,
        HISTORY_RETENTION_PERIOD = 5 YEARS ) );
```

Review the list of required elements, and make sure you identify them in the code. Also observe the optional elements used here to define the period columns as hidden, and an automated retention policy of five years.

Assuming the history table doesn't exist when you run this code, SQL Server creates it for you. If you do not specify a name for the table, SQL Server assigns one for you using the form *MSSQL_ TemporalHistoryFor_<object_id>*, where *object_id* is the object ID of the current table. To find the exact name that SQL Server assigned, you can browse the object tree in Object Explorer. SQL Server creates the history table with a mirrored schema of the current table, but with the following differences:

- No primary key

- A clustered index on (*<endcol>*, *<startcol>*), with page compression if possible

- Period columns that are not marked with any special options, like *GENERATED ALWAYS AS ROW START/END* or *HIDDEN*

- No designation of the period columns with the option *PERIOD FOR SYSTEM_TIME*

- The history table is not marked with the option *SYSTEM_VERSIONING*

If the history table already exists when you create the current table, SQL Server validates the consistency of both the schema (as just described) and the data (with no overlapping periods). If the history table doesn't pass the consistency checks, SQL Server will produce an error at DDL time and won't create the current table. You can optionally indicate you do not want SQL Server to perform the data-consistency check. Usually this is done when you're certain that the data is consistent and you cannot allow the time required for the verification of the data.

If you browse the object tree in Object Explorer in SQL Server Management Studio (SSMS), you'll find the *Employees* table marked as (System-Versioned) and below it the linked *EmployeesHistory* table marked as (History), as shown in Figure 9-1.

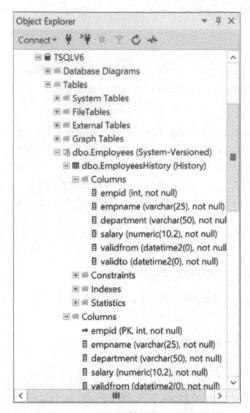

FIGURE 9-1 Temporal table and associated history table in SSMS

You can also turn an existing nontemporal table that already has data into a temporal one. For example, suppose you have a table called *Employees* in your database and you want to turn it into a temporal table. You first alter the table, adding the period columns and designating them as such using the following code (but don't actually run the code because our *Employees* table is already temporal):

```
ALTER TABLE dbo.Employees ADD
  validfrom DATETIME2(0) GENERATED ALWAYS AS ROW START HIDDEN NOT NULL
    CONSTRAINT DFT_Employees_validfrom DEFAULT('19000101'),
  validto DATETIME2(0) GENERATED ALWAYS AS ROW END HIDDEN NOT NULL
    CONSTRAINT DFT_Employees_validto DEFAULT('99991231 23:59:59'),
  PERIOD FOR SYSTEM_TIME (validfrom, validto);
```

Notice the defaults that set the validity period for the existing rows. You decide what you want the start time of the validity period to be, as long as it's not in the future. The end has to be the maximum supported value in the type.

You then alter the table to enable system versioning, link it to a history table, and define a retention policy using the following code (again, don't actually run this code):

```
ALTER TABLE dbo.Employees
  SET ( SYSTEM_VERSIONING = ON
      ( HISTORY_TABLE = dbo.EmployeesHistory,
        HISTORY_RETENTION_PERIOD = 5 YEARS ) );
```

Remember that if you marked the period columns as hidden, when you query the table with *SELECT* * SQL Server won't return them. Try this with our *Employees* table by running the following code:

```
SELECT *
FROM dbo.Employees;
```

You get the following output:

```
empid  empname  department  salary
------ -------- ----------- ---------
```

If you do want to return the period columns, mention them explicitly in the *SELECT* list, like so:

```
SELECT empid, empname, department, salary, validfrom, validto
FROM dbo.Employees;
```

You get the following output:

```
empid  empname  department  salary    validfrom            validto
------ -------- ----------- --------- -------------------- --------------------
```

SQL Server supports making schema changes to a temporal table without needing to disable system versioning first. You issue the schema change to the current table, and SQL Server applies it to both the current and history tables. Naturally, if you want to add a non-nullable column, you'll need to add it with a default constraint. For example, suppose you want to add a non-nullable column called *hiredate* to our *Employees* table and use the date January 1st, 1900, as the default. You do so by running the following code:

```
ALTER TABLE dbo.Employees
  ADD hiredate DATE NOT NULL
    CONSTRAINT DFT_Employees_hiredate DEFAULT('19000101');
```

You can then update the hire date of existing employees as needed.

Query the *Employees* table after adding the *hiredate* column:

```
SELECT *
FROM dbo.Employees;
```

You get the following output:

```
empid  empname  department  salary    hiredate
------ -------- ----------- --------- ----------
```

Query the *EmployeesHistory* table:

```
SELECT *
FROM dbo.EmployeesHistory;
```

Notice the output has the *hiredate* column in this table as well:

```
empid  empname  department  salary  validfrom             validto              hiredate
------ -------- ----------- ------- --------------------- -------------------- ----------
```

SQL Server added the *hiredate* column to both tables, but the default constraint was added only in the current table. Still, if there had been any rows in the history table, SQL Server would have assigned the default value to the *hiredate* column in those rows.

Suppose you want to drop the *hiredate* column from both tables. First you drop the default constraint from the current table by running the following code:

```
ALTER TABLE dbo.Employees
  DROP CONSTRAINT DFT_Employees_hiredate;
```

Second, you drop the column from the current table by running the following code:

```
ALTER TABLE dbo.Employees
  DROP COLUMN hiredate;
```

SQL Server drops the column from both tables.

Note that if you want to drop a system-versioned table, you need to first disable system versioning with an *ALTER TABLE* command, and then manually drop the current and history tables.

Modifying data

Modifying temporal tables is similar to modifying regular tables. You modify only the current table with *INSERT, UPDATE, DELETE,* and *MERGE* statements. (There's no support for *TRUNCATE* in SQL Server 2022 for temporal tables.) Behind the scenes, SQL Server updates the period columns and moves rows to the history table as needed. Remember that the period columns reflect the validity period of the row in the UTC time zone.

If you defined the period columns as hidden, like in our case, you simply ignore them in *INSERT* statements. If you didn't define them as hidden, as long as you follow best practices and explicitly mention the target column names, you can still ignore them. If you didn't define them as hidden and you do not mention the target column names, you'll need to specify the keyword *DEFAULT* as the value for them.

In the following examples, I'll demonstrate modifications against the *Employees* table and mention the point in time in the UTC time zone at which I apply them. Naturally, the modification times will be different for you when you run the code samples, so it might be a good idea for you to make a note of those times when you submit them. You can query the *SYSUTCDATETIME* function to get this information.

Run the following code to add a few rows to the *Employees* table (the time was 2022-02-16 17:08:41 when I ran it):

```
INSERT INTO dbo.Employees(empid, empname, department, salary)
  VALUES(1, 'Sara', 'IT'        , 50000.00),
        (2, 'Don' , 'HR'        , 45000.00),
        (3, 'Judy', 'Sales'     , 55000.00),
        (4, 'Yael', 'Marketing', 55000.00),
        (5, 'Sven', 'IT'        , 45000.00),
        (6, 'Paul', 'Sales'     , 40000.00);
```

Query the data in both the current and history tables to see what SQL Server did behind the scenes:

```
SELECT empid, empname, department, salary, validfrom, validto
FROM dbo.Employees;

SELECT empid, empname, department, salary, validfrom, validto
FROM dbo.EmployeesHistory;
```

The current table has the six new rows, with the *validfrom* column reflecting the modification time and *validto* holding the maximum possible value in the type with the chosen precision:

empid	empname	department	salary	validfrom	validto
1	Sara	IT	50000.00	2022-02-16 17:08:41	9999-12-31 23:59:59
2	Don	HR	45000.00	2022-02-16 17:08:41	9999-12-31 23:59:59
3	Judy	Sales	55000.00	2022-02-16 17:08:41	9999-12-31 23:59:59
4	Yael	Marketing	55000.00	2022-02 16 17:08:41	9999-12-31 23:59:59
5	Sven	IT	45000.00	2022-02-16 17:08:41	9999-12-31 23:59:59
6	Paul	Sales	40000.00	2022-02-16 17:08:41	9999-12-31 23:59:59

The validity period indicates that the rows are considered valid since the time they were inserted and with no end limit.

The history table is empty at this point:

empid	empname	department	salary	validfrom	validto

Run the following code to delete the row where the employee ID is 6 (the time was 2022-02-16 17:15:26 when I ran it):

```
DELETE FROM dbo.Employees
WHERE empid = 6;
```

SQL Server moves the deleted row to the history table, setting its *validto* value to the deletion time. Following is the content of the current table at this point:

empid	empname	department	salary	validfrom	validto
1	Sara	IT	50000.00	2022-02-16 17:08:41	9999-12-31 23:59:59
2	Don	HR	45000.00	2022-02-16 17:08:41	9999-12-31 23:59:59
3	Judy	Sales	55000.00	2022-02-16 17:08:41	9999-12-31 23:59:59
4	Yael	Marketing	55000.00	2022-02-16 17:08:41	9999-12-31 23:59:59
5	Sven	IT	45000.00	2022-02-16 17:08:41	9999-12-31 23:59:59

Following is the content of the history table:

```
empid  empname  department   salary     validfrom             validto
------ -------- ------------ --------- --------------------- ---------------------
6      Paul     Sales        40000.00  2022-02-16 17:08:41   2022-02-16 17:15:26
```

An update of a row is treated as a delete plus an insert. SQL Server moves the old version of the row to the history table with the transaction time as the period end time, and it keeps the current version of the row in the current table with the transaction time as the period start time and the maximum value in the type as the period end time. For example, run the following update to increase the salary of all IT employees by 5 percent (the time was 2022-02-16 17:20:02 when I ran it):

```
UPDATE dbo.Employees
  SET salary *= 1.05
WHERE department = 'IT';
```

Following is the content of the current table after the update:

```
empid  empname  department   salary     validfrom             validto
------ -------- ------------ --------- --------------------- ---------------------
1      Sara     IT           52500.00  2022-02-16 17:20:02   9999-12-31 23:59:59
2      Don      HR           45000.00  2022-02-16 17:08:41   9999-12-31 23:59:59
3      Judy     Sales        55000.00  2022-02-16 17:08:41   9999-12-31 23:59:59
4      Yael     Marketing    55000.00  2022-02-16 17:08:41   9999-12-31 23:59:59
5      Sven     IT           47250.00  2022-02-16 17:20:02   9999-12-31 23:59:59
```

Notice the values in the *salary* and period columns for the IT employees.

Following is the content of the history table:

```
empid  empname  department   salary     validfrom             validto
------ -------- ------------ --------- --------------------- ---------------------
6      Paul     Sales        40000.00  2022-02-16 17:08:41   2022-02-16 17:15:26
1      Sara     IT           50000.00  2022-02-16 17:08:41   2022-02-16 17:20:02
5      Sven     IT           45000.00  2022-02-16 17:08:41   2022-02-16 17:20:02
```

> **Tip** Curiously, if you don't care about keeping older states of modified rows to enable time-travel queries, but you do need to be able to tell when was the last time that the row was inserted or updated, SQL Server supports such a scenario. You create the current temporal table with the *SYSTEM_VERSIONING* option set to *OFF* and without a history table. You will still be required to have both the period start and the period end columns, even though only the former is really meaningful. As you insert and update rows into the table, SQL Server records the last time the row was inserted or updated in the period start column. It records the maximum supported value in the type in the period end column.

The modification times that SQL Server records in the period columns reflect the transaction start time. If you have a long-running transaction that started at point in time T1 and ended at T2, SQL Server will record T1 as the modification time for all statements. For example, run this code to open an explicit transaction and change the department of employee 5 to Sales (the time was 2022-02-16 17:28:10 when I ran it):

```
BEGIN TRAN;

UPDATE dbo.Employees
  SET department = 'Sales'
WHERE empid = 5;
```

Wait a few seconds, and then run the following code to change the department of employee 3 to IT (the time was 2022-02-16 17:29:22 when I ran it):

```
UPDATE dbo.Employees
  SET department = 'IT'
WHERE empid = 3;

COMMIT TRAN;
```

The *BEGIN TRAN* statement opens a transaction, and the *COMMIT TRAN* statement closes it by committing its changes.

Following is the content of the current table after running this transaction:

```
empid  empname  department  salary    validfrom            validto
-----  -------  ----------  --------  -------------------  -------------------
1      Sara     IT          52500.00  2022-02-16 17:20:02  9999-12-31 23:59:59
2      Don      HR          45000.00  2022-02-16 17:08:41  9999-12-31 23:59:59
3      Judy     IT          55000.00  2022-02-16 17:28:10  9999-12-31 23:59:59
4      Yael     Marketing   55000.00  2022-02-16 17:08:41  9999-12-31 23:59:59
5      Sven     Sales       47250.00  2022-02-16 17:28:10  9999-12-31 23:59:59
```

Following is the content of the history table at this point:

```
empid  empname  department  salary    validfrom            validto
-----  -------  ----------  --------  -------------------  -------------------
6      Paul     Sales       40000.00  2022-02-16 17:08:41  2022-02-16 17:15:26
1      Sara     IT          50000.00  2022-02-16 17:08:41  2022-02-16 17:20:02
5      Sven     IT          45000.00  2022-02-16 17:08:41  2022-02-16 17:20:02
3      Judy     Sales       55000.00  2022-02-16 17:08:41  2022-02-16 17:28:10
5      Sven     IT          47250.00  2022-02-16 17:20:02  2022-02-16 17:28:10
```

Observe that for all modified rows, the modification time (*validfrom* for current rows and *validto* for history rows) reflects the transaction start time.

The fact that the modification time reflects the transaction start time can lead to some noteworthy situations. One of those is that if you update the same row multiple times in the same transaction, you'll end up with the in-between versions (between the oldest and newest in the series of updates) having zero-length validity periods. Both the *validfrom* and the *validto* values in those rows will be the same, both reflecting the transaction start time. Such intervals are known as *degenerate intervals*. When you query temporal tables using the *FOR SYSTEM_TIME* clause to perform time-travel queries, SQL Server automatically discards rows whose validity period is a degenerate interval.

Another noteworthy situation develops if you perform a sequence of events such as the one described in Table 9-1 from two different sessions (I'll refer to them as session 1 and session 2).

TABLE 9-1 Noteworthy modification sequence

point in time	session 1	session 2
T1	Begin tran A	
T2		Begin tran B
T3		Update some row R in a system-versioned table (recorded modification time is T2)
T4		Commit tran B
T5	Update the same row R (recorded modification time is T1, which is earlier than the last recorded modification time T2!)	
T6	Commit tran A	

As you can see, with this sequence of events, session 2 updates row R first, recording modification time T2, and later session 1 attempts to update the same row R, recording an earlier modification time T1 than the one already recorded T2. SQL Server doesn't allow the second update to materialize, and at point in time T5 when the second update is attempted, SQL Server fails it, generating the following error:

```
Msg 13535, Level 16, State 0, Line 4
Data modification failed on system-versioned table 'TSQLV6.dbo.Employees' because transaction time was earlier than period start time for affected records.
The statement has been terminated.
```

SQL Server keeps transaction A open despite the error, so you would still want to make sure you have error handling code present to deal with such a situation. You can find more information on transactions in Chapter 10 and on error handling in Chapter 12.

Can you change history?

As mentioned and demonstrated in this section, the system versioning feature allows users to submit direct data modifications only against the current table. Normally, only SQL Server is allowed to internally write to the history table older versions of rows to account for user updates and deletes against the current table. The thinking behind this restriction is that some companies might be using the system versioning feature for auditing purposes and for legal reasons. In such a case you don't want users to be able to change the history. Still, you probably want to be able to purge historic data periodically. SQL Server supports a number of ways to achieve this, such as the retention policy option covered earlier, partitioning, and others. For details, see "Manage retention of historical data in system-versioned temporal tables" in the product documentation here: *https://learn.microsoft.com/en-us/sql/relational-databases/tables/manage-retention-of-historical-data-in-system-versioned-temporal-tables.*

What's very important to understand is that the restriction that prevents users from applying direct modifications against the history table is only applicable when the system versioning option is enabled. At any point, the DBA can disable versioning with the statement *ALTER TABLE TargetTable SET (SYSTEM_VERSIONING = OFF)*. Once it is disabled, you can apply direct modifications against both the current and the history table, and then the DBA can re-enable versioning with the statement *ALTER TABLE TargetTable SET (SYSTEM_VERSIONING = ON)*. So the company cannot really attest to interested parties like auditors that the data hasn't been tampered with. For companies dealing with very sensitive data and who do need such a guarantee, you can use a feature called *ledger*, available in SQL Server 2022 and later and in Azure SQL Database. This feature is built on top of the system-versioning technology, extending it further by relying on blockchain technology. It uses Merkle hash trees to provide tamper evidence. Based on this evidence you can cryptographically attest to interested parties that the data hasn't been tampered with. You can use updateable ledger tables with tamper-evidence capabilities, or you can even use append-only ledger tables, which allow only inserting new rows. For more details on the ledger feature, see "Ledger overview" here: *https://learn.microsoft.com/en-us/sql/relational-databases/security/ledger/ledger-overview.*

Querying data

Querying data in temporal tables is simple and elegant. If you want to query the current state of the data, you simply query the current table as you would query a normal table. If you want to query a past state of the data, you still query the current table, but you add a clause called *FOR SYSTEM_TIME* and a subclause that indicates the validity point or period of time you're interested in.

Before examining the specifics of querying temporal tables, run the following code to re-create the *Employees* and *EmployeesHistory* tables and to populate them with the same sample data as in my environment, including the values in the period columns:

```
USE TSQLV6;

-- Drop tables if exist
IF OBJECT_ID(N'dbo.Employees', N'U') IS NOT NULL
BEGIN
  IF OBJECTPROPERTY(OBJECT_ID(N'dbo.Employees', N'U'), N'TableTemporalType') = 2
    ALTER TABLE dbo.Employees SET ( SYSTEM_VERSIONING = OFF );
  DROP TABLE IF EXISTS dbo.EmployeesHistory, dbo.Employees;
END;
GO
```

```
-- Create and populate Employees table
CREATE TABLE dbo.Employees
(
  empid       INT          NOT NULL
    CONSTRAINT PK_Employees PRIMARY KEY,
  empname     VARCHAR(25)  NOT NULL,
  department  VARCHAR(50)  NOT NULL,
  salary      NUMERIC(10, 2) NOT NULL,
  validfrom   DATETIME2(0) NOT NULL,
  validto     DATETIME2(0) NOT NULL
);

INSERT INTO dbo.Employees(empid, empname, department, salary, validfrom, validto) VALUES
  (1 , 'Sara', 'IT'       , 52500.00, '2022-02-16 17:20:02', '9999-12-31 23:59:59'),
  (2 , 'Don' , 'HR'       , 45000.00, '2022-02-16 17:08:41', '9999-12-31 23:59:59'),
  (3 , 'Judy', 'IT'       , 55000.00, '2022-02-16 17:28:10', '9999-12-31 23:59:59'),
  (4 , 'Yael', 'Marketing', 55000.00, '2022-02-16 17:08:41', '9999-12-31 23:59:59'),
  (5 , 'Sven', 'Sales'    , 47250.00, '2022-02-16 17:28:10', '9999-12-31 23:59:59');

-- Create and populate EmployeesHistory table
CREATE TABLE dbo.EmployeesHistory
(
  empid       INT          NOT NULL,
  empname     VARCHAR(25)  NOT NULL,
  department  VARCHAR(50)  NOT NULL,
  salary      NUMERIC(10, 2) NOT NULL,
  validfrom   DATETIME2(0) NOT NULL,
  validto     DATETIME2(0) NOT NULL,
  INDEX ix_EmployeesHistory CLUSTERED(validto, validfrom)
    WITH (DATA_COMPRESSION = PAGE)
);

INSERT INTO dbo.EmployeesHistory(empid, empname, department, salary, validfrom, validto) VALUES
  (6 , 'Paul', 'Sales' , 40000.00, '2022-02-16 17:08:41', '2022-02-16 17:15:26'),
  (1 , 'Sara', 'IT'    , 50000.00, '2022-02-16 17:08:41', '2022-02-16 17:20:02'),
  (5 , 'Sven', 'IT'    , 45000.00, '2022-02-16 17:08:41', '2022-02-16 17:20:02'),
  (3 , 'Judy', 'Sales' , 55000.00, '2022-02-16 17:08:41', '2022-02-16 17:28:10'),
  (5 , 'Sven', 'IT'    , 47250.00, '2022-02-16 17:20:02', '2022-02-16 17:28:10');

-- Enable system versioning
ALTER TABLE dbo.Employees ADD PERIOD FOR SYSTEM_TIME (validfrom, validto);

ALTER TABLE dbo.Employees ALTER COLUMN validfrom ADD HIDDEN;
ALTER TABLE dbo.Employees ALTER COLUMN validto ADD HIDDEN;

ALTER TABLE dbo.Employees
  SET ( SYSTEM_VERSIONING = ON
        ( HISTORY_TABLE = dbo.EmployeesHistory,
          HISTORY_RETENTION_PERIOD = 5 YEARS ) );
```

This way, the outputs of the queries in your environment will be the same as in the book. Just remember that when a query has no *ORDER BY* clause, there's no guarantee for any specific presentation order in the output. So it is possible that the order of the rows you'll get when you run the queries will be different than in the book.

As mentioned, if you want to query the current state of the rows, simply query the current table:

```
SELECT *
FROM dbo.Employees;
```

This query generates the following output:

```
empid  empname  department   salary
------ -------- ------------ ---------
1      Sara     IT           52500.00
2      Don      HR           45000.00
3      Judy     IT           55000.00
4      Yael     Marketing    55000.00
5      Sven     Sales        47250.00
```

Remember that because the period columns are defined as hidden, a *SELECT* * query doesn't return them. Here I use *SELECT* * for illustration purposes, but I remind you that the best practice is to be explicit about the column list in production code. The same applies to *INSERT* statements. If you do follow best practices, whether the period columns were defined as hidden or not shouldn't really matter to you.

If you want to see a past state of the data, correct to a certain point or period of time, you query the current table followed by the *FOR SYSTEM_TIME* clause, plus a subclause that indicates more specifics. SQL Server will retrieve the data from both the current and history tables as needed. Conveniently, you can specify the *FOR SYSTEM_TIME* clause when querying views, and the clause definition is propagated to underlying objects.

Following is the syntax for using the *FOR SYSTEM_TIME* clause:

```
SELECT ... FROM <table_or_view> FOR SYSTEM_TIME <subclause> AS <alias>;
```

Of the five subclauses that the *SYSTEM_TIME* clause supports, you'll probably use the *AS OF* subclause most often. You use it to request to see the data correct to a specific point in time you specify. The syntax of this subclause is *FOR SYSTEM_TIME AS OF <datetime2 value>*. The input can be a constant, a variable, or a parameter. Say the input is a variable called *@datetime*. You'll get back the rows where *@datetime* is on or after *validfrom* and before *validto*. In other words, the validity period starts on or before *@datetime* and ends after *@datetime*. The following predicate identifies the qualifying rows:

```
validfrom <= @datetime AND validto > @datetime
```

Run the following code to return the employee rows correct to the point in time 2022-02-16 17:00:00:

```
SELECT *
FROM dbo.Employees FOR SYSTEM_TIME AS OF '2022-02-16 17:00:00';
```

You'll get an empty result because the first insert you issued against the table happened at 2022-02-16 17:08:41:

```
empid  empname  department   salary
------ -------- ------------ ---------
```

Query the table again, this time as of 2022-02-16 17:10:00:

```
SELECT *
FROM dbo.Employees FOR SYSTEM_TIME AS OF '2022-02-16 17:10:00';
```

You get the following output:

```
empid  empname  department   salary
------ -------- ------------ ---------
2      Don      HR           45000.00
4      Yael     Marketing    55000.00
6      Paul     Sales        40000.00
1      Sara     IT           50000.00
5      Sven     IT           45000.00
3      Judy     Sales        55000.00
```

You can also query multiple instances of the same table, comparing different states of the data at different points in time. For example, the following query returns the percentage of increase of salary of employees who had a salary increase between two different points in time:

```
SELECT T2.empid, T2.empname,
  CAST( (T2.salary / T1.salary - 1.0) * 100.0 AS NUMERIC(10, 2) ) AS pct
FROM dbo.Employees FOR SYSTEM_TIME AS OF '2022-02-16 17:10:00' AS T1
  INNER JOIN dbo.Employees FOR SYSTEM_TIME AS OF '2022-02-16 17:25:00' AS T2
    ON T1.empid = T2.empid
    AND T2.salary > T1.salary;
```

This code generates the following output:

```
empid  empname  pct
------ -------- -----
1      Sara     5.00
5      Sven     5.00
```

The subclause *FROM @start TO @end* returns the rows that satisfy the predicate *validfrom < @end AND validto > @start*. In other words, it returns the rows with a validity period that starts before the input interval ends and that ends after the input interval starts. The following query demonstrates using this subclause:

```
SELECT empid, empname, department, salary, validfrom, validto
FROM dbo.Employees
  FOR SYSTEM_TIME FROM '2022-02-16 17:15:26' TO '2022-02-16 17:20:02';
```

This query generates the following output:

```
empid  empname  department   salary     validfrom             validto
------ -------- ------------ ---------  --------------------  --------------------
2      Don      HR           45000.00   2022-02-16 17:08:41   9999-12-31 23:59:59
4      Yael     Marketing    55000.00   2022-02-16 17:08:41   9999-12-31 23:59:59
1      Sara     IT           50000.00   2022-02-16 17:08:41,  2022-02-16 17:20:02
5      Sven     IT           45000.00   2022-02-16 17:08:41   2022-02-16 17:20:02
3      Judy     Sales        55000.00   2022-02-16 17:08:41   2022-02-16 17:28:10
```

Notice that rows with a *validfrom* value of 2022-02-16 17:20:02 are not included in the output. If you need the input *@end* value to be inclusive, use the *BETWEEN* subclause instead of the *FROM* subclause. The syntax of the *BETWEEN* subclause is BETWEEN *@start* AND *@end*, and it returns the rows that satisfy the predicate *validfrom <= @end AND validto > @start*. It returns the rows with a validity period that starts *on or before* the input interval ends and that ends after the input interval starts. The following query demonstrates using this subclause with the same input values as in the previous query:

```
SELECT empid, empname, department, salary, validfrom, validto
FROM dbo.Employees
  FOR SYSTEM_TIME BETWEEN '2022-02-16 17:15:26' AND '2022-02-16 17:20:02';
```

You get the following output, this time including rows with a *validfrom* value of 2022-02-16 17:20:02:

empid	empname	department	salary	validfrom	validto
1	Sara	IT	52500.00	2022-02-16 17:20:02	9999-12-31 23:59:59
2	Don	HR	45000.00	2022-02-16 17:08:41	9999-12-31 23:59:59
4	Yael	Marketing	55000.00	2022-02-16 17:08:41	9999-12-31 23:59:59
1	Sara	IT	50000.00	2022-02-16 17:08:41	2022-02-16 17:20:02
5	Sven	IT	45000.00	2022-02-16 17:08:41	2022-02-16 17:20:02
3	Judy	Sales	55000.00	2022-02-16 17:08:41	2022-02-16 17:28:10
5	Sven	IT	47250.00	2022-02-16 17:20:02	2022-02-16 17:28:10

The subclause *FOR SYSTEM_TIME CONTAINED IN(@start, @end)* returns the rows that satisfy the predicate *validfrom >= @start AND validto <= @end*. It returns the rows with a validity period that starts on or after the input interval starts and that ends on or before the input interval ends. In other words, the validity period needs to be completely contained in the input period.

Here's an example demonstrating the use of this clause:

```
SELECT empid, empname, department, salary, validfrom, validto
FROM dbo.Employees
  FOR SYSTEM_TIME CONTAINED IN('2022-02-16 17:00:00', '2022-02-16 18:00:00');
```

This query generates the following output:

empid	empname	department	salary	validfrom	validto
6	Paul	Sales	10000.00	2022-02-16 17:08:41	2022-02-16 17:15:26
1	Sara	IT	50000.00	2022-02-16 17:08:41	2022-02-16 17:20:02
5	Sven	IT	45000.00	2022-02-16 17:08:41	2022-02-16 17:20:02
3	Judy	Sales	55000.00	2022-02-16 17:08:41	2022-02-16 17:28:10
5	Sven	IT	47250.00	2022-02-16 17:20:02	2022-02-16 17:28:10

Table 9-2 summarizes the aforementioned subclauses and the predicates that represent the qualifying rows.

TABLE 9-2 Qualifying rows for *FOR SYSTEM_TIME* subclauses

Subclause	Qualifying rows
AS OF @datetime	*validfrom <= @datetime AND validto > @datetime*
FROM @start TO @end	*validfrom < @end AND validto > @start*
BETWEEN @start AND @end	*validfrom <= @end AND validto > @start*
CONTAINED IN(@start, @end)	*validfrom >= @start AND validto <= @end*

Figure 9-2 has a similar summary of the subclauses, with a graphical depiction of the predicates and qualifying rows.

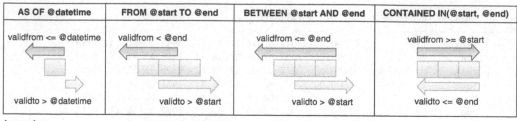

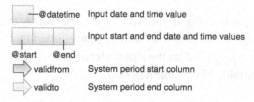

Legend:

@datetime	Input date and time value
Input start and end date and time values	
@start @end	
validfrom	System period start column
validto	System period end column

FIGURE 9-2 Illustrations of *FOR SYSTEM_TIME* subclauses

T-SQL also supports the *ALL* subclause, which simply returns all rows from both tables. The following query demonstrates the use of this subclause:

```
SELECT empid, empname, department, salary, validfrom, validto
FROM dbo.Employees FOR SYSTEM_TIME ALL
WHERE empid = 5;
```

This query generates the following output:

```
empid  empname  department  salary    validfrom            validto
------ -------- ----------- --------- -------------------- --------------------
5      Sven     Sales       47250.00  2022-02-16 17:28:10  9999-12-31 23:59:59
5      Sven     IT          45000.00  2022-02-16 17:08:41  2022-02-16 17:20:02
5      Sven     IT          47250.00  2022-02-16 17:20:02  2022-02-16 17:28:10
```

Remember that the period columns reflect the validity period of the row as *datetime2* values in the UTC time zone. If you want to return those as *datetimeoffset* values in a desired time zone, you can use the *AT TIME ZONE* function, which was covered in Chapter 2. You'll need to use the function twice: once to convert the input to *datetimeoffset*, indicating that it's in the UTC time zone, and another to convert the value to the target time zone—for example, *validfrom AT TIME ZONE 'UTC' AT TIME ZONE 'Pacific Standard Time'*. If you use only one conversion straight to the target time zone, the function will assume that the source value is already in the target time zone and won't perform the desired switching.

Another thing to consider is that for the *validto* column, if the value is the maximum in the type, you'll just want to consider it as using the UTC time zone so that it won't overflow. Otherwise, you'll want to convert it to the target time zone, as with the *validfrom* column. You can use a *CASE* expression to apply this logic.

As an example, the following query returns all rows and presents the period columns in the time zone Pacific Standard Time:

```
SELECT empid, empname, department, salary,
  validfrom AT TIME ZONE 'UTC' AT TIME ZONE 'Pacific Standard Time' AS validfrom,
  CASE
    WHEN validto = '9999-12-31 23:59:59'
      THEN validto AT TIME ZONE 'UTC'
    ELSE validto AT TIME ZONE 'UTC' AT TIME ZONE 'Pacific Standard Time'
  END AS validto
FROM dbo.Employees FOR SYSTEM_TIME ALL;
```

This query generates the following output:

```
empid  empname  department  salary    validfrom                   validto
------ -------- ----------- --------- --------------------------- ---------------------------
1      Sara     IT          52500.00  2022-02-16 09:20:02 -08:00  9999-12-31 23:59:59 +00:00
2      Don      HR          45000.00  2022-02-16 09:08:41 -08:00  9999-12-31 23:59:59 +00:00
3      Judy     IT          55000.00  2022-02-16 09:28:10 -08:00  9999-12-31 23:59:59 +00:00
4      Yael     Marketing   55000.00  2022-02-16 09:08:41 -08:00  9999-12-31 23:59:59 +00:00
5      Sven     Sales       47250.00  2022-02-16 09:28:10 -08:00  9999-12-31 23:59:59 +00:00
6      Paul     Sales       40000.00  2022-02-16 09:08:41 -08:00  2022-02-16 09:15:26 -08:00
1      Sara     IT          50000.00  2022-02-16 09:08:41 -08:00  2022-02-16 09:20:02 -08:00
5      Sven     IT          45000.00  2022-02-16 09:08:41 -08:00  2022-02-16 09:20:02 -08:00
3      Judy     Sales       55000.00  2022-02-16 09:08:41 -08:00  2022-02-16 09:28:10 -08:00
5      Sven     IT          47250.00  2022-02-16 09:20:02 -08:00  2022-02-16 09:28:10 -08:00
```

When you're done experimenting with the data, run the following code for cleanup:

```
IF OBJECT_ID(N'dbo.Employees', N'U') IS NOT NULL
BEGIN
  IF OBJECTPROPERTY(OBJECT_ID(N'dbo.Employees', N'U'), N'TableTemporalType') = 2
    ALTER TABLE dbo.Employees SET ( SYSTEM_VERSIONING = OFF );
  DROP TABLE IF EXISTS dbo.EmployeesHistory, dbo.Employees;
END;
```

Conclusion

SQL Server's support for system-versioned temporal tables is very powerful. In the past, many systems implemented their own customized solutions to address the same need. With built-in support, the solutions are much simpler and more efficient. This chapter explained how to create, modify, and query temporal tables. Remember that with system-version temporal tables, the system transaction time determines the validity period of the row. I hope that in the future we'll see support in SQL Server for application-time period tables where the application can define the validity period, including setting it to a future one, plus bitemporal support, which combines the two types.

Exercises

This section provides exercises to help you familiarize yourself with the subjects discussed in Chapter 9.

Exercise 1

In this exercise, you create a system-versioned temporal table and identify it in SSMS.

Exercise 1-1

Create a system-versioned temporal table called *Departments* with an associated history table called *DepartmentsHistory* in the database *TSQLV6*. The table should have the following columns: *deptid INT*, *deptname VARCHAR(25)*, and *mgrid INT*, all disallowing *NULLs*. Also include columns called *validfrom* and *validto* that define the validity period of the row. Define those with precision zero (1 second), and make them hidden. Define a history retention policy of six months.

Exercise 1-2

Browse the object tree in Object Explorer in SSMS, and identify the *Departments* table and its associated history table.

Exercise 2

In this exercise, you'll modify data in the table *Departments*. Note the point in time in UTC when you submit each statement, and mark those as P1, P2, and so on. You can do so by invoking the *SYSUTCDATETIME* function in the same batch in which you submit the modification. Another option is to query the *Departments* table and its associated history table to obtain the point in time from the *validfrom* and *validto* columns.

Exercise 2-1

Insert four rows to the table *Departments* with the following details, and note the time when you apply this insert (call it P1):

- *deptid*: 1, *deptname*: HR, *mgrid*: 7

- *deptid*: 2, *deptname*: IT, *mgrid*: 5

- *deptid*: 3, *deptname*: Sales, *mgrid*: 11

- *deptid*: 4, *deptname*: Marketing, *mgrid*: 13

Exercise 2-2

In one transaction, update the name of department 3 to Sales and Marketing and delete department 4. Call the point in time when the transaction starts P2.

Exercise 2-3

Update the manager ID of department 3 to 13. Call the point in time when you apply this update P3.

Exercise 3

In this exercise, you'll query data from the table *Departments*.

Exercise 3-1

Query the current state of the table *Departments*:

- Desired output:

```
deptid       deptname                      mgrid
-----------  ----------------------------  -----------
1            HR                            7
2            IT                            5
3            Sales and Marketing           13
```

Exercise 3-2

Query the state of the table *Departments* at a point in time of your choosing after P2 and before P3:

- Desired output:

```
deptid       deptname                      mgrid
-----------  ----------------------------  -----------
1            HR                            7
2            IT                            5
3            Sales and Marketing           11
```

Exercise 3-3

Query the state of the table *Departments* in the period between P2 and P3. Be explicit about the column names in the *SELECT* list, and include the *validfrom* and *validto* columns:

- Desired output (with *validfrom* and *validto* reflecting your modification times):

```
deptid  deptname               mgrid  validfrom             validto
-------  ---------------------  ------  --------------------  --------------------
1        HR                     7       2022-02-18 10:26:07   9999-12-31 23:59:59
2        IT                     5       2022-02-18 10:26:07   9999-12-31 23:59:59
3        Sales and Marketing    13      2022-02-18 10:30:40   9999-12-31 23:59:59
3        Sales and Marketing    11      2022-02-18 10:28:27   2022-02-18 10:30:40
```

Exercise 4

Drop the table *Departments* and its associated history table.

Solutions

This section provides solutions to the Chapter 9 exercises.

Exercise 1

This exercise is split into two parts. The following sections provide the solutions to those parts.

Exercise 1-1

The following code creates the *Departments* table as a system-versioned temporal table with an associated history table called *DepartmentsHistory*:

```
USE TSQLV6;

CREATE TABLE dbo.Departments
(
  deptid    INT                               NOT NULL
    CONSTRAINT PK_Departments PRIMARY KEY,
  deptname  VARCHAR(25)                        NOT NULL,
  mgrid INT                                    NOT NULL,
  validfrom DATETIME2(0)
    GENERATED ALWAYS AS ROW START HIDDEN NOT NULL,
  validto   DATETIME2(0)
    GENERATED ALWAYS AS ROW END   HIDDEN NOT NULL,
  PERIOD FOR SYSTEM_TIME (validfrom, validto)
)
WITH ( SYSTEM_VERSIONING = ON
       ( HISTORY_TABLE = dbo.DepartmentsHistory,
         HISTORY_RETENTION_PERIOD = 6 MONTHS ) );
```

Following are the requirements for creating a system-versioned temporal table as they are applied to the *Departments* table:

- A primary key: defined based on the *deptid* column.

- The table option *SYSTEM_VERSIONING* set to *ON*.

- Two non-nullable *DATETIME2* columns, with any precision (in our case 0), representing the start and end of the row's validity period; in our table, the columns are named *validfrom* and *validto*.

- The start column (*validfrom*) marked with the option *GENERATED ALWAYS AS ROW START*.

- The end column (*validto*) marked with the option *GENERATED ALWAYS AS ROW END*.

- A designation of the period columns: *PERIOD FOR SYSTEM_TIME (validfrom, validto)*.

- A linked history table called *DepartmentsHistory* (which SQL Server creates for you) to hold the past states of modified rows.

The code also uses optional elements, as instructed, to set the period columns to be hidden and to define an automated history retention policy of six months.

Exercise 1-2

In Object Explorer, navigate to Databases, then to the *TSQLV6* database, and then to Tables. Below Tables, you'll find the *Departments* table marked as System-Versioned and, below it, the *DepartmentsHistory* table marked as *History*, as shown in Figure 9-3.

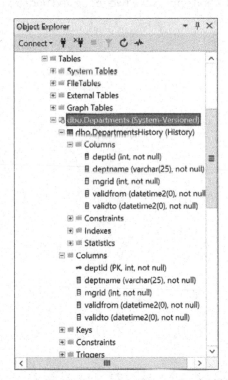

FIGURE 9-3 The *Departments* temporal table and associated history table in SSMS

Exercise 2

This exercise is split into three parts. The following sections provide the solutions to those parts.

Exercise 2-1

The following code identifies the current point in time as P1 and adds the four requested rows:

```
SELECT CAST(SYSUTCDATETIME() AS DATETIME2(0)) AS P1;

INSERT INTO dbo.Departments(deptid, deptname, mgrid)
  VALUES(1, 'HR'        , 7 ),
        (2, 'IT'        , 5 ),
        (3, 'Sales'     , 11),
        (4, 'marketing' , 13);
```

When I ran this code, I got the following output:

```
P1
---------------------------
2022-02-18 10:26:07
```

Make a note of P1 in your execution, which will be different than in mine.

Exercise 2-2

The following code identifies the current point in time as P2 and applies the two requested updates in a transaction:

```
SELECT CAST(SYSUTCDATETIME() AS DATETIME2(0)) AS P2;

BEGIN TRAN;

UPDATE dbo.Departments
  SET deptname = 'Sales and Marketing'
WHERE deptid = 3;

DELETE FROM dbo.Departments
WHERE deptid = 4;

COMMIT TRAN;
```

I got the following output when I ran this code:

```
P2
---------------------------
2022-02-18 10:28:27
```

Again, make a note of P2 in your execution.

Exercise 2-3

The following code identifies the current point in time as P3 and applies the requested update:

```
SELECT CAST(SYSUTCDATETIME() AS DATETIME2(0)) AS P3;

UPDATE dbo.Departments
  SET mgrid = 13
WHERE deptid = 3;
```

I got the following output when I ran this code:

```
P3
---------------------------
2022-02-18 10:30:40
```

Make a note of P3 in your execution.

At this point, I recommend you query both tables, with an explicit reference to the *validfrom* and *validto* columns. Make sure you understand why the values in those columns are what they are.

Exercise 3

This exercise is split into three parts. The following sections provide the solutions to those parts.

Exercise 3-1

Run the following code to query the current state of the table *Departments*, without explicitly referring to the *validfrom* and *validto* columns (using *):

```
SELECT *
FROM dbo.Departments;
```

You get the following output:

```
deptid      deptname                   mgrid
----------- -------------------------- -----------
1           HR                         7
2           IT                         5
3           Sales and Marketing        13
```

Exercise 3-2

Run the following code to query the state of the table *Departments* at a point in time after P2 and before P3 (replace the point in time in this code with one that appears after P2 and before P3 that you recorded):

```
SELECT *
FROM dbo.Departments
  FOR SYSTEM_TIME AS OF '2022-02-18 10:29:00'; -- replace this with your time
```

You get the following output:

```
deptid       deptname                      mgrid
----------   --------------------------    -----------
1            HR                            7
2            IT                            5
3            Sales and Marketing          11
```

Notice that the name of department 3 is the new name Sales and Marketing, which was updated at P2. However, the manager ID of department 3 is still 11, because the change to 13 happened at P3.

Exercise 3-3

Run the following code to query the state of the table *Departments* in the period between P2 and P3 (replace the points in time in this code with P2 and P3 that you recorded):

```
SELECT deptid, deptname, mgrid, validfrom, validto
FROM dbo.Departments
  FOR SYSTEM_TIME BETWEEN '2022-02-18 10:28:27'  -- replace this with your P2
                      AND '2022-02-18 10:30:40'; -- replace this with your P3
```

You get the following output (with *validfrom* and *validto* reflecting your modification times):

```
deptid  deptname                mgrid  validfrom             validto
-------  --------------------    ------  -------------------   -------------------
1        HR                      7       2022-02-18 10:26:07   9999-12-31 23:59:59
2        IT                      5       2022-02-18 10:26:07   9999-12-31 23:59:59
3        Sales and Marketing     13      2022-02-18 10:30:40   9999-12-31 23:59:59
3        Sales and Marketing     11      2022-02-18 10:28:27   2022-02-18 10:30:40
```

This output shows rows that were valid during the period in which *validfrom* is on or before P3 and *validto* is after P2.

Exercise 4

As mentioned earlier, you cannot drop tables that take part in an enabled system-versioning relationship. You'll need to disable system versioning first. Here's the code to achieve this with the tables in our exercises:

```
ALTER TABLE dbo.Departments SET ( SYSTEM_VERSIONING = OFF );
DROP TABLE dbo.DepartmentsHistory, dbo.Departments;
```

Transactions and concurrency

This chapter covers transactions and their properties and describes how Microsoft SQL Server handles users who are concurrently trying to access the same data. I explain how SQL Server uses locks to isolate inconsistent data, how you can troubleshoot blocking situations, and how you can control the level of consistency when you're querying data with isolation levels. This chapter also covers deadlocks and ways to mitigate their occurrence.

Because this is a book about fundamentals, this chapter focuses on concurrency aspects of traditional data representation in disk-based tables. SQL Server supports a memory-optimized database engine called *In-Memory OLTP*, which holds the data in memory-optimized tables. The handling of concurrency for memory-optimized tables is very different than with disk-based tables. Because this feature is an advanced performance-centric feature, it's outside the scope of this book. You can find coverage of the In-Memory OLTP feature in the product documentation here: *https://learn.microsoft.com/en-us/sql/relational-databases/in-memory-oltp*.

Transactions

A *transaction* is a unit of work that might include multiple activities that query and modify data and that can also change the data definition.

You can define transaction boundaries either explicitly or implicitly. You define the beginning of a transaction explicitly with a *BEGIN TRAN* (or *BEGIN TRANSACTION*) statement. You define the end of a transaction explicitly with a *COMMIT TRAN* statement if you want to commit it and with a *ROLLBACK TRAN* (or *ROLLBACK TRANSACTION*) statement if you want to undo its changes. Here's an example of marking the boundaries of a transaction with two *INSERT* statements (don't actually try running this code, since the tables involved don't exist in the sample database):

```
BEGIN TRAN;
  INSERT INTO dbo.T1(keycol, col1, col2) VALUES(4, 101, 'C');
  INSERT INTO dbo.T2(keycol, col1, col2) VALUES(4, 201, 'X');
COMMIT TRAN;
```

If you do not mark the boundaries of a transaction explicitly, by default, SQL Server treats each individual statement as a transaction; in other words, by default, SQL Server automatically begins a transaction before each statement starts and commits the transaction at the end of each statement. This mode is known as an auto-commit mode. You can change the way SQL Server handles implicit transactions so that it won't auto-commit by turning on a session option called *IMPLICIT_TRANSACTIONS*. This option is turned off by default. When this option is turned on, you do not have to specify the *BEGIN TRAN* statement to mark the beginning of a transaction, but you have to mark the transaction's end with a *COMMIT TRAN* or *ROLLBACK TRAN* statement.

After one transaction commits or rolls back, unless you open another explicit transaction, the next statement executed implicitly begins another transaction.

Transactions have four properties—atomicity, consistency, isolation, and durability—abbreviated with the acronym *ACID*:

- **Atomicity** A transaction is an atomic unit of work. Either all changes in the transaction take place or none do. If the system fails before a transaction is completed (before the commit instruction is recorded in the transaction log), upon restart, SQL Server undoes the changes that took place. Also, if errors are encountered during the transaction and the error is considered severe enough, such as the target filegroup being full when you try to insert data, SQL Server automatically rolls back the transaction. Some errors, such as primary-key violations and lock-expiration timeouts (discussed later in this chapter, in the "Troubleshooting blocking" section), are not considered severe enough to justify an automatic rollback of the transaction. If you want all errors to abort execution and cause any open transaction to roll back, you can enable a session option called *XACT_ABORT*. You can use error-handling code to capture such errors and apply some course of action (for example, log the error and roll back the transaction). Chapter 12, "Programmable objects," provides an overview of error handling.

> **Tip** At any point in your code, you can tell programmatically whether you're in an open transaction by querying a function called *@@TRANCOUNT*. This function returns *0* if you're not in an open transaction and returns a value greater than 0 if you are.

- **Consistency** The term *consistency* refers to the state of the data that the relational database management system (RDBMS) gives you access to as concurrent transactions modify and query it. As you can probably imagine, consistency is a subjective term, which depends on your application's needs. The "Isolation levels" section later in this chapter explains the level of consistency that SQL Server provides by default and how you can control it if the default behavior is not suitable for your application. Consistency also refers to the fact that the database must adhere to all integrity rules that have been defined within it by constraints (such as primary keys, unique constraints, and foreign keys). The transaction transitions the database from one consistent state to another.

- **Isolation** *Isolation* ensures that transactions access only consistent data. You control what consistency means to your transactions through a mechanism called *isolation levels*. With disk-based tables, SQL Server supports two different models to handle isolation: one based purely on locking, and another based on a combination of locking and row versioning. For simplicity, I'll refer to the latter as just *row versioning*. The model based on locking is the default in a box product. In this model, readers require shared locks. If the current state of the data is inconsistent, readers are blocked until the state of the data becomes consistent. The model based on row versioning is the default in Azure SQL Database. In this model, readers don't take shared locks and don't need to wait. If the current state of the data is inconsistent, the reader gets an older consistent state. The "Isolation levels" section later in this chapter provides more details about both ways of handling isolation.

- **Durability** The *durability* property means that once a commit instruction is acknowledged by the database engine, the transaction's changes are guaranteed to be durable—or in other words, persist—in the database. A commit is acknowledged by getting control back to the application and running the next line of code. The mechanism that guarantees the durability property in SQL Server depends on the recovery architecture that is in effect. There's the more traditional architecture used prior to SQL Server 2019. There's a newer architecture that is available in SQL Server 2019 or later if you enable a feature called Accelerated Data Recovery (ADR) to support a faster recovery process. The traditional architecture is simpler and involves fewer components. Data changes are always written to the database's transaction log on disk before they are written to the data portion of the database on disk. After the commit instruction is recorded in the transaction log on disk, the transaction is considered durable even if the change hasn't yet made it to the data portion on disk. When the system starts, either normally or after a system failure, SQL Server runs a recovery process in each database that involves analyzing the log, then applying a redo phase, and then applying an undo phase. The redo phase involves rolling forward (replaying) all the changes from any transaction whose commit instruction is written to the log but whose changes haven't yet made it to the data portion. The undo phase involves rolling back (undoing) the changes from any transaction whose commit instruction was not recorded in the log. If you do enable ADR, the architecture of recovery is more sophisticated, involving additional components and a more sophisticated process. You can find details on ADR in the product documentation here: *https://learn.microsoft.com/en-us/sql/relational-databases/accelerated-database-recovery-concepts*. Whether relying on the traditional recovery architecture or the newer one, you get the same transaction durability guarantee upon the acknowledgement of your commit instruction, just with different mechanics beneath the covers.

For example, the following code defines a transaction that records information about a new order in the *TSQLV6* database:

```
USE TSQLV6;

-- Start a new transaction
BEGIN TRAN;

  -- Declare a variable
  DECLARE @neworderid AS INT;

  -- Insert a new order into the Sales.Orders table
  INSERT INTO Sales.Orders
      (custid, empid, orderdate, requireddate, shippeddate,
       shipperid, freight, shipname, shipaddress, shipcity,
       shippostalcode, shipcountry)
```

```
    VALUES
        (85, 5, '20220212', '20220301', '20220216',
         3, 32.38, N'Ship to 85-B', N'6789 rue de l''Abbaye', N'Reims',
         N'10345', N'France');

    -- Save the new order ID in a variable
    SET @neworderid = SCOPE_IDENTITY();

    -- Return the new order ID
    SELECT @neworderid AS neworderid;

    -- Insert order lines for the new order into Sales.OrderDetails
    INSERT INTO Sales.OrderDetails
        (orderid, productid, unitprice, qty, discount)
      VALUES(@neworderid, 11, 14.00, 12, 0.000),
            (@neworderid, 42, 9.80, 10, 0.000),
            (@neworderid, 72, 34.80, 5, 0.000);

-- Commit the transaction
COMMIT TRAN;
```

The transaction's code inserts a row with the order header information into the *Sales.Orders* table and a few rows with the order lines information into the *Sales.OrderDetails* table. The new order ID is produced automatically by SQL Server because the *orderid* column has an identity property. Immediately after the code inserts the new row into the *Sales.Orders* table, it stores the newly generated order ID in a local variable, and then it uses that local variable when inserting rows into the *Sales.OrderDetails* table. For test purposes, I added a *SELECT* statement that returns the order ID of the newly generated order. Here's the output from the *SELECT* statement after the code runs:

```
neworderid
-----------
11078
```

Note that this example has no error handling and does not make any provision for a *ROLLBACK* in case of an error. To handle errors, you can enclose a transaction in a *TRY/CATCH* construct. You can find an overview of error handling in Chapter 12.

When you're done, run the following code for cleanup:

```
DELETE FROM Sales.OrderDetails
WHERE orderid > 11077;

DELETE FROM Sales.Orders
WHERE orderid > 11077;
```

Locks and blocking

By default, a SQL Server box product uses a pure locking model to enforce the isolation property of transactions. The following sections provide details about locking and explain how to troubleshoot blocking situations that are caused by conflicting lock requests.

As mentioned, Azure SQL Database uses the row-versioning model by default. If you're testing the code in this chapter on Azure SQL Database, you need to turn off the database property *READ_COMMITTED_SNAPSHOT* to switch to the locking model as the default. Use the following code to achieve this:

```
ALTER DATABASE TSQLV6 SET READ_COMMITTED_SNAPSHOT OFF;
```

If you're connected to the *TSQLV6* database, you can alternatively use the keyword *CURRENT* instead of the database name. Also, by default, connections to Azure SQL Database time out quite quickly. So if a demo you're running doesn't work as expected, it could be that a connection involved in that demo timed out.

Locks

Locks are control resources obtained by a transaction to guard data resources, preventing conflicting or incompatible access by other transactions. I'll first cover the important lock modes supported by SQL Server and their compatibility, and then I'll describe the lockable resource types.

Lock modes and compatibility

As you start learning about transactions and concurrency, you should first familiarize yourself with two main lock modes: *exclusive* and *shared*.

When you try to modify data, your transaction requests an exclusive lock on the data resource, regardless of your isolation level. (You'll learn more about isolation levels later in this chapter.) If granted, the exclusive lock is held until the end of the transaction. For single-statement transactions, this means that the lock is held until the statement completes. For multistatement transactions, this means that the lock is held until all statements complete and the transaction is ended by a *COMMIT TRAN* or *ROLLBACK TRAN* command.

Exclusive locks are called "exclusive" because you cannot obtain an exclusive lock on a resource if another transaction is holding any lock mode on the resource, and no lock mode can be obtained on a resource if another transaction is holding an exclusive lock on the resource. This is the way modifications behave by default, and this default behavior cannot be changed—not In terms of the lock mode required to modify a data resource (exclusive) and not in terms of the duration of the lock (until the end of the transaction). In practical terms, this means that if one transaction modifies rows, until the transaction is completed, another transaction cannot modify the same rows. However, whether another transaction can read the same rows or not depends on its isolation level.

As for reading data, the defaults are different for a SQL Server box product and Azure SQL Database. In SQL Server, the default isolation level is called *READ COMMITTED*. In this isolation, when you try to read data, by default your transaction requests a shared lock on the data resource and releases the lock as soon as the read statement is done with that resource. This lock mode is called "shared" because multiple transactions can hold shared locks on the same data resource simultaneously. Although you cannot change the lock mode and duration required when you're modifying data, you can control the way locking is handled when you're reading data by changing your isolation level. As mentioned, I will elaborate on this later in this chapter.

In Azure SQL Database, the default isolation level is called *READ COMMITTED SNAPSHOT*. Instead of relying only on locking, this isolation level relies on a combination of locking and row versioning. Under this isolation level, readers do not require shared locks, and therefore they never wait; they rely on the row-versioning technology to provide the expected isolation. In practical terms, this means that under the *READ COMMITTED* isolation level, if a transaction modifies rows, until the transaction completes, another transaction can't read the same rows. This approach to concurrency control is known as the *pessimistic concurrency* approach. Under the *READ COMMITTED SNAPSHOT* isolation level, if a transaction modifies rows, another transaction trying to read the data will get the last committed state of the rows that was available when the statement started. This approach to concurrency control is known as the *optimistic concurrency* approach.

This lock interaction between transactions is known as *lock compatibility*. Table 10-1 shows the lock compatibility of exclusive and shared locks (when you're working with an isolation level that generates these locks). The columns represent granted lock modes, and the rows represent requested lock modes.

TABLE 10-1 Lock compatibility of exclusive and shared locks

Requested mode	Granted Exclusive (X)	Granted Shared (S)
Exclusive	No	No
Shared	No	Yes

A "No" in the intersection means that the locks are incompatible and the requested mode is denied; the requester must wait. A "Yes" in the intersection means that the locks are compatible and the requested mode is accepted.

The following summarizes lock interaction between transactions in simple terms: data that was modified by one transaction can be neither modified nor read (at least by default in a SQL Server box product) by another transaction until the first transaction finishes. And while data is being read by one transaction, it cannot be modified by another (at least by default in a SQL Server box product).

Lockable resource types

SQL Server can lock different types of resources. Those include rows (RID in a heap, key in an index), pages, objects (for example, tables), databases, and others. Rows reside within pages, and pages are the physical data blocks that contain table or index data. You should first familiarize yourself with these resource types, and at a more advanced stage, you might want to familiarize yourself with other lockable resource types such as extents, allocation units, and heaps or B-trees.

To obtain a lock on a certain resource type, your transaction must first obtain intent locks of the same mode on higher levels of granularity. For example, to get an exclusive lock on a row, your transaction must first acquire intent exclusive locks on the table and the page where the row resides. Similarly, to get a shared lock on a certain level of granularity, your transaction first needs to acquire intent shared locks on higher levels of granularity. The purpose of intent locks is to efficiently detect incompatible lock requests on higher levels of granularity and prevent the granting of those. For example, if one transaction holds a lock on a row and another asks for an incompatible lock mode on the whole page or table where that row resides, it's easy for SQL Server to identify the conflict because of the intent locks that the first transaction acquired on the page and table. Intent locks do not interfere with requests for locks on lower levels of granularity. For example, an intent lock on a page doesn't prevent other transactions from acquiring incompatible lock modes on rows within the page. Table 10-2 expands on the lock compatibility table shown in Table 10-1, adding intent exclusive and intent shared locks.

TABLE 10-2 Lock compatibility including intent locks

Requested mode	Granted Exclusive (X)	Granted Shared (S)	Granted Intent Exclusive (IX)	Granted Intent Shared (IS)
Exclusive	No	No	No	No
Shared	No	Yes	No	Yes
Intent Exclusive	No	No	Yes	Yes
Intent Shared	No	Yes	Yes	Yes

SQL Server determines dynamically which resource types to lock. Naturally, for ideal concurrency, it's best to lock only what needs to be locked—namely, only the affected rows. However, locks require memory resources and internal management overhead. So SQL Server considers both concurrency and system resources when it's choosing which resource types to lock. When SQL Server estimates that a transaction will interact with a small number of rows, it tends to use row locks. With larger numbers of rows, SQL Server tends to use page locks.

SQL Server might first acquire fine-grained locks (such as row or page locks) and, in certain circum- stances, try to escalate the fine-grained locks to a table lock to preserve memory. Lock escalation is triggered when a single statement acquires at least 5,000 locks against the same object. Lock escala- tion checking occurs first when a transaction holds 2,500 locks, and then for every 1,250 new locks.

You can set a table option called *LOCK_ESCALATION* by using the *ALTER TABLE* statement to control the way lock escalation behaves. You can disable lock escalation if you like, or you can determine whether escalation takes place at a table level (default) or a partition level. (A table can be physically organized into multiple smaller units called *partitions*.)

Troubleshooting blocking

When one transaction holds a lock on a data resource and another transaction requests an incompat- ible lock on the same resource, the request is blocked and the requester enters a wait state. By default, the blocked request keeps waiting until the blocker releases the interfering lock. Later in this section, I'll explain how you can define a lock expiration time out in your session if you want to restrict the amount of time that a blocked request waits before it times out.

Blocking is normal in a system as long as requests are satisfied within a reasonable amount of time. However, if some requests end up waiting too long, you might need to troubleshoot the blocking situation and see whether you can do something to prevent such long latencies. For example, long- running transactions result in locks being held for long periods. You can try to shorten such transac- tions, moving activities that are not supposed to be part of the unit of work outside the transaction.

A bug in the application might result in a transaction that remains open in certain circumstances. If you identify such a bug, you can fix it and ensure that the transaction is closed in all circumstances.

The next example demonstrates a blocking situation and how to troubleshoot it. I'm assuming that you're running under the isolation level *READ COMMITTED*. Open three separate query windows in SQL Server Management Studio. (For this example, I'll refer to them as Connection 1, Connection 2, and Connection 3.) Make sure that in all of them you are connected to the sample database *TSQLV6*:

```
USE TSQLV6;
```

Run the following code in Connection 1 to update a row in the *Production.Products* table, adding 1.00 to the current unit price of 19.00 for product 2:

```
BEGIN TRAN;

  UPDATE Production.Products
    SET unitprice += 1.00
  WHERE productid = 2;
```

To update the row, your session had to acquire an exclusive lock, and if the update was successful, SQL Server granted your session the lock. Recall that exclusive locks are kept until the end of the transaction. Because no *COMMIT TRAN* or *ROLLBACK TRAN* statement was submitted yet, the transaction remains open, and the lock is still held.

Run the following code in Connection 2 to try to query the same row:

```
SELECT productid, unitprice
FROM Production.Products
WHERE productid = 2;
```

Your session needs a shared lock to read the data, but because the row is exclusively locked by the other session, and a shared lock is incompatible with an exclusive lock, your session is blocked and has to wait.

Assuming that such a blocking situation happens in your system, and the blocked session ends up waiting for a long time, you probably want to troubleshoot the situation. The rest of this section provides queries against dynamic management objects (objects providing dynamic information about various aspects of your system), including views and functions, that you should run from Connection 3 when you troubleshoot the blocking situation.

To get lock information, including both locks that are currently granted to sessions and locks that sessions are waiting for, query the dynamic management view (DMV) *sys.dm_tran_locks* in Connection 3:

```
SELECT -- use * to explore other available attributes
  request_session_id              AS sid,
  resource_type                   AS restype,
  resource_database_id            AS dbid,
  DB_NAME(resource_database_id)   AS dbname,
  resource_description            AS res,
  resource_associated_entity_id   AS resid,
  request_mode                    AS mode,
  request_status                  AS status
FROM sys.dm_tran_locks;
```

When I run this code in my system (with no other query window open), I get the following output:

sid	restype	dbid	dbname	res	resid	mode	status
53	DATABASE	8	TSQLV6		0	S	GRANT
52	DATABASE	8	TSQLV6		0	S	GRANT
51	DATABASE	8	TSQLV6		0	S	GRANT
54	DATABASE	8	TSQLV6		0	S	GRANT
53	PAGE	8	TSQLV6	1:127	72057594038845440	IS	GRANT
52	PAGE	8	TSQLV6	1:127	72057594038845440	IX	GRANT
53	OBJECT	8	TSQLV6		133575514	IS	GRANT
52	OBJECT	8	TSQLV6		133575514	IX	GRANT
52	KEY	8	TSQLV6	(020068e8b274)	72057594038845440	X	GRANT
53	KEY	8	TSQLV6	(020068e8b274)	72057594038845440	S	WAIT

Each session is identified by a unique session ID. You can determine your session's ID by querying the function @@SPID. If you're working with SQL Server Management Studio, you'll find the session ID in parentheses to the right of the login name in the status bar at the bottom of the query window that has the focus, and also in the caption of the connected query window. For example, Figure 10-1 shows a screenshot of SQL Server Management Studio (SSMS), where the session ID 52 appears to the right of the login name SHIRE\Gandalf.

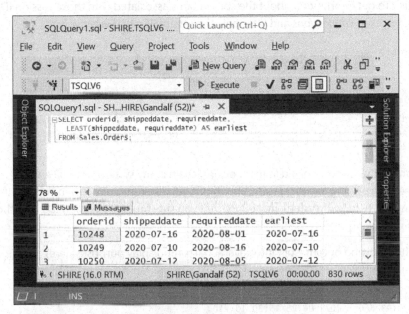

FIGURE 10-1 The session ID shown in SQL Server Management Studio

As you can see in the output of the query against *sys.dm_tran_locks*, four sessions (51, 52, 53, and 54) are currently holding locks. You can see the following:

- The resource type that is locked (for example, *KEY* for a row in an index)

- The ID of the database in which it is locked, which you can translate to the database name by using the *DB_NAME* function

- The resource and resource ID

- The lock mode

- Whether the lock was granted or the session is waiting for it

Note that this is only a subset of the view's attributes; I recommend that you explore the other attributes of the view to learn what other information about locks is available.

In the output from my query, you can observe that session 53 is waiting for a shared lock on a row in the sample database *TSQLV6*. Notice that session 52 is holding an exclusive lock on the same row. You can determine this by observing that both sessions lock a row with the same *res* and *resid* values. You can figure out which table is involved by moving upward in the lock hierarchy for either session 52 or 53 and inspecting the intent locks on the object (table) where the row resides. You can use the *OBJECT_NAME* function to translate the object ID (133575514, in this example) that appears under the *resid* attribute in the object lock. You will find that the table involved is *Production.Products*.

The *sys.dm_tran_locks* view gives you information about the IDs of the sessions involved in the blocking chain. A *blocking chain* is a chain of two or more sessions that are involved in the blocking situation. You could have session *x* blocking session *y*, session *y* blocking session *z*, and so on—hence the use of the term *chain*. To get information about the connections associated with those session IDs, query a view called *sys.dm_exec_connections* and filter only the session IDs that are involved:

```
SELECT -- use * to explore
  session_id AS sid,
  connect_time,
  last_read,
  last_write,
  most_recent_sql_handle
FROM sys.dm_exec_connections
WHERE session_id IN(52, 53);
```

Note that the session IDs that were involved in the blocking chain in my system were 52 and 53. Depending on what else you're doing in your system, you might get different ones. When you run the queries that I demonstrate here in your system, make sure that you substitute the session IDs with those you find involved in your blocking chain.

This query returns the following output (split into several parts for display purposes here):

```
sid    connect_time             last_read
------ ------------------------ ------------------------
52     2022-06-25 15:20:03.360  2022-06-25 15:20:15.750
53     2022-06-25 15:20:07.300  2022-06-25 15:20:20.950


sid    last_write               most_recent_sql_handle
------ ------------------------ -----------------------------------------------------
52     2022-06-25 15:20:15.817  0x01000800DE2DB71FB0936F0500000000000000000000000000
53     2022-06-25 15:20:07.327  0x0200000063FC7D052E09844778CDD615CFE7A2D1FB411802
```

The information that this query gives you about the connections includes

- The time they connected.

- The time of their last read and write.

- A binary value holding a handle to the most recent SQL batch run by the connection. You provide this handle as an input parameter to a table function called *sys.dm_exec_sql_text*, and the function returns the batch of code represented by the handle. You can query the table function passing the binary handle explicitly, but you'll probably find it more convenient to use the *APPLY* table operator described in Chapter 5, "Table expressions," to apply the table function to each connection row like this (run in Connection 3):

```
SELECT session_id, text
FROM sys.dm_exec_connections
  CROSS APPLY sys.dm_exec_sql_text(most_recent_sql_handle) AS ST
WHERE session_id IN(52, 53);
```

When I run this query, I get the following output, showing the last batch of code invoked by each connection involved in the blocking chain:

```
session_id  text
----------- --------------------------------------
52          BEGIN TRAN;

               UPDATE Production.Products
                 SET unitprice += 1.00
               WHERE productid = 2;

53             (@1 tinyint)
               SELECT [productid],[unitprice]
               FROM [Production].[Products]
               WHERE [productid]=@1
```

The blocked session—53—shows the query that is waiting because that's the last thing the session ran. As for the blocker, in this example, you can see the statement that caused the problem, but keep in mind that in other situations the blocker might continue working and that the last thing you see in the code isn't necessarily the statement that caused the trouble.

Starting with SQL Server 2016, you can use the function *sys.dm_exec_input_buffer* instead of *sys. dm_exec_sql_text* to get the code that the sessions of interest submitted last. The function accepts a session ID and request ID (from *sys.dm_exec_requests*, which is described shortly), or a *NULL* instead of a request ID if the ID is not relevant. Here's the code to replace the last example using the new function:

```
SELECT session_id, event_info
FROM sys.dm_exec_connections
  CROSS APPLY sys.dm_exec_input_buffer(session_id, NULL) AS IB
WHERE session_id IN(52, 53);
```

You can also find a lot of useful information about the sessions involved in a blocking situation in the DMV *sys.dm_exec_sessions*. The following query returns only a small subset of the attributes available about those sessions:

```
SELECT -- use * to explore
  session_id AS sid,
  login_time,
  host_name,
  program_name,
  login_name,
  nt_user_name,
  last_request_start_time,
  last_request_end_time
FROM sys.dm_exec_sessions
WHERE session_id IN(52, 53);
```

This query returns the following output in this example, split here into several parts:

```
sid  login_time               host_name
----  -----------------------  ---------
52   2022-06-25 15:20:03.407   K2
53   2022-06-25 15:20:07.303   K2

sid   program_name                                     login_name
------  -----------------------------------------------  ---------------
52     Microsoft SQL Server Management Studio - Query   K2\Gandalf
53     Microsoft SQL Server Management Studio - Query   K2\Gandalf

sid   nt_user_name    last_request_start_time   last_request_end_time
------  --------------  ------------------------  -----------------------
52     Gandalf         2022-06-25 15:20:15.703   2022-06-25 15:20:15.750
53     Gandalf         2022-06-25 15:20:20.693   2022-06-25 15:20:07.320
```

This output contains information such as the session's logon time, the host name, the program name, the login name, the Windows user name (the *nt_user_name* column), the time that the last request started, and the time that the last request ended. This kind of information gives you a good idea of what those sessions are doing.

Another DMV you'll probably find useful for troubleshooting blocking situations is *sys.dm_exec_requests*. This view has a row for each active request, including blocked requests. In fact, you can easily isolate blocked requests because the attribute *blocking_session_id* is greater than zero. For example, the following query filters only blocked requests:

```
SELECT -- use * to explore
  session_id AS sid,
  blocking_session_id,
  command,
  sql_handle,
  database_id,
  wait_type,
  wait_time,
  wait_resource
FROM sys.dm_exec_requests
WHERE blocking_session_id > 0;
```

This query returns the following output, split across several lines:

```
sid     blocking_session_id     command
------  ---------------------   -------
53      52                      SELECT

sid     sql_handle                                              database_id
------  ------------------------------------------------------  -----------
53      0x0200000063FC7D052E09844778CDD615CFE7A2D1FB411802       8

sid     wait_type    wait_time    wait_resource
------  -----------  -----------  ---------------------------------------
53      LCK_M_S      1383760      KEY: 8:72057594038845440 (020068e8b274)
```

You can easily identify the sessions that participate in the blocking chain, the resource in dispute, how long the blocked session is waiting in milliseconds, and more.

Alternatively, you can query a DMV called *sys.dm_os_waiting_tasks*, which has only tasks that are currently waiting. It also has an attribute called *blocking_session_id*, and to troubleshoot blocking you'll filter only the waiting tasks where this attribute is greater than zero. Some information in this view overlaps with that in the *sys.dm_exec_requests* view, but it does provide a few attributes that are unique to it with some more information, like the resource description that is in conflict.

If you need to terminate the blocker—for example, if you realize that as a result of a bug in the application the transaction remained open and nothing in the application can close it—you can do so by using the *KILL <session_id>* command. (Don't do so yet.)

Earlier, I mentioned that by default the session has no lock timeout set. If you want to restrict the amount of time your session waits for a lock, you can set a session option called *LOCK_TIMEOUT*. You specify a value in milliseconds—such as 5000 for 5 seconds, 0 for an immediate timeout, and –1 for no timeout (which is the default). To see how this option works, first stop the query in Connection 2 by choosing Cancel Executing Query from the Query menu (or by pressing Alt+Break). Note that if you had an explicit transaction open, canceling the executing query wouldn't cancel the transaction automatically. Run the following code to set the lock timeout to five seconds, and run the query again:

```
SET LOCK_TIMEOUT 5000;

SELECT productid, unitprice
FROM Production.Products
WHERE productid = 2;
```

The query is still blocked because Connection 1 hasn't yet ended the update transaction, but if after 5 seconds the lock request is not satisfied, SQL Server terminates the query and you get the following error:

```
Msg 1222, Level 16, State 51, Line 3
Lock request time out period exceeded.
```

Note that lock timeouts do not roll back transactions.

To remove the lock timeout value, set it back to the default (no timeout), and issue the query again. Run the following code in Connection 2 to achieve this:

```
SET LOCK_TIMEOUT -1;

SELECT productid, unitprice
FROM Production.Products
WHERE productid = 2;
```

To terminate the update transaction in Connection 1, run the following code from Connection 3:

```
KILL 52;
```

This statement causes a rollback of the transaction in Connection 1, meaning that the price change of product 2 from 19.00 to 20.00 is undone, and the exclusive lock is released. Go to Connection 2. The query that was blocked until now is able to acquire the lock, and you get the data after the change is undone—namely, before the price change:

```
productid    unitprice
-----------  --------------------
2            19.00
```

 Note If you try to close a query window while a transaction is still open, SSMS will prompt you to choose to either commit or roll back the open transaction.

Isolation levels

Isolation levels determine the level of consistency you get when you interact with data. In the default isolation level in a box product, a reader uses shared locks on the target resources and a writer uses exclusive locks. You cannot control the way writers behave in terms of the locks they acquire and the duration of the locks, but you can control the way readers behave. Also, as a result of controlling the behavior of readers, you can have an implicit influence on the behavior of writers. You do so by setting the isolation level, either at the session level with a session option or at the query level with a table hint, which is an instruction you specify after the table name as part of the query.

SQL Server supports four isolation levels that are based on the pure locking model: *READ UNCOMMITTED*, *READ COMMITTED* (the default in a SQL Server box product), *REPEATABLE READ*, and *SERIALIZABLE*. SQL Server also supports two isolation levels that are based on a combination of locking and row versioning: *SNAPSHOT* and *READ COMMITTED SNAPSHOT* (the default in Azure SQL Database). *SNAPSHOT* and *READ COMMITTED SNAPSHOT* are in a sense the row-versioning counterparts of *READ COMMITTED* and *SERIALIZABLE*, respectively.

Some texts refer to *READ COMMITTED* and *READ COMMITTED SNAPSHOT* as one isolation level with two different semantic treatments.

You can set the isolation level of the whole session by using the following command:

```
SET TRANSACTION ISOLATION LEVEL <isolation name>;
```

You can use a table hint to set the isolation level of a query:

```
SELECT ... FROM <table> WITH (<isolationname>);
```

> **Note** You cannot explicitly set the isolation level name *READ COMMITTED SNAPSHOT* as a session or query option. To use this isolation level, you need a database flag to be enabled. I provide details on this later in the chapter, in the section "Isolation levels based on row versioning."

With the session option, you specify a space between the words in case the name of the isolation level is made of more than one word, such as *REPEATABLE READ*. With the query hint, you don't specify a space between the words—for example, *WITH (REPEATABLEREAD)*. Also, some isolation-level names used as table hints have synonyms. For example, *NOLOCK* is the equivalent of specifying *READUN-COMMITTED*, and *HOLDLOCK* is the equivalent of specifying *SERIALIZABLE*.

By changing the isolation level, you affect both the concurrency of the database users and the consistency they get from the data.

With the first four isolation levels, the higher the isolation level, the stricter the locks are that readers request and the longer their duration is; therefore, the higher the isolation level is, the higher the consistency is and the lower the concurrency is.

With the two row-versioning-based isolation levels, SQL Server is able to store previous committed versions of rows in a version store. Readers do not request shared locks; instead, if the current version of the rows is not what they are supposed to see, SQL Server provides them with an older version.

The following sections describe each of the six supported isolation levels and demonstrate their behavior.

The *READ UNCOMMITTED* isolation level

READ UNCOMMITTED is the lowest available isolation level. In this isolation level, a reader doesn't ask for a shared lock. A reader that doesn't ask for a shared lock can never be in conflict with a writer that is holding an exclusive lock. This means that the reader can read uncommitted changes (also known as *dirty reads*). It also means the reader won't interfere with a writer that asks for an exclusive lock. In other words, a writer can change data while a reader that is running under the *READ UNCOMMITTED* isolation level reads data.

To see how an uncommitted read (dirty read) works, open two query windows. (I'll refer to them as Connection 1 and Connection 2.) Make sure that in all connections your database context is that of the sample database *TSQLV6*. To avoid confusion, make sure that this is the only activity in the instance.

Run the following code in Connection 1 to open a transaction, update the unit price of product 2 by adding 1.00 to its current price (19.00), and then query the product's row:

```
BEGIN TRAN;

  UPDATE Production.Products
    SET unitprice += 1.00
  WHERE productid = 2;

  SELECT productid, unitprice
  FROM Production.Products
  WHERE productid = 2;
```

Note that the transaction remains open, meaning that the product's row is locked exclusively by Connection 1. The code in Connection 1 returns the following output showing the product's new price:

```
productid   unitprice
----------- ----------------------
2           20.00
```

In Connection 2, run the following code to set the isolation level to *READ UNCOMMITTED* and query the row for product 2:

```
SET TRANSACTION ISOLATION LEVEL READ UNCOMMITTED;

SELECT productid, unitprice
FROM Production.Products
WHERE productid = 2;
```

Because the query did not request a shared lock, it was not in conflict with the other transaction. This query returned the state of the row after the change, even though the change was not committed:

```
productid   unitprice
----------- ----------------------
2           20.00
```

Keep in mind that Connection 1 might apply further changes to the row later in the transaction or even roll back at some point. For example, run the following code in Connection 1 to roll back the transaction:

```
ROLLBACK TRAN;
```

This rollback undoes the update of product 2, changing its price back to 19.00. The value 20.00 that the reader got was never committed. That's an example of a dirty read.

The *READ COMMITTED* isolation level

If you want to prevent readers from reading uncommitted changes, you need to use a stronger isolation level. The lowest isolation level that prevents dirty reads is *READ COMMITTED*, which is also the default isolation level in SQL Server (the box product). As the name indicates, this isolation level allows readers to read only committed changes. It prevents uncommitted reads by requiring a reader to obtain a shared lock. This means that if a writer is holding an exclusive lock, the reader's shared lock request will be in conflict with the writer, and it has to wait. As soon as the writer commits the transaction, the reader can get its shared lock, but what it reads are necessarily only committed changes.

The following example demonstrates that, in this isolation level, a reader can read only committed changes.

Run the following code in Connection 1 to open a transaction, update the price of product 2, and query the row to show the new price:

```
BEGIN TRAN;

  UPDATE Production.Products
    SET unitprice += 1.00
  WHERE productid = 2;

  SELECT productid, unitprice
  FROM Production.Products
  WHERE productid = 2;
```

This code returns the following output:

```
productid    unitprice
-----------  ---------------------
2            20.00
```

Connection 1 now locks the row for product 2 exclusively.

Run the following code in Connection 2 to set the session's isolation level to *READ COMMITTED* and query the row for product 2:

```
SET TRANSACTION ISOLATION LEVEL READ COMMITTED;

SELECT productid, unitprice
FROM Production.Products
WHERE productid = 2;
```

Keep in mind that this isolation level is the default, so unless you previously changed the session's isolation level, you don't need to set it explicitly. The *SELECT* statement is currently blocked because it needs a shared lock to be able to read the row, and this shared lock request is in conflict with the exclusive lock held by the writer in Connection 1.

Next, run the following code in Connection 1 to commit the transaction:

```
COMMIT TRAN;
```

Now go to Connection 2 and notice that you get the following output:

```
productid    unitprice
-----------  ---------------------
2            20.00
```

Unlike in *READ UNCOMMITTED*, in the *READ COMMITTED* isolation level, you don't get dirty reads. Instead, you can read only committed changes.

In terms of the duration of locks, in the *READ COMMITTED* isolation level, a reader holds the shared lock only until it's done with the resource. It doesn't keep the lock until the end of the transaction; in fact, it doesn't even keep the lock until the end of the statement. This means that in between two reads of the same data resource in the same transaction, no lock is held on the resource. Therefore, another transaction can modify the resource in between those two reads, and the reader might get different values in each read. This phenomenon is called *nonrepeatable reads* or *inconsistent analysis*. For many applications, this phenomenon is acceptable, but for some it isn't.

When you're done, run the following code for cleanup in any of the open connections:

```
UPDATE Production.Products
  SET unitprice = 19.00
WHERE productid = 2;
```

Also, ensure any open transactions in all windows are closed.

The *REPEATABLE READ* isolation level

If you want to ensure that no one can change values in between reads that take place in the same transaction, you need to move up in the isolation levels to *REPEATABLE READ*. In this isolation level, not only does a reader need a shared lock to be able to read, but it also holds the lock until the end of the transaction. This means that as soon as the reader acquires a shared lock on a data resource to read it, no one can obtain an exclusive lock to modify that resource until the reader ends the transaction. This way, you're guaranteed to get repeatable reads, or consistent analysis.

The following example demonstrates getting repeatable reads. Run the following code in Connection 1 to set the session's isolation level to *REPEATABLE READ*, open a transaction, and read the row for product 2:

```
SET TRANSACTION ISOLATION LEVEL REPEATABLE READ;

BEGIN TRAN;

  SELECT productid, unitprice
  FROM Production.Products
  WHERE productid = 2;
```

This code returns the following output showing the current price of product 2:

```
productid   unitprice
----------- ---------------------
2           19.00
```

Connection 1 still holds a shared lock on the row for product 2 because in *REPEATABLE READ*, shared locks are held until the end of the transaction. Run the following code from Connection 2 to try to modify the row for product 2:

```
UPDATE Production.Products
   SET unitprice += 1.00
WHERE productid = 2;
```

Notice that the attempt is blocked because the modifier's request for an exclusive lock is in conflict with the reader's granted shared lock. If the reader was running under the *READ UNCOMMITTED* or *READ COMMITTED* isolation level, it wouldn't hold the shared lock at this point, and the attempt to modify the row would be successful.

Back in Connection 1, run the following code to read the row for product 2 a second time and commit the transaction:

```
SELECT productid, unitprice
FROM Production.Products
WHERE productid = 2;

COMMIT TRAN;
```

This code returns the following output:

```
productid    unitprice
-----------  --------------------
2            19.00
```

Notice that the second read got the same unit price for product 2 as the first read. Now that the reader's transaction has been committed and the shared lock is released, the modifier in Connection 2 can obtain the exclusive lock it was waiting for and update the row.

Another phenomenon prevented by *REPEATABLE READ* but not by lower isolation levels is called a *lost update*. A lost update happens when two transactions read a value, make calculations based on what they read, and then update the value. Because in isolation levels lower than *REPEATABLE READ* no lock is held on the resource after the read, both transactions can update the value, and whichever transaction updates the value last "wins," overwriting the other transaction's update. In *REPEATABLE READ*, both sides keep their shared locks after the first read, so neither can acquire an exclusive lock later in order to update. The situation results in a deadlock, and the update conflict is prevented. I'll provide more details on deadlocks later in this chapter, in the "Deadlocks" section.

When you're done, run the following code for cleanup:

```
UPDATE Production.Products
   SET unitprice = 19.00
WHERE productid = 2;
```

The *SERIALIZABLE* isolation level

Running under the *REPEATABLE READ* isolation level, readers keep shared locks until the end of the transaction. Therefore, you're guaranteed to get a repeatable read of the rows that you read the first time in the transaction. However, your transaction locks only resources (for example, rows) that the query found the first time it ran, not rows that weren't there when the query ran. Therefore, a second read in the same transaction might return new rows as well. Those new rows are called *phantoms*, and such reads are called *phantom reads*. This happens if, in between the reads, another transaction inserts new rows that satisfy the reader's query filter.

To prevent phantom reads, you need to move up in the isolation levels to *SERIALIZABLE*. For the most part, the *SERIALIZABLE* isolation level behaves similarly to *REPEATABLE READ*: namely, it requires a reader to obtain a shared lock to be able to read, and it keeps the lock until the end of the transaction. But the *SERIALIZABLE* isolation level adds another facet—logically, this isolation level causes a reader to lock the whole range of keys that qualify for the query's filter. This means that the reader locks not only the existing rows that qualify for the query's filter, but also future ones. Or, more accurately, it blocks attempts made by other transactions to add rows that qualify for the reader's query filter.

The following example demonstrates that the *SERIALIZABLE* isolation level prevents phantom reads. Run the following code in Connection 1 to set the transaction isolation level to *SERIALIZABLE*, open a transaction, and query all products with category 1:

```
SET TRANSACTION ISOLATION LEVEL SERIALIZABLE;

BEGIN TRAN

  SELECT productid, productname, categoryid, unitprice
  FROM Production.Products
  WHERE categoryid = 1;
```

You get the following output, showing 12 products in category 1:

```
productid   productname      categoryid  unitprice
----------- ---------------- ----------- --------------------
1           Product HHYDP    1           18.00
2           Product RECZE    1           19.00
24          Product QOGNU    1           4.50
34          Product SWNJY    1           14.00
35          Product NEVTJ    1           18.00
38          Product QDOMO    1           263.50
39          Product LSOFL    1           18.00
43          Product ZZZHR    1           46.00
67          Product XLXQF    1           14.00
70          Product TOONT    1           15.00
75          Product BWRLG    1           7.75
76          Product JYGFE    1           18.00

(12 rows affected)
```

From Connection 2, run the following code in an attempt to insert a new product with category 1:

```
INSERT INTO Production.Products
    (productname, supplierid, categoryid,
     unitprice, discontinued)
  VALUES('Product ABCDE', 1, 1, 20.00, 0);
```

In all isolation levels that are lower than *SERIALIZABLE*, such an attempt would be successful. In the *SERIALIZABLE* isolation level, the attempt is blocked.

Back in Connection 1, run the following code to query products with category 1 a second time and commit the transaction:

```
SELECT productid, productname, categoryid, unitprice
FROM Production.Products
WHERE categoryid = 1;
```

```
COMMIT TRAN;
```

You get the same output as before, with no phantoms. Now that the reader's transaction is committed and the shared key-range lock is released, the modifier in Connection 2 can obtain the exclusive lock it was waiting for, insert the row, and auto-commit. If at this point you rerun the code to query the products in category 1 from a new transaction, you will get 13 rows in the output.

When you're done, run the following code for cleanup:

```
DELETE FROM Production.Products
WHERE productid > 77;
```

Run the following code in all open connections to set the isolation level back to the default:

```
SET TRANSACTION ISOLATION LEVEL READ COMMITTED;
```

Isolation levels based on row versioning

With the row-versioning technology, SQL Server can store previous versions of committed rows in a version store. If the Accelerated Database Recovery (ADR) feature, which I mentioned earlier when discussing durability, is not enabled in the database, the version store resides in the *tempdb* database. If ADR is enabled, the version store resides in the user database in question. SQL Server supports two isolation levels, called *SNAPSHOT* and *READ COMMITTED SNAPSHOT*, that are based on this row-versioning technology. The *SNAPSHOT* isolation level is logically similar to the *SERIALIZABLE* isolation level in terms of the types of consistency problems that can or cannot happen; the *READ COMMITTED SNAPSHOT* isolation level is similar to the *READ COMMITTED* isolation level. However, readers using isolation levels based on row versioning do not acquire shared locks, so they don't wait when the requested data is exclusively locked. In other words, readers don't block writers and writers don't block readers. Readers still get levels of consistency similar to *SERIALIZABLE* and *READ COMMITTED*. SQL Server provides readers with an older version of the row if the current version is not the one they are supposed to see.

Note that if you enable any of the row-versioning-based isolation levels (which are enabled in Azure SQL Database by default), the *DELETE* and *UPDATE* statements need to copy the version of the row before the change to the version store; *INSERT* statements don't need to write anything to the version store, because no earlier version of the row exists. But it's important to be aware that enabling any of the isolation levels that are based on row versioning might have a negative impact on the performance of updates and deletes. The performance of readers usually improves, sometimes dramatically, because they do not acquire shared locks and don't need to wait when data is exclusively locked or its version is not the expected one.

The *SNAPSHOT* isolation level

Under the *SNAPSHOT* isolation level, when the reader is reading data, it's guaranteed to get the last committed version of the row that was available when the transaction started. This means you're guaranteed to get committed reads and repeatable reads, and you're also guaranteed not to get phantom reads—just as in the *SERIALIZABLE* isolation level. But instead of using shared locks, this isolation level relies on row versioning.

As mentioned, row versioning incurs a performance penalty, mainly when updating and deleting data, regardless of whether or not the modification is executed from a session running under one of the row-versioning-based isolation levels. For this reason, to allow your transactions to work with the *SNAPSHOT* isolation level in a SQL Server box product instance (a behavior that is enabled by default in Azure SQL Database), you need to first enable the option at the database level by running the following code in any open query window:

```
ALTER DATABASE TSQLV6 SET ALLOW_SNAPSHOT_ISOLATION ON;
```

The following example demonstrates the behavior of the *SNAPSHOT* isolation level. Run the following code from Connection 1 to open a transaction, update the price of product 2 by adding 1.00 to its current price of 19.00, and query the product's row to show the new price:

```
BEGIN TRAN;

  UPDATE Production.Products
    SET unitprice += 1.00
  WHERE productid = 2;

  SELECT productid, unitprice
  FROM Production.Products
  WHERE productid = 2;
```

Here the output of this code shows that the product's price was updated to 20.00:

```
productid    unitprice
-----------  ----------------------
2            20.00
```

Note that even if the transaction in Connection 1 runs under the *READ COMMITTED* isolation level, SQL Server has to copy the version of the row before the update (with the price of 19.00) to the version store. That's because the *SNAPSHOT* isolation level is enabled at the database level. If someone begins a transaction using the *SNAPSHOT* isolation level, that session can request the version before the update. For example, run the following code from Connection 2 to set the isolation level to *SNAPSHOT*, open a transaction, and query the row for product 2:

```
SET TRANSACTION ISOLATION LEVEL SNAPSHOT;

BEGIN TRAN;

  SELECT productid, unitprice
  FROM Production.Products
  WHERE productid = 2;
```

If your transaction were under the *SERIALIZABLE* isolation level, the query would be blocked. But because it's running under *SNAPSHOT*, you get the last committed version of the row that was available when the transaction started. That version (with the price of 19.00) is not the current version (with the price of 20.00), so SQL Server pulls the appropriate version from the version store, and the code returns the following output:

```
productid   unitprice
----------- --------------------
2           19.00
```

Go back to Connection 1, and commit the transaction that modified the row:

```
COMMIT TRAN;
```

At this point, the current version of the row with the price of 20.00 is a committed version. However, if you read the data again in Connection 2, you should still get the last committed version of the row that was available when the transaction started (with a price of 19.00). Run the following code in Connection 2 to read the data again, and then commit the transaction:

```
  SELECT productid, unitprice
  FROM Production.Products
  WHERE productid = 2;

COMMIT TRAN;
```

As expected, you get the following output with a price of 19.00:

```
productid   unitprice
----------- --------------------
2           19.00
```

Run the following code in Connection 2 to open a new transaction, query the data, and commit the transaction:

```
BEGIN TRAN

  SELECT productid, unitprice
  FROM Production.Products
  WHERE productid = 2;

COMMIT TRAN;
```

This time, the last committed version of the row that was available when the transaction started is the one with a price of 20.00. Therefore, you get the following output:

```
productid    unitprice
-----------  --------------------
2            20.00
```

Now that no transaction needs the version of the row with the price of 19.00, next time a cleanup thread will run, it can remove the row version from the version store. As you can imagine, very long transactions prevent SQL Server from being able to clean up row versions, and can cause the version store to expand.

When you're done, run the following code for cleanup:

```
UPDATE Production.Products
  SET unitprice = 19.00
WHERE productid = 2;
```

Conflict detection

The *SNAPSHOT* isolation level prevents update conflicts, but unlike the *REPEATABLE READ* and *SERIALIZABLE* isolation levels that do so by generating a deadlock, the *SNAPSHOT* isolation level generates a more specific error, indicating that an update conflict was detected. The *SNAPSHOT* isolation level can detect update conflicts by examining the version store. It can figure out whether another transaction modified the data between a read and a write that took place in your transaction. In other words, *REPEATABLE READ*, *SERIALIZABLE*, and *SNAPSHOT* all prevent lost updates; however, only *SNAPSHOT* generates a specific error indicating that it detected an update conflict as opposed to the more generalized deadlock error, which could happen for other reasons as well. For this reason, Table 10-3, shown later, in the section "Summary of isolation levels," indicates that *SNAPSHOT* isolation detects update conflicts, but that *REPEATABLE READ* and *SERIALIZABLE* don't.

The following example demonstrates a scenario with no update conflict, followed by an example of a scenario with an update conflict.

Run the following code in Connection 1 to set the transaction isolation level to *SNAPSHOT*, open a transaction, and read the row for product 2:

```
SET TRANSACTION ISOLATION LEVEL SNAPSHOT;

BEGIN TRAN;

  SELECT productid, unitprice
  FROM Production.Products
  WHERE productid = 2;
```

You get the following output:

```
productid    unitprice
-----------  --------------------
2            19.00
```

Assuming you made some calculations based on what you read, run the following code while still in Connection 1 to update the price of the product you queried previously to 20.00, and commit the transaction:

```
UPDATE Production.Products
   SET unitprice = 20.00
WHERE productid = 2;
```

COMMIT TRAN;

No other transaction modified the row between your read, calculation, and write; therefore, there was no update conflict and SQL Server allowed the update to take place.

Run the following code to modify the price of product 2 back to 19.00:

```
UPDATE Production.Products
   SET unitprice = 19.00
WHERE productid = 2;
```

Next, run the following code in Connection 1, again, to open a transaction, and read the row for product 2:

```
BEGIN TRAN;

   SELECT productid, unitprice
   FROM Production.Products
   WHERE productid = 2;
```

You get the following output, indicating that the price of the product is 19.00:

```
productid    unitprice
----------- ---------------------
2            19.00
```

This time, run the following code in Connection 2 to update the price of product 2 to 25.00:

```
UPDATE Production.Products
   SET unitprice = 25.00
WHERE productid = 2;
```

Assume you made calculations in Connection 1 based on the price of 19.00 that you read. Based on your calculations, try to update the price of the product to 20.00 in Connection 1:

```
UPDATE Production.Products
   SET unitprice = 20.00
WHERE productid = 2;
```

SQL Server detected that this time another transaction modified the data between your read and write; therefore, it fails your transaction with the following error:

```
Msg 3960, Level 16, State 2, Line 1
Snapshot isolation transaction aborted due to update conflict. You cannot use snapshot isolation
to access table 'Production.Products' directly or indirectly in database 'TSQLV6' to update,
delete, or insert the row that has been modified or deleted by another transaction. Retry the
transaction or change the isolation level for the update/delete statement.
```

Of course, you can use error-handling code to retry the whole transaction when an update conflict is detected.

When you're done, run the following code for cleanup:

```
UPDATE Production.Products
  SET unitprice = 19.00
WHERE productid = 2;
```

Close all connections. Note that if all connections aren't closed, your example results might not match those in the chapter examples.

The *READ COMMITTED SNAPSHOT* isolation level

The *READ COMMITTED SNAPSHOT* isolation level is also based on row versioning. It differs from the *SNAPSHOT* isolation level in that instead of providing a reader with a transaction-level consistent view of the data, it provides the reader with a statement-level consistent view of the data. The *READ COM-MITTED SNAPSHOT* isolation level also does not detect update conflicts. This results in logical behavior similar to the *READ COMMITTED* isolation level, except that readers do not acquire shared locks and do not wait when the requested resource is exclusively locked. If under *READ COMMITTED SNAPSHOT* you want a reader to acquire a shared lock, you need to add a table hint called *READCOMMITTEDLOCK* to your *SELECT* statements, as in *SELECT * FROM dbo.T1 WITH (READCOMMITTEDLOCK)*.

To enable the use of the *READ COMMITTED SNAPSHOT* isolation level in a SQL Server box product (a behavior that is enabled by default in Azure SQL Database), you need to turn on a database option called *READ_COMMITTED_SNAPSHOT*. Run the following code to enable this option in the *TSQLV6* database:

```
ALTER DATABASE TSQLV6 SET READ_COMMITTED_SNAPSHOT ON;
```

Note that for this code to run successfully, you need exclusive access to the *TSQLV6* database.

An interesting aspect of enabling this database flag is that, unlike with the *SNAPSHOT* isolation level, this flag actually changes the meaning, or semantics, of the *READ COMMITTED* isolation level to *READ COMMITTED SNAPSHOT.* This means that when this database flag is turned on, unless you explicitly change the session's isolation level, *READ COMMITTED SNAPSHOT* is the default.

For a demonstration of using the *READ COMMITTED SNAPSHOT* isolation level, open two connec-tions. Run the following code in Connection 1 to open a transaction, update the row for product 2, and read the row, leaving the transaction open:

```
USE TSQLV6;

BEGIN TRAN;

  UPDATE Production.Products
    SET unitprice += 1.00
  WHERE productid = 2;

  SELECT productid, unitprice
  FROM Production.Products
  WHERE productid = 2;
```

You get the following output, indicating that the product's price was changed to 20.00:

```
productid    unitprice
-----------  ----------------------
2            20.00
```

In Connection 2, open a transaction and read the row for product 2, leaving the transaction open:

```
BEGIN TRAN;

  SELECT productid, unitprice
  FROM Production.Products
  WHERE productid = 2;
```

You get the last committed version of the row that was available when the statement started (19.00):

```
productid    unitprice
-----------  ----------------------
2            19.00
```

Run the following code in Connection 1 to commit the transaction:

```
COMMIT TRAN;
```

Now run the code in Connection 2 to read the row for product 2 again, and commit the transaction:

```
  SELECT productid, unitprice
  FROM Production.Products
  WHERE productid = 2;

COMMIT TRAN;
```

If this code were running under the *SNAPSHOT* isolation level, you would get a price of 19.00; however, because the code is running under the *READ COMMITTED SNAPSHOT* isolation level, you get the last committed version of the row that was available when the statement started (20.00) and not when the transaction started (19.00):

```
productid    unitprice
-----------  ----------------------
2            20.00
```

Recall that this phenomenon is called a nonrepeatable read, or inconsistent analysis.

When you're done, run the following code for cleanup:

```
UPDATE Production.Products
  SET unitprice = 19.00
WHERE productid = 2;
```

Close all connections. Open a new connection, and run the following code to disable the isolation levels that are based on row versioning in the *TSQLV6* database:

```
ALTER DATABASE TSQLV6 SET ALLOW_SNAPSHOT_ISOLATION OFF;
ALTER DATABASE TSQLV6 SET READ_COMMITTED_SNAPSHOT OFF;
```

Summary of isolation levels

Table 10-3 provides a summary of the logical consistency problems that can or cannot happen in each isolation level, and it indicates whether the isolation level detects update conflicts for you and whether the isolation level uses row versioning.

TABLE 10-3 Isolation level properties

Isolation level	Allows uncommitted reads?	Allows nonrepeatable reads?	Allows lost updates?	Allows phantom reads?	Detects update conflicts?	Uses row versioning?
READ UNCOMMITTED	Yes	Yes	Yes	Yes	No	No
READ COMMITTED	No	Yes	Yes	Yes	No	No
READ COMMITTED SNAPSHOT	No	Yes	Yes	Yes	No	Yes
REPEATABLE READ	No	No	No	Yes	No	No
SERIALIZABLE	No	No	No	No	No	No
SNAPSHOT	No	No	No	No	Yes	Yes

Deadlocks

A *deadlock* is a situation in which two or more sessions block each other. An example of a two-session deadlock is when session A blocks session B and session B blocks session A. An example of a deadlock involving more than two sessions is when session A blocks session B, session B blocks session C, and session C blocks session A. In any of these cases, SQL Server detects the deadlock and intervenes by terminating one of the transactions. If SQL Server did not intervene, the sessions involved would remain deadlocked forever.

Unless otherwise specified, SQL Server chooses to terminate the transaction that did the least work (based on the activity written to the transaction log), because rolling that transaction's work back is the cheapest option. However, with SQL Server you can set a session option called *DEADLOCK_PRIORITY* to one of 21 values in the range *–10* through *10*. The session with the lowest deadlock priority is chosen as the deadlock "victim" regardless of how much work is done; in the event of a tie, the amount of work is used as a tiebreaker. If the same amount of work is estimated for all sessions involved, the system chooses the victim randomly.

The following example demonstrates a simple deadlock. After presenting the example, I'll explain how you can mitigate deadlock occurrences in the system.

Open two connections, and make sure you're connected to the *TSQLV6* database in both. Run the following code in Connection 1 to open a new transaction, update a row in the *Production.Products* table for product 2, and leave the transaction open:

```
USE TSQLV6;

BEGIN TRAN;

  UPDATE Production.Products
    SET unitprice += 1.00
  WHERE productid = 2;
```

Run the following code in Connection 2 to open a new transaction, update a row in the *Sales.OrderDetails* table for product 2, and leave the transaction open:

```
BEGIN TRAN;

  UPDATE Sales.OrderDetails
    SET unitprice += 1.00
  WHERE productid = 2;
```

At this point, the transaction in Connection 1 is holding an exclusive lock on the row for product 2 in the *Production.Products* table, and the transaction in Connection 2 is now holding locks on the rows for product 2 in the *Sales.OrderDetails* table. Both queries succeed, and no blocking has occurred yet.

Run the following code in Connection 1 to attempt to query the rows for product 2 in the *Sales.OrderDetails* table, and commit the transaction:

```
SELECT orderid, productid, unitprice
FROM Sales.OrderDetails
WHERE productid = 2;

COMMIT TRAN;
```

The transaction in Connection 1 needs a shared lock to be able to perform its read. Because the other transaction holds an exclusive lock on the same resource, the transaction in Connection 1 is blocked. At this point, you have a blocking situation, not yet a deadlock. Of course, a chance remains that Connection 2 will end the transaction, releasing all locks and allowing the transaction in Connection 1 to get the requested locks.

Next, run the following code in Connection 2 to attempt to query the row for product 2 in the *Production.Products* table and commit the transaction:

```
SELECT productid, unitprice
FROM Production.Products
WHERE productid = 2;

COMMIT TRAN;
```

To be able to perform its read, the transaction in Connection 2 needs a shared lock on the row for product 2 in the *Production.Products* table, so this request is now in conflict with the exclusive lock held on the same resource by Connection 1. Each of the sessions blocks the other—you have a deadlock. SQL Server identifies the deadlock (typically within a few seconds), chooses one of the sessions involved as the deadlock victim, and terminates its transaction with the following error:

```
Msg 1205, Level 13, State 51, Line 1
Transaction (Process ID 52) was deadlocked on lock resources with another process and has been
chosen as the deadlock victim. Rerun the transaction.
```

In this example, SQL Server chose to terminate the transaction in Connection 1 (shown here as process ID 52). Because you didn't set a deadlock priority and both transactions did a similar amount of work, either transaction could have been terminated.

Deadlocks are expensive because they involve undoing work that has already been done and then, usually with some error-handling logic, redoing the work. You can follow a few practices to mitigate deadlock occurrences in your system.

Obviously, the longer the transactions are, the longer locks are kept, increasing the probability of deadlocks. You should try to keep transactions as short as possible, taking activities out of the transaction that aren't logically supposed to be part of the same unit of work. For example, don't use transactions that require user input to finish!

One typical deadlock, also called a *deadly embrace* deadlock, happens when transactions access resources in inverse order. In the example just given, Connection 1 first accessed a row in *Production. Products* and then accessed a row in *Sales.OrderDetails*, whereas Connection 2 first accessed a row in *Sales.OrderDetails* and then accessed a row in *Production.Products*. This type of deadlock can't happen if both transactions access resources in the same order. By swapping the order in one of the transactions, you can prevent this type of deadlock from happening—assuming that it makes no logical difference to your application.

The deadlock example has a real logical conflict because both sides try to access the same rows. However, deadlocks often happen when there is no real logical conflict, because of a lack of good indexing to support query filters. For example, suppose both statements in the transaction in Connection 2 filtered product 5. Now that the statements in Connection 1 handle product 2 and the statements in Connection 2 handle product 5, there shouldn't be any conflict. However, if you don't have indexes defined on the *productid* column in the tables to support the filter, SQL Server has to scan (and lock) all rows in the table. This, of course, can lead to a deadlock. In short, good index design can help mitigate the occurrences of deadlocks that have no real logical conflict.

Another option to consider to mitigate deadlock occurrences is the choice of isolation level. The *SELECT* statements in the example needed shared locks because they ran under the *READ COMMITTED* isolation level. If you use the *READ COMMITTED SNAPSHOT* isolation level, readers will not need shared locks, and deadlocks that evolve because of the involvement of shared locks can be eliminated.

When you're done, run the following code for cleanup in any connection:

```
UPDATE Production.Products
  SET unitprice = 19.00
WHERE productid = 2;

UPDATE Sales.OrderDetails
  SET unitprice = 19.00
WHERE productid = 2
  AND orderid >= 10500;

UPDATE Sales.OrderDetails
  SET unitprice = 15.20
WHERE productid = 2
  AND orderid < 10500;
```

Conclusion

This chapter introduced you to transactions and concurrency. I described what transactions are and how SQL Server manages them. I explained how SQL Server isolates data accessed by one transaction from inconsistent use by other transactions, and how to troubleshoot blocking scenarios. I described how you can control the level of consistency you get from the data by choosing an isolation level, and the impact your choice has on concurrency. I described four isolation levels that do not rely on row versioning and two that do. Finally, I covered deadlocks and explained practices you can follow to reduce the frequency of their occurrence.

To practice what you learned, perform the following exercises.

Exercises

This section provides exercises to help you familiarize yourself with the subjects discussed in this chapter. The exercises for most of the previous chapters involve requests for which you have to figure out a solution in the form of a T-SQL query or statement. The exercises for this chapter are different. You'll be provided with instructions to follow to troubleshoot blocking and deadlock situations, and to observe the behavior of different isolation levels. Therefore, this chapter's exercises have no separate "Solutions" section as in other chapters. Exercises 1, 2, and 3 are independent of each other.

For all exercises in this chapter, make sure you're connected to the *TSQLV6* sample database by running the following code:

```
USE TSQLV6;
```

Exercise 1

Exercises 1-1 through 1-6 deal with blocking. They assume you're using the isolation level *READ COMMITTED* (locking). Remember that this is the default isolation level in a SQL Server box product. To perform these exercises on Azure SQL Database, you need to turn versioning off.

Exercise 1-1

Open three connections in SQL Server Management Studio. (The exercises will refer to them as Connection 1, Connection 2, and Connection 3.) Run the following code in Connection 1 to open a transaction and update rows in *Sales.OrderDetails*:

```
BEGIN TRAN;

  UPDATE Sales.OrderDetails
    SET discount = 0.05
  WHERE orderid = 10249;
```

Exercise 1-2

Run the following code in Connection 2 to query *Sales.OrderDetails*; Connection 2 will be blocked:

```
SELECT orderid, productid, unitprice, qty, discount
FROM Sales.OrderDetails
WHERE orderid = 10249;
```

Exercise 1-3

Run the following code in Connection 3, and identify the locks and session IDs involved in the blocking chain:

```
SELECT -- use * to explore
  request_session_id            AS sid,
  resource_type                 AS restype,
  resource_database_id          AS dbid,
  resource_description          AS res,
  resource_associated_entity_id AS resid,
  request_mode                  AS mode,
  request_status                AS status
FROM sys.dm_tran_locks;
```

Exercise 1-4

Replace the session IDs 52 and 53 with the ones you found to be involved in the blocking chain in the previous exercise. Run the following code to obtain connection, session, and blocking information about the processes involved in the blocking chain:

```
-- Connection info:
SELECT -- use * to explore
  session_id AS sid,
  connect_time,
  last_read,
  last_write,
  most_recent_sql_handle
FROM sys.dm_exec_connections
WHERE session_id IN(52, 53);
```

```
-- Session info
SELECT -- use * to explore
  session_id AS sid,
  login_time,
  host_name,
  program_name,
  login_name,
  nt_user_name,
  last_request_start_time,
  last_request_end_time
FROM sys.dm_exec_sessions
WHERE session_id IN(52, 53);

-- Blocking
SELECT -- use * to explore
  session_id AS sid,
  blocking_session_id,
  command,
  sql_handle,
  database_id,
  wait_type,
  wait_time,
  wait_resource
FROM sys.dm_exec_requests
WHERE blocking_session_id > 0;
```

Exercise 1-5

Run the following code to obtain the SQL text of the connections involved in the blocking chain:

```
SELECT session_id, text
FROM sys.dm_exec_connections
  CROSS APPLY sys.dm_exec_sql_text(most_recent_sql_handle) AS ST
WHERE session_id IN(52, 53);
```

Exercise 1-6

Run the following code in Connection 1 to roll back the transaction.

```
ROLLBACK TRAN;
```

Observe in Connection 2 that the *SELECT* query returned the two order detail rows, and that those rows were not modified—namely, their discounts remained 0.000.

Remember that if you need to terminate the blocker's transaction, you can use the KILL command. Close all connections.

Exercise 2

Exercises 2-1 through 2-6 deal with isolation levels.

Exercise 2-1

In this exercise, you'll practice using the *READ UNCOMMITTED* isolation level.

Exercise 2-1a

Open two new connections. (This exercise will refer to them as Connection 1 and Connection 2.) As a reminder, make sure that you're connected to the sample database *TSQLV6*.

Exercise 2-1b

Run the following code in Connection 1 to open a transaction, update rows in *Sales.OrderDetails*, and query it:

```
BEGIN TRAN;

  UPDATE Sales.OrderDetails
    SET discount += 0.05
  WHERE orderid = 10249;

  SELECT orderid, productid, unitprice, qty, discount
  FROM Sales.OrderDetails
  WHERE orderid = 10249;
```

Exercise 2-1c

Run the following code in Connection 2 to set the isolation level to *READ UNCOMMITTED* and query *Sales.OrderDetails*:

```
SET TRANSACTION ISOLATION LEVEL READ UNCOMMITTED;

SELECT orderid, productid, unitprice, qty, discount
FROM Sales.OrderDetails
WHERE orderid = 10249;
```

Notice that you get the modified, uncommitted version of the rows.

Exercise 2-1d

Run the following code in Connection 1 to roll back the transaction:

```
ROLLBACK TRAN;
```

Exercise 2-2

In this exercise, you'll practice using the *READ COMMITTED* isolation level.

Exercise 2-2a

Run the following code in Connection 1 to open a transaction, update rows in *Sales.OrderDetails*, and query it:

```
BEGIN TRAN;

  UPDATE Sales.OrderDetails
    SET discount += 0.05
  WHERE orderid = 10249;

  SELECT orderid, productid, unitprice, qty, discount
  FROM Sales.OrderDetails
  WHERE orderid = 10249;
```

Exercise 2-2b

Run the following code in Connection 2 to set the isolation level to *READ COMMITTED* and query *Sales.OrderDetails*:

```
SET TRANSACTION ISOLATION LEVEL READ COMMITTED;

SELECT orderid, productid, unitprice, qty, discount
FROM Sales.OrderDetails
WHERE orderid = 10249;
```

Notice that you're now blocked.

Exercise 2-2c

Run the following code in Connection 1 to commit the transaction:

```
COMMIT TRAN;
```

Exercise 2-2d

Go to Connection 2, and notice that you get the modified, committed version of the rows.

Exercise 2-2e

Run the following code for cleanup:

```
UPDATE Sales.OrderDetails
  SET discount = 0.00
WHERE orderid = 10249;
```

Exercise 2-3

In this exercise, you'll practice using the *REPEATABLE READ* isolation level.

Exercise 2-3a

Run the following code in Connection 1 to set the isolation level to *REPEATABLE READ*, open a transaction, and read data from *Sales.OrderDetails*:

```
SET TRANSACTION ISOLATION LEVEL REPEATABLE READ;

BEGIN TRAN;

  SELECT orderid, productid, unitprice, qty, discount
  FROM Sales.OrderDetails
  WHERE orderid = 10249;
```

You get two rows with discount values of 0.00.

Exercise 2-3b

Run the following code in Connection 2, and notice that you're blocked:

```
UPDATE Sales.OrderDetails
  SET discount += 0.05
WHERE orderid = 10249;
```

Exercise 2-3c

Run the following code in Connection 1 to read the data again and commit the transaction:

```
  SELECT orderid, productid, unitprice, qty, discount
  FROM Sales.OrderDetails
  WHERE orderid = 10249;

COMMIT TRAN;
```

You get the two rows with discount values of 0.00 again, giving you repeatable reads. Note that if your code were running under a lower isolation level (such as *READ UNCOMMITTED* or *READ COMMITTED*), the *UPDATE* statement wouldn't be blocked and you would get nonrepeatable reads.

Exercise 2-3d

Go to Connection 2, and notice that the update has finished.

Exercise 2-3e

Run the following code for cleanup:

```
UPDATE Sales.OrderDetails
  SET discount = 0.00
WHERE orderid = 10249;
```

Exercise 2-4

In this exercise, you'll practice using the *SERIALIZABLE* isolation level.

Exercise 2-4a

Run the following code in Connection 1 to set the isolation level to *SERIALIZABLE* and query *Sales.OrderDetails*:

```
SET TRANSACTION ISOLATION LEVEL SERIALIZABLE;

BEGIN TRAN;

  SELECT orderid, productid, unitprice, qty, discount
  FROM Sales.OrderDetails
  WHERE orderid = 10249;
```

Exercise 2-4b

Run the following code in Connection 2 to attempt to insert a row to *Sales.OrderDetails* with the same order ID that is filtered by the previous query, and notice that you're blocked:

```
INSERT INTO Sales.OrderDetails
    (orderid, productid, unitprice, qty, discount)
  VALUES(10249, 2, 19.00, 10, 0.00);
```

Note that in lower isolation levels (such as *READ UNCOMMITTED*, *READ COMMITTED*, or *REPEATABLE READ*), this *INSERT* statement wouldn't be blocked.

Exercise 2-4c

Run the following code in Connection 1 to query *Sales.OrderDetails* again and commit the transaction:

```
  SELECT orderid, productid, unitprice, qty, discount
  FROM Sales.OrderDetails
  WHERE orderid = 10249;

COMMIT TRAN;
```

You get the same result set you got from the previous query in the same transaction, and because the *INSERT* statement was blocked, you get no phantom reads.

Exercise 2-4d

Go back to Connection 2, and notice that the *INSERT* statement has finished.

Exercise 2-4e

Run the following code for cleanup:

```
DELETE FROM Sales.OrderDetails
WHERE orderid = 10249
  AND productid = 2;
```

Exercise 2-4f

Run the following code in both Connection 1 and Connection 2 to set the isolation level to the default:

```
SET TRANSACTION ISOLATION LEVEL READ COMMITTED;
```

Exercise 2-5

In this exercise, you'll practice using the *SNAPSHOT* isolation level.

Exercise 2-5a

Run the following code to allow the *SNAPSHOT* isolation level in the *TSQLV6* database:

```
ALTER DATABASE TSQLV6 SET ALLOW_SNAPSHOT_ISOLATION ON;
```

Exercise 2-5b

Run the following code in Connection 1 to open a transaction, update rows in *Sales.OrderDetails*, and query it:

```
BEGIN TRAN;

  UPDATE Sales.OrderDetails
    SET discount += 0.05
  WHERE orderid = 10249;

  SELECT orderid, productid, unitprice, qty, discount
  FROM Sales.OrderDetails
  WHERE orderid = 10249;
```

Exercise 2-5c

Run the following code in Connection 2 to set the isolation level to *SNAPSHOT* and query *Sales.OrderDetails*. Notice that you're not blocked—instead, you get an earlier, consistent version of the data that was available when the transaction started (with discount values of 0.00):

```
SET TRANSACTION ISOLATION LEVEL SNAPSHOT;

BEGIN TRAN;

  SELECT orderid, productid, unitprice, qty, discount
  FROM Sales.OrderDetails
  WHERE orderid = 10249;
```

Exercise 2-5d

Go to Connection 1 and commit the transaction:

```
COMMIT TRAN;
```

Exercise 2-5e

Go to Connection 2 and query the data again; notice that you still get discount values of 0.00:

```
SELECT orderid, productid, unitprice, qty, discount
FROM Sales.OrderDetails
WHERE orderid = 10249;
```

Exercise 2-5f

In Connection 2, commit the transaction and query the data again; notice that now you get discount values of 0.05:

```
COMMIT TRAN;

SELECT orderid, productid, unitprice, qty, discount
FROM Sales.OrderDetails
WHERE orderid = 10249;
```

Exercise 2-5g

Run the following code for cleanup:

```
UPDATE Sales.OrderDetails
  SET discount = 0.00
WHERE orderid = 10249;
```

Close all connections.

Exercise 2-6

In this exercise, you'll practice using the *READ COMMITTED SNAPSHOT* isolation level.

Exercise 2-6a

Turn on *READ_COMMITTED_SNAPSHOT* in the *TSQLV6* database by running the following code in any connection:

```
ALTER DATABASE TSQLV6 SET READ_COMMITTED_SNAPSHOT ON;
```

Exercise 2-6b

Open two new connections. (This exercise will refer to them as Connection 1 and Connection 2.)

Exercise 2-6c

Run the following code in Connection 1 to open a transaction, update rows in *Sales.OrderDetails*, and query it:

```
BEGIN TRAN;

  UPDATE Sales.OrderDetails
    SET discount += 0.05
  WHERE orderid = 10249;

  SELECT orderid, productid, unitprice, qty, discount
  FROM Sales.OrderDetails
  WHERE orderid = 10249;
```

Exercise 2-6d

Run the following code in Connection 2, which is now running under the *READ COMMITTED SNAP-SHOT* isolation level because the database flag *READ_COMMITTED_SNAPSHOT* is turned on. Notice that you're not blocked—instead, you get an earlier, consistent version of the data that was available when the statement started (with discount values of 0.00):

```
BEGIN TRAN;

  SELECT orderid, productid, unitprice, qty, discount
  FROM Sales.OrderDetails
  WHERE orderid = 10249;
```

Exercise 2-6e

Go to Connection 1 and commit the transaction:

```
COMMIT TRAN;
```

Exercise 2-6f

Go to Connection 2, query the data again, and commit the transaction. Notice that you get the new discount values of 0.05:

```
  SELECT orderid, productid, unitprice, qty, discount
  FROM Sales.OrderDetails
  WHERE orderid = 10249;

COMMIT TRAN;
```

Exercise 2-6g

Run the following code for cleanup:

```
UPDATE Sales.OrderDetails
  SET discount = 0.00
WHERE orderid = 10249;
```

Close all connections.

Exercise 2-6h

Change the database flags back to the defaults in a box product, disabling isolation levels based on row versioning:

```
ALTER DATABASE TSQLV6 SET ALLOW_SNAPSHOT_ISOLATION OFF;
ALTER DATABASE TSQLV6 SET READ_COMMITTED_SNAPSHOT OFF;
```

Note that if you want to change these settings back to the defaults in Azure SQL Database, you'll need to set both to ON.

Exercise 3

Exercise 3 (steps 1 through 7) deals with deadlocks. It assumes that versioning is turned off.

Exercise 3-1

Open two new connections. (This exercise will refer to them as Connection 1 and Connection 2.)

Exercise 3-2

Run the following code in Connection 1 to open a transaction and update the row for product 2 in *Production.Products*:

```
BEGIN TRAN;

  UPDATE Production.Products
    SET unitprice += 1.00
  WHERE productid = 2;
```

Exercise 3-3

Run the following code in Connection 2 to open a transaction and update the row for product 3 in *Production.Products*:

```
BEGIN TRAN;

  UPDATE Production.Products
    SET unitprice += 1.00
  WHERE productid = 3;
```

Exercise 3-4

Run the following code in Connection 1 to query product 3. You will be blocked.

```
  SELECT productid, unitprice
  FROM Production.Products
  WHERE productid = 3;

COMMIT TRAN;
```

Exercise 3-5

Run the following code in Connection 2 to query product 2. You will be blocked, and a deadlock error will be generated either in Connection 1 or Connection 2:

```
SELECT productid, unitprice
FROM Production.Products
WHERE productid = 2;

COMMIT TRAN;
```

Exercise 3-6

Can you suggest a way to prevent this deadlock? Refer back to what you read in the "Deadlocks" section—specifically, ways to mitigate deadlock occurrences.

Exercise 3-7

Run the following code for cleanup:

```
UPDATE Production.Products
  SET unitprice = 19.00
WHERE productid = 2;

UPDATE Production.Products
  SET unitprice = 10.00
WHERE productid = 3;
```

SQL Graph

The SQL Graph feature provides an alternative way to model and query your data compared to traditional modeling and querying. It was introduced in SQL Server 2017 and later further enhanced. The modeling part involves using specialized *node* and *edge* tables to store the data, with the nodes representing the vertices of the graph and the edges connecting pairs of nodes. The querying part involves a specialized syntax in which you list the objects involved and use a *MATCH* clause to indicate how they connect.

If you are considering a graph-based design, I recommend reading this chapter very carefully. You need to understand the pros and cons compared to the traditional design, and make a decision whether the pros justify the different model and coding—even more so if you are considering migrating an existing traditional implementation to a SQL Graph-based one, in light of the refactoring overhead.

For simple, typical querying needs where you're just connecting nodes with edges, I find that using the SQL Graph feature often results in more concise and intuitive queries compared to the more traditional queries, where you would use tools like joins instead. But for such needs alone, it would probably be hard to justify the departure from the traditional modeling and querying. The potential for the SQL Graph feature to really shine is in complex needs like finding the shortest path between graph nodes, producing the transitive closure of a graph, traversing arbitrary-length paths, and so on. Some of these capabilities are already available in T-SQL, but not all are. As more of these capabilities are added to T-SQL, the more appealing the use of the SQL Graph option becomes.

This chapter starts by comparing traditional and graph-based models for a fictitious social network, including creating and populating the tables using both models. The chapter continues to querying graph tables using the *MATCH* clause, including recursive queries, as well as the use of the *SHORTEST_PATH* option. The chapter then covers data modification considerations.

 Note In order to be able to run all code samples and work on all exercises in this chapter, you will need to use SQL Server 2019 or later or Azure SQL Database.

Creating tables

The scenario that I use for the examples in this chapter is that of a fictitious social network. I'll start by presenting the entities involved and the interactions among them. I'll then show how to design and implement the data using traditional modeling, followed by graph-based modeling.

The entities involved in our social network are:

- Accounts. These could be personal or company accounts. An account has an ID, a name, a join date, and reputation points.

- Posts. These could be status messages or news items by a single poster. A post has an ID, a posting date and time, and the post text.

- Publications. These are books, articles, and blogs authored by one or more accounts. A publication has an ID, a publication date, and a title. Normally you would want to store more information about publications, but for simplicity's sake, assume that's sufficient information for us.

These entities interact in the following ways:

- Two accounts befriend each other. That's a two-way relationship where one account requests a friendship and another confirms. Once the relationship is established, the two accounts are friends and have access to certain items that are restricted to friends only. You need to record the friendship's start date.

- One account follows another account to automatically get their news feed. That's a one-way relationship. Account A may follow account B without account B also following account A. You need to record who's the follower and who's the followee, as well as the relationship's start date.

- A post is posted by some account.

- A post may have a parent post, in which case it's a reply.

- An account likes a post. You need to record the date and time of the like.

- A publication is authored by one or more accounts.

To make a clear distinction between the normal modeling tables and the graph-based tables, I'll place each set of tables in its own schema. I'll name the schemas *Norm* and *Graph*, respectively. Run the following code to create both schemas in the *TSQLV6* sample database:

```
USE TSQLV6;
GO
CREATE SCHEMA Norm; -- schema for traditional modeling
GO
CREATE SCHEMA Graph; -- schema for graph modeling
```

If you're up to it, before looking at my suggested design, try to come up with your own design based on traditional modeling for our social network, representing the aforementioned entities and interactions among them.

Traditional modeling

Figure 11-1 has a diagram with a suggested design for our fictitious social network based on traditional modeling. It shows the tables involved, their columns, primary keys, and foreign keys.

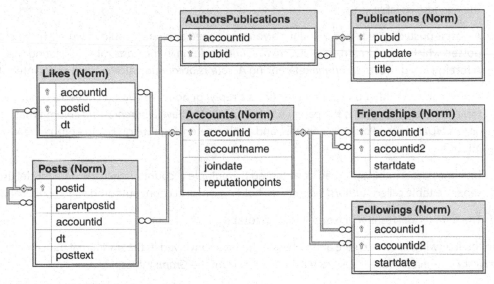

FIGURE 11-1 Traditional data model

The design is pretty straightforward and self-explanatory. Still, I'd like to point out a few design choices here that are based on traditional modeling and that, as you will soon see, are handled differently in the graph modeling:

- A common point for debates related to data modeling is whether to use the singular or plural form for table names. Remember that a table is SQL's counterpart to a relation (from relational theory), and just as a relation's body is a set of tuples, a table's body is a set of rows. So it seems to me more appropriate to use the plural form for table names under traditional modeling: *Accounts*, *Posts*, *Publications*, and so on.

- In a friendship relationship the two accounts have equivalent roles. Saying that account A is friends with account B is equivalent to saying that account B is friends with account A. This makes the relationship *commutative*. Using traditional modeling, if you want to record the fact that the accounts whose IDs are 71 and 379 are friends, technically you have two options in terms of what you store in the table *Friendships*. You either store a row with *accountid1* being 71 and *accountid2* being 379, or the other way around. Storing two rows with both arrangements would be redundant. There's a trick to prevent the redundancy. You can introduce a check constraint to the table, with the predicate *accountid1 < accountid2*, and of course ensure that when you populate the tables, you provide the account IDs in the right order to avoid a constraint violation.

- Contrary to a friendship relationship, a follow relationship isn't commutative. Account A could follow account B without account B necessarily following account A. And if they do follow each other, it could be that account A started following account B on one date and account B started following account A on another date. So you want to store each follow relationship in the *Followings* table as a separate row, with *accountid1* representing the follower and *accountid2* representing the followee, and avoid introducing a check constraint as you did in the *Friendships* table.

■ A post is posted by only one account, so you don't need a separate table to store which account posted which post. Instead, you have an *accountid* column in the *Posts* table indicating this. A foreign key on *Posts.accountid* referencing *Accounts.accountid* enforces referential integrity.

■ A post can have either one parent post (if it's a reply) or none, so you don't need a separate table to hold which post is the parent of which post. You have a *parentpostid* column that allows *NULLs* in the *Posts* table for this, and a self-referencing foreign key to enforce referential integrity.

■ Unlike a post, a publication can be authored by multiple accounts; hence the data model uses a separate table called *AuthorsPublications*, holding which account authored which publication.

■ The data model resulted in seven tables in total.

Use the following code to create and populate the tables involved in the traditional data model (all in the *Norm* schema to make it easy to tell them apart from the *Graph* tables):

```
-- Accounts
CREATE TABLE Norm.Accounts
(
  accountid        INT          NOT NULL,
  accountname      NVARCHAR(50) NOT NULL,
  joindate         DATE         NOT NULL
    CONSTRAINT DFT_Accounts_joindate DEFAULT(SYSDATETIME()),
  reputationpoints INT          NOT NULL
    CONSTRAINT DFT_Accounts_reputationpoints DEFAULT(0),
  CONSTRAINT PK_Accounts PRIMARY KEY(accountid)
);

INSERT INTO Norm.Accounts
  (accountid, accountname, joindate, reputationpoints) VALUES
  (641, N'Inka'  , '20200801',  5),
  ( 71, N'Miko'  , '20210514',  8),
  (379, N'Tami'  , '20211003',  5),
  (421, N'Buzi'  , '20210517',  8),
  (661, N'Alma'  , '20210119', 13),
  (  2, N'Orli'  , '20220202',  2),
  (941, N'Stav'  , '20220105',  1),
  (953, N'Omer'  , '20220315',  0),
  (727, N'Mitzi' , '20200714',  3),
  (883, N'Yatzek', '20210217',  3),
  (199, N'Lilach', '20220112',  1);
```

```
-- Posts
CREATE TABLE Norm.Posts
(
  postid        INT          NOT NULL,
  parentpostid  INT          NULL,
  accountid     INT          NOT NULL,
  dt            DATETIME2(0)  NOT NULL
    CONSTRAINT DFT_Posts_dt DEFAULT(SYSDATETIME()),
  posttext      NVARCHAR(1000) NOT NULL,
  CONSTRAINT PK_Posts PRIMARY KEY(postid),
  CONSTRAINT FK_Posts_Accounts FOREIGN KEY(accountid)
    REFERENCES Norm.Accounts(accountid),
  CONSTRAINT FK_Posts_Posts FOREIGN KEY(parentpostid)
    REFERENCES Norm.Posts(postid)
);

INSERT INTO Norm.Posts
  (postid, parentpostid, accountid, dt, posttext) VALUES
  (  13, NULL, 727,  '20200921 13:09:46' ,
  N'Got a new kitten. Any suggestions for a name?'),
  ( 109, NULL,  71,  '20210515 17:00:00' ,
  N'Starting to hike the PCT today. Wish me luck!'),
  ( 113, NULL, 421,  '20210517 10:21:33' ,
  N'Buzi here. This is my first post.'),
  ( 149, NULL, 421,  '20210519 14:05:45' ,
  N'Buzi here. This is my second post.'
     + N' Aren''t. my posts exciting?'),
  ( 179, NULL, 421,  '20210520 09:12:17' ,
  N'Buzi here. Guess what; this is my third post!'),
  ( 199, NULL,  71,  '20210802 15:56:02' ,
  N'Made it to Oregon!'),
  ( 239, NULL, 883,  '20220219 09:31:23' ,
  N'I''m thinking of growing a mustache,'
     + N' but am worried about milk drinking...'),
  ( 281, NULL, 953,  '20220318 08:14:24' ,
  N'Burt Shavits: "A good day is when no one shows up'
     + N' and you don''t have to go anywhere."'),
  ( 449,   13, 641,  '20200921 13:10:30' ,
  N'Maybe Pickle?'),
  ( 677,   13, 883,  '20200921 13:12:22' ,
  N'Ambrosius?'),
  ( 857,  109, 883,  '20210515 17:02:13' ,
  N'Break a leg. I mean, don''t!'),
  ( 859,  109, 379,  '20210515 17:04:21' ,
  N'The longest I''ve seen you hike was...'
     + N'wait, I''ve never seen you hike ;)'),
  ( 883,  109, 199,  '20210515 17:23:43' ,
  N'Ha ha ha!'),
  (1021,  449,   2,  '20200921 13:44:17' ,
  N'It does look a bit sour faced :)'),
  (1031,  449, 379,  '20200921 14:02:03' ,
  N'How about Gherkin?'),
  (1051,  883,  71,  '20210515 17:24:35' ,
  N'Jokes aside, is 95lbs reasonable for my backpack?'),
  (1061, 1031, 727,  '20200921 14:07:51' ,
  N'I love Gherkin!'),
  (1151, 1051, 379,  '20210515 18:40:12' ,
```

```
    N'Short answer, no! Long answer, nooooooo!!!'),
  (1153, 1051, 883,  '20210515 18:47:17' ,
   N'Say what!?'),
  (1187, 1061, 641,  '20200921 14:07:52' ,
   N'So you don''t like Pickle!? I''M UNFRIENDING YOU!!!'),
  (1259, 1151,  71,  '20210515 19:05:54' ,
   N'Did I say that was without water?');

-- Publications
CREATE TABLE Norm.Publications
(
  pubid    INT          NOT NULL,
  pubdate  DATE         NOT NULL,
  title    NVARCHAR(100) NOT NULL,
  CONSTRAINT PK_Publications PRIMARY KEY(pubid)
);

INSERT INTO Norm.Publications(pubid, pubdate, title) VALUES
  (23977, '20200912' , N'When Mitzi met Inka'),
  ( 4967, '20210304' , N'When Mitzi left Inka'),
  (27059, '20210401' , N'It''s actually Inka who left Mitzi'),
  (14563, '20210802' ,
   N'Been everywhere, seen it all; there''s no place like home!'),
  (46601, '20220119' , N'Love at first second');

-- Friendships
CREATE TABLE Norm.Friendships
(
  accountid1 INT  NOT NULL,
  accountid2 INT  NOT NULL,
  startdate  DATE NOT NULL
    CONSTRAINT DFT_Friendships_startdate DEFAULT(SYSDATETIME()),
  CONSTRAINT PK_Friendships PRIMARY KEY(accountid1, accountid2),
  -- undirected graph; don't allow mirrored pair
  CONSTRAINT CHK_Friendships_act1_lt_act2
    CHECK(accountid1 < accountid2),
  CONSTRAINT FK_Friendships_Accounts_act1 FOREIGN KEY(accountid1)
    REFERENCES Norm.Accounts(accountid),
  CONSTRAINT FK_Friendships_Accounts_act2 FOREIGN KEY(accountid2)
    REFERENCES Norm.Accounts(accountid)
);

INSERT INTO Norm.Friendships
  (accountid1, accountid2, startdate) VALUES
  (  2, 379, '20220202'),
  (  2, 641, '20220202'),
  (  2, 727, '20220202'),
  ( 71, 199, '20220112'),
  ( 71, 379, '20211003'),
  ( 71, 661, '20210514'),
  ( 71, 883, '20210514'),
  ( 71, 953, '20220315'),
  (199, 661, '20220112'),
  (199, 883, '20220112'),
  (199, 941, '20220112'),
  (199, 953, '20220315'),
  (379, 421, '20211003'),
```

```
  (379, 641, '20211003'),
  (421, 661, '20210517'),
  (421, 727, '20210517'),
  (641, 727, '20200801'),
  (661, 883, '20210217'),
  (661, 941, '20220105'),
  (727, 883, '20210217'),
  (883, 953, '20220315');

-- Followings
CREATE TABLE Norm.Followings
(
  accountid1 INT  NOT NULL,
  accountid2 INT  NOT NULL,
  startdate  DATE NOT NULL
    CONSTRAINT DFT_Followings_startdate DEFAULT(SYSDATETIME()),
  CONSTRAINT PK_Followings PRIMARY KEY(accountid1, accountid2),
  CONSTRAINT FK_Followings_Accounts_act1 FOREIGN KEY(accountid1)
    REFERENCES Norm.Accounts(accountid),
  CONSTRAINT FK_Followings_Accounts_act2 FOREIGN KEY(accountid2)
    REFERENCES Norm.Accounts(accountid)
);

INSERT INTO Norm.Followings
  (accountid1, accountid2, startdate) VALUES
  (641, 727, '20200802'),
  (883, 199, '20220113'),
  ( 71, 953, '20220316'),
  (661, 421, '20210518'),
  (199, 941, '20220114'),
  ( 71, 883, '20210516'),
  (199, 953, '20220317'),
  (661, 941, '20220106'),
  (953,  71, '20220316'),
  (379,   2, '20220202'),
  (421, 661, '20210518'),
  (661,  71, '20210516'),
  (  2, 727, '20220202'),
  (  2, 379, '20220203'),
  (379, 641, '20211004'),
  (941, 199, '20220112'),
  (727, 421, '20210518'),
  (379,  71, '20211005'),
  (941, 661, '20220105'),
  (641,   2, '20220204'),
  (953, 199, '20220316'),
  (727, 883, '20210218'),
  (421, 379, '20211004'),
  ( 71, 379, '20211004'),
  (641, 379, '20211003'),
  (199, 883, '20220114'),
  (727,   2, '20220203'),
  (199,  71, '20220113'),
  (953, 883, '20220317'),
  ( 71, 661, '20210514');
```

```
-- Likes
CREATE TABLE Norm.Likes
(
  accountid INT          NOT NULL,
  postid    INT          NOT NULL,
  dt        DATETIME2(0) NOT NULL
    CONSTRAINT DFT_Likes_dt DEFAULT(SYSDATETIME()),
  CONSTRAINT PK_Likes PRIMARY KEY(accountid, postid),
  CONSTRAINT FK_Likes_Accounts FOREIGN KEY(accountid)
    REFERENCES Norm.Accounts(accountid),
  CONSTRAINT FK_Likes_Posts FOREIGN KEY(postid)
    REFERENCES Norm.Posts(postid)
);

INSERT INTO Norm.Likes(accountid, postid, dt) VALUES
  (  2,   13, '2020-09-21 15:33:46'),
  (199,  109, '2021-05-16 03:24:00'),
  (379,  109, '2021-05-15 21:48:00'),
  (379,  113, '2021-05-19 04:45:33'),
  (661,  113, '2021-05-17 21:33:33'),
  (727,  113, '2021-05-18 09:33:33'),
  (379,  179, '2021-05-21 10:00:17'),
  (661,  179, '2021-05-20 22:00:17'),
  (727,  179, '2021-05-21 00:24:17'),
  (199,  199, '2021-08-02 22:20:02'),
  ( 71,  239, '2022-02-20 07:55:23'),
  (199,  239, '2022-02-21 04:43:23'),
  (661,  239, '2022-02-19 12:43:23'),
  (727,  239, '2022-02-20 21:31:23'),
  (  2,  449, '2020-09-21 20:22:30'),
  (379,  449, '2020-09-22 12:22:30'),
  (727,  449, '2020-09-21 19:34:30'),
  ( 71,  677, '2020-09-23 08:24:22'),
  (199,  677, '2020-09-23 12:24:22'),
  (661,  677, '2020-09-23 05:12:22'),
  (727,  677, '2020-09-21 17:12:22'),
  (953,  677, '2020-09-23 11:36:22'),
  ( 71,  857, '2021-05-16 09:50:13'),
  (199,  857, '2021-05-17 00:14:13'),
  (661,  857, '2021-05-16 08:14:13'),
  (727,  857, '2021-05-17 07:26:13'),
  (953,  857, '2021-05-16 11:26:13'),
  (  2,  859, '2021-05-15 21:52:21'),
  ( 71,  859, '2021-05-17 05:04:21'),
  (421,  859, '2021-05-17 11:28:21'),
  ( 71,  883, '2021-05-17 03:47:43'),
  (379, 1021, '2020-09-22 20:56:17'),
  (641, 1021, '2020-09-23 04:56:17'),
  (  2, 1031, '2020-09-21 16:26:03'),
  ( 71, 1031, '2020-09-23 00:26:03'),
  (421, 1031, '2020-09-23 10:02:03'),
  (199, 1051, '2021-05-17 12:36:35'),
  (  2, 1061, '2020-09-22 08:31:51'),
  (421, 1061, '2020-09-23 06:07:51'),
  (641, 1061, '2020-09-21 18:55:51'),
  (883, 1061, '2020-09-21 20:31:51'),
  (  2, 1151, '2021-05-17 13:04:12'),
```

```
( 71, 1151, '2021-05-16 22:40:12'),
(421, 1151, '2021-05-16 01:04:12'),
(641, 1151, '2021-05-15 22:40:12'),
(  2, 1187, '2020-09-23 13:19:52'),
(379, 1187, '2020-09-22 13:19:52');

-- AuthorsPublications
CREATE TABLE Norm.AuthorsPublications
(
  accountid INT NOT NULL,
  pubid     INT NOT NULL,
  CONSTRAINT PK_AuthorsPublications PRIMARY KEY(pubid, accountid),
  CONSTRAINT FK_AuthorsPublications_Accounts FOREIGN KEY(accountid)
    REFERENCES Norm.Accounts(accountid),
  CONSTRAINT FK_AuthorsPublications_Publications FOREIGN KEY(pubid)
    REFERENCES Norm.Publications(pubid)
);

INSERT INTO Norm.AuthorsPublications(accountid, pubid) VALUES
  (727, 23977),
  (641, 23977),
  (727,  4967),
  (641, 27059),
  (883, 14563),
  (883, 46601),
  (199, 46601);
```

Browse the code that creates and populates the tables, and see that you can identify the aforementioned items, such as the check constraint on the *Friendships* table, the primary keys, the foreign keys, and so on.

Graph modeling

In graph-based modeling you have two main types of entities: *nodes* and *edges*. Nodes represent the vertices, or endpoints, of a relationship. An edge represents the way one node, known as the *from node*, relates to the other node, known as the *to node*.

With the SQL Graph feature you define a table for each node and for each edge, marking the tables with the clauses *AS NODE* and *AS EDGE*, respectively. When you query the data, instead of using joins to connect nodes via edges, you use a clause called *MATCH*, and within it form an arrow between the *from node* and the *to node* via an edge using ASCII art-style syntax, like so:

```
from_node-(edge)->to_node
```

Here's an example for such an arrow connecting an *Account* node with a *Post* node via a *Likes* edge:

```
Account-(Likes)->Post
```

As you can see, you can actually read the code in English, which makes it intuitive.

In graph-based modeling it's customary to name nodes using a noun in the singular form—for example, *Account*, *Post*, and *Publication*. As for edges, it's customary to use a verb in the third-person singular form—for example, *Follows*. I also try to address the time aspect in the edge naming. If an edge represents a relationship that is currently relevant, I like to use present tense, such as *Likes* or *Follows*. If a relationship represents something that took place in the past, I like to use past tense, such as *Posted* or *Authored*. Sometimes it even makes sense to precede the verb in the edge name with an auxiliary verb like *is* and sometimes to follow it with a preposition like *with*, *to*, or *of*, such as *IsReplyTo* or *IsFriendOf*. Think English and intuitive phrasing of relationships.

With this in mind, I was able to identify three nodes and six edges for the graph-based data model of our fictitious social network, as shown in Figure 11-2.

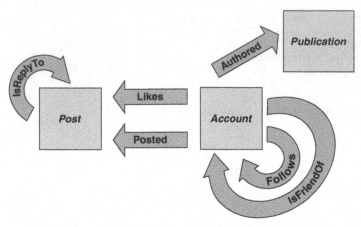

FIGURE 11-2 Graph nodes and edges

As you can see, it's convenient to represent nodes as rectangles and edges as arrows.

Both nodes and edges are implemented as tables in the database. Figure 11-3 shows the detailed graph-based data model for our fictitious social network.

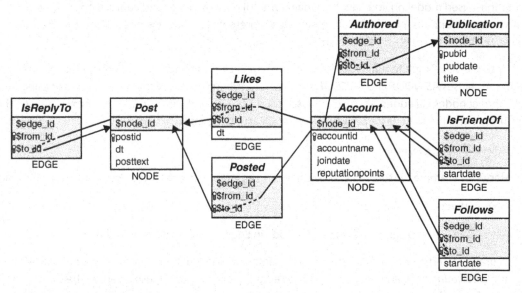

FIGURE 11-3 Graph data model

A few things to note about the graph-based data model:

- Node tables have a column called *$node_id*. This column is created by SQL Server in addition to the user-defined columns, and it uniquely identifies a given node in the database. It is generated as a combination of the object ID of the table in question and an automatically generated *BIGINT* value known as the graph ID. If you query the *$node_id* column, you get a computed JSON string representation of the value.

- Similarly to node tables having an automatically created implicit *$node_id* column that uniquely identifies a node in the database, edge tables have an automatically created implicit *$edge_id* column that uniquely identifies an edge in the database. It is also created as a combination of the object ID of the table in question and an automatically generated *BIGINT* graph ID value. Also with the *$edge_id* column, if you query it, you get a computed JSON string representation of the value.

- Remember that an edge connects two nodes—the *from node* and the *to node*. Therefore, every edge table has a pair of columns called *$from_node* and *$to_node* to store the node IDs of the two nodes that a given edge is connecting. When you add a row to an edge table, you are responsible for acquiring the node IDs of the *from node* and the *to node* that the edge in question is supposed to connect, and store them in the *$from_id* and *$to_id* columns, respectively.

- An edge table may or may not have additional user-defined columns beyond the mandatory system-created *$edge_id*, *$from_node*, and *$to_node* columns. For example, the edge table *Follows* has a user-defined column called *startdate*, but the edge table *IsReplyTo* doesn't have any user-defined columns.

- Recall that in the traditional data model the *Posts* table has a *parentpostid* column linking a post to a parent post if relevant. Notice that in the graph model, the *Post* node table does not have a similar *parentpostid* column; instead, you have a separate edge table called *IsReplyTo* that connects a child post to its parent post. Similarly, the *Posts* table in the traditional data model has an *accountid* column indicating the ID of the account that posted the post. Conversely, in the graph model you store the information about which account posted which post in a separate edge table named *Posted*. As a tip, foreign key relationships in traditional modeling usually translate to edge tables in graph modeling.

- To be able to conveniently identify and query a node row based on user-defined means, I like to introduce a user-defined key in my node tables. Notice the column *accountid* in the table *Account*, *postid* in *Post*, and so on. Theoretically, you could rely on the system-generated graph ID value as part of the *$node_id* column, but it's a bit awkward to work with it. Moreover, if for whatever reason you need to remove a node row and later reintroduce it into the table, it gets a new graph ID value.

- The graph-based data model resulted in nine tables in total, compared to seven tables in the traditional data model.

Creating node tables

To create a node table, you specify the clause *AS NODE* at the end of the table definition. You provide the definitions of columns as usual, with their names, data types, NULLability, and so on. You do not provide the *$node_id* column definition, remember that SQL Server creates this column implicitly.

Use the following code to create the *Account* table in the *Graph* schema:

```
CREATE TABLE Graph.Account
(
  accountid          INT           NOT NULL,
  accountname        NVARCHAR(50)  NOT NULL,
  joindate           DATE          NOT NULL
    CONSTRAINT DFT_Account_joindate DEFAULT(SYSDATETIME()),
  reputationpoints   INT           NOT NULL
    CONSTRAINT DFT_Account_reputationpoints DEFAULT(0),
  CONSTRAINT PK_Account PRIMARY KEY(accountid)
) AS NODE;
```

Use the following code to populate the table:

```
INSERT INTO Graph.Account
  (accountid, accountname, joindate, reputationpoints) VALUES
  (641, N'Inka'  , '20200801',  5),
  ( 71, N'Miko'  , '20210514',  8),
  (379, N'Tami'  , '20211003',  5),
  (421, N'Buzi'  , '20210517',  8),
  (661, N'Alma'  , '20210119', 13),
  (  2, N'Orli'  , '20220202',  2),
  (941, N'Stav'  , '20220105',  1),
  (953, N'Omer'  , '20220315',  0),
  (727, N'Mitzi' , '20200714',  3),
  (883, N'Yatzek', '20210217',  3),
  (199, N'Lilach', '20220112',  1);
```

Use the following code to query the table:

```
SELECT * FROM Graph.Account;
```

This code generates the following output (formatted to fit the page):

```
$node_id_778BA26000F9442194D5F7A4EFC932A0
------------------------------------------------------------
{"type":"node","schema":"Graph","table":"Account","id":5}
{"type":"node","schema":"Graph","table":"Account","id":1}
{"type":"node","schema":"Graph","table":"Account","id":10}
{"type":"node","schema":"Graph","table":"Account","id":2}
{"type":"node","schema":"Graph","table":"Account","id":3}
{"type":"node","schema":"Graph","table":"Account","id":0}
{"type":"node","schema":"Graph","table":"Account","id":4}
{"type":"node","schema":"Graph","table":"Account","id":8}
{"type":"node","schema":"Graph","table":"Account","id":9}
{"type":"node","schema":"Graph","table":"Account","id":6}
{"type":"node","schema":"Graph","table":"Account","id":7}
```

```
accountid   accountname   joindate     reputationpoints
---------   -----------   ----------   ----------------
2           Orli          2022-02-02   2
71          Miko          2021-05-14   8
199         Lilach        2022-01-12   1
379         Tami          2021-10-03   5
421         Buzi          2021-05-17   8
641         Inka          2020-08-01   5
661         Alma          2021-01-19   13
727         Mitzi         2020-07-14   3
883         Yatzek        2021-02-17   3
941         Stav          2022-01-05   1
953         Omer          2022-03-15   0
```

As mentioned, when you query the $node_id column (here as part of the SELECT * request), you get a JSON string representation of the column and not its actual internal representation. Observe that the auto-generated BIGINT graph ID values start with 0 (assigned to the row with accountid value 641, which was specified first in the INSERT statement). Note, though, that unlike with the identity property, if you truncate a node table and repopulate it, the graph ID is not reset to 0, but rather continues. Also unlike with identity, there's no way for you to provide your own explicit graph ID values.

Use the following code to create and populate the remaining node tables Post and Publication:

```
-- Post
CREATE TABLE Graph.Post
(
  postid     INT            NOT NULL,
  dt         DATETIME2(0)   NOT NULL
    CONSTRAINT DFT_Post_dt DEFAULT(SYSDATETIME()),
  posttext   NVARCHAR(1000) NOT NULL,
  CONSTRAINT PK_Post PRIMARY KEY(postid)
) AS NODE;

INSERT INTO Graph.Post(postid, dt, posttext) VALUES
  ( 13, '20200921 13:09:46' ,
   N'Got a new kitten. Any suggestions for a name?'),
  ( 109, '20210515 17:00:00' ,
   N'Starting to hike the PCT today. Wish me luck!'),
  ( 113, '20210517 10:21:33' ,
   N'Buzi here. This is my first post.'),
  ( 149, '20210519 14:05:45' ,
   N'Buzi here. This is my second post.'
     + N' Aren''t my posts exciting?'),
  ( 179, '20210520 09:12:17' ,
   N'Buzi here. Guess what; this is my third post!'),
  ( 199, '20210802 15:56:02' ,
   N'Made it to Oregon!'),
  ( 239, '20220219 09:31:23' ,
   N'I''m thinking of growing a mustache,'
     + N' but am worried about milk drinking...'),
  ( 281, '20220318 08:14:24' ,
   N'Burt Shavits: "A good day is when no one shows up'
     + N' and you don''t have to go anywhere."'),
  ( 449, '20200921 13:10:30' ,
   N'Maybe Pickle?'),
```

```
( 677, '20200921 13:12:22' ,
 N'Ambrosius?'),
( 857, '20210515 17:02:13' ,
 N'Break a leg. I mean, don''t!'),
( 859, '20210515 17:04:21' ,
 N'The longest I''ve seen you hike was...'
    + N'wait, I''ve never seen you hike ;)'),
( 883, '20210515 17:23:43' ,
 N'Ha ha ha!'),
(1021, '20200921 13:44:17' ,
 N'It does look a bit sour faced :)'),
(1031, '20200921 14:02:03' ,
 N'How about Gherkin?'),
(1051, '20210515 17:24:35' ,
 N'Jokes aside, is 95lbs reasonable for my backpack?'),
(1061, '20200921 14:07:51' ,
 N'I love Gherkin!'),
(1151, '20210515 18:40:12' ,
 N'Short answer, no! Long answer, nooooooo!!!'),
(1153, '20210515 18:47:17' ,
 N'Say what!?'),
(1187, '20200921 14:07:52' ,
 N'So you don''t like Pickle!? I''M UNFRIENDING YOU!!!'),
(1259, '20210515 19:05:54' ,
 N'Did I say that was without water?');

-- Publication
CREATE TABLE Graph.Publication
(
  pubid    INT          NOT NULL,
  pubdate  DATE         NOT NULL,
  title    NVARCHAR(100) NOT NULL,
  CONSTRAINT PK_Publication PRIMARY KEY(pubid)
) AS NODE;

INSERT INTO Graph.Publication(pubid, pubdate, title) VALUES
  (23977, '20200912' , N'When Mitzi met Inka'),
  ( 4967, '20210304' , N'When Mitzi left Inka'),
  (27059, '20210401' , N'It''s actually Inka who left Mitzi'),
  (14563, '20210802' ,
  N'Been everywhere, seen it all; there''s no place like home!'),
  (46601, '20220119' , N'Love at first second');
```

Feel free to query the tables to evaluate their contents.

Creating edge tables

Just as with node tables, you use the *CREATE TABLE* statement to create an edge table. You specify the table name, the definition in parentheses (user columns and constraints), and the *AS EDGE* clause at the end of the table definition. You do not provide the definitions of the columns *$node_id*, *$from_id*, and *$to_id*; remember that SQL Server creates them implicitly. If you don't need to define your own columns and constraints, you just provide the table name followed by the *AS EDGE* clause, like so:

```
CREATE TABLE <table_name>  AS EDGE;
```

If you do need to define your own columns and constraints, you provide their specification in parentheses as usual, like so:

```
CREATE TABLE <table_name>  (<columns_and_constraints>) AS EDGE;
```

If you're using SQL Server 2019 or later, or Azure SQL Database, you can restrict which node tables an edge table can connect by using an *edge constraint*. Edge constraints help you avoid having orphaned edge rows that are based on nonexisting nodes.

The syntax for an edge constraint goes like so:

```
[CONSTRAINT <constraint_name>]
  CONNECTION (<from_node_table_1> TO <to_node_table_1>
           [ ... , <from_node_table_n> TO <to_node_table_n>])
  [ON DELETE <referential_action>]
```

The delete referential action can be NO ACTION or CASCADE. The former means that you want SQL Server to reject an attempt to delete a node that has connecting edges. The latter means that when you delete a node, you want SQL Server to automatically delete all connecting edges. There's no support for an update referential action, simply because you're not allowed to update the *$node_id* column of a node row anyway.

Use the following code to create the *IsReplyTo* edge table:

```
CREATE TABLE Graph.IsReplyTo
(
  CONSTRAINT EC_IsReplyTo CONNECTION (Graph.Post TO Graph.Post)
    ON DELETE NO ACTION
) AS EDGE;
```

Remember that an edge stored in the *IsReplyTo* table is supposed to connect a child post to its parent post. Here you use an edge constraint to restrict the connection from the *Post* node table representing the child post to the *Post* node table representing the parent post. Since the *IsReplyTo* edge table doesn't have any user-defined columns, the table definition has only the edge constraint definition.

You cannot define foreign key constraints on the *$from_id* and *$to_id* columns of an edge table to reference *$node_id* columns of the corresponding node tables. There's a reason for this restriction. What if you want to use one edge table to store edges that connect nodes from more than one pair of node tables? Two different foreign key constraints would conflict with each other. An edge constraint is more sophisticated than a foreign key constraint in that it supports specifying multiple pairs of *from node table – to node table* in one constraint. If you want to support such a case, be sure to use a syntax similar to the following:

```
CREATE TABLE MyEdgeTable
(
  CONSTRAINT MyConstraint
    CONNECTION (MyFromNode1 TO MyToNode1, MyFromNode2 TO MyToNode2, …)
      ON DELETE NO ACTION
) AS EDGE;
```

Here, *any* of the constraints must be satisfied per pair of nodes, meaning that your edge table will support pairs of nodes from all specified pairs of node tables.

Do not specify a separate edge constraint for each pair:

```
CREATE TABLE MyEdgeTable
(
  CONSTRAINT MyConstraint1
    CONNECTION (MyFromNode1 TO MyToNode1)
      ON DELETE NO ACTION,
  CONSTRAINT MyConstraint2
    CONNECTION (MyFromNode2 TO MyToNode2)
      ON DELETE NO ACTION,
  ...
) AS EDGE;
```

Here, just like you would have with multiple foreign keys had they been supported, *all* of the constraints must be satisfied per pair of nodes, which would typically not be possible.

To prevent adding duplicate edge rows in terms of having the same *from node* and *to node* pairs, it might be a good idea to introduce a unique constraint based on the *$from_id* and *$to_id* columns. It can't be a primary key constraint, since the columns are nullable. Use the following code to introduce such a unique constraint to our *IsReplyTo* edge table:

```
ALTER TABLE Graph.IsReplyTo
  ADD CONSTRAINT UNQ_IsReplyTo_fromid_toid UNIQUE($from_id, $to_id);
```

Next, you need to insert edge rows into the *IsReplyTo* table to connect the pairs of posts with the following *postid* values:

```
postid of from node postid of to node
------------------- ------------------
449                 13
677                 13
857                 109
859                 109
883                 109
1021                449
1031                449
1051                883
1061                1031
1151                1051
1153                1051
1187                1061
1259                1151
```

However, the way the SQL Graph feature works is that you're supposed to store the *$node_id* values of the *from node* and *to node* in the *$from_node* and *$to_node* columns of the edge row, respectively. You're responsible for extracting the relevant *$node_id* values from the relevant node tables. One way to achieve this, albeit a bit verbose, is to use a scalar subquery for each node where you query the node table, filtering the row with the given *postid* value, and returning the respective *$node_id* value, like so:

```
INSERT INTO Graph.IsReplyTo($from_id, $to_id) VALUES
  ( (SELECT $node_id FROM Graph.Post WHERE postid =  449),
    (SELECT $node_id FROM Graph.Post WHERE postid =   13) ),
  ( (SELECT $node_id FROM Graph.Post WHERE postid =  677),
    (SELECT $node_id FROM Graph.Post WHERE postid =   13) ),
  ( (SELECT $node_id FROM Graph.Post WHERE postid =  857),
    (SELECT $node_id FROM Graph.Post WHERE postid =  109) ),
  ( (SELECT $node_id FROM Graph.Post WHERE postid =  859),
    (SELECT $node_id FROM Graph.Post WHERE postid =  109) ),
  ( (SELECT $node_id FROM Graph.Post WHERE postid =  883),
    (SELECT $node_id FROM Graph.Post WHERE postid =  109) ),
  ( (SELECT $node_id FROM Graph.Post WHERE postid = 1021),
    (SELECT $node_id FROM Graph.Post WHERE postid =  449) ),
  ( (SELECT $node_id FROM Graph.Post WHERE postid = 1031),
    (SELECT $node_id FROM Graph.Post WHERE postid =  449) ),
  ( (SELECT $node_id FROM Graph.Post WHERE postid = 1051),
    (SELECT $node_id FROM Graph.Post WHERE postid =  883) ),
  ( (SELECT $node_id FROM Graph.Post WHERE postid = 1061),
    (SELECT $node_id FROM Graph.Post WHERE postid = 1031) ),
  ( (SELECT $node_id FROM Graph.Post WHERE postid = 1151),
    (SELECT $node_id FROM Graph.Post WHERE postid = 1051) ),
  ( (SELECT $node_id FROM Graph.Post WHERE postid = 1153),
    (SELECT $node_id FROM Graph.Post WHERE postid = 1051) ),
  ( (SELECT $node_id FROM Graph.Post WHERE postid = 1187),
    (SELECT $node_id FROM Graph.Post WHERE postid = 1061) ),
  ( (SELECT $node_id FROM Graph.Post WHERE postid = 1259),
    (SELECT $node_id FROM Graph.Post WHERE postid = 1151) );
```

Query the *IsReplyTo* table to see what got stored there:

```
SELECT * FROM Graph.IsReplyTo;
```

This code generates the following output (again, formatted to fit the page):

```
$edge_id_0C951A35BF65467D9DC10CFB020A005B
----------   ----------------------------------------------------
{"type":"edge","schema":"Graph","table":"IsReplyTo","id":0}
{"type":"edge","schema":"Graph","table":"IsReplyTo","id":1}
{"type":"edge","schema":"Graph","table":"IsReplyTo","id":2}
{"type":"edge","schema":"Graph","table":"IsReplyTo","id":3}
{"type":"edge","schema":"Graph","table":"IsReplyTo","id":4}
{"type":"edge","schema":"Graph","table":"IsReplyTo","id":5}
{"type":"edge","schema":"Graph","table":"IsReplyTo","id":6}
{"type":"edge","schema":"Graph","table":"IsReplyTo","id":7}
{"type":"edge","schema":"Graph","table":"IsReplyTo","id":8}
{"type":"edge","schema":"Graph","table":"IsReplyTo","id":9}
{"type":"edge","schema":"Graph","table":"IsReplyTo","id":10}
{"type":"edge","schema":"Graph","table":"IsReplyTo","id":11}
{"type":"edge","schema":"Graph","table":"IsReplyTo","id":12}
```

$from_id_6B162D7BAC56496E8F5D005313C07BEC

{"type":"node","schema":"Graph","table":"Post","id":8}
{"type":"node","schema":"Graph","table":"Post","id":9}
{"type":"node","schema":"Graph","table":"Post","id":10}
{"type":"node","schema":"Graph","table":"Post","id":11}
{"type":"node","schema":"Graph","table":"Post","id":12}
{"type":"node","schema":"Graph","table":"Post","id":13}
{"type":"node","schema":"Graph","table":"Post","id":14}
{"type":"node","schema":"Graph","table":"Post","id":15}
{"type":"node","schema":"Graph","table":"Post","id":16}
{"type":"node","schema":"Graph","table":"Post","id":17}
{"type":"node","schema":"Graph","table":"Post","id":18}
{"type":"node","schema":"Graph","table":"Post","id":19}
{"type":"node","schema":"Graph","table":"Post","id":20}

$to_id_2EBB26F1CACA47AE8F0278E019472C7F

{"type":"node","schema":"Graph","table":"Post","id":0}
{"type":"node","schema":"Graph","table":"Post","id":0}
{"type":"node","schema":"Graph","table":"Post","id":1}
{"type":"node","schema":"Graph","table":"Post","id":1}
{"type":"node","schema":"Graph","table":"Post","id":1}
{"type":"node","schema":"Graph","table":"Post","id":8}
{"type":"node","schema":"Graph","table":"Post","id":8}
{"type":"node","schema":"Graph","table":"Post","id":12}
{"type":"node","schema":"Graph","table":"Post","id":14}
{"type":"node","schema":"Graph","table":"Post","id":15}
{"type":"node","schema":"Graph","table":"Post","id":15}
{"type":"node","schema":"Graph","table":"Post","id":16}
{"type":"node","schema":"Graph","table":"Post","id":17}

As with new node rows, new edge rows get assigned with internally generated graph ID values starting with 0 in the table. Here, we got graph ID values in the range 0 through 12, since we have 13 edges. Remember that you cannot provide your own explicit graph ID values, and if you delete or truncate rows, the graph ID values do not get reset—rather, they continue where the last insertion left off. As for the $from_id and $to_id values, those were obtained from the respective *Post* node table rows.

> **Note** At the time of this writing you cannot update the $from_id and $to_id column values of an existing edge row. If you need to apply a change to an existing edge row in terms of which nodes it connects, you need to delete the row and reinsert a new one. This will create a new graph ID value as part of the new $edge_id value.

There's a more concise technique to insert a set of edge rows based on pairs of user-defined node keys (*postid* values, in our case). Define a table-value constructor (for details, refer to the section "The *INSERT VALUES* statement" in Chapter 8) with the pairs of user-supplied keys and join it with the two relevant node tables to obtain the respective *$node_id* values. The following code applies this technique to reinsert the edge rows (after first truncating the table of course):

```
TRUNCATE TABLE Graph.IsReplyTo;

INSERT INTO Graph.IsReplyTo($from_id, $to_id)
  SELECT FP.$node_id AS fromid, TP.$node_id AS toid
  FROM (VALUES( 449,    13),
             ( 677,    13),
             ( 857,   109),
             ( 859,   109),
             ( 883,   109),
             (1021,   449),
             (1031,   449),
             (1051,   883),
             (1061,  1031),
             (1151,  1051),
             (1153,  1051),
             (1187,  1061),
             (1259,  1151)) AS D(frompostid, topostid)
    INNER JOIN Graph.Post AS FP
      ON D.frompostid = FP.postid
    INNER JOIN Graph.Post AS TP
      ON D.topostid = TP.postid;
```

Query the table again:

```
SELECT * FROM Graph.IsReplyTo;
```

This code generates the following output:

```
$edge_id_9638455E25A24E77B56C525D5B51294F
------------------------------------------------------------
{"type":"edge","schema":"Graph","table":"IsReplyTo","id":13}
{"type":"edge","schema":"Graph","table":"IsReplyTo","id":14}
{"type":"edge","schema":"Graph","table":"IsReplyTo","id":15}
{"type":"edge","schema":"Graph","table":"IsReplyTo","id":16}
{"type":"edge","schema":"Graph","table":"IsReplyTo","id":17}
{"type":"edge","schema":"Graph","table":"IsReplyTo","id":18}
{"type":"edge","schema":"Graph","table":"IsReplyTo","id":19}
{"type":"edge","schema":"Graph","table":"IsReplyTo","id":20}
{"type":"edge","schema":"Graph","table":"IsReplyTo","id":21}
{"type":"edge","schema":"Graph","table":"IsReplyTo","id":22}
{"type":"edge","schema":"Graph","table":"IsReplyTo","id":23}
{"type":"edge","schema":"Graph","table":"IsReplyTo","id":24}
{"type":"edge","schema":"Graph","table":"IsReplyTo","id":25}

$from_id_88C5F44AF3614A819FA26AFD5302DFF2
------------------------------------------------------------
{"type":"node","schema":"Graph","table":"Post","id":8}
{"type":"node","schema":"Graph","table":"Post","id":9}
{"type":"node","schema":"Graph","table":"Post","id":10}
{"type":"node","schema":"Graph","table":"Post","id":11}
{"type":"node","schema":"Graph","table":"Post","id":12}
{"type":"node","schema":"Graph","table":"Post","id":13}
{"type":"node","schema":"Graph","table":"Post","id":14}
```

{"type":"node","schema":"Graph","table":"Post","id":15}
{"type":"node","schema":"Graph","table":"Post","id":16}
{"type":"node","schema":"Graph","table":"Post","id":17}
{"type":"node","schema":"Graph","table":"Post","id":18}
{"type":"node","schema":"Graph","table":"Post","id":19}
{"type":"node","schema":"Graph","table":"Post","id":20}

$to_id_AE36188F967349FE85D008F44EEFCC49

{"type":"node","schema":"Graph","table":"Post","id":0}
{"type":"node","schema":"Graph","table":"Post","id":0}
{"type":"node","schema":"Graph","table":"Post","id":1}
{"type":"node","schema":"Graph","table":"Post","id":1}
{"type":"node","schema":"Graph","table":"Post","id":1}
{"type":"node","schema":"Graph","table":"Post","id":8}
{"type":"node","schema":"Graph","table":"Post","id":8}
{"type":"node","schema":"Graph","table":"Post","id":12}
{"type":"node","schema":"Graph","table":"Post","id":14}
{"type":"node","schema":"Graph","table":"Post","id":15}
{"type":"node","schema":"Graph","table":"Post","id":15}
{"type":"node","schema":"Graph","table":"Post","id":16}
{"type":"node","schema":"Graph","table":"Post","id":17}

Of course, the *$from_id* and *$to_id* values remain the same as before, since you are connecting the same pairs of nodes as before; however, notice that the graph ID values as part of the *$edge_id* values are new. This time they start with 13 (continuing after the maximum 12 generated in the previous batch) and go up to 25.

If you are migrating the data from an already existing implementation that is based on traditional modeling to a new implementation that is based on graph modeling, you use the following process:

1. Create node tables.

2. Populate each node table using *INSERT SELECT* from the respective source table, letting SQL Server create the new *$node_id* values.

3. Create edge tables.

4. Populate each edge table using *INSERT SELECT* from the source table with pairs of connected keys, joined with already existing graph-based node tables to obtain the respective *$node_id* values.

Steps 1, 2, and 3 are straightforward. Suppose that you already applied those in our database. Here's the code implementing step 4 to populate the target *Graph.IsReplyTo* edge table with the data from the source *Norm.Posts* table (again, after first truncating what it had previously):

```
TRUNCATE TABLE Graph.IsReplyTo;

INSERT INTO Graph.IsReplyTo($from_id, $to_id)
  SELECT FP.$node_id AS fromid, TP.$node_id AS toid
  FROM Norm.Posts AS P
    INNER JOIN Graph.Post AS FP
      ON P.postid = FP.postid
    INNER JOIN Graph.Post AS TP
      ON P.parentpostid = TP.postid;
```

Query the *IsReplyTo* table:

```
SELECT * FROM Graph.IsReplyTo;
```

This code generates the following output:

```
$edge_id_9638455E25A24E77B56C525D5B51294F
-------------------------------------------------------------
{"type":"edge","schema":"Graph","table":"IsReplyTo","id":26}
{"type":"edge","schema":"Graph","table":"IsReplyTo","id":27}
{"type":"edge","schema":"Graph","table":"IsReplyTo","id":28}
{"type":"edge","schema":"Graph","table":"IsReplyTo","id":29}
{"type":"edge","schema":"Graph","table":"IsReplyTo","id":30}
{"type":"edge","schema":"Graph","table":"IsReplyTo","id":31}
{"type":"edge","schema":"Graph","table":"IsReplyTo","id":32}
{"type":"edge","schema":"Graph","table":"IsReplyTo","id":33}
{"type":"edge","schema":"Graph","table":"IsReplyTo","id":34}
{"type":"edge","schema":"Graph","table":"IsReplyTo","id":35}
{"type":"edge","schema":"Graph","table":"IsReplyTo","id":36}
{"type":"edge","schema":"Graph","table":"IsReplyTo","id":37}
{"type":"edge","schema":"Graph","table":"IsReplyTo","id":38}


$from_id_88C5F44AF3614A819FA26AFD5302DFF2
-------------------------------------------------------------
{"type":"node","schema":"Graph","table":"Post","id":8}
{"type":"node","schema":"Graph","table":"Post","id":9}
{"type":"node","schema":"Graph","table":"Post","id":10}
{"type":"node","schema":"Graph","table":"Post","id":11}
{"type":"node","schema":"Graph","table":"Post","id":12}
{"type":"node","schema":"Graph","table":"Post","id":13}
{"type":"node","schema":"Graph","table":"Post","id":14}
{"type":"node","schema":"Graph","table":"Post","id":15}
{"type":"node","schema":"Graph","table":"Post","id":16}
{"type":"node","schema":"Graph","table":"Post","id":17}
{"type":"node","schema":"Graph","table":"Post","id":18}
{"type":"node","schema":"Graph","table":"Post","id":19}
{"type":"node","schema":"Graph","table":"Post","id":20}


$to_id_AE36188F967349FE85D008F44EEFCC49
-------------------------------------------------------------
{"type":"node","schema":"Graph","table":"Post","id":0}
{"type":"node","schema":"Graph","table":"Post","id":0}
{"type":"node","schema":"Graph","table":"Post","id":1}
{"type":"node","schema":"Graph","table":"Post","id":1}
{"type":"node","schema":"Graph","table":"Post","id":1}
{"type":"node","schema":"Graph","table":"Post","id":8}
{"type":"node","schema":"Graph","table":"Post","id":8}
{"type":"node","schema":"Graph","table":"Post","id":12}
{"type":"node","schema":"Graph","table":"Post","id":14}
{"type":"node","schema":"Graph","table":"Post","id":15}
{"type":"node","schema":"Graph","table":"Post","id":15}
{"type":"node","schema":"Graph","table":"Post","id":16}
{"type":"node","schema":"Graph","table":"Post","id":17}
```

Naturally, the edges connect the same *$from_id* and *$to_id* values as before, but got new graph ID values in the range 26 through 38 as part of the *$edge_id* values.

Hopefully, you now have a good idea of how to create and populate edge tables.

Use the following code to create and populate the remaining edge tables in our graph data model (*Posted, IsFriendOf, Follows, Likes,* and *Authored*):

```
-- Posted
CREATE TABLE Graph.Posted
(
  CONSTRAINT EC_Posted CONNECTION (Graph.Account TO Graph.Post)
    ON DELETE NO ACTION
) AS EDGE;

ALTER TABLE Graph.Posted
  ADD CONSTRAINT UNQ_Posted_fromid_toid UNIQUE($from_id, $to_id);

INSERT INTO Graph.Posted($from_id, $to_id)
  SELECT A.$node_id AS fromid, P.$node_id AS toid
  FROM (VALUES(727,    13),
              ( 71,   109),
              (421,   113),
              (421,   149),
              (421,   179),
              ( 71,   199),
              (883,   239),
              (953,   281),
              (641,   449),
              (883,   677),
              (883,   857),
              (379,   859),
              (199,   883),
              (  2,  1021),
              (379,  1031),
              ( 71,  1051),
              (727,  1061),
              (379,  1151),
              (883,  1153),
              (641,  1187),
              ( 71,  1259)) AS D(accountid, postid)
    INNER JOIN Graph.Account AS A
      ON D.accountid = A.accountid
    INNER JOIN Graph.Post AS P
      ON D.postid = P.postid;

-- IsFriendOf
CREATE TABLE Graph.IsFriendOf
(
  startdate   DATE NOT NULL
    CONSTRAINT DFT_Friendships_startdate DEFAULT(SYSDATETIME()),
  CONSTRAINT EC_IsFriendOf CONNECTION (Graph.Account TO Graph.Account)
    ON DELETE NO ACTION
) AS EDGE;

ALTER TABLE Graph.IsFriendOf
  ADD CONSTRAINT UNQ_IsFriendOf_fromid_toid UNIQUE($from_id, $to_id);
```

```
INSERT INTO Graph.IsFriendOf($from_id, $to_id, startdate)
  SELECT A1.$node_id AS fromid, A2.$node_id AS toid, D.startdate
  FROM (VALUES(  2, 379, '20220202'),
              (  2, 641, '20220202'),
              (  2, 727, '20220202'),
              ( 71, 199, '20220112'),
              ( 71, 379, '20211003'),
              ( 71, 661, '20210514'),
              ( 71, 883, '20210514'),
              ( 71, 953, '20220315'),
              (199, 661, '20220112'),
              (199, 883, '20220112'),
              (199, 941, '20220112'),
              (199, 953, '20220315'),
              (379, 421, '20211003'),
              (379, 641, '20211003'),
              (421, 661, '20210517'),
              (421, 727, '20210517'),
              (641, 727, '20200801'),
              (661, 883, '20210217'),
              (661, 941, '20220105'),
              (727, 883, '20210217'),
              (883, 953, '20220315'),
              (379,   2, '20220202'),
              (641,   2, '20220202'),
              (727,   2, '20220202'),
              (199,  71, '20220112'),
              (379,  71, '20211003'),
              (661,  71, '20210514'),
              (883,  71, '20210514'),
              (953,  71, '20220315'),
              (661, 199, '20220112'),
              (883, 199, '20220112'),
              (941, 199, '20220112'),
              (953, 199, '20220315'),
              (421, 379, '20211003'),
              (641, 379, '20211003'),
              (661, 421, '20210517'),
              (727, 421, '20210517'),
              (727, 641, '20200801'),
              (883, 661, '20210217'),
              (941, 661, '20220105'),
              (883, 727, '20210217'),
              (953, 883, '20220315'))
          AS D(accountid1, accountid2, startdate)
      INNER JOIN Graph.Account AS A1
        ON D.accountid1 = A1.accountid
      INNER JOIN Graph.Account AS A2
        ON D.accountid2 = A2.accountid;

-- Follows
CREATE TABLE Graph.Follows
(
  startdate  DATE NOT NULL
    CONSTRAINT DFT_Follows_startdate DEFAULT(SYSDATETIME()),
```

```
        CONSTRAINT EC_Follows CONNECTION (Graph.Account TO Graph.Account)
          ON DELETE NO ACTION
) AS EDGE;

ALTER TABLE Graph.Follows
  ADD CONSTRAINT UNQ_Follows_fromid_toid UNIQUE($from_id, $to_id);

INSERT INTO Graph.Follows($from_id, $to_id, startdate)
  SELECT A1.$node_id AS fromid, A2.$node_id AS toid, D.startdate
  FROM (VALUES(641, 727, '20200802'),
              (883, 199, '20220113'),
              ( 71, 953, '20220316'),
              (661, 421, '20210518'),
              (199, 941, '20220114'),
              ( 71, 883, '20210516'),
              (199, 953, '20220317'),
              (661, 941, '20220106'),
              (953,  71, '20220316'),
              (379,   2, '20220202'),
              (421, 661, '20210518'),
              (661,  71, '20210516'),
              (  2, 727, '20220202'),
              (  2, 379, '20220203'),
              (379, 641, '20211004'),
              (941, 199, '20220112'),
              (727, 421, '20210518'),
              (379,  71, '20211005'),
              (941, 661, '20220105'),
              (641,   2, '20220204'),
              (953, 199, '20220316'),
              (727, 883, '20210218'),
              (421, 379, '20211004'),
              ( 71, 379, '20211004'),
              (641, 379, '20211003'),
              (199, 883, '20220114'),
              (727,   2, '20220203'),
              (199,  71, '20220113'),
              (953, 883, '20220317'),
              ( 71, 661, '20210514'))
         AS D(accountid1, accountid2, startdate)
     INNER JOIN Graph.Account AS A1
       ON D.accountid1 = A1.accountid
     INNER JOIN Graph.Account AS A2
       ON D.accountid2 = A2.accountid;

-- Likes
CREATE TABLE Graph.Likes
(
  dt DATETIME2(0) NOT NULL
    CONSTRAINT DFT_Likes_dt DEFAULT(SYSDATETIME()),
  CONSTRAINT EC_Likes CONNECTION (Graph.Account TO Graph.Post)
    ON DELETE NO ACTION
) AS EDGE;

ALTER TABLE Graph.Likes
  ADD CONSTRAINT UNQ_Likes_fromid_toid UNIQUE($from_id, $to_id);
```

```
INSERT INTO Graph.Likes($from_id, $to_id, dt)
  SELECT A.$node_id AS fromid, P.$node_id AS toid, D.dt
  FROM (VALUES(  2,    13, '2020-09-21 15:33:46'),
              (199,   109, '2021-05-16 03:24:00'),
              (379,   109, '2021-05-15 21:48:00'),
              (379,   113, '2021-05-19 04:45:33'),
              (661,   113, '2021-05-17 21:33:33'),
              (727,   113, '2021-05-18 09:33:33'),
              (379,   179, '2021-05-21 10:00:17'),
              (661,   179, '2021-05-20 22:00:17'),
              (727,   179, '2021-05-21 00:24:17'),
              (199,   199, '2021-08-02 22:20:02'),
              ( 71,   239, '2022-02-20 07:55:23'),
              (199,   239, '2022-02-21 04:43:23'),
              (661,   239, '2022-02-19 12:43:23'),
              (727,   239, '2022-02-20 21:31:23'),
              (  2,   449, '2020-09-21 20:22:30'),
              (379,   449, '2020-09-22 12:22:30'),
              (727,   449, '2020-09-21 19:34:30'),
              ( 71,   677, '2020-09-23 08:24:22'),
              (199,   677, '2020-09-23 12:24:22'),
              (661,   677, '2020-09-23 05:12:22'),
              (727,   677, '2020-09-21 17:12:22'),
              (953,   677, '2020-09-23 11:36:22'),
              ( 71,   857, '2021-05-16 09:50:13'),
              (199,   857, '2021-05-17 00:14:13'),
              (661,   857, '2021-05-16 08:14:13'),
              (727,   857, '2021-05-17 07:26:13'),
              (953,   857, '2021-05-16 11:26:13'),
              (  2,   859, '2021-05-15 21:52:21'),
              ( 71,   859, '2021-05-17 05:04:21'),
              (421,   859, '2021-05-17 11:28:21'),
              ( 71,   883, '2021-05-17 03:47:43'),
              (379,  1021, '2020-09-22 20:56:17'),
              (641,  1021, '2020-09-23 04:56:17'),
              (  2,  1031, '2020-09-21 16:26:03'),
              ( 71,  1031, '2020-09-23 00:26:03'),
              (421,  1031, '2020-09-23 10:02:03'),
              (199,  1051, '2021-05-17 12:36:35'),
              (  2,  1061, '2020-09-22 08:31:51'),
              (421,  1061, '2020-09-23 06:07:51'),
              (641,  1061, '2020-09-21 18:55:51'),
              (883,  1061, '2020-09-21 20:31:51'),
              (  2,  1151, '2021-05-17 13:04:12'),
              ( 71,  1151, '2021-05-16 22:40:12'),
              (421,  1151, '2021-05-16 01:04:12'),
              (641,  1151, '2021-05-15 22:40:12'),
              (  2,  1187, '2020-09-23 13:19:52'),
              (379,  1187, '2020-09-22 13:19:52'))
         AS D(accountid, postid, dt)
    INNER JOIN Graph.Account AS A
      ON D.accountid = A.accountid
    INNER JOIN Graph.Post AS P
      ON D.postid = P.postid;
```

```
-- Authored
CREATE TABLE Graph.Authored
(
  CONSTRAINT EC_Authored CONNECTION
    (Graph.Account TO Graph.Publication)
    ON DELETE NO ACTION
) AS EDGE;

ALTER TABLE Graph.Authored
  ADD CONSTRAINT UNQ_Authored_fromid_toid UNIQUE($from_id, $to_id);

INSERT INTO Graph.Authored($from_id, $to_id)
  SELECT A.$node_id AS fromid, P.$node_id AS toid
  FROM (VALUES(727, 23977),
             (641, 23977),
             (727,  4967),
             (641, 27059),
             (883, 14563),
             (883, 46601),
             (199, 46601)) AS D(accountid, pubid)
    INNER JOIN Graph.Account AS A
      ON D.accountid = A.accountid
    INNER JOIN Graph.Publication AS P
      ON D.pubid = P.pubid;
```

Again, feel free to query the newly created edge tables to examine their contents.

Querying metadata

SQL Server provides you with catalog views and system functions to query metadata about your graph objects.

The *sys.tables* view has a pair of columns called *is_node* and *is_edge* indicating whether a given table is a node table or an edge table, respectively. A value of 1 in the column means true and 0 means false. As an example, the following query returns all node and edge tables in the current database:

```
SELECT SCHEMA_NAME(schema_id) + N'.' + name AS tablename,
  CASE
    WHEN is_node = 1 THEN 'NODE'
    WHEN is_edge = 1 THEN 'EDGE'
    ELSE 'Not SQLGraph table'
  END AS tabletype
FROM sys.tables
WHERE is_node = 1 OR is_edge = 1;
```

This query generates the following output:

```
tablename           tabletype
------------------  ----------
Graph.Account       NODE
Graph.Post          NODE
Graph.Publication   NODE
Graph.IsReplyTo     EDGE
Graph.Posted        EDGE
Graph.IsFriendOf    EDGE
```

```
Graph.Follows      EDGE
Graph.Likes        EDGE
Graph.Authored     EDGE
```

The *sys.columns* view has two columns called *graph_type* and *graph_type_desc*, providing a numeric graph type and a textual descriptive graph type, respectively, for columns with a special meaning for graph objects. For example, the following query returns metadata information about the columns in the *Graph.Account* node table, including the two columns with the graph-specific information:

```
SELECT name, TYPE_NAME(user_type_id) AS typename, max_length,
  graph_type, graph_type_desc
FROM sys.columns
WHERE object_id = OBJECT_ID('Graph.Account');
```

This query generates the following output:

```
name
-------------------------------------------
graph_id_E386DEE1CFDA4AF7B5384DF1581D3EB7
$node_id_C3736967DCB2474D966CA368C2D8AD4A
accountid
accountname
joindate
reputationpoints
```

typename	max_length	graph_type	graph_type_desc
bigint	8	1	GRAPH_ID
nvarchar	2000	2	GRAPH_ID_COMPUTED
int	4	NULL	NULL
nvarchar	100	NULL	NULL
date	3	NULL	NULL
int	4	NULL	NULL

There are two graph-specific columns in every node table—one internal and one exposed to the user:

- *graph_id* (with a lengthy suffix) is an internal column that holds a system-generated *BIGINT* graph ID, which is unique per graph object (node, in this case) in the table. You cannot query this column directly, but there is a way to extract it indirectly with a function, as I will demonstrate shortly.

- *$node_id* (with a lengthy suffix) is a computed column with a JSON string representation of the node ID, and it is unique per graph object (node, in this case) in the database. The JSON string holds the type of object (node or edge), schema, table, and graph ID. You can query this column directly. When you do so, you just refer to it as *$node_id* without the suffix.

The following query returns metadata information about the columns in the *Graph.Posted* edge table:

```
SELECT name, TYPE_NAME(user_type_id) AS typename, max_length,
  graph_type, graph_type_desc
FROM sys.columns
WHERE object_id = OBJECT_ID('Graph.Posted');
```

This query generates the following output:

```
name
-----------------------------------------------
graph_id_C6C5CC1CFB9148AB15F67A888B8B019
$edge_id_9402E3E10FEB4C2097023334CDD93EFD
from_obj_id_921F3A63A5BD4363A7BF162B36E42F15
from_id_73466ABF0B1348C8A2A20706E0BFEAAA
$from_id_ED1EDE58038C45489E5A8346676CE7C6
to_obj_id_C8CD294E3DDF45308E3594490186AA69
to_id_91D22669EFCC4AF4A6C2A6877F28E1AA
$to_id_EB455237A45E4194A933F5F00B376C93
```

```
typename    max_length  graph_type  graph_type_desc
---------   ----------  ----------  ----------------------
bigint      8           1           GRAPH_ID
nvarchar    2000        2           GRAPH_ID_COMPUTED
int         4           4           GRAPH_FROM_OBJ_ID
bigint      8           3           GRAPH_FROM_ID
nvarchar    2000        5           GRAPH_FROM_ID_COMPUTED
int         4           7           GRAPH_TO_OBJ_ID
bigint      8           6           GRAPH_TO_ID
nvarchar    2000        8           GRAPH_TO_ID_COMPUTED
```

As you can see, an edge table has eight columns with graph-specific meaning. Some are internal and not accessible to the user directly and some are exposed to the user for direct querying. Here are the eight columns (lengthy suffix part omitted) and their roles:

- *graph_id* is an internal column that holds the system-generated *BIGINT* graph ID, which is unique to an edge in the table.

- *$edge_id* is an exposed computed column holding the JSON string representation of the edge ID, which is unique to a graph object in the database.

- *$from_id* is an exposed computed column holding the *$node_id* value of the *from node* in the edge. The *from_obj_id* and *from_id* columns are internal columns that hold the raw object ID and graph ID values of the *from node*, respectively.

- *$to_id* is an exposed computed column holding the *$node_id* value of the *to node* in the edge. The *to_obj_id* and *to_id* columns are internal columns that hold the raw object ID and graph ID values of the *to node*, respectively.

When you query graph tables, you can directly query the column *$node_id* in node tables, and the columns *$edge_id*, *$from_id*, and *$to_id* in edge tables. All four are computed columns with a JSON string representation of some graph object, consisting of the object type (node or edge), schema, table, and graph ID. T-SQL provides you with system functions that enable you to extract the raw graph ID and object ID values from the above four columns, as well as to construct node ID and edge ID values from input raw graph ID and object ID values. Table 11-1 lists the supported functions and their purpose.

TABLE 11-1 System functions

Function	Purpose
OBJECT_ID_FROM_NODE_ID	Extract the *object_id* from a *node_id*.
GRAPH_ID_FROM_NODE_ID	Extract the *graph_id* from a *node_id*.
NODE_ID_FROM_PARTS	Construct a *node_id* from an *object_id* and a *graph_id*.
OBJECT_ID_FROM_EDGE_ID	Extract *object_id* from *edge_id*.
GRAPH_ID_FROM_EDGE_ID	Extract identity from *edge_id*.
EDGE_ID_FROM_PARTS	Construct *edge_id* from *object_id* and identity.

As an example, the following query extracts the object ID and graph ID values from the *$node_id* values of the nodes stored in the *Account* table:

```
SELECT $node_id,
  OBJECT_ID_FROM_NODE_ID($node_id) AS obj_id,
  GRAPH_ID_FROM_NODE_ID($node_id) AS graph_id
FROM Graph.Account;
```

This query generates the following output:

```
$node_id_40D6A9476A244872A6BFC576723DC0E8                        obj_id       graph_id
--------------------------------------------------------------- -----------  ---------
{"type":"node","schema":"Graph","table":"Account","id":0}       1275151588   0
{"type":"node","schema":"Graph","table":"Account","id":1}       1275151588   1
{"type":"node","schema":"Graph","table":"Account","id":2}       1275151588   2
{"type":"node","schema":"Graph","table":"Account","id":3}       1275151588   3
{"type":"node","schema":"Graph","table":"Account","id":4}       1275151588   4
{"type":"node","schema":"Graph","table":"Account","id":5}       1275151588   5
{"type":"node","schema":"Graph","table":"Account","id":6}       1275151588   6
{"type":"node","schema":"Graph","table":"Account","id":7}       1275151588   7
{"type":"node","schema":"Graph","table":"Account","id":8}       1275151588   8
{"type":"node","schema":"Graph","table":"Account","id":9}       1275151588   9
{"type":"node","schema":"Graph","table":"Account","id":10}      1275151588   10
```

As mentioned earlier, I prefer to introduce my own node key columns in node tables, such as the *accountid* column in the *Account* table. This makes it easy and convenient to identify a node with a filter based on my own key. However, if you do decide to rely on the system-generated graph ID value, it then becomes very useful to work with the *GRAPH_ID_FROM_NODE_ID* function, since, as a reminder, you do not have direct access to the internal *graph_id* column. You just saw in the last query how to use this function to extract the graph ID value of a given node based on its *$node_id* value. Similarly, you can use this function in a *WHERE* filter predicate to identify a node based on a given graph ID value. For example, this query identifies the account whose internal graph ID value is 3:

```
SELECT $node_id, accountid, accountname
FROM Graph.Account
WHERE GRAPH_ID_FROM_NODE_ID($node_id) = 3;
```

This query generates the following output:

```
$node_id_40D6A9476A244872A6BFC576723DC0E8                 accountid   accountname
-------------------------------------------------------- ----------- -----------
{"type":"node","schema":"Graph","table":"Account","id":3} 421        Buzi
```

The following query shows an example for using the *NODE_ID_FROM_PARTS* function to build a node ID from given raw object ID and graph ID values:

```
SELECT NODE_ID_FROM_PARTS(OBJECT_ID(N'Graph.Account'), 3);
```

This query returns the following node ID value:

```
{"type":"node","schema":"Graph","table":"Account","id":3}
```

Just like you manipulate node objects with the functions *OBJECT_ID_FROM_NODE_ID*, *GRAPH_ID_FROM_NODE_ID*, and *NODE_ID_FROM_PARTS*, you apply similar manipulation to edge objects with the functions *OBJECT_ID_FROM_EDGE_ID*, *GRAPH_ID_FROM_EDGE_ID*, and *EDGE_ID_FROM_PARTS*.

Querying data

Querying graph data is one of the main perks of the SQL Graph feature. Using specialized graph language extensions to T-SQL, you typically end up writing elegant, intuitive, and more concise queries compared to using the more traditional T-SQL tools, like joins. Hopefully, Microsoft is going to keep investing in SQL Graph by adding more such extensions to make your investment in working with this feature worthwhile. I'll describe here what's available in T-SQL at the time of this writing, and also mention examples for strong potential additions in the future.

Using the *MATCH* clause

The main language extension that you get for querying graph data is a clause called *MATCH*. Here I'll describe how to use it in *SELECT* queries. Later in the chapter I'll describe how to use it in modification statements. The general syntax for a *SELECT* query against graph objects goes like this:

```
SELECT <select_list>
FROM <commalist of graph objects>
WHERE MATCH(<match_specification_1>) [ ... AND MATCH(<match_specification_n>)];
```

The match specification part defines the relationships between the graph objects using elegant ASCII art-style syntax. It can also have more sophisticated elements, like the *SHORTEST_PATH* option I'll describe later.

Probably the best way to learn about the syntax is to delve straight into querying examples. Initially I'll compare traditional querying with graph querying, but once you get the point, I'll focus primarily on the graph-querying syntax. Of course, in those cases where I show only the graph syntax, feel free to attempt to come up with the traditional querying alternative as an exercise. This will give you an appreciation for the benefits of the specialized graph language extensions.

Let's start with a very basic example. Suppose that you need to match accounts with their respective posts. Here's the way you would achieve this against the traditional data model using a join:

```
SELECT A.accountid, A.accountname, P.postid, P.posttext
FROM Norm.Accounts AS A
  INNER JOIN Norm.Posts AS P
    ON A.accountid = P.accountid;
```

This query generates the following output (post text truncated to fit the page):

```
accountid  accountname  postid  posttext
---------  -----------  ------  ---------------------------------------
727        Mitzi        13      Got a new kitten. Any suggestions f...
71         Miko         109     Starting to hike the PCT today. Wis...
421        Buzi         113     Buzi here. This is my first post.
421        Buzi         149     Buzi here. This is my second post. ...
421        Buzi         179     Buzi here. Guess what; this is my t...
71         Miko         199     Made it to Oregon!
883        Yatzek       239     I'm thinking of growing a mustache,...
953        Omer         281     Burt Shavits: "A good day is when n...
641        Inka         449     Maybe Pickle?
883        Yatzek       677     Ambrosius?
883        Yatzek       857     Break a leg. I mean, don't!
379        Tami         859     The longest I've seen you hike was....
199        Lilach       883     Ha ha ha!
2          Orli         1021    It does look a bit sour faced :)
379        Tami         1031    How about Gherkin?
71         Miko         1051    Jokes aside, is 95lbs reasonable to...
727        Mitzi        1061    I love Gherkin!
379        Tami         1151    Short answer, no! long answer, nooo...
883        Yatzek       1153    Say what!?
641        Inka         1187    So you don't like Pickle!? I'M UNFR...
71         Miko         1259    Did I say that was without water?
```

Recall earlier that under the traditional data model the way you connect an account to its posts is by keeping an *accountid* column in the *Posts* table. You're able to use this design without an additional junction table because a given post has only one related account. The relationship is *one-to-one* from the *Posts* side to the *Accounts* side, and *one-to-many* from the *Accounts* side to the *Posts* side. Had the relationship been *many-to-many*, you would have needed a third junction table, and the query would have needed two joins instead of one.

With graph modeling, you connect nodes through edges, so you normally use a third table (the edge table) to connect two nodes. That's irrespective of the nature of the relationship between the nodes, including a one-to-one relationship such as the one between *Post* and *Account*. The edge table connecting the two nodes in our case is the *Posted* table.

So to match accounts with their respective posts, using graph syntax against the graph objects, you will need to list all three objects in the query's *FROM* clause, separated by commas, like so,

```
FROM Graph.Account, Graph.Posted, Graph.Post
```

The next part is the *WHERE* clause. You need to figure out the ASCII art-style syntax that you should provide in the *MATCH* clause as part of the match specification. The basic syntax for connecting two nodes via an edge is using the following match pattern:

```
from_node-(edge)->to_node
```

What's important here is the direction of the arrow. You could express the very same relationship by reversing both the arrow direction and the order in which you specify the nodes, like so:

```
to_node<-(edge)-from_node
```

With such a simple example it doesn't really matter which of the two options you use. However, as you will later see, the ability to define the arrow direction either to the right or to the left becomes very handy when you need to define more elaborate and sophisticated relationships. So the *WHERE* clause in our query should look like this:

```
WHERE MATCH(Account-(Posted)->Post)
```

What's left is just to add the *SELECT* clause with the desired columns that you need to return. Here's our complete query:

```
SELECT accountid, accountname, postid, posttext
FROM Graph.Account, Graph.Posted, Graph.Post
WHERE MATCH(Account-(Posted)->Post);
```

You can assign aliases to graph tables in the *FROM* clause. If you do, you need to also use the aliases in the *MATCH* clause and not the original table names. For example, if you assign the alias *Act* to the *Graph.Account* table, the match specification would then need to be Act-(Posted)->Post. Here's the complete query:

```
SELECT accountid, accountname, postid, posttext
FROM Graph.Account AS Act, Graph.Posted, Graph.Post
WHERE MATCH(Act-(Posted)->Post);
```

In this simple example there's no good reason to assign an alias. However, as you will later see, if you need to query multiple instances of the same table, you have to work with table aliases.

Earlier I provided a traditional query that used an inner join to match posts with their respective accounts, as well as the graph-based query alternative. This probably implied that the two are logically equivalent. In actuality, the semantics that the graph query uses are closer to an outer join query, with the edge table as the preserved side. Using a graph query with the path Account-(Posted)->Post against the graph data model is actually closer to using the following query against the traditional data model:

```
SELECT A.accountid, A.accountname, P.postid, P.posttext
FROM Norm.Posts AS P
  LEFT OUTER JOIN Norm.Accounts AS A
    ON P.accountid = A.accountid;
```

The thing is, you would normally have constraints that ensure that an edge connects existing nodes. In the traditional modeling you would use foreign keys for this, and in the graph modeling you use edge constraints. If you can trust that you cannot have orphaned edges that rely on nonexisting nodes, when you convert a graph path to a join-based alternative, both the inner and the outer join versions return the same results anyway.

So far, I've shown traditional T-SQL queries against the traditional data model and graph queries against the graph model. If you're curious whether you can use traditional T-SQL syntax based on joins against the graph data model, this is a fully supported scenario. In our example, you simply join the three relevant tables (the edge table with the two node tables) using outer joins if you want the true logical equivalent to the graph path, marking the edge table as the preserved side. In the join predicates you explicitly match the *$from_id* and *$to_id* columns from the edge table with the *$node_id* columns of the respective node tables, like so:

```
SELECT
  Account.accountid, Account.accountname,
  Post.postid, Post.posttext
FROM Graph.Posted
  LEFT OUTER JOIN Graph.Account
    ON Posted.$from_id = Account.$node_id
  LEFT OUTER JOIN Graph.Post
    ON Posted.$to_id = Post.$node_id;
```

There are two main benefits that I see in being able to use traditional T-SQL syntax against graph objects. One is for troubleshooting purposes to make sure that the match specification's graph paths mean what you think they mean. Another is that there are cases where the graph syntax isn't supported against the graph objects, such as when writing recursive queries, as I'll explain in the next section. Otherwise, when the specialized graph syntax is supported, it's typically preferred to the traditional syntax in terms of its elegance and conciseness. Note that whereas you can use traditional syntax against graph objects, you cannot use graph syntax against traditional objects.

Your next querying task is to return accounts and their publications. Let's start with traditional modeling. The relationship between accounts (stored in the *Accounts* table) and their publications (stored in the *Publications* table) is a many-to-many relationship. So the traditional data model uses a third table called *AuthorsPublications* to connect the other two. You achieve the task with a three-way join, like so:

```
SELECT A.accountid, A.accountname, P.pubid, P.title
FROM Norm.Accounts AS A
  INNER JOIN Norm.AuthorsPublications AS AP
    ON A.accountid = AP.accountid
  INNER JOIN Norm.Publications AS P
    ON AP.pubid = P.pubid;
```

This query generates the following output:

```
accountid  accountname  pubid
---------- ------------ ------
727        Mitzi        4967
883        Yatzek       14563
641        Inka         23977
727        Mitzi        23977
641        Inka         27059
199        Lilach       46601
883        Yatzek       46601

title
----------------------------------------------------------
When Mitzi left Inka
Been everywhere, seen it all; there's no place like home!
When Mitzi met Inka
When Mitzi met Inka
It's actually Inka who left Mitzi
Love at first second
Love at first second
```

With graph querying you list the graph tables *Account* (node), *Authored* (edge), and *Publication* (node) in the query's *FROM* clause, and specify the pattern Account-(Authored)->Publication in the *MATCH* clause as part of the *WHERE* filter, like so:

```
SELECT accountid, accountname, pubid, title
FROM Graph.Account, Graph.Authored, Graph.Publication
WHERE MATCH(Account-(Authored)->Publication);
```

Again, I used inner joins in my traditional query, but as mentioned, graph queries use outer join semantics. Here's a traditional query using outer joins that is a closer logical equivalent to the above graph query:

```
SELECT A.accountid, A.accountname, P.pubid, P.title
FROM Norm.AuthorsPublications AS AP
  LEFT OUTER JOIN Norm.Accounts AS A
    ON AP.accountid = A.accountid
  LEFT OUTER JOIN Norm.Publications AS P
    ON AP.pubid = P.pubid;
```

I mentioned that with edge constraints in place to maintain graph data integrity you can't have orphaned edges. In such a case you won't see any outer rows in the results of your graph queries. However, if you don't have edge constraints in place, SQL Server won't prevent orphaned edges, and if those exist, your graph queries can return outer rows. Their presence is an indication for inconsistencies in your data. To demonstrate this with our data, you will first need to temporarily disable integrity enforcement of edge constraints. Use the following code to disable the edge constraint *EC_Authored* in the *Authored* edge table:

```
ALTER TABLE Graph.Authored NOCHECK CONSTRAINT EC_Authored;
```

When active, this constraint ensures that authored edges connect existing author nodes with existing publication nodes.

Next, run the following code to insert a few edges, where some of the node IDs are ones that don't exist in the respective node table:

```
INSERT INTO Graph.Authored($from_id, $to_id)
  VALUES(NODE_ID_FROM_PARTS(OBJECT_ID(N'Graph.Account'), -1),
         NODE_ID_FROM_PARTS(OBJECT_ID(N'Graph.Publication'), -1));
INSERT INTO Graph.Authored($from_id, $to_id)
  VALUES(NODE_ID_FROM_PARTS(OBJECT_ID(N'Graph.Account'), -1),
         NODE_ID_FROM_PARTS(OBJECT_ID(N'Graph.Publication'), 0));
INSERT INTO Graph.Authored($from_id, $to_id)
  VALUES(NODE_ID_FROM_PARTS(OBJECT_ID(N'Graph.Account'), 0),
         NODE_ID_FROM_PARTS(OBJECT_ID(N'Graph.Publication'), -1));
```

Recall that SQL Server automatically generates node IDs in node tables starting with the value 0. I'm using –1 as a clearly orphaned node ID in the edge table. But it could be any node ID value in the edge table that perhaps used to be a nonorphaned one in the past, but became orphaned. This could be due to the deletion of the corresponding node row, with no edge constraint in place to prevent this.

Run the graph query that returns accounts and their publications again:

```
SELECT accountid, accountname, pubid, title
FROM Graph.Account, Graph.Authored, Graph.Publication
WHERE MATCH(Account-(Authored)->Publication);
```

This time the output includes outer rows representing orphaned edges, with *NULLs* used as placeholders for the attributes of the nonexisting respective nodes:

```
accountid  accountname  pubid
---------- ------------ ---------
NULL       NULL         NULL
NULL       NULL         23977
641        Inka         NULL
641        Inka         23977
641        Inka         27059
727        Mitzi        23977
727        Mitzi        4967
883        Yatzek       14563
883        Yatzek       46601
199        Lilach       46601

title
-----------------------------------------------------------
NULL
When Mitzi met Inka
NULL
When Mitzi met Inka
It's actually Inka who left Mitzi
When Mitzi met Inka
When Mitzi left Inka
Been everywhere, seen it all; there's no place like home!
Love at first second
Love at first second
```

Observe that you can have an edge with an orphaned account node ID, an orphaned publication node ID, or both. Clearly it's a good idea to maintain integrity with edge constraints.

When you're done, run the following code to delete the orphaned edges:

```
DELETE FROM Graph.Authored
WHERE -1 IN (GRAPH_ID_FROM_NODE_ID($from_id),
             GRAPH_ID_FROM_NODE_ID($to_id));
```

Then run the following code to re-enable the edge constraint:

```
ALTER TABLE Graph.Authored WITH CHECK CHECK CONSTRAINT EC_Authored;
```

Let's proceed to graph querying with a bit more elaborate match patterns. Your next querying task is to return all posts—some of which are replies to other posts, mind you—and their direct replies. For both the post and the reply you need to return the posting account name and the post text.

There are three relationships that you need to express in your graph query:

1. Account 1 posted post 1.

2. Account 2 posted post 2.

3. Post 2 is a reply to post 1.

The account node, the posted edge, and the post node each play two different roles in the relationships above. So you need to list each of the respective graph tables twice in the query's *FROM* clause, and use different aliases to distinguish the two.

Starting with the two occurrences of the *Account* node table, you can alias them *Account1* and *Account2*. As for the two occurrences of the *Post* node table, one represents the parent post, so you can just keep the name *Post* for it, and the other represents the reply post, so you can alias it as *Reply*. As for the two occurrences of the *Posted* edge table, you can keep the name *Posted* for the one connecting *Account1* with *Post*, and alias the other, which connects *Account2* with *Reply*, as *RepliedWith*.

You also need to list the *IsReplyTo* edge table in the *FROM* clause, but since it plays only one role in the above relationships, you need to specify it only once and there's no need to alias it.

So your query's *FROM* clause should look like this:

```
FROM Graph.Account AS Account1, Graph.Posted, Graph.Post,
  Graph.Account AS Account2, Graph.Posted AS RepliedWith,
  Graph.Post AS Reply, Graph.IsReplyTo
```

Next, translating the aforementioned three relationships to base match patterns, you get the following:

1. Account1-(Posted)->Post

2. Account2-(RepliedWith)->Reply

3. Reply-(IsReplyTo)->Post

T-SQL gives you flexibility in the syntax when you need to express multiple relationships such as the ones above. You can merge two patterns into one when they share the same node table. You just need to maintain the correct arrow directions based on the role that the node plays in each of the relationships. For example, consider the patterns N1-(E1)->N2 and N1-(E2)->N3. The node table *N1* plays a *from node* role in both patterns. So you can form one merged pattern with *N1* at the center, and two arrows coming out of it going in both the left and right directions to express the two original base patterns. You can express the merged pattern as either N3<-(E2)-N1-(E1)->N2 or as N2<-(E1)-N1-(E2)->N3. Both have the same meaning.

If the same node plays a *to node* role in two patterns, you can merge them by having both arrows pointing to it. For example, you can merge the patterns N2-(E1)->N1 and N3-(E2)->N1 either as N3-(E2)->N1<-(E1)-N2 or as N2-(E1)->N1<-(E2)-N3.

You could also have a node playing a *from node* role in one pattern and a *to node* role in another. To merge the two base patterns, you form a pattern with one arrow going into the shared node and one coming out of it. For example, to merge N2-(E1)->N1 and N1-(E2)->N3, you use either N2-(E1)->N1-(E2)->N3 or N3<-(E2)-N1<-(E1)-N2.

Based on these merger and acquisition strategies, there are two mergers that you can perform in our querying task. Pattern 1 (`Account1-(Posted)->Post`) and pattern 3 (`Reply-(IsReplyTo)->Post`) both share the same *Post* node table, which plays a *to node* role in both patterns. So you can merge the two into one pattern: `Account1-(Posted)->Post<-(IsReplyTo)-Reply`. You can then apply another merger between this merged pattern and pattern 2 (`Account2-(RepliedWith)->Reply`). The *Reply* node table plays the rightmost *from node* role in the former pattern and the *to node* role in the latter pattern, so you can form the merged pattern `Account1-(Posted)->Post<-(IsReplyTo)-Reply<-(RepliedWith)-Account2`.

Now that you've figured out both how to list the tables in the query's FROM clause and how to express the match pattern, you can produce the following complete solution query:

```
SELECT Account1.accountname AS account1, Post.posttext,
  Account2.accountname AS account2, Reply.posttext AS replytext
FROM Graph.Account AS Account1, Graph.Posted, Graph.Post,
  Graph.Account AS Account2, Graph.Posted AS RepliedWith,
  Graph.Post AS Reply, Graph.IsReplyTo
WHERE MATCH(Account1-(Posted)->Post<-(IsReplyTo)-Reply
  <-(RepliedWith)-Account2) -- white spaces are ignored
ORDER BY Post.dt, Post.postid, Reply.dt;
```

This query generates the following output (formatted as staggered lines for clarity and to fit the page):

```
account1   posttext
  account2   replytext
---------- --------------------------------------------------
Mitzi      Got a new kitten. Any suggestions for a name?
  Inka       Maybe Pickle?
Mitzi      Got a new kitten. Any suggestions for a name?
  Yatzek     Ambrosius?
```

```
Inka     Maybe Pickle?
  Orli     It does look a bit sour faced :)
Inka     Maybe Pickle?
  Tami     How about Gherkin?
Tami     How about Gherkin?
  Mitzi     I love Gherkin!
Mitzi    I love Gherkin!
  Inka     So you don't like Pickle!? I'M UNFRIENDING YOU!!!
Miko     Starting to hike the PCT today. Wish me luck!
  Yatzek    Break a leg. I mean, don't!
Miko     Starting to hike the PCT today. Wish me luck!
  Tami     The longest I've seen you hike was...wait,
            I've never seen you hike ;)
Miko     Starting to hike the PCT today. Wish me luck!
  Lilach    Ha ha ha!
Lilach   Ha ha ha!
  Miko     Jokes aside, is 95lbs reasonable for my backpack?
Miko     Jokes aside, is 95lbs reasonable for my backpack?
  Tami     Short answer, no! Long answer, nooooooo!!!
Miko     Jokes aside, is 95lbs reasonable for my backpack?
  Yatzek    Say what!?
Tami     Short answer, no! Long answer, nooooooo!!!
  Miko     Did I say that was without water?
```

But what if you're not comfortable with a single lengthy, elaborate pattern? T-SQL allows you to express a match specification as a conjunction of multiple base patterns separated by *AND* operators, still using one *MATCH* clause, like so:

```
SELECT Account1.accountname AS account1, Post.posttext,
  Account2.accountname AS account2, Reply.posttext AS replytext
FROM Graph.Account AS Account1, Graph.Posted, Graph.Post,
  Graph.Account AS Account2, Graph.Posted AS RepliedWith,
  Graph.Post AS Reply, Graph.IsReplyTo
WHERE MATCH(Account1-(Posted)->Post
       AND Account2-(RepliedWith)->Reply
       AND Reply-(IsReplyTo)->Post)
ORDER BY Post.dt, Post.postid, Reply.dt;
```

Yet another option is to specify a conjunction of predicates in the *WHERE* clause, each with a separate *MATCH* clause with its own base pattern, separated by *AND* operators, like so:

```
SELECT Account1.accountname AS account1, Post.posttext,
  Account2.accountname AS account2, Reply.posttext AS replytext
FROM Graph.Account AS Account1, Graph.Posted, Graph.Post,
  Graph.Account AS Account2, Graph.Posted AS RepliedWith,
  Graph.Post AS Reply, Graph.IsReplyTo
WHERE MATCH(Account1-(Posted)->Post)
  AND MATCH(Account2-(RepliedWith)->Reply)
  AND MATCH(Reply-(IsReplyTo)->Post)
ORDER BY Post.dt, Post.postid, Reply.dt;
```

All three options are logically equivalent. Behind the scenes they are all treated the same by SQL Server. The good news is that you can even combine the three techniques as needed. You need to figure out what works best for you and your team in terms of code clarity and maintainability.

Let's add another requirement to the last task. Like before, you need to return posts and their direct replies; only this time, the replying account must be one who follows the account that posted the parent post. Suppose that you prefer the format with the single lengthy pattern. The single pattern form from the previous query is Account1-(Posted)->Post<-(IsReplyTo)-Reply<-(RepliedWith)-Account2. You now need to add the base pattern Account2-(Follows)->Account1. Based on the aforementioned rules, it's quite natural to merge the two into the pattern Account1-(Posted)->Post<-(IsReplyTo)-Reply<-(RepliedWith)-Account2-(Follows)->Account1. There's the added edge table *Follows* in the new pattern, so you should add it to the *FROM* clause. Here's the complete solution query:

```
SELECT Account1.accountname AS account1, Post.posttext,
  Account2.accountname AS account2, Reply.posttext AS replytext
FROM Graph.Account AS Account1, Graph.Posted, Graph.Post,
  Graph.Account AS Account2, Graph.Posted AS RepliedWith,
  Graph.Post AS Reply, Graph.IsReplyTo, Graph.Follows
WHERE MATCH(Account1-(Posted)->Post<-(IsReplyTo)-Reply
  <-(RepliedWith)-Account2-(Follows)->Account1)
ORDER BY Post.dt, Post.postid, Reply.dt;
```

Observe that *Account1* appears twice in the merged pattern, and that's perfectly valid.

Now you have four base relationships involved in the pattern. The more relationships you have, the more the graph-based syntax with the match pattern saves you coding compared to the more traditional syntax. For the sake of comparison, here's a solution using traditional join-based syntax (using inner joins for simplicity) against the graph objects:

```
SELECT Account1.accountname AS account1, Post.posttext,
  Account2.accountname AS account2, Reply.posttext AS replytext
FROM Graph.Account AS Account1
  INNER JOIN Graph.Posted
    ON Posted.$from_id = Account1.$node_id
  INNER JOIN Graph.Post
    ON Posted.$to_id = Post.$node_id
  INNER JOIN Graph.IsReplyTo
    ON IsReplyTo.$to_id = Post.$node_id
  INNER JOIN Graph.Post AS Reply
    ON IsReplyTo.$from_id = Reply.$node_id
  INNER JOIN Graph.Posted AS RepliedWith
    ON RepliedWith.$to_id = Reply.$node_id
  INNER JOIN Graph.Account AS Account2
    ON RepliedWith.$from_id = Account2.$node_id
  INNER JOIN Graph.Follows
    ON Follows.$from_id = Account2.$node_id
    AND Follows.$to_id = Account1.$node_id
ORDER BY Post.dt, Post.postid, Reply.dt;
```

Beyond being more concise, the graph-based syntax is more natural, enabling you to read the pattern in English. You just read each of the base patterns in the direction of the arrow. The pattern Account1-(Posted)->Post<-(IsReplyTo)-Reply<-(RepliedWith)-Account2-(Follows)->Account1 can be read as "Account 1 posted a post. The reply is a reply to that post. Account 2 replied with that reply. Account 2 follows account 1." Conversely, attempting to analyze the join-based solution is not that natural. It doesn't translate as well to English. If you think about it, one of the goals of the designers of SQL was to create a declarative, English-like language that is as close as possible to the way people speak when they express requests. The graph-based syntax seems to be closer to achieving this goal than does the more traditional syntax.

Note that at the time of this writing, you're allowed to combine base match patterns only by using *AND* logic—whether it be by using a single *MATCH* clause with multiple base patterns separated by *AND* operators, or by using multiple *MATCH* clauses separated by *AND* operators, or by using a single merged match pattern, or any combination of those three options. Currently, T-SQL supports neither combining base patterns using *OR* logic directly nor negating patterns using *NOT* logic directly.

So how do you deal with the need for handling *OR* and *NOT* logic? One option is to use set operators like *UNION* instead of *OR* and *EXCEPT* instead of *NOT*. Another option is to use the *OR* and *NOT* operators combined with an *EXISTS* predicate that is based on a subquery, which apparently is supported, though this is not common knowledge. The subquery approach tends to be the more concise of the two, and to me is the more natural to use.

As an example, let's further extend the last task. You need to return posts and their direct replies only if the account who replied follows *or* is a friend of the account who posted the parent post.

Using set operators, you handle *OR* logic with a *UNION* operator. You basically form two queries, each with its own match pattern, and apply a *UNION* operator between them. The two match patterns repeat all of the *AND*ed logic and differ only in the part that is *OR*ed. In our case, one query's match pattern is `Account1-(Posted)->Post<-(IsReplyTo)-Reply<-(RepliedWith)-Account2-(Follows)->Account1`, and the other is `Account1-(Posted)->Post<-(IsReplyTo)-Reply<-(RepliedWith)-Account2-(IsFriendOf)->Account1`. The table list in the two queries will slightly differ. The query involving the `Account2-(Follows)->Account1` pattern will naturally list the *Follows* edge table, and the query involving the `Account2-(IsFriendOf)->Account1` pattern will list the *IsFriendOf* edge table.

Here's the complete solution code:

```
SELECT Account1.accountname AS account1, Post.posttext,
  Account2.accountname AS account2, Reply.posttext AS replytext
FROM Graph.Account AS Account1, Graph.Posted, Graph.Post,
  Graph.Account AS Account2, Graph.Posted AS RepliedWith,
  Graph.Post AS Reply, Graph.IsReplyTo, Graph.Follows
WHERE MATCH(Account1-(Posted)->Post<-(IsReplyTo)-Reply
  <-(RepliedWith)-Account2-(Follows)->Account1)

UNION

SELECT Account1.accountname AS account1, Post.posttext,
  Account2.accountname AS account2, Reply.posttext AS replytext
FROM Graph.Account AS Account1, Graph.Posted, Graph.Post,
  Graph.Account AS Account2, Graph.Posted AS RepliedWith,
  Graph.Post AS Reply, Graph.IsReplyTo, Graph.IsFriendOf
WHERE MATCH(Account1-(Posted)->Post<-(IsReplyTo)-Reply
  <-(RepliedWith)-Account2-(IsFriendOf)->Account1);
```

The main issue that I see with this solution is that there's a lot of repetition of code, resulting in a lengthy solution. Remember that one of the points in using graph-based syntax is to reduce the amount of needed code.

The other option is to use the *EXISTS* predicate and subqueries. The idea is to have the outer query use a pattern that is based on all of the *AND*ed logic, and of course list all relevant tables that appear in its base patterns in its *FROM* clause. Then, for each of the *OR*ed parts, you use an *EXISTS* predicate with a subquery, and apply a normal *OR* operator between these *EXISTS* predicates. Each of the subqueries explicitly refers to only the new table in the currently handled base pattern, since you have access to all of the outer query's tables via correlations, and specifies the relevant base match pattern in the *WHERE* clause.

Here's the complete solution code:

```
SELECT Account1.accountname AS account1, Post.posttext,
  Account2.accountname AS account2, Reply.posttext AS replytext
FROM Graph.Account AS Account1, Graph.Posted, Graph.Post,
  Graph.Account AS Account2, Graph.Posted AS RepliedWith,
  Graph.Post AS Reply, Graph.IsReplyTo
WHERE MATCH(Account1-(Posted)->Post<-(IsReplyTo)-Reply
  <-(RepliedWith)-Account2)
  AND (EXISTS (SELECT * FROM Graph.Follows
              WHERE MATCH(Account2-(Follows)->Account1))
      OR
      EXISTS (SELECT * FROM Graph.IsFriendOf
              WHERE MATCH(Account2-(IsFriendOf)->Account1)));
```

Notice the references in the subqueries to the outer node tables *Account1* and *Account2*. These are essentially correlations.

The last two examples demonstrated how to handle *OR* logic. Handling *NOT* logic is very similar. As an example, suppose that your task is to return posts and their direct replies only if the account who replied *didn't* also like the post.

With a solution that is based on set operators, this time you use the *EXCEPT* operator, like so:

```
SELECT Account1.accountname AS account1, Post.posttext,
  Account2.accountname AS account2, Reply.posttext AS replytext
FROM Graph.Account AS Account1, Graph.Posted, Graph.Post,
  Graph.Account AS Account2, Graph.Posted AS RepliedWith,
  Graph.Post AS Reply, Graph.IsReplyTo
WHERE MATCH(Account1-(Posted)->Post<-(IsReplyTo)-Reply
  <-(RepliedWith)-Account2)

EXCEPT

SELECT Account1.accountname AS account1, Post.posttext,
  Account2.accountname AS account2, Reply.posttext AS replytext
FROM Graph.Account AS Account1, Graph.Posted, Graph.Post,
  Graph.Account AS Account2, Graph.Posted AS RepliedWith,
  Graph.Post AS Reply, Graph.IsReplyTo, Graph.Likes
WHERE MATCH(Account1-(Posted)->Post<-(IsReplyTo)-Reply
  <-(RepliedWith)-Account2-(Likes)->Post);
```

With a solution that is based on the *EXISTS* predicate, this time you use the *NOT EXISTS* predicate, like so:

```
SELECT Account1.accountname AS account1, Post.posttext,
  Account2.accountname AS account2, Reply.posttext AS replytext
FROM Graph.Account AS Account1, Graph.Posted, Graph.Post,
  Graph.Account AS Account2, Graph.Posted AS RepliedWith,
  Graph.Post AS Reply, Graph.IsReplyTo
WHERE MATCH(Account1-(Posted)->Post<-(IsReplyTo)-Reply
  <-(RepliedWith)-Account2)
  AND NOT EXISTS
    (SELECT *
     FROM Graph.Likes
     WHERE MATCH(Account2-(Likes)->Post));
```

I find this technique pretty neat. It essentially allows you to handle *OR* and *NOT* logic using *OR* and *NOT* operators, even though they are not supported directly in match patterns or in combining multiple match patterns.

Recursive queries

Before the SQL Graph feature was added to T-SQL, people often used recursive queries based on recursive CTEs to handle graph data stored in traditional tables. (Recursive queries are covered in Chapter 5, "Table expressions.") That was especially the case when you needed to traverse graph structures with arbitrary length paths. Examples for tasks involving such structures include obtaining a subgraph of an input node (return the subtree of posts starting with an input post), obtaining the chain of nodes that lead to an input node (return the path of ancestor posts leading to the input post), and so on. At the time of this writing, the SQL Graph feature doesn't support normal match patterns that handle arbitrary length paths; it only supports such patterns when using the specialized *SHORTEST_PATH* option, which I'll get to later in this chapter. In the meanwhile, many use recursive queries and other iterative solutions to traverse graphs with arbitrary length paths stored in SQL Graph tables. In this section I explain how to use recursive queries against graph objects, including limitations of the syntax and workarounds to those limitations. Hopefully, T-SQL will add support for normal match patterns that handle arbitrary-length paths, substantially reducing the need to use recursive queries and other iterative solutions.

A typical task that you would expect to handle using recursive queries is returning the subgraph of an input node. As an example, given an input post ID (we'll use a local variable called *@postid* for this purpose), you're supposed to return the input post, as well as all of the posts below the input one—direct and indirect. That is, all direct replies, replies to replies, and so on. For each post you need to return the parent post ID, post ID, and post text.

Assuming you are familiar with recursive queries but haven't yet used them to query graph objects, you're likely to come up with the following solution as your first attempt (using the sample input post ID 13):

```
DECLARE @postid AS INT = 13;

WITH C AS
(
  SELECT NULL AS parentpostid, postid, posttext
  FROM Graph.Post
  WHERE postid = @postid

  UNION ALL

  SELECT ParentPost.postid AS parentpostid,
    ChildPost.postid, ChildPost.posttext
  FROM C AS ParentPost, Graph.IsReplyTo, Graph.Post AS ChildPost
  WHERE MATCH(ChildPost-(IsReplyTo)->ParentPost)
)
SELECT parentpostid, postid, posttext
FROM C;
```

The anchor query returns a row for the input post, with a *NULL* as the parent post ID because it represents the root of the subgraph that you're about to return. The recursive query then attempts to use graph-based syntax with a basic match pattern (`ChildPost-(IsReplyTo)->ParentPost`) to return the direct replies to the posts from the previous iteration. The posts from the previous iteration are represented by a recursive reference to the CTE name (`C AS ParentPost`). The thing is, at the time of this writing, the *MATCH* clause doesn't support using a recursive reference to the CTE name in lieu of a graph object in the match pattern. Attempting to run this solution fails with the following error:

```
Msg 13940, Level 16, State 1, Line 1373
Cannot use a derived table 'ParentPost' in a MATCH clause.
```

At this point many give up on using graph-based syntax in the recursive query, assuming it's simply not supported. Instead, they proceed to use a join-based syntax where you handle the graph object relationships explicitly via the join predicates. I'll cover such solutions shortly. A little-known fact is that there is a simple workaround, though it does require you to add a table to the recursive query, so it comes at a certain cost. The idea is that instead of considering the recursive reference to the CTE name as a node table, you add the relevant node table to the query (*Graph.Post AS ParentPost*, in our case), and use the recursive reference to the CTE name as a proxy, matching the IDs of the two in the query's *WHERE* clause. You can then safely use the alias you assigned to the node table (*ParentPost*, in our case) as part of your match pattern. Here's how you apply this technique to our solution:

```
DECLARE @postid AS INT = 13;

WITH C AS
(
  SELECT NULL AS parentpostid, postid, posttext
  FROM Graph.Post
  WHERE postid = @postid
```

```
UNION ALL

SELECT ParentPost.postid AS parentpostid,
  ChildPost.postid, ChildPost.posttext
FROM C, Graph.Post AS ParentPost, Graph.IsReplyTo,
  Graph.Post AS ChildPost
WHERE ParentPost.postid = C.postid -- recursive ref used as proxy
  AND MATCH(ChildPost-(IsReplyTo)->ParentPost)
)
SELECT parentpostid, postid, posttext
FROM C;
```

This code generates the following output:

```
parentpostid postid      posttext
------------ ----------- -------------------------------------------------
NULL         13          Got a new kitten. Any suggestions for a name?
13           449         Maybe Pickle?
13           677         Ambrosius?
449          1021        It does look a bit sour faced :)
449          1031        How about Gherkin?
1031         1061        I love Gherkin!
1061         1187        So you don't like Pickle!? I'M UNFRIENDING YOU!!!
```

Alternatively, you can always use traditional join-based syntax in your recursive query, like so:

```
DECLARE @postid AS INT = 13;

WITH C AS
(
  SELECT $node_id AS nodeid, NULL AS parentpostid, postid, posttext
  FROM Graph.Post
  WHERE postid = @postid

  UNION ALL

  SELECT CP.$node_id AS nodeid, PP.postid AS parentpostid,
    CP.postid, CP.posttext
  FROM C AS PP -- parent post
    INNER JOIN Graph.IsReplyTo AS R
      ON R.$to_id = PP.nodeid
    INNER JOIN Graph.Post AS CP -- child post
      ON R.$from_id = CP.$node_id
)
SELECT parentpostid, postid, posttext
FROM C;
```

The benefit of the traditional syntax is that you have one less table involved, since you don't need the proxy trick here, and therefore it is a bit more efficient. We discussed the benefits of the graph-based syntax earlier—it tends to be more natural and more concise. If you do like the graph-based syntax better, I'd recommend testing it to see if its performance is satisfactory despite the extra table involved.

Adding sorting and indentation

Often when you need to return a subgraph, you want to sort the result in what's known as *topological order*. That is, a parent node should be returned before its descendants. Also, if node N1 sorts before its sibling N2, all descendants of node N1 should sort after N1 and before N2. It's also common to need to add a visual effect that involves pushing some attribute of the returned node (say, the post text in our case) in a manner that is proportional to its level in the subtree. With the sorting and indentation effects you can get a very clear and appealing representation of the relationships between the returned nodes.

Before I explain how you handle the sorting and indentation requirements, it would a good idea for you to look ahead at the output of the solution, to understand what we're trying to achieve here.

As for the solution's code, you can start with the graph-based solution to the subgraph task, using the recursive CTE name as a proxy to the parent post node table. Of course, you can use the more traditional join-based syntax if that's what you prefer, but I'll demonstrate the solution using the graph-based syntax. You add a column called *lvl* representing the level of the node in the subgraph (0 for the input root node, 1 for the direct replies, and so on). In the anchor query you simply assign the constant 0 as the *lvl* column (`0 AS lvl`). In the recursive query, you add one to the level of the parent post using the reference to the recursive CTE name (`C.lvl + 1 AS lvl`). You add another column called *sortkey* representing a character-string-based sort value of the node in the output. In the anchor query you set *sortkey* to the constant '.'. In the recursive query, you concatenate the parent post's *sortkey* value with the current post ID and '.'. Take post ID 1061 as an example. Its parent post ID is 1031, whose parent post ID in turn is 449, whose parent post ID is 13—the input post ID in our example. The code should generate the *sortkey* value '.449.1031.1061.' for post 1061. The outer query can achieve the desired sorting by ordering the output by *sortkey*. It can achieve the indentation by replicating some string, say ' | ', *lvl* times, and concatenating the desired attribute (*posttext*). Here's the complete solution code:

```
DECLARE @postid AS INT = 13;

WITH C AS
(
  SELECT NULL AS parentpostid, postid, posttext,
    0 AS lvl,
    CAST('.' AS VARCHAR(MAX)) AS sortkey
  FROM Graph.Post
  WHERE postid = @postid

  UNION ALL

  SELECT ParentPost.postid AS parentpostid,
    ChildPost.postid, ChildPost.posttext,
    C.lvl + 1 AS lvl,
    CONCAT(C.sortkey, ChildPost.postid, '.') AS sortkey
  FROM C, Graph.Post AS ParentPost, Graph.IsReplyTo,
    Graph.Post AS ChildPost
  WHERE ParentPost.postid = C.postid -- recursive ref used as proxy
    AND MATCH(ChildPost-(IsReplyTo)->ParentPost)
)
SELECT
  REPLICATE(' | ', lvl) + posttext AS post
FROM C
ORDER BY sortkey;
```

This code generates the following output:

```
post
------------------------------------------------------------------
Got a new kitten. Any suggestions for a name?
 | Maybe Pickle?
 |  | It does look a bit sour faced :)
 |  | How about Gherkin?
 |  |  | I love Gherkin!
 |  |  |  | So you don't like Pickle!? I'M UNFRIENDING YOU!!!
 | Ambrosius?
```

If the techniques used in this solution are not completely clear yet, it could be helpful to run the code again with a *SELECT *** in the outer query and inspect the *lvl* and *sortkey* columns.

Using the SHORTEST_PATH option

Finding the shortest path between two nodes is a classic need in graph handling. Think about tasks like identifying the shortest path between two locations on a map, or in our scenario, the shortest friendship path between two accounts, or the shortest followings path between two accounts. Often you want the shortest path irrespective of the number of hops, or levels, you need to go through, but sometimes you want to be able to restrict the number of hops. T-SQL enables you to handle such needs with graph-based querying syntax using the *SHORTEST_PATH* subclause of the *MATCH* clause. This subclause is available starting with SQL Server 2019 and in Azure SQL Database. At the time of this writing, T-SQL doesn't yet support finding a weighted shortest path. An example for a weighted shortest path task is finding the shortest route in terms of total mileage between two cities. Using the *SHORTEST_PATH* option, you can currently find the route that involves the fewest road/highway segments (hops), but not the shortest route in terms of total mileage. Hopefully T-SQL will add such capabilities in the future.

You can use the *SHORTEST_PATH* option to find the shortest path between a single source node and multiple target nodes, between two specific nodes, and between multiple source nodes and multiple target nodes. I'll start with a task involving finding the shortest paths between a single source node and multiple target nodes. For example, suppose that you need to find the shortest friendship paths between Orli and her direct and indirect friends.

You already know how to identify an account's direct friends using a *simple match pattern*, like so:

```
SELECT Account1.accountname AS account1,
  Account2.accountname AS account2
FROM Graph.Account AS Account1, Graph.IsFriendOf,
  Graph.Account AS Account2
WHERE MATCH(Account1-(IsFriendOf)->Account2)
  AND Account1.accountname = N'Orli';
```

This code generates the following output:

```
account1    account2
----------- -----------
Orli        Inka
Orli        Tami
Orli        Mitzi
```

You need the *SHORTEST_PATH* option to cover the indirect friendship relationships. The *SHORTEST_PATH* option allows you to specify an arbitrary length match pattern using the following syntax: MATCH(SHORTEST_PATH(`arbitrary_length_pattern`)). The pattern including the *SHORTEST_PATH* clause itself is known as an *arbitrary length match pattern*. The pattern specified inside the *SHORTEST_PATH* clause is known as an *arbitrary length pattern*. An arbitrary length pattern is essentially an extension of a simple match pattern. It involves a part that is considered once and a part that needs to be repeated. Take for example the simple match pattern from the above query identifying direct friendship relationships:

```
Account1-(IsFriendOf)->Account2
```

Remember that normally with a simple match pattern you list all relevant graph tables and their aliases in the query's *FROM* clause, and specify the table names/aliases in the pattern in the *MATCH* clause, with no part of the pattern being considered repeatedly. In our shortest path task, you want to extend the simple match pattern to an arbitrary-length one to also support indirect friendship relationships, since those can be of any arbitrary length. The starting part of the pattern is the first *from node* in the relationships, which is the node table alias *Account1* in our case. This part needs to be considered only once. So you specify the source table name and alias Graph.Account AS Account1 as usual in the query's *FROM* clause, and the alias *Account1* as the starting part of the pattern. So far that's the same as the simple match pattern. Now comes the part that is different—the part that needs to be repeated. You want to continue the pattern with an arrow pointing to the *to node*, which is *Account2* in our case, through the edge table *IsFriendOf*. In a simple match pattern, you would express this part as -(IsFriendOf)->Account2. In our arbitrary-length pattern, you somehow want to express the fact that this part needs to be considered repeatedly. This is achieved by applying the following:

- In the query's *FROM* clause, specify the graph tables from the repeating part of the pattern, each followed by the *FOR PATH* clause, followed by an alias.

- Specify the repeating part of the pattern in parentheses followed by a regular expression-based quantifier. Use the quantifier + to not limit the number of hops, and the quantifier {1, N}, where N is a positive integer value of your choosing, to limit the number of hops to N.

Considering the part that needs to be repeated in our pattern, in the query's *FROM* clause you add Graph.IsFriendOf FOR PATH AS IFO (or any other alias of your choosing) and Graph.Account FOR PATH AS Account2. As for the pattern itself, you add the part that needs to be repeated: (-(IFO)->Account2)+. You use the quantifier + to indicate that you don't want to limit the number of hops. You get the arbitrary-length pattern Account1(-(IFO)->Account2)+. The arbitrary-length match pattern then becomes SHORTEST_PATH(Account1(-(IFO)->Account2)+), and this goes into a *MATCH* clause as part of the query's *WHERE* filter. You still need to filter Orli's account as the only first *from node* of interest in our query by using another filter predicate in the *WHERE* clause.

At this point you have the query's *FROM* and *WHERE* clauses figured out:

```
FROM
  Graph.Account AS Account1,
  Graph.IsFriendOf FOR PATH AS IFO,
  Graph.Account FOR PATH AS Account2
WHERE MATCH(SHORTEST_PATH(Account1(-(IFO)->Account2)+))
  AND Account1.accountname = N'Orli'
```

There is one more thing left—the *SELECT* clause. There's something special about the rows that are delivered to the *SELECT* phase of the query's logical processing in shortest-path graph queries with an arbitrary-length match pattern. In normal graph queries, each result column value in each result row in the *SELECT* phase represents a single value. That's still the case with shortest-path queries for all columns that belong to graph objects that participate in the part of the pattern that is considered only once, such as *Account1* in our pattern. You interact with such columns in the *SELECT* clause as usual. For example, if you want to return the *accountname* column from *Account1*, you use the expression Account1.accountname. As for graph objects from the repeating part of the pattern, such as *IFO* and *Account2*, each of their column values in each result row is considered an *ordered collection*, with the order being the *graph path* order. This is probably best understood with a visual aid. Suppose that one of the shortest paths that our query found is Orli->Tami->Miko->Omer (account names shown in the path). Figure 11-4 depicts the values of the columns *Account1.accountname* (singular) and *Account2.accountname* (ordered collection) in the respective result row.

Account1.accountname	Account2.accountname
	Tami
Orli	Miko
	Omer

FIGURE 11-4 Singular versus ordered collection values from one result row

It's clear why there shouldn't be any special issues using the expression *Account1.accountname* in the *SELECT* list, since it represents a singular value per row, and indeed there are none. As for a column value representing a collection—well, that's different. Normally T-SQL requires expressions in the *SELECT* list to return singular column values per result row. For example, try running the following query:

```
SELECT Account1.accountname, Account2.accountname
FROM
  Graph.Account AS Account1,
  Graph.IsFriendOf FOR PATH AS IFO,
  Graph.Account FOR PATH AS Account2
WHERE MATCH(SHORTEST_PATH(Account1(-(IFO)->Account2)+))
  AND Account1.accountname = N'Orli';
```

The reference to *Account2.accountname* is invalid, since the column value in each result row represents a collection. You get the following error:

```
Msg 13961, Level 16, State 1, Line 1572
The alias or identifier 'Account2.accountname' cannot be used in the select list, order by,
group by, or having context.
```

T-SQL requires you to apply some manipulation to the collection-based value so that the outcome will be a singular value. To achieve this, T-SQL provides you with specialized aggregate functions known as *graph path aggregate functions*, which include *STRING_AGG, LAST_VALUE, SUM, COUNT, AVG, MIN*, and *MAX*. You provide an expression involving the collection-based column as input to the function and add the order clause *WITHIN GROUP (GRAPH PATH)*.

As an example, to form a character string-based path with the names of the accounts in the shortest friendship paths in our query, you can use the expression Account1.accountname + N'->' + STRING_AGG(Account2.accountname, N'->') WITHIN GROUP(GRAPH PATH). You start the path with *Account1.accountname* because it's not part of the *Account2.accountname* ordered collection. You then add the separator '->' or any other separator of your liking. You then concatenate the result of the *STRING_AGG* graph path aggregate applied to *Account2.accountname*, again, using '->' as the separator.

So you now have the complete solution query for our task:

```
SELECT
  Account1.accountname + N'->'
    + STRING_AGG(Account2.accountname, N'->')
        WITHIN GROUP(GRAPH PATH) AS friendships
FROM
  Graph.Account AS Account1,
  Graph.IsFriendOf FOR PATH AS IFO,
  Graph.Account FOR PATH AS Account2
WHERE MATCH(SHORTEST_PATH(Account1(-(IFO)->Account2)+))
  AND Account1.accountname = N'Orli';
```

This code generates the following output:

```
friendships
----------------------------
Orli->Inka
Orli->Tami
Orli->Mitzi
Orli->Tami->Miko
Orli->Tami->Buzi
Orli->Mitzi->Orli
Orli->Mitzi->Yatzek
Orli->Tami->Buzi->Alma
Orli->Tami->Miko->Omer
Orli->Mitzi->Yatzek->Lilach
Orli->Tami->Buzi->Alma->Stav
```

Observe that the output includes friendship paths in which the first and last nodes are the same. I'll show how to eliminate such paths from the output shortly.

As you can imagine, there could be multiple shortest paths between two nodes. An arbitrary-length match pattern is designed to return any one of them. Currently, you don't have control over which one you will get as part of the pattern.

In the above query you used the regex quantifier + to indicate that you don't want to restrict the number of hops in the shortest paths. Recall that you can use the quantifier {1, N} to restrict the number of hops to N. Here's an example for adjusting the last query to return only shortest paths with up to two hops:

```
SELECT
  Account1.accountname + N'->'
    + STRING_AGG(Account2.accountname, N'->')
        WITHIN GROUP(GRAPH PATH) AS friendships
```

```
FROM
  Graph.Account AS Account1,
  Graph.IsFriendOf FOR PATH AS IFO,
  Graph.Account FOR PATH AS Account2
WHERE MATCH(SHORTEST_PATH(Account1(-(IFO)->Account2){1, 2}))
  AND Account1.accountname = N'Orli';
```

This code generates the following output:

```
friendships
-------------------------------
Orli->Inka
Orli->Tami
Orli->Mitzi
Orli->Tami->Miko
Orli->Tami->Buzi
Orli->Mitzi->Orli
Orli->Mitzi->Yatzek
```

Note that arbitrary-length patterns don't have to start with the part that is considered only once and continue with the part that is considered repeatedly. You position each in the pattern wherever it makes sense, depending on the given task. For example, suppose that instead of returning the shortest paths *from* Orli you need to return the shortest paths *to* Orli. In order to achieve this, you will need to make a few changes to the query that finds all paths from Orli. One of the changes is to form an arbitrary-length pattern that starts with the repeating part (Account1-(IFO)->)+, and ends with Account2 as the part that is considered once, giving you the pattern (Account1-(IFO)->)+Account2. Another change is to filter the *Account2.accountname* Orli in the *WHERE* clause. I'll describe a few more changes in the upcoming paragraphs.

It would appear that when using such a pattern with the first part being the repeating part, the collection is returned in what you might consider the reversed path order. For example, *Account2. accountname* is the singular-value Orli in this example. *Account1.accountname* is the collection-based value (Tami, Miko, Alma, Stav) in this example, in this specific order. From a physical processing perspective, it is naturally sensible to start with the singular part, which is the end of the graph path in this case, and traverse the path going backward, if you will, toward the beginning. That's very likely why the collection has the items in the order that it does. To form a correct character string-based representation of the path, you could start with *Account2.accountname*. Then concatenate a left-direction arrow '<-' as a separator. Then concatenate the result of the *STRING_AGG* function applied to *Account1. accountname*, based on the graph path order, with a left-direction arrow '<-' as a separator as well. Here's the complete solution query:

```
SELECT
  Account2.accountname + N'<-'
    + STRING_AGG(Account1.accountname, N'<-')
      WITHIN GROUP(GRAPH PATH) AS friendships
FROM
  Graph.Account FOR PATH AS Account1,
  Graph.IsFriendOf FOR PATH AS IFO,
  Graph.Account AS Account2
WHERE MATCH(SHORTEST_PATH((Account1-(IFO)->)+Account2))
  AND Account2.accountname = N'Orli';
```

This query generates the following output:

```
friendships
------------------------------
Orli<-Inka
Orli<-Tami
Orli<-Mitzi
Orli<-Tami<-Miko
Orli<-Tami<-Buzi
Orli<-Mitzi<-Orli
Orli<-Mitzi<-Yatzek
Orli<-Tami<-Miko<-Alma
Orli<-Mitzi<-Yatzek<-Omer
Orli<-Mitzi<-Yatzek<-Lilach
Orli<-Tami<-Miko<-Alma<-Stav
```

And no, currently there's no support for specifying a *DESCENDING* graph path order direction.

The next task is to return the shortest path between two specific nodes—for example, return the shortest friendship path between Orli and Stav. To return a direct friendship relationship between the two, if one exists, you would use the following query with a simple match pattern, and two basic filter predicates looking for these specific account names:

```
SELECT Account1.accountname AS account1,
  Account2.accountname AS account2
FROM Graph.Account AS Account1, Graph.IsFriendOf,
  Graph.Account AS Account2
WHERE MATCH(Account1-(IsFriendOf)->Account2)
  AND Account1.accountname = N'Orli'
  AND Account2.accountname = N'Stav';
```

Apparently, Orli and Stav are not direct friends, so you get an empty set as the output of this query:

```
account1     account2
---------    -----------

(0 rows affected)
```

Next, you want to extend the query to use the *SHORTEST_PATH* option. As a starting point, you can use the same query that looked for the shortest path between Orli and her direct and indirect friends using the arbitrary-length pattern Account1(-(IFO)->Account2)+. In that query, you used the filter predicate Account1.accountname = N'Orli'. You might be tempted to now add the filter predicate Account2.accountname = N'Stav', like so:

```
SELECT
  Account1.accountname + N'->'
    + STRING_AGG(Account2.accountname, N'->')
        WITHIN GROUP(GRAPH PATH) AS friendships
FROM
  Graph.Account AS Account1,
  Graph.IsFriendOf FOR PATH AS IFO,
  Graph.Account FOR PATH AS Account2
WHERE MATCH(SHORTEST_PATH(Account1(-(IFO)->Account2)+))
  AND Account1.accountname = N'Orli'
  AND Account2.accountname = N'Stav'; -- not allowed
```

However, this attempt is invalid, since *Account2.accountname* is a collection. This query fails with the following error:

```
Msg 13961, Level 16, State 1, Line 1573
The alias or identifier 'Account2.accountname' cannot be used in the select list, order by,
group by, or having context.
```

What you really want to do is extract the last account name value from the *Account2.accountname* collection, and filter the row where that name is Stav. You can use the *LAST_VALUE* function based on graph path order for this purpose. You do so in the query's *SELECT* list and assign an alias to the result column—say, *lastnode*. You can still filter *Account1.accountname* being Orli in this query. You then define a table expression such as a CTE based on this query, and filter the row where the last node is Stav in the outer query. Here's the complete solution code:

```
WITH C AS
(
  SELECT
    Account1.accountname + N'->'
      + STRING_AGG(Account2.accountname, N'->')
          WITHIN GROUP(GRAPH PATH) AS friendships,
    LAST_VALUE(Account2.accountname)
      WITHIN GROUP (GRAPH PATH) AS lastnode -- to access last node
  FROM
    Graph.Account AS Account1,
    Graph.IsFriendOf FOR PATH AS IFO,
    Graph.Account FOR PATH AS Account2
  WHERE MATCH(SHORTEST_PATH(Account1(-(IFO)->Account2)+))
    AND Account1.accountname = N'Orli'
)
SELECT friendships
FROM C
WHERE lastnode = N'Stav';
```

This code generates the following output, showing that there is a friendship path between Orli and Stav:

```
friendships
-----------------------------
Orli->Tami->Buzi->Alma->Stav
```

Back to the task of returning all paths that lead to Orli, only getting those in correct graph path order as opposed to the reversed one, you achieve this with a minor change to the above query. Remove the inner query filter on *Account1.accountname*, and have the outer query filter be `lastnode = N'Orli'`, like so:

```
WITH C AS
(
  SELECT
    Account1.accountname + N'->'
      + STRING_AGG(Account2.accountname, N'->')
          WITHIN GROUP(GRAPH PATH) AS friendships,
    LAST_VALUE(Account2.accountname)
      WITHIN GROUP (GRAPH PATH) AS lastnode
```

```
FROM
    Graph.Account AS Account1,
    Graph.IsFriendOf FOR PATH AS IFO,
    Graph.Account FOR PATH AS Account2
  WHERE MATCH(SHORTEST_PATH(Account1(-(IFO)->Account2)+))
)
SELECT friendships
FROM C
WHERE lastnode = N'Orli';
```

This code generates the following output:

```
Friendships
----------------------------
Inka->Orli
Tami->Orli
Mitzi->Orli
Miko->Tami->Orli
Buzi->Tami->Orli
Orli->Mitzi->Orli
Yatzek->Mitzi->Orli
Alma->Miko->Tami->Orli
Omer->Yatzek->Mitzi->Orli
Lilach->Yatzek->Mitzi->Orli
Stav->Alma->Miko->Tami->Orli
```

As for returning the shortest paths between multiple source nodes and multiple target nodes, such as the shortest friendship paths between all source and target accounts, you achieve this by simply removing both account name filters. Also, if you don't need to return or filter by the last node, you don't need the CTE anymore. Here's the solution query:

```
SELECT
    Account1.accountname + N'->'
      + STRING_AGG(Account2.accountname, N'->')
          WITHIN GROUP(GRAPH PATH) AS friendships
FROM
    Graph.Account AS Account1,
    Graph.IsFriendOf FOR PATH AS IFO,
    Graph.Account FOR PATH AS Account2
WHERE MATCH(SHORTEST_PATH(Account1(-(IFO)->Account2)+));
```

This code generates the following output, shown here in abbreviated form:

```
Friendships
----------------------------
Inka->Tami
Inka->Orli
Inka->Mitzi
...
Inka->Orli->Inka
Inka->Tami->Miko
Inka->Tami->Buzi
Inka->Mitzi->Yatzek
Miko->Tami->Inka
Miko->Tami->Miko
```

```
Miko->Alma->Buzi
Miko->Tami->Orli
Miko->Alma->Stav
Miko->Yatzek->Mitzi
...
Stav->Alma->Miko->Tami->Inka
Stav->Alma->Buzi->Mitzi->Orli
```

```
(121 rows affected)
```

At this point you're very close to handling a very classic task in graph theory—returning the transitive closure of a graph. The *transitive closure* of an input graph *G* is a new graph *TC* with an output pair of nodes for every input pair of nodes that has a path, direct or indirect, between the source and target nodes. For example, the transitive closure of our friendships graph is a graph with all pairs of accounts that have a direct or indirect friendship relationship. This is achieved using our multi-multi shortest paths solution, returning only the first and last nodes from each shortest path, like so:

```
SELECT
  Account1.accountname AS firstnode,
  LAST_VALUE(Account2.accountname)
    WITHIN GROUP (GRAPH PATH) AS lastnode
FROM
  Graph.Account AS Account1,
  Graph.IsFriendOf FOR PATH AS IFO,
  Graph.Account FOR PATH AS Account2
WHERE MATCH(SHORTEST_PATH(Account1(-(IFO)->Account2)+));
```

This code generates the following output, shown here in abbreviated form:

```
firstnode  lastnode
---------- ---------
Inka       Tami
Inka       Orli
Inka       Mitzi
Miko       Tami
Miko       Alma
Miko       Omer
Miko       Yatzek
Miko       Lilach
Tami       Inka
Tami       Miko
...
Inka       Inka
Inka       Miko
Inka       Buzi
Inka       Yatzek
Miko       Inka
Miko       Miko
Miko       Buzi
Miko       Orli
Miko       Stav
Miko       Mitzi
...
```

```
Omer      Inka
Omer      Buzi
Omer      Orli
Mitzi     Stav
Lilach    Inka
Lilach    Orli
Inka      Stav
Orli      Stav
Stav      Inka
Stav      Orli
```

(121 rows affected)

Note that the above output includes self-pairs such as (Inka, Inka), as well as mirrored pairs such as (Inka, Miko) and (Miko, Inka). If you wish to remove those, you can add a filter that keeps only the pairs where *firstnode < lastnode*. You will need to use a table expression like you did before to be able to refer to the aliases of the computation results *firstnode* and *lastnode* in the outer query filter. If you also want to count the number of hops in the shortest paths, you can use the COUNT function based on graph path order. Here's the complete solution query including both the filtering part and the part that counts hops:

```
WITH C AS
(
  SELECT
    Account1.accountname AS firstnode,
    COUNT(Account2.accountid)
      WITHIN GROUP(GRAPH PATH) AS hops,
    LAST_VALUE(Account2.accountname)
      WITHIN GROUP (GRAPH PATH) AS lastnode
  FROM
    Graph.Account AS Account1,
    Graph.IsFriendOf FOR PATH AS IFO,
    Graph.Account FOR PATH AS Account2
  WHERE MATCH(SHORTEST_PATH(Account1(-(IFO)->Account2)+))
)
SELECT firstnode AS account1, lastnode AS account2, hops
FROM C
WHERE firstnode < lastnode;
```

This code generates the following output:

```
account1    account2    hops
----------- ----------- -----
Inka        Tami        1
Inka        Orli        1
Inka        Mitzi       1
Miko        Tami        1
Miko        Omer        1
Miko        Yatzek      1
Buzi        Tami        1
Buzi        Mitzi       1
Alma        Miko        1
Alma        Buzi        1
Alma        Stav        1
```

```
Alma      Yatzek     1
Alma      Lilach     1
Orli      Tami       1
Omer      Yatzek     1
Mitzi     Orli       1
Mitzi     Yatzek     1
Lilach    Miko       1
Lilach    Stav       1
Lilach    Omer       1
Lilach    Yatzek     1
Inka      Miko       2
Inka      Yatzek     2
Miko      Orli       2
Miko      Stav       2
Miko      Mitzi      2
Tami      Yatzek     2
Buzi      Inka       2
Buzi      Miko       2
Buzi      Orli       2
Buzi      Stav       2
Buzi      Yatzek     2
Buzi      Lilach     2
Alma      Tami       2
Alma      Omer       2
Alma      Mitzi      2
Orli      Yatzek     2
Stav      Yatzek     2
Omer      Tami       2
Omer      Stav       2
Mitzi     Tami       2
Mitzi     Omer       2
Lilach    Tami       2
Lilach    Mitzi      2
Inka      Omer       3
Inka      Lilach     3
Buzi      Omer       3
Alma      Inka       3
Alma      Orli       3
Stav      Tami       3
Omer      Orli       3
Mitzi     Stav       3
Lilach    Orli       3
Inka      Stav       4
Orli      Stav       4
```

Using the *LAST_NODE* function

The *LAST_NODE* function is designed to enable you to chain multiple arbitrary-length patterns. You use the function as part of an arbitrary-length pattern within the *SHORTEST_PATH* option. You apply it to some node table as input, and it represents the last node in the shortest path. You can use it to chain the end of one shortest path with the beginning of another, or to chain shortest paths at their ends.

For example, suppose that you need to identify the shortest friendship chain going from Orli to Yatzek through Stav, without Orli or Yatzek being intermediary accounts in the path. The first shortest path starts with Orli and ends with Stav, not including Yatzek as an intermediary. The second shortest path starts with Stav and ends with Yatzek, not including Orli as an intermediary. Here you need three references to the *Graph.Account* node table. One reference represents a singular node (call it *Account1*) that starts the first shortest path. A second reference represents a *for path* collection (call it *Account2*) that continues and ends the first shortest path and starts the second. You can use a derived table that filters all accounts but Yatzek as *Account2*. A third reference represents a *for path* collection (call it *Account3*) that continues and ends the second shortest path. You can use a derived table that filters all accounts but Orli as *Account3*. You also need two *for path* references to the *Graph.IsFriendOf* edge table: one to connect *Account1* with *Account2* (call it *IFO1*) and another to connect *Account2* with *Account3* (call it *IFO2*). The arbitrary-length pattern for the first shortest path is, as expected, Account1(-(IFO1)->Account2)+. The arbitrary-length pattern for the second shortest path is similar, only it starts with the *LAST_NODE* function applied to *Account2*, giving you the pattern LAST_NODE(Account2)(-(IFO2)->Account3)+. You specify each of the above arbitrary-length paths inside a *SHORTEST_PATH* option, and separate the two with an *AND* operator. You use a CTE like before, and this time you apply three account name filters. You can apply the filter predicate Account1.accountname = N'Orli' in the inner query. You use the *LAST_VALUE* function to extract the last node in the first shortest path (call it *midnode*), as well as the last node in the second path (call it *lastnode*). Then in the outer query you filter *midnode* being Stav and *lastnode* being Yatzek.

Here's the complete solution code:

```
WITH C AS
(
  SELECT
    Account1.accountname + N'->'
      + STRING_AGG(Account2.accountname, N'->')
          WITHIN GROUP(GRAPH PATH) + N'->'
      + STRING_AGG(Account3.accountname, N' >')
          WITHIN GROUP(GRAPH PATH) AS friendships,
    LAST_VALUE(Account2.accountname)
      WITHIN GROUP (GRAPH PATH) AS midnode,
    LAST_VALUE(Account3.accountname)
      WITHIN GROUP (GRAPH PATH) AS lastnode
  FROM
    Graph.Account AS Account1,
    ( SELECT * FROM Graph.Account
      WHERE accountname <> N'Yatzek' ) FOR PATH AS Account2,
    ( SELECT * FROM Graph.Account
      WHERE accountname <> N'Orli') FOR PATH AS Account3,
    Graph.IsFriendOf FOR PATH AS IFO1,
    Graph.IsFriendOf FOR PATH AS IFO2
  WHERE MATCH(SHORTEST_PATH(Account1(-(IFO1)->Account2)+)
            AND SHORTEST_PATH(LAST_NODE(Account2)(-(IFO2)->Account3)+))
    AND Account1.accountname = N'Orli'
)
SELECT friendships
FROM C
WHERE midnode = N'Stav'
  AND lastnode = N'Yatzek';
```

This code generates the following output, showing that there's a path from Orli to Yatzek through Stav, not including Orli or Yatzek as intermediate accounts:

```
friendships
-----------------------------------------------
Orli->Tami->Buzi->Alma->Stav->Lilach->Yatzek
```

Suppose that you need to return all accounts that connect Orli and Yatzek, without Orli and Yatzek as intermediaries, and the shortest path that connects the three, the third one being the friend that connects the two chains, this time not necessarily Stav. Again, the account needs to end the shortest path that starts with Orli, without Yatzek appearing as an intermediary. The same account needs to start the shortest path that ends with Yatzek, without Orli appearing as an intermediary.

To achieve this, you can use the above query as your starting point. Remove the *midnode* filter from the outer query, and add a filter to ensure that the connecting node (*midnode*) is different than both the first node and the last node. Here's the complete solution code:

```
WITH C AS
(
  SELECT
    Account1.accountname AS firstnode,
    Account1.accountname + N'->'
      + STRING_AGG(Account2.accountname, N'->')
        WITHIN GROUP(GRAPH PATH) + N'->'
      + STRING_AGG(Account3.accountname, N'->')
        WITHIN GROUP(GRAPH PATH) AS friendships,
    LAST_VALUE(Account2.accountname)
      WITHIN GROUP (GRAPH PATH) AS midnode,
    LAST_VALUE(Account3.accountname)
      WITHIN GROUP (GRAPH PATH) AS lastnode
  FROM
    Graph.Account AS Account1,
    ( SELECT * FROM Graph.Account
      WHERE accountname <> N'Yatzek' ) FOR PATH AS Account2,
    ( SELECT * FROM Graph.Account
      WHERE accountname <> N'Orli') FOR PATH AS Account3,
    Graph.IsFriendOf FOR PATH AS IFO1,
    Graph.IsFriendOf FOR PATH AS IFO2
  WHERE MATCH(SHORTEST_PATH(Account1(-(IFO1)->Account2)+)
            AND SHORTEST_PATH(LAST_NODE(Account2)(-(IFO2)->Account3)+))
    AND Account1.accountname = N'Orli'
)
SELECT friendships, midnode
FROM C
WHERE lastnode = N'Yatzek'
  AND midnode NOT IN (firstnode, lastnode);
```

This code generates the following output:

```
friendships                                    midnode
---------------------------------------------- --------
Orli->Tami->Miko->Yatzek                       Miko
Orli->Tami->Buzi->Alma->Yatzek                 Alma
Orli->Tami->Miko->Omer->Yatzek                 Omer
```

```
Orli->Mitzi->Yatzek                         Mitzi
Orli->Mitzi->Yatzek->Lilach->Yatzek         Lilach
Orli->Inka->Mitzi->Yatzek                   Inka
Orli->Tami->Miko->Yatzek                    Tami
Orli->Tami->Buzi->Alma->Yatzek              Buzi
Orli->Tami->Buzi->Alma->Stav->Lilach->Yatzek Stav
```

Let's proceed to chaining shortest paths at their ends. Suppose that you need to pair shortest paths where one starts with Orli, another with Yatzek, and both end with the same account. Orli and Yatzek cannot appear as intermediaries. Here's the solution query for this task:

```
WITH C AS
(
  SELECT
    Account1.accountname AS firstnode1,
    Account1.accountname + N'->'
      + STRING_AGG(Account2.accountname, N'->')
          WITHIN GROUP(GRAPH PATH) + N'<-'
      + STRING_AGG(Account3.accountname, N'<-')
          WITHIN GROUP(GRAPH PATH) AS friendships,
    LAST_VALUE(Account2.accountname)
      WITHIN GROUP (GRAPH PATH) AS midnode,
    LAST_VALUE(Account3.accountname)
      WITHIN GROUP (GRAPH PATH) AS firstnode2
  FROM
    Graph.Account AS Account1,
    ( SELECT * FROM Graph.Account
      WHERE accountname <> N'Yatzek' ) FOR PATH AS Account2,
    ( SELECT * FROM Graph.Account
      WHERE accountname <> N'Orli') FOR PATH AS Account3,
    Graph.IsFriendOf FOR PATH AS IFO1,
    Graph.IsFriendOf FOR PATH AS IFO2
  WHERE MATCH(SHORTEST_PATH(Account1(-(IFO1)->Account2)+)
          AND SHORTEST_PATH((Account3-(IFO2)->)+LAST_NODE(Account2)))
    AND Account1.accountname = N'Orli'
)
SELECT friendships, midnode
FROM C
WHERE firstnode2 = N'Yatzek'
  AND midnode NOT IN (firstnode1, firstnode2);
```

Observe how LAST_NODE(Account2) this time ends the second arbitrary-length pattern as opposed to starting it. Also observe the left-direction arrow used as the separator in the second path. It's also interesting to note that applying the *LAST_VALUE* function to *Account3.accountname* based on graph path order effectively returns the account name of the first node in the second shortest path, since that's the last node visited by the second arbitrary-length path. This query generates the following output:

```
friendships                                 midnode
------------------------------------------- --------
Orli->Tami->Miko<-Yatzek                    Miko
Orli->Tami->Buzi->Alma<-Yatzek              Alma
Orli->Tami->Miko->Omer<-Yatzek              Omer
Orli->Mitzi<-Yatzek                         Mitzi
```

```
Orli->Mitzi->Lilach<-Yatzek          Lilach
Orli->Inka<-Mitzi<-Yatzek            Inka
Orli->Tami<-Miko<-Yatzek             Tami
Orli->Tami->Buzi<-Alma<-Yatzek       Buzi
Orli->Tami->Buzi->Alma->Stav<-Lilach<-Yatzek  Stav
```

This output looks suspiciously similar to the previous output, other than the reversed direction of the arrow in the second path. Recall that a friendship relationship between two accounts is undirected; namely, if Buzi is friends with Alma, it also means that Alma is friends with Buzi. Consequently, chaining pairs of shortest paths where the end of one is the beginning of the other is effectively the same as chaining pairs of shortest paths where both end with the same node. But that's the case only when the graph is undirected. Try applying the same two solutions to a directed graph (aka *digraph*), such as follow relationships instead of friendship relationships, and they will have different meanings and can certainly produce different results.

Here's the first solution returning the shortest follow relationships between Orli and Yatzek through the same intermediate account, without Orli or Yatzek being intermediaries:

```
WITH C AS
(
  SELECT
    Account1.accountname AS firstnode,
    Account1.accountname + N'->'
      + STRING_AGG(Account2.accountname, N'->')
          WITHIN GROUP(GRAPH PATH) + N'->'
      + STRING_AGG(Account3.accountname, N'->')
          WITHIN GROUP(GRAPH PATH) AS followings,
    LAST_VALUE(Account2.accountname)
      WITHIN GROUP (GRAPH PATH) AS midnode,
    LAST_VALUE(Account3.accountname)
      WITHIN GROUP (GRAPH PATH) AS lastnode
  FROM
    Graph.Account AS Account1,
    ( SELECT * FROM Graph.Account
      WHERE accountname <> N'Yatzek' ) FOR PATH AS Account2,
    ( SELECT * FROM Graph.Account
      WHERE accountname <> N'Orli') FOR PATH AS Account3,
    Graph.Follows FOR PATH AS Follows1,
    Graph.Follows FOR PATH AS Follows2
  WHERE MATCH(SHORTEST_PATH(Account1(-(Follows1)->Account2)+)
              AND SHORTEST_PATH(LAST_NODE(Account2)(-(Follows2)->Account3)+))
    AND Account1.accountname = N'Orli'
)
SELECT followings, midnode
FROM C
WHERE lastnode = N'Yatzek'
  AND midnode NOT IN (firstnode, lastnode);
```

This code generates the following output:

```
followings                                     midnode
---------------------------------------------- --------
Orli->Tami->Miko->Yatzek                       Miko
Orli->Tami->Miko->Omer->Yatzek                 Omer
```

```
Orli->Mitzi->Yatzek                              Mitzi
Orli->Mitzi->Lilach->Yatzek                      Lilach
Orli->Tami->Inka->Mitzi->Yatzek                  Inka
Orli->Tami->Miko->Yatzek                         Tami
Orli->Mitzi->Buzi->Alma->Miko->Yatzek            Alma
Orli->Mitzi->Buzi->Alma->Stav->Lilach->Yatzek    Stav
Orli->Mitzi->Buzi->Tami->Miko->Yatzek            Buzi
```

Here's the second solution returning pairs of shortest follow relationships, one starting with Orli and the other with Yatzek, both ending with the same account, without Orli or Yatzek being intermediaries:

```
WITH C AS
(
  SELECT
    Account1.accountname AS firstnode1,
    Account1.accountname + N'->'
      + STRING_AGG(Account2.accountname, N'->')
        WITHIN GROUP(GRAPH PATH) + N'<-'
      + STRING_AGG(Account3.accountname, N'<-')
        WITHIN GROUP(GRAPH PATH) AS followings,
    LAST_VALUE(Account2.accountname)
      WITHIN GROUP (GRAPH PATH) AS midnode,
    LAST_VALUE(Account3.accountname)
      WITHIN GROUP (GRAPH PATH) AS firstnode2
  FROM
    Graph.Account AS Account1,
    ( SELECT * FROM Graph.Account
      WHERE accountname <> N'Yatzek' ) FOR PATH AS Account2,
    ( SELECT * FROM Graph.Account
      WHERE accountname <> N'Orli') FOR PATH AS Account3,
    Graph.Follows FOR PATH AS Follows1,
    Graph.Follows FOR PATH AS Follows2
  WHERE MATCH(SHORTEST_PATH(Account1(-(Follows1)->Account2)+)
              AND SHORTEST_PATH((Account3-(Follows2)->)+LAST_NODE(Account2)))
    AND Account1.accountname = N'Orli'
)
SELECT followings, midnode
FROM C
WHERE firstnode2 = N'Yatzek'
  AND midnode NOT IN (firstnode1, firstnode2);
```

This code generates the following output:

```
followings                                       midnode
------------------------------------------------ --------
Orli->Mitzi->Lilach<-Yatzek                      Lilach
Orli->Tami->Miko<-Lilach<-Yatzek                 Miko
Orli->Mitzi->Buzi->Alma->Stav<-Lilach<-Yatzek    Stav
Orli->Tami->Miko->Omer<-Lilach<-Yatzek           Omer
Orli->Tami<-Miko<-Lilach<-Yatzek                 Tami
Orli->Mitzi->Buzi->Alma<-Miko<-Lilach<-Yatzek    Alma
Orli->Tami->Inka<-Tami<-Miko<-Lilach<-Yatzek     Inka
Orli->Mitzi->Buzi<-Alma<-Miko<-Lilach<-Yatzek    Buzi
Orli->Mitzi<-Inka<-Tami<-Miko<-Lilach<-Yatzek    Mitzi
```

Suppose that you want to return pairs of shortest friendship and follow relationship chains that start and end with the same pair of accounts, and return for both their respective account name paths from left to right. For this purpose, T-SQL allows you to compare two *LAST_NODE* function calls, like so:

```
SELECT
  Account1.accountname + N'->'
    + STRING_AGG(Account2.accountname, N'->')
      WITHIN GROUP(GRAPH PATH) AS friendships,
  Account1.accountname + N'->'
    + STRING_AGG(Account3.accountname, N'->')
      WITHIN GROUP(GRAPH PATH) AS followings,
  Account1.accountname AS firstnode
FROM
  Graph.Account AS Account1,
  Graph.Account FOR PATH AS Account2,
  Graph.Account FOR PATH AS Account3,
  Graph.IsFriendOf FOR PATH AS IFO,
  Graph.Follows FOR PATH AS FLO
WHERE MATCH(SHORTEST_PATH(Account1(-(IFO)->Account2)+)
            AND SHORTEST_PATH(Account1(-(FLO)->Account3)+)
            AND LAST_NODE(Account2) = LAST_NODE(Account3));
```

Notice that both arbitrary-length patterns start with *Account1*, so you don't need to apply a filter saying the two paths start with the same account.

This code generates the following output, shown here in abbreviated form:

```
friendships                      followings
-----------------------------    ----------------------------------------
Inka->Tami                       Inka->Tami
Inka->Orli                       Inka->Orli
Inka->Mitzi                      Inka->Mitzi
Miko->Tami                       Miko->Tami
Miko->Alma                       Miko->Alma
Miko->Omer                       Miko->Omer
Miko->Yatzek                     Miko->Yatzek
Tami->Inka                       Tami->Inka
Tami->Miko                       Tami->Miko
Tami->Orli                       Tami->Orli
...
Orli->Tami->Buzi->Alma->Stav     Orli->Tami->Miko->Alma->Stav
Stav->Alma->Miko->Tami->Inka     Stav->Alma->Miko->Tami->Inka
Stav->Alma->Buzi->Mitzi->Orli    Stav->Alma->Miko->Tami->Orli
Omer->Yatzek->Mitzi              Omer->Miko->Tami->Inka->Mitzi
Yatzek->Mitzi->Inka              Yatzek->Lilach->Miko->Tami->Inka
Yatzek->Alma->Buzi               Yatzek->Lilach->Miko->Alma->Buzi
Yatzek->Mitzi->Orli              Yatzek->Lilach->Miko->Tami->Orli
Lilach->Yatzek->Mitzi            Lilach->Miko->Tami->Inka->Mitzi
Stav->Alma->Buzi->Mitzi          Stav->Alma->Miko->Tami->Inka->Mitzi
Yatzek->Mitzi                    Yatzek->Lilach->Miko->Tami->Inka->Mitzi

(121 rows affected)
```

You can achieve the same result without the *LAST_NODE* function by using two calls to the *LAST_VALUE* function to extract the account names of the last nodes in the two paths, and filtering only the paths where the two are the same. You would need a CTE to apply the filtering indirectly like you did before. Here's the complete solution code:

```
WITH C AS
(
  SELECT
    Account1.accountname + N'->'
      + STRING_AGG(Account2.accountname, N'->')
          WITHIN GROUP(GRAPH PATH) AS friendships,
    Account1.accountname + N'->'
      + STRING_AGG(Account3.accountname, N'->')
          WITHIN GROUP(GRAPH PATH) AS followings,
    Account1.accountname AS firstnode,
    LAST_VALUE(Account2.accountname)
      WITHIN GROUP (GRAPH PATH) AS lastnode1,
    LAST_VALUE(Account3.accountname)
      WITHIN GROUP (GRAPH PATH) AS lastnode2
  FROM
    Graph.Account AS Account1,
    Graph.Account FOR PATH AS Account2,
    Graph.Account FOR PATH AS Account3,
    Graph.IsFriendOf FOR PATH AS IFO,
    Graph.Follows FOR PATH AS FLO
  WHERE MATCH(SHORTEST_PATH(Account1(-(IFO)->Account2)+)
          AND SHORTEST_PATH(Account1(-(FLO)->Account3)+))
)
SELECT friendships, followings
FROM C
WHERE lastnode1 = lastnode2;
```

SQL Graph querying features that are still missing

As mentioned, a big part of the appeal of using the SQL Graph feature is the brevity and intuitiveness of its code compared to using traditional T-SQL code. Using match patterns saves a lot of coding that you would otherwise handle with tools like joins, subqueries, and sometimes even iterative constructs like loops. There's potential for more improvements that would make the SQL Graph feature even more appealing. Here I'll mention a couple of examples to give you a sense, but there's room for more. I'll talk about the need for weighted shortest path searches and for using arbitrary-length patterns that are not related to shortest path searches.

When describing the SHORTEST_PATH option, I explained that currently T-SQL relies on the number of hops as the only defining criterion for which path is the shortest. In reality, many shortest path problems are weighted ones. A classic use case for finding weighted shortest paths is tasks involving travel between locations. For example, suppose that you have a node table called *Location* holding locations like cities and towns, with a column called *locationname*, and an edge table called *Road* holding road segments between locations, with columns called *distance* and *avgspeed*. You want to be able to write a query that identifies the shortest path between two locations in terms of total distance or total travel time. What would be great is if the SHORTEST_PATH option allowed you to specify an expression that defines the weight alongside the specified edge. Here's a possible syntax using an imaginary *WEIGHT BY* clause for identifying the shortest path between Seattle and San Francisco in terms of total distance:

```
WITH C AS
(
  SELECT
    Location1.locationname + N'->'
      + STRING_AGG(location2.locationname, N'->')
        WITHIN GROUP(GRAPH PATH) AS route,
    LAST_VALUE(location2.locationname)
      WITHIN GROUP (GRAPH PATH) AS lastlocation
  FROM
    Location AS Location1,
    Road FOR PATH AS IsConnectedTo,
    Location FOR PATH AS Location2
  WHERE
    MATCH(SHORTEST_PATH(
      Location1(-(IsConnectedTo WEIGHT BY SUM(distance))->Location2)+))
    AND Location1.locationname = N'Seattle'
)
SELECT route
FROM C
WHERE lastlocation = N'San Francisco';
```

Note that this syntax doesn't exist. I invented it for the sake of illustration. Observe how you specify the *WEIGHT BY* clause alongside the edge alias *IsConnectedTo* that connects *Location1* to *Location2*. For the weight, you apply some aggregate to some expression. Usually the weight would be a sum of some attribute from the edge table. In the above query, the expression is SUM(distance), obviously giving you the total distance. But it could be more elaborate, such as SUM(distance * avgspeed). The default, if unspecified, is essentially equivalent to COUNT(*), which counts hops. Again, this syntax is just an example. If Microsoft will entertain the idea of adding support for a weighted shortest path, it could be that they will consider an entirely different syntax. Whatever the syntax may be, such support would be an important addition to the SQL Graph feature.

Another potentially useful feature would be allowing the use of arbitrary-length patterns even when not using the *SHORTEST_PATH* option, returning a separate row for each match as opposed to an ordered collection. Each result row would represent one *from node*–edge–*to node* match, and allow returning attributes from all three tables. Such a feature would be very handy for handling classic graph tasks such as subgraph and path without the need to resort to recursive queries or other iterative solutions. An example for a subgraph request is returning all direct and indirect replies to some input post. Currently, you can achieve this using the following recursive query (using a local variable *@postid* initialized to 13 as the input post, where the poster asks for name suggestions for a new kitten):

```
DECLARE @postid AS INT = 13;

WITH C AS
(
  SELECT ParentPost.postid AS parentpostid,
    ChildPost.postid, ChildPost.posttext
```

```
FROM Graph.Post AS ChildPost, Graph.IsReplyTo,
  Graph.Post AS ParentPost
WHERE ParentPost.postid = @postid
  AND MATCH(ChildPost-(IsReplyTo)->ParentPost)

UNION ALL

SELECT ParentPost.postid AS parentpostid,
  ChildPost.postid, ChildPost.posttext
FROM Graph.Post AS ChildPost, Graph.IsReplyTo,
  C, Graph.Post AS ParentPost
WHERE ParentPost.postid = C.postid
  AND MATCH(ChildPost-(IsReplyTo)->ParentPost)
)
SELECT parentpostid, postid, posttext
FROM C;
```

This code generates the following output:

```
parentpostid postid      posttext
------------ ----------- -------------------------------------------------
13           449         Maybe Pickle?
13           677         Ambrosius?
449          1021        It does look a bit sour faced :)
449          1031        How about Gherkin?
1031         1061        I love Gherkin!
1061         1187        So you don't like Pickle!? I'M UNFRIENDING YOU!!!
```

What would be good is if we could express the same request with an arbitrary-length pattern without the need to write so much code. Here's an example for what such code might look like:

```
DECLARE @postid AS INT = 13;

SELECT ParentPost.postid AS parentpostid,
  ChildPost.postid, ChildPost.posttext
FROM Graph.Post AS ChildPost, Graph.IsReplyTo,
  (SELECT * FROM Graph.Post WHERE postid = @postid) AS ParentPost
WHERE MATCH((ChildPost-(IsReplyTo)->)+ParentPost);
```

Remember that this code is just wishful thinking and is not currently supported, so don't try this at home. The thinking is that the arbitrary-length pattern (ChildPost-(IsReplyTo)->)+ParentPost should be internally translated into a loop that in each round handles one base ChildPost-(IsReplyTo)->ParentPost pattern. The first iteration uses the derived table representing the input post as *ParentPost* in the pattern. The remaining iterations use the previous iteration's *ChildPost* as the current iteration's *ParentPost*. The rows from the different iterations are unified. You can see the similarity here to the logic used by recursive queries, only this syntax is much more concise. Again, don't get hung up on this specific syntax; it's just an example of what's theoretically possible. The point is that there is a need for concise syntax that allows the expression of arbitrary-length patterns elsewhere than in shortest path queries, to help reduce the need for lengthy recursive queries and other iterative solutions.

Data modification considerations

Earlier in the chapter I covered various ways to insert data into node and edge graph tables, and the considerations involved. In this section I continue the coverage of data modification considerations involving graph tables, addressing deleting, updating, and merging data.

Deleting and updating data

Deleting and updating node table rows, where you need to identify the target rows based on your own provided user-defined keys, is not really special in any way. What requires a bit more effort is deleting and updating rows in edge tables, where you need to identify the edge rows based on the pair of user-defined keys of the respective *from node* and *to node* that the edge row connects. Remember that the edge row does not have the user-defined keys of the nodes it connects; rather, it has the internal system-generated keys. You will need to add a bit of logic to obtain the system-generated keys based on the user-defined ones that you will typically get as inputs.

Before I demonstrate deleting and updating graph data, run the following query to return current follow relationships where Alma is the follower:

```
SELECT
  Account1.accountid AS actid1, Account1.accountname AS actname1,
  Account2.accountid AS actid2, Account2.accountname AS actname2,
  Follows.startdate
FROM Graph.Account AS Account1, Graph.Follows,
  Graph.Account AS Account2
WHERE MATCH(Account1-(Follows)->Account2)
  AND Account1.accountid = 661; -- follower is Alma
```

This code generates the following output showing that Alma follows three accounts:

```
actid1  actname1  actid2     actname2  startdate
------- --------- ---------- --------- ----------
661     Alma      71         Miko      2021-05-16
661     Alma      421        Buzi      2021-05-18
661     Alma      941        Stav      2022-01-06
```

Suppose that Alma stops following Buzi and you need to delete the corresponding follow relationship from the *Graph.Follows* table. You get the two user-defined keys of the nodes involved as inputs. We'll use the local variables @actid1 = 661 (Alma) and @actid2 = 421 (Buzi) in our ad-hoc example for simplicity. Normally, you would have a stored procedure handling the task, with @*actid1* and @*actid2* defined as the procedure's input parameters. The *DELETE* statement is the same whether the inputs are variables in an ad-hoc example or parameters passed to a stored procedure.

One way to achieve the task is to use subqueries. You issue the *DELETE* statement against the *Graph.Follows* edge table. In the statement's filter, you compare the *$from_id* and *$to_id* columns with the results of scalar subqueries against the *Graph.Account* table that convert the input user-defined keys to the system-generated ones.

The following code handles the deletion and re-queries the data to show the post-delete follow relationships where Alma is the follower:

```
BEGIN TRAN;

DECLARE @actid1 AS INT = 661, @actid2 AS INT = 421;

DELETE FROM Graph.Follows
WHERE $from_id = (SELECT $node_id FROM Graph.Account
                    WHERE accountid = @actid1)
  AND $to_id = (SELECT $node_id FROM Graph.Account
                    WHERE accountid = @actid2);

SELECT
  Account1.accountid AS actid1, Account1.accountname AS actname1,
  Account2.accountid AS actid2, Account2.accountname AS actname2,
  Follows.startdate
FROM Graph.Account AS Account1, Graph.Follows,
  Graph.Account AS Account2
WHERE MATCH(Account1-(Follows)->Account2)
  AND Account1.accountid = 661;

ROLLBACK TRAN;
```

> **Note** I'm using a transaction here for demo purposes only. Using a transaction, you can easily revert the data back to its pre-delete state after examining the effect of the change. The code opens a transaction, applies the change, queries the data to verify what got deleted based on what's left, and then rolls the transaction back to undo the deletion. Obviously, normally you will want the change committed.

This code generates the following output showing that Alma stopped following Buzi:

actid1	actname1	actid2	actname2	startdate
661	Alma	71	Miko	2021-05-10
661	Alma	941	Stav	2022-01-06

Another way to achieve the task, which is probably a bit more elegant, is to use a match pattern. You use one *FROM* clause in the *DELETE* statement to list the tables involved in the match pattern and their aliases. In our case, you have Graph.Account AS Account1, Graph.Account AS Account2, and Graph.Follows. In the statement's *WHERE* clause you specify the *MATCH* clause with the pattern Account1-(Follows)->Account2; plus, you filter *Account1.accountid* being equal to *@actid1*, and *Account2.accountid* being equal to *@actid2*. Finally, you use a second *DELETE* clause at the top of the statement to specify that the *Follows* table is the target of the deletion.

Here's the complete solution code, followed by a query to verify the change, again encapsulated in a transaction that you roll back to undo the change:

```
BEGIN TRAN;

DECLARE @actid1 AS INT = 661, @actid2 AS INT = 421;

DELETE FROM Follows
FROM Graph.Account AS Account1, Graph.Account AS Account2,
  Graph.Follows
WHERE MATCH(Account1-(Follows)->Account2)
  AND Account1.accountid = @actid1
  AND Account2.accountid = @actid2;

SELECT
  Account1.accountid AS actid1, Account1.accountname AS actname1,
  Account2.accountid AS actid2, Account2.accountname AS actname2,
  Follows.startdate
FROM Graph.Account AS Account1, Graph.Follows,
  Graph.Account AS Account2
WHERE MATCH(Account1-(Follows)->Account2)
  AND Account1.accountid = 661;

ROLLBACK TRAN;
```

This code generates the following output, showing that Alma stopped following Buzi:

```
actid1   actname1   actid2        actname2   startdate
-------  ---------  ------------  ---------  ----------
661      Alma       71            Miko       2021-05-16
661      Alma       941           Stav       2022-01-06
```

As for updating edge tables, T-SQL does not support updating the *$from_node* and *$to_node* columns. If you need to update which nodes are involved in a given edge, you'll basically need to delete the existing edge row and introduce a new one. As for updating other attributes of an edge, you handle such updates similarly to the way you handle deletions, in terms of identifying the right rows based on given user-defined node keys.

As an example, suppose that you need to change the start date of the follow relationship between Alma and Buzi to August 2, 2021. The following code shows how to achieve the task using subqueries, only this time I use the *OUTPUT* clause to return what changed:

```
BEGIN TRAN;

DECLARE @actid1 AS INT = 661, @actid2 AS INT = 421,
  @startdate AS DATE = '20210802';

UPDATE Graph.Follows
  SET startdate = @startdate
OUTPUT deleted.startdate AS olddate, inserted.startdate AS newdate
WHERE $from_id = (SELECT $node_id FROM Graph.Account
                  WHERE accountid = @actid1)
  AND $to_id = (SELECT $node_id FROM Graph.Account
                WHERE accountid = @actid2);
```

```
ROLLBACK TRAN;
```

This code generates the following output:

```
olddate     newdate
----------  ----------
2021-05-18  2021-08-02
```

Just as with deletions, you can alternatively use a more elegant solution based on a match pattern, like so:

```
BEGIN TRAN;

DECLARE @actid1 AS INT = 661, @actid2 AS INT = 421,
  @startdate AS DATE = '20210802';

UPDATE Follows
  SET startdate = @startdate
OUTPUT deleted.startdate AS olddate, inserted.startdate AS newdate
FROM Graph.Account AS Account1, Graph.Account AS Account2,
  Graph.Follows
WHERE MATCH(Account1-(Follows)->Account2)
  AND Account1.accountid = @actid1
  AND Account2.accountid = @actid2;

ROLLBACK TRAN;
```

This code generates the same output:

```
olddate     newdate
----------  ----------
2021-05-18  2021-08-02
```

Merging data

T-SQL allows you to use the *MATCH* clause in the *MERGE* statement to identify the merge matching status, and accordingly activate the right action. This capability is available starting with SQL Server 2019 and in Azure SQL Database.

Before I demonstrate this, first use the following query to return the current follow relationships where Alma is the follower or Yatzek is the followee:

```
SELECT
  Account1.accountid AS actid1, Account1.accountname AS actname1,
  Account2.accountid AS actid2, Account2.accountname AS actname2,
  Follows.startdate
FROM Graph.Account AS Account1, Graph.Follows,
  Graph.Account AS Account2
WHERE MATCH(Account1-(Follows)->Account2)
  AND (Account1.accountid = 661 -- follower is Alma
       OR Account2.accountid = 883); -- followee is Yatzek
```

This code generates the following output:

```
actid1   actname1   actid2   actname2   startdate
-------  ---------  ------   ---------   ----------
661      Alma       421      Buzi        2021-05-18
71       Miko       883      Yatzek      2021-05-16
661      Alma       941      Stav        2022-01-06
661      Alma       71       Miko        2021-05-16
727      Mitzi      883      Yatzek      2021-02-18
199      Lilach     883      Yatzek      2022-01-14
953      Omer       883      Yatzek      2022-03-17

(7 rows affected)
```

Your task is to merge an input follow relationship represented by the variables *@actid1*, *@actid2*, and *@startdate* into the *Graph.Follows* table. I'll assign the following values to the variables in my first example: *@actid1* = 661 (Alma), *@actid2* = 421 (Buzi), `@startdate` = `'20210802'`. If the input follow relationship doesn't already exist, you're supposed to insert a new edge row representing it. Otherwise, you're supposed to update the existing edge row's *startdate* column to the new value provided in *@startdate*.

The target table you specify in the *MERGE* statement's *INTO* clause is *Graph.Follows*, of course.

As for the source for the merge activity, you're supposed to provide it in the *MERGE* statement's *USING* clause. Recall that this clause is designed similarly to a query's *FROM* clause in that it allows you to use table operators like joins. The source for our merge activity should involve two instances of the *Graph.Account* node table—one representing the *from node* of the input edge, specifically the row represented by *@actid1*, and another representing the *to node*, specifically the row represented by *@actid2*. To achieve this, you can start by forming a derived table with a single row that is based on the input variables using the syntax (SELECT @actid1, @actid2, @startdate) AS SRC(actid1, actid2, startdate). Then, use inner joins connecting *SRC* with two instances of the *Graph.Account* table to get the respective node rows.

Then, as the merge predicate in the *MERGE* statement's *ON* clause, specify a *MATCH* clause with the match pattern *Account1-(Follows)->Account2*. The nodes are defined as the source of the *MERGE* statement and the edge is defined as the target.

What's left is to apply an *UPDATE* action in the *WHEN MATCHED* clause and an *INSERT* action in the *WHEN NOT MATCHED* clause.

Here's the complete *MERGE* statement handling our task—again, using a transaction that is followed by a query that examines the data and then rolls back the change:

```
BEGIN TRAN;

DECLARE @actid1 AS INT = 661, @actid2 AS INT = 421,
  @startdate AS DATE = '20210802';

MERGE INTO Graph.Follows
USING (SELECT @actid1, @actid2, @startdate)
    AS SRC(actid1, actid2, startdate)
```

```
  INNER JOIN Graph.Account AS Account1
    ON SRC.actid1 = Account1.accountid
  INNER JOIN Graph.Account AS Account2
    ON SRC.actid2 = Account2.accountid
  ON MATCH(Account1-(Follows)->Account2)
WHEN MATCHED THEN UPDATE
  SET startdate = SRC.startdate
WHEN NOT MATCHED THEN INSERT($from_id, $to_id, startdate)
  VALUES(Account1.$node_id, Account2.$node_id, SRC.startdate);

SELECT
  Account1.accountid AS actid1, Account1.accountname AS actname1,
  Account2.accountid AS actid2, Account2.accountname AS actname2,
  Follows.startdate
FROM Graph.Account AS Account1, Graph.Follows,
  Graph.Account AS Account2
WHERE MATCH(Account1-(Follows)->Account2)
  AND (Account1.accountid = 661
      OR Account2.accountid = 883);

ROLLBACK TRAN;
```

This code generates the following output:

```
actid1  actname1  actid2  actname2  startdate
-------  --------- ------  --------- ----------
661      Alma      421     Buzi      2021-08-02
71       Miko      883     Yatzek    2021-05-16
661      Alma      941     Stav      2022-01-06
661      Alma      71      Miko      2021-05-16
727      Mitzi     883     Yatzek    2021-02-18
199      Lilach    883     Yatzek    2022-01-14
953      Omer      883     Yatzek    2022-03-17

(7 rows affected)
```

Notice that the relationship between Alma and Buzi, which already existed prior to running this code, has a changed start date.

Run another merge task, this time with a nonexistent edge where Alma (account ID 661) follows Yatzek (account ID 883), with a start date of August 2, 2021:

```
BEGIN TRAN;

DECLARE @actid1 AS INT = 661, @actid2 AS INT = 883,
  @startdate AS DATE = '20210802';

MERGE INTO Graph.Follows
USING (SELECT @actid1, @actid2, @startdate)
     AS SRC(actid1, actid2, startdate)
  INNER JOIN Graph.Account AS Account1
    ON SRC.actid1 = Account1.accountid
  INNER JOIN Graph.Account AS Account2
    ON SRC.actid2 = Account2.accountid
  ON MATCH(Account1-(Follows)->Account2)
```

```
WHEN MATCHED THEN UPDATE
  SET startdate = SRC.startdate
WHEN NOT MATCHED THEN INSERT($from_id, $to_id, startdate)
  VALUES(Account1.$node_id, Account2.$node_id, SRC.startdate);

SELECT
  Account1.accountid AS actid1, Account1.accountname AS actname1,
  Account2.accountid AS actid2, Account2.accountname AS actname2,
  Follows.startdate
FROM Graph.Account AS Account1, Graph.Follows,
  Graph.Account AS Account2
WHERE MATCH(Account1-(Follows)->Account2)
  AND (Account1.accountid = 661
      OR Account2.accountid = 883);

ROLLBACK TRAN;
```

This time a new row is inserted into the *Graph.Follows* table, as shown in the output generated by this code:

```
actid1  actname1  actid2 actname2  startdate
-------  --------- ------ --------- ----------
661     Alma      421    Buzi      2021-05-18
71      Miko      883    Yatzek    2021-05-16
661     Alma      941    Stav      2022-01-06
661     Alma      71     Miko      2021-05-16
727     Mitzi     883    Yatzek    2021-02-18
199     Lilach    883    Yatzek    2022-01-14
953     Omer      883    Yatzek    2022-03-17
661     Alma      883    Yatzek    2021-08-02

(8 rows affected)
```

Conclusion

SQL Graph is an intriguing feature. It demonstrates that you can model the same data in different ways and that traditional relational modeling is not the only option. At the same time, you do need to take into account the fact that SQL Graph-based modeling is quite a departure from traditional modeling. This means migrating existing data, using alternative syntax, and other challenges. One benefit of the SQL Graph feature is that it tends to result in less verbose queries. Another is that for some scenarios, graph-based modeling could be more intuitive. You will need to ask yourself whether using a more specialized model is worth the tradeoff. Certainly, the more functionality Microsoft adds to this feature compared to traditional modeling, the more appealing it becomes. I described a couple of examples of missing capabilities that could add more value.

To practice what you learned, perform the following exercises.

Exercises

This section provides exercises to help you familiarize yourself with the subjects discussed in Chapter 11. All exercises require you to be connected to the sample database *TSQLV6*.

Exercise 1

In this exercise, you'll query data from the tables *Graph.Account* and *Graph.Follows*.

Exercise 1-1

Write a query that identifies who follows Stav.

- Desired output:

```
accountname
--------------
Alma
Lilach

(2 rows affected)
```

Exercise 1-2

Write a query that identifies who follows Stav, Yatzek, or both.

- Desired output:

```
accountname     follows
--------------  ----------
Miko            Yatzek
Alma            Stav
Omer            Yatzek
Mitzi           Yatzek
Lilach          Stav
Lilach          Yatzek

(6 rows affected)
```

Exercise 1-3

Write a query that identifies who follows both Stav and Yatzek.

- Desired output:

```
accountname
--------------
Lilach
```

Exercise 1-4

Write a query that identifies who follows Stav but not Yatzek.

- Desired output:

```
accountname
--------------
Alma
```

Exercise 2

In this exercise, you'll query data from the tables *Graph.Account*, *Graph.IsFriendOf*, and *Graph.Follows*.

Exercise 2-1

Write a query that returns relationships where the first account is a friend of the second account, follows the second account, or both.

- Desired output:

actid1	act1	actid2	act2
2	Orli	379	Tami
2	Orli	641	Inka
2	Orli	727	Mitzi
71	Miko	199	Lilach
71	Miko	379	Tami
71	Miko	661	Alma
71	Miko	883	Yatzek
71	Miko	953	Omer
199	Lilach	71	Miko
199	Lilach	661	Alma
199	Lilach	883	Yatzek
199	Lilach	941	Stav
199	Lilach	953	Omer
379	Tami	2	Orli
379	Tami	71	Miko
379	Tami	421	Buzi
379	Tami	641	Inka
421	Buzi	379	Tami
421	Buzi	661	Alma
421	Buzi	727	Mitzi
641	Inka	2	Orli
641	Inka	379	Tami
641	Inka	727	Mitzi
661	Alma	71	Miko
661	Alma	199	Lilach
661	Alma	421	Buzi
661	Alma	883	Yatzek
661	Alma	941	Stav
727	Mitzi	2	Orli
727	Mitzi	421	Buzi
727	Mitzi	641	Inka
727	Mitzi	883	Yatzek
883	Yatzek	71	Miko
883	Yatzek	199	Lilach
883	Yatzek	661	Alma

```
883    Yatzek  727    Mitzi
883    Yatzek  953    Omer
941    Stav    199    Lilach
941    Stav    661    Alma
953    Omer    71     Miko
953    Omer    199    Lilach
953    Omer    883    Yatzek

(42 rows affected)
```

Exercise 2-2

Write a query that returns relationships where the first account is a friend of, but doesn't follow, the second account.

- Desired output:

```
actid1  act1    actid2  act2
-------  -------  -------  -------
2       Orli    641    Inka
71      Miko    199    Lilach
199     Lilach  661    Alma
379     Tami    421    Buzi
421     Buzi    727    Mitzi
661     Alma    199    Lilach
661     Alma    883    Yatzek
727     Mitzi   641    Inka
883     Yatzek  71     Miko
883     Yatzek  661    Alma
883     Yatzek  727    Mitzi
883     Yatzek  953    Omer

(12 rows affected)
```

Exercise 3

Given an input post ID, possibly representing a reply to another post, return the chain of posts leading to the input one. Use a recursive query.

- Tables involved: *Graph.Post* and *Graph.IsReplyTo*

- Desired output for input post ID 1187 as an example:

```
postid  posttext
-------  --------------------------------------------------
13      Got a new kitten. Any suggestions for a name?
449     Maybe Pickle?
1031    How about Gherkin?
1061    I love Gherkin!
1187    So you don't like Pickle!? I'M UNFRIENDING YOU!!!

(5 rows affected)
```

Exercise 4

Solve Exercise 3 again, only this time using the *SHORTEST_PATH* option.

Solutions

This section provides solutions to the Chapter 11 exercises.

Exercise 1

This exercise is split into four parts. The following sections provide the solutions to those parts.

Exercise 1-1

To identify who follows Stav, you need to query two instances of the node table *Account*, assign them different aliases—for example, *Account1* and *Account2*—and connect them with the edge table *Follows*. In the query filter you use the *MATCH* clause with the match pattern `Account2-(Follows)->Account1`. You also filter the account name in the instance *Account1* being Stav.

Here's the complete solution query:

```
SELECT Account2.accountname
FROM Graph.Account AS Account1, Graph.Account AS Account2,
  Graph.Follows
WHERE MATCH(Account2-(Follows)->Account1)
  AND Account1.accountname = N'Stav';
```

Exercise 1-2

The solution to this exercise is very similar to the solution to Exercise 1-1, with a minor change to the query filter. Simply revise the filter predicate `Account1.accountname = N'Stav'` to `Account1.accountname IN (N'Stav', N'Yatzek')`, like so:

```
SELECT Account2.accountname, Account1.accountname AS follows
FROM Graph.Account AS Account1, Graph.Account AS Account2,
  Graph.Follows
WHERE MATCH(Account2-(Follows)->Account1)
  AND Account1.accountname IN (N'Stav', N'Yatzek');
```

Exercise 1-3

This time the solution is not as trivial as the solution for Exercise 1-2 due to the requirement that the follower follows both Stav and Yatzek, as opposed to following either one or both. To satisfy the new requirement you need to query three instances of the node table *Account*—one representing Stav as the followee (aliased *Account1*), one representing Yatzek as the followee (aliased *Account2*), and one representing the follower (aliased *Account3*). You also need two instances of the edge table *Follows*—one aliased *Follows1* connecting *Account3* with *Account1*, and another aliased *Follows2* connecting *Account3* with *Account2*. Since *Account3* is the *from node* in both relationships, you can express the two relationships using a match pattern with *Account3* at the center, with arrows going in both directions toward *Account2* and *Account1* via the respective edge table aliases: `Account2<-(Follows2)-Account3-(Follows1)->Account1`. You also need additional predicates to filter Stav as the account name from *Account1* and Yatzek as the account name from *Account2*.

Here's the complete solution query:

```sql
SELECT Account3.accountname
FROM Graph.Account AS Account1, Graph.Account AS Account2,
  Graph.Account AS Account3, Graph.Follows AS Follows1,
  Graph.Follows AS Follows2
WHERE MATCH(Account2<-(Follows2)-Account3-(Follows1)->Account1)
  AND Account1.accountname = N'Stav'
  AND Account2.accountname = N'Yatzek';
```

Exercise 1-4

Remember that T-SQL doesn't currently support directly negating match predicates. However, it does support negating the *EXISTS* predicate, which in turn can have a subquery—even a correlated one—with a match predicate. With this in mind, you can achieve the task as follows:

- Have the outer query handle the part that identifies who follows Stav, similarly to the way you handled Exercise 1-1. I'll use the aliases *Account3* for the follower node, *Account1* for the followee node (Stav), and *Follows1* for the connecting edge.

- Use a *NOT EXISTS* predicate with a correlated subquery that handles the part with the account not following Yatzek. I'll use a correlation to *Account3* for the follower node, the alias *Account2* for the followee node (Yatzek), and *Follows2* for the connecting edge.

Here's the complete solution query:

```sql
SELECT Account3.accountname
FROM Graph.Account AS Account1,
  Graph.Account AS Account3, Graph.Follows AS Follows1
WHERE MATCH(Account3-(Follows1)->Account1)
  AND Account1.accountname = N'Stav'
  AND NOT EXISTS(SELECT *
                 FROM Graph.Account AS Account2,
                   Graph.Follows AS Follows2
                 WHERE MATCH(Account3-(Follows2)->Account2)
                   AND Account2.accountname = N'Yatzek');
```

Exercise 2

This exercise is split into two parts. The following sections provide the solutions to those parts.

Exercise 2-1

T-SQL doesn't currently support directly expressing a disjunction of match predicates (predicates separated by *OR* operators). You have to come up with a workaround. The long way to achieve the task is as follows:

- Write one query that identifies friendships.

- Write another query that identifies follow relationships.

- Apply a *UNION* set operator between the two queries.

Here's the complete solution code:

```
SELECT
  Account1.accountid AS actid1, Account1.accountname AS act1,
  Account2.accountid AS actid2, Account2.accountname AS act2
FROM Graph.Account AS Account1, Graph.Account AS Account2,
  Graph.IsFriendOf
WHERE MATCH(Account1-(IsFriendOf)->Account2)

UNION

SELECT
  Account1.accountid AS actid1, Account1.accountname AS act1,
  Account2.accountid AS actid2, Account2.accountname AS act2
FROM Graph.Account AS Account1, Graph.Account AS Account2,
  Graph.Follows
WHERE MATCH(Account1-(Follows)->Account2);
```

The short way to achieve the task is as follows:

- Write an outer query that interacts with two instances of the *Account* node table, aliased *Account1* and *Account2*.

- In the outer query's *WHERE* clause, use a disjunction of two *EXISTS* predicates with correlated subqueries: one connecting *Account1* and *Account2* via the *IsFriendOf* edge table, and the other connecting the two via the *Follows* edge table.

Here's the complete solution code:

```
SELECT
  Account1.accountid AS actid1, Account1.accountname AS act1,
  Account2.accountid AS actid2, Account2.accountname AS act2
FROM Graph.Account AS Account1, Graph.Account AS Account2
WHERE EXISTS (SELECT * FROM Graph.IsFriendOf
              WHERE MATCH(Account1-(IsFriendOf)->Account2))
   OR EXISTS (SELECT * FROM Graph.Follows
              WHERE MATCH(Account1-(Follows)->Account2));
```

Exercise 2-2

The solutions to this exercise are similar to the solutions to Exercise 2-1, with minor changes. The solution that uses a set operator needs to be changed to use the EXCEPT operator instead of the UNION operator, like so:

```
SELECT
  Account1.accountid AS actid1, Account1.accountname AS act1,
  Account2.accountid AS actid2, Account2.accountname AS act2
FROM Graph.Account AS Account1, Graph.Account AS Account2,
  Graph.IsFriendOf
WHERE MATCH(Account1-(IsFriendOf)->Account2)
```

```
EXCEPT

SELECT
  Account1.accountid AS actid1, Account1.accountname AS act1,
  Account2.accountid AS actid2, Account2.accountname AS act2
FROM Graph.Account AS Account1, Graph.Account AS Account2,
  Graph.Follows
WHERE MATCH(Account1-(Follows)->Account2);
```

As for the solution that uses correlated subqueries, replace the use of the *OR* operator with *AND NOT*, like so:

```
SELECT
  Account1.accountid AS actid1, Account1.accountname AS act1,
  Account2.accountid AS actid2, Account2.accountname AS act2
FROM Graph.Account AS Account1, Graph.Account AS Account2
WHERE EXISTS (SELECT * FROM Graph.IsFriendOf
               WHERE MATCH(Account1-(IsFriendOf)->Account2))
  AND NOT EXISTS (SELECT * FROM Graph.Follows
                    WHERE MATCH(Account1-(Follows)->Account2));
```

Exercise 3

Remember that using a recursive CTE you typically have an anchor member and a recursive member. To handle our task the anchor member should return the row for the input post from the *Post* node table, possibly assigning the constant 0 to a result column as a sort key. The recursive member should refer to the CTE name representing the child post from the previous round and connect it via the *IsReplyTo* edge to an instance of the node table *Post* representing the parent post. However, as a reminder, T-SQL doesn't support treating the recursive reference to the CTE name as a node table in a match pattern. The workaround is to add a reference to another instance of the node table representing the child node, and use the recursive member reference as a proxy to that instance, matching the keys of the two. Also, adding 1 to the sort key from the previous round can produce the sort key in the recursive member.

Here's the complete solution code applied to the input post 1187 in this example:

```
DECLARE @postid AS INT = 1187;

WITH C AS
(
  SELECT postid, posttext, 0 AS sortkey
  FROM Graph.Post
  WHERE postid = @postid

  UNION ALL

  SELECT ParentPost.postid, ParentPost.posttext,
    C.sortkey + 1 AS sortkey
  FROM C, Graph.Post AS ParentPost, Graph.IsReplyTo,
    Graph.Post AS ChildPost
  WHERE ChildPost.postid = C.postid -- recursive ref used as proxy
    AND MATCH(ChildPost-(IsReplyTo)->ParentPost)
)
```

```
SELECT postid, posttext
FROM C
ORDER BY sortkey DESC;
```

Alternatively, you can use explicit joins in the recursive member, matching the recursive CTE *nodeid* column with the edge table's *$from_id* column, and the edge table's *$to_id* column with the parent node's *$node_id* column.

Here's the complete solution code:

```
DECLARE @postid AS INT = 1187;

WITH C AS
(
  SELECT $node_id AS nodeid, postid, posttext, 0 AS sortkey
  FROM Graph.Post
  WHERE postid = @postid

  UNION ALL

  SELECT PP.$node_id AS nodeid, PP.postid, PP.posttext,
    CP.sortkey + 1 AS sortkey
  FROM C AS CP
    INNER JOIN Graph.IsReplyTo AS R
      ON R.$from_id = CP.nodeid
    INNER JOIN Graph.Post AS PP
      ON R.$to_id = PP.$node_id
)
SELECT postid, posttext
FROM C
ORDER BY sortkey DESC;
```

The tradeoff here is that the first solution allows you to use the native graph syntax, but at the cost of adding another table to the query and therefore some performance penalty. You can test both solutions and see if the penalty is small enough for you to justify using the native syntax.

Exercise 4

To solve the task using the *SHORTEST_PATH* option you can apply the following steps:

- Write a simple query that returns the row from the *Post* node table for the input post, assigning the constant 0 as the sort key.

- Write a graph query using the *SHORTEST_PATH* option to get all ancestor posts of the input post:

  - Query one instance of *Post* as the instance *Reply*, the *IsReplyTo* edge table with the *FOR PATH* option aliased as *IRT*, and a second instance of *Post* with the *FOR PATH* option aliased as *Post*. Use a match pattern with the *SHORTEST_PATH* option based on an arbitrary-length path that starts with *Reply*, and continues with the repeating pattern *(-(IRT)->Post)+*. Remember that the plus (+) quantifier represents one or more matches. That's how you keep going until you run out of ancestor posts.

In this query filter, the *Reply.postid* column is equal to the input *@postid*.

- Use the *LAST_VALUE* function to return the *postid* and *posttext* values of the last node in the graph path. Use the *COUNT* function to compute the sort key.

■ Unify the two queries from the previous two steps using a *UNION ALL* operator and define a CTE based on this code.

■ Have the outer query return the *postid* and *posttext* values from the CTE, and order the rows based on the sort key.

Here's the complete solution code:

```
DECLARE @postid AS INT = 1187;

WITH C AS
(
    SELECT postid, posttext, 0 AS sortkey
    FROM Graph.Post
    WHERE postid = @postid

    UNION ALL

    SELECT
      LAST_VALUE(Post.postid)   WITHIN GROUP (GRAPH PATH) AS postid,
      LAST_VALUE(Post.posttext) WITHIN GROUP (GRAPH PATH) AS posttext,
      COUNT(Post.postid)        WITHIN GROUP (GRAPH PATH) AS sortkey
    FROM
      Graph.Post AS Reply,
      Graph.IsReplyTo FOR PATH AS IRT,
      Graph.Post FOR PATH AS Post
    WHERE MATCH(SHORTEST_PATH(Reply(-(IRT)->Post)+))
      AND Reply.postid = @postid
)
SELECT postid, posttext
FROM C
ORDER BY sortkey DESC;
```

Note that none of the queries in the CTE is a recursive query.

Cleanup

When you're done reading the module and working on the exercises, run the following code for cleanup:

```
DROP TABLE IF EXISTS
  Norm.Friendships,
  Norm.Followings,
  Norm.Likes,
  Norm.AuthorsPublications,
  Norm.Posts,
  Norm.Accounts,
  Norm.Publications;

DROP TABLE IF EXISTS
  Graph.IsReplyTo,
  Graph.IsFriendOf,
  Graph.Follows,
  Graph.Posted,
  Graph.Likes,
  Graph.Authored,
  Graph.Post,
  Graph.Account,
  Graph.Publication;
GO

DROP SCHEMA IF EXISTS Norm;
DROP SCHEMA IF EXISTS Graph;
```

CHAPTER 12

Programmable objects

This chapter provides a brief overview of programmable objects to familiarize you with the capabilities of T-SQL in this area and with the concepts involved. The chapter covers variables; batches; flow elements; cursors; temporary tables; dynamic SQL; routines such as user-defined functions, stored procedures, and triggers; and error handling.

This chapter is designed, in part, to be used as a reference for describing programmability-related language elements that are mentioned earlier in the book. To be consistent with the book's focus, which is T-SQL fundamentals, and the goal to make this book accessible, this chapter was not designed to be an exhaustive guide for T-SQL programmability. Some important programmability topics are outside the scope of this book—for example, XML and JSON capabilities. If you need coverage of such topics, you can find them in other sources, such as the product documentation here:

- XML: *https://learn.microsoft.com/en-us/sql/t-sql/xml*

- JSON: *https://learn.microsoft.com/en-us/sql/relational-databases/json*

Variables

You use variables to temporarily store data values for later use in the same batch in which they were declared. I describe batches later in this chapter, but for now, the important thing for you to know is that a batch is one or more T-SQL statements sent to Microsoft SQL Server for execution as a single unit.

Use a *DECLARE* statement to declare one or more variables, and use a *SET* statement to assign a value to a single variable. For example, the following code declares a variable called @i of an *INT* data type and assigns it the value *10*:

```
DECLARE @i AS INT;
SET @i = 10;
```

Alternatively, you can declare and initialize a variable in the same statement, like this:

```
DECLARE @i AS INT = 10;
```

When you assign a value to a scalar variable, the value must be the result of a scalar expression. The expression can be a scalar subquery. For example, the following code declares a variable called

@*empname* and assigns it the result of a scalar subquery that returns the full name of the employee with an ID of 3:

```
USE TSQLV6;

DECLARE @empname AS NVARCHAR(61);

SET @empname = (SELECT firstname + N' ' + lastname
                FROM HR.Employees
                WHERE empid = 3);

SELECT @empname AS empname;
```

This code returns the following output:

```
empname
----------
Judy Lew
```

The *SET* statement can operate on only one variable at a time, so if you need to assign values to multiple variables, you need to use multiple *SET* statements. This approach can involve unnecessary overhead when you need to pull multiple attribute values from the same row. For example, the following code uses two separate *SET* statements to pull both the first and last names of the employee with an ID of 3 to two separate variables:

```
DECLARE @firstname AS NVARCHAR(20), @lastname AS NVARCHAR(40);

SET @firstname = (SELECT firstname
                         FROM HR.Employees
                         WHERE empid = 3);
SET @lastname = (SELECT lastname
                        FROM HR.Employees
                        WHERE empid = 3);

SELECT @firstname AS firstname, @lastname AS lastname;
```

This code returns the following output:

```
firstname  lastname
---------- ---------
Judy       Lew
```

T-SQL also supports a nonstandard assignment *SELECT* statement, which you use to query data and assign multiple values obtained from the same row to multiple variables by using a single statement. Here's an example:

```
DECLARE @firstname AS NVARCHAR(20), @lastname AS NVARCHAR(40);

SELECT
  @firstname = firstname,
  @lastname  = lastname
FROM HR.Employees
WHERE empid = 3;

SELECT @firstname AS firstname, @lastname AS lastname;
```

The assignment *SELECT* has predictable behavior when exactly one row qualifies. However, note that if the query has more than one qualifying row, the code doesn't fail. The assignments take place per qualifying row, and with each row accessed, the values from the current row overwrite the existing values in the variables. When the assignment *SELECT* finishes, the values in the variables are those from the last row that SQL Server happened to access. For example, the following assignment *SELECT* has two qualifying rows:

```
DECLARE @empname AS NVARCHAR(61);

SELECT @empname = firstname + N' ' + lastname
FROM HR.Employees
WHERE mgrid = 2;

SELECT @empname AS empname;
```

The employee information that ends up in the variable after the assignment *SELECT* finishes depends on the order in which SQL Server happens to access those rows—and you have no control over this order. When I ran this code, I got the following output:

```
empname
---------------
Sven Mortensen
```

But theoretically, I could have gotten Judy Lew.

The *SET* statement is safer than the assignment *SELECT* because it requires you to use a scalar subquery to pull data from a table. Remember that a scalar subquery fails at run time if it returns more than one value. For example, the following code fails:

```
DECLARE @empname AS NVARCHAR(61);

SET @empname = (SELECT firstname + N' ' + lastname
                FROM HR.Employees
                WHERE mgrid = 2);

SELECT @empname AS empname;
```

Because the variable was not assigned a value, it remains *NULL*, which is the default for variables that were not initialized. This code returns the following output:

```
Msg 512, Level 16, State 1, Line 71
Subquery returned more than 1 value. This is not permitted when the subquery follows =, !=, <,
<= , >, >= or when the subquery is used as an expression.
empname
--------
NULL
```

Batches

A batch is one or more T-SQL statements sent by a client application to SQL Server for execution as a single unit. The batch undergoes parsing (syntax checking), resolution/binding (checking the existence of referenced objects and columns, permissions checking), and optimization as a unit.

Don't confuse *transactions* and *batches*. A transaction is an atomic unit of work. A batch can have multiple transactions, and a transaction can be submitted in parts as multiple batches. When a transaction is canceled or rolled back, SQL Server undoes the partial activity that has taken place since the beginning of the transaction, regardless of where the batch began.

Client application programming interfaces (APIs) such as ADO.NET provide you with methods for submitting a batch of code to SQL Server for execution. SQL Server utilities such as SQL Server Management Studio (SSMS), Azure Data Studio (ADS), SQLCMD, and OSQL provide a client tool command called *GO* that signals the end of a batch. Note that the *GO* command is a client tool command and not a T-SQL server command. And unlike with T-SQL statements, which you're supposed to terminate with a semicolon as a best practice, you do not terminate the *GO* command, since that's not part of its syntax.

A batch as a unit of parsing

A batch is a set of commands that are parsed and executed as a unit. If the parsing is successful, SQL Server then attempts to execute the batch. In the event of a syntax error in the batch, the whole batch is not submitted to SQL Server for execution. For example, the following code has three batches, the second of which has a syntax error (*FOM* instead of *FROM* in the second query):

```
-- Valid batch
PRINT 'First batch';
USE TSQLV6;
GO
-- Invalid batch
PRINT 'Second batch';
SELECT custid FROM Sales.Customers;
SELECT orderid FOM Sales.Orders;
GO
-- Valid batch
PRINT 'Third batch';
SELECT empid FROM HR.Employees;
```

Because the second batch has a syntax error, the whole batch is not submitted to SQL Server for execution. The first and third batches pass syntax validation and therefore are submitted for execution. This code produces the following output showing that the whole second batch was not executed:

```
First batch
Msg 102, Level 15, State 1, Line 91
Incorrect syntax near 'Sales'.
Third batch
empid
-----------
2
7
```

```
1
5
6
8
3
9
4
```

```
(9 rows affected)
```

Batches and variables

A variable is local to the batch in which it's defined. If you refer to a variable that was defined in another batch, you'll get an error saying that the variable was not defined. For example, the following code declares a variable and prints its content in one batch, and then it tries to print its content from another batch:

```
DECLARE @i AS INT;
SET @i = 10;
-- Succeeds
PRINT @i;
GO

-- Fails
PRINT @i;
```

The reference to the variable in the first *PRINT* statement is valid because it appears in the same batch where the variable was declared, but the second reference is invalid. Therefore, the first *PRINT* statement returns the variable's value (*10*), whereas the second fails. Here's the output returned from this code:

```
10
Msg 137, Level 15, State 2, Line 106
Must declare the scalar variable "@i".
```

Statements that cannot be combined in the same batch

The following statements cannot be combined with other statements in the same batch: *CREATE DEFAULT, CREATE FUNCTION, CREATE PROCEDURE, CREATE RULE, CREATE SCHEMA, CREATE TRIGGER*, and *CREATE VIEW*. For example, the following code has a *DROP* statement followed by a *CREATE VIEW* statement in the same batch and therefore is invalid:

```
DROP VIEW IF EXISTS Sales.MyView;

CREATE VIEW Sales.MyView
AS

SELECT YEAR(orderdate) AS orderyear, COUNT(*) AS numorders
FROM Sales.Orders
GROUP BY YEAR(orderdate);
GO
```

An attempt to run this code generates the following error:

```
Msg 111, Level 15, State 1, Line 113
'CREATE VIEW' must be the first statement in a query batch.
```

To get around the problem, separate the *DROP VIEW* and *CREATE VIEW* statements into different batches by adding a *GO* command after the *DROP VIEW* statement.

A batch as a unit of resolution

A batch is a unit of resolution (also known as *binding*). This means that checking the existence of objects and columns happens at the batch level. Keep this fact in mind when you're designing batch boundaries. When you apply schema changes to an object and try to manipulate the object data in the same batch, SQL Server might not be aware of the schema changes yet and fail the data-manipulation statement with a resolution error. I'll demonstrate the problem through an example and then recommend best practices.

Run the following code to create a table called *T1* in the current database, with one column called *col1*:

```
DROP TABLE IF EXISTS dbo.T1;
CREATE TABLE dbo.T1(col1 INT);
```

Next, try to add a column called *col2* to *T1* and query the new column in the same batch:

```
ALTER TABLE dbo.T1 ADD col2 INT;
SELECT col1, col2 FROM dbo.T1;
```

Even though the code might seem to be perfectly valid, the batch fails during the resolution phase with the following error:

```
Msg 207, Level 16, State 1, Line 130
Invalid column name 'col2'.
```

At the time the *SELECT* statement was resolved, *T1* had only one column, and the reference to the *col2* column caused the error. One best practice you can follow to avoid such problems is to separate data definition language (DDL) and data manipulation language (DML) statements into different batches, as in the following example:

```
ALTER TABLE dbo.T1 ADD col2 INT;
GO
SELECT col1, col2 FROM dbo.T1;
```

The *GO n* option

The *GO* command is not really a T-SQL command; it's actually a command used by SQL Server's client tools, such as SSMS, to denote the end of a batch. This command supports an argument indicating how many times you want to execute the batch. To see how the *GO* command with the argument works, first create the table *T1* by using the following code:

```
DROP TABLE IF EXISTS dbo.T1;
CREATE TABLE dbo.T1(col1 INT IDENTITY);
```

The *col1* column gets its values automatically from an identity property. Note that the demo works just as well if you use a default constraint to generate values from a sequence object. Next, run the following code to suppress the default output produced by DML statements that indicates how many rows were affected:

```
SET NOCOUNT ON;
```

Finally, run the following code to define a batch with an *INSERT DEFAULT VALUES* statement and to execute the batch 100 times:

```
INSERT INTO dbo.T1 DEFAULT VALUES;
GO 100
```

```
SELECT * FROM dbo.T1;
```

The query returns 100 rows with the values *1* through *100* in *col1*.

Flow elements

You use flow elements to control the flow of your code. T-SQL provides basic forms of control with flow elements, including the *IF . . . ELSE* element and the *WHILE* element.

The *IF . . . ELSE* flow element

You use the *IF . . . ELSE* element to control the flow of your code based on the result of a predicate. You specify a statement or statement block that is executed if the predicate is *TRUE*, and optionally a statement or statement block that is executed if the predicate is *FALSE* or *UNKNOWN*.

For example, the following code checks whether today is the last day of the year (in other words, whether today's year is different than tomorrow's year). If this is true, the code prints a message saying that today is the last day of the year; if it's not true ("else"), the code prints a message saying that today is not the last day of the year:

```
IF YEAR(SYSDATETIME()) <> YEAR(DATEADD(day, 1, SYSDATETIME()))
  PRINT 'Today is the last day of the year.';
ELSE
  PRINT 'Today is not the last day of the year.';
```

In this example, I use *PRINT* statements to demonstrate which parts of the code were executed and which weren't, but of course you can specify other statements as well.

Keep in mind that T-SQL uses three-valued logic and that the *ELSE* block is activated when the predicate is either *FALSE* or *UNKNOWN*. In cases for which both *FALSE* and *UNKNOWN* are possible outcomes of the predicate (for example, when *NULLs* are involved) and you need different treatment for each case, make sure you have an explicit test for *NULLs* with the *IS NULL* predicate.

If the flow you need to control involves more than two cases, you can nest *IF . . . ELSE* elements. For example, the next code I'll show you handles the following three cases differently:

- Today is the last day of the year.

- Today is the last day of the month but not the last day of the year.

- Today is not the last day of the month.

```
IF YEAR(SYSDATETIME()) <> YEAR(DATEADD(day, 1, SYSDATETIME()))
  PRINT 'Today is the last day of the year.';
ELSE
  IF MONTH(SYSDATETIME()) <> MONTH(DATEADD(day, 1, SYSDATETIME()))
    PRINT 'Today is the last day of the month but not the last day of the year.';
  ELSE
    PRINT 'Today is not the last day of the month.';
```

If you need to run more than one statement in the *IF* or *ELSE* sections, you need to use a statement block. You mark the boundaries of a statement block with the *BEGIN* and *END* keywords. For example, the following code shows how to run one type of process if it's the first day of the month and another type of process if it isn't:

```
IF DAY(SYSDATETIME()) = 1
BEGIN
  PRINT 'Today is the first day of the month.';
  PRINT 'Starting first-of-month-day process.';
  /* ... process code goes here ... */
  PRINT 'Finished first-of-month-day database process.';
END;
ELSE
BEGIN
  PRINT 'Today is not the first day of the month.';
  PRINT 'Starting non-first-of-month-day process.';
  /* ... process code goes here ... */
  PRINT 'Finished non-first-of-month-day process.';
END;
```

The *WHILE* flow element

T-SQL provides the *WHILE* element, which you can use to execute code in a loop. The *WHILE* element executes a statement or statement block repeatedly while the predicate you specify after the *WHILE* keyword is *TRUE*. When the predicate is *FALSE* or *UNKNOWN*, the loop terminates.

T-SQL doesn't provide a built-in looping element that executes a predetermined number of times, but it's easy to mimic such an element with a *WHILE* loop and a variable. For example, the following code demonstrates how to write a loop that iterates 10 times:

```
DECLARE @i AS INT = 1;
WHILE @i <= 10
BEGIN
  PRINT @i;
  SET @i = @i + 1;
END;
```

The code declares an integer variable called @*i* that serves as the loop counter and initializes it with the value *1*. The code then enters a loop that iterates while the variable is smaller than or equal to *10*. In each iteration, the code in the loop's body prints the current value of @*i* and then increments it by 1. This code returns the following output showing that the loop iterated 10 times:

```
1
2
3
4
5
6
7
8
9
10
```

If at some point in the loop's body you want to break out of the current loop and proceed to execute the statement that appears after the loop's body, use the *BREAK* command. For example, the following code breaks from the loop if the value of @*i* is equal to 6:

```
DECLARE @i AS INT = 1;
WHILE @i <= 10
BEGIN
  IF @i = 6 BREAK;
  PRINT @i;
  SET @i = @i + 1;
END;
```

This code produces the following output showing that the loop iterated five times and terminated at the beginning of the sixth iteration:

```
1
2
3
4
5
```

Of course, this code is not very sensible; if you want the loop to iterate only five times, you should simply specify the predicate @*i* <= 5. Here I just wanted to demonstrate the use of the *BREAK* command with a simple example.

If at some point in the loop's body you want to skip the rest of the activity in the current iteration and evaluate the loop's predicate again, use the *CONTINUE* command. For example, the following code demonstrates how to skip the activity of the sixth iteration of the loop from the point where the *IF* statement appears and until the end of the loop's body:

```
DECLARE @i AS INT = 0;
WHILE @i < 10
BEGIN
  SET @i = @i + 1;
  IF @i = 6 CONTINUE;
  PRINT @i;
END;
```

The output of this code shows that the value of @*i* was printed in all iterations except the sixth:

```
1
2
3
4
5
7
8
9
10
```

As another example of using a *WHILE* loop, the following code creates a table called *dbo.Numbers* and populates it with 1,000 rows with the values *1* through *1,000* in the column *n*:

```
SET NOCOUNT ON;
DROP TABLE IF EXISTS dbo.Numbers;
CREATE TABLE dbo.Numbers(n INT NOT NULL PRIMARY KEY);
GO

DECLARE @i AS INT = 1;
WHILE @i <= 1000
BEGIN
  INSERT INTO dbo.Numbers(n) VALUES(@i);
  SET @i = @i + 1;
END;
```

Cursors

In Chapter 2, "Single-table queries," I explained that a query without an *ORDER BY* clause returns a set (or a multiset), whereas a query with an *ORDER BY* clause returns what standard SQL calls a *cursor*—a nonrelational result with order guaranteed among rows. In the context of the discussion in Chapter 2, the use of the term "cursor" was conceptual. SQL and T-SQL also support an object called *cursor* you can use to process rows from a result of a query one at a time and in a requested order. This is in contrast to using set-based queries—normal queries without a cursor for which you manipulate the set or multiset as a whole and cannot rely on order.

I want to stress that your default choice should be to use set-based queries; only when you have a compelling reason to do otherwise should you consider using cursors. This recommendation is based on several factors, including the following:

- First and foremost, when you use cursors you pretty much go against the relational model, which is based on set theory.

- The record-by-record manipulation done by the cursor has overhead. A certain extra cost is associated with each record manipulation by the cursor compared to set-based manipulation. Given a set-based query and cursor code that do similar physical processing behind the scenes, the cursor code is usually many times slower than the set-based code.

- With cursors, you write imperative solutions—in other words, you're responsible for defining how to process the data (declaring the cursor, opening it, looping through the cursor records, closing the cursor, and deallocating the cursor). With set-based solutions, you write declarative code where you mainly focus on the logical aspects of the solution—in other words, on what to get instead of on how to get it. Therefore, cursor solutions tend to be longer, less readable, and harder to maintain than set-based solutions.

For most people, it's not simple to think in relational terms immediately when they start learning SQL. It's more intuitive for most people to think in terms of cursors—processing one record at a time in a certain order. As a result, cursors are widely used, and in most cases they are misused; that is, they are used even when much better set-based solutions exist. Make a conscious effort to adopt the set-based state of mind and to truly think in terms of sets. It can take time—in some cases years—but as long as you're working with a language that is based on the relational model, that's the right way to think.

Every rule has exceptions. One example is when you need to apply a certain task to each row from some table or view. For example, you might need to execute some administrative task for each index or table in your database. In such a case, it makes sense to use a cursor to iterate through the index or table names one at a time and execute the relevant task for each of those.

Another example of when you should consider cursors is when your set-based solution performs badly and you exhaust your tuning efforts using the set-based approach. As mentioned, set-based solutions tend to be much faster, but in some exceptional cases the cursor solution is faster. One such example is computing running aggregates using T-SQL code that is compatible with legacy versions of SQL Server that don't support the frame option in window functions. Relational solutions to running aggregates using joins or subqueries are extremely slow. An iterative solution, such as one based on a cursor, is usually the optimal one. If there are no compatibility restrictions, using a relational solution with window functions is the optimal way to compute running totals.

Working with a cursor generally involves the following steps:

1. Declare the cursor based on a query.

2. Open the cursor.

3. Fetch attribute values from the first cursor record into variables.

4. As long as you haven't reached the end of the cursor (while the value of a function called @@FETCH_STATUS is 0), loop through the cursor records; in each iteration of the loop, perform the processing needed for the current row, and then fetch the attribute values from the next row into the variables.

5. Close the cursor.

6. Deallocate the cursor.

The following example with cursor code calculates the running total quantity for each customer and month from the *Sales.CustOrders* view:

```
-- Suppress messages indicating how many rows were affected
SET NOCOUNT ON;

-- Declare table variable to hold the final result
DECLARE @Result AS TABLE
(
  custid     INT,
  ordermonth DATE,
  qty        INT,
  runqty     INT,
  PRIMARY KEY(custid, ordermonth)
);

-- Declare local variables that are used to store intermediate values
DECLARE
  @custid    AS INT,
  @prvcustid AS INT,
  @ordermonth AS DATE,
  @qty       AS INT,
  @runqty    AS INT;

-- Step 1: Declare the cursor based on a query
DECLARE C CURSOR FAST_FORWARD /* read only, forward only */ FOR
  SELECT custid, ordermonth, qty
  FROM Sales.CustOrders
  ORDER BY custid, ordermonth;

-- Step 2: Open the cursor
OPEN C;

-- Step 3: Fetch attribute values from the first cursor record into variables
FETCH NEXT FROM C INTO @custid, @ordermonth, @qty;

-- Initialize variables
SELECT @prvcustid = @custid, @runqty = 0;

-- Step 4: Loop through the cursor records while last fetch was successful
--         In each iteration:
--             Reset variables if customer ID changes
--             Compute current running total and insert into table variable
--             Fetch next cursor record
WHILE @@FETCH_STATUS = 0
BEGIN
```

```
  IF @custid <> @prvcustid
    SELECT @prvcustid = @custid, @runqty = 0;

  SET @runqty = @runqty + @qty;

  INSERT INTO @Result VALUES(@custid, @ordermonth, @qty, @runqty);

  FETCH NEXT FROM C INTO @custid, @ordermonth, @qty;
END;

-- Step 5: Close the cursor
CLOSE C;

-- Step 6: Deallocate the cursor
DEALLOCATE C;

-- Enable showing messages indicating how many rows were affected
SET NOCOUNT OFF;

-- Query the table variable to return the final result
SELECT
  custid,
  CONVERT(VARCHAR(7), ordermonth, 121) AS ordermonth,
  qty,
  runqty
FROM @Result
ORDER BY custid, ordermonth;
```

Let's examine this code based on the aforementioned steps:

1. Declare the cursor based on a query.

    The code starts by declaring a table variable that will hold the final result as well as some local variables that are used to store intermediate values. The code then uses the *DECLARE CURSOR* command to declare a cursor called C based on a query that returns the rows from the *CustOrders* view ordered by customer ID and order month.

2. Open the cursor.

    The code then opens cursor C using the *OPEN* command.

3. Fetch attribute values from the first cursor record into variables.

    The code then fetches the values from the first cursor record using the *FETCH* command into local variables.

4. Loop through cursor records.

    The code proceeds to initialize local variables. Then it loops through the cursor records while the last fetch was successful. In each iteration, the code resets variables if the customer ID changes, computes the current running total and inserts it into the table variable, and fetches the next cursor record with a *FETCH* command.

5. Close the cursor.

The code then closes cursor C using the *CLOSE* command.

6. Deallocate the cursor.

Finally, the code deallocates cursor C using the *DEALLOCATE* command, re-enables showing how many rows were affected, and queries the table variable to return the final result.

Here's the output returned by this code, shown in abbreviated form:

```
custid       ordermonth qty        runqty
-----------  ---------- ---------- -----------
1            2021-08    38         38
1            2021-10    41         79
1            2022-01    17         96
1            2022-03    18         114
1            2022-04    60         174
2            2020-09    6          6
2            2021-08    18         24
2            2021-11    10         34
2            2022-03    29         63
3            2020-11    24         24
3            2021-04    30         54
3            2021-05    80         134
3            2021-06    83         217
3            2021-09    102        319
3            2022-01    40         359
...
89           2020-07    80         80
89           2020-11    105        185
89           2021-03    142        327
89           2021-04    59         386
89           2021-07    59         445
89           2021-10    164        609
89           2021-11    94         703
89           2022-01    140        843
89           2022-02    50         893
89           2022-04    90         983
89           2022-05    80         1063
90           2021-07    5          5
90           2021-09    15         20
90           2021-10    34         54
90           2022-02    82         136
90           2022-04    12         148
91           2020-12    45         45
91           2021-07    31         76
91           2021-12    28         104
91           2022-02    20         124
91           2022-04    81         205

(636 rows affected)
```

As explained in Chapter 7, "T-SQL for data analysis," T-SQL supports window functions you can use to provide elegant and highly efficient solutions to running aggregates, freeing you from needing to use cursors. Here's how you address the same task with a window function:

```
SELECT custid, ordermonth, qty,
  SUM(qty) OVER(PARTITION BY custid
                ORDER BY ordermonth
                ROWS UNBOUNDED PRECEDING) AS runqty
FROM Sales.CustOrders
ORDER BY custid, ordermonth;
```

Temporary tables

When you need to temporarily store data in tables, in certain cases you might prefer not to work with permanent tables. Suppose you need the data to be visible only to the current session, or even only to the current batch. As an example, suppose you need to store temporary data during data processing, as in the cursor example in the previous section. Another case where people use temporary tables is when they don't have permissions to create permanent tables in a user database.

SQL Server supports three kinds of temporary tables you might find more convenient to work with than permanent tables in such cases: local temporary tables, global temporary tables, and table variables. The following sections describe the three kinds and demonstrate their use with code samples.

Local temporary tables

You create a local temporary table by naming it with a single number sign (#) as a prefix, such as #T1. All three kinds of temporary tables are created in the *tempdb* database.

A local temporary table is visible only to the session that created it, in the creating level and all inner levels in the call stack (inner procedures, triggers, and dynamic batches). A local temporary table is destroyed automatically by SQL Server when the creating level in the call stack goes out of scope. For example, suppose a stored procedure called *Proc1* calls a procedure called *Proc2*, which in turn calls a procedure called *Proc3*, which in turn calls a procedure called *Proc4*. *Proc2* creates a temporary table called #T1 before calling *Proc3*. The table #T1 is visible to *Proc2*, *Proc3*, and *Proc4* but not to *Proc1*, and it's destroyed automatically by SQL Server when *Proc2* finishes. If the temporary table is created in an ad-hoc batch in the outermost nesting level of the session (in other words, when the value of the @@NESTLEVEL function is 0), it's visible to all subsequent batches as well and is destroyed by SQL Server automatically only when the creating session disconnects.

You might wonder how SQL Server prevents name conflicts when two sessions create local temporary tables with the same name. SQL Server internally adds a suffix to the table name that makes it unique in *tempdb*. As a developer, you shouldn't care—you refer to the table using the name you provided without the internal suffix, and only your session has access to your table.

One obvious scenario for which local temporary tables are useful is when you have a process that needs to store intermediate results temporarily—such as during a loop—and later query the data.

Another scenario is when you need to access the result of some expensive processing multiple times. For example, suppose you need to join the *Sales.Orders* and *Sales.OrderDetails* tables, aggregate order quantities by order year, and join two instances of the aggregated data to compare each year's total quantity with the previous year. The *Orders* and *OrderDetails* tables in the sample database are very small, but in real-life situations such tables can have millions of rows. One option is to use table expressions, but remember that table expressions are virtual. The expensive work involving scanning all the data, joining the *Orders* and *OrderDetails* tables, and aggregating the data would have to happen twice with table expressions. Instead, it makes sense to do all the expensive work only once—storing the result in a local temporary table—and then join two instances of the temporary table, especially because the result of the expensive work is a tiny set with only one row per order year.

The following code illustrates this scenario using a local temporary table:

```
DROP TABLE IF EXISTS #MyOrderTotalsByYear;
GO

CREATE TABLE #MyOrderTotalsByYear
(
  orderyear INT NOT NULL PRIMARY KEY,
  qty       INT NOT NULL
);

INSERT INTO #MyOrderTotalsByYear(orderyear, qty)
  SELECT
    YEAR(O.orderdate) AS orderyear,
    SUM(OD.qty) AS qty
  FROM Sales.Orders AS O
    INNER JOIN Sales.OrderDetails AS OD
      ON OD.orderid = O.orderid
  GROUP BY YEAR(orderdate);

SELECT Cur.orderyear, Cur.qty AS curyearqty, Prv.qty AS prvyearqty
FROM #MyOrderTotalsByYear AS Cur
  LEFT OUTER JOIN #MyOrderTotalsByYear AS Prv
    ON Cur.orderyear = Prv.orderyear + 1;
```

This code produces the following output:

```
orderyear   curyearqty  prvyearqty
----------- ----------- -----------
2020        9581        NULL
2021        25489       9581
2022        16247       25489
```

To verify that the local temporary table is visible only to the creating session, try accessing it from another session:

```
SELECT orderyear, qty FROM #MyOrderTotalsByYear;
```

You get the following error:

```
Msg 208, Level 16, State 0, Line 1
Invalid object name '#MyOrderTotalsByYear'.
```

When you're done, go back to the original session and drop the temporary table:

```
DROP TABLE IF EXISTS #MyOrderTotalsByYear;
```

It's generally recommended that you clean up resources as soon as you're done working with them.

Global temporary tables

When you create a global temporary table, it's visible to all other sessions. Global temporary tables are destroyed automatically by SQL Server when the creating session disconnects and there are no active references to the table. You create a global temporary table by naming it with a double number sign (##) as a prefix, such as *##T1*.

Global temporary tables are useful when you want to share temporary data with everyone. No special permissions are required, and everyone has full DDL and DML access. That's the case even if you populate global temporary tables with data from sources that the target users don't have permissions to access. Of course, the fact that everyone has full access means that anyone can change or even drop the table, so consider the alternatives carefully.

For example, the following code creates a global temporary table called *##Globals* with columns called *id* and *val*:

```
CREATE TABLE ##Globals
(
  id   sysname      NOT NULL PRIMARY KEY,
  val SQL_VARIANT NOT NULL
);
```

The table in this example is intended to mimic global variables, which are not supported in T-SQL. The *id* column is of a *sysname* data type (the type that SQL Server uses internally to represent identifiers), and the *val* column is of a *SQL_VARIANT* data type (a generic type that can store within it a value of almost any base type).

Anyone can insert rows into the table. For example, run the following code to insert a row representing a variable called *i* and initialize it with the integer value *10*:

```
INSERT INTO ##Globals(id, val) VALUES(N'I', CAST(10 AS INT));
```

Anyone can modify and retrieve data from the table. For example, run the following code from any session to query the current value of the variable *i*:

```
SELECT val FROM ##Globals WHERE id = N'I';
```

This code returns the following output:

```
val
-----------
10
```

Note Keep in mind that as soon as the session that created the global temporary table disconnects and there are no active references to the table, SQL Server automatically destroys the table.

If you want a global temporary table to be created every time SQL Server starts, and you don't want SQL Server to try to destroy it automatically, you need to create the table from a stored procedure that is marked as a startup procedure. (For details, see "sp_procoption" in the product documentation at the following URL: *https://learn.microsoft.com/en-us/sql/relational-databases/system-stored-procedures/sp-procoption-transact-sql*.)

Run the following code from any session to explicitly destroy the global temporary table:

```
DROP TABLE IF EXISTS ##Globals;
```

Table variables

Table variables are similar to local temporary tables in some ways and different in others. You declare table variables much like you declare other variables, by using the *DECLARE* statement.

As with local temporary tables, table variables have a physical presence as a table in the *tempdb* database, contrary to the common misconception that they exist only in memory. Like local temporary tables, table variables are visible only to the creating session, but because they are variables they have a more limited scope: only the current batch. Table variables are visible neither to inner batches in the call stack nor to subsequent batches in the session.

If an explicit transaction is rolled back, changes made to temporary tables in that transaction are rolled back as well; however, changes made to table variables by statements that completed in the transaction aren't rolled back. Only changes made by the active statement that failed or that was terminated before completion are undone.

Temporary tables and table variables also have optimization differences, but those topics are outside the scope of this book. For now, I'll just say that in terms of performance, usually it makes more sense to use table variables with small volumes of data (only a few rows) and to use local temporary tables otherwise.

For example, the following code uses a table variable instead of a local temporary table to compare total order quantities of each order year with the year before:

```
DECLARE @MyOrderTotalsByYear TABLE
(
  orderyear INT NOT NULL PRIMARY KEY,
  qty       INT NOT NULL
);

INSERT INTO @MyOrderTotalsByYear(orderyear, qty)
  SELECT
    YEAR(O.orderdate) AS orderyear,
```

```
    SUM(OD.qty) AS qty
FROM Sales.Orders AS O
  INNER JOIN Sales.OrderDetails AS OD
    ON OD.orderid = O.orderid
GROUP BY YEAR(orderdate);

SELECT Cur.orderyear, Cur.qty AS curyearqty, Prv.qty AS prvyearqty
FROM @MyOrderTotalsByYear AS Cur
  LEFT OUTER JOIN @MyOrderTotalsByYear AS Prv
    ON Cur.orderyear = Prv.orderyear + 1;
```

This code returns the following output:

```
orderyear    curyearqty   prvyearqty
-----------  -----------  -----------
2020         9581         NULL
2021         25489        9581
2022         16247        25489
```

Note that instead of using a table variable or a temporary table and a self-join here, this particular task can be handled alternatively with the *LAG* function, like this:

```
SELECT
  YEAR(O.orderdate) AS orderyear,
  SUM(OD.qty) AS curyearqty,
  LAG(SUM(OD.qty)) OVER(ORDER BY YEAR(orderdate)) AS prvyearqty
FROM Sales.Orders AS O
  INNER JOIN Sales.OrderDetails AS OD
    ON OD.orderid = O.orderid
GROUP BY YEAR(orderdate);
```

Table types

You can use a table type to preserve a table definition, or metadata, as an object in the database. Later you can reuse it as the table definition of table variables and input parameters of stored procedures and user-defined functions. Table types are required for table-valued parameters (TVPs).

For example, the following code creates a table type called *dbo.OrderTotalsByYear* in the current database:

```
DROP TYPE IF EXISTS dbo.OrderTotalsByYear;

CREATE TYPE dbo.OrderTotalsByYear AS TABLE
(
  orderyear INT NOT NULL PRIMARY KEY,
  qty       INT NOT NULL
);
```

After the table type is created, whenever you need to declare a table variable based on the table type's definition, you won't need to repeat the code—instead, you can simply specify *dbo.OrderTotalsByYear* as the variable's type, like this:

```
DECLARE @MyOrderTotalsByYear AS dbo.OrderTotalsByYear;
```

As a more complete example, the following code declares a variable called *@MyOrderTotalsByYear* of the new table type, queries the *Orders* and *OrderDetails* tables to calculate total order quantities by order year, stores the result of the query in the table variable, and queries the variable to present its contents:

```
DECLARE @MyOrderTotalsByYear AS dbo.OrderTotalsByYear;

INSERT INTO @MyOrderTotalsByYear(orderyear, qty)
  SELECT
    YEAR(O.orderdate) AS orderyear,
    SUM(OD.qty) AS qty
  FROM Sales.Orders AS O
    INNER JOIN Sales.OrderDetails AS OD
      ON OD.orderid = O.orderid
  GROUP BY YEAR(orderdate);

SELECT orderyear, qty FROM @MyOrderTotalsByYear;
```

This code returns the following output:

```
orderyear   qty
----------- -----------
2020        9581
2021        25489
2022        16247
```

The benefit of the table type feature extends beyond just helping you shorten your code. As I mentioned, you can use it as the type of input parameters of stored procedures and functions, which is a useful capability.

Dynamic SQL

With SQL Server, you can construct a batch of T-SQL code as a character string and then execute that batch. This capability is called *dynamic SQL*. SQL Server provides two ways of executing dynamic SQL: using the *EXEC* (short for *EXECUTE*) command and using the *sp_executesql* stored procedure. I will explain the difference between the two and provide examples for using each.

Dynamic SQL is useful for several purposes, including the following ones:

- **Automating administrative tasks**   For example, querying metadata and constructing and executing a *BACKUP DATABASE* statement for each database in the instance

- **Improving performance of certain tasks**   For example, constructing parameterized ad-hoc queries that can reuse previously cached execution plans (more on this later)

- **Constructing elements of the code based on querying the actual data**   For example, constructing a *PIVOT* query dynamically when you don't know ahead of time which elements should appear in the *IN* clause of the *PIVOT* operator

> **Note** Be extremely careful when concatenating user input as part of your code. Hackers can attempt to inject code you did not intend to run. The best measure you can take against SQL injection is to avoid concatenating user input as part of your code (for example, by using parameters). If you do concatenate user input as part of your code, make sure you thoroughly inspect the input and look for SQL injection attempts. You can find an article on the subject in the product documentation at the following URL: *https://learn.microsoft.com/en-us/sql/relational-databases/security/sql-injection*.

The *EXEC* command

The *EXEC* command accepts a character string in parentheses as input and executes the batch of code within the character string. *EXEC* supports both regular and Unicode character strings as input. This command can also be used to execute a stored procedure, as I will demonstrate later in the chapter.

The following example stores a character string with a *PRINT* statement in the variable *@sql* and then uses the *EXEC* command to invoke the batch of code stored within the variable:

```
DECLARE @sql AS VARCHAR(100);
SET @sql = 'PRINT ''This message was printed by a dynamic SQL batch.'';';
EXEC(@sql);
```

Notice the use of two single quotes to represent one single quote in a string within a string. This code returns the following output:

```
This message was printed by a dynamic SQL batch.
```

The *sp_executesql* stored procedure

The *sp_executesql* stored procedure is an alternative tool to the *EXEC* command for executing dynamic SQL code. It's more secure and more flexible in the sense that it has an interface; that is, it supports input and output parameters. Note that unlike *EXEC*, *sp_executesql* supports only Unicode character strings as the input batch of code.

The fact that you can use input and output parameters in your dynamic SQL code can help you write more secure and more efficient code. In terms of security, parameters that appear in the code cannot be considered part of the code—they can only be considered operands in expressions. So by using parameters, you can eliminate your exposure to SQL injection.

The *sp_executesql* stored procedure can perform better than *EXEC* because its parameterization aids in reusing cached execution plans, which incur cost when SQL Server needs to create them anew. An execution plan is the physical processing plan SQL Server produces for a query, with the set of instructions describing which objects to access, in what order, which indexes to use, how to access them, which join algorithms to use, and so on. One of the requirements for reusing a previously cached plan is that the query string be the same as the one for which the cached plan was created. The best way to efficiently reuse query execution plans is to use stored procedures with parameters. This way, even when parameter values change, the query string remains the same. But if you decide to use ad-hoc code instead of stored procedures, at least you can still work with parameters if you use *sp_executesql* and therefore increase the chances for plan reuse.

The *sp_executesql* procedure has two input parameters and an assignments section. You specify the Unicode character string holding the batch of code you want to run in the first parameter, which is called *@stmt*. You provide a Unicode character string holding the declarations of input and output parameters in the second input parameter, which is called *@params*. Then you specify the assignments of input and output parameters separated by commas.

The following example constructs a batch of code with a query against the *Sales.Orders* table. The example uses an input parameter called *@orderid* in the query's filter:

```
DECLARE @sql AS NVARCHAR(100);

SET @sql = N'SELECT orderid, custid, empid, orderdate
FROM Sales.Orders
WHERE orderid = @orderid;';

EXEC sp_executesql
  @stmt = @sql,
  @params = N'@orderid AS INT',
  @orderid = 10248;
```

This code generates the following output:

```
orderid     custid      empid       orderdate
----------- ----------- ----------- -----------
10248       85          5           2020-07-04
```

The code assigns the value *10248* to the input parameter, but even if you run it again with a different value, the code string remains the same. This way, you increase the chances for reusing a previously cached plan.

Using *PIVOT* with Dynamic SQL

In Chapter 7, I explained how to use the *PIVOT* operator to pivot data. I mentioned that in a static query, you have to know ahead of time which values to specify in the *IN* clause of the *PIVOT* operator. Following is an example of a static query with the *PIVOT* operator:

```
SELECT *
FROM (SELECT shipperid, YEAR(orderdate) AS orderyear, freight
      FROM Sales.Orders) AS D
  PIVOT(SUM(freight) FOR orderyear IN([2020],[2021],[2022])) AS P;
```

This example queries the *Sales.Orders* table and pivots the data so that it returns shipper IDs in the rows, order years in the columns, and the total freight in the intersection of each shipper and order year. This code returns the following output:

```
shipperid   2020          2021           2022
----------- ------------- -------------- -------------
3           4233.78       11413.35       4865.38
1           2297.42       8681.38        5206.53
2           3748.67       12374.04       12122.14
```

With the static query, you have to know ahead of time which values (order years, in this case) to specify in the *IN* clause of the *PIVOT* operator. This means you need to revise the code every year. Instead, you can query the distinct order years from the data, construct a batch of dynamic SQL code based on the years you queried, and execute the dynamic SQL batch like this:

```
DECLARE @sql AS NVARCHAR(1000) = N'SELECT *
FROM (SELECT shipperid, YEAR(orderdate) AS orderyear, freight
      FROM Sales.Orders) AS D
  PIVOT(SUM(freight) FOR orderyear IN('

  + (SELECT STRING_AGG(QUOTENAME(orderyear), N',') WITHIN GROUP(ORDER BY orderyear)
     FROM (SELECT DISTINCT(YEAR(orderdate)) AS orderyear FROM Sales.Orders) AS D)

  + N')) AS P;';

EXEC sys.sp_executesql @stmt = @sql;
```

As you can see, the code uses the *STRING_AGG* function, which was covered in Chapter 2, to concatenate the distinct order years that are currently present in the *Sales.Orders* table. The purpose of the *QUOTENAME* function is to convert the integer year into a Unicode character string; the function also adds square brackets to make it a valid column identifier. With the current data in the queried table, the subquery with the *STRING_AGG* function generates the Unicode string N'[2020],[2021],[2022]'. With the static pieces of code added before and after this piece, you get the complete *PIVOT* query string stored in the variable *@sql*. The code then uses the *sp_executesql* stored procedure to execute the code stored in the *@sql* variable.

Routines

Routines are programmable objects that encapsulate code to calculate a result or to execute activity. SQL Server supports three types of routines: user-defined functions, stored procedures, and triggers.

With SQL Server, you can choose whether to develop a routine with T-SQL or with Microsoft .NET code based on the CLR integration in the product. Because this book's focus is T-SQL, the examples here use T-SQL. When the task at hand mainly involves data manipulation, T-SQL is usually a better choice. When the task is more about iterative logic, string manipulation, or computationally intensive operations, .NET code is usually a better choice.

User-defined functions

The purpose of a user-defined function (UDF) is to encapsulate logic that calculates something, possibly based on input parameters, and return a result.

SQL Server supports scalar and table-valued UDFs. *Scalar UDFs* return a single value; *table-valued UDFs* return a table. One benefit of using UDFs is that you can incorporate them into queries. Scalar UDFs can appear anywhere in the query where an expression that returns a single value can appear (for example, in the *SELECT* list). Table UDFs can appear in the *FROM* clause of a query. The example in this section is a scalar UDF.

UDFs are not allowed to have any side effects. This obviously means UDFs are not allowed to apply any schema or data changes in the database. But other ways of causing side effects are less obvious.

For example, invoking the *RAND* function to return a random value or the *NEWID* function to return a globally unique identifier (GUID) has side effects. Whenever you invoke the *RAND* function without specifying a seed, SQL Server generates a random seed that is based on the previous invocation of *RAND*. For this reason, SQL Server needs to store information internally whenever you invoke the *RAND* function. Similarly, whenever you invoke the *NEWID* function, the system needs to set some information aside to be taken into consideration in the next invocation of *NEWID*. Because *RAND* and *NEWID* have side effects, you're not allowed to use them in your UDFs.

For example, the following code creates a UDF called *dbo.GetAge* that returns the age of a person with a specified birth date (*@birthdate argument*) at a specified event date (*@eventdate argument*):

```
CREATE OR ALTER FUNCTION dbo.GetAge
(
  @birthdate AS DATE,
  @eventdate AS DATE
)
RETURNS INT
AS
BEGIN
  RETURN
    DATEDIFF(year, @birthdate, @eventdate)
    - CASE WHEN 100 * MONTH(@eventdate) + DAY(@eventdate)
             < 100 * MONTH(@birthdate) + DAY(@birthdate)
           THEN 1 ELSE 0
      END;
END;
GO
```

The function calculates the age as the difference, in terms of years, between the birth year and the event year, minus 1 year in cases where the event month and day are smaller than the birth month and day. The expression *100 * month + day* is simply a trick to concatenate the month and day. For example, for the twelfth day in the month of February, the expression yields the integer 212.

Note that a function can have more than just a *RETURN* clause in its body. It can have code with flow elements, calculations, and more. But the function must have a *RETURN* clause that returns a value.

To demonstrate using a UDF in a query, the following code queries the *HR.Employees* table and invokes the *GetAge* function in the *SELECT* list to calculate the age of each employee today:

```
SELECT
  empid, firstname, lastname, birthdate,
  dbo.GetAge(birthdate, SYSDATETIME()) AS age
FROM HR.Employees;
```

For example, if you were to run this query on February 12, 2022, you would get the following output:

```
empid       firstname  lastname              birthdate  age
----------- ---------- -------------------- ---------- -----------
1           Sara       Davis                 1968-12-08 53
2           Don        Funk                  1972-02-19 49
3           Judy       Lew                   1983-08-30 38
4           Yael       Peled                 1957-09-19 64
5           Sven       Mortensen             1975-03-04 46
6           Paul       Suurs                 1983-07-02 38
7           Russell    King                  1980-05-29 41
8           Maria      Cameron               1978-01-09 44
9           Patricia   Doyle                 1986-01-27 36

(9 rows affected)
```

Naturally if you run the query in your system, the values you get in the age column depend on the date on which you run the query.

There's an important performance improvement called scalar UDF inlining that is available starting with SQL Server 2019 and Azure SQL Database, assuming that the database compatibility level is set to 150 or higher and that the function meets certain requirements. With this feature in effect, SQL Server inlines the scalar UDF in the outer query, effectively merging the UDF's code with the outer query's code before fully optimizing it. Without inlining, when you use a scalar UDF in a query and you pass columns from the outer tables as inputs to the UDF, you typically pay a pretty hefty performance penalty for the invocation of the UDF per row. With scalar UDF inlining in effect, you typically experience a significant performance improvement. Performance coverage is outside the scope of this book, but if you want to get more details on this feature and its requirements, consult the product documentation at the following URL: *https://learn.microsoft.com/en-us/sql/relational-databases/user-defined-functions/scalar-udf-inlining*.

Stored procedures

Stored procedures are routines that encapsulate code. They can have input and output parameters, they can return result sets of queries, and they are allowed to have side effects. Not only can you modify data through stored procedures, you can also apply schema changes through them.

Compared to using ad-hoc code, the use of stored procedures gives you many benefits:

- **Stored procedures encapsulate logic.**   If you need to change the implementation of a stored procedure, you apply the change in one place using the *ALTER PROC* command, and all users of the procedure will use the new version from that point.

- **Stored procedures give you better control of security.** You can grant a user permissions to execute the procedure without granting the user direct permissions to perform the underlying activities. For example, suppose you want to allow certain users to delete a customer from the database, but you don't want to grant them direct permissions to delete rows from the *Customers* table. You want to ensure that requests to delete a customer are validated—for example, by checking whether the customer has open orders or open debts—and you might also want to audit the requests. By not granting direct permissions to delete rows from the *Customers* table but instead granting permissions to execute a procedure that handles the task, you ensure that all the required validations and auditing always take place. In addition, stored procedures with parameters can help prevent SQL injection, especially when they replace ad-hoc SQL submitted from the client application.

- **You can incorporate all error-handling code within a procedure, silently taking corrective action where relevant.** I discuss error handling later in this chapter.

- **Stored procedures give you performance benefits.** Earlier I talked about reuse of previously cached execution plans. Queries in stored procedures are usually parameterized and therefore have a high likelihood of reusing previously cached plans. Another performance benefit of using stored procedures is a reduction in network traffic. The client application needs to submit only the procedure name and its arguments to SQL Server. The server processes all the procedure's code and returns only the output back to the caller. No back-and-forth traffic is associated with intermediate steps of the procedure.

As a simple example, the following code creates a stored procedure called *Sales.GetCustomerOrders*. The procedure accepts a customer ID (*@custid*) and a date range (*@fromdate* and *@todate*) as inputs. The procedure returns rows from the *Sales.Orders* table representing orders placed by the requested customer in the requested date range as a result set, and the number of affected rows as an output parameter (*@numrows*):

```
CREATE OR ALTER PROC Sales.GetCustomerOrders
  @custid   AS INT,
  @fromdate AS DATETIME = '19000101',
  @todate   AS DATETIME = '99991231',
  @numrows  AS INT OUTPUT
AS
SET NOCOUNT ON;

SELECT orderid, custid, empid, orderdate
FROM Sales.Orders
WHERE custid = @custid
  AND orderdate >= @fromdate
  AND orderdate < @todate;

SET @numrows = @@rowcount;
GO
```

When executing the procedure, if you don't specify a value in the *@fromdate* parameter, the procedure will use the default *19000101*, and if you don't specify a value in the *@todate* parameter, the procedure will use the default *99991231*. Notice the use of the keyword *OUTPUT* to indicate that the parameter *@numrows* is an output parameter. The *SET NOCOUNT ON* command is used to suppress messages indicating how many rows were affected by DML statements, such as the *SELECT* statement within the procedure.

Here's an example of executing the procedure, requesting information about orders placed by the customer with the ID of 1 in the year 2021. The code absorbs the value of the output parameter *@numrows* in the local variable *@rc* and returns it to show how many rows were affected by the query:

```
DECLARE @rc AS INT;

EXEC Sales.GetCustomerOrders
    @custid   = 1,
    @fromdate = '20210101',
    @todate   = '20220101',
    @numrows  = @rc OUTPUT;

SELECT @rc AS numrows;
```

The code returns the following output, showing three qualifying orders:

```
orderid     custid      empid       orderdate
----------- ----------- ----------- -----------
10643       1           6           2021-08-25
10692       1           4           2021-10-03
10702       1           4           2021-10-13


numrows
-----------
3
```

Run the code again, providing a customer ID that doesn't exist in the *Orders* table (for example, customer ID 100). You get the following output, indicating that there are zero qualifying orders:

```
orderid     custid      empid       orderdate
----------- ----------- ----------- -----------------------


numrows
-----------
0
```

Triggers

A *trigger* is a special kind of stored procedure—one that cannot be executed explicitly. Instead, it's attached to an event. Whenever the event takes place, the trigger fires and the trigger's code runs. SQL Server supports the association of triggers with two kinds of events: data manipulation events (DML triggers) such as *INSERT*, and data definition events (DDL triggers) such as *CREATE TABLE*.

You can use triggers for many purposes, including auditing, enforcing integrity rules that cannot be enforced with constraints, and enforcing policies.

A trigger is considered part of the transaction that includes the event that caused the trigger to fire. Issuing a *ROLLBACK TRAN* command within the trigger's code causes a rollback of all changes that took place in the trigger, and also of all changes that took place in the transaction associated with the trigger.

Triggers in SQL Server fire per statement and not per modified row.

DML triggers

SQL Server supports two kinds of DML triggers: *after* and *instead of*. An *after* trigger fires after the event it's associated with finishes and can be defined only on permanent tables. An *instead of* trigger fires instead of the event it's associated with and can be defined on permanent tables and views.

In the trigger's code, you can access pseudo tables called *inserted* and *deleted* that contain the rows that were affected by the modification that caused the trigger to fire. The inserted table holds the new image of the affected rows in the case of *INSERT* and *UPDATE* actions. The deleted table holds the old image of the affected rows in the case of *DELETE* and *UPDATE* actions. Remember that *INSERT*, *UPDATE*, and *DELETE* actions can be invoked by the *INSERT*, *UPDATE*, and *DELETE* statements, as well as by the *MERGE* statement. In the case of *instead of* triggers, the inserted and deleted tables contain the rows that were supposed to be affected by the modification that caused the trigger to fire.

The following simple example of an *after* trigger audits inserts to a table. Run the following code to create a table called *dbo.T1* in the current database, and a table called *dbo.T1_Audit* that holds audit information for insertions to *T1*:

```
DROP TABLE IF EXISTS dbo.T1_Audit, dbo.T1;

CREATE TABLE dbo.T1
(
  keycol  INT          NOT NULL PRIMARY KEY,
  datacol VARCHAR(10) NOT NULL
);

CREATE TABLE dbo.T1_Audit
(
  audit_lsn  INT          NOT NULL IDENTITY PRIMARY KEY,
  dt         DATETIME2(3) NOT NULL DEFAULT(SYSDATETIME()),
  login_name sysname      NOT NULL DEFAULT(ORIGINAL_LOGIN()),
  keycol     INT          NOT NULL,
  datacol    VARCHAR(10)  NOT NULL
);
```

In the audit table, the *audit_lsn* column has an identity property and represents an audit log serial number. The *dt* column represents the date and time of the insertion, using the default expression *SYSDATETIME()*. The *login_name* column represents the name of the login that performed the insertion, using the default expression *ORIGINAL_LOGIN()*.

Next, run the following code to create the *AFTER INSERT* trigger *trg_T1_insert_audit* on the *T1* table to audit insertions:

```
CREATE OR ALTER TRIGGER trg_T1_insert_audit ON dbo.T1 AFTER INSERT
AS
SET NOCOUNT ON;

INSERT INTO dbo.T1_Audit(keycol, datacol)
  SELECT keycol, datacol FROM inserted;
GO
```

As you can see, the trigger simply inserts into the audit table the result of a query against the inserted table. The values of the columns in the audit table that are not listed explicitly in the *INSERT* statement are generated by the default expressions described earlier. To test the trigger, run the following code:

```
INSERT INTO dbo.T1(keycol, datacol) VALUES(10, 'a');
INSERT INTO dbo.T1(keycol, datacol) VALUES(30, 'x');
INSERT INTO dbo.T1(keycol, datacol) VALUES(20, 'g');
```

The trigger fires after each statement. Next, query the audit table:

```
SELECT audit_lsn, dt, login_name, keycol, datacol
FROM dbo.T1_Audit;
```

You get the following output, only with *dt* and *login_name* values that reflect the date and time when you ran the inserts and the login you used to connect to SQL Server:

```
audit_lsn   dt                       login_name        keycol      datacol
----------- ------------------------ ----------------- ----------- ----------
1           2022-02-12 09:04:27.713  SHIRE\Gandalf     10          a
2           2022-02-12 09:04:27.733  SHIRE\Gandalf     30          x
3           2022-02-12 09:04:27.733  SHIRE\Gandalf     20          g
```

When you're done, run the following code for cleanup:

```
DROP TABLE dbo.T1_Audit, dbo.T1;
```

DDL triggers

SQL Server supports DDL triggers, which can be used for purposes such as auditing, policy enforcement, and change management. SQL Server box product supports the creation of DDL triggers at two scopes, the database scope and the server scope, depending on the scope of the event. Azure SQL Database currently supports only database triggers.

You create a *database* trigger for events with a database scope, such as *CREATE TABLE*. You create an *all server* trigger for events with a server scope, such as *CREATE DATABASE*. SQL Server supports only *after* DDL triggers; it doesn't support *instead of* DDL triggers.

Within the trigger, you obtain information about the event that caused the trigger to fire by querying a function called *EVENTDATA*, which returns the event information as an XML instance. You can use XQuery expressions to extract event attributes such as post time, event type, and login name from the XML instance.

The following code creates the *dbo.AuditDDLEvents* table, which holds the audit information:

```
DROP TABLE IF EXISTS dbo.AuditDDLEvents;

CREATE TABLE dbo.AuditDDLEvents
(
  audit_lsn          INT          NOT NULL IDENTITY,
  posttime           DATETIME2(3) NOT NULL,
  eventtype          sysname      NOT NULL,
  loginname          sysname      NOT NULL,
  schemaname         sysname      NOT NULL,
  objectname         sysname      NOT NULL,
  targetobjectname   sysname      NULL,
  eventdata          XML          NOT NULL,
  CONSTRAINT PK_AuditDDLEvents PRIMARY KEY(audit_lsn)
);
```

Notice that the table has a column called *eventdata* that has an XML data type. In addition to the individual attributes that the trigger extracts from the event information and stores in individual attributes, it also stores the full event information in the *eventdata* column.

Run the following code to create the *trg_audit_ddl_events* audit trigger on the database by using the event group *DDL_DATABASE_LEVEL_EVENTS*, which represents all DDL events at the database level:

```
CREATE OR ALTER TRIGGER trg_audit_ddl_events
  ON DATABASE FOR DDL_DATABASE_LEVEL_EVENTS
AS
SET NOCOUNT ON;

DECLARE @eventdata AS XML = eventdata();

INSERT INTO dbo.AuditDDLEvents(
  posttime, eventtype, loginname, schemaname,
  objectname, targetobjectname, eventdata)
  VALUES(
    @eventdata.value('(/EVENT_INSTANCE/PostTime)[1]', 'VARCHAR(23)'),
    @eventdata.value('(/EVENT_INSTANCE/EventType)[1]', 'sysname'),
    @eventdata.value('(/EVENT_INSTANCE/LoginName)[1]', 'sysname'),
    @eventdata.value('(/EVENT_INSTANCE/SchemaName)[1]', 'sysname'),
    @eventdata.value('(/EVENT_INSTANCE/ObjectName)[1]', 'sysname'),
    @eventdata.value('(/EVENT_INSTANCE/TargetObjectName)[1]', 'sysname'),
    @eventdata);
GO
```

The trigger's code first stores the event information obtained from the *EVENTDATA* function in the *@eventdata* variable. The code then inserts a row into the audit table with the attributes extracted by using XQuery expressions by the *.value* method from the event information, plus the XML instance with the full event information. (For details about the XQuery language, see the following Wikipedia article: *https://en.wikipedia.org/wiki/XQuery*.)

To test the trigger, run the following code, which contains a few DDL statements:

```
CREATE TABLE dbo.T1(col1 INT NOT NULL PRIMARY KEY);
ALTER TABLE dbo.T1 ADD col2 INT NULL;
ALTER TABLE dbo.T1 ALTER COLUMN col2 INT NOT NULL;
CREATE NONCLUSTERED INDEX idx1 ON dbo.T1(col2);
```

Next, run the following code to query the audit table:

```
SELECT * FROM dbo.AuditDDLEvents;
```

You get the following output (split here into two sections for display purposes), but with values in the *posttime* and *loginname* attributes that reflect the post time and login name in your environment:

audit_lsn	posttime	eventtype	loginname
1	2022-02-12 09:06:18.293	CREATE_TABLE	SHIRE\Gandalf
2	2022-02-12 09:06:18.413	ALTER_TABLE	SHIRE\Gandalf
3	2022-02-12 09:06:18.423	ALTER_TABLE	SHIRE\Gandalf
4	2022-02-12 09:06:18.423	CREATE_INDEX	SHIRE\Gandalf

audit_lsn	schemaname	objectname	targetobjectname	eventdata
1	dbo	T1	NULL	<EVENT_INSTANCE>...
2	dbo	T1	NULL	<EVENT_INSTANCE>...
3	dbo	T1	NULL	<EVENT_INSTANCE>...
4	dbo	idx1	T1	<EVENT_INSTANCE>...

When you're done, run the following code for cleanup:

```
DROP TRIGGER IF EXISTS trg_audit_ddl_events ON DATABASE;
DROP TABLE IF EXISTS dbo.AuditDDLEvents, dbo.T1;
```

Error handling

SQL Server provides you with tools to handle errors in your T-SQL code. The main tool used for error handling is a construct called *TRY...CATCH*. SQL Server also provides a set of functions you can invoke to get information about the error. I'll start with a basic example demonstrating the use of *TRY...CATCH*, followed by a more detailed example demonstrating the use of the error functions.

You work with the *TRY...CATCH* construct by placing the usual T-SQL code in a *TRY* block (between the *BEGIN TRY* and *END TRY* keywords) and placing all the error-handling code in the adjacent *CATCH* block (between the *BEGIN CATCH* and *END CATCH* keywords). If the *TRY* block has no error, the *CATCH* block is simply skipped. If the *TRY* block has an error, control is passed to the corresponding *CATCH* block. Note that if a *TRY...CATCH* block captures and handles an error, as far as the caller is concerned, there was no error.

Run the following code to demonstrate a case with no error in the *TRY* block:

```
BEGIN TRY
  PRINT 10/2;
  PRINT 'No error';
END TRY
BEGIN CATCH
  PRINT 'Error';
END CATCH;
```

All code in the *TRY* block completed successfully; therefore, the *CATCH* block was skipped. This code generates the following output:

```
5
No error
```

Next, run similar code, but this time divide by zero. An error occurs:

```
BEGIN TRY
  PRINT 10/0;
  PRINT 'No error';
END TRY
BEGIN CATCH
  PRINT 'Error';
END CATCH;
```

When the *divide by zero* error happened in the first *PRINT* statement in the *TRY* block, control was passed to the corresponding *CATCH* block. The second *PRINT* statement in the *TRY* block was not executed. Therefore, this code generates the following output:

```
Error
```

Typically, error handling involves some work in the *CATCH* block investigating the cause of the error and taking a course of action. SQL Server gives you information about the error via a set of functions. The *ERROR_NUMBER* function returns an integer with the number of the error. The *CATCH* block usually includes flow code that inspects the error number to determine what course of action to take. The *ERROR_MESSAGE* function returns error-message text. To get the list of error numbers and messages, query the *sys.messages* catalog view. The *ERROR_SEVERITY* and *ERROR_STATE* functions return the error severity and state. The *ERROR_LINE* function returns the line number in the code where the error happened. Finally, the *ERROR_PROCEDURE* function returns the name of the procedure in which the error happened and returns *NULL* if the error did not happen within a procedure.

To demonstrate a more detailed error-handling example, including the use of the error functions, first run the following code, which creates a table called *dbo.Employees* in the current database:

```
DROP TABLE IF EXISTS dbo.Employees;

CREATE TABLE dbo.Employees
(
  empid    INT         NOT NULL,
  empname  VARCHAR(25) NOT NULL,
  mgrid    INT         NULL,
```

```
CONSTRAINT PK_Employees PRIMARY KEY(empid),
CONSTRAINT CHK_Employees_empid CHECK(empid > 0),
CONSTRAINT FK_Employees_Employees
  FOREIGN KEY(mgrid) REFERENCES dbo.Employees(empid)
);
```

The following code inserts a new row into the *Employees* table in a *TRY* block, and if an error occurs, shows how to identify the error by inspecting the *ERROR_NUMBER* function in the *CATCH* block. The code uses flow control to identify and handle errors you want to deal with in the *CATCH* block, and it re-throws the error otherwise.

The code also prints the values of the other error functions simply to show what information is available to you when an error occurs:

```
BEGIN TRY

  INSERT INTO dbo.Employees(empid, empname, mgrid)
    VALUES(1, 'Emp1', NULL);
  -- Also try with empid = 0, 'A', NULL

END TRY
BEGIN CATCH

  IF ERROR_NUMBER() = 2627
  BEGIN
    PRINT '   Handling PK violation...';
  END;
  ELSE IF ERROR_NUMBER() = 547
  BEGIN
    PRINT '   Handling CHECK/FK constraint violation...';
  END;
  ELSE IF ERROR_NUMBER() = 515
  BEGIN
    PRINT '   Handling NULL violation...';
  END;
  ELSE IF ERROR_NUMBER() = 245
  BEGIN
    PRINT '   Handling conversion error...';
  END;
  ELSE
  BEGIN
    PRINT 'Re-throwing error...';
    THROW;
  END;

  PRINT '   Error Number  : ' + CAST(ERROR_NUMBER() AS VARCHAR(10));
  PRINT '   Error Message : ' + ERROR_MESSAGE();
  PRINT '   Error Severity: ' + CAST(ERROR_SEVERITY() AS VARCHAR(10));
  PRINT '   Error State   : ' + CAST(ERROR_STATE() AS VARCHAR(10));
  PRINT '   Error Line    : ' + CAST(ERROR_LINE() AS VARCHAR(10));
  PRINT '   Error Proc    : ' + COALESCE(ERROR_PROCEDURE(), 'Not within proc');

END CATCH;
```

When you run this code for the first time, the new row is inserted into the *Employees* table successfully, and therefore the *CATCH* block is skipped. You get the following output:

```
(1 row affected)
```

When you run the same code a second time, the *INSERT* statement fails, control is passed to the *CATCH* block, and a primary-key-violation error is identified. You get the following output:

```
Handling PK violation...
Error Number  : 2627
Error Message : Violation of PRIMARY KEY constraint 'PK_Employees'. Cannot insert
duplicate key in object 'dbo.Employees'...
Error Severity: 14
Error State   : 1
Error Line    : 3
Error Proc    : Not within proc
```

To see other errors, run the code with the values *0*, '*A*', and *NULL* as the employee ID.

Here, for demonstration purposes, I used *PRINT* statements as the actions when an error was identified. Of course, error handling usually involves more than just printing a message indicating that the error was identified.

Note that you can create a stored procedure that encapsulates reusable error-handling code like this:

```
CREATE OR ALTER PROC dbo.ErrInsertHandler
AS
SET NOCOUNT ON;

IF ERROR_NUMBER() = 2627
BEGIN
  PRINT 'Handling PK violation...';
END;
ELSE IF ERROR_NUMBER() = 547
BEGIN
  PRINT 'Handling CHECK/FK constraint violation...';
END;
ELSE IF ERROR_NUMBER() = 515
BEGIN
  PRINT 'Handling NULL violation...';
END;
ELSE IF ERROR_NUMBER() = 245
BEGIN
  PRINT 'Handling conversion error...';
END;

PRINT 'Error Number  : ' + CAST(ERROR_NUMBER() AS VARCHAR(10));
PRINT 'Error Message : ' + ERROR_MESSAGE();
PRINT 'Error Severity: ' + CAST(ERROR_SEVERITY() AS VARCHAR(10));
PRINT 'Error State   : ' + CAST(ERROR_STATE() AS VARCHAR(10));
PRINT 'Error Line    : ' + CAST(ERROR_LINE() AS VARCHAR(10));
PRINT 'Error Proc    : ' + COALESCE(ERROR_PROCEDURE(), 'Not within proc');
GO
```

In your *CATCH* block, you check whether the error number is one of those you want to deal with locally. If it is, you simply execute the stored procedure; otherwise, you re-throw the error:

```
BEGIN TRY

  INSERT INTO dbo.Employees(empid, empname, mgrid)
    VALUES(1, 'Emp1', NULL);

END TRY
BEGIN CATCH

  IF ERROR_NUMBER() IN (2627, 547, 515, 245)
    EXEC dbo.ErrInsertHandler;
  ELSE
    THROW;

END CATCH;
```

This way, you can maintain the reusable error-handling code in one place.

Conclusion

This chapter provided a high-level overview of programmable objects and therefore doesn't include an exercises section. Its goal is to make you aware of SQL Server's programmability capabilities. This chapter covered variables, batches, flow elements, cursors, temporary tables, dynamic SQL, user-defined functions, stored procedures, triggers, and error handling—quite a few subjects. This chapter also concludes the book. T-SQL and its foundations are very deep topics. You can spend a lifetime writing T-SQL code and still keep learning new things all the time. As you probably realize, this book is just the beginning...

Getting started

The purpose of this appendix is to help you get started and set up your environment so that you have everything you need to get the most out of this book.

You can run the code samples in this book either on a Microsoft SQL Server box flavor (on premises) or on a cloud flavor such as Azure SQL Database or Azure SQL Managed Instance. For details about the differences between the flavors, see the section "SQL Server architecture" in Chapter 1, "Background to T-SQL querying and programming."

The first section in this appendix, "Getting started with Azure SQL," provides a link to the website where you can find the information you need to get started with the cloud option.

The second section, "Installing a SQL Server box product," assumes you want to connect to a SQL Server box product instance to run the code samples in this book, and that you don't have an instance to connect to already. This section walks you through the installation process for a SQL Server 2022 instance. If you already have an instance of SQL Server to connect to, feel free to skip this section.

The third section, "Downloading and installing SQL Server Management Studio," provides instructions to download and install SQL Server Management Studio (SSMS).

The fourth section, "Downloading source code and installing the sample database," points you to the website where you can get the downloadable source code for the book and provides instructions for installing the book's sample database.

The fifth section, "Working with SQL Server Management Studio," explains how to develop and execute T-SQL code in SQL Server by using SSMS.

The last section, "Working with the SQL Server product documentation," explains how to get information about SQL Server-related topics, including T-SQL.

Getting started with Azure SQL

If you already have access to Azure SQL Database or Azure SQL Managed instance, you can run the code samples in this book against those. If you don't and you would like to explore this option, you can find the information that you need here: *https://azure.microsoft.com/en-us/products/azure-sql/*.

Installing a SQL Server box product

This section is relevant for those who want to run the code samples in this book and practice the exercises against a SQL Server box product and don't already have access to one. You can use any edition of SQL Server 2022 or later. Assuming you don't already have an instance of SQL Server to connect to, the following sections describe where you can obtain SQL Server and how to install it.

1. Obtain SQL Server installation software

As mentioned, you can use any edition of SQL Server 2022 or later to practice the materials in this book. If you don't already have SQL Server installed, I recommend downloading and installing SQL Server 2022 Developer edition. It has the same feature set as the Enterprise edition, but you're only allowed to use it for a development and test database in a non-production environment. You can find the SQL Server 2022 Developer edition download here: *https://www.microsoft.com/en-us/sql-server/sql-server-downloads*.

1. Follow the above URL to get to the SQL Server downloads website. Click "Download now" in the Developer edition download section. This will download a small file named SQL2022-SSEI-Dev. exe to your Downloads folder.

2. Open the file. You will be presented with a screen asking you to choose an installation type.

3. Choose Custom. At this point you will be asked to provide a target folder for the installation media.

4. Keep the default folder provided or specify a custom folder of your choice, then proceed by clicking Install. Now you need to wait for the installation media to be downloaded to the specified folder.

   Once the download is complete, the installation process will automatically start the setup.exe program from the target folder to kick off the SQL Server installation process. You should see the SQL Server Installation Center, as shown in Figure A-1.

5. You could proceed to installing SQL Server at this point. Note, though, that if you prefer to continue with the installation later, you don't have to go through the process of downloading the installation media again. Feel free at this point to close the SQL Server Installation Center. When you're ready to install the database engine, just start the setup.exe application from the installation media folder, and it will load the SQL Server Installation Center again. This is described in the next section, "Install the database engine."

2. Install the database engine

Assuming you have the SQL Server installation software available, you can proceed to installing the product.

To install the database engine

1. Start the setup.exe application from the SQL Server installation folder. You should see the SQL Server Installation Center, as shown in Figure A-1.

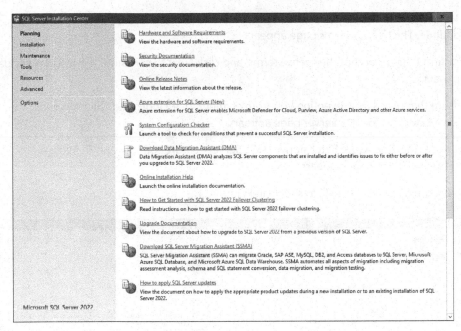

FIGURE A-1 SQL Server Installation Center

2. In the left pane, choose Installation. Note that the screen changes.

3. In the right pane, choose "New SQL Server standalone installation or add features to an existing installation." The Edition page appears, as shown in Figure A-2.

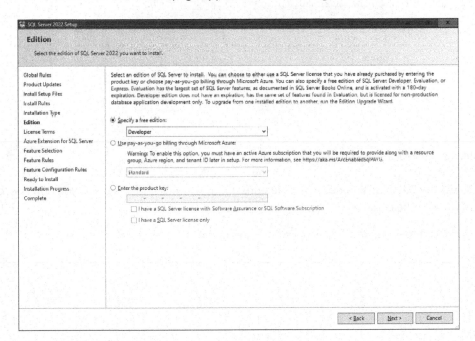

FIGURE A-2 The Edition page

4. Make sure that Developer is selected in the "Specify a free edition" menu, and click Next to continue. The License Terms page appears.

5. Confirm that you accept the license terms, and click Next to continue. The Install Rules page appears.

6. Ensure that no errors preventing you from continuing are indicated. Click Next to continue. The Azure Extension for SQL Server page appears.

7. Deselect the "The Azure Extension for SQL Server Feature" option, and then press Next. The Feature Selection page appears.

8. Select the features to install, as shown in Figure A-3.

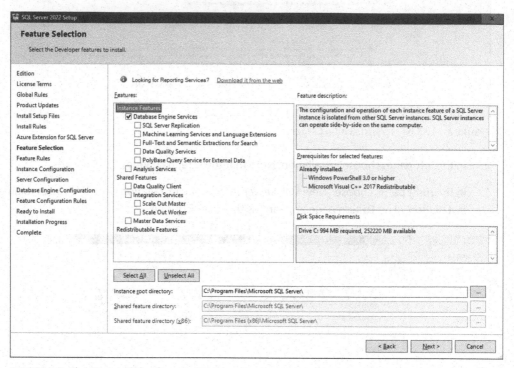

FIGURE A-3 The Feature Selection page

Select the Database Engine Services feature. For the purposes of this book, you don't need any of the other features.

9. Click Next to continue. The Instance Configuration page appears, as shown in Figure A-4.

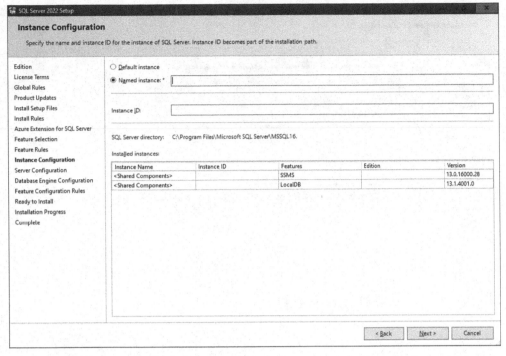

FIGURE A-4 The Instance Configuration page

If you're not familiar with the concept of SQL Server instances, you can find details in Chapter 1, in the "SQL Server architecture" section.

10. If a default instance of SQL Server is not installed on your computer and you would like to configure the new instance as the default, select the Default Instance option. If you want to configure the new instance as a named instance, make sure the "Named instance" option is selected and that you specify a name for the new instance (for example, **SQL2022**). When you later connect to SQL Server, you'll specify only the computer name for a default instance (for example, **SHIRE**) or the computer name\instance name for a named instance (for example, **SHIRE\SQL2022**).

11. Click Next to continue. The Server Configuration page appears.

For the purposes of this book, you do not need to change the default choices in the Service Accounts and Collation tabs. If you want to know more about collation, you can find details in Chapter 2, "Single-table queries," in the "Working with character data" section.

12. Click Next to continue. The Database Engine Configuration page appears.

13. On the Server Configuration tab, ensure that under Authentication Mode the "Windows authentication mode" option is selected. Under "Specify SQL Server administrators," click Add Current User to assign the current logged-in user the System Administrator (sysadmin) server role, as shown in Figure A-5. SQL Server administrators have unrestricted access to the SQL Server database engine.

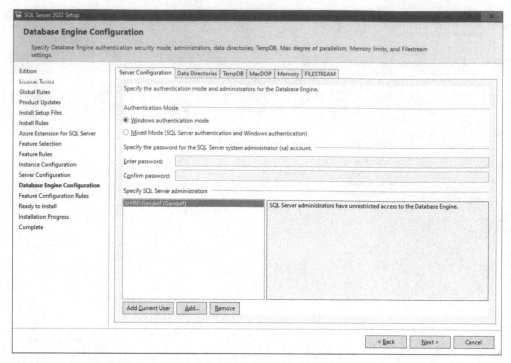

FIGURE A-5 The Database Engine Configuration page

Of course, your current user name will appear instead of *SHIRE\Gandalf*.

If you want to change the setup program's defaults in terms of data directories, you can do so on the Data Directories tab. For the purposes of the book, you don't need to configure anything on the TempDB, MaxDOP, Memory, and FILESTREAM tabs.

14. Click Next to continue. The Ready To Install page appears with a summary of the installation choices.

15. Ensure that the summary indicates your choices correctly, and click Install to start the installation process. The Installation Progress page appears and remains open throughout the remainder of the installation process. This page provides a general progress bar as well as indicating the status of each feature that is being installed. (See Figure A-6.)

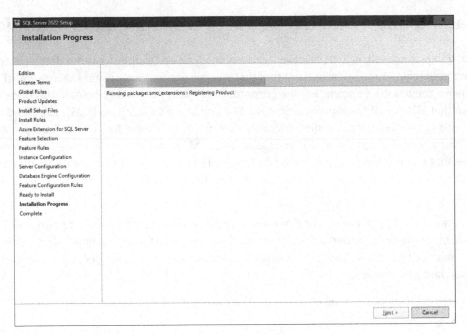

FIGURE A-6 The Installation Progress page

16. When the installation is complete, the Complete page appears, as shown in Figure A-7.

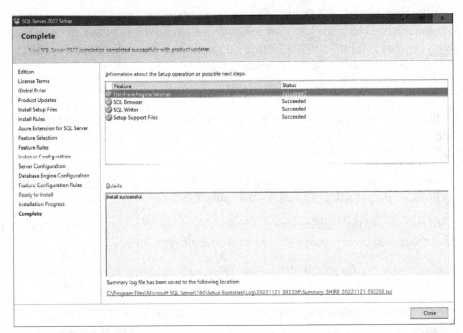

FIGURE A-7 The Complete page

This page should indicate the successful completion of the installation.

17. Click Close to finish.

Downloading and installing SQL Server Management Studio

Whether you plan to work with SQL Server or one of the Azure SQL options as the database engine, you need to download and install a client tool that you will use to develop and execute your T-SQL code against the database engine. For the purposes of running the code samples in this book you can use either SQL Server Management Studio (SSMS) or Azure Data Studio (ADS). You can download SSMS at *https://learn.microsoft.com/en-us/sql/ssms*. You can download Azure Data Studio at *https://learn.microsoft.com/en-us/sql/azure-data-studio*. I use SSMS primarily, so when I need to provide examples that involve the client tool, I provide those using SSMS. But keep in mind that the focus of this book is the language and not the tools, so feel free to use any client tool that you feel comfortable with.

Once the download completes, run the setup program. With the SSMS setup program, you just need to confirm the target folder and click the Install button. Once the installation is done, click the Close button. With the ADS installation there's a bit more user input required, but it's all pretty straightforward and intuitive.

From here on, examples that involve the client tool assume that you're using SSMS.

Downloading source code and installing the sample database

To download the source code, visit Pearson's book page here: *https://microsoftpressstore.com/TSQLFund4e/downloads*. This page has a link to download a single compressed file with the book's source code, as well as a script file called TSQLV6.sql that creates the sample database. Extract the files to a local folder (for example, C:\TSQLFundamentals).

You'll find up to three .sql script files associated with each chapter of the book:

- One file contains the source code for the corresponding chapter. It's provided for your convenience, in case you don't want to type the code that appears in the book. The name of this file matches the title of the corresponding chapter.

- A second file contains the exercises for the chapter. The name of this file also matches the title of the corresponding chapter but includes the suffix "Exercises."

- A third file contains the solutions to the chapter's exercises. The name of this file matches the title of the corresponding chapter but includes the suffix "Solutions."

While reading the book, use your preferred client tool, such as SSMS, to open the files and run the relevant part of the code they contain. The next section explains how to work with SSMS.

You'll also find a text file called orders.txt, which you can use when practicing the materials from Chapter 8, "Data modification." Also included is a script file called TSQLV6.sql, which creates the book's sample database, *TSQLV6*.

To create the sample database in an instance of a SQL Server box product, you simply need to run this script file while you're connected to the target SQL Server instance. If you aren't familiar with running script files in SQL Server, you can follow these steps to complete the database creation.

To create and populate the sample database in a SQL Server box product:

1. Double-click the TSQLV6.sql file name in File Explorer to open the file in SSMS. The Connect to Database Engine dialog box appears.

2. In the "Server name" box, ensure that the name of the instance you want to connect to appears. For example, you would type the name **SHIRE** if your instance was installed as the default instance in a computer called **SHIRE**, or **SHIRE\SQL2022** if your instance was installed as a named instance called *SQL2022* in a computer called *SHIRE*.

3. In the Authentication box, make sure Windows Authentication is selected. Click Connect. Note that the Connect to Database Engine dialog box might appear twice. In such a case, one occurrence represents the Object Explorer's connection to the server, and the other represents the query window's connection to the server. If this happens, simply follow the instructions in this step for both occurrences.

4. When you're connected to SQL Server, ensure that your cursor is positioned somewhere in the query window with no code selected, and press F5 to run the script. When the execution is done, the Command(s) Completed Successfully message should appear in the Messages pane. You should see the *TSQLV6* database in the Available Databases box.

5. When you're done, you can close SSMS.

To create and populate the sample database in Azure SQL Database:

1. Double-click the TSQLV6.sql file name in File Explorer to open the file in SSMS. The Connect to Database Engine dialog box appears.

2. In the Server Name box, ensure that the name of the Azure SQL Database server you want to connect to appears—for example, *myserver.database.windows.net*.

3. In the Authentication box, make sure that the correct authentication option and credentials are entered. Click Options.

4. On the Connection Properties tab, type **master** in the Connect to database text box, and then click Connect. Note that the Connect to Database Engine dialog box might appear twice. In such a case, one occurrence represents the Object Explorer's connection to the server, and the other represents the query window's connection to the server. If this happens, simply follow the instructions in this step for both occurrences.

5. Skip the instructions under Section A in the script (for a SQL Server box product).

6. At this point you need to manually create an empty database called *TSQLV6* in your Azure SQL Database server. You can either use the Azure portal (portal.azure.com) for this or follow the

instructions in the script file in Section B to run code directly in SSMS. Using the Azure portal, you get a GUI-based interface to choose the various options for your database specification. If indeed you prefer this option, go to the portal, choose the target Azure SQL Database server, choose Create Database, and select your desired options.

If you prefer the SSMS option, follow the instructions under Section B in the script, to run code directly to create the empty database. The most important instruction is the one telling you to run the following command to create the *TSQLV6* database:

```
CREATE DATABASE TSQLV6;
```

Note that if you run this statement as is, the database will be configured based on the default specifications. You can be explicit with the *CREATE DATABASE* command options if you want to configure the database with specifications that are different from the default, such as your preferred edition options and others. You can find the *CREATE DATABASE* command syntax for Azure SQL Database here: *https://learn.microsoft.com/en-us/sql/t-sql/statements/create-database-transact-sql?view=azuresqldb-current*.

Whether you used the Azure portal or ran the *CREATE DATABASE* command in SSMS, you should now have a new, empty database called *TSQLV6* in your Azure SQL Database server.

7. Back in SSMS, right-click any empty area in the query pane, and choose Connection | Change Connection. The Connect to Database Engine dialog box appears. Click Options, specify **TSQLV6** as the database to connect to, and click Connect. You should see the *TSQLV6* database in the Available Databases box.

   As an alternative, you can simply select the *TSQLV6* database from the Available Databases box.

8. Highlight the code in Section C (beginning with Create Schemas and continuing all the way to the end of the script file). Press F5 to run the script. When the execution is done, the Command(s) Completed Successfully message should appear in the Messages pane. Note that on slow connections it might take the code a few minutes to complete.

9. When you're done, you can close SSMS.

The data model of the *TSQLV6* database is provided in Figure A-8 for your convenience.

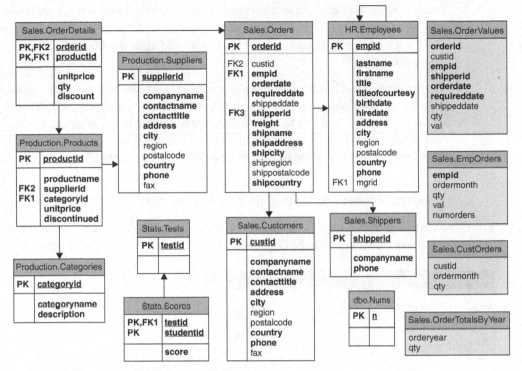

FIGURE A-8 The data model of the *TSQLV6* database

Working with SQL Server Management Studio

SQL Server Management Studio (SSMS) is one of the client tools you can use to develop and execute T-SQL code against SQL Server. The purpose of this section is not to provide a complete guide to working with SSMS, but rather just to help you get started.

> **Note** SSMS is updated periodically, so your experience might vary from the screenshots in this appendix. And your experience will of course be different if you use a different client tool, like ADS.

To start working with SSMS

1. Type **SSMS** in the Windows Start menu and choose SQL Server Management Studio.

2. If this is the first time you have run SSMS, I recommend specifying the startup options so that the environment is set up the way you want it.

   A. If a Connect to Server dialog box appears, click Cancel for now.

B.   Choose the Tools | Options menu item to open the Options dialog box. Under Environment | Startup, set the At Startup option to "Open Object Explorer and query window." This choice tells SSMS that whenever it starts, it should open the Object Explorer and a new query window.

The Object Explorer is the tool you use to manage SQL Server and graphically inspect object definitions, and a query window is where you develop and execute T-SQL code against SQL Server. Feel free to navigate the tree to explore the options you can set, but few of them are likely to mean much at this point. After you gain some experience with SSMS, you'll find many of the options more meaningful and probably want to change some of them.

C.   When you're done exploring the Options dialog box, click OK to confirm your choices.

3.   Close SSMS and start it again to verify that it actually opens the Object Explorer and a new query window. You should see the Connect to Server dialog box, as shown in Figure A-9.

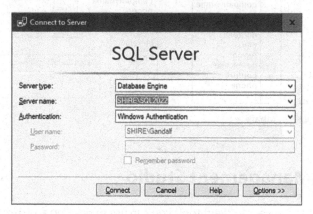

FIGURE A-9 The Connect to Server dialog box

In this dialog box, you specify the details of the SQL Server instance you want to connect to.

4.   Type the name of the server you want to connect to in the Server Name box, or select it from the list if you've already connected to it successfully in the past. For Azure SQL Database you will need to specify the full DNS server name in the form *yourserver.database.windows.net* (replacing *yourserver* with your server name).

5.   Choose the authentication mode in the Authentication list box according to the type of login you are connecting with (Windows Authentication or SQL Server Authentication). If you use the former (recommended), you don't need to specify the login name and password. If you use the latter, specify the SQL authenticated login name and password information. For Azure SQL Database, also click Options and specify **TSQLV6** in the "Connect to dataset" box in the Connection Properties tab.

6.   Click Connect. SSMS should start, as shown in Figure A-10.

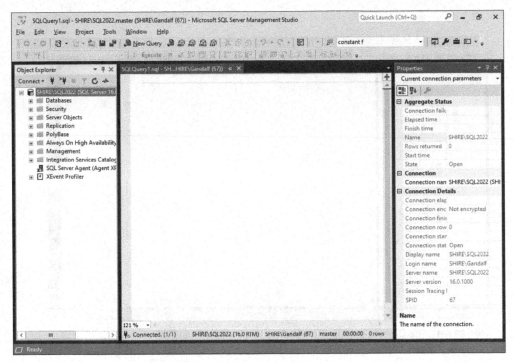

FIGURE A-10 The opening screen of SSMS

The Object Explorer window appears on the left, the query window appears to the right of Object Explorer, and the Properties window is to the right of the query window. If the Properties window is not open, you can open it by pressing the F4 key. You can hide the Properties window by clicking the Auto Hide button (in the upper-right corner of the window, to the left of the X). Adjust the sizes of the Object Explorer pane and the query window as convenient to you. Although the focus of this book is on developing T-SQL code and not on SQL Server management, I urge you to explore the Object Explorer by navigating the tree and by right-clicking the various nodes. You'll find the Object Explorer to be a convenient tool for graphically inspecting your databases and database objects, as shown in Figure A-11.

Note that you can drag items from the Object Explorer to the query window.

Tip If you drag the Columns folder of a table from the Object Explorer to the query window, SQL Server will list all table columns separated by commas.

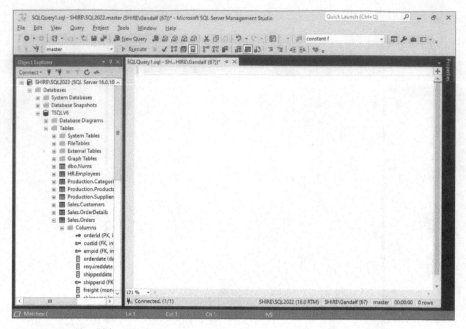

FIGURE A-11 The Object Explorer

In the query window, you develop and execute T-SQL code. The code you run is executed against the database you're connected to. You can choose the database you want to connect to from the Available Databases combo box, as shown in Figure A-12.

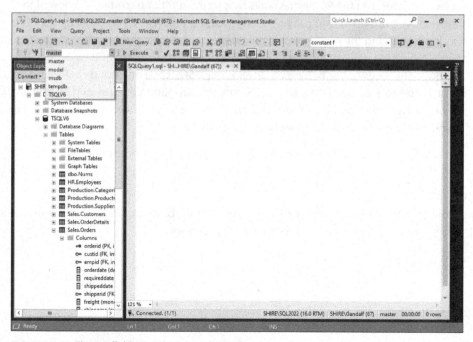

FIGURE A-12 The Available Databases combo box

7. Make sure you're currently connected to the *TSQLV6* sample database.

Note that, at any point, you can change the server and database you're connected to by right-clicking an empty area in the query window and then choosing Connection | Change Connection.

8. You're now ready to start developing T-SQL code. Type the following code into the query window:

```
SELECT orderid, orderdate FROM Sales.Orders;
```

9. Press F5 to execute the code. Alternatively, you can click Execute (the icon with the green triangle facing right). You'll get the output of the code in the Results pane, as shown in Figure A-13.

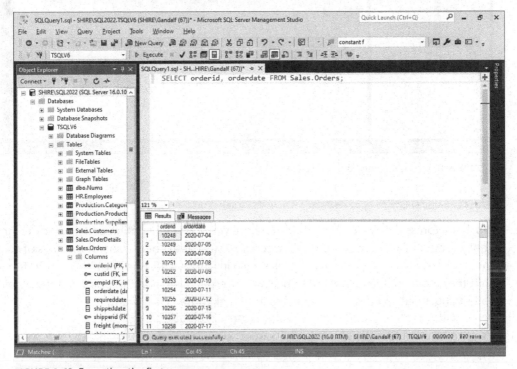

FIGURE A-13 Executing the first query

You can control the target of the results from the Query | Results To menu item or by clicking the corresponding icons in the SQL Editor toolbar. You have the following options: Results To Grid (default), Results To Text, and Results To File.

Note that if some of the code is highlighted, as shown in Figure A-14, when you execute the code, SQL Server executes only the selected part. SQL Server executes all code in the script only if no code is highlighted.

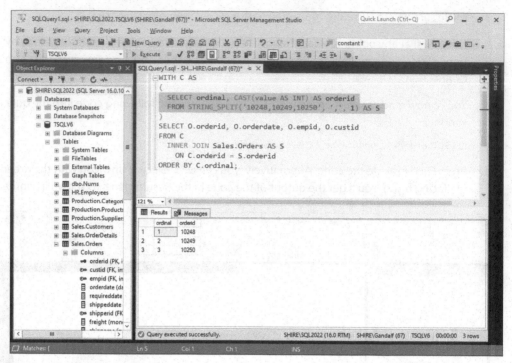

FIGURE A-14 Executing only selected code

Tip If you press and hold the Alt button before you start highlighting code, you can high-light a rectangular block that doesn't necessarily start at the beginning of the lines of code, for purposes of copying or executing, as shown in Figure A-15. Pressing Tab or Shift+Tab will shift the whole rectangle forward or backward, respectively. If at this point you start typing something, what you type gets repeated in all highlighted lines. Try it!

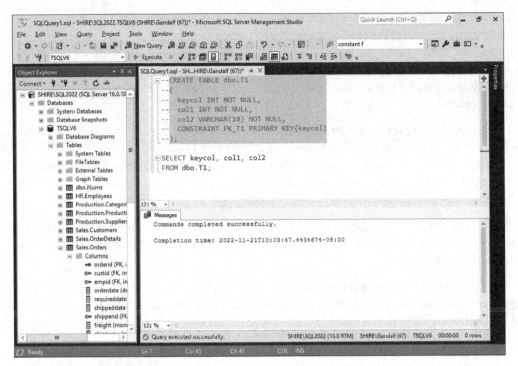

FIGURE A-15 Highlighting a rectangular block

Finally, before I leave you to your own explorations, I remind you that all the source code for the book is available for download from Pearson's book web page. A previous section in this appendix, "Downloading source code and installing the sample database," provides the details. Assuming you downloaded the source code and extracted the compressed files to a local folder, you can open the script file you want to work with from File | Open | File or by clicking the Open File icon on the standard toolbar. Alternatively, you can double-click the script file's name in File Explorer to open the script file within SSMS.

Working with the SQL Server product documentation

The Microsoft SQL Server product documentation contains a huge amount of useful information. When you're developing T-SQL code, think of the product documentation as your best friend.

You can access the product documentation from the Help menu in SSMS by clicking View Help. By default, SSMS goes to the internet to get help content, which is most people's preferred option. You can also install and access help locally from the Help Viewer, which you start by choosing Add and Remove Help Content from the Help menu, or by clicking Ctrl+Alt+F1. You can install new content by adding items from the Manage Content tab and clicking Update. I installed the items with SQL in their name and the product versions that I'm using.

Learning to use the product documentation is not rocket science, and I don't want to insult anyone's intelligence by explaining the obvious. Dedicating a section to using the product documentation in this appendix is more about making you aware of its existence and emphasizing its importance rather than explaining how to use it. Too often, people ask others for help about a topic related to SQL Server when they can easily find the answer if they only put a little effort into searching for it in the product documentation.

I'll explain a few of the ways to get information from the product documentation. If you are using the internet, the easiest option to find help on a T-SQL feature is probably to type T-SQL *<your desired feature>* in a search engine. For example, when I search for the term T-SQL PIVOT, the first article I find is at *https://learn.microsoft.com/en-us/sql/t-sql/queries/from-using-pivot-and-unpivot*, which happens to be the official product documentation article on the topic.

If you do prefer the offline option, as mentioned, you will use the Help Viewer. One of the windows I use most in Help Viewer to search for information is the Index tab at the bottom left of the Help window, shown in Figure A-16.

Type what you're looking for in the search box. As you type the letters of the subject you're looking for (for example, **window function**), Help Viewer places the first qualifying item at the top of the ordered list of subjects. You can type T-SQL keywords for which you need syntax information, for example, or any other subject of interest.

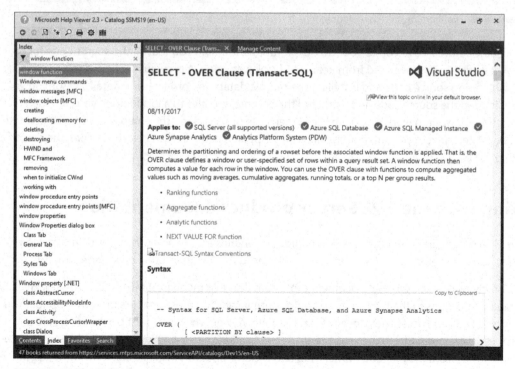

FIGURE A-16 The Help Viewer Index window

You can add the topic to the Help Favorites by clicking the Add To Favorites button from the toolbar, making it easy to get back to later. You can also sync the current help item with the respective topic on the Content tab by clicking the Show Topic In Contents button.

You can also look for an item through the Contents tab by navigating the tree of topics, as shown in Figure A-17.

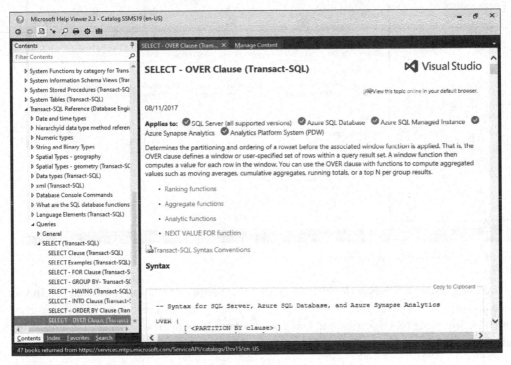

FIGURE A-17 The Help Viewer Contents window

If you just want to explore what's available in T-SQL, navigate the Transact-SQL Reference folder tree, which can be found under the Reference folder, under the SQL Server Documentation folder. The online alternative can be found at *https://learn.microsoft.com/en-us/sql/t-sql/language-reference*.

Another useful tool is the Help Viewer's Search tab, which is shown in Figure A-18.

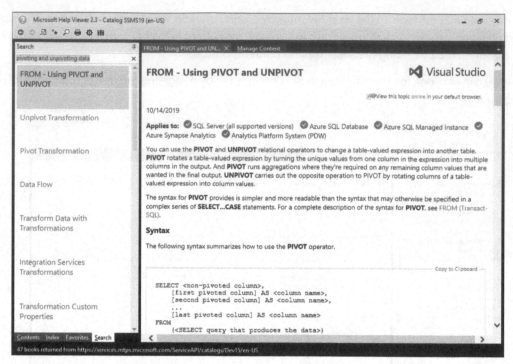

FIGURE A-18 The Help Viewer Search tab

You use the search box when looking for articles that contain words you're looking for. This search is more abstract than a search on the Index tab—somewhat similar to a search performed by an internet search engine. Note that if you want to find a certain word in an open article, click the Find In Topic button on the toolbar or press Ctrl+F to activate the Find bar.

> **Tip** Finally, let me add a last tip. If you need help with a syntax element while writing code in SQL Server Management Studio, make sure your cursor is positioned somewhere in that code element and then press F1. This will open the syntax help page for that element, assuming that such a Help item exists.

Index

Symbols and Numbers

Plug into learning at

MicrosoftPressStore.com

The Microsoft Press Store by Pearson offers:

- Free U.S. shipping

- Buy an eBook, get three formats – Includes PDF, EPUB, and MOBI to use with your computer, tablet, and mobile devices

- Print & eBook Best Value Packs

- eBook Deal of the Week – Save up to 50% on featured title

- Newsletter – Be the first to hear about new releases, announcements, special offers, and more

- Register your book – Find companion files, errata, and product updates, plus receive a special coupon* to save on your next purchase

 Pearson